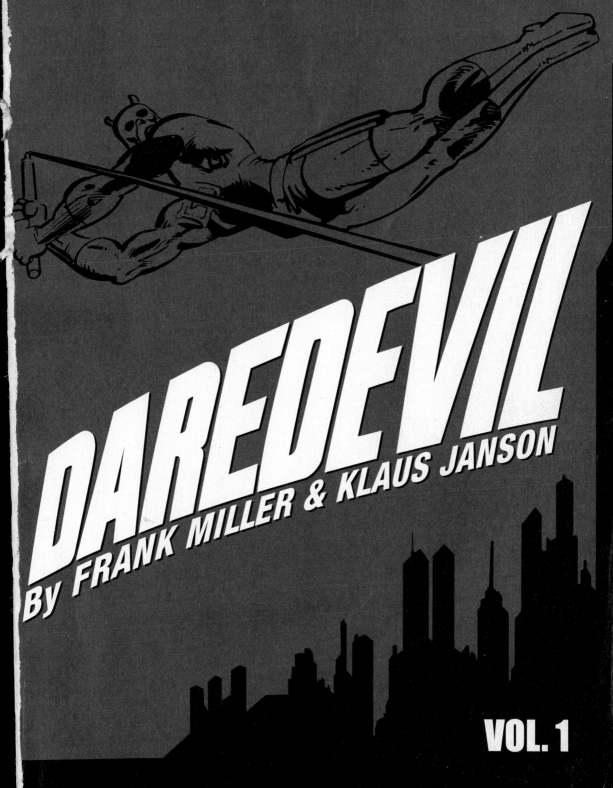

DAREDEVIL

By FRANK MILLER & KLAUS JANSON

VOL. 1

DAREDEVIL BY FRANK MILLER & KLAUS JANSON VOL. 1. Contains material originally published in magazine form as PETER PARKER, THE SPECTACULAR SPIDER-MAN #27-28, and DAREDEVIL #158-161 and #163-172. Fifth printing 2015. ISBN# 978-0-7851-3473-2. Published by MARVEL WORLDWIDE, INC., a subsidiary of MARVEL ENTERTAINMENT, LLC. OFFICE OF PUBLICATION: 135 West 50th Street, New York, NY 10020. Copyright © 2008 MARVEL No similarity between any of the names, characters, persons, and/or institutions in this magazine with those of any living or dead person or institution is intended, and any such similarity which may exist is purely coincidental. **Printed in the U.S.A.** ALAN FINE, President, Marvel Entertainment; DAN BUCKLEY, President, TV, Publishing and Brand Management; JOE QUESADA, Chief Creative Officer; TOM BREVOORT, SVP of Publishing; DAVID BOGART, SVP of Operations & Procurement, Publishing; C.B. CEBULSKI, VP of International Development & Brand Management; DAVID GABRIEL, SVP Print, Sales & Marketing; JIM O'KEEFE, VP of Operations & Logistics; DAN CARR, Executive Director of Publishing Technology; SUSAN CRESPI, Editorial Operations Manager; ALEX MORALES, Publishing Operations Manager; STAN LEE, Chairman Emeritus. For information regarding advertising in Marvel Comics or on Marvel.com, please contact Jonathan Rheingold, VP of Custom Solutions & Ad Sales, at jrheingold@marvel.com. For Marvel subscription inquiries, please call 800-217-9158. **Manufactured between 6/3/2015 and 7/6/2015 by R.R. DONNELLEY, INC., SALEM, VA, USA.**

1 0 9 8 7 6 5

DAREDEVIL

BY FRANK MILLER & KLAUS JANSON

WRITERS: **Frank Miller** (Nos. 165-191; What If…? No. 28)
Roger McKenzie (Nos. 158-161, 163-166)
David Michelinie (No. 167)
Bill Mantlo (Peter Parker, the Spectacular Spider-Man Nos. 27-28)

PENCILER: **Frank Miller**

INKERS: **Klaus Janson** (Nos. 158-161, 163-172)
Frank Springer (Peter Parker, the Spectacular Spider-Man Nos. 27-28)
Joe Rubinstein (No. 163)

LETTERERS: **Denise Wohl** (Peter Parker, the Spectacular Spider-Man Nos. 27-28)
Joe Rosen (Nos. 158, 160, 165-172)
Jim Novak (Nos. 159, 163)
Diana Albers (No. 161)
John Costanza (No. 164)

COLORISTS: **Bob Sharen** (Peter Parker, the Spectacular Spider-Man No. 27; No. 165)
Mario Sen (Peter Parker, the Spectacular Spider-Man No. 28)
George Roussos (No. 158)
Glynis Wein (Nos. 159-161, 163-164, 166-167, 169-172)
"Dr. Martin" (No. 168)

EDITORS: **Mary Jo Duffy** (Peter Parker, the Spectacular Spider-Man No. 27; Nos. 159-163)
Al Milgrom (Nos. 158-161)
Denny O'Neil (Nos. 163-172)

COVER ART: **Frank Miller**

COLOR RECONSTRUCTION: **Marie Javins with Colorgraphix/ Velazquez/Giarrusso/Herrera; Steve Buccellato with Clarissa Marrero, Rob Tokar and Brian Buccellato; Jerron Quality Color & Tom Smith**

SPECIAL THANKS TO: **Tom Brevoort, Ralph Macchio, Klaus Janson, Harris Miller & Hildy Mesnik**

COLLECTION EDITOR: **Mark D. Beazley**
ASSISTANT EDITOR: **Sarah Brunstad**
ASSOCIATE MANAGING EDITOR: **Alex Starbuck**
EDITOR, SPECIAL PROJECTS: **Jennifer Grünwald**
SENIOR EDITOR, SPECIAL PROJECTS: **Jeff Youngquist**
PRODUCTION: **Jerry Kalinowski & Jerron Quality Color**
SVP PRINT, SALES & MARKETING: **David Gabriel**

BOOK DESIGNERS: **Patrick McGrath & Spring Hoteling**

EDITOR IN CHIEF: **Axel Alonso**
CHIEF CREATIVE OFFICER: **Joe Quesada**
PUBLISHER: **Dan Buckley**
EXECUTIVE PRODUCER: **Alan Fine**

CONTENTS

INTRODUCTION

It was a jolly time to be working at Marvel Comics. You couldn't walk through the Bullpen without running into other artists and joining them in round or three of show-and-tell, poring over bristol boards to see the latest inks by Joe Rubinstein or Bob Wiacek or Terry Austin, the newest pencils by Herb Trimpe or John Buscema or John Byrne. Just to name a few. It was quite possible to wander into an editor's office and find yourself kibitzing with the writer over the next plot course for Dr. Strange.

There was electricity in the air. Jim Shooter, at the top of his form, had (not gently) used his new authority as editor in chief to increase the sense of competition among talent and bring renewed focus to the sprawling pantheon of Marvel super heroes.

I'd been banging around the offices for months, snapping up the occasional fill-in job, eagerly devouring the advice of Al Milgrom, John Romita Sr., Marie Severin…veteran talents, all generous with their advice to the struggling newcomer from Vermont.

My guardian angel was writer and staffer Jo Duffy. Ever patient, she guided me past many a rocky professional shoal. When Gene Colan decided to end his historic run on Daredevil, it was Jo I sought out.

I wanted the job. Boy, did I want that job. I'd always been intrigued by the notion of a hero whose defining attribute is a disability – a blind protagonist in a purely visual medium – and, most importantly, Daredevil offered up a chance to draw the kind of spooky crime comics I'd always wanted to do.

Jo didn't laugh at my feigned confidence. Sure, I recall her raising a startled eyebrow, but she didn't laugh. She put my name in to Jim Shooter, who agreed to take the chance, and, of course, proceeded to kibitz ferociously.

Things got better yet. Klaus Janson agreed to stay on the book as inker. Klaus had to sand down many a rough edge, and rescue many a panel outright. Across time, we developed a creative rapport that bordered on the psychic. Roger McKenzie and I babbled our way through countless afternoons, figuring out what new way we'd push things to the edge of what the Comics Code would allow, as well as what editorial could tolerate, and conspiring to steal away as many *Spider-Man* villains as we could.

Nobody – from Klaus to Roger – to wizard colorist Glynis Oliver to editors Milgrom and Duffy to Shooter – held back their best.

We had a blast.

Frank Miller
2000

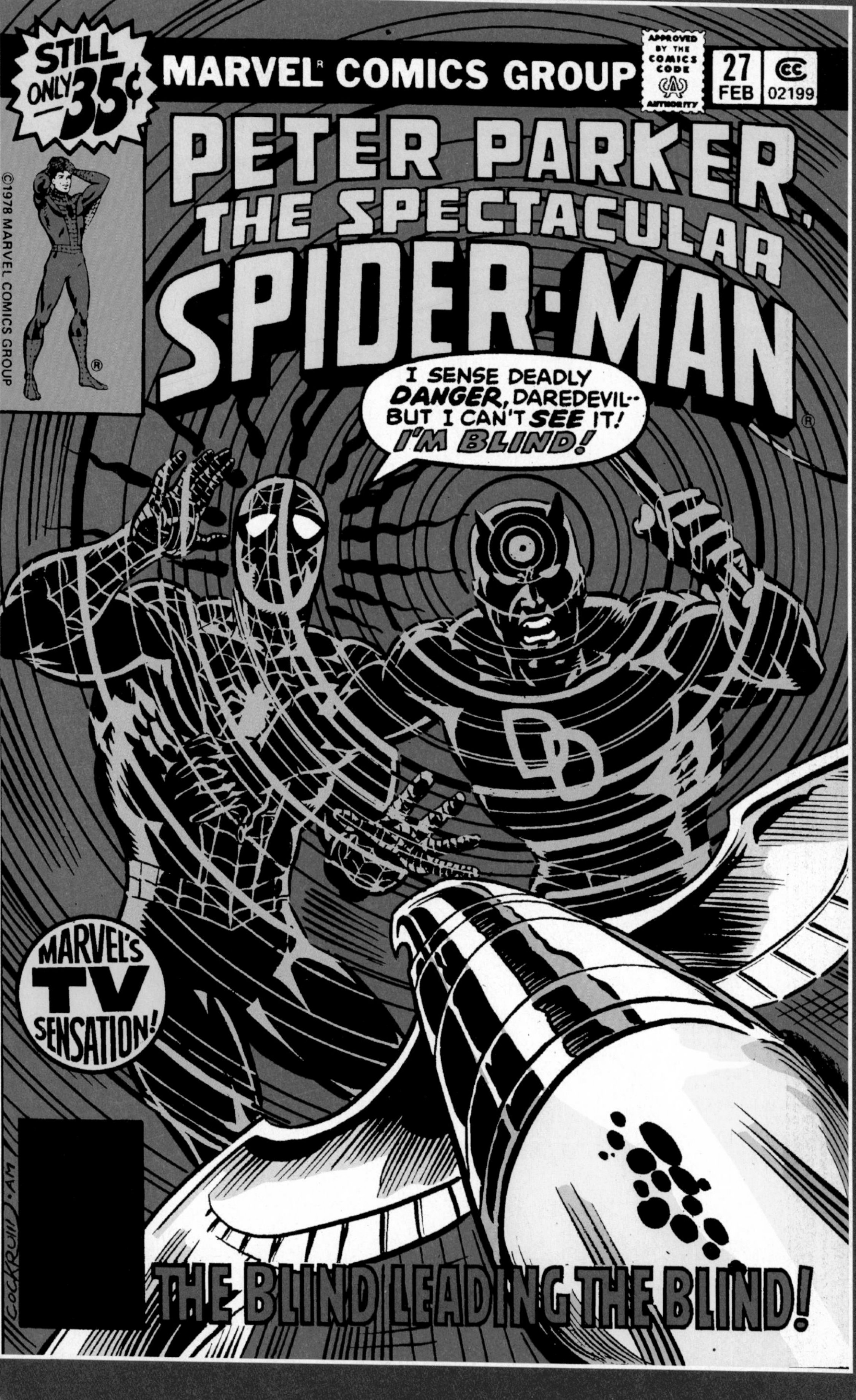
STILL ONLY 35¢
MARVEL® COMICS GROUP
APPROVED BY THE COMICS CODE AUTHORITY
27 FEB
CC 02199
©1978 MARVEL COMICS GROUP
PETER PARKER, THE SPECTACULAR SPIDER-MAN®
I SENSE DEADLY DANGER, DAREDEVIL-- BUT I CAN'T SEE IT! I'M BLIND!
MARVEL'S TV SENSATION!
THE BLIND LEADING THE BLIND!

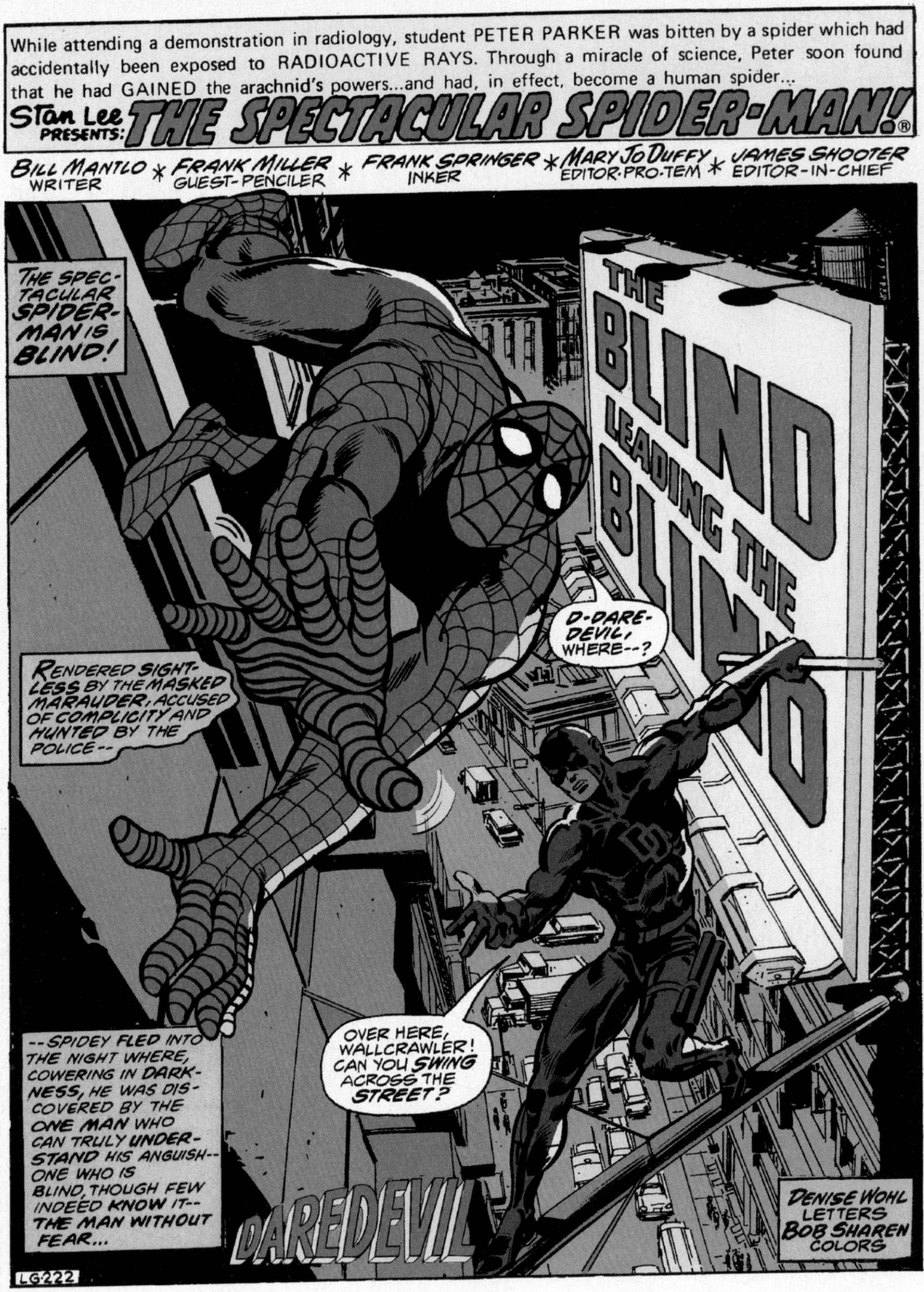
While attending a demonstration in radiology, student PETER PARKER was bitten by a spider which had accidentally been exposed to RADIOACTIVE RAYS. Through a miracle of science, Peter soon found that he had GAINED the arachnid's powers...and had, in effect, become a human spider...
Stan Lee PRESENTS: THE SPECTACULAR SPIDER-MAN!®
BILL MANTLO WRITER * FRANK MILLER GUEST-PENCILER * FRANK SPRINGER INKER * MARY JO DUFFY EDITOR-PRO-TEM * JAMES SHOOTER EDITOR-IN-CHIEF
THE SPECTACULAR SPIDER-MAN IS BLIND!
THE BLIND LEADING THE BLIND
RENDERED SIGHTLESS BY THE MASKED MARAUDER, ACCUSED OF COMPLICITY AND HUNTED BY THE POLICE--
D-DARE-DEVIL, WHERE--?
--SPIDEY FLED INTO THE NIGHT WHERE, COWERING IN DARKNESS, HE WAS DISCOVERED BY THE ONE MAN WHO CAN TRULY UNDERSTAND HIS ANGUISH--ONE WHO IS BLIND, THOUGH FEW INDEED KNOW IT--THE MAN WITHOUT FEAR...
OVER HERE, WALLCRAWLER! CAN YOU SWING ACROSS THE STREET?
DAREDEVIL
DENISE WOHL LETTERS
BOB SHAREN COLORS
LG-222

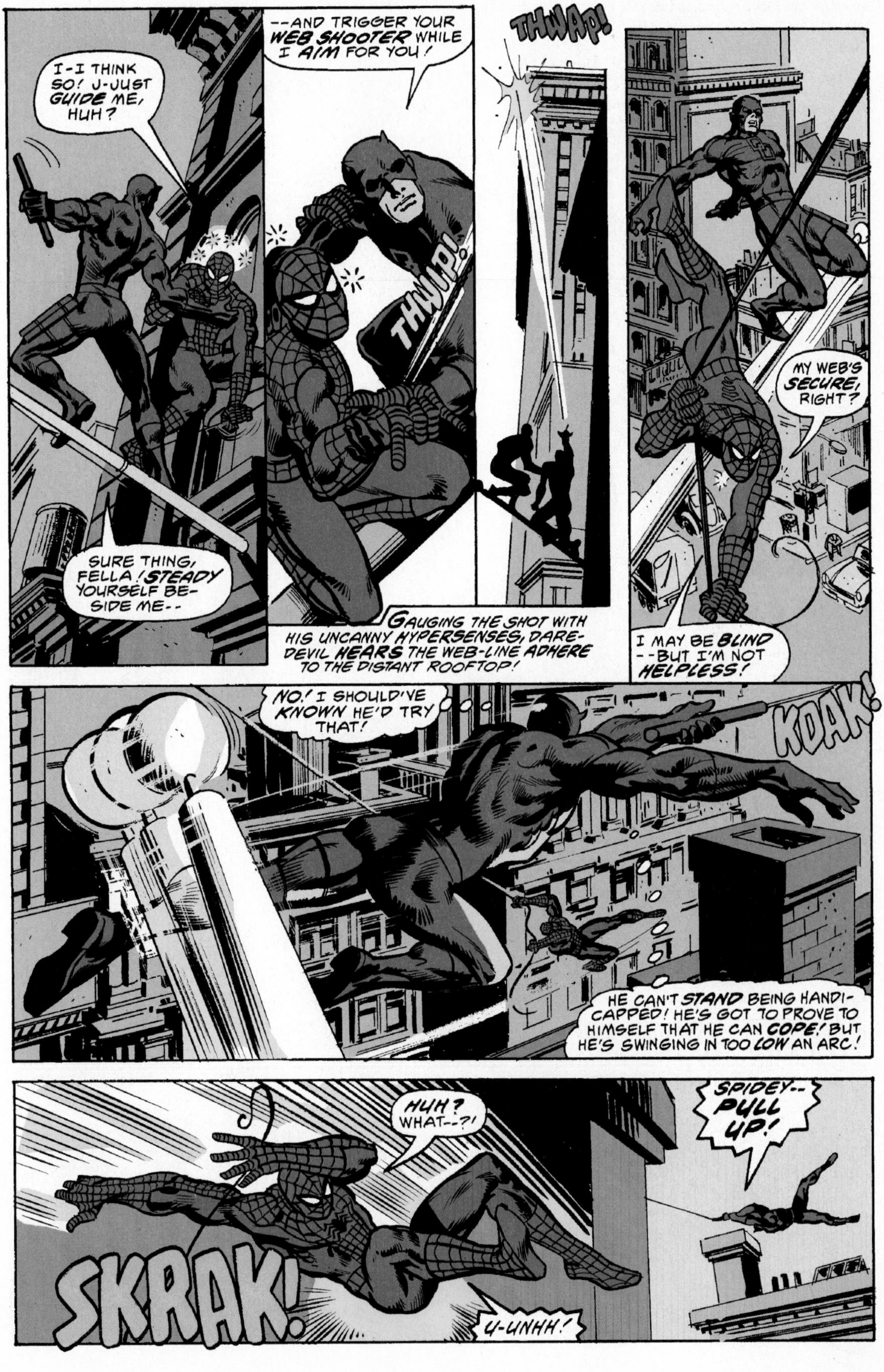
I-I THINK SO! J-JUST GUIDE ME, HUH?
SURE THING, FELLA! STEADY YOURSELF BESIDE ME--
--AND TRIGGER YOUR WEB SHOOTER WHILE I AIM FOR YOU!
THWIP!
THWAP!
GAUGING THE SHOT WITH HIS UNCANNY HYPERSENSES, DAREDEVIL HEARS THE WEB-LINE ADHERE TO THE DISTANT ROOFTOP!
MY WEB'S SECURE, RIGHT?
I MAY BE BLIND --BUT I'M NOT HELPLESS!
NO! I SHOULD'VE KNOWN HE'D TRY THAT!
KDAK!
HE CAN'T STAND BEING HANDICAPPED! HE'S GOT TO PROVE TO HIMSELF THAT HE CAN COPE! BUT HE'S SWINGING IN TOO LOW AN ARC!
HUH? WHAT--?!
SPIDEY-- PULL UP!
SKRAK!
U-UNHH!

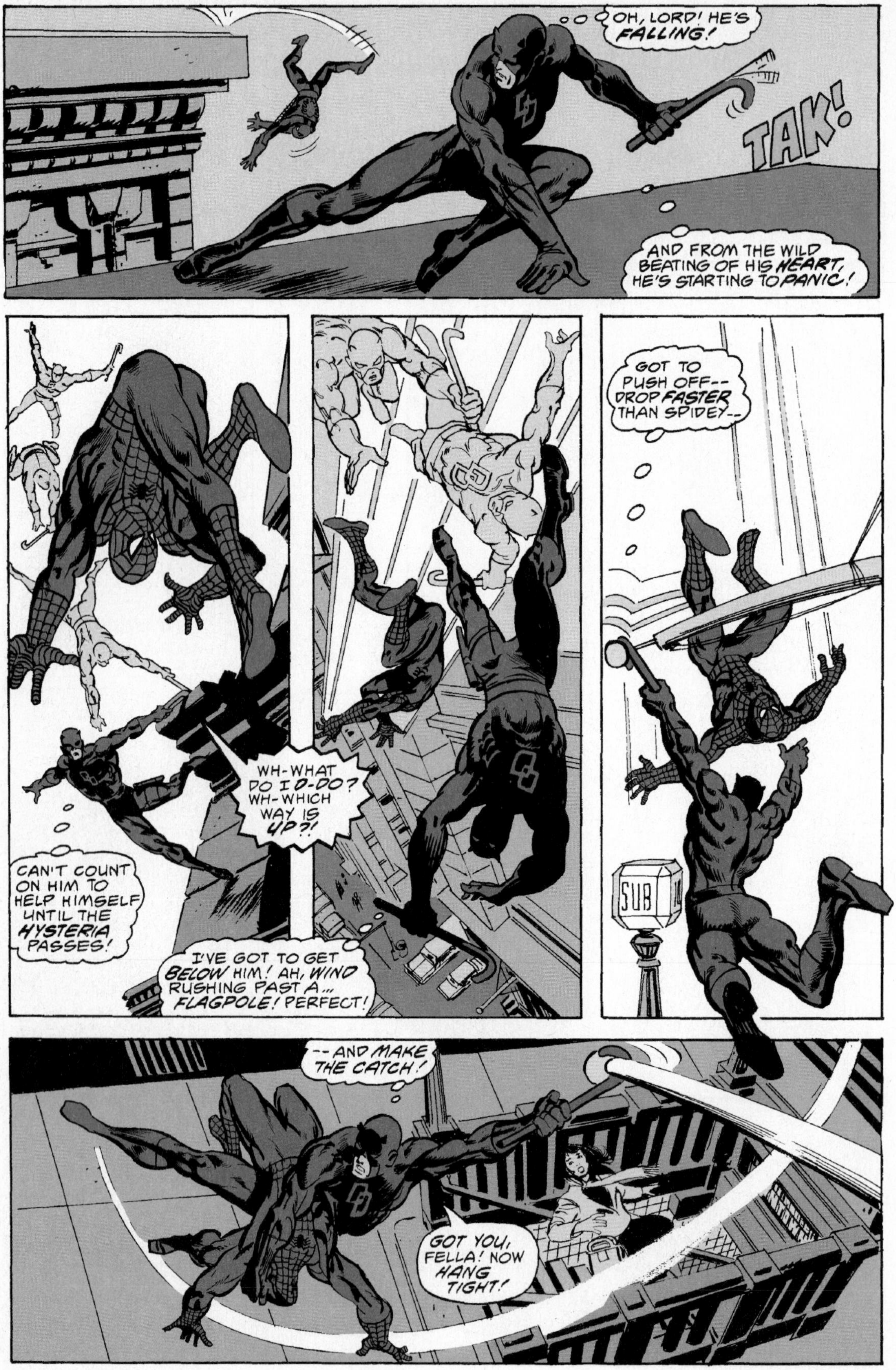
OH, LORD! HE'S FALLING!
TAK!
AND FROM THE WILD BEATING OF HIS HEART, HE'S STARTING TO PANIC!
WH-WHAT DO I D-DO? WH-WHICH WAY IS UP?!
CAN'T COUNT ON HIM TO HELP HIMSELF UNTIL THE HYSTERIA PASSES!
I'VE GOT TO GET BELOW HIM! AH, WIND RUSHING PAST A... FLAGPOLE! PERFECT!
GOT TO PUSH OFF-- DROP FASTER THAN SPIDEY--
SUB
--AND MAKE THE CATCH!
GOT YOU, FELLA! NOW HANG TIGHT!

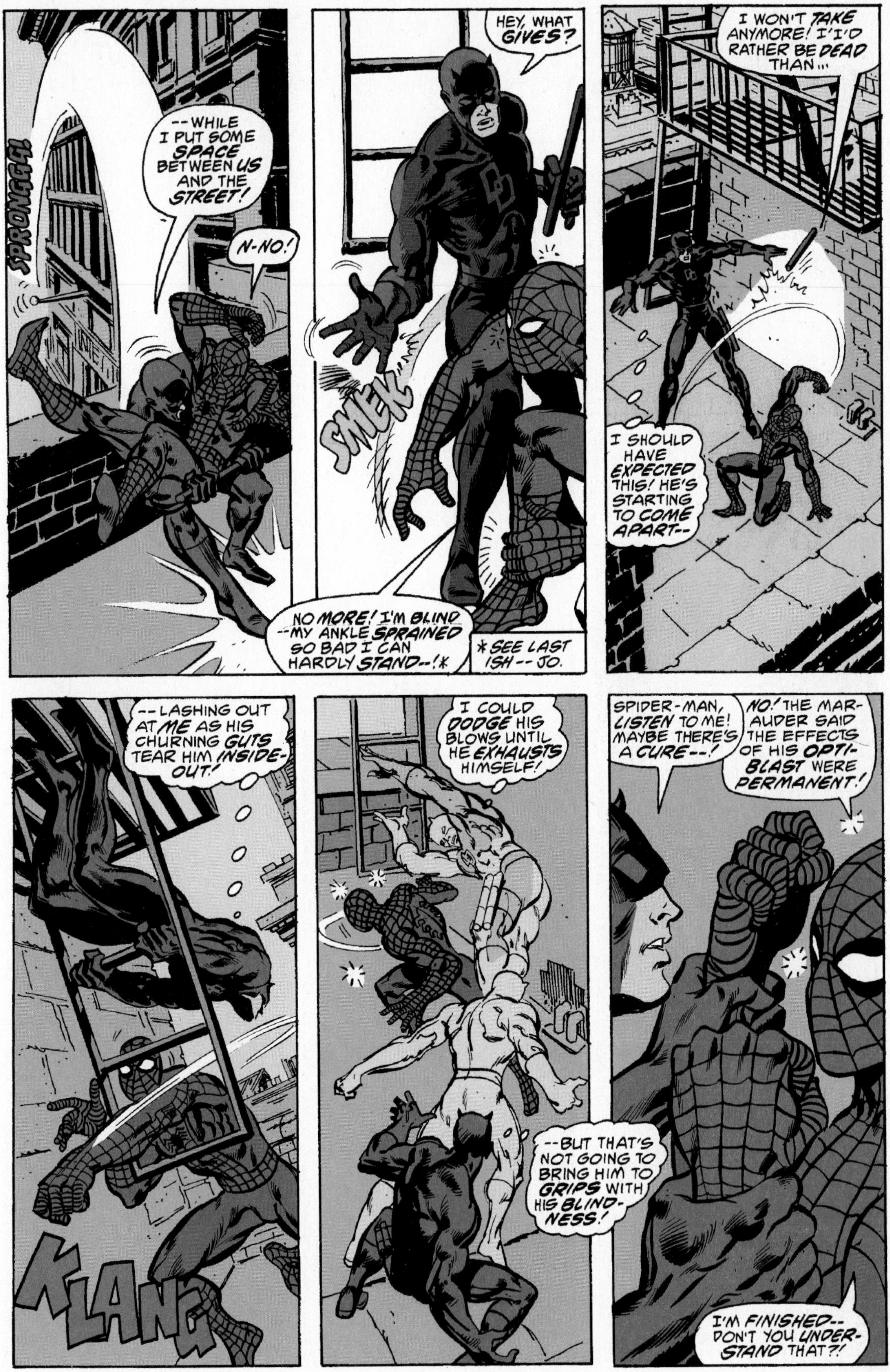
SPRONGG!
--WHILE I PUT SOME SPACE BETWEEN US AND THE STREET!
N-NO!
HEY, WHAT GIVES?
SMICK
NO MORE! I'M BLIND --MY ANKLE SPRAINED SO BAD I CAN HARDLY STAND--!*
*SEE LAST ISH -- JO.
I WON'T TAKE ANYMORE! I'D RATHER BE DEAD THAN...
I SHOULD HAVE EXPECTED THIS! HE'S STARTING TO COME APART--
--LASHING OUT AT ME AS HIS CHURNING GUTS TEAR HIM INSIDE-OUT!
KLANG
I COULD DODGE HIS BLOWS UNTIL HE EXHAUSTS HIMSELF!
--BUT THAT'S NOT GOING TO BRING HIM TO GRIPS WITH HIS BLINDNESS!
SPIDER-MAN, LISTEN TO ME! MAYBE THERE'S A CURE--!
NO! THE MARAUDER SAID THE EFFECTS OF HIS OPTI-BLAST WERE PERMANENT!
I'M FINISHED-- DON'T YOU UNDERSTAND THAT?!

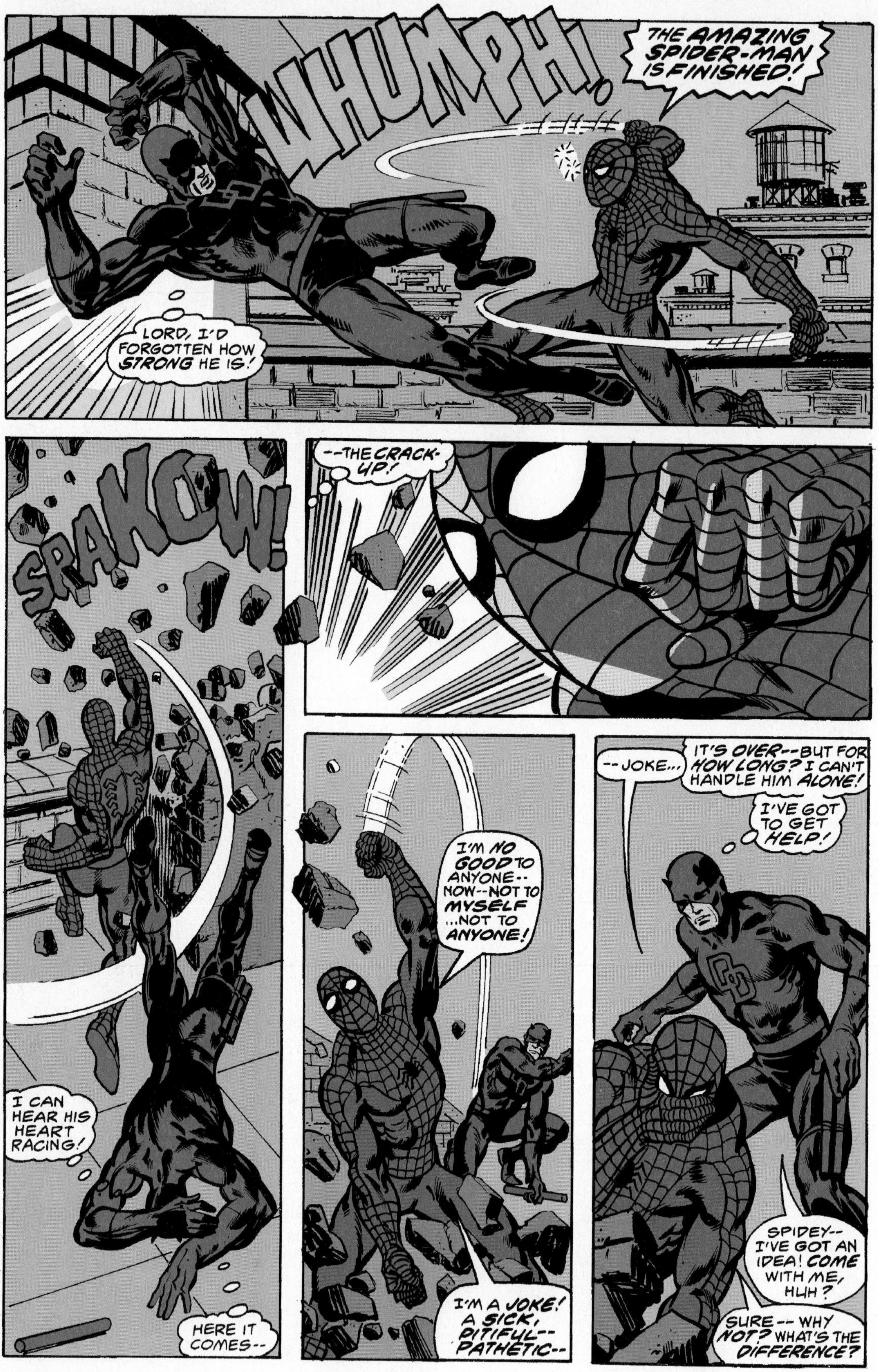
WHUMPH!
THE AMAZING SPIDER-MAN IS FINISHED!
LORD, I'D FORGOTTEN HOW STRONG HE IS!
SPAKOW!
--THE CRACK-UP!
I CAN HEAR HIS HEART RACING!
HERE IT COMES--
I'M NO GOOD TO ANYONE-- NOW--NOT TO MYSELF ...NOT TO ANYONE!
I'M A JOKE! A SICK, PITIFUL-- PATHETIC--
--JOKE...
IT'S OVER--BUT FOR HOW LONG? I CAN'T HANDLE HIM ALONE!
I'VE GOT TO GET HELP!
SPIDEY-- I'VE GOT AN IDEA! COME WITH ME, HUH?
SURE -- WHY NOT? WHAT'S THE DIFFERENCE?

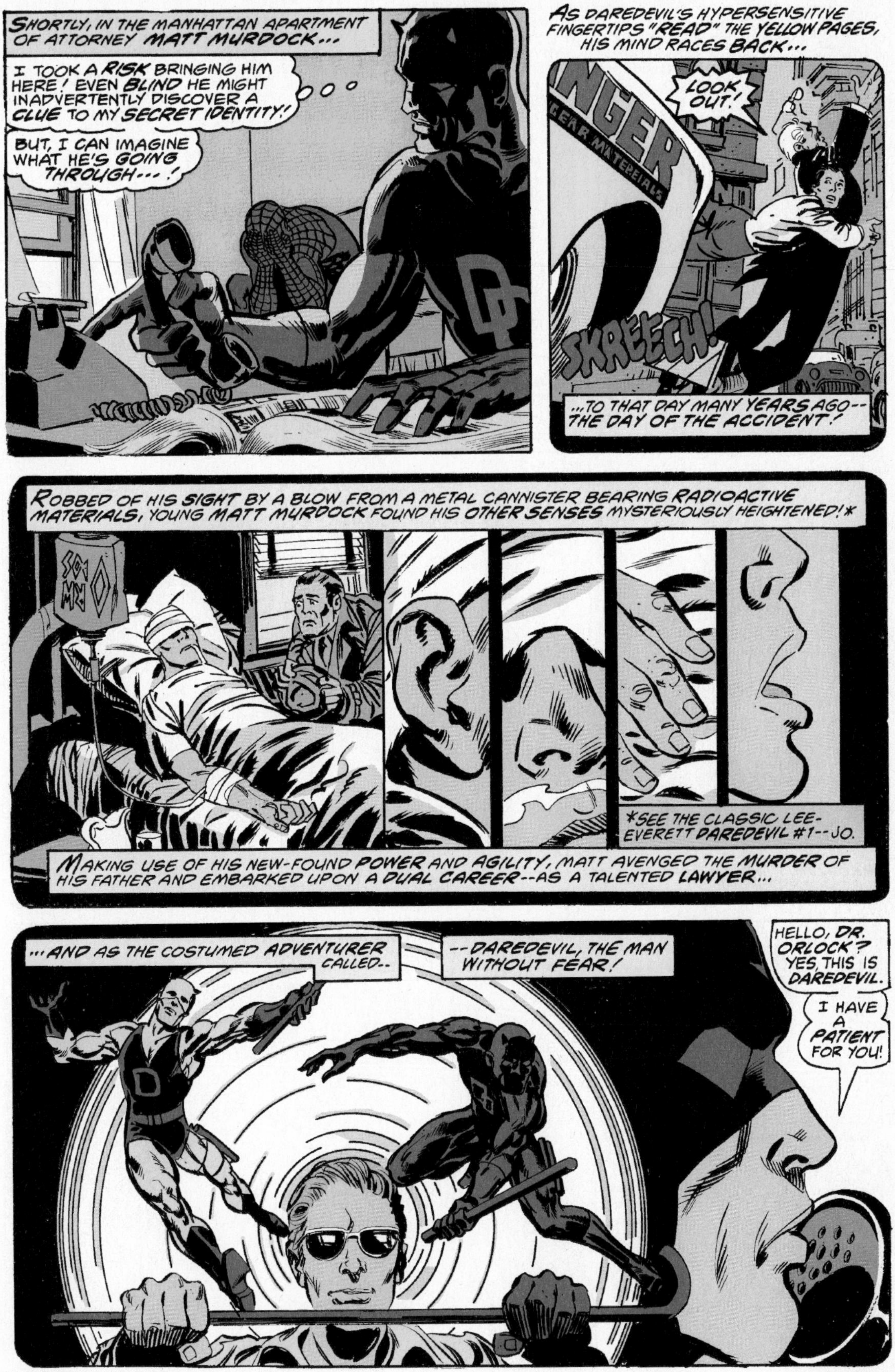
SHORTLY, IN THE MANHATTAN APARTMENT OF ATTORNEY MATT MURDOCK...
I TOOK A RISK BRINGING HIM HERE! EVEN BLIND HE MIGHT INADVERTENTLY DISCOVER A CLUE TO MY SECRET IDENTITY!
BUT, I CAN IMAGINE WHAT HE'S GOING THROUGH...!
AS DAREDEVIL'S HYPERSENSITIVE FINGERTIPS "READ" THE YELLOW PAGES, HIS MIND RACES BACK...
LOOK OUT!
SKREECH!
...TO THAT DAY MANY YEARS AGO-- THE DAY OF THE ACCIDENT!
ROBBED OF HIS SIGHT BY A BLOW FROM A METAL CANNISTER BEARING RADIOACTIVE MATERIALS, YOUNG MATT MURDOCK FOUND HIS OTHER SENSES MYSTERIOUSLY HEIGHTENED!*
*SEE THE CLASSIC LEE-EVERETT DAREDEVIL #1--JO.
MAKING USE OF HIS NEW-FOUND POWER AND AGILITY, MATT AVENGED THE MURDER OF HIS FATHER AND EMBARKED UPON A DUAL CAREER--AS A TALENTED LAWYER...
...AND AS THE COSTUMED ADVENTURER CALLED..
--DAREDEVIL, THE MAN WITHOUT FEAR!
HELLO, DR. ORLOCK? YES, THIS IS DAREDEVIL.
I HAVE A PATIENT FOR YOU!

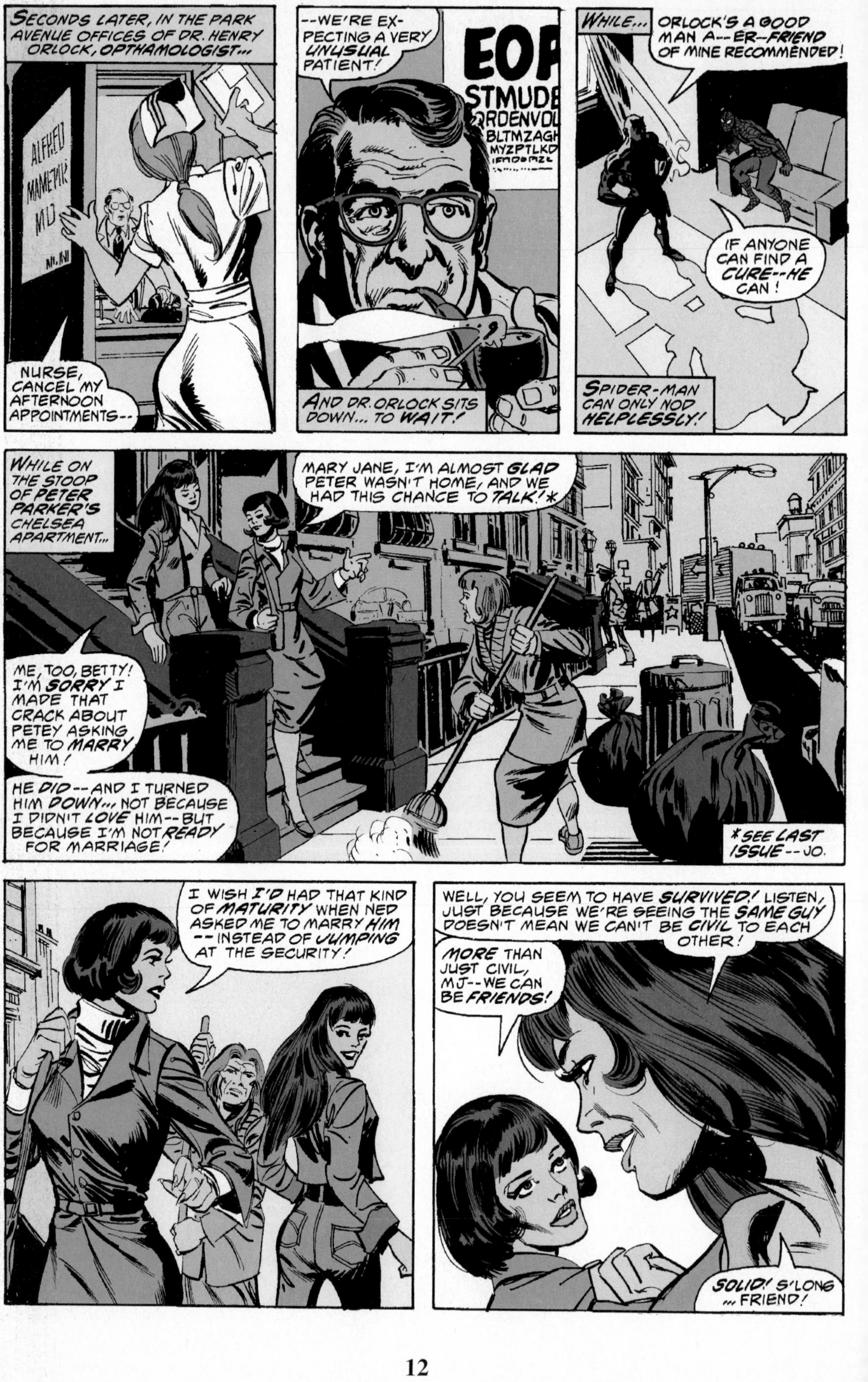
SECONDS LATER, IN THE PARK AVENUE OFFICES OF DR. HENRY ORLOCK, OPTHAMOLOGIST...
NURSE, CANCEL MY AFTERNOON APPOINTMENTS--
--WE'RE EXPECTING A VERY UNUSUAL PATIENT!
AND DR. ORLOCK SITS DOWN... TO WAIT!
WHILE...
ORLOCK'S A GOOD MAN A--ER--FRIEND OF MINE RECOMMENDED!
IF ANYONE CAN FIND A CURE--HE CAN!
SPIDER-MAN CAN ONLY NOD HELPLESSLY!
WHILE ON THE STOOP OF PETER PARKER'S CHELSEA APARTMENT...
MARY JANE, I'M ALMOST GLAD PETER WASN'T HOME, AND WE HAD THIS CHANCE TO TALK!*
ME, TOO, BETTY! I'M SORRY I MADE THAT CRACK ABOUT PETEY ASKING ME TO MARRY HIM!
HE DID--AND I TURNED HIM DOWN... NOT BECAUSE I DIDN'T LOVE HIM--BUT BECAUSE I'M NOT READY FOR MARRIAGE!
*SEE LAST ISSUE--JO.
I WISH I'D HAD THAT KIND OF MATURITY WHEN NED ASKED ME TO MARRY HIM--INSTEAD OF JUMPING AT THE SECURITY!
WELL, YOU SEEM TO HAVE SURVIVED! LISTEN, JUST BECAUSE WE'RE SEEING THE SAME GUY DOESN'T MEAN WE CAN'T BE CIVIL TO EACH OTHER!
MORE THAN JUST CIVIL, MJ--WE CAN BE FRIENDS!
SOLID! S'LONG ...FRIEND!

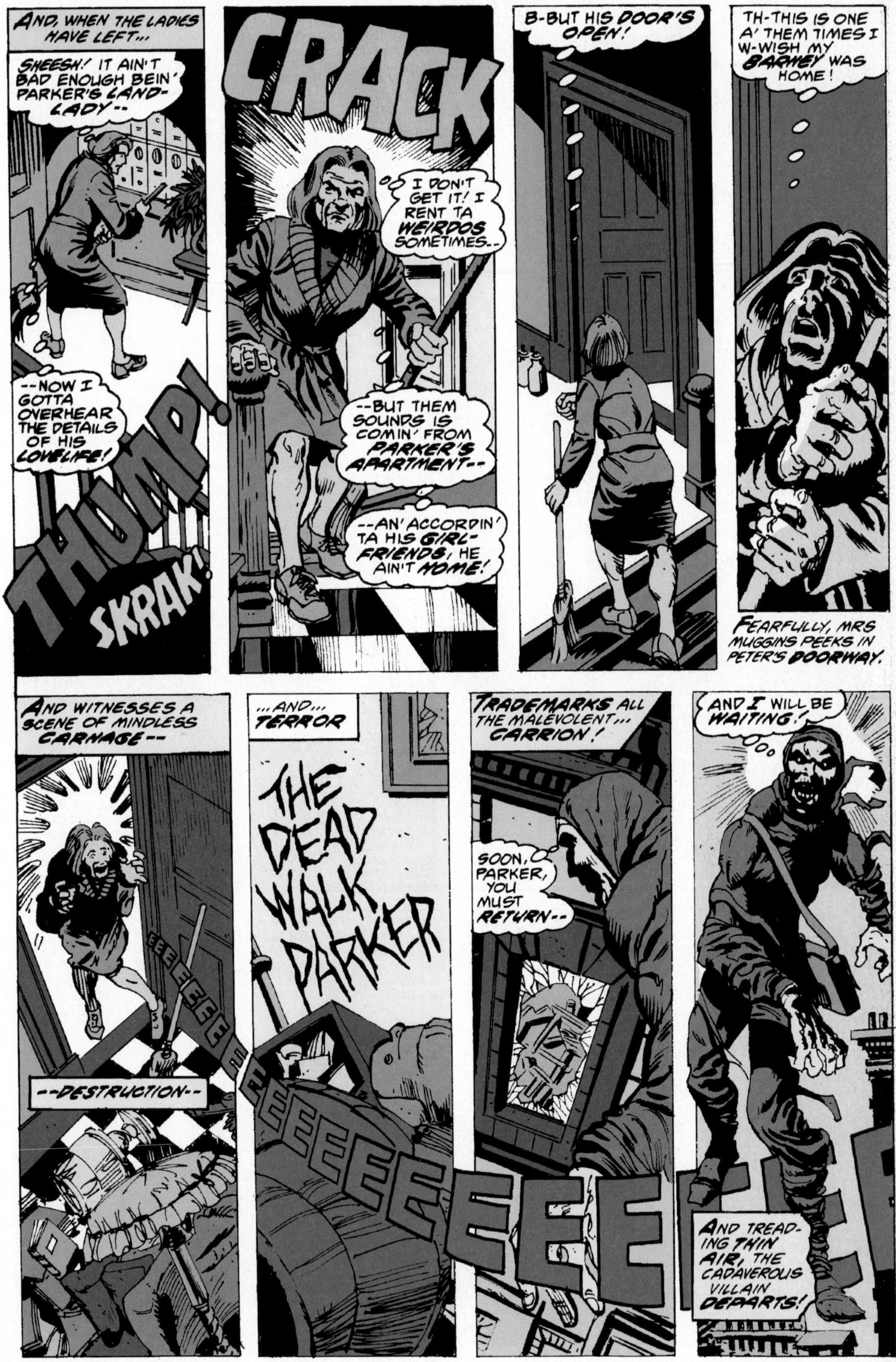
AND, WHEN THE LADIES HAVE LEFT...
SHEESH! IT AIN'T BAD ENOUGH BEIN' PARKER'S LAND-LADY--
--NOW I GOTTA OVERHEAR THE DETAILS OF HIS LOVELIFE!
THUMP!
SKRAK!
CRACK
I DON'T GET IT! I RENT TA WEIRDOS SOMETIMES--
--BUT THEM SOUNDS IS COMIN' FROM PARKER'S APARTMENT--
--AN' ACCORDIN' TA HIS GIRL-FRIENDS, HE AIN'T HOME!
B-BUT HIS DOOR'S OPEN!
TH-THIS IS ONE A' THEM TIMES I W-WISH MY BARNEY WAS HOME!
FEARFULLY, MRS MUGGINS PEEKS IN PETER'S DOORWAY.
AND WITNESSES A SCENE OF MINDLESS CARNAGE--
--DESTRUCTION--
...AND... TERROR
THE DEAD WALK PARKER
TRADEMARKS ALL THE MALEVOLENT... CARRION!
SOON, PARKER, YOU MUST RETURN--
AND I WILL BE WAITING!
AND TREADING THIN AIR, THE CADAVEROUS VILLAIN DEPARTS!

MANY HOURS LATER...

I DON'T *UNDERSTAND!* THEY SHOULD HAVE BEEN HERE BY *NOW!*

DOCTOR ORLOCK-- THEY *ARE* HERE!

SORRY IT TOOK US SO *LONG,* SIR! I THOUGHT IT BEST TO WAIT 'TIL AFTER *NIGHTFALL!*

DAREDEVIL-- HELPING *SPIDER-MAN?!* B-BUT... THAT *CITICORP ROBBERY!* THE POLICE!

--ARE OFTEN *MIS-TAKEN* NURSE WILLS--

--AND *WE* WILL RESPECT THE *CONFIDENTIALITY* OF OUR...*PATIENT!*

THANKS, DOC! AS I EXPLAINED ON THE *PHONE*...

IT'S ALRIGHT, *DD!* LET ME TELL HIM!

I WAS HIT BY SOMETHING CALLED AN *OPTI-BLAST,* DOC-- A *RAY* USED TO *PARA-LYZE* THE OPTIC NERVE.

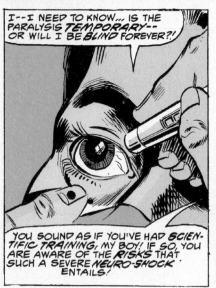

I--I NEED TO KNOW... IS THE PARALYSIS *TEMPORARY*-- OR WILL I BE *BLIND* FOREVER?!

YOU SOUND AS IF YOU'VE HAD *SCIEN-TIFIC* TRAINING, MY BOY! IF SO, YOU ARE AWARE OF THE *RISKS* THAT SUCH A SEVERE *NEURO-SHOCK* ENTAILS!

STILL, THE OPTIC FIBERS SEEM TO BE *WHOLE*... AND SEEM TO BE *RECUPERATING* WITH ASTONISHING SPEED!

SPIDER-MAN'S EXTRAORDINARY *PHYSIOLOGY* COULD ACCOUNT FOR THAT...!

BUT WILL IT BE A *COMPLETE RECOVERY??*

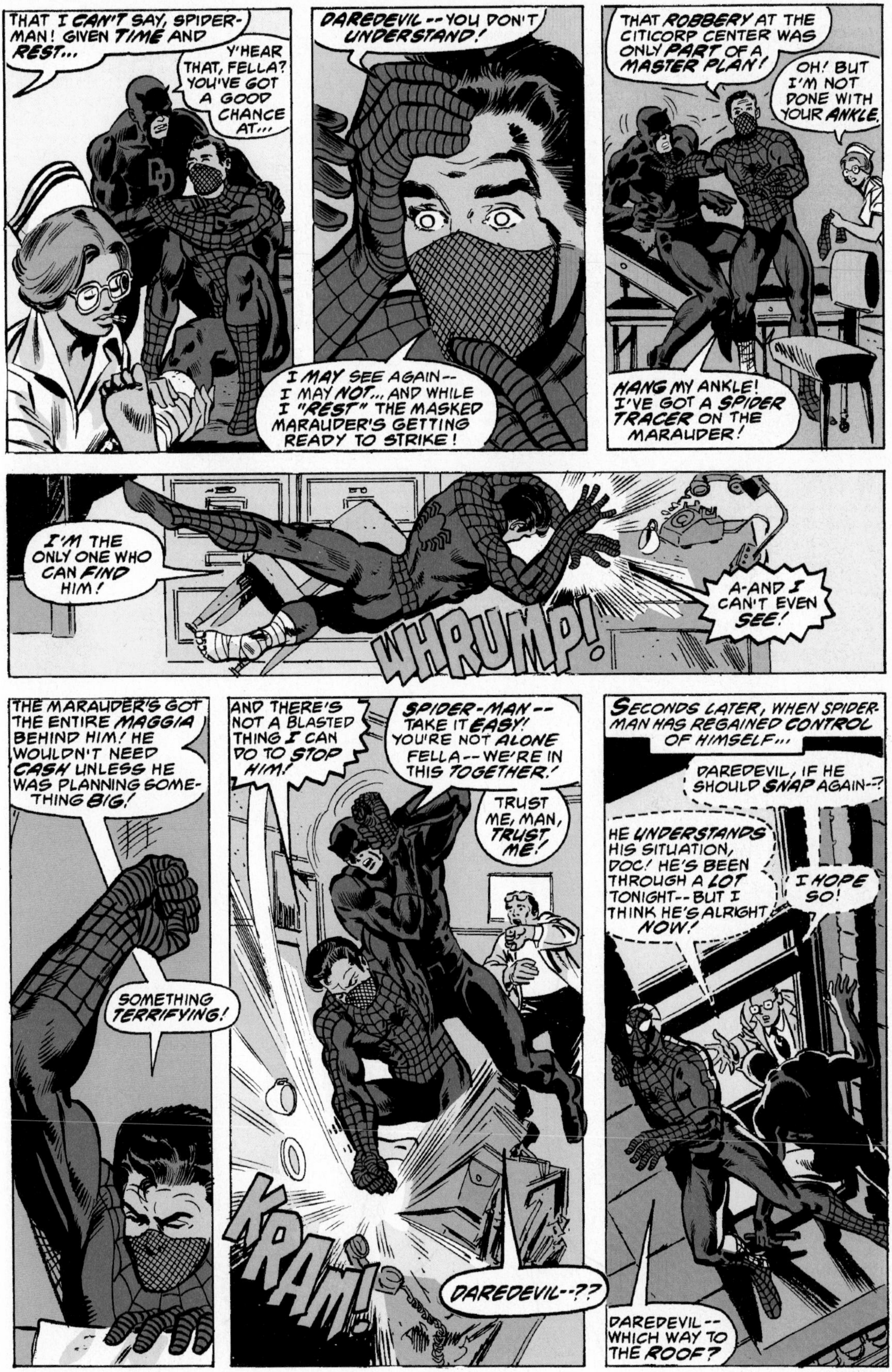
THAT I CAN'T SAY, SPIDER-MAN! GIVEN TIME AND REST...
Y'HEAR THAT, FELLA? YOU'VE GOT A GOOD CHANCE AT...
DAREDEVIL -- YOU DON'T UNDERSTAND!
I MAY SEE AGAIN -- I MAY NOT... AND WHILE I "REST" THE MASKED MARAUDER'S GETTING READY TO STRIKE!
THAT ROBBERY AT THE CITICORP CENTER WAS ONLY PART OF A MASTER PLAN!
OH! BUT I'M NOT DONE WITH YOUR ANKLE.
HANG MY ANKLE! I'VE GOT A SPIDER TRACER ON THE MARAUDER!
I'M THE ONLY ONE WHO CAN FIND HIM!
WHRUMP!
A-AND I CAN'T EVEN SEE!
THE MARAUDER'S GOT THE ENTIRE MAGGIA BEHIND HIM! HE WOULDN'T NEED CASH UNLESS HE WAS PLANNING SOMETHING BIG!
SOMETHING TERRIFYING!
AND THERE'S NOT A BLASTED THING I CAN DO TO STOP HIM!
SPIDER-MAN -- TAKE IT EASY! YOU'RE NOT ALONE FELLA -- WE'RE IN THIS TOGETHER!
TRUST ME, MAN, TRUST ME!
KRAM!
DAREDEVIL--??
SECONDS LATER, WHEN SPIDER-MAN HAS REGAINED CONTROL OF HIMSELF...
DAREDEVIL, IF HE SHOULD SNAP AGAIN--?
HE UNDERSTANDS HIS SITUATION, DOC! HE'S BEEN THROUGH A LOT TONIGHT-- BUT I THINK HE'S ALRIGHT NOW!
I HOPE SO!
DAREDEVIL -- WHICH WAY TO THE ROOF?

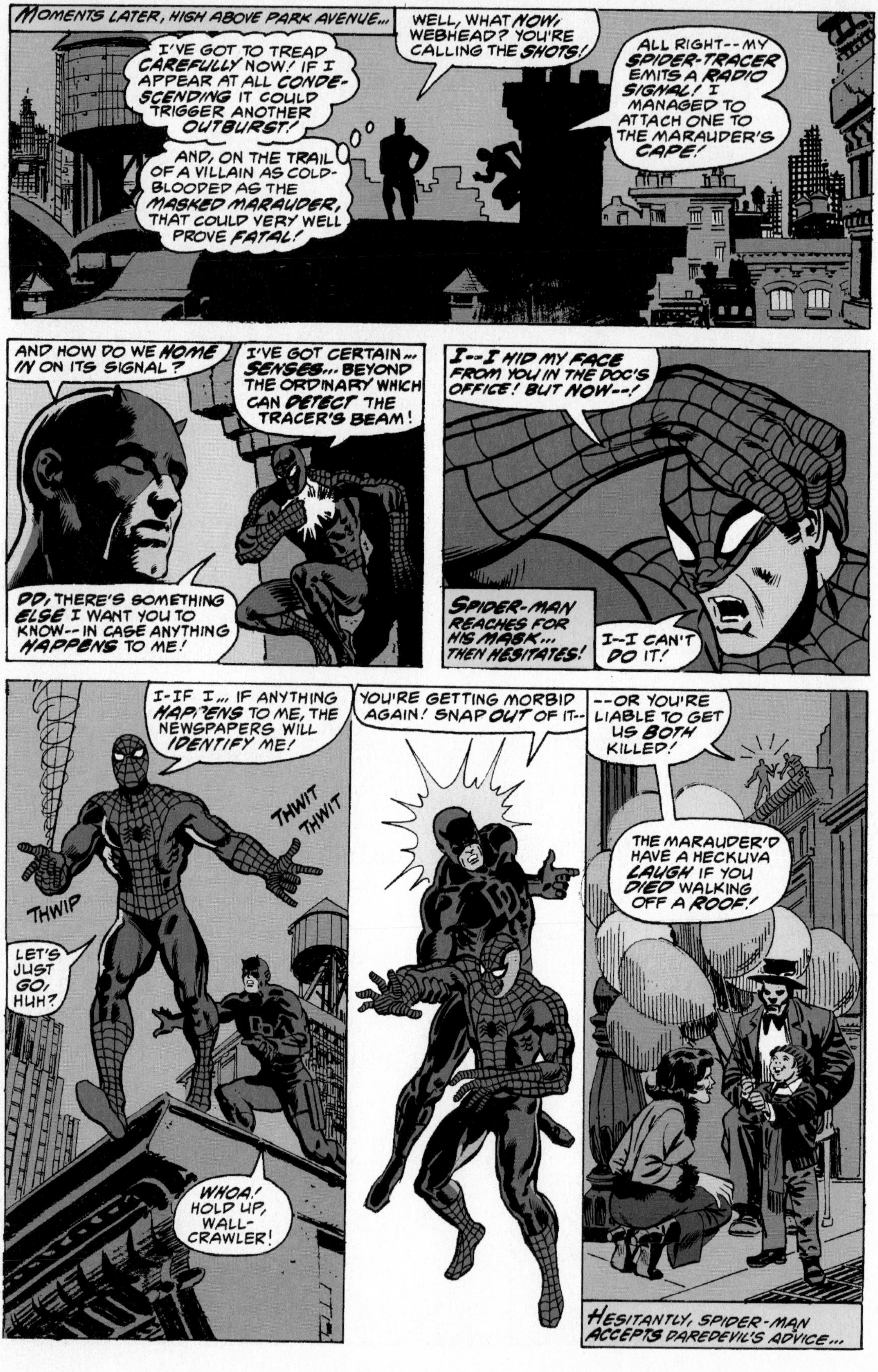
MOMENTS LATER, HIGH ABOVE PARK AVENUE...
I'VE GOT TO TREAD CAREFULLY NOW! IF I APPEAR AT ALL CONDESCENDING IT COULD TRIGGER ANOTHER OUTBURST!
AND, ON THE TRAIL OF A VILLAIN AS COLD-BLOODED AS THE MASKED MARAUDER, THAT COULD VERY WELL PROVE FATAL!
WELL, WHAT NOW, WEBHEAD? YOU'RE CALLING THE SHOTS!
ALL RIGHT--MY SPIDER-TRACER EMITS A RADIO SIGNAL! I MANAGED TO ATTACH ONE TO THE MARAUDER'S CAPE!
AND HOW DO WE HOME IN ON ITS SIGNAL?
I'VE GOT CERTAIN... SENSES... BEYOND THE ORDINARY WHICH CAN DETECT THE TRACER'S BEAM!
DD, THERE'S SOMETHING ELSE I WANT YOU TO KNOW--IN CASE ANYTHING HAPPENS TO ME!
I--I HID MY FACE FROM YOU IN THE DOC'S OFFICE! BUT NOW--!
SPIDER-MAN REACHES FOR HIS MASK... THEN HESITATES!
I--I CAN'T DO IT!
I-IF I... IF ANYTHING HAPPENS TO ME, THE NEWSPAPERS WILL IDENTIFY ME!
THWIT THWIT
THWIP
LET'S JUST GO, HUH?
WHOA! HOLD UP, WALL-CRAWLER!
YOU'RE GETTING MORBID AGAIN! SNAP OUT OF IT--
--OR YOU'RE LIABLE TO GET US BOTH KILLED!
THE MARAUDER'D HAVE A HECKUVA LAUGH IF YOU DIED WALKING OFF A ROOF!
HESITANTLY, SPIDER-MAN ACCEPTS DAREDEVIL'S ADVICE...

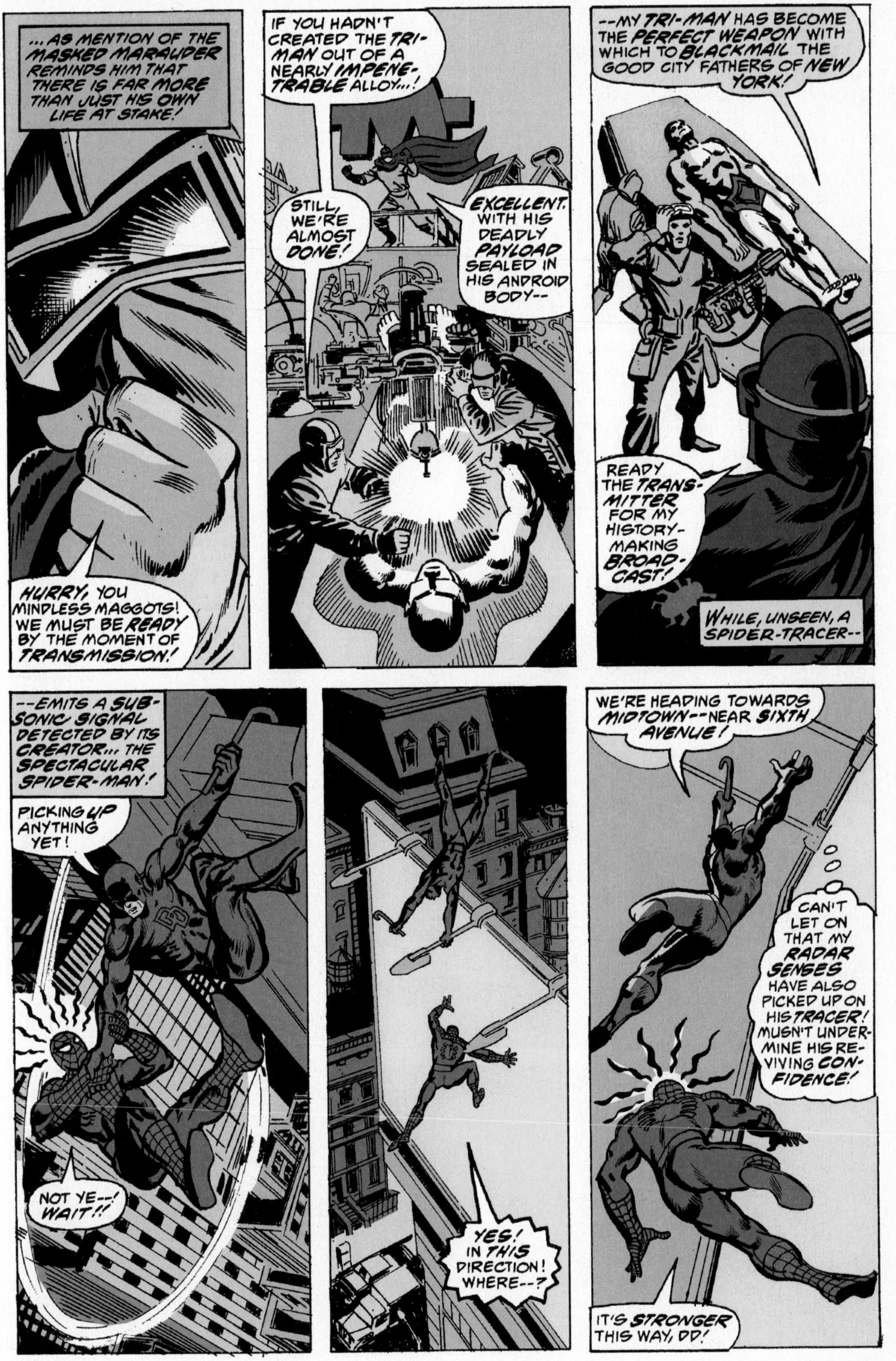
...AS MENTION OF THE MASKED MARAUDER REMINDS HIM THAT THERE IS FAR MORE THAN JUST HIS OWN LIFE AT STAKE!
HURRY, YOU MINDLESS MAGGOTS! WE MUST BE READY BY THE MOMENT OF TRANSMISSION!
IF YOU HADN'T CREATED THE TRI-MAN OUT OF A NEARLY IMPENETRABLE ALLOY...!
STILL, WE'RE ALMOST DONE!
EXCELLENT. WITH HIS DEADLY PAYLOAD SEALED IN HIS ANDROID BODY--
--MY TRI-MAN HAS BECOME THE PERFECT WEAPON WITH WHICH TO BLACKMAIL THE GOOD CITY FATHERS OF NEW YORK!
READY THE TRANSMITTER FOR MY HISTORY-MAKING BROADCAST!
WHILE, UNSEEN, A SPIDER-TRACER--
--EMITS A SUB-SONIC SIGNAL DETECTED BY ITS CREATOR... THE SPECTACULAR SPIDER-MAN!
PICKING UP ANYTHING YET!
NOT YE--! WAIT!!
YES! IN THIS DIRECTION! WHERE--?
WE'RE HEADING TOWARDS MIDTOWN--NEAR SIXTH AVENUE!
CAN'T LET ON THAT MY RADAR SENSES HAVE ALSO PICKED UP ON HIS TRACER! MUSN'T UNDERMINE HIS REVIVING CONFIDENCE!
IT'S STRONGER THIS WAY, DD!

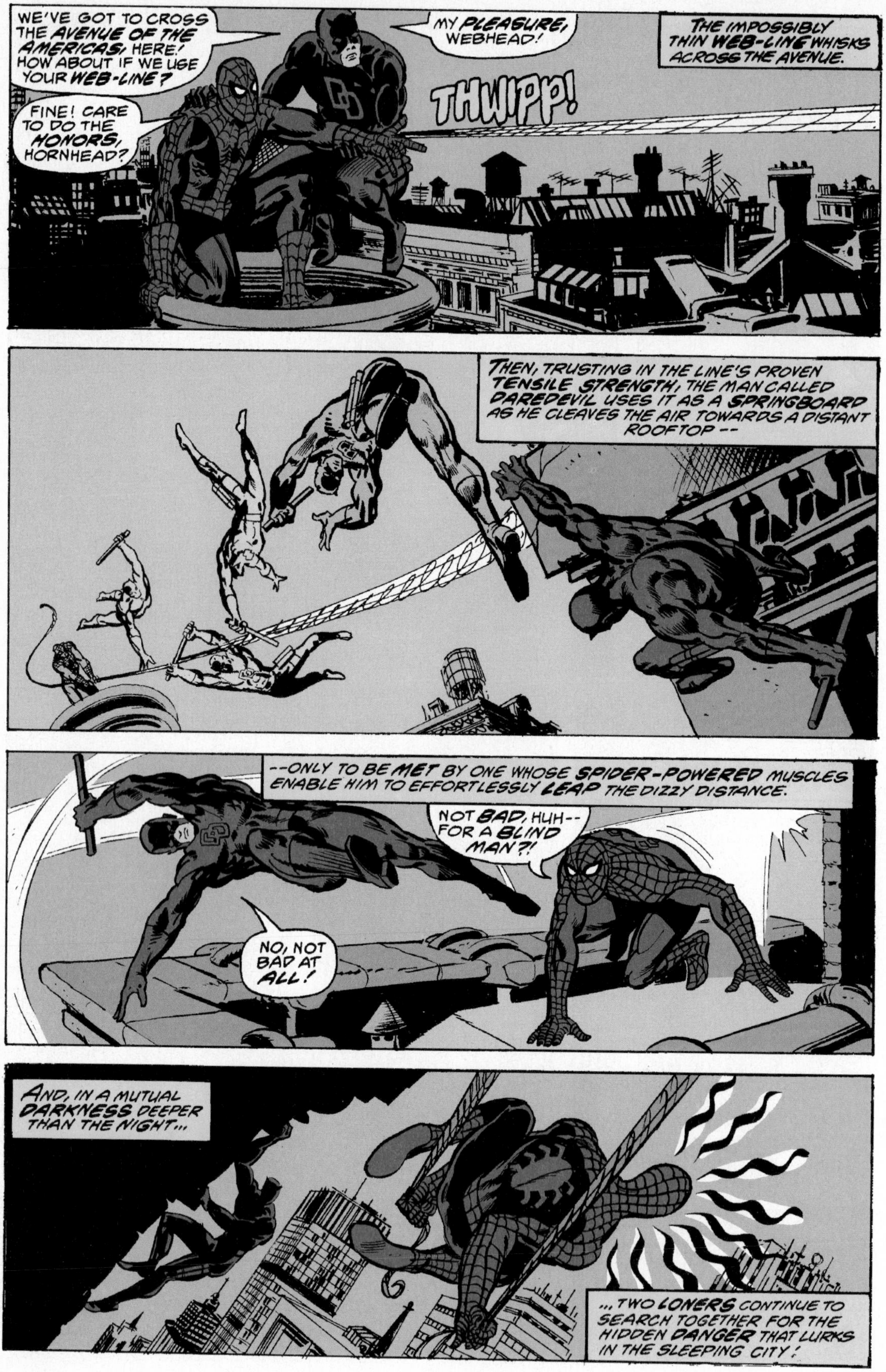
WE'VE GOT TO CROSS THE AVENUE OF THE AMERICAS, HERE! HOW ABOUT IF WE USE YOUR WEB-LINE?
FINE! CARE TO DO THE HONORS, HORNHEAD?
MY PLEASURE, WEBHEAD!
THE IMPOSSIBLY THIN WEB-LINE WHISKS ACROSS THE AVENUE.
THWIPP!
THEN, TRUSTING IN THE LINE'S PROVEN TENSILE STRENGTH, THE MAN CALLED DAREDEVIL USES IT AS A SPRINGBOARD AS HE CLEAVES THE AIR TOWARDS A DISTANT ROOFTOP --
--ONLY TO BE MET BY ONE WHOSE SPIDER-POWERED MUSCLES ENABLE HIM TO EFFORTLESSLY LEAP THE DIZZY DISTANCE.
NOT BAD, HUH-- FOR A BLIND MAN?!
NO, NOT BAD AT ALL!
AND, IN A MUTUAL DARKNESS DEEPER THAN THE NIGHT...
...TWO LONERS CONTINUE TO SEARCH TOGETHER FOR THE HIDDEN DANGER THAT LURKS IN THE SLEEPING CITY!

SOON...

WE'RE *CLOSE,* HORNHEAD --REAL *CLOSE!*

SWEEPING THE SKY- LINE WITH HIS UNCANNY *RADAR SENSE...*

...THE MAN WITHOUT *FEAR* IS INUNDATED WITH LITERALLY *THOU- SANDS* OF BROAD- CAST *SIGNALS!*

GOT TO *NARROW* MY FOCUS! SPIDER-MAN'S *ATTUNED* TO THE *TRACER* SIGNAL BECAUSE OF HIS *SPIDER-SENSE* --

--BUT *I'VE* GOT TO *SORT IT OUT* FROM AMONGST ALL THE *REST!*

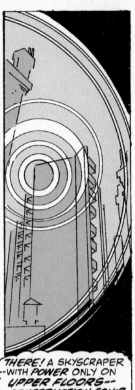

THERE! A SKYSCRAPER --WITH *POWER* ONLY ON *UPPER FLOORS* -- CONSTRUCTION EQUIP- MENT SCATTERED AROUND THE SIDEWALK BELOW!

THAT'S THE ONE -- THAT UNFINISHED *BUILDING* ON 47th STREET! THE PENT- HOUSE FLOORS ARE FILLED WITH *MEN* AND *MACHINES!*

AT *THIS* TIME OF NIGHT, IT'S *GOT* TO BE THE *MARAUDER* AND HIS *MAGGIA GOONS!*

OKAY, MY JOB'S DONE! GO GET 'EM, *DD!*

I WOULDN'T BE MUCH *USE* IN A *FIGHT!*

DROP THE *SOB-SISTER* ROUTINE, FELLA! I'VE SAID THIS BEFORE-- I'LL SAY IT *AGAIN!*

H-HEY--?!

KDAK

WE'RE IN THIS TOGETHER!

I ONLY HOPE WE COME *OUT* OF IT THAT WAY!

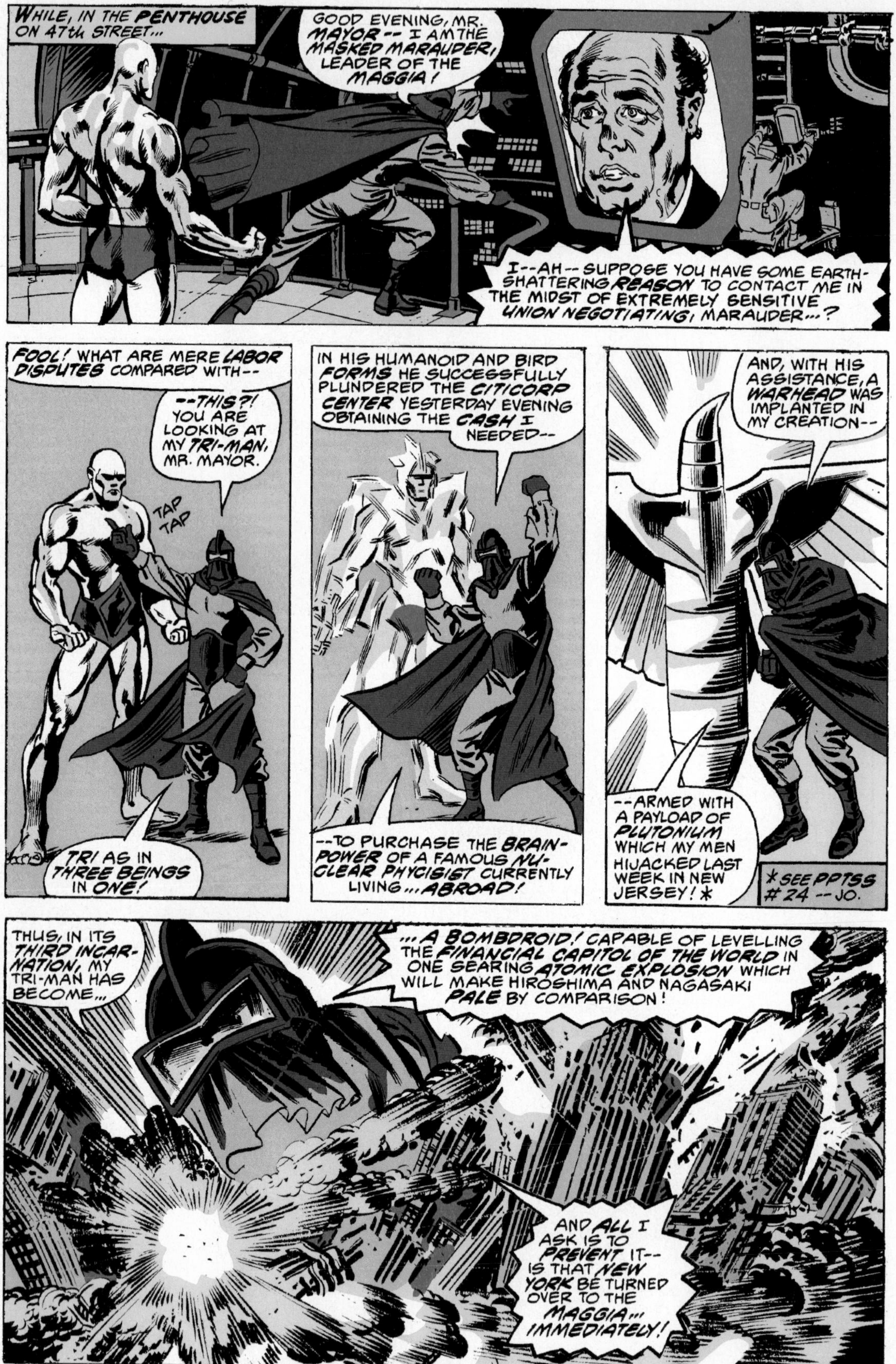
WHILE, IN THE PENTHOUSE ON 47th STREET...
GOOD EVENING, MR. MAYOR -- I AM THE MASKED MARAUDER, LEADER OF THE MAGGIA!
I--AH--SUPPOSE YOU HAVE SOME EARTH-SHATTERING REASON TO CONTACT ME IN THE MIDST OF EXTREMELY SENSITIVE UNION NEGOTIATING, MARAUDER...?
FOOL! WHAT ARE MERE LABOR DISPUTES COMPARED WITH--
--THIS?! YOU ARE LOOKING AT MY TRI-MAN, MR. MAYOR.
TAP TAP
TRI AS IN THREE BEINGS IN ONE!
IN HIS HUMANOID AND BIRD FORMS HE SUCCESSFULLY PLUNDERED THE CITICORP CENTER YESTERDAY EVENING OBTAINING THE CASH I NEEDED--
--TO PURCHASE THE BRAIN-POWER OF A FAMOUS NU-CLEAR PHYCISIST CURRENTLY LIVING...ABROAD!
AND, WITH HIS ASSISTANCE, A WARHEAD WAS IMPLANTED IN MY CREATION--
--ARMED WITH A PAYLOAD OF PLUTONIUM WHICH MY MEN HIJACKED LAST WEEK IN NEW JERSEY! *
* SEE PPTSS #24 --JO.
THUS, IN ITS THIRD INCAR-NATION, MY TRI-MAN HAS BECOME...
...A BOMBDROID! CAPABLE OF LEVELLING THE FINANCIAL CAPITOL OF THE WORLD IN ONE SEARING ATOMIC EXPLOSION WHICH WILL MAKE HIROSHIMA AND NAGASAKI PALE BY COMPARISON!
AND ALL I ASK IS TO PREVENT IT-- IS THAT NEW YORK BE TURNED OVER TO THE MAGGIA... IMMEDIATELY!

BUT, EVEN AS THE MAYOR GASPS IN HORROR...

THAT'S WHAT I *LIKE* ABOUT YOU, MARAUDER --YOU *AIM* FOR THE *SKIES!*

CHOK!

SKRASH!

DAREDEVIL?! HERE?!!

SURE! DID YOU EXPECT ME TO *STAY AWAY* ONCE I LEARNED FROM *SPIDER-MAN*--

KTANSSSG

--THAT *YOU* WERE UP TO YOUR *OLD TRICKS?*

KLUGGGGG

WHUNFF!

I'M *SHOCKED!* WE KNOW EACH OTHER *BETTER* THAN THAT!

TOO WELL, YOU CRIMSON CRETIN! IT WILL GIVE ME GREAT *PLEASURE* TO DESTROY YOU--

--IN THE *SAME* INSTANT THAT I *CREMATE* THE CITY OF NEW YORK!

VROOSH!

YOU *MADMAN!* LAUNCH THE *TRI-MAN* AND YOU DOOM *YOURSELF* AS WELL!

NO CHANCE, HERO! THE BOSS HAS AN *ESCAPE ROUTE* ALL SET! A *TELEPORTER!*

21

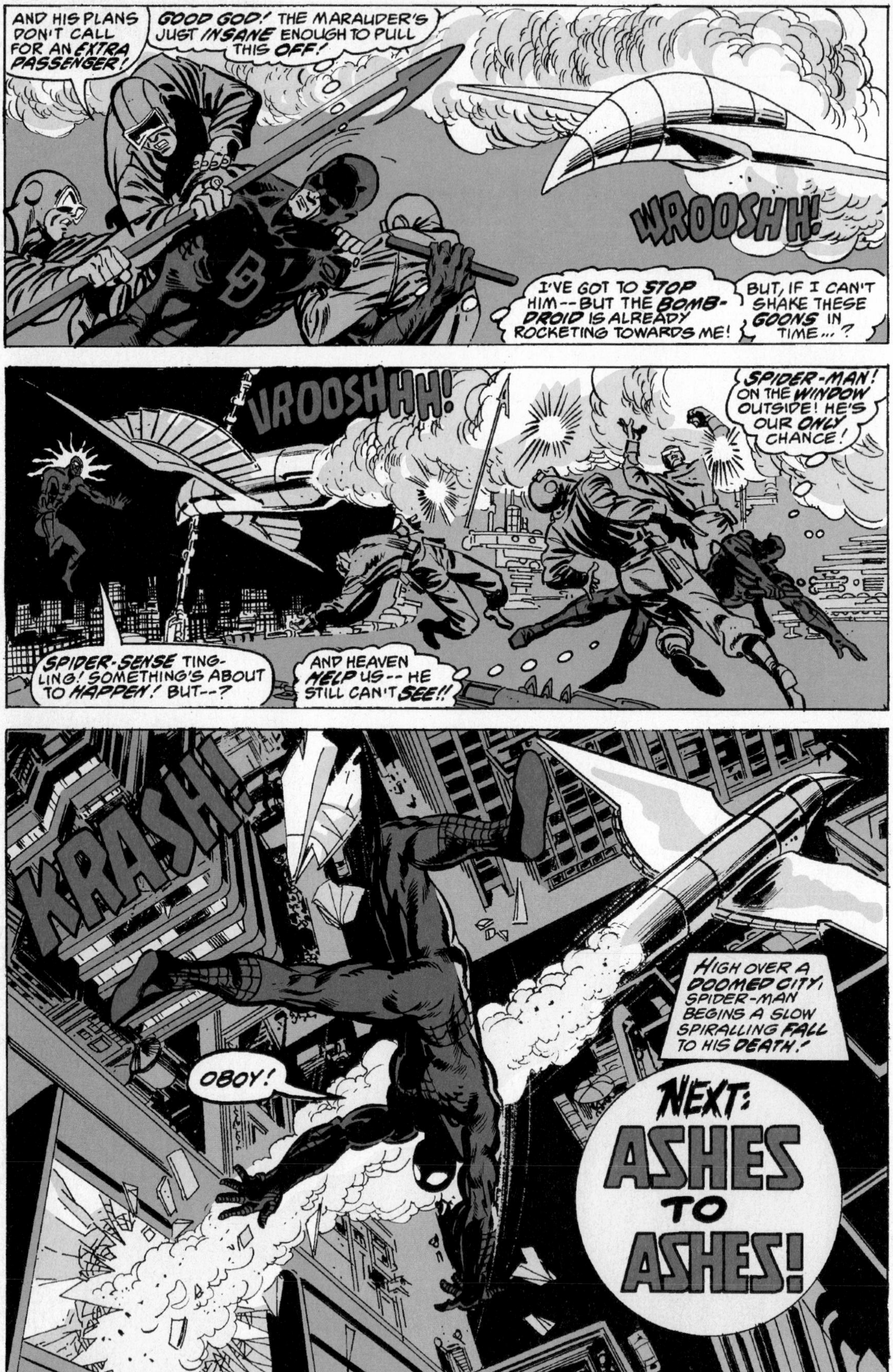
AND HIS PLANS DON'T CALL FOR AN EXTRA PASSENGER!
GOOD GOD! THE MARAUDER'S JUST INSANE ENOUGH TO PULL THIS OFF!
WROOSHH!
I'VE GOT TO STOP HIM--BUT THE BOMB-DROID IS ALREADY ROCKETING TOWARDS ME!
BUT, IF I CAN'T SHAKE THESE GOONS IN TIME...?
VROOSHHH!
SPIDER-MAN! ON THE WINDOW OUTSIDE! HE'S OUR ONLY CHANCE!
SPIDER-SENSE TINGLING! SOMETHING'S ABOUT TO HAPPEN! BUT--?
AND HEAVEN HELP US-- HE STILL CAN'T SEE!!
KRASH!
HIGH OVER A DOOMED CITY, SPIDER-MAN BEGINS A SLOW SPIRALLING FALL TO HIS DEATH!
OBOY!
NEXT: ASHES TO ASHES!

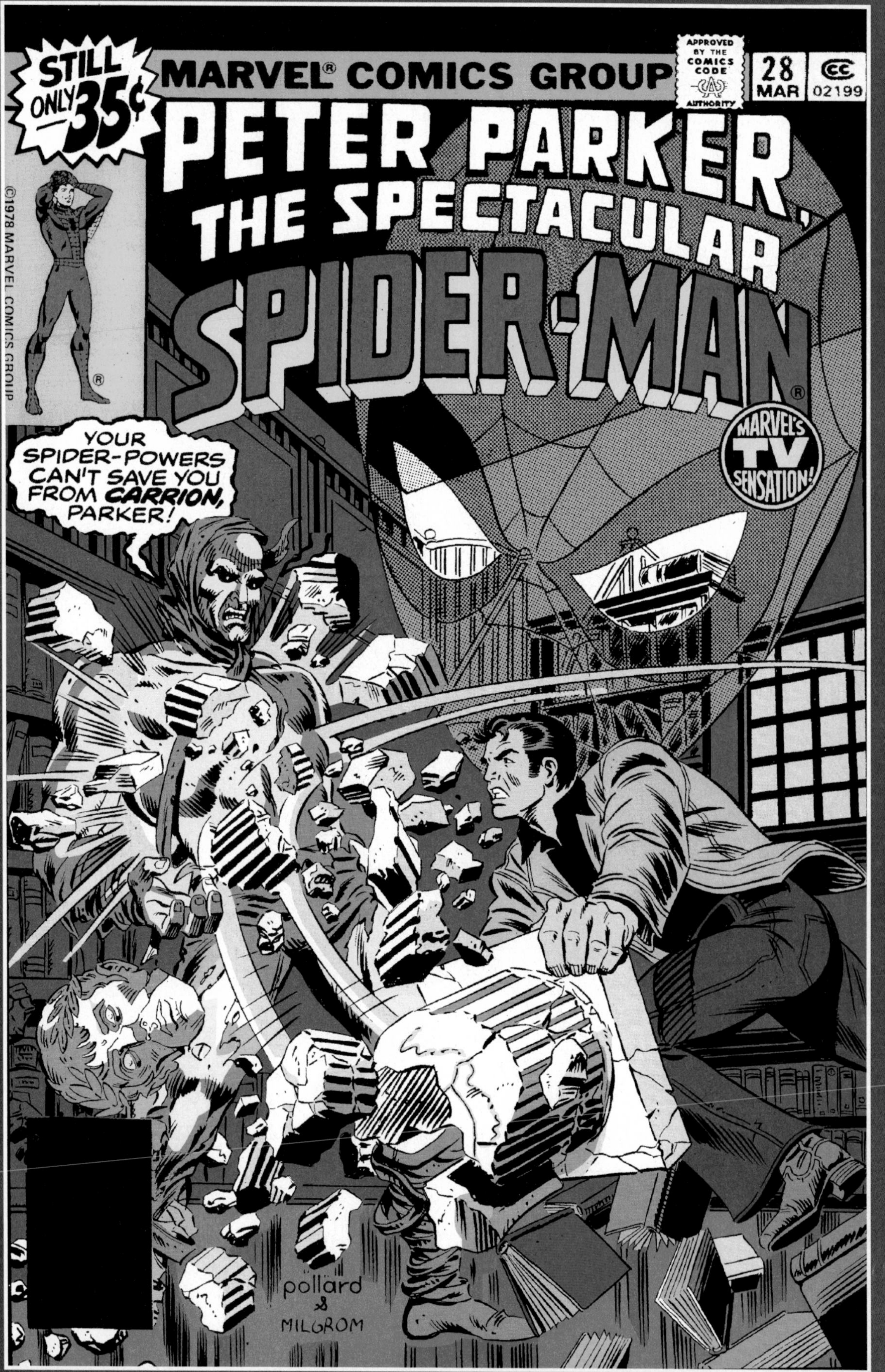
STILL ONLY 35¢
MARVEL® COMICS GROUP
APPROVED BY THE COMICS CODE AUTHORITY
28 MAR
CC 02199
PETER PARKER, THE SPECTACULAR SPIDER-MAN®
©1978 MARVEL COMICS GROUP
MARVEL'S TV SENSATION!
YOUR SPIDER-POWERS CAN'T SAVE YOU FROM CARRION, PARKER!
pollard & MILGROM

While attending a demonstration in radiology, student PETER PARKER was bitten by a spider which had accidentally been exposed to RADIOACTIVE RAYS. Through a miracle of science, Peter soon found that he had GAINED the arachnid's powers...and had, in effect, become a human spider...

Stan Lee PRESENTS: **THE SPECTACULAR SPIDER-MAN!** ®

HIGH ABOVE NEW YORK, A SIGHTLESS SPIDER-MAN BEGINS A SLOW SPIRAL-LING FALL TO HIS DEATH--

KKRASH!

VROOARR

OBOY!!

--WHILE THE MASKED MARAUDER'S BOMBDROID CARRIES ITS PLUTONIUM PAYLOAD OVER THE DOOMED CITY!

DAREDEVIL MUST NOT'VE BEEN ABLE TO STOP THE MARAUDER FROM LAUNCHING THE BIRDROID! I DON'T KNOW THE GAME PLAN--

--BUT I'M BETTING IT'S IMPORTANT THAT METAL MENACE BE STOPPED!

AND BLIND OR NOT-- STOP IT I WILL!

ALSO FEATURING: THE CADAVEROUS CARRION!!

ASHES to ASHES!

LG285

BILL MANTLO	FRANK MILLER and FRANK SPRINGER	DENISE WOHL and ELAINE HEINL	MARIO SEN	ALLEN MILGROM	JIM SHOOTER
WRITER	ARTISTS	LETTERERS	COLORIST	EDITOR	EDITOR-IN-CHIEF

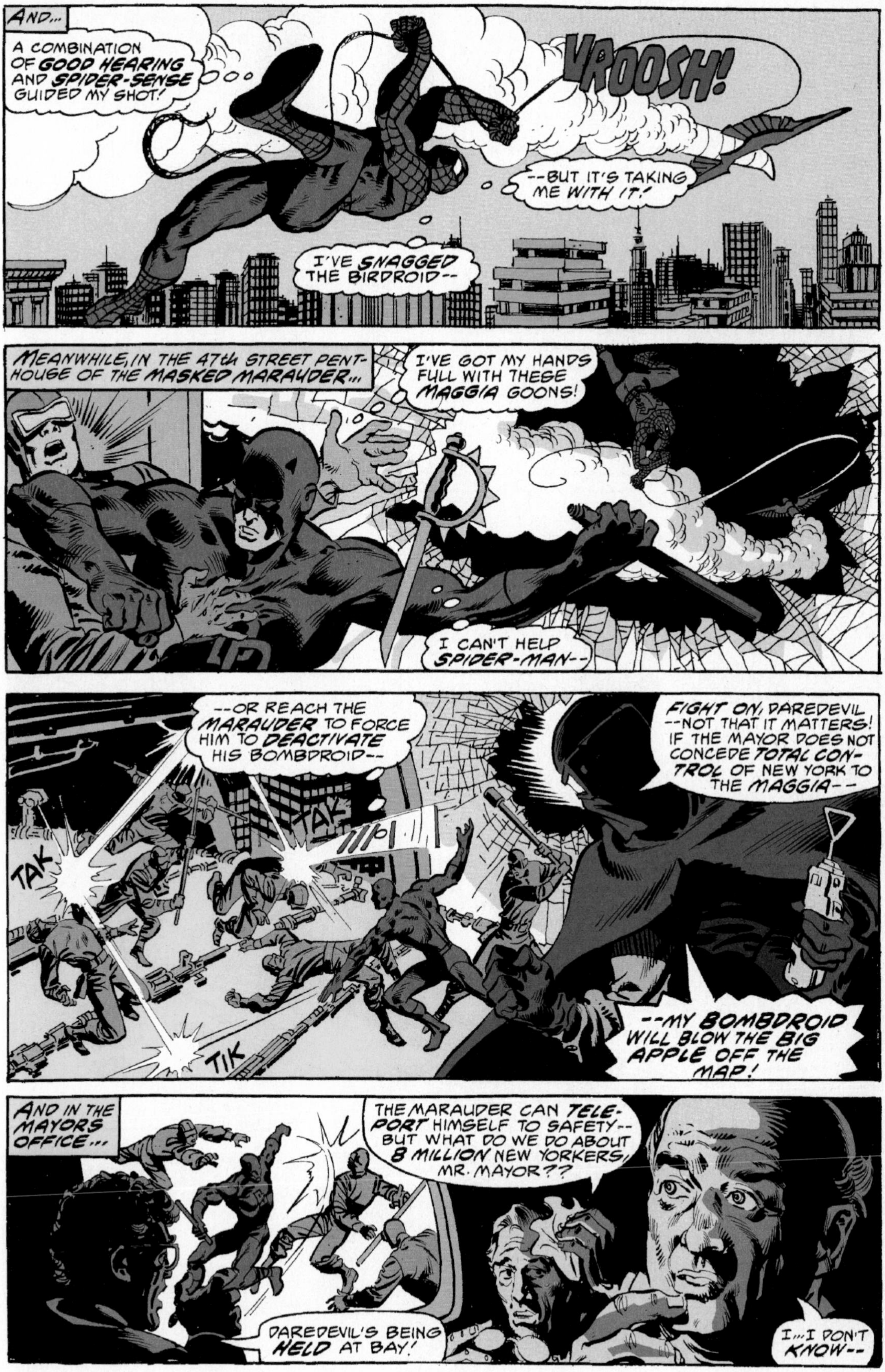
AND...
A COMBINATION OF GOOD HEARING AND SPIDER-SENSE GUIDED MY SHOT!
VROOSH!
I'VE SNAGGED THE BIRDROID--
--BUT IT'S TAKING ME WITH IT!
MEANWHILE, IN THE 47th STREET PENTHOUSE OF THE MASKED MARAUDER...
I'VE GOT MY HANDS FULL WITH THESE MAGGIA GOONS!
I CAN'T HELP SPIDER-MAN--
--OR REACH THE MARAUDER TO FORCE HIM TO DEACTIVATE HIS BOMBDROID--
TAK
TAK
TIK
FIGHT ON, DAREDEVIL --NOT THAT IT MATTERS! IF THE MAYOR DOES NOT CONCEDE TOTAL CONTROL OF NEW YORK TO THE MAGGIA--
--MY BOMBDROID WILL BLOW THE BIG APPLE OFF THE MAP!
AND IN THE MAYORS OFFICE...
DAREDEVIL'S BEING HELD AT BAY!
THE MARAUDER CAN TELEPORT HIMSELF TO SAFETY-- BUT WHAT DO WE DO ABOUT 8 MILLION NEW YORKERS, MR. MAYOR??
I...I DON'T KNOW--

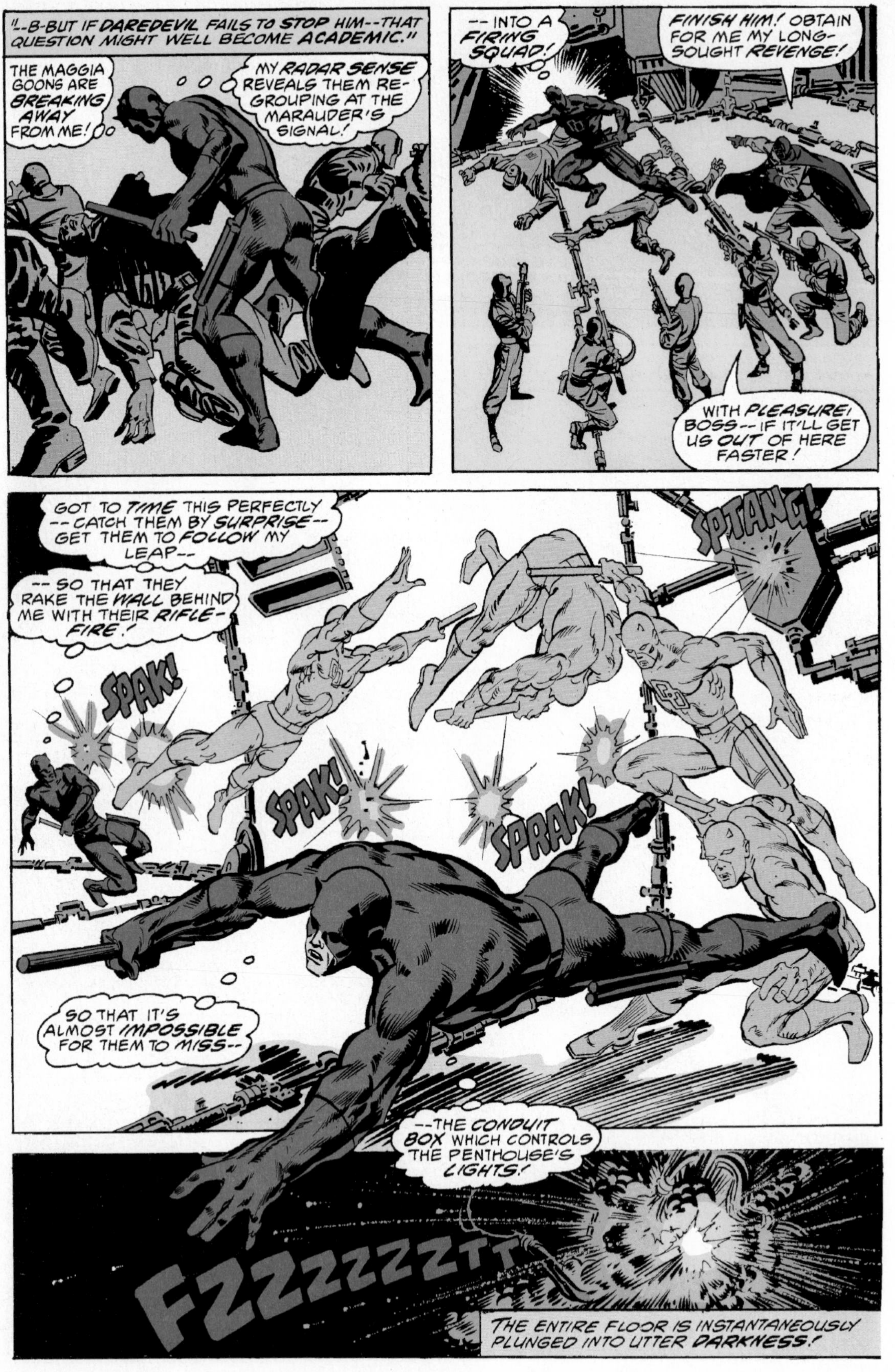
"--B-BUT IF DAREDEVIL FAILS TO STOP HIM--THAT QUESTION MIGHT WELL BECOME ACADEMIC."
THE MAGGIA GOONS ARE BREAKING AWAY FROM ME!
MY RADAR SENSE REVEALS THEM RE-GROUPING AT THE MARAUDER'S SIGNAL!
--INTO A FIRING SQUAD!
FINISH HIM! OBTAIN FOR ME MY LONG-SOUGHT REVENGE!
WITH PLEASURE, BOSS--IF IT'LL GET US OUT OF HERE FASTER!
GOT TO TIME THIS PERFECTLY --CATCH THEM BY SURPRISE-- GET THEM TO FOLLOW MY LEAP--
--SO THAT THEY RAKE THE WALL BEHIND ME WITH THEIR RIFLE-FIRE!
SPTANG!
SPAK!
SPAK!
SPRAK!
SO THAT IT'S ALMOST IMPOSSIBLE FOR THEM TO MISS--
--THE CONDUIT BOX WHICH CONTROLS THE PENTHOUSE'S LIGHTS!
FZZZZZZZTT
THE ENTIRE FLOOR IS INSTANTANEOUSLY PLUNGED INTO UTTER DARKNESS!

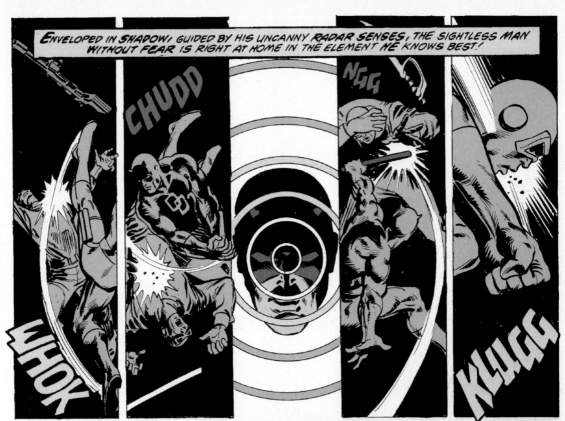

ENVELOPED IN SHADOW, GUIDED BY HIS UNCANNY *RADAR SENSES*, THE SIGHTLESS MAN WITHOUT FEAR IS RIGHT AT HOME IN THE ELEMENT *HE* KNOWS BEST!

CHUDD

NGG

WHOK

KLUGG

THAT'S THE *LAST* OF YOUR FLUNKIES, MARAUDER...

DAREDEVIL'S *MASK* MUST BE EQUIPPED--AS MINE IS--WITH *INFRARED LENSES*, ENABLING HIM TO SEE IN THE DARK! BUT IF HE THINKS ME *BLIND*....*HELPLESS*...AT HIS *MERCY*--

--HOW *LITTLE* HE HAS LEARNED OF MY *POWER* OVER THE YEARS!

SHKROW!

YEEAGGHH!!

THE IMPACT OF MY *EYE-BLASTS* IS *PHYSICAL* AS WELL AS OPTICAL, YOU COSTUMED CRETIN!

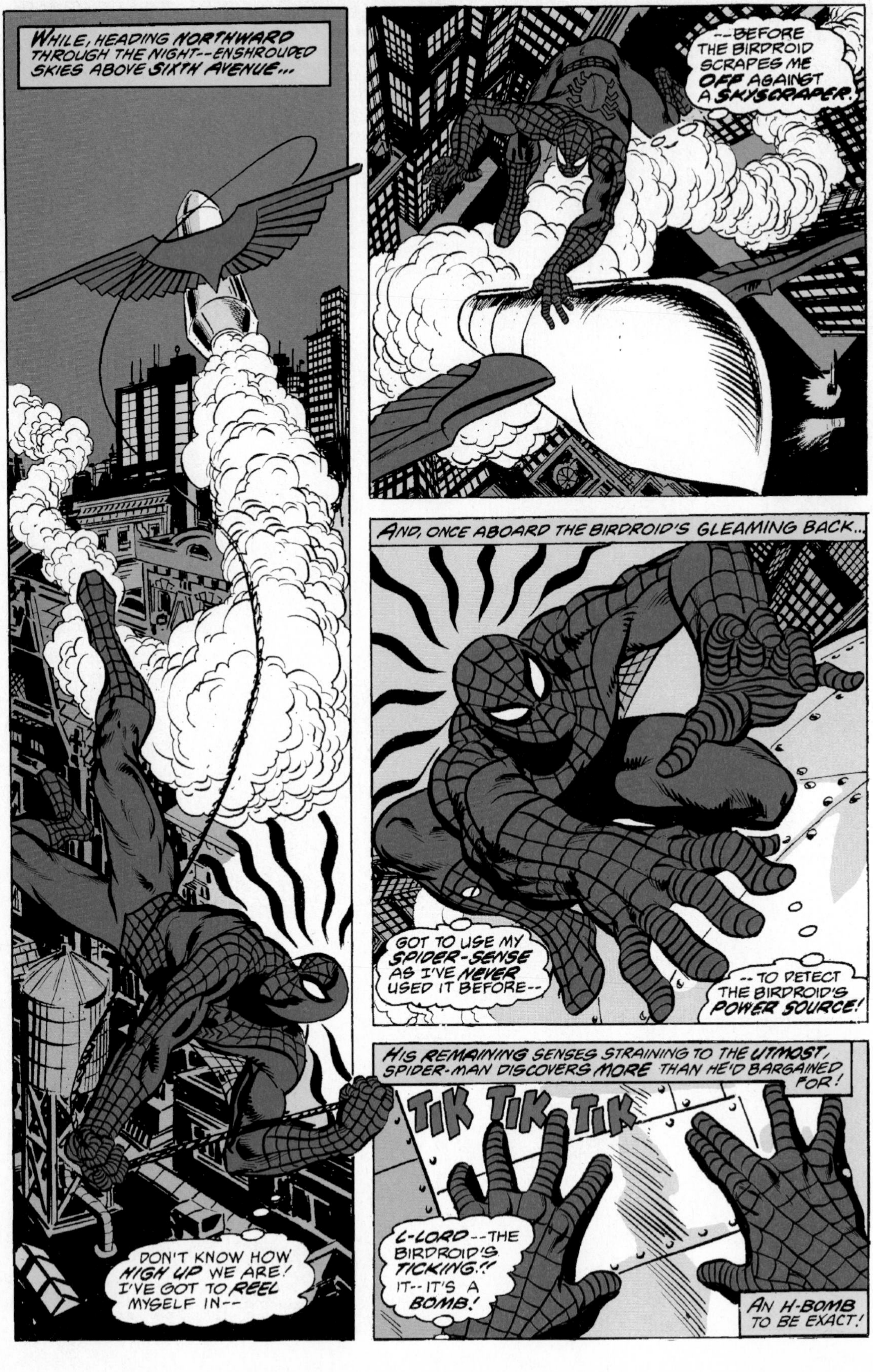
WHILE, HEADING NORTHWARD THROUGH THE NIGHT--ENSHROUDED SKIES ABOVE SIXTH AVENUE...
DON'T KNOW HOW HIGH UP WE ARE! I'VE GOT TO REEL MYSELF IN--
--BEFORE THE BIRDROID SCRAPES ME OFF AGAINST A SKYSCRAPER.
AND, ONCE ABOARD THE BIRDROID'S GLEAMING BACK...
GOT TO USE MY SPIDER-SENSE AS I'VE NEVER USED IT BEFORE--
--TO DETECT THE BIRDROID'S POWER SOURCE!
HIS REMAINING SENSES STRAINING TO THE UTMOST, SPIDER-MAN DISCOVERS MORE THAN HE'D BARGAINED FOR!
TIK TIK TIK
L-LORD--THE BIRDROID'S TICKING?! IT--IT'S A BOMB!
AN H-BOMB TO BE EXACT!

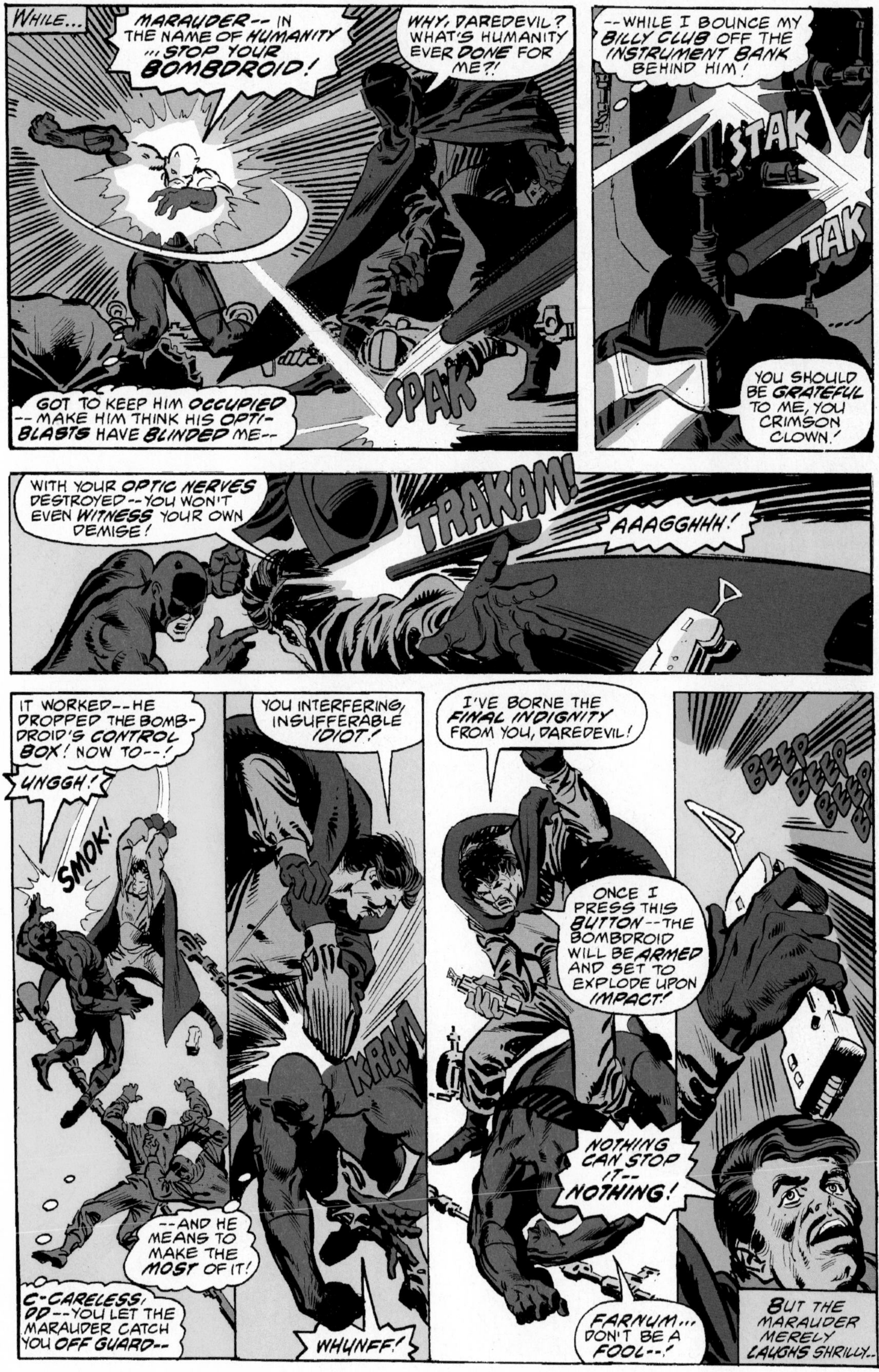
WHILE...
MARAUDER-- IN THE NAME OF HUMANITY ...STOP YOUR BOMBDROID!
WHY, DAREDEVIL? WHAT'S HUMANITY EVER DONE FOR ME?!
GOT TO KEEP HIM OCCUPIED -- MAKE HIM THINK HIS OPTI-BLASTS HAVE BLINDED ME--
SPAK
--WHILE I BOUNCE MY BILLY CLUB OFF THE INSTRUMENT BANK BEHIND HIM!
STAK
TAK
YOU SHOULD BE GRATEFUL TO ME, YOU CRIMSON CLOWN!
WITH YOUR OPTIC NERVES DESTROYED--YOU WON'T EVEN WITNESS YOUR OWN DEMISE!
TRAKAM!
AAAGGHHH!
IT WORKED--HE DROPPED THE BOMB-DROID'S CONTROL BOX! NOW TO--!
UNGGH!
SMOK!
--AND HE MEANS TO MAKE THE MOST OF IT!
C-CARELESS, DD--YOU LET THE MARAUDER CATCH YOU OFF GUARD--
YOU INTERFERING, INSUFFERABLE IDIOT!
KRAM
WHUNFF!
I'VE BORNE THE FINAL INDIGNITY FROM YOU, DAREDEVIL!
ONCE I PRESS THIS BUTTON--THE BOMBDROID WILL BE ARMED AND SET TO EXPLODE UPON IMPACT!
NOTHING CAN STOP IT-- NOTHING!
FARNUM... DON'T BE A FOOL--!
BEEP BEEP BEEP
BUT THE MARAUDER MERELY LAUGHS SHRILLY...

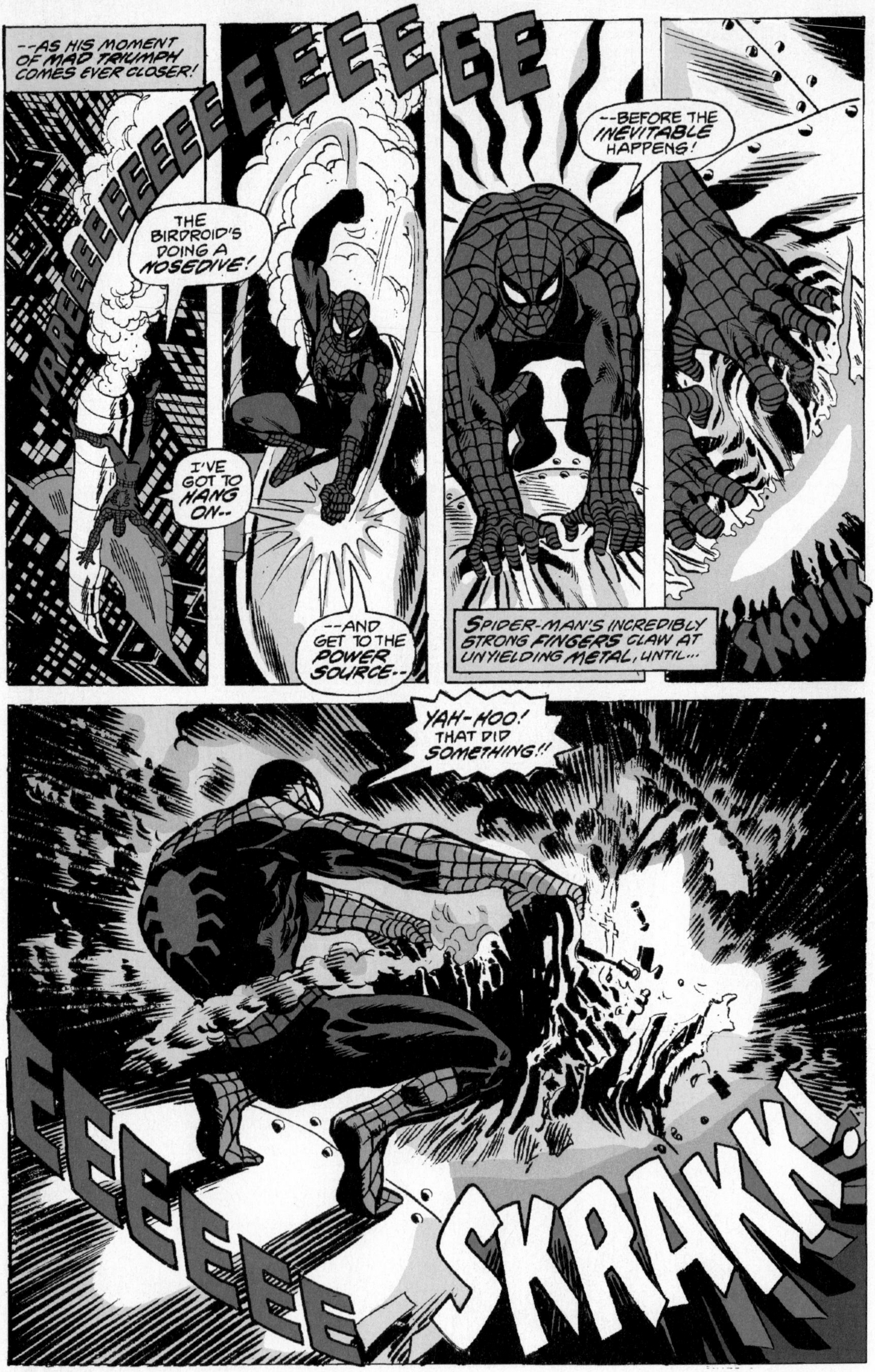
--AS HIS MOMENT OF MAD TRIUMPH COMES EVER CLOSER!
VREEEEEEEEEEEEEEE
THE BIRDROID'S DOING A NOSEDIVE!
I'VE GOT TO HANG ON--
--AND GET TO THE POWER SOURCE--
--BEFORE THE INEVITABLE HAPPENS!
SPIDER-MAN'S INCREDIBLY STRONG FINGERS CLAW AT UNYIELDING METAL, UNTIL...
SKRIIK
YAH-HOO! THAT DID SOMETHING!!
EEEEEE
SKRAKK!

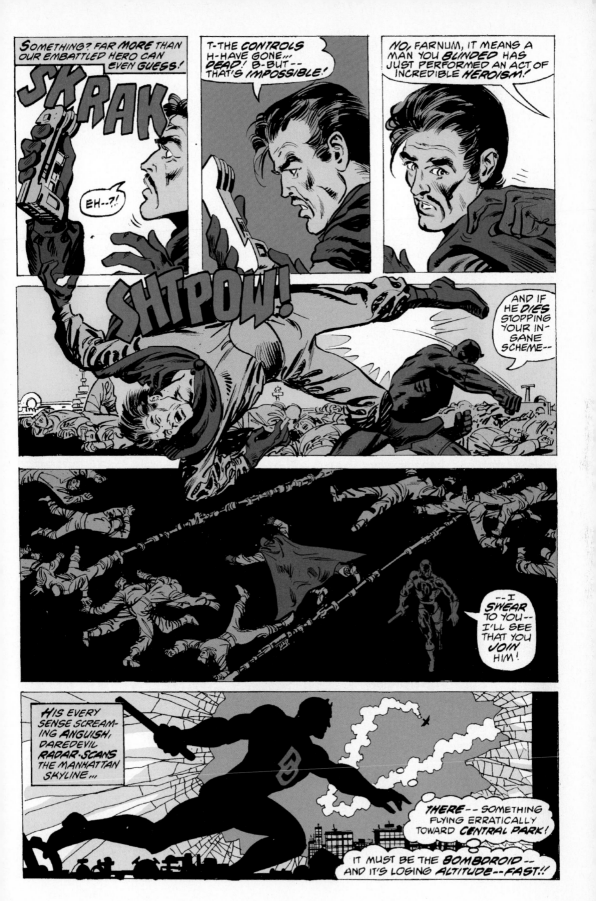

SOMETHING? FAR MORE THAN OUR EMBATTLED HERO CAN EVEN GUESS!

SKRAK

EH--?!

T-THE CONTROLS H-HAVE GONE... DEAD! B-BUT-- THAT'S IMPOSSIBLE!

NO, FARNUM, IT MEANS A MAN YOU BLINDED HAS JUST PERFORMED AN ACT OF INCREDIBLE HEROISM!

SHTPOW!

AND IF HE DIES STOPPING YOUR INSANE SCHEME--

--I SWEAR TO YOU-- I'LL SEE THAT YOU JOIN HIM!

HIS EVERY SENSE SCREAMING ANGUISH, DAREDEVIL RADAR-SCANS THE MANHATTAN SKYLINE...

THERE-- SOMETHING FLYING ERRATICALLY TOWARD CENTRAL PARK!

IT MUST BE THE BOMBOROID-- AND IT'S LOSING ALTITUDE--FAST!!

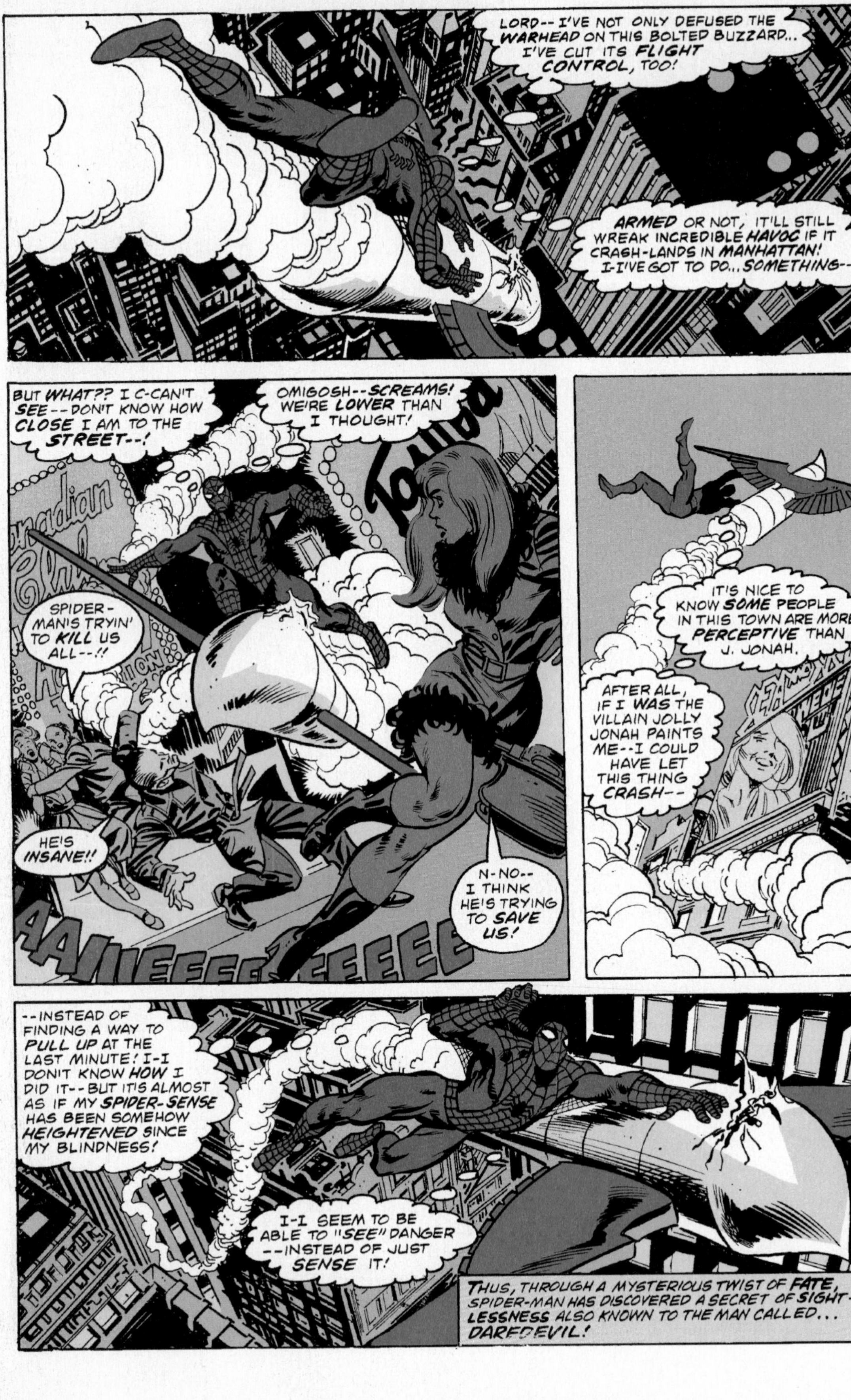
LORD-- I'VE NOT ONLY DEFUSED THE WARHEAD ON THIS BOLTED BUZZARD... I'VE CUT ITS FLIGHT CONTROL, TOO!
ARMED OR NOT, IT'LL STILL WREAK INCREDIBLE HAVOC IF IT CRASH-LANDS IN MANHATTAN! I-I'VE GOT TO DO... SOMETHING--!
BUT WHAT?? I C-CAN'T SEE--DON'T KNOW HOW CLOSE I AM TO THE STREET--!
OMIGOSH--SCREAMS! WE'RE LOWER THAN I THOUGHT!
SPIDER-MAN'S TRYIN' TO KILL US ALL--!!
HE'S INSANE!!
N-NO-- I THINK HE'S TRYING TO SAVE US!
IT'S NICE TO KNOW SOME PEOPLE IN THIS TOWN ARE MORE PERCEPTIVE THAN J. JONAH.
AFTER ALL, IF I WAS THE VILLAIN JOLLY JONAH PAINTS ME--I COULD HAVE LET THIS THING CRASH--
--INSTEAD OF FINDING A WAY TO PULL UP AT THE LAST MINUTE! I-I DON'T KNOW HOW I DID IT--BUT IT'S ALMOST AS IF MY SPIDER-SENSE HAS BEEN SOMEHOW HEIGHTENED SINCE MY BLINDNESS!
I-I SEEM TO BE ABLE TO "SEE" DANGER --INSTEAD OF JUST SENSE IT!
THUS, THROUGH A MYSTERIOUS TWIST OF FATE, SPIDER-MAN HAS DISCOVERED A SECRET OF SIGHT-LESSNESS ALSO KNOWN TO THE MAN CALLED... DAREDEVIL!

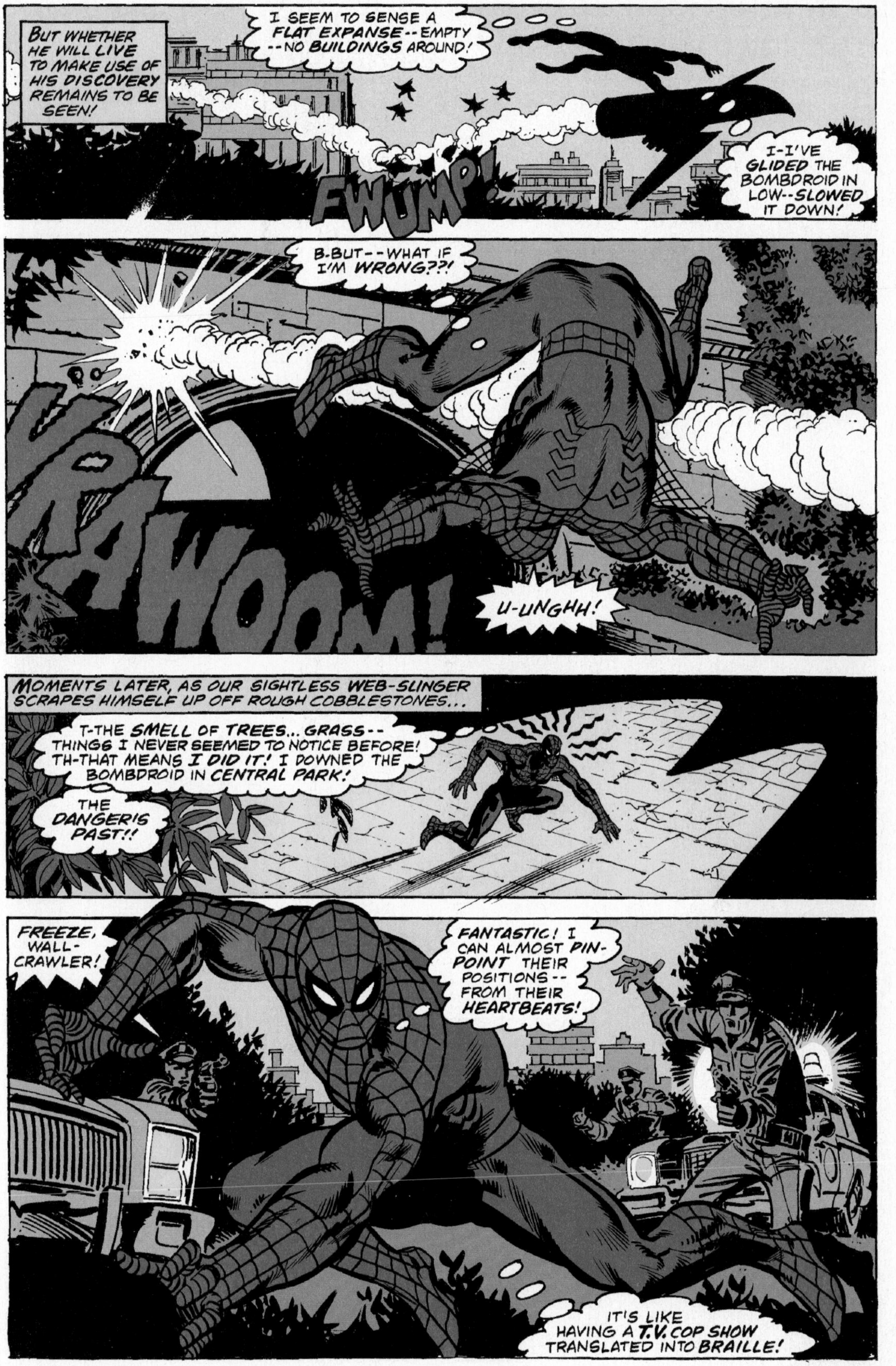
BUT WHETHER HE WILL LIVE TO MAKE USE OF HIS DISCOVERY REMAINS TO BE SEEN!
I SEEM TO SENSE A FLAT EXPANSE--EMPTY --NO BUILDINGS AROUND!
I-I'VE GLIDED THE BOMBDROID IN LOW--SLOWED IT DOWN!
FWUMP!
B-BUT--WHAT IF I'M WRONG??!
KRAWOOM!
U-UNGHH!
MOMENTS LATER, AS OUR SIGHTLESS WEB-SLINGER SCRAPES HIMSELF UP OFF ROUGH COBBLESTONES...
T-THE SMELL OF TREES... GRASS-- THINGS I NEVER SEEMED TO NOTICE BEFORE! TH-THAT MEANS I DID IT! I DOWNED THE BOMBDROID IN CENTRAL PARK!
THE DANGER'S PAST!!
FREEZE, WALL-CRAWLER!
FANTASTIC! I CAN ALMOST PIN-POINT THEIR POSITIONS-- FROM THEIR HEARTBEATS!
IT'S LIKE HAVING A T.V. COP SHOW TRANSLATED INTO BRAILLE!

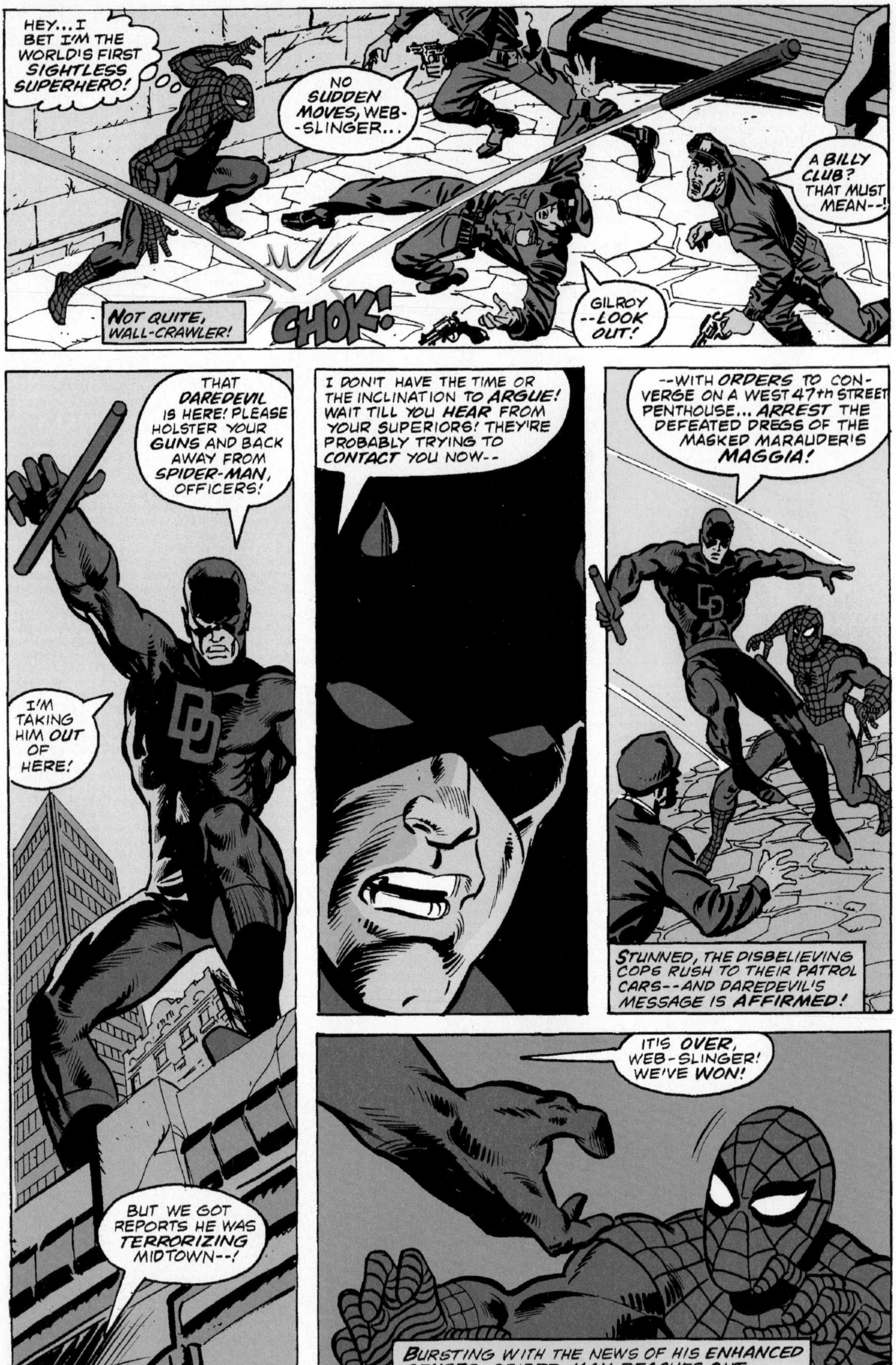
HEY...I BET I'M THE WORLD'S FIRST SIGHTLESS SUPERHERO!
NO SUDDEN MOVES, WEB-SLINGER...
A BILLY CLUB? THAT MUST MEAN--!
NOT QUITE, WALL-CRAWLER!
CHOK!
GILROY--LOOK OUT!
THAT DAREDEVIL IS HERE! PLEASE HOLSTER YOUR GUNS AND BACK AWAY FROM SPIDER-MAN, OFFICERS!
I'M TAKING HIM OUT OF HERE!
BUT WE GOT REPORTS HE WAS TERRORIZING MIDTOWN--!
I DON'T HAVE THE TIME OR THE INCLINATION TO ARGUE! WAIT TILL YOU HEAR FROM YOUR SUPERIORS! THEY'RE PROBABLY TRYING TO CONTACT YOU NOW--
--WITH ORDERS TO CONVERGE ON A WEST 47th STREET PENTHOUSE... ARREST THE DEFEATED DREGS OF THE MASKED MARAUDER'S MAGGIA!
STUNNED, THE DISBELIEVING COPS RUSH TO THEIR PATROL CARS--AND DAREDEVIL'S MESSAGE IS AFFIRMED!
IT'S OVER, WEB-SLINGER! WE'VE WON!
BURSTING WITH THE NEWS OF HIS ENHANCED SENSES, SPIDER-MAN REACHES OUT--

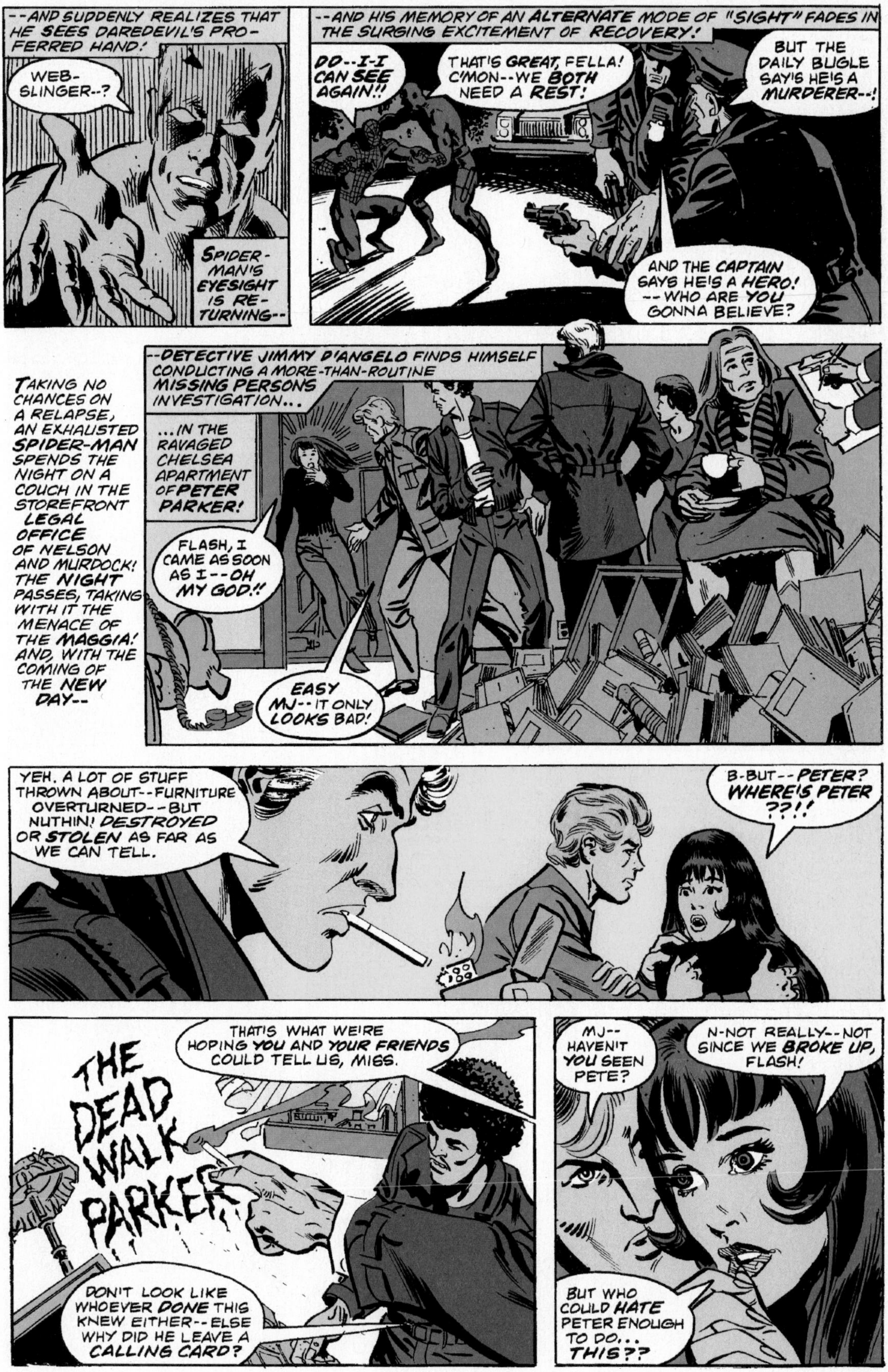
--AND SUDDENLY REALIZES THAT HE SEES DAREDEVIL'S PRO- FERRED HAND!
WEB- SLINGER--?
SPIDER- MAN'S EYESIGHT IS RE- TURNING--
--AND HIS MEMORY OF AN ALTERNATE MODE OF "SIGHT" FADES IN THE SURGING EXCITEMENT OF RECOVERY!
DO--I-I CAN SEE AGAIN!!
THAT'S GREAT, FELLA! C'MON--WE BOTH NEED A REST!
BUT THE DAILY BUGLE SAY'S HE'S A MURDERER--!
AND THE CAPTAIN SAYS HE'S A HERO! --WHO ARE YOU GONNA BELIEVE?
TAKING NO CHANCES ON A RELAPSE, AN EXHAUSTED SPIDER-MAN SPENDS THE NIGHT ON A COUCH IN THE STOREFRONT LEGAL OFFICE OF NELSON AND MURDOCK! THE NIGHT PASSES, TAKING WITH IT THE MENACE OF THE MAGGIA! AND, WITH THE COMING OF THE NEW DAY--
--DETECTIVE JIMMY D'ANGELO FINDS HIMSELF CONDUCTING A MORE-THAN-ROUTINE MISSING PERSONS INVESTIGATION...
...IN THE RAVAGED CHELSEA APARTMENT OF PETER PARKER!
FLASH, I CAME AS SOON AS I--OH MY GOD!!
EASY MJ--IT ONLY LOOKS BAD!
YEH. A LOT OF STUFF THROWN ABOUT--FURNITURE OVERTURNED--BUT NUTHIN' DESTROYED OR STOLEN AS FAR AS WE CAN TELL.
B-BUT--PETER? WHERE'S PETER ??!!
THE DEAD WALK PARKER
THAT'S WHAT WE'RE HOPING YOU AND YOUR FRIENDS COULD TELL US, MISS.
DON'T LOOK LIKE WHOEVER DONE THIS KNEW EITHER--ELSE WHY DID HE LEAVE A CALLING CARD?
MJ-- HAVEN'T YOU SEEN PETE?
N-NOT REALLY--NOT SINCE WE BROKE UP, FLASH!
BUT WHO COULD HATE PETER ENOUGH TO DO... THIS??

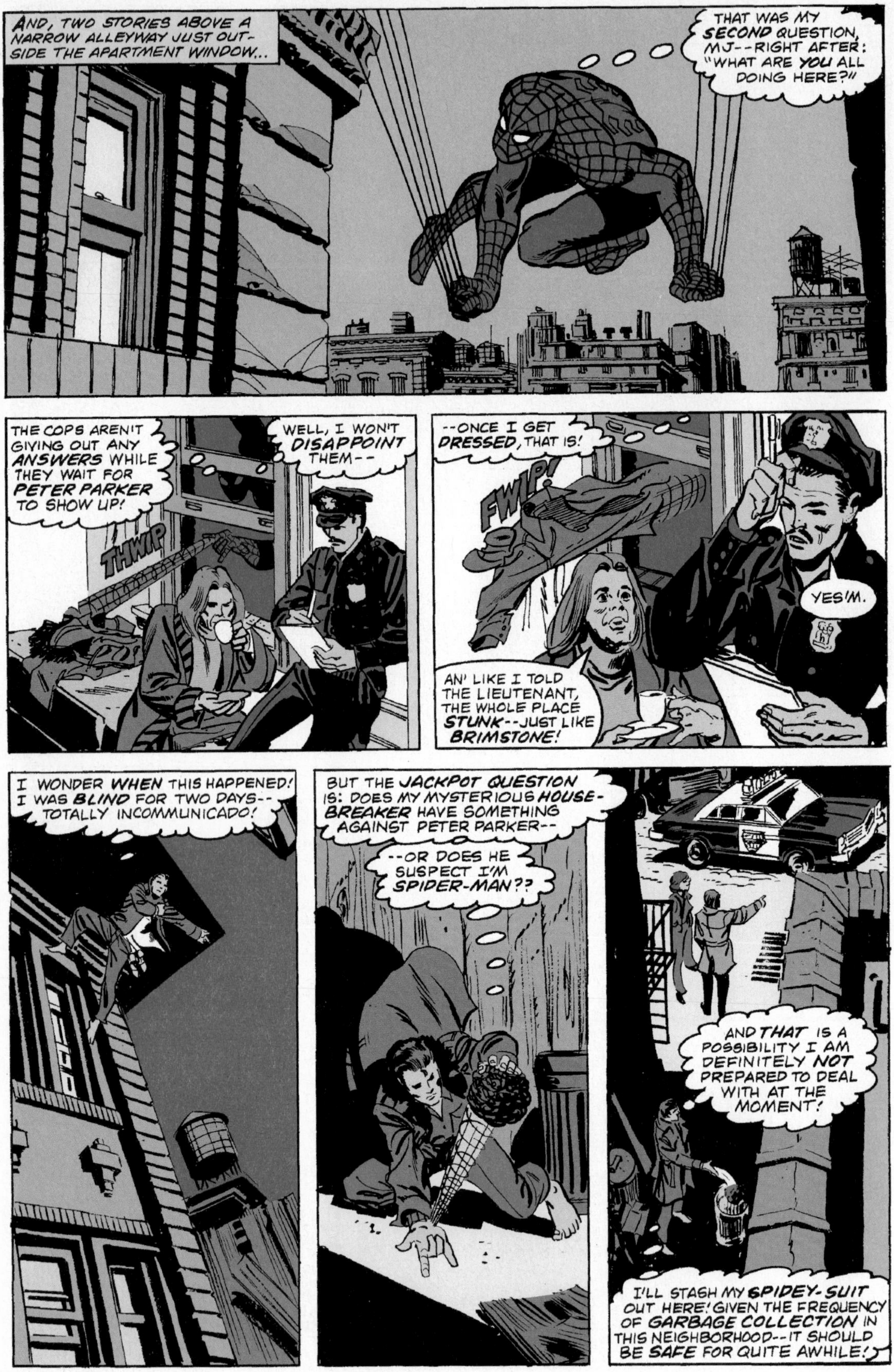
AND, TWO STORIES ABOVE A NARROW ALLEYWAY JUST OUTSIDE THE APARTMENT WINDOW...
THAT WAS MY SECOND QUESTION, MJ--RIGHT AFTER: "WHAT ARE YOU ALL DOING HERE?"
THE COPS AREN'T GIVING OUT ANY ANSWERS WHILE THEY WAIT FOR PETER PARKER TO SHOW UP!
WELL, I WON'T DISAPPOINT THEM--
THWIP
--ONCE I GET DRESSED, THAT IS!
FWIP!
YES'M.
AN' LIKE I TOLD THE LIEUTENANT, THE WHOLE PLACE STUNK--JUST LIKE BRIMSTONE!
I WONDER WHEN THIS HAPPENED! I WAS BLIND FOR TWO DAYS--TOTALLY INCOMMUNICADO!
BUT THE JACKPOT QUESTION IS: DOES MY MYSTERIOUS HOUSE-BREAKER HAVE SOMETHING AGAINST PETER PARKER--
--OR DOES HE SUSPECT I'M SPIDER-MAN??
AND THAT IS A POSSIBILITY I AM DEFINITELY NOT PREPARED TO DEAL WITH AT THE MOMENT!
I'LL STASH MY SPIDEY-SUIT OUT HERE! GIVEN THE FREQUENCY OF GARBAGE COLLECTION IN THIS NEIGHBORHOOD--IT SHOULD BE SAFE FOR QUITE AWHILE!

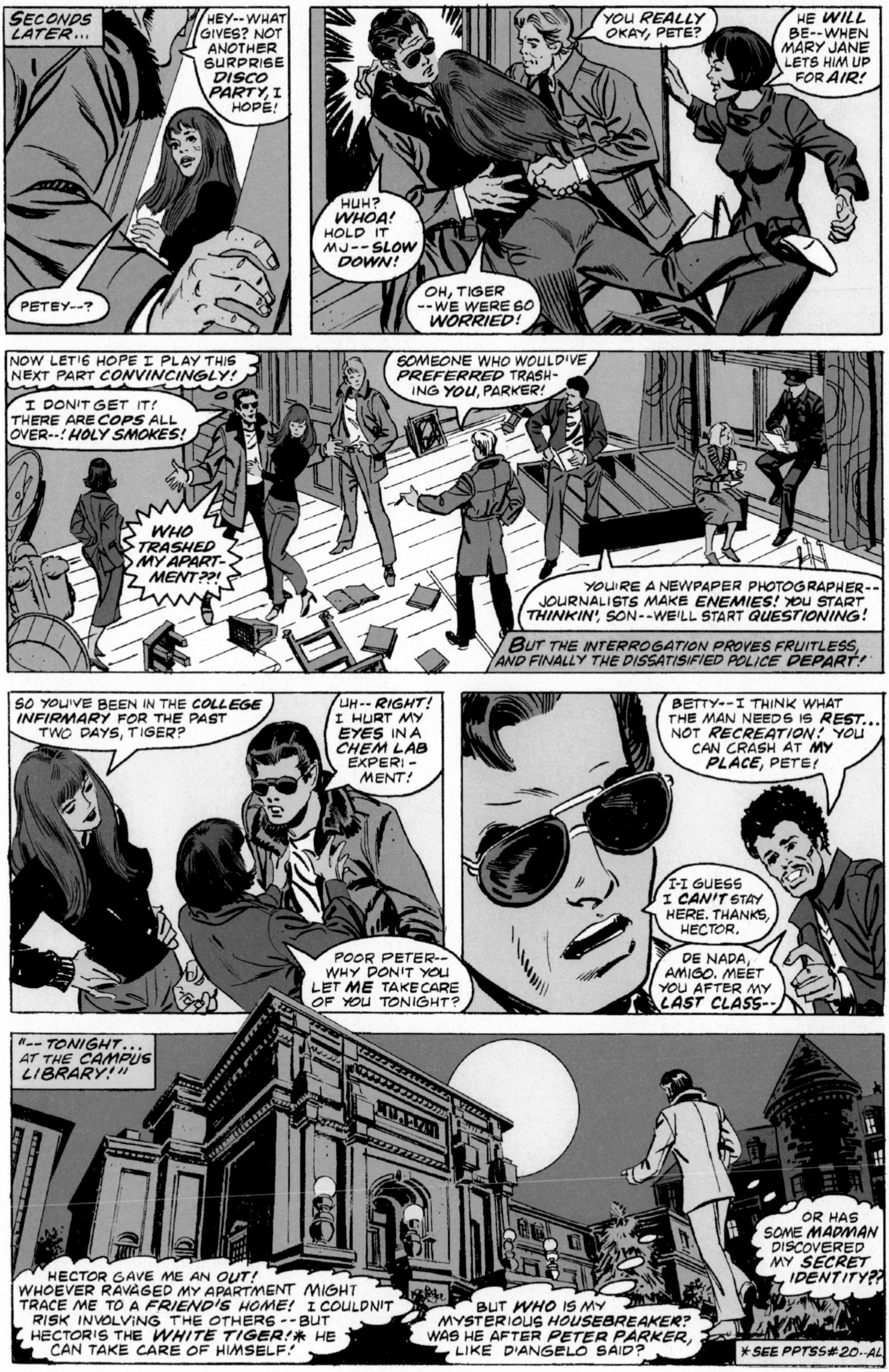

SECONDS LATER...
HEY--WHAT GIVES? NOT ANOTHER SURPRISE DISCO PARTY, I HOPE!
PETEY--?
YOU REALLY OKAY, PETE?
HE WILL BE--WHEN MARY JANE LETS HIM UP FOR AIR!
HUH? WHOA! HOLD IT MJ--SLOW DOWN!
OH, TIGER --WE WERE SO WORRIED!
NOW LET'S HOPE I PLAY THIS NEXT PART CONVINCINGLY!
I DON'T GET IT! THERE ARE COPS ALL OVER--! HOLY SMOKES!
WHO TRASHED MY APARTMENT??!
SOMEONE WHO WOULD'VE PREFERRED TRASHING YOU, PARKER!
YOU'RE A NEWPAPER PHOTOGRAPHER-- JOURNALISTS MAKE ENEMIES! YOU START THINKIN', SON--WE'LL START QUESTIONING!
BUT THE INTERROGATION PROVES FRUITLESS, AND FINALLY THE DISSATISIFIED POLICE DEPART!
SO YOU'VE BEEN IN THE COLLEGE INFIRMARY FOR THE PAST TWO DAYS, TIGER?
UH--RIGHT! I HURT MY EYES IN A CHEM LAB EXPERIMENT!
POOR PETER-- WHY DON'T YOU LET ME TAKE CARE OF YOU TONIGHT?
BETTY--I THINK WHAT THE MAN NEEDS IS REST... NOT RECREATION! YOU CAN CRASH AT MY PLACE, PETE!
I-I GUESS I CAN'T STAY HERE. THANKS, HECTOR.
DE NADA, AMIGO. MEET YOU AFTER MY LAST CLASS--
"--TONIGHT... AT THE CAMPUS LIBRARY!"
HECTOR GAVE ME AN OUT! WHOEVER RAVAGED MY APARTMENT MIGHT TRACE ME TO A FRIEND'S HOME! I COULDN'T RISK INVOLVING THE OTHERS--BUT HECTOR'S THE WHITE TIGER!* HE CAN TAKE CARE OF HIMSELF!
BUT WHO IS MY MYSTERIOUS HOUSEBREAKER? WAS HE AFTER PETER PARKER, LIKE D'ANGELO SAID?
OR HAS SOME MADMAN DISCOVERED MY SECRET IDENTITY??
*SEE PPTSS#20--AL

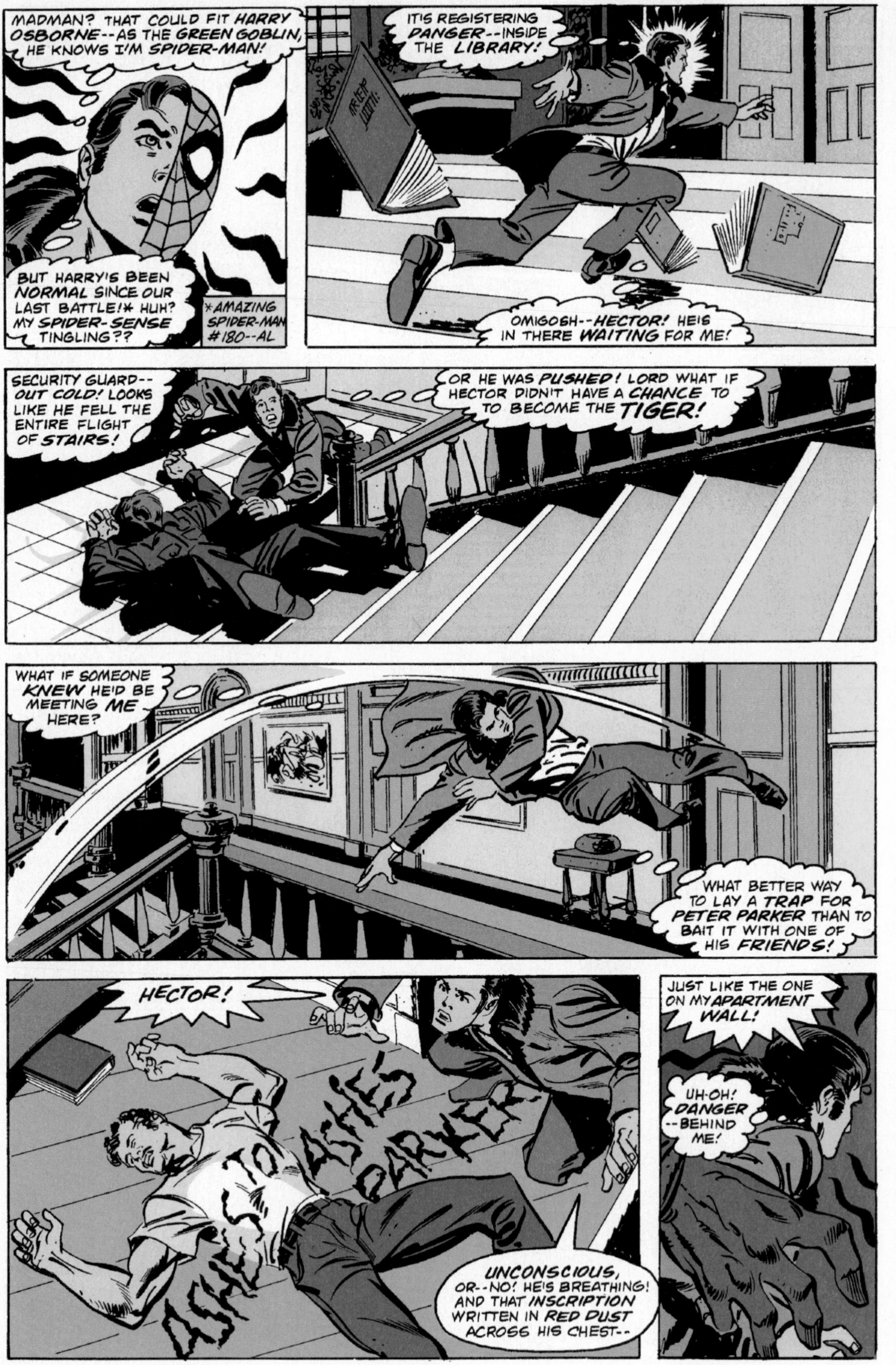
MADMAN? THAT COULD FIT HARRY OSBORNE--AS THE GREEN GOBLIN, HE KNOWS I'M SPIDER-MAN!
BUT HARRY'S BEEN NORMAL SINCE OUR LAST BATTLE!* HUH? MY SPIDER-SENSE TINGLING??
*AMAZING SPIDER-MAN #180--AL
IT'S REGISTERING DANGER--INSIDE THE LIBRARY!
OMIGOSH--HECTOR! HE'S IN THERE WAITING FOR ME!
SECURITY GUARD--OUT COLD! LOOKS LIKE HE FELL THE ENTIRE FLIGHT OF STAIRS!
OR HE WAS PUSHED! LORD WHAT IF HECTOR DIDN'T HAVE A CHANCE TO TO BECOME THE TIGER!
WHAT IF SOMEONE KNEW HE'D BE MEETING ME HERE?
WHAT BETTER WAY TO LAY A TRAP FOR PETER PARKER THAN TO BAIT IT WITH ONE OF HIS FRIENDS!
HECTOR!
ASHES TO ASHES PARKER
UNCONSCIOUS, OR--NO! HE'S BREATHING! AND THAT INSCRIPTION WRITTEN IN RED DUST ACROSS HIS CHEST--
JUST LIKE THE ONE ON MY APARTMENT WALL!
UH-OH! DANGER--BEHIND ME!

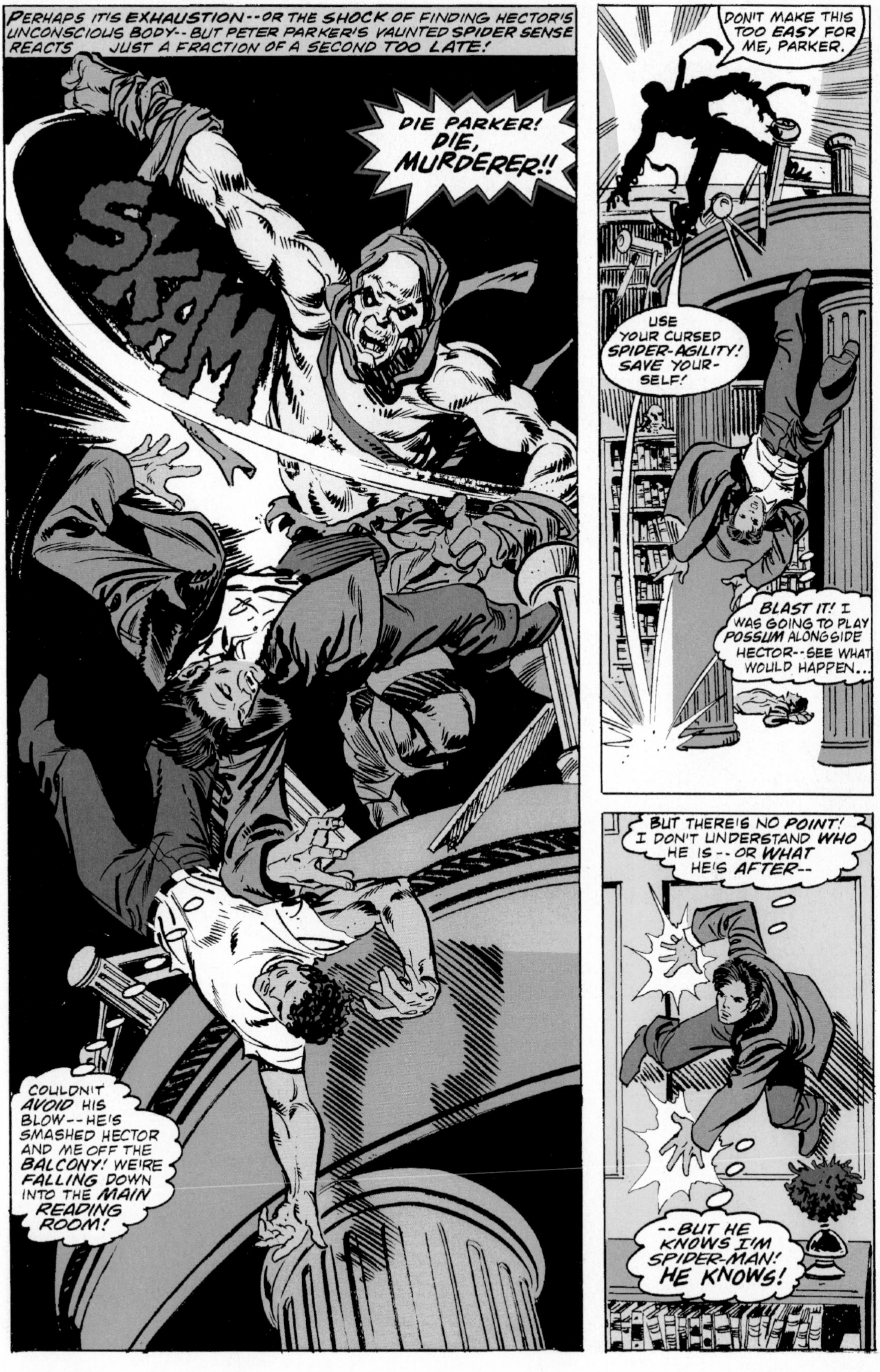
PERHAPS IT'S EXHAUSTION--OR THE SHOCK OF FINDING HECTOR'S UNCONSCIOUS BODY--BUT PETER PARKER'S VAUNTED SPIDER SENSE REACTS JUST A FRACTION OF A SECOND TOO LATE!
DIE PARKER! DIE, MURDERER!!
SLAM
COULDN'T AVOID HIS BLOW--HE'S SMASHED HECTOR AND ME OFF THE BALCONY! WE'RE FALLING DOWN INTO THE MAIN READING ROOM!
DON'T MAKE THIS TOO EASY FOR ME, PARKER.
USE YOUR CURSED SPIDER-AGILITY! SAVE YOURSELF!
BLAST IT! I WAS GOING TO PLAY POSSUM ALONGSIDE HECTOR--SEE WHAT WOULD HAPPEN...
BUT THERE'S NO POINT! I DON'T UNDERSTAND WHO HE IS--OR WHAT HE'S AFTER--
--BUT HE KNOWS I'M SPIDER-MAN! HE KNOWS!

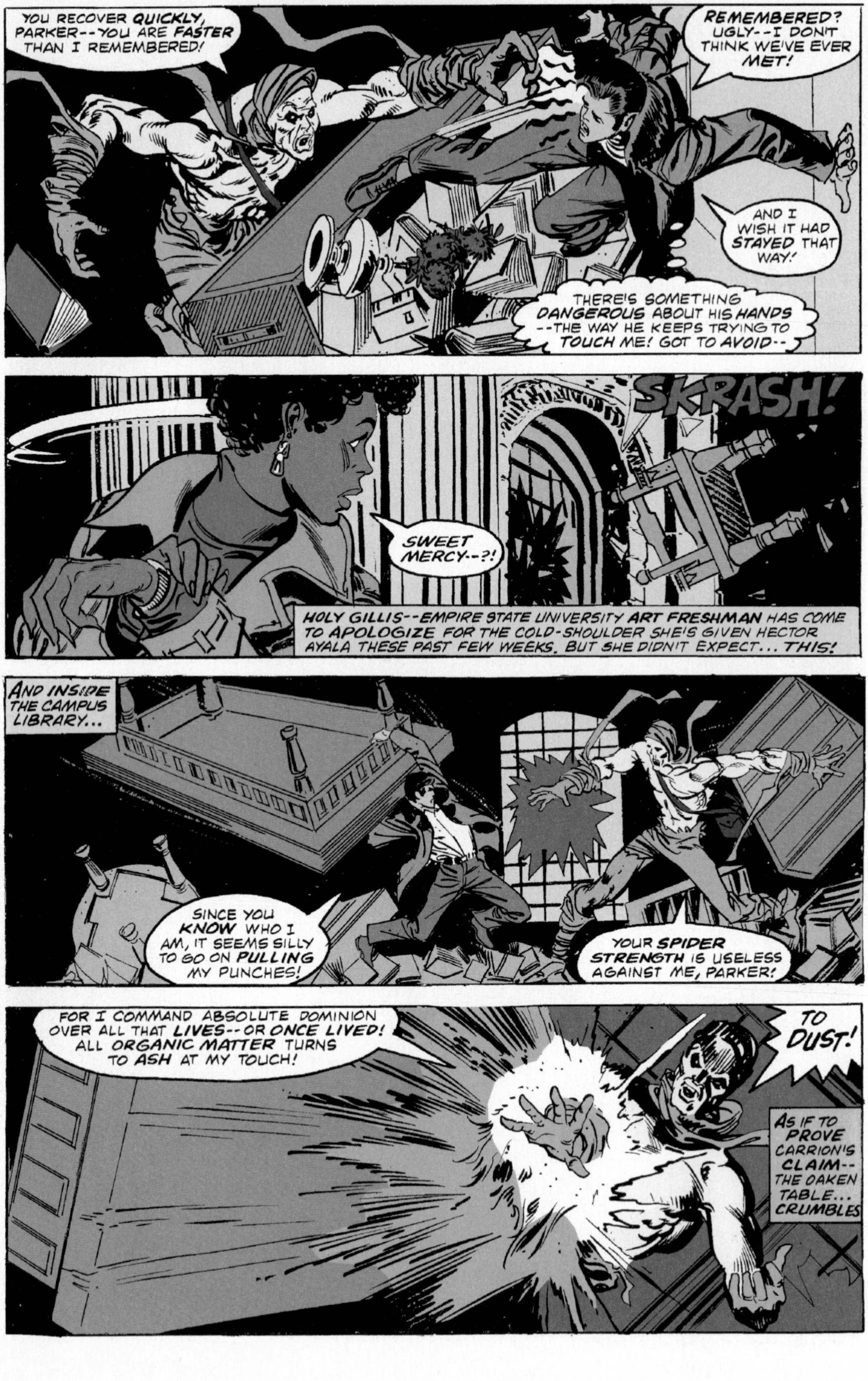
YOU RECOVER QUICKLY, PARKER--YOU ARE FASTER THAN I REMEMBERED!
REMEMBERED? UGLY--I DON'T THINK WE'VE EVER MET!
AND I WISH IT HAD STAYED THAT WAY!
THERE'S SOMETHING DANGEROUS ABOUT HIS HANDS--THE WAY HE KEEPS TRYING TO TOUCH ME! GOT TO AVOID--
SKRASH!
SWEET MERCY--?!
HOLY GILLIS--EMPIRE STATE UNIVERSITY ART FRESHMAN HAS COME TO APOLOGIZE FOR THE COLD-SHOULDER SHE'S GIVEN HECTOR AYALA THESE PAST FEW WEEKS. BUT SHE DIDN'T EXPECT... THIS!
AND INSIDE THE CAMPUS LIBRARY...
SINCE YOU KNOW WHO I AM, IT SEEMS SILLY TO GO ON PULLING MY PUNCHES!
YOUR SPIDER STRENGTH IS USELESS AGAINST ME, PARKER!
FOR I COMMAND ABSOLUTE DOMINION OVER ALL THAT LIVES--OR ONCE LIVED! ALL ORGANIC MATTER TURNS TO ASH AT MY TOUCH!
TO DUST!
AS IF TO PROVE CARRION'S CLAIM--THE OAKEN TABLE... CRUMBLES

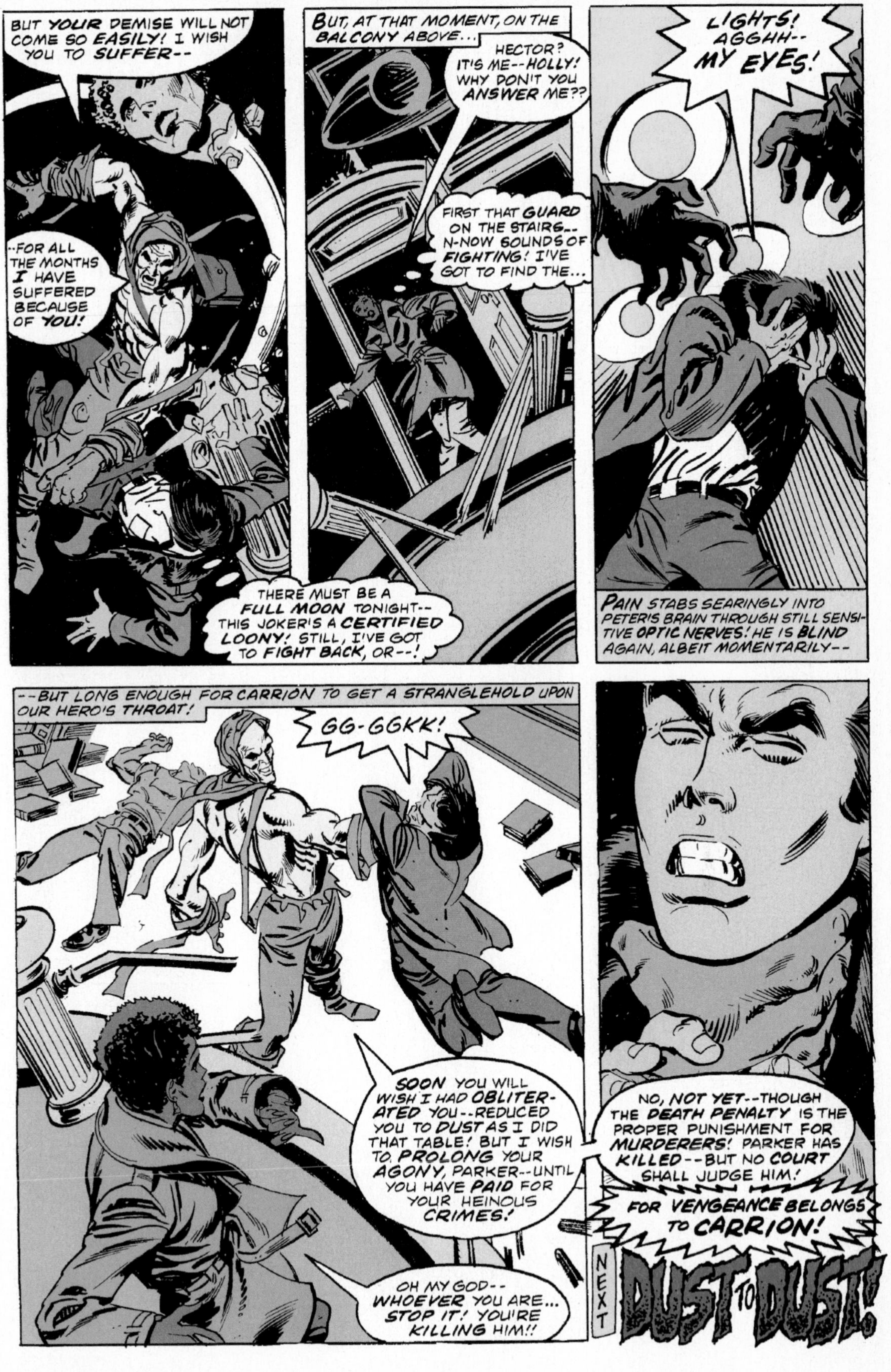
BUT YOUR DEMISE WILL NOT COME SO EASILY! I WISH YOU TO SUFFER--
--FOR ALL THE MONTHS I HAVE SUFFERED BECAUSE OF YOU!
THERE MUST BE A FULL MOON TONIGHT-- THIS JOKER'S A CERTIFIED LOONY! STILL, I'VE GOT TO FIGHT BACK, OR--!
BUT, AT THAT MOMENT, ON THE BALCONY ABOVE...
HECTOR? IT'S ME--HOLLY! WHY DON'T YOU ANSWER ME??
FIRST THAT GUARD ON THE STAIRS-- N-NOW SOUNDS OF FIGHTING! I'VE GOT TO FIND THE...
LIGHTS! AGGHH-- MY EYES!
PAIN STABS SEARINGLY INTO PETER'S BRAIN THROUGH STILL SENSITIVE OPTIC NERVES! HE IS BLIND AGAIN, ALBEIT MOMENTARILY--
--BUT LONG ENOUGH FOR CARRION TO GET A STRANGLEHOLD UPON OUR HERO'S THROAT!
GG-GGKK!
SOON YOU WILL WISH I HAD OBLITERATED YOU--REDUCED YOU TO DUST AS I DID THAT TABLE! BUT I WISH TO PROLONG YOUR AGONY, PARKER--UNTIL YOU HAVE PAID FOR YOUR HEINOUS CRIMES!
OH MY GOD-- WHOEVER YOU ARE... STOP IT! YOU'RE KILLING HIM!!
NO, NOT YET--THOUGH THE DEATH PENALTY IS THE PROPER PUNISHMENT FOR MURDERERS! PARKER HAS KILLED--BUT NO COURT SHALL JUDGE HIM!
FOR VENGEANCE BELONGS TO CARRION!
NEXT
DUST TO DUST!

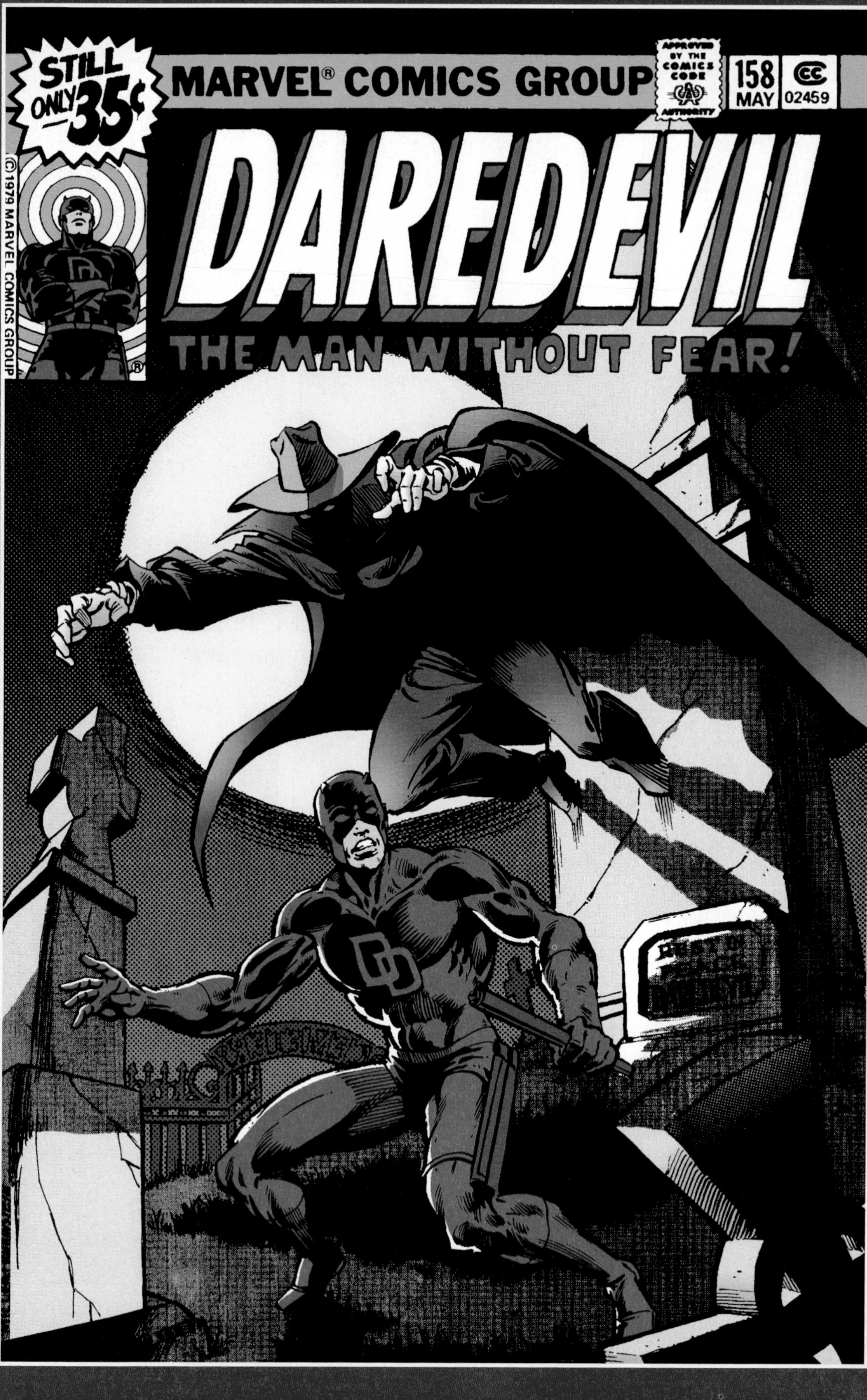
STILL ONLY 35¢
MARVEL® COMICS GROUP
APPROVED BY THE COMICS CODE AUTHORITY
158 MAY
CC 02459
DAREDEVIL
THE MAN WITHOUT FEAR!
© 1979 MARVEL COMICS GROUP

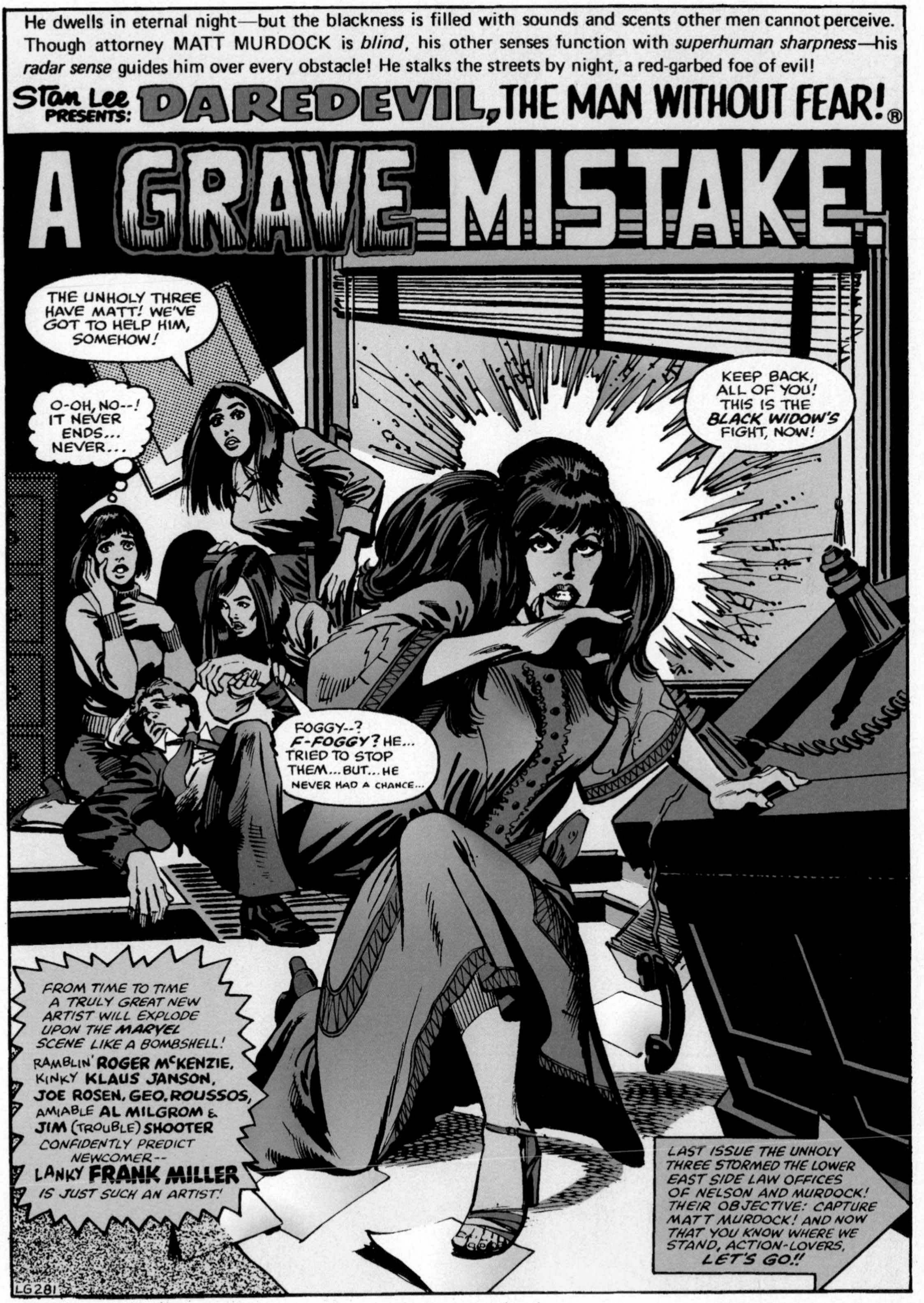
He dwells in eternal night—but the blackness is filled with sounds and scents other men cannot perceive. Though attorney MATT MURDOCK is *blind*, his other senses function with *superhuman sharpness*—his *radar sense* guides him over every obstacle! He stalks the streets by night, a red-garbed foe of evil!
Stan Lee PRESENTS: DAREDEVIL, THE MAN WITHOUT FEAR!®
A GRAVE MISTAKE!
THE UNHOLY THREE HAVE MATT! WE'VE GOT TO HELP HIM, SOMEHOW!
O-OH, NO--! IT NEVER ENDS... NEVER...
KEEP BACK, ALL OF YOU! THIS IS THE BLACK WIDOW'S FIGHT, NOW!
FOGGY--? F-FOGGY? HE... TRIED TO STOP THEM... BUT... HE NEVER HAD A CHANCE...
FROM TIME TO TIME A TRULY GREAT NEW ARTIST WILL EXPLODE UPON THE MARVEL SCENE LIKE A BOMBSHELL! RAMBLIN' ROGER McKENZIE, KINKY KLAUS JANSON, JOE ROSEN, GEO. ROUSSOS, AMIABLE AL MILGROM & JIM (TROUBLE) SHOOTER CONFIDENTLY PREDICT NEWCOMER-- LANKY FRANK MILLER IS JUST SUCH AN ARTIST!
LAST ISSUE THE UNHOLY THREE STORMED THE LOWER EAST SIDE LAW OFFICES OF NELSON AND MURDOCK! THEIR OBJECTIVE: CAPTURE MATT MURDOCK! AND NOW THAT YOU KNOW WHERE WE STAND, ACTION-LOVERS, LET'S GO!!
LG281

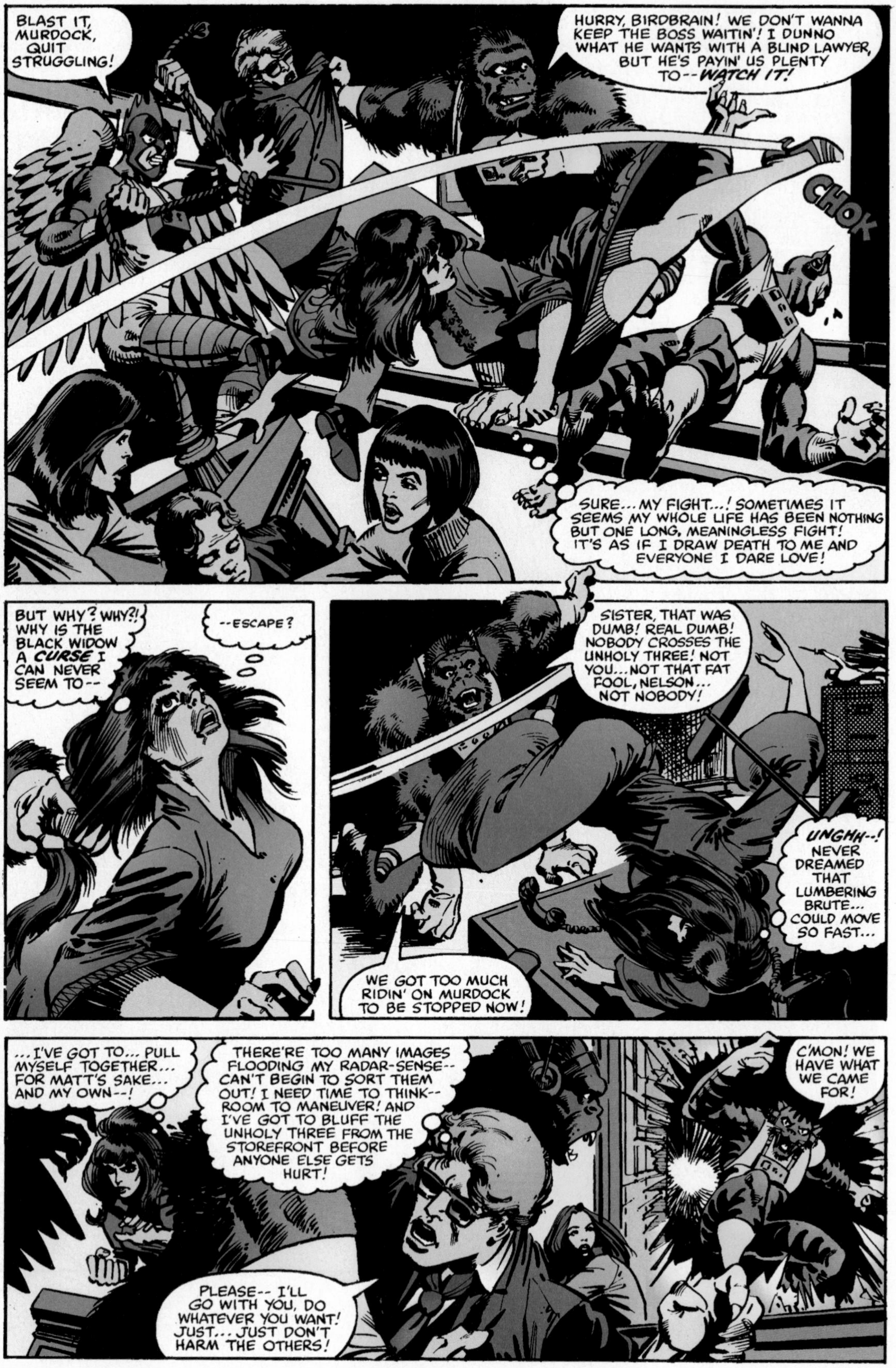

BLAST IT, MURDOCK, QUIT STRUGGLING!
HURRY, BIRDBRAIN! WE DON'T WANNA KEEP THE BOSS WAITIN'! I DUNNO WHAT HE WANTS WITH A BLIND LAWYER, BUT HE'S PAYIN' US PLENTY TO--WATCH IT!
CHOK
SURE... MY FIGHT...! SOMETIMES IT SEEMS MY WHOLE LIFE HAS BEEN NOTHING BUT ONE LONG, MEANINGLESS FIGHT! IT'S AS IF I DRAW DEATH TO ME AND EVERYONE I DARE LOVE!
BUT WHY? WHY?! WHY IS THE BLACK WIDOW A CURSE I CAN NEVER SEEM TO--
--ESCAPE?
SISTER, THAT WAS DUMB! REAL DUMB! NOBODY CROSSES THE UNHOLY THREE! NOT YOU... NOT THAT FAT FOOL, NELSON... NOT NOBODY!
WE GOT TOO MUCH RIDIN' ON MURDOCK TO BE STOPPED NOW!
UNGHH--! NEVER DREAMED THAT LUMBERING BRUTE... COULD MOVE SO FAST...
...I'VE GOT TO... PULL MYSELF TOGETHER... FOR MATT'S SAKE... AND MY OWN--!
THERE'RE TOO MANY IMAGES FLOODING MY RADAR-SENSE-- CAN'T BEGIN TO SORT THEM OUT! I NEED TIME TO THINK-- ROOM TO MANEUVER! AND I'VE GOT TO BLUFF THE UNHOLY THREE FROM THE STOREFRONT BEFORE ANYONE ELSE GETS HURT!
C'MON! WE HAVE WHAT WE CAME FOR!
PLEASE-- I'LL GO WITH YOU, DO WHATEVER YOU WANT! JUST... JUST DON'T HARM THE OTHERS!

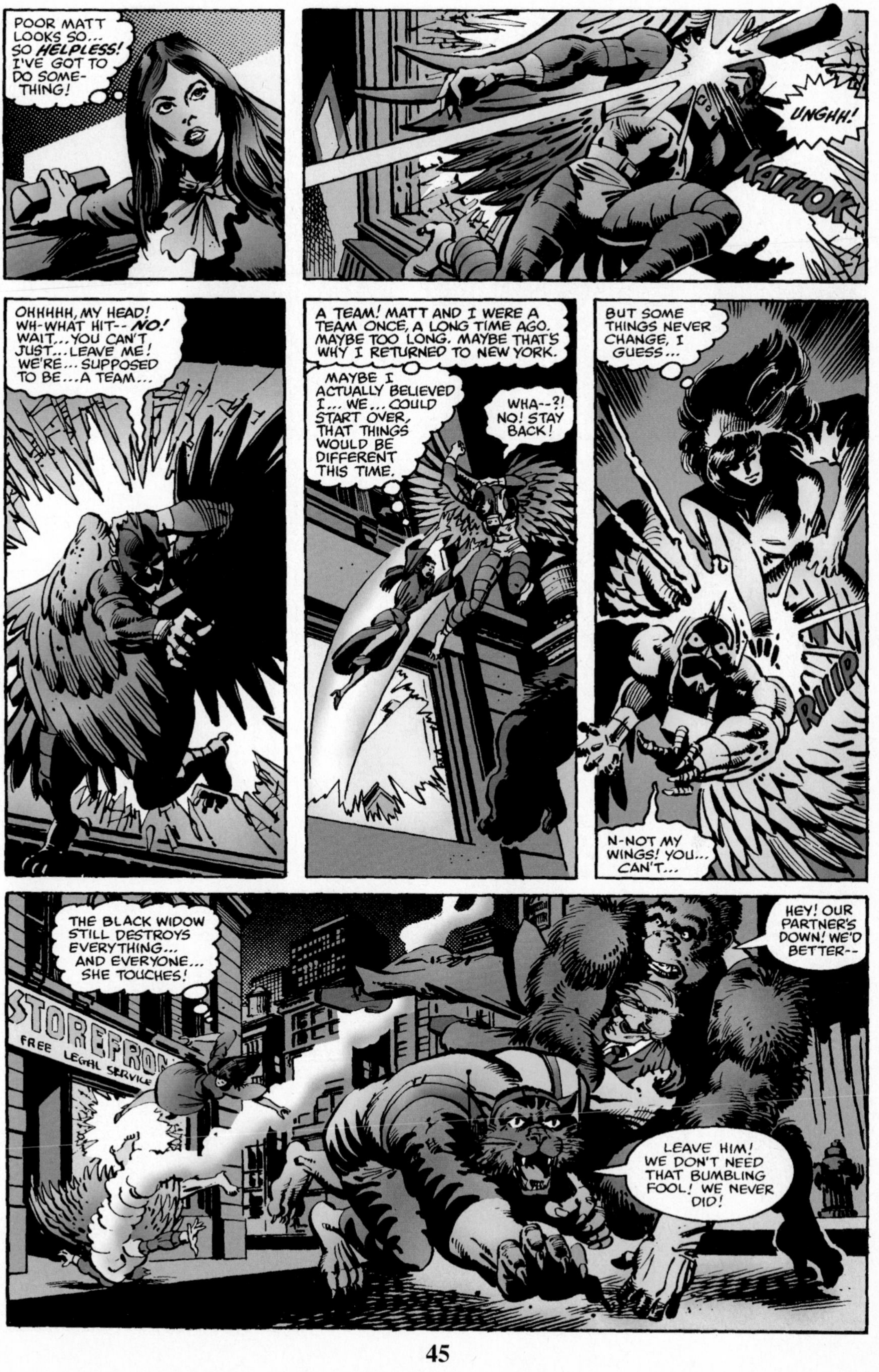
POOR MATT LOOKS SO... SO HELPLESS! I'VE GOT TO DO SOME-THING!
UNGHH!
KATHOK
OHHHHH, MY HEAD! WH-WHAT HIT-- NO! WAIT... YOU CAN'T JUST... LEAVE ME! WE'RE... SUPPOSED TO BE... A TEAM...
A TEAM! MATT AND I WERE A TEAM ONCE, A LONG TIME AGO. MAYBE TOO LONG. MAYBE THAT'S WHY I RETURNED TO NEW YORK.
MAYBE I ACTUALLY BELIEVED I... WE... COULD START OVER, THAT THINGS WOULD BE DIFFERENT THIS TIME.
WHA--?! NO! STAY BACK!
BUT SOME THINGS NEVER CHANGE, I GUESS...
RIIIP
N-NOT MY WINGS! YOU... CAN'T...
THE BLACK WIDOW STILL DESTROYS EVERYTHING... AND EVERYONE... SHE TOUCHES!
HEY! OUR PARTNER'S DOWN! WE'D BETTER--
STOREFRON
FREE LEGAL SERVICE
LEAVE HIM! WE DON'T NEED THAT BUMBLING FOOL! WE NEVER DID!

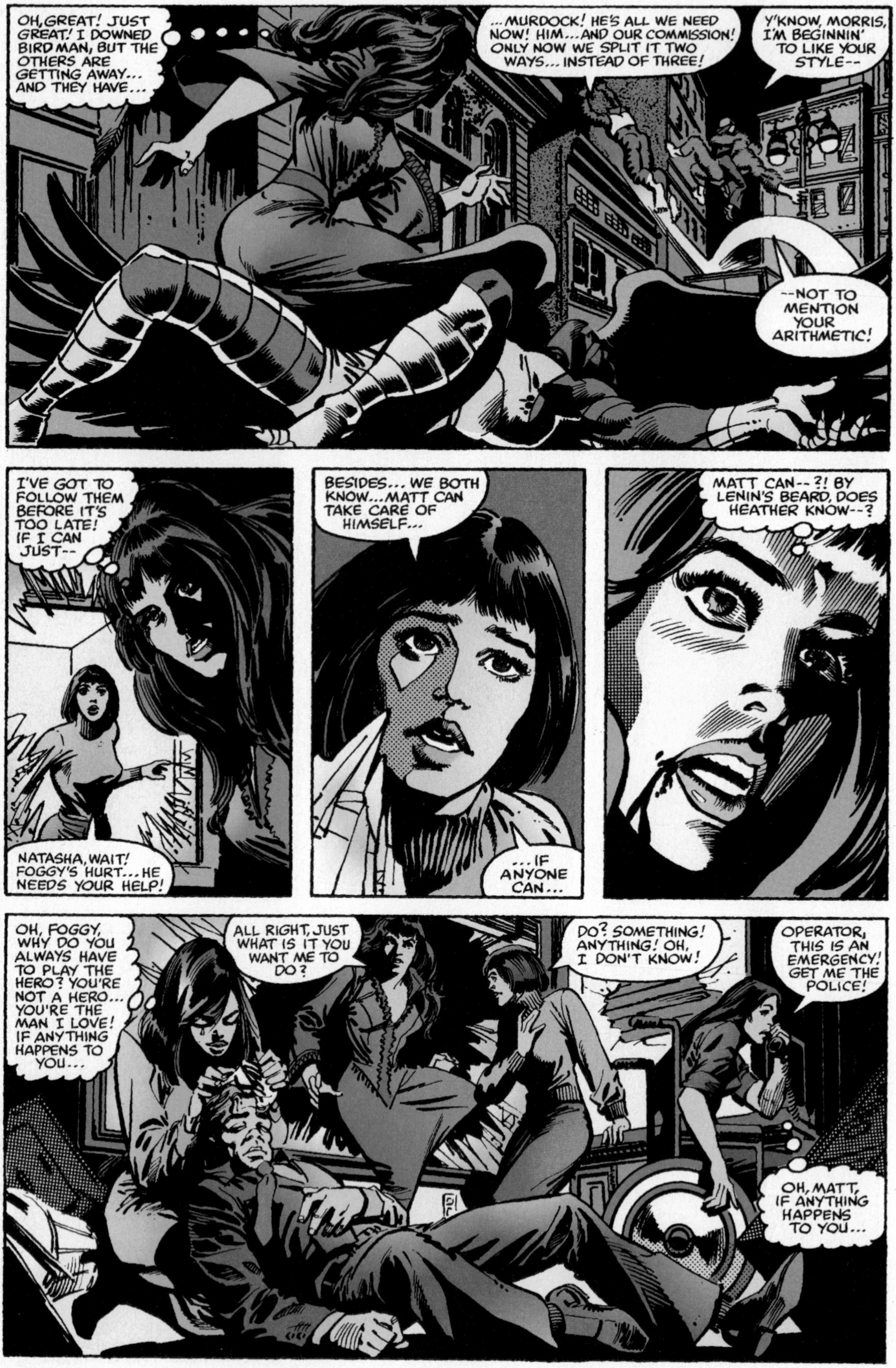
OH, GREAT! JUST GREAT! I DOWNED BIRD MAN, BUT THE OTHERS ARE GETTING AWAY... AND THEY HAVE...
...MURDOCK! HE'S ALL WE NEED NOW! HIM...AND OUR COMMISSION! ONLY NOW WE SPLIT IT TWO WAYS... INSTEAD OF THREE!
Y'KNOW, MORRIS, I'M BEGINNIN' TO LIKE YOUR STYLE--
--NOT TO MENTION YOUR ARITHMETIC!
I'VE GOT TO FOLLOW THEM BEFORE IT'S TOO LATE! IF I CAN JUST--
NATASHA, WAIT! FOGGY'S HURT... HE NEEDS YOUR HELP!
BESIDES... WE BOTH KNOW...MATT CAN TAKE CARE OF HIMSELF...
...IF ANYONE CAN...
MATT CAN--?! BY LENIN'S BEARD, DOES HEATHER KNOW--?
OH, FOGGY, WHY DO YOU ALWAYS HAVE TO PLAY THE HERO? YOU'RE NOT A HERO... YOU'RE THE MAN I LOVE! IF ANYTHING HAPPENS TO YOU...
ALL RIGHT, JUST WHAT IS IT YOU WANT ME TO DO?
DO? SOMETHING! ANYTHING! OH, I DON'T KNOW!
OPERATOR, THIS IS AN EMERGENCY! GET ME THE POLICE!
OH, MATT, IF ANYTHING HAPPENS TO YOU...

MURDOCK, YOU DON'T KNOW IT YET, BUT YOU'RE GONNA MAKE US RICH MEN! VERY RICH MEN! AND THIS'S ONLY THE BEGINNIN'! WITH THESE *SPECIAL OUTFITS* THERE AIN'T NOTHIN' WE CAN'T DO--

YEAH, WELL IF YOU DON'T HOLD STILL I'M JUST LIABLE TO DROP YOU! DEATH-STALKER NEVER SAID HE WANTED YOU ALIVE, ANYHOW!

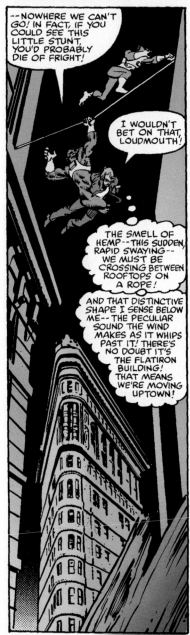

--NOWHERE WE CAN'T GO! IN FACT, IF YOU COULD SEE THIS LITTLE STUNT, YOU'D PROBABLY DIE OF FRIGHT!

I WOULDN'T BET ON THAT, LOUDMOUTH!

THE SMELL OF HEMP--THIS SUDDEN, RAPID SWAYING-- WE MUST BE CROSSING BETWEEN ROOFTOPS ON A ROPE!

AND THAT DISTINCTIVE SHAPE I SENSE BELOW ME-- THE PECULIAR SOUND THE WIND MAKES AS IT WHIPS PAST IT! THERE'S NO DOUBT IT'S THE FLATIRON BUILDING! THAT MEANS WE'RE MOVING UPTOWN!

DEATH-STALKER--?!

YOU'VE GOT TO LISTEN TO ME! DEATH-STALKER'S A KILLER! A COLD-BLOODED, INHUMAN KILLER! HE'S JUST USING YOU! AND WHEN YOU'VE SERVED HIS PURPOSE, HE'LL--!

NICE TRY, SHYSTER, BUT IT WON'T WASH! WHAT COULD A STUFFED SHIRT LIKE YOU KNOW ABOUT HIM ANYWAY? BESIDES...

WE'RE HERE!

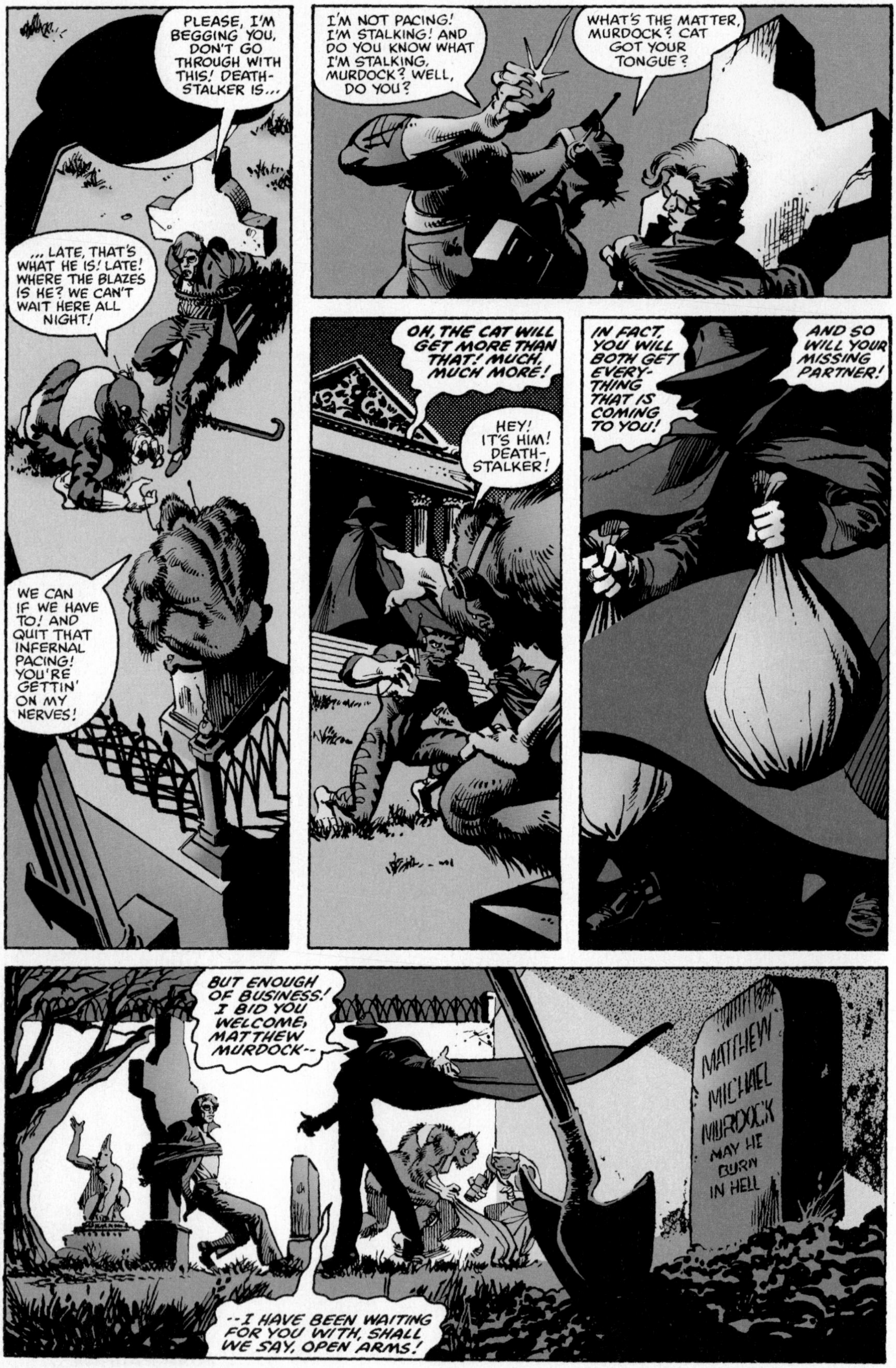
PLEASE, I'M BEGGING YOU, DON'T GO THROUGH WITH THIS! DEATH-STALKER IS...
...LATE, THAT'S WHAT HE IS! LATE! WHERE THE BLAZES IS HE? WE CAN'T WAIT HERE ALL NIGHT!
WE CAN IF WE HAVE TO! AND QUIT THAT INFERNAL PACING! YOU'RE GETTIN' ON MY NERVES!
I'M NOT PACING! I'M STALKING! AND DO YOU KNOW WHAT I'M STALKING, MURDOCK? WELL, DO YOU?
WHAT'S THE MATTER, MURDOCK? CAT GOT YOUR TONGUE?
OH, THE CAT WILL GET MORE THAN THAT! MUCH, MUCH MORE!
HEY! IT'S HIM! DEATH-STALKER!
IN FACT, YOU WILL BOTH GET EVERY-THING THAT IS COMING TO YOU!
AND SO WILL YOUR MISSING PARTNER!
BUT ENOUGH OF BUSINESS! I BID YOU WELCOME, MATTHEW MURDOCK--
MATTHEW MICHAEL MURDOCK MAY HE BURN IN HELL
--I HAVE BEEN WAITING FOR YOU WITH, SHALL WE SAY, OPEN ARMS!

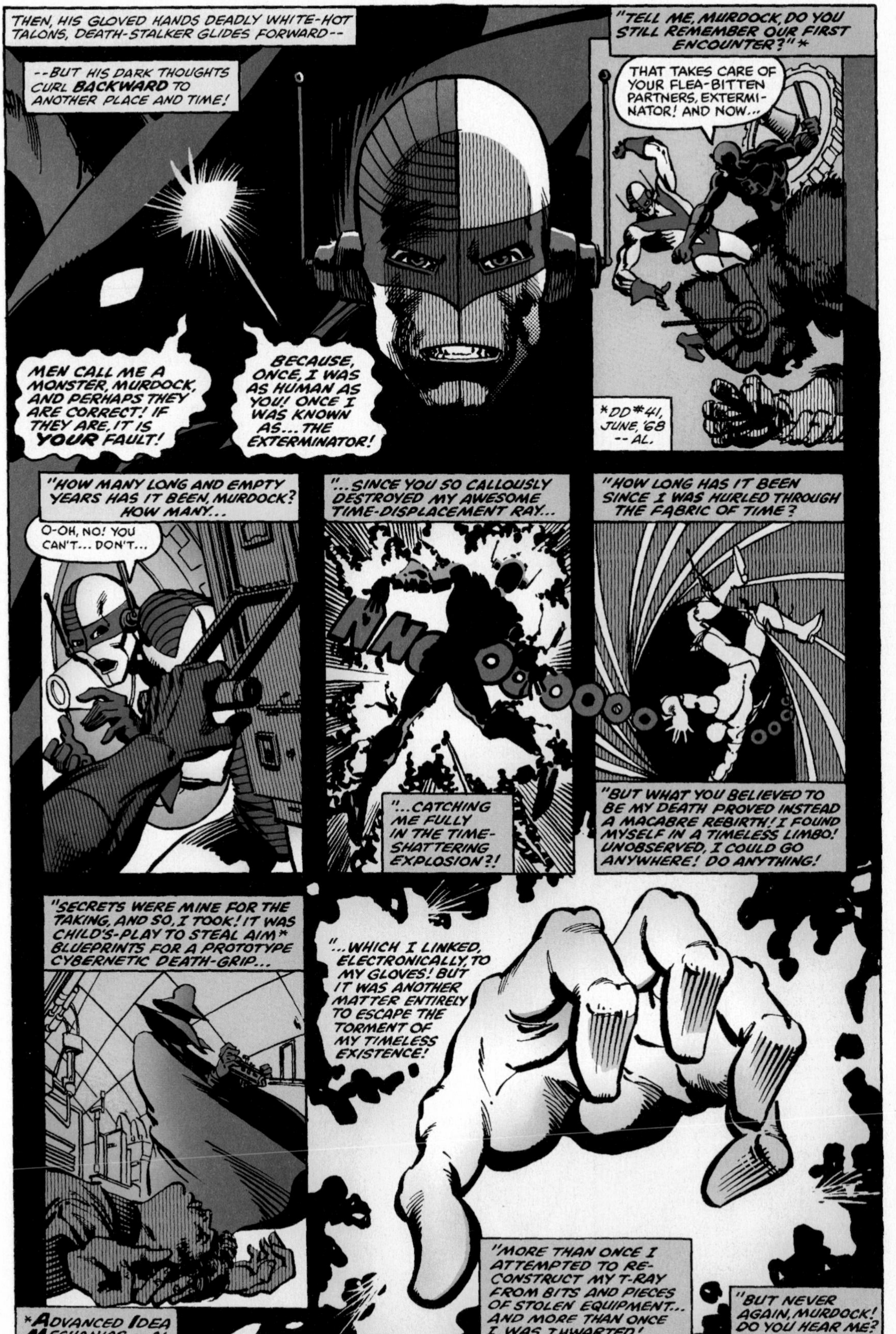
THEN, HIS GLOVED HANDS DEADLY WHITE-HOT TALONS, DEATH-STALKER GLIDES FORWARD--
--BUT HIS DARK THOUGHTS CURL BACKWARD TO ANOTHER PLACE AND TIME!
MEN CALL ME A MONSTER, MURDOCK, AND PERHAPS THEY ARE CORRECT! IF THEY ARE, IT IS YOUR FAULT!
BECAUSE, ONCE, I WAS AS HUMAN AS YOU! ONCE I WAS KNOWN AS... THE EXTERMINATOR!
"TELL ME, MURDOCK, DO YOU STILL REMEMBER OUR FIRST ENCOUNTER?"*
THAT TAKES CARE OF YOUR FLEA-BITTEN PARTNERS, EXTERMINATOR! AND NOW...
*DD #41, JUNE, '68 --AL.
"HOW MANY LONG AND EMPTY YEARS HAS IT BEEN, MURDOCK? HOW MANY...
O-OH, NO! YOU CAN'T... DON'T...
"...SINCE YOU SO CALLOUSLY DESTROYED MY AWESOME TIME-DISPLACEMENT RAY...
NNOOOOOOOOO
"...CATCHING ME FULLY IN THE TIME-SHATTERING EXPLOSION?!
"HOW LONG HAS IT BEEN SINCE I WAS HURLED THROUGH THE FABRIC OF TIME?
"BUT WHAT YOU BELIEVED TO BE MY DEATH PROVED INSTEAD A MACABRE REBIRTH! I FOUND MYSELF IN A TIMELESS LIMBO! UNOBSERVED, I COULD GO ANYWHERE! DO ANYTHING!
"SECRETS WERE MINE FOR THE TAKING, AND SO, I TOOK! IT WAS CHILD'S-PLAY TO STEAL AIM* BLUEPRINTS FOR A PROTOTYPE CYBERNETIC DEATH-GRIP...
*ADVANCED IDEA MECHANICS --AL.
"...WHICH I LINKED, ELECTRONICALLY, TO MY GLOVES! BUT IT WAS ANOTHER MATTER ENTIRELY TO ESCAPE THE TORMENT OF MY TIMELESS EXISTENCE!
"MORE THAN ONCE I ATTEMPTED TO RE-CONSTRUCT MY T-RAY FROM BITS AND PIECES OF STOLEN EQUIPMENT... AND MORE THAN ONCE I WAS THWARTED!
"BUT NEVER AGAIN, MURDOCK! DO YOU HEAR ME? NEVER AGAIN!

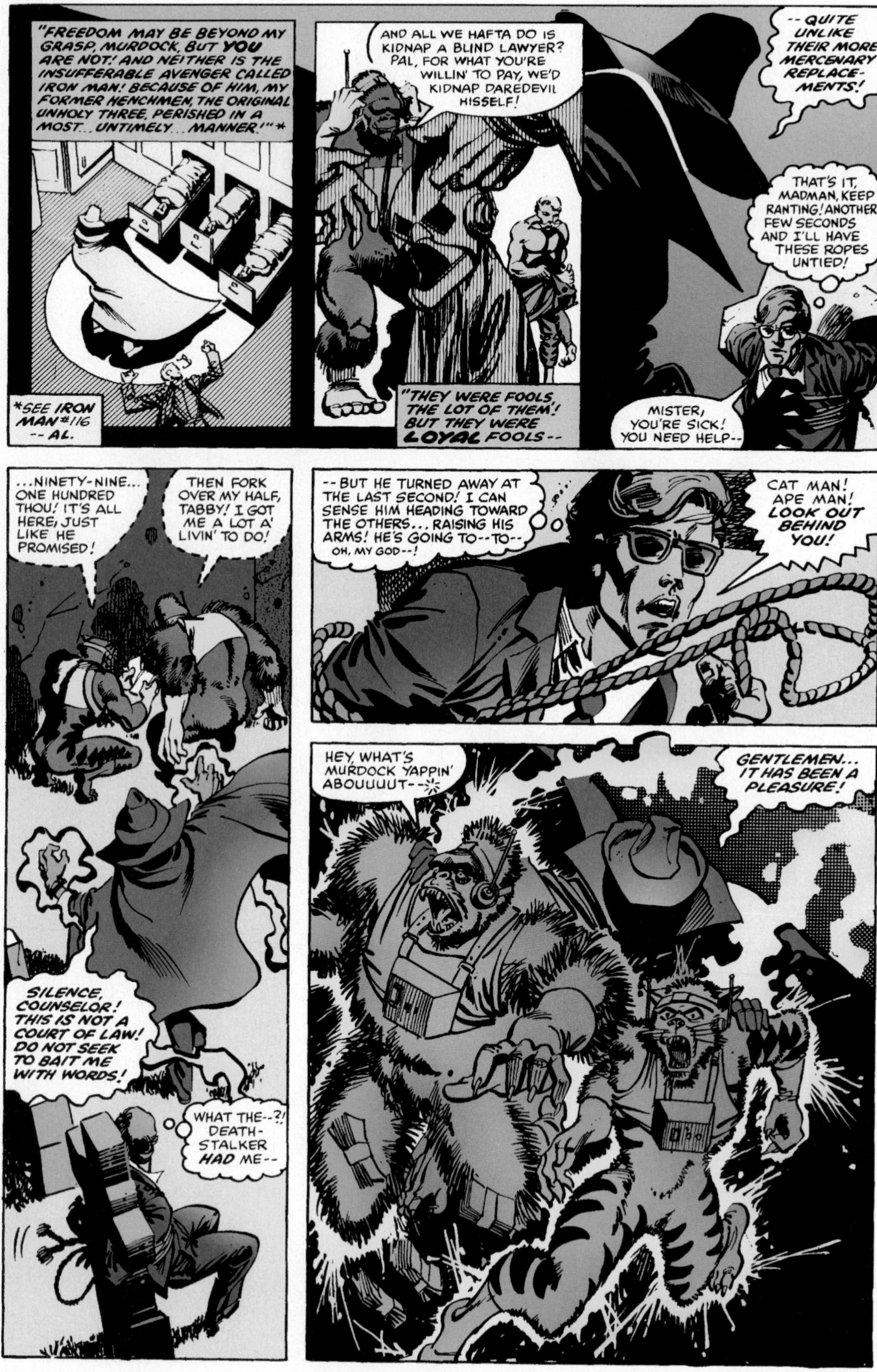
"FREEDOM MAY BE BEYOND MY GRASP, MURDOCK, BUT YOU ARE NOT! AND NEITHER IS THE INSUFFERABLE AVENGER CALLED IRON MAN! BECAUSE OF HIM, MY FORMER HENCHMEN, THE ORIGINAL UNHOLY THREE, PERISHED IN A MOST... UNTIMELY... MANNER!" *
*SEE IRON MAN #116 --AL.
AND ALL WE HAFTA DO IS KIDNAP A BLIND LAWYER? PAL, FOR WHAT YOU'RE WILLIN' TO PAY, WE'D KIDNAP DAREDEVIL HISSELF!
"THEY WERE FOOLS, THE LOT OF THEM! BUT THEY WERE LOYAL FOOLS--
--QUITE UNLIKE THEIR MORE MERCENARY REPLACEMENTS!
THAT'S IT, MADMAN, KEEP RANTING! ANOTHER FEW SECONDS AND I'LL HAVE THESE ROPES UNTIED!
MISTER, YOU'RE SICK! YOU NEED HELP--
...NINETY-NINE... ONE HUNDRED THOU! IT'S ALL HERE, JUST LIKE HE PROMISED!
THEN FORK OVER MY HALF, TABBY! I GOT ME A LOT A' LIVIN' TO DO!
SILENCE, COUNSELOR! THIS IS NOT A COURT OF LAW! DO NOT SEEK TO BAIT ME WITH WORDS!
WHAT THE--?! DEATH-STALKER HAD ME--
--BUT HE TURNED AWAY AT THE LAST SECOND! I CAN SENSE HIM HEADING TOWARD THE OTHERS... RAISING HIS ARMS! HE'S GOING TO--TO-- OH, MY GOD--!
CAT MAN! APE MAN! LOOK OUT BEHIND YOU!
HEY, WHAT'S MURDOCK YAPPIN' ABOUUUUT--
GENTLEMEN... IT HAS BEEN A PLEASURE!

I'M TOO LATE! HE MURDERED THEM IN COLD BLOOD! BUT WHY? HE HAD NOTHING TO GAIN BY THEIR DEATHS... EXCEPT...

DEATH-STALKER! YOU GAVE ME THE TIME I NEEDED TO FREE MYSELF! BUT YOU KNEW I WOULD! THAT'S WHAT YOU WANTED ALL ALONG!

NO, MURDOCK! I WANT DAREDEVIL!

I... SEE...

IT HAD TO COME DOWN TO THIS SOONER OR LATER, DIDN'T IT?

POK

TAK

YES...!

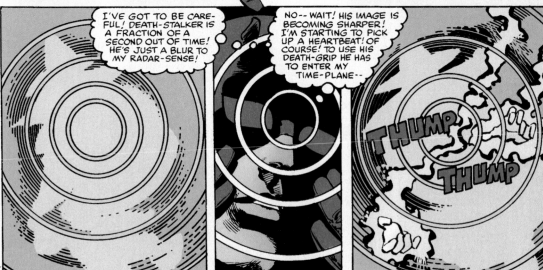

I'VE GOT TO BE CARE-FUL! DEATH-STALKER IS A FRACTION OF A SECOND OUT OF TIME! HE'S JUST A BLUR TO MY RADAR-SENSE!

NO-- WAIT! HIS IMAGE IS BECOMING SHARPER! I'M STARTING TO PICK UP A HEARTBEAT! OF COURSE! TO USE HIS DEATH-GRIP HE HAS TO ENTER MY TIME-PLANE--

THUMP

THUMP

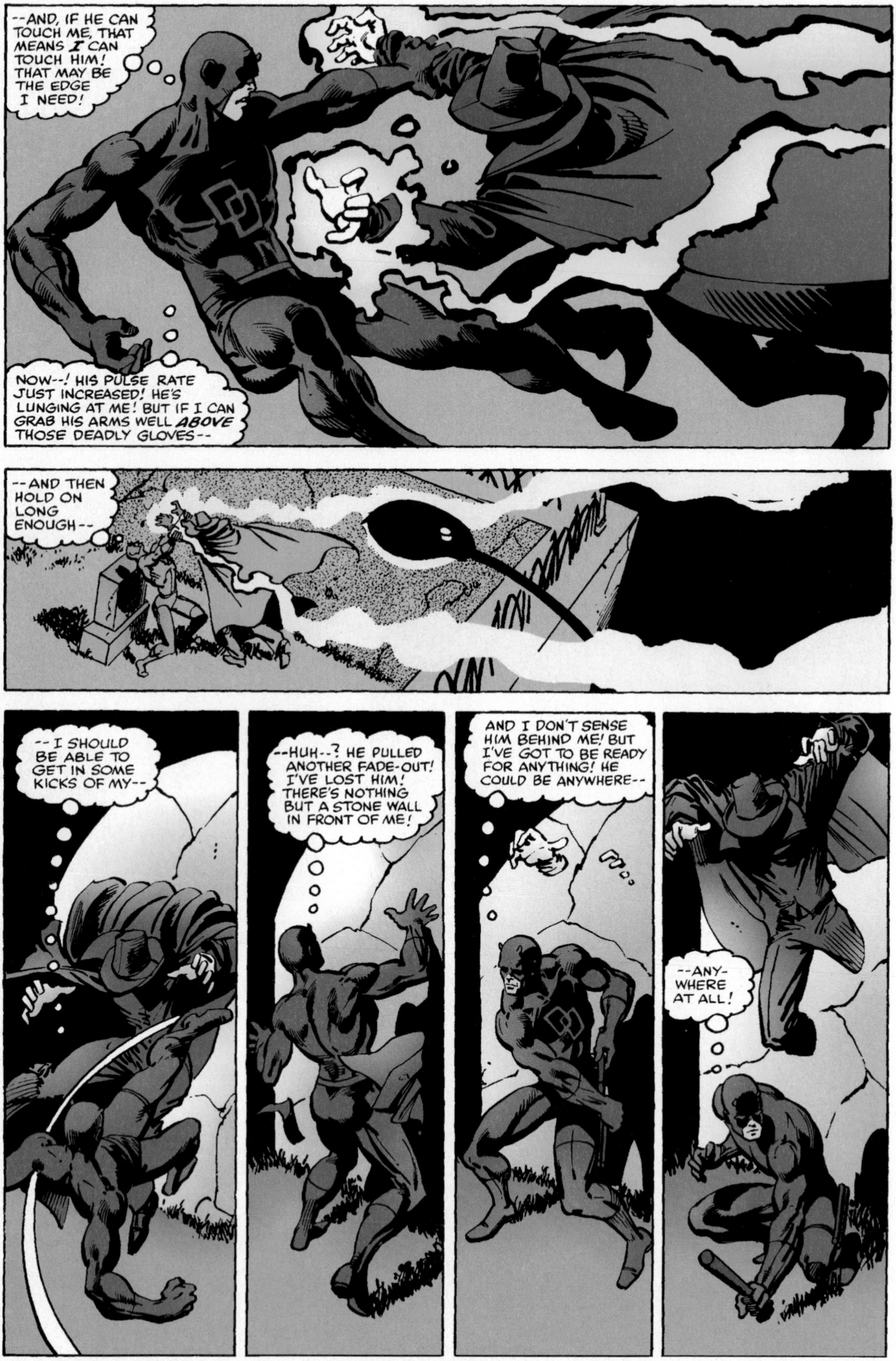
--AND, IF HE CAN TOUCH ME, THAT MEANS I CAN TOUCH HIM! THAT MAY BE THE EDGE I NEED!
NOW--! HIS PULSE RATE JUST INCREASED! HE'S LUNGING AT ME! BUT IF I CAN GRAB HIS ARMS WELL ABOVE THOSE DEADLY GLOVES--
--AND THEN HOLD ON LONG ENOUGH--
--I SHOULD BE ABLE TO GET IN SOME KICKS OF MY--
--HUH--? HE PULLED ANOTHER FADE-OUT! I'VE LOST HIM! THERE'S NOTHING BUT A STONE WALL IN FRONT OF ME!
AND I DON'T SENSE HIM BEHIND ME! BUT I'VE GOT TO BE READY FOR ANYTHING! HE COULD BE ANYWHERE--
--ANY-WHERE AT ALL!

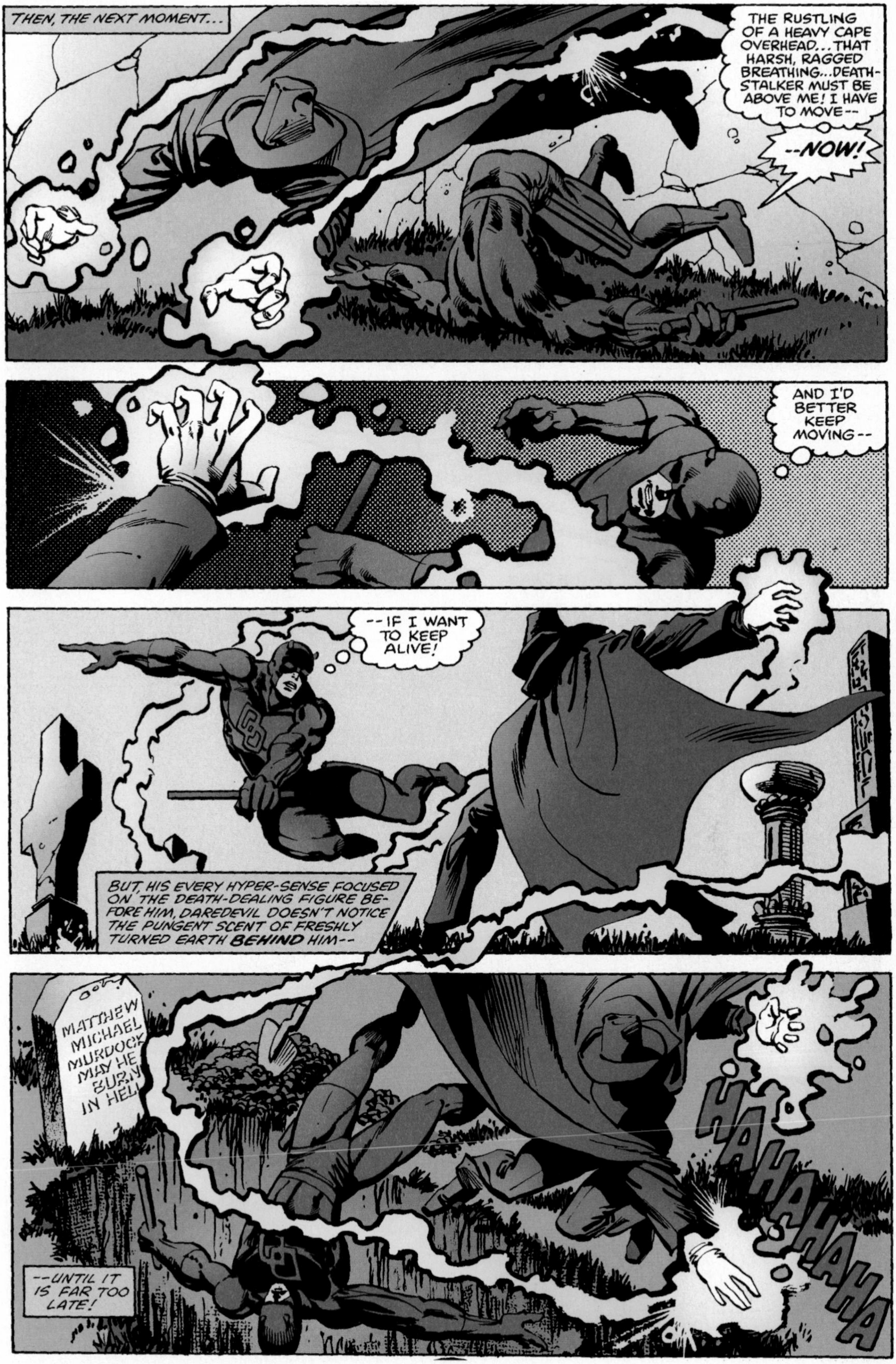

THEN, THE NEXT MOMENT...
THE RUSTLING OF A HEAVY CAPE OVERHEAD... THAT HARSH, RAGGED BREATHING... DEATH-STALKER MUST BE ABOVE ME! I HAVE TO MOVE--
--NOW!
AND I'D BETTER KEEP MOVING--
--IF I WANT TO KEEP ALIVE!
BUT, HIS EVERY HYPER-SENSE FOCUSED ON THE DEATH-DEALING FIGURE BEFORE HIM, DAREDEVIL DOESN'T NOTICE THE PUNGENT SCENT OF FRESHLY TURNED EARTH BEHIND HIM--
MATTHEW MICHAEL MURDOCK MAY HE BURN IN HELL
HAHAHAHAHAHA
--UNTIL IT IS FAR TOO LATE!

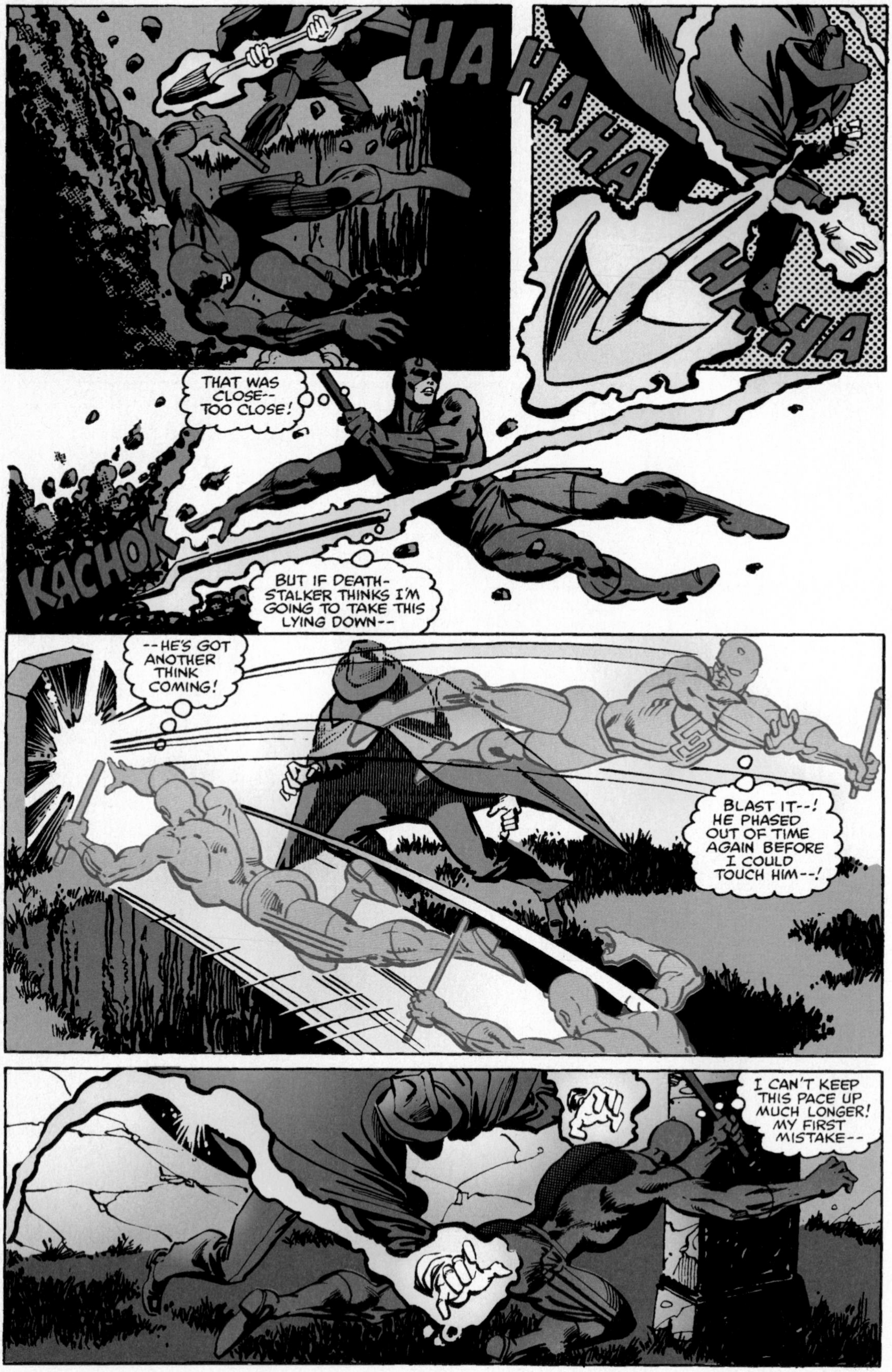
HA HA
HA
HA
HA
HA HA
THAT WAS CLOSE-- TOO CLOSE!
KACHOK
BUT IF DEATH-STALKER THINKS I'M GOING TO TAKE THIS LYING DOWN--
--HE'S GOT ANOTHER THINK COMING!
BLAST IT--! HE PHASED OUT OF TIME AGAIN BEFORE I COULD TOUCH HIM--!
I CAN'T KEEP THIS PACE UP MUCH LONGER! MY FIRST MISTAKE--

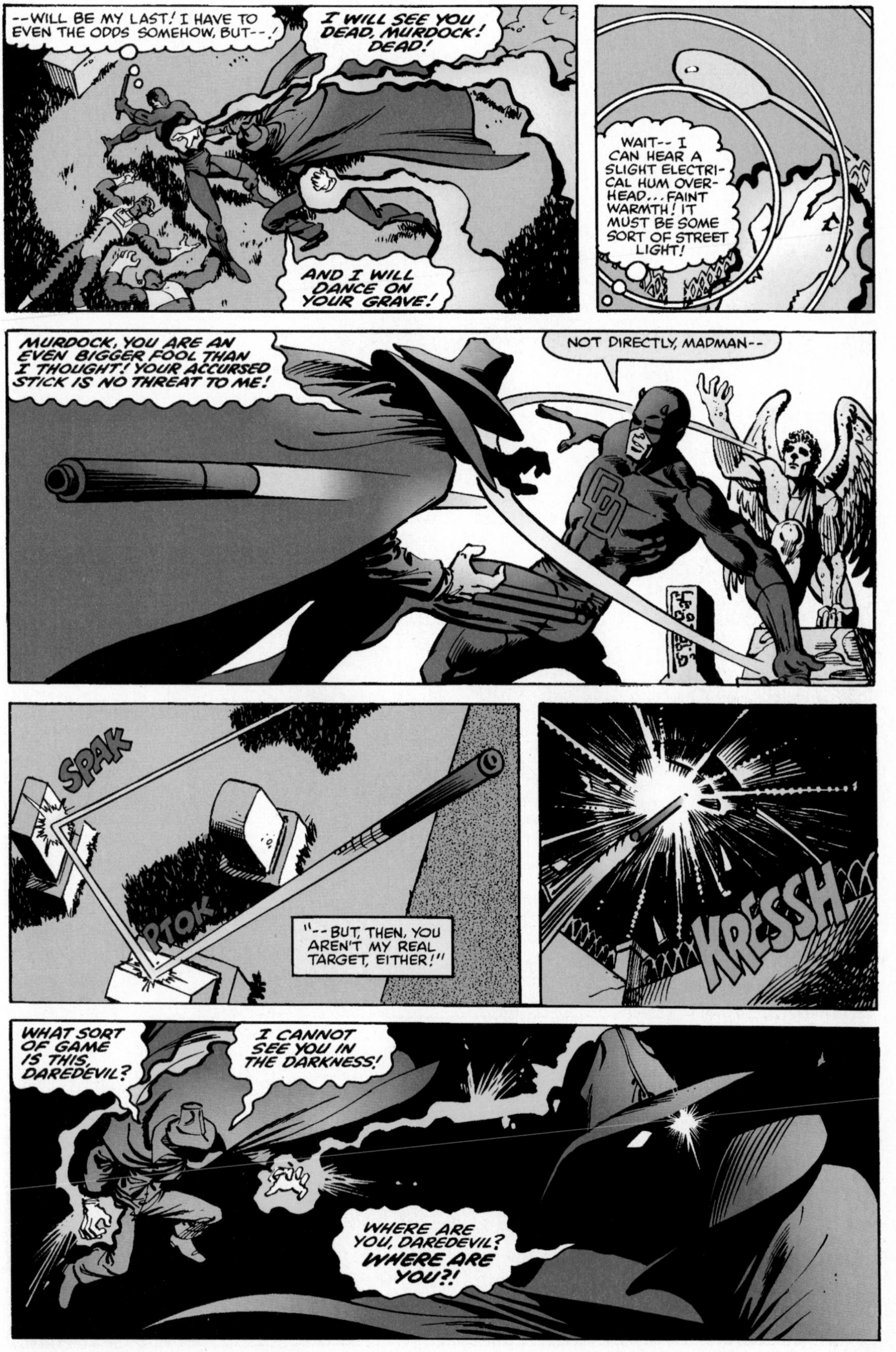
--WILL BE MY LAST! I HAVE TO EVEN THE ODDS SOMEHOW, BUT--!
I WILL SEE YOU DEAD, MURDOCK! DEAD!
AND I WILL DANCE ON YOUR GRAVE!
WAIT-- I CAN HEAR A SLIGHT ELECTRICAL HUM OVERHEAD... FAINT WARMTH! IT MUST BE SOME SORT OF STREET LIGHT!
MURDOCK, YOU ARE AN EVEN BIGGER FOOL THAN I THOUGHT! YOUR ACCURSED STICK IS NO THREAT TO ME!
NOT DIRECTLY, MADMAN--
SPAK
PTOK
"--BUT, THEN, YOU AREN'T MY REAL TARGET, EITHER!"
KRESSH
WHAT SORT OF GAME IS THIS, DAREDEVIL?
I CANNOT SEE YOU IN THE DARKNESS!
WHERE ARE YOU, DAREDEVIL? WHERE ARE YOU?!

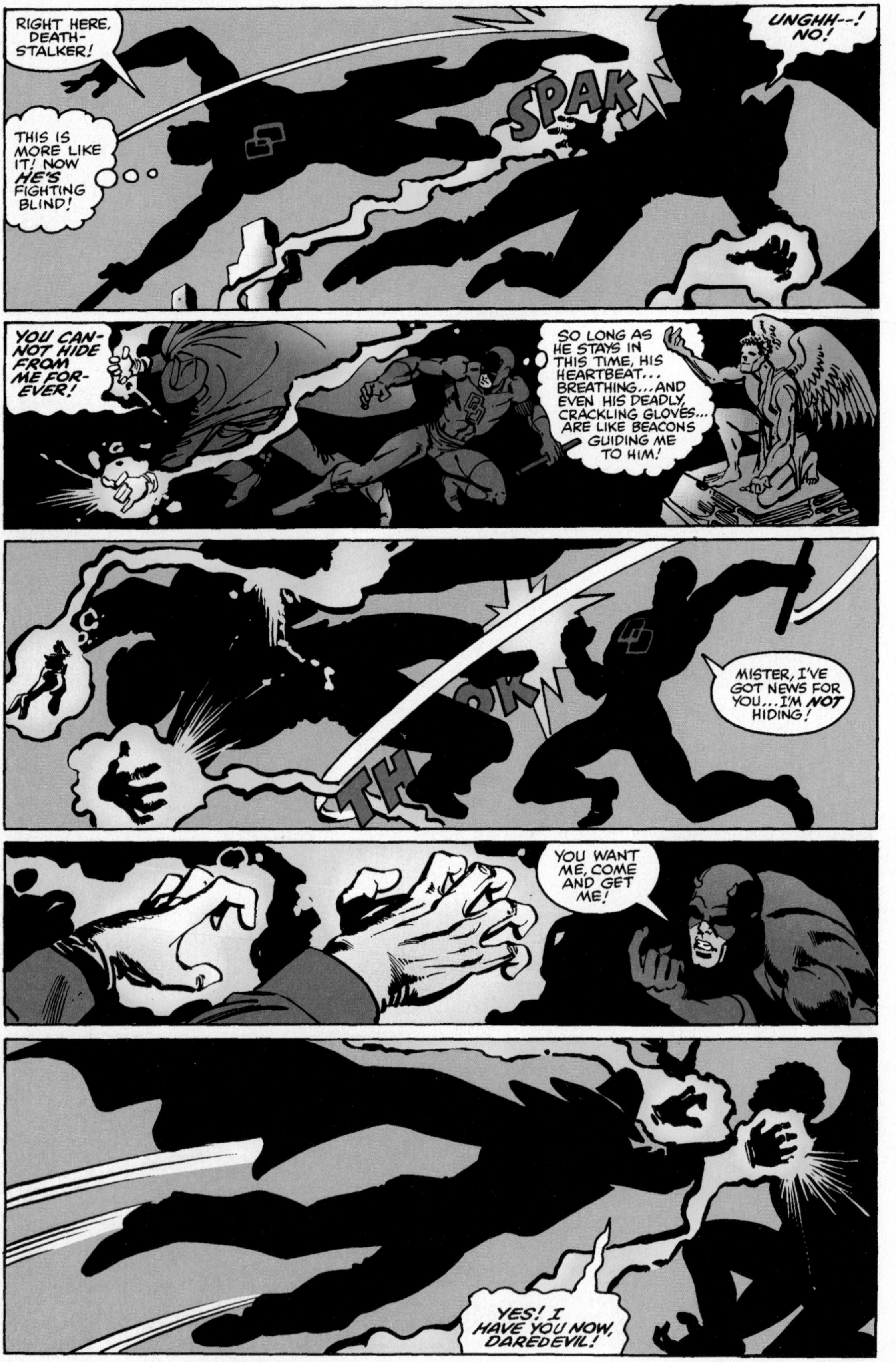

RIGHT HERE, DEATH-STALKER!
THIS IS MORE LIKE IT! NOW HE'S FIGHTING BLIND!
SPAK
UNGHH--! NO!
YOU CAN-NOT HIDE FROM ME FOR-EVER!
SO LONG AS HE STAYS IN THIS TIME, HIS HEARTBEAT... BREATHING... AND EVEN HIS DEADLY, CRACKLING GLOVES... ARE LIKE BEACONS GUIDING ME TO HIM!
MISTER, I'VE GOT NEWS FOR YOU... I'M NOT HIDING!
YOU WANT ME, COME AND GET ME!
YES! I HAVE YOU NOW, DAREDEVIL!

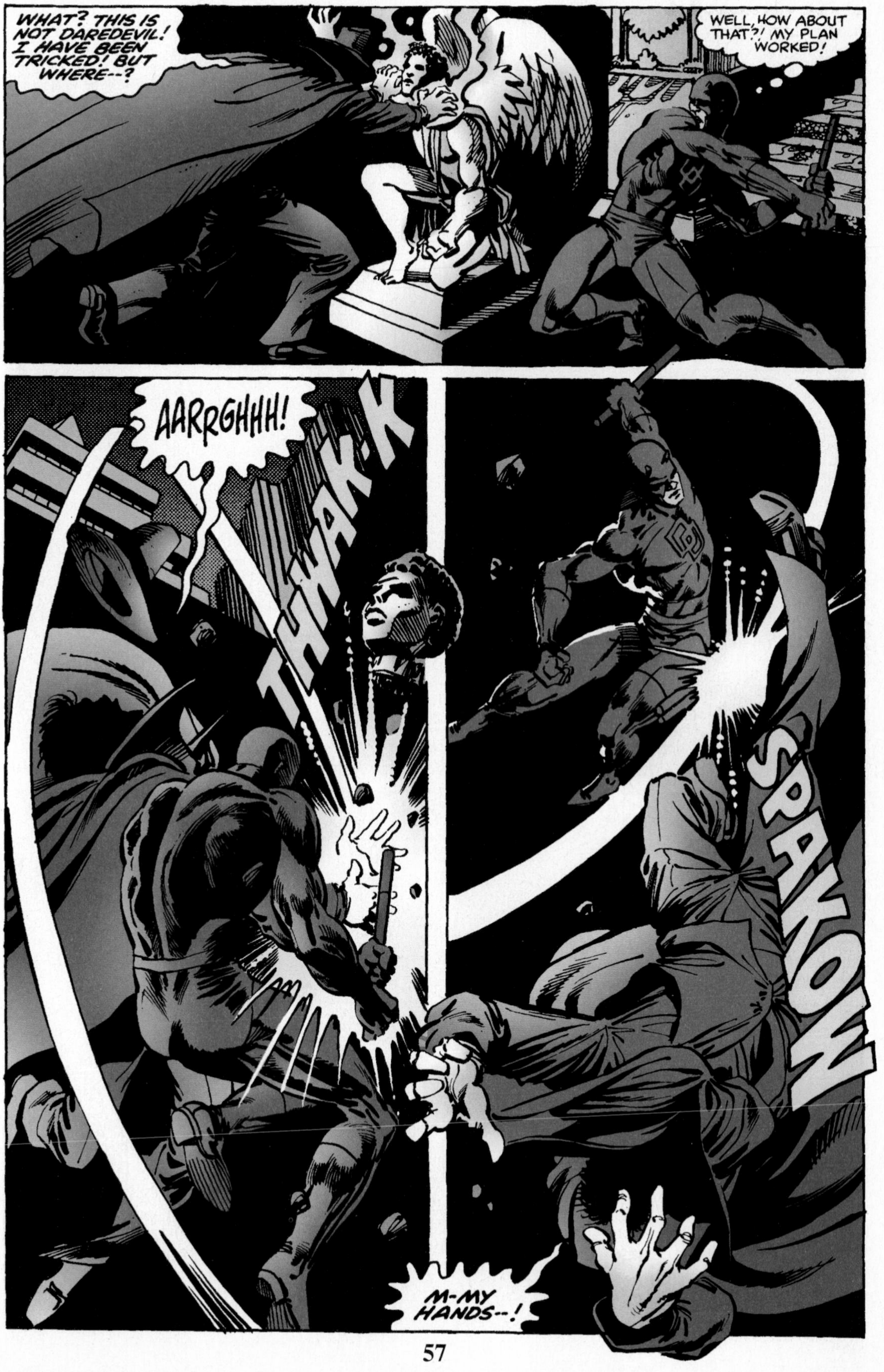
WHAT? THIS IS NOT DAREDEVIL! I HAVE BEEN TRICKED! BUT WHERE--?
WELL, HOW ABOUT THAT?! MY PLAN WORKED!
AARRGHHH!
THWAK-K
SPAKOW
M-MY HANDS--!

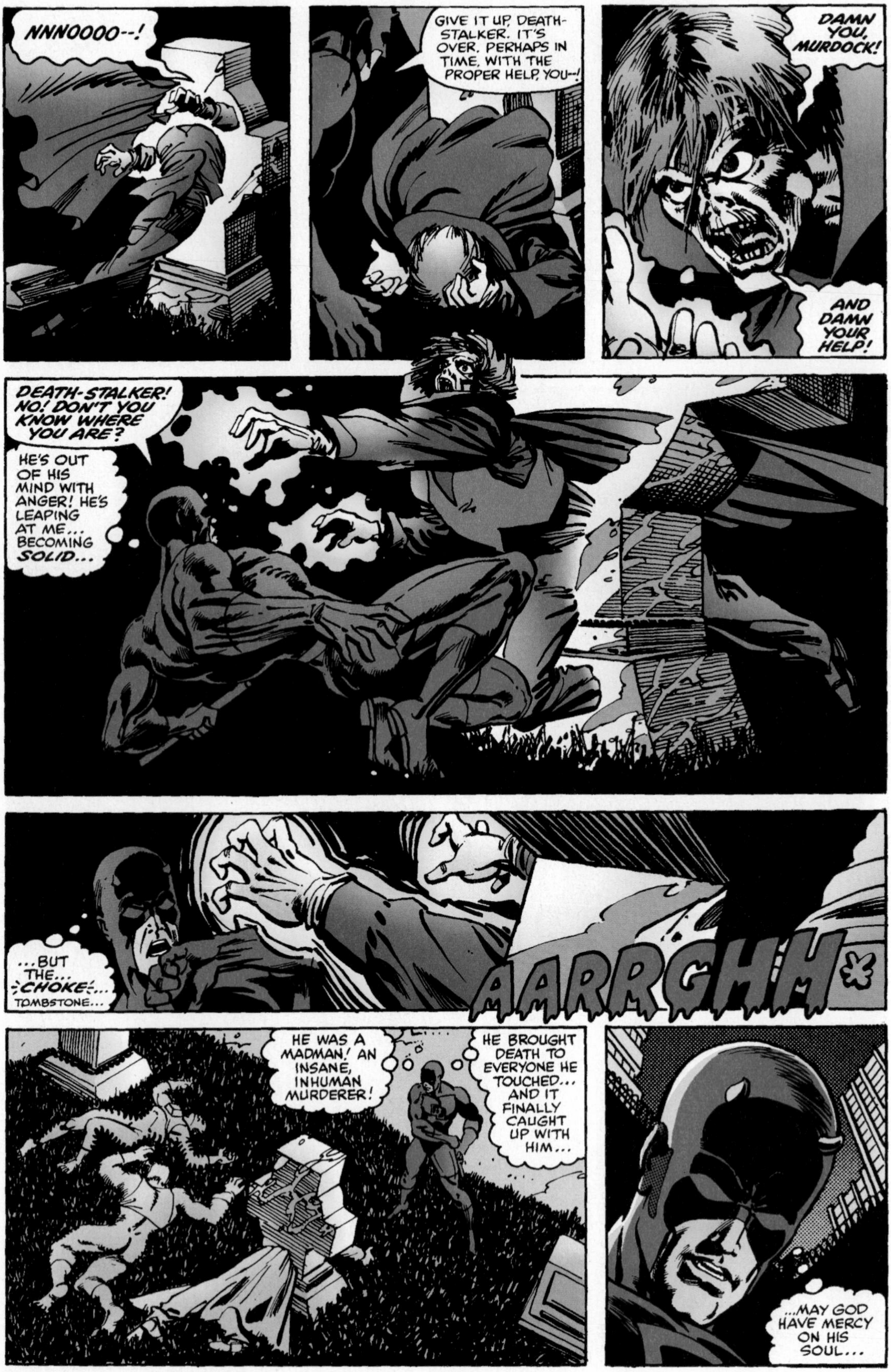
NNNOOOO--!
GIVE IT UP, DEATH-STALKER. IT'S OVER. PERHAPS IN TIME, WITH THE PROPER HELP, YOU--!
DAMN YOU, MURDOCK!
AND DAMN YOUR HELP!
DEATH-STALKER! NO! DON'T YOU KNOW WHERE YOU ARE?
HE'S OUT OF HIS MIND WITH ANGER! HE'S LEAPING AT ME... BECOMING SOLID...
...BUT THE... *CHOKE*... TOMBSTONE...
AARRGHH
HE WAS A MADMAN! AN INSANE, INHUMAN MURDERER!
HE BROUGHT DEATH TO EVERYONE HE TOUCHED... AND IT FINALLY CAUGHT UP WITH HIM...
...MAY GOD HAVE MERCY ON HIS SOUL...

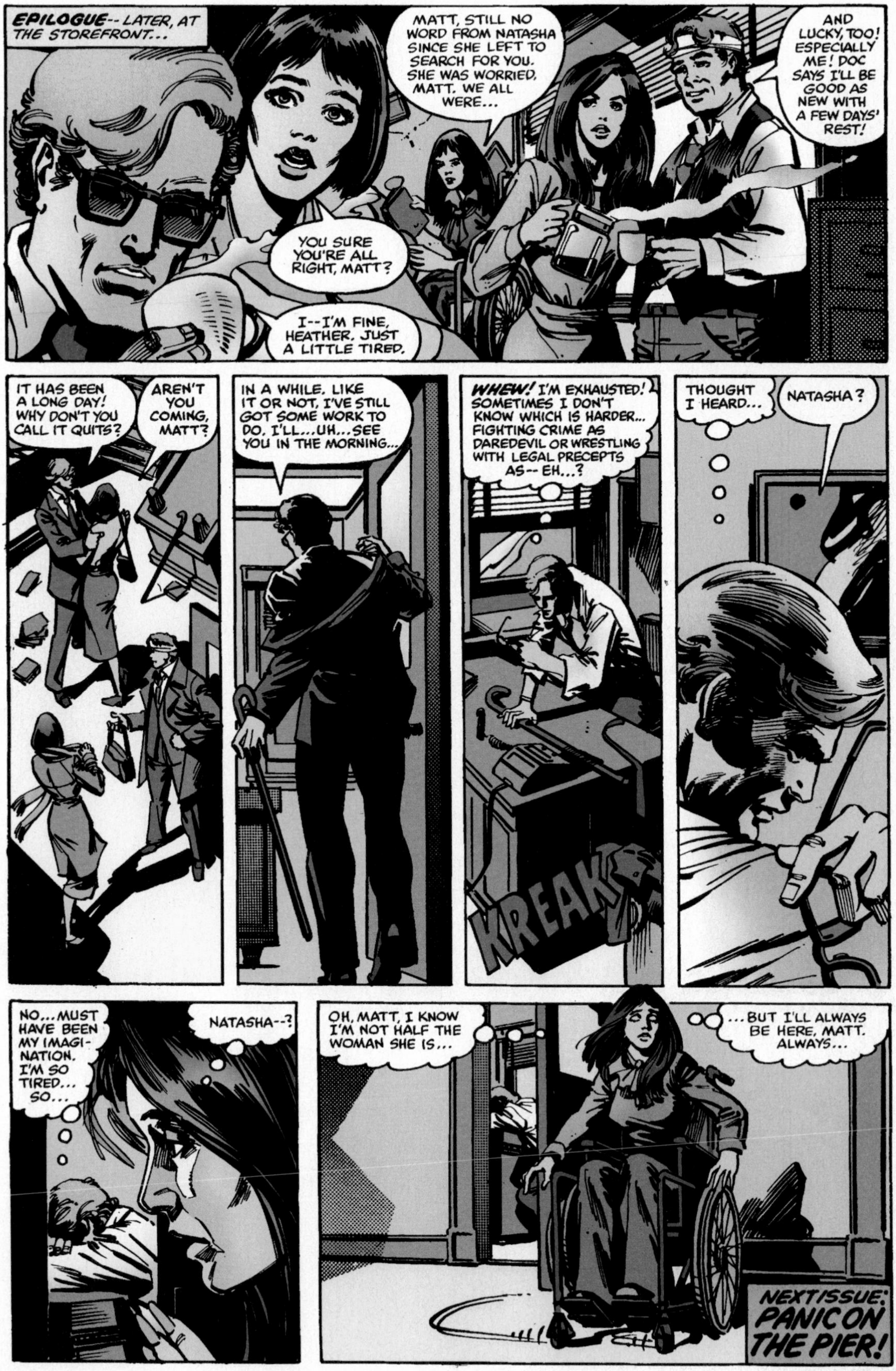
EPILOGUE-- LATER, AT THE STOREFRONT...
MATT, STILL NO WORD FROM NATASHA SINCE SHE LEFT TO SEARCH FOR YOU. SHE WAS WORRIED, MATT. WE ALL WERE...
AND LUCKY, TOO! ESPECIALLY ME! DOC SAYS I'LL BE GOOD AS NEW WITH A FEW DAYS' REST!
YOU SURE YOU'RE ALL RIGHT, MATT?
I--I'M FINE, HEATHER. JUST A LITTLE TIRED.
IT HAS BEEN A LONG DAY! WHY DON'T YOU CALL IT QUITS?
AREN'T YOU COMING, MATT?
IN A WHILE. LIKE IT OR NOT, I'VE STILL GOT SOME WORK TO DO. I'LL...UH...SEE YOU IN THE MORNING...
WHEW! I'M EXHAUSTED! SOMETIMES I DON'T KNOW WHICH IS HARDER... FIGHTING CRIME AS DAREDEVIL OR WRESTLING WITH LEGAL PRECEPTS AS-- EH...?
KREAK
THOUGHT I HEARD...
NATASHA?
NO... MUST HAVE BEEN MY IMAGI-NATION. I'M SO TIRED... SO...
NATASHA--?
OH, MATT, I KNOW I'M NOT HALF THE WOMAN SHE IS...
...BUT I'LL ALWAYS BE HERE, MATT. ALWAYS...
NEXT ISSUE: PANIC ON THE PIER!

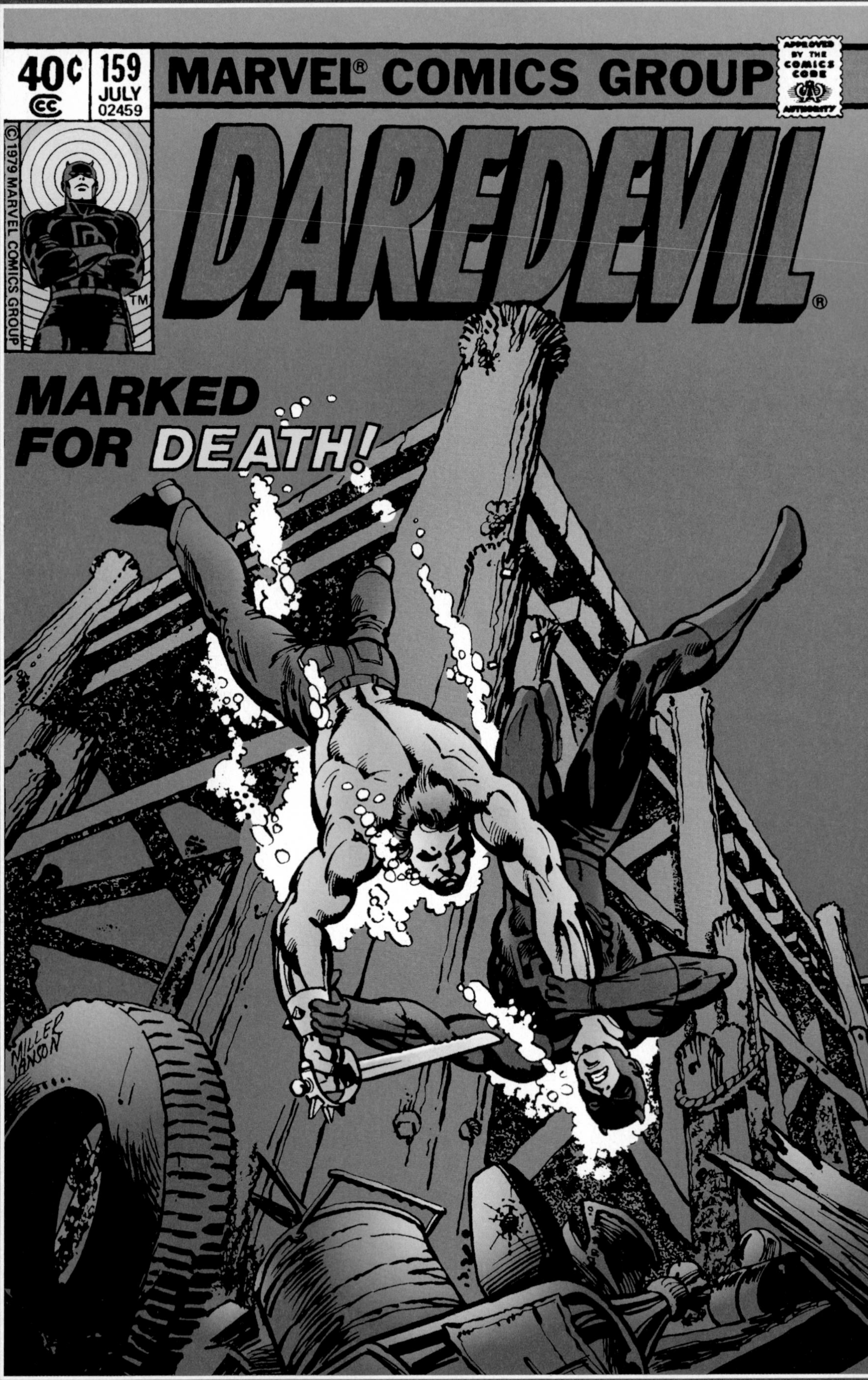

40¢
159
JULY
02459
MARVEL® COMICS GROUP
APPROVED BY THE COMICS CODE AUTHORITY
© 1979 MARVEL COMICS GROUP
DAREDEVIL®
MARKED FOR DEATH!
MILLER JANSON

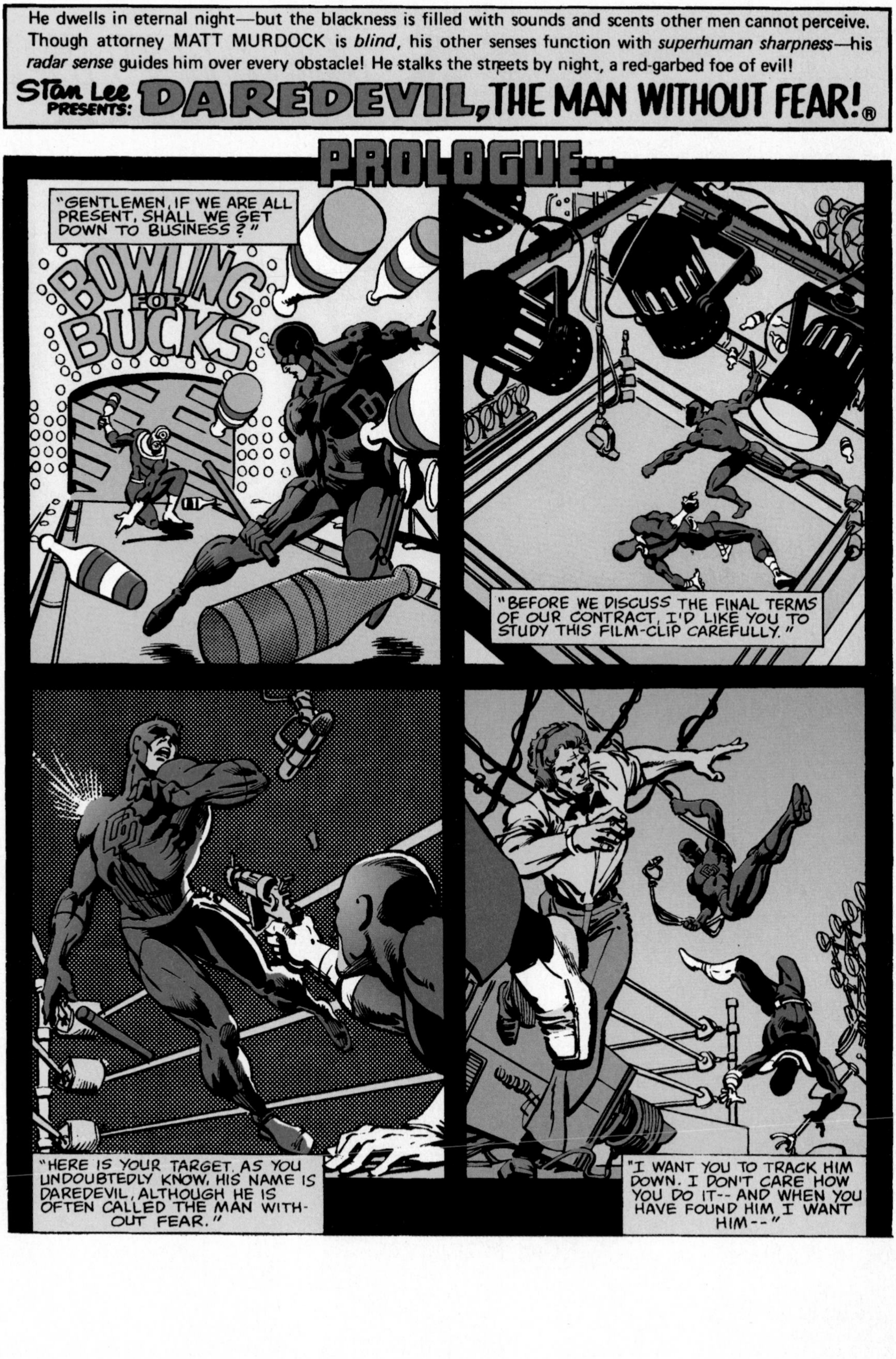
He dwells in eternal night—but the blackness is filled with sounds and scents other men cannot perceive. Though attorney MATT MURDOCK is *blind*, his other senses function with *superhuman sharpness*—his *radar sense* guides him over every obstacle! He stalks the streets by night, a red-garbed foe of evil!
Stan Lee PRESENTS: DAREDEVIL, THE MAN WITHOUT FEAR!®
PROLOGUE..
"GENTLEMEN, IF WE ARE ALL PRESENT, SHALL WE GET DOWN TO BUSINESS?"
BOWLING FOR BUCKS
"BEFORE WE DISCUSS THE FINAL TERMS OF OUR CONTRACT, I'D LIKE YOU TO STUDY THIS FILM-CLIP CAREFULLY."
"HERE IS YOUR TARGET. AS YOU UNDOUBTEDLY KNOW, HIS NAME IS DAREDEVIL, ALTHOUGH HE IS OFTEN CALLED THE MAN WITH-OUT FEAR."
"I WANT YOU TO TRACK HIM DOWN. I DON'T CARE HOW YOU DO IT-- AND WHEN YOU HAVE FOUND HIM I WANT HIM--"

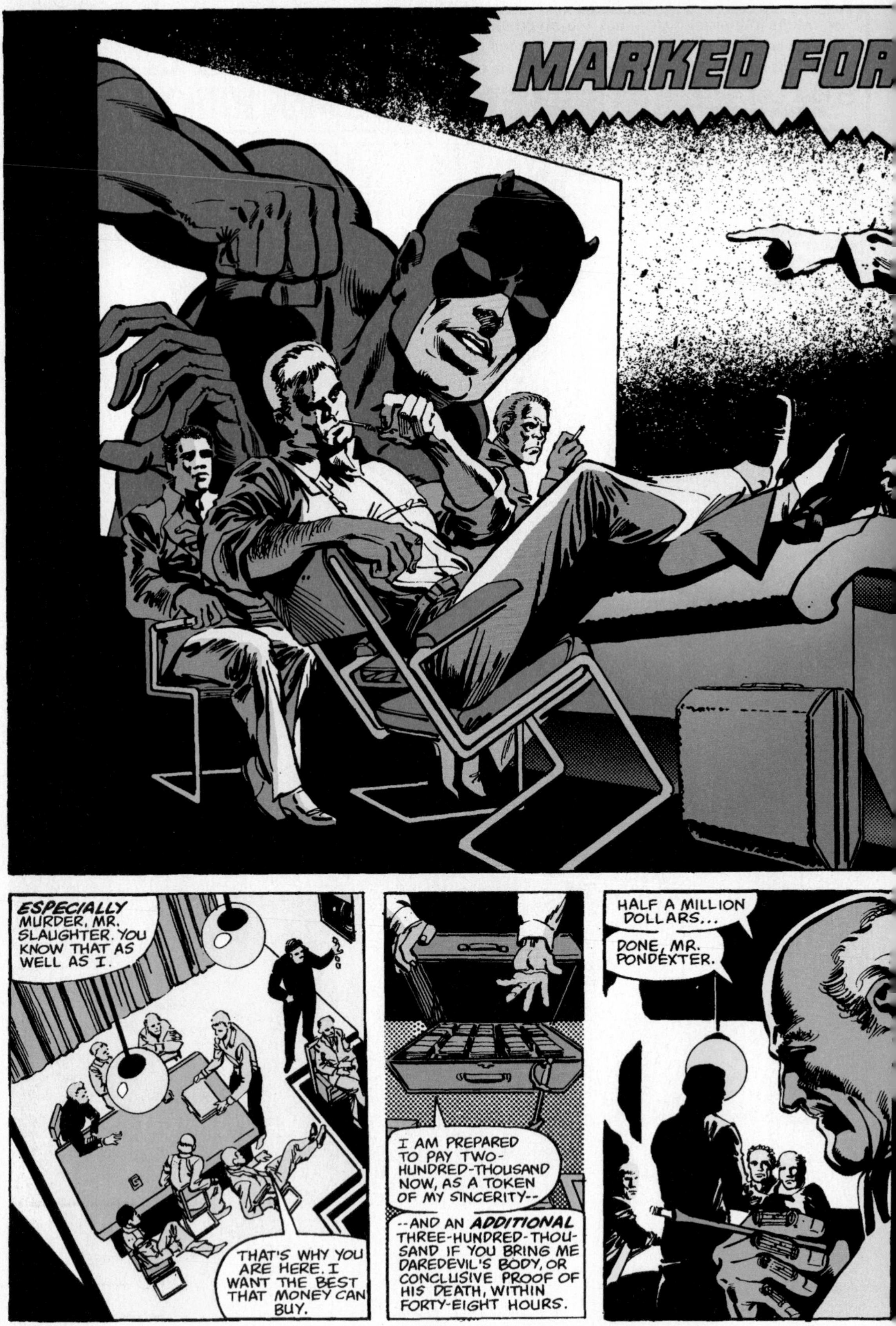
MARKED FOR
ESPECIALLY MURDER, MR. SLAUGHTER. YOU KNOW THAT AS WELL AS I.
THAT'S WHY YOU ARE HERE. I WANT THE BEST THAT MONEY CAN BUY.
I AM PREPARED TO PAY TWO-HUNDRED-THOUSAND NOW, AS A TOKEN OF MY SINCERITY--
--AND AN ADDITIONAL THREE-HUNDRED-THOUSAND IF YOU BRING ME DAREDEVIL'S BODY, OR CONCLUSIVE PROOF OF HIS DEATH, WITHIN FORTY-EIGHT HOURS.
HALF A MILLION DOLLARS...
DONE, MR. PONDEXTER.

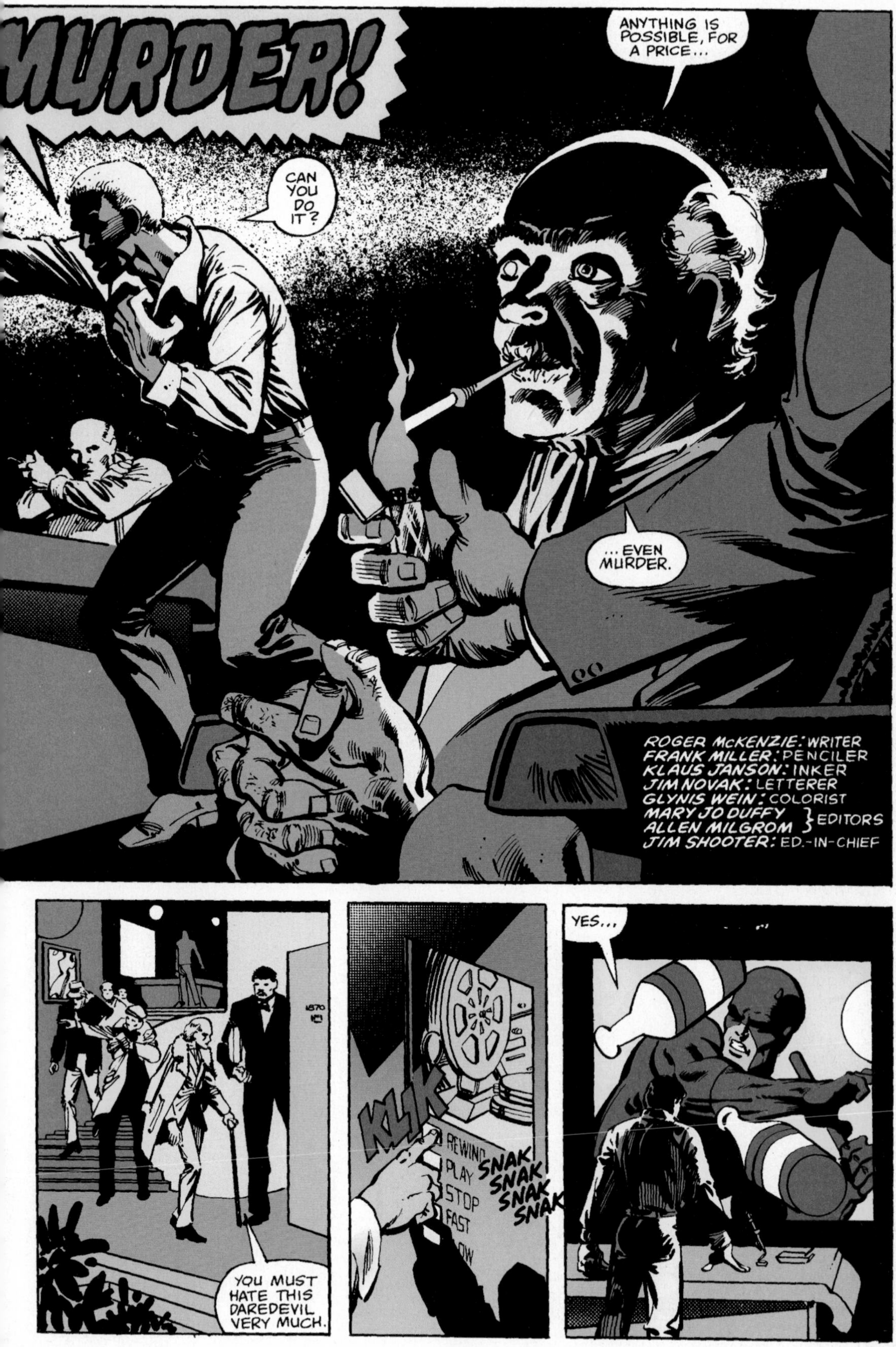
MURDER!
CAN YOU DO IT?
ANYTHING IS POSSIBLE, FOR A PRICE...
...EVEN MURDER.
ROGER McKENZIE: WRITER
FRANK MILLER: PENCILER
KLAUS JANSON: INKER
JIM NOVAK: LETTERER
GLYNIS WEIN: COLORIST
MARY JO DUFFY
ALLEN MILGROM } EDITORS
JIM SHOOTER: ED.-IN-CHIEF
YOU MUST HATE THIS DAREDEVIL VERY MUCH.
KLIK
REWIN
PLAY
STOP
FAST
SNAK SNAK SNAK SNAK
YES...

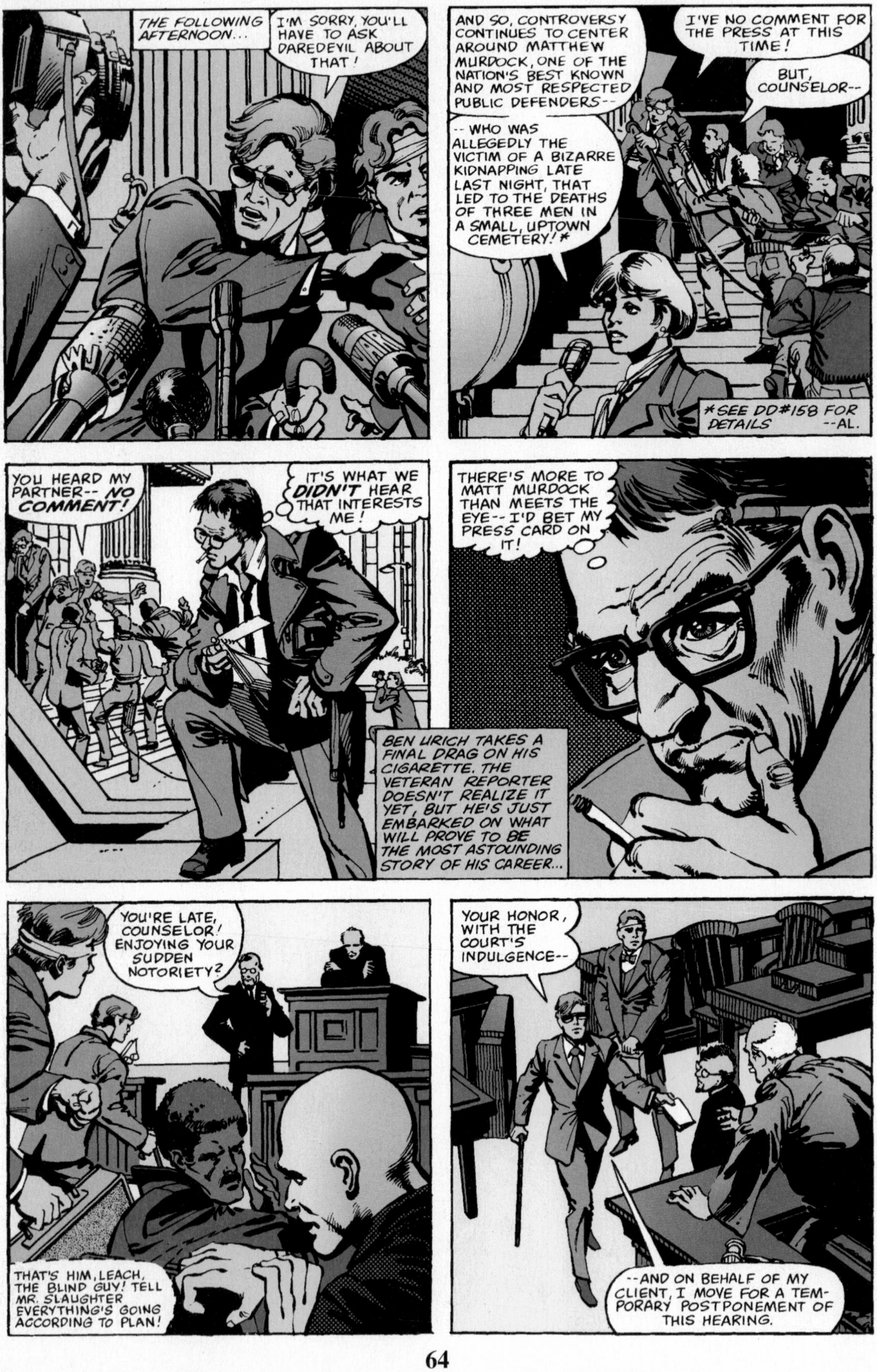
THE FOLLOWING AFTERNOON...
I'M SORRY, YOU'LL HAVE TO ASK DAREDEVIL ABOUT THAT!
AND SO, CONTROVERSY CONTINUES TO CENTER AROUND MATTHEW MURDOCK, ONE OF THE NATION'S BEST KNOWN AND MOST RESPECTED PUBLIC DEFENDERS--
I'VE NO COMMENT FOR THE PRESS AT THIS TIME!
BUT, COUNSELOR--
--WHO WAS ALLEGEDLY THE VICTIM OF A BIZARRE KIDNAPPING LATE LAST NIGHT, THAT LED TO THE DEATHS OF THREE MEN IN A SMALL, UPTOWN CEMETERY!*
*SEE DD #158 FOR DETAILS --AL.
YOU HEARD MY PARTNER-- NO COMMENT!
IT'S WHAT WE DIDN'T HEAR THAT INTERESTS ME!
BEN URICH TAKES A FINAL DRAG ON HIS CIGARETTE. THE VETERAN REPORTER DOESN'T REALIZE IT YET, BUT HE'S JUST EMBARKED ON WHAT WILL PROVE TO BE THE MOST ASTOUNDING STORY OF HIS CAREER...
THERE'S MORE TO MATT MURDOCK THAN MEETS THE EYE-- I'D BET MY PRESS CARD ON IT!
YOU'RE LATE, COUNSELOR! ENJOYING YOUR SUDDEN NOTORIETY?
THAT'S HIM, LEACH, THE BLIND GUY! TELL MR. SLAUGHTER EVERYTHING'S GOING ACCORDING TO PLAN!
YOUR HONOR, WITH THE COURT'S INDULGENCE--
--AND ON BEHALF OF MY CLIENT, I MOVE FOR A TEMPORARY POSTPONEMENT OF THIS HEARING.

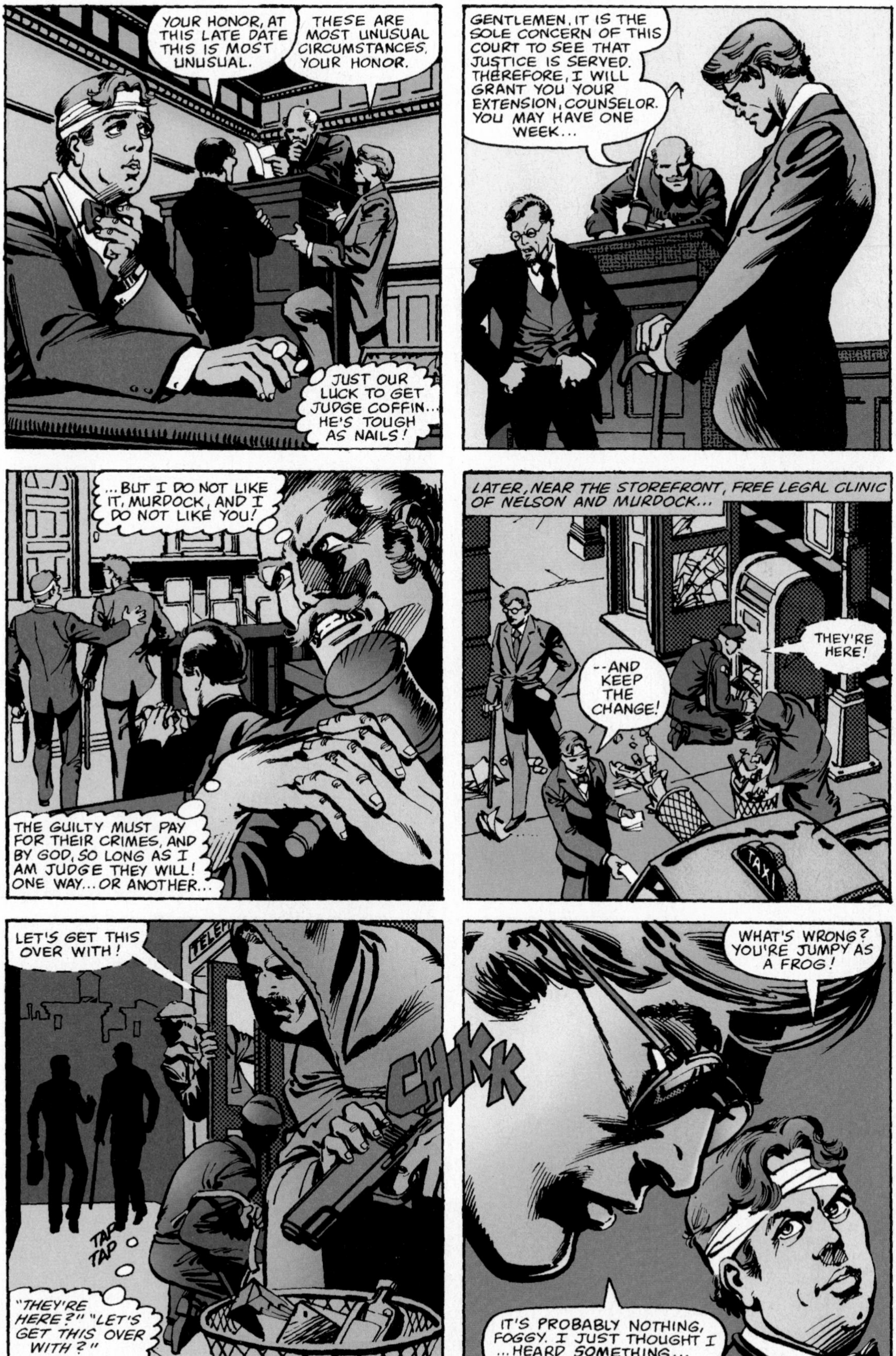
YOUR HONOR, AT THIS LATE DATE THIS IS MOST UNUSUAL.
THESE ARE MOST UNUSUAL CIRCUMSTANCES, YOUR HONOR.
JUST OUR LUCK TO GET JUDGE COFFIN... HE'S TOUGH AS NAILS!
GENTLEMEN, IT IS THE SOLE CONCERN OF THIS COURT TO SEE THAT JUSTICE IS SERVED. THEREFORE, I WILL GRANT YOU YOUR EXTENSION, COUNSELOR. YOU MAY HAVE ONE WEEK...
...BUT I DO NOT LIKE IT, MURDOCK, AND I DO NOT LIKE YOU!
THE GUILTY MUST PAY FOR THEIR CRIMES, AND BY GOD, SO LONG AS I AM JUDGE THEY WILL! ONE WAY... OR ANOTHER...
LATER, NEAR THE STOREFRONT, FREE LEGAL CLINIC OF NELSON AND MURDOCK...
THEY'RE HERE!
--AND KEEP THE CHANGE!
TAXI
LET'S GET THIS OVER WITH!
CHIKK
TAP TAP
"THEY'RE HERE?" "LET'S GET THIS OVER WITH?"
WHAT'S WRONG? YOU'RE JUMPY AS A FROG!
IT'S PROBABLY NOTHING, FOGGY. I JUST THOUGHT I ...HEARD SOMETHING...

WELL, ALL *I* CAN HEAR IS MY BELLY GROWLING! I'M STARVED! HONESTLY, MATT--

--MY STOMACH THINKS MY THROAT'S BEEN CUT!

THIS NEW DIET DEBBIE PUT ME ON IS JUST... MUR... MUR...

MURDOCK!

UH... I DON'T HAVE MUCH MONEY ON ME RIGHT N-NOW...

...DO... DO YOU TAKE MASTER CHARGE?

WHO ARE YOU? WHAT DO YOU WANT? FOGGY, ARE YOU ALL RIGHT?

HE WILL BE MURDOCK... *IF* YOU FOLLOW ORDERS!

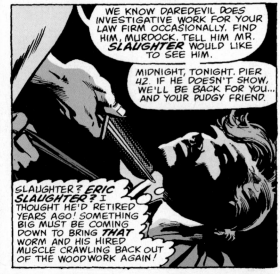

WE KNOW DAREDEVIL DOES INVESTIGATIVE WORK FOR YOUR LAW FIRM OCCASIONALLY. FIND HIM, MURDOCK. TELL HIM MR. *SLAUGHTER* WOULD LIKE TO SEE HIM.

MIDNIGHT, TONIGHT. PIER 42. IF HE DOESN'T SHOW, WE'LL BE BACK FOR YOU... AND YOUR PUDGY FRIEND.

SLAUGHTER? *ERIC SLAUGHTER?* I THOUGHT HE'D RETIRED YEARS AGO! SOMETHING BIG MUST BE COMING DOWN TO BRING *THAT* WORM AND HIS HIRED MUSCLE CRAWLING BACK OUT OF THE WOODWORK AGAIN!

:*WHEW!*: WHAT WAS THAT ALL ABOUT, MATT?

MATT?

MIDNIGHT. THE WITCHING HOUR. BUT IT ISN'T A WITCH THAT PROWLS HELL'S KITCHEN THIS NIGHT.

IT IS A DEVIL...

...A GRIM AND *SIGHTLESS* DEVIL THAT GLIDES AS SILENTLY AS A MOONCAST SHADOW ACROSS DARK ROOFTOPS...

...AND DOWN DIRTY, CHEERLESS BACKSTREETS TOWARD THE FOG-SHROUDED WATERS OF THE HUDSON RIVER AND...

PIER 42--! I'LL GIVE SLAUGHTER CREDIT, HE COULDN'T HAVE CHOSEN A LONELIER OR MORE FOREBODING LOCALE!

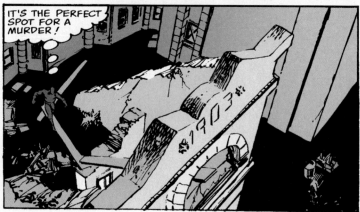

IT'S THE PERFECT SPOT FOR A MURDER!

67

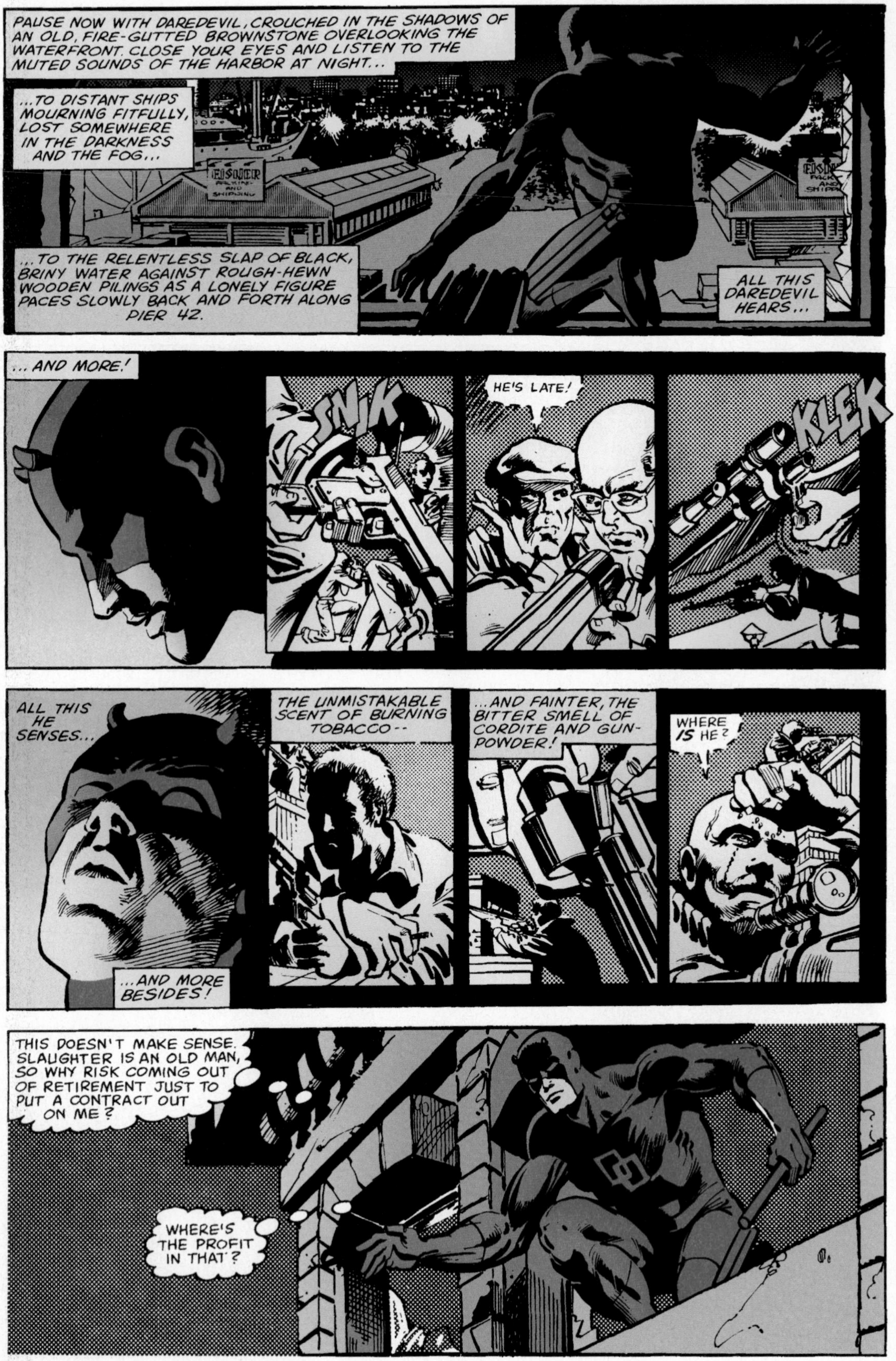
PAUSE NOW WITH DAREDEVIL, CROUCHED IN THE SHADOWS OF AN OLD, FIRE-GUTTED BROWNSTONE OVERLOOKING THE WATERFRONT. CLOSE YOUR EYES AND LISTEN TO THE MUTED SOUNDS OF THE HARBOR AT NIGHT...
...TO DISTANT SHIPS MOURNING FITFULLY, LOST SOMEWHERE IN THE DARKNESS AND THE FOG...
...TO THE RELENTLESS SLAP OF BLACK, BRINY WATER AGAINST ROUGH-HEWN WOODEN PILINGS AS A LONELY FIGURE PACES SLOWLY BACK AND FORTH ALONG PIER 42.
ALL THIS DAREDEVIL HEARS...
...AND MORE!
SNIK
HE'S LATE!
KLEK
ALL THIS HE SENSES...
...AND MORE BESIDES!
THE UNMISTAKABLE SCENT OF BURNING TOBACCO--
...AND FAINTER, THE BITTER SMELL OF CORDITE AND GUN-POWDER!
WHERE IS HE?
THIS DOESN'T MAKE SENSE. SLAUGHTER IS AN OLD MAN, SO WHY RISK COMING OUT OF RETIREMENT JUST TO PUT A CONTRACT OUT ON ME?
WHERE'S THE PROFIT IN THAT?

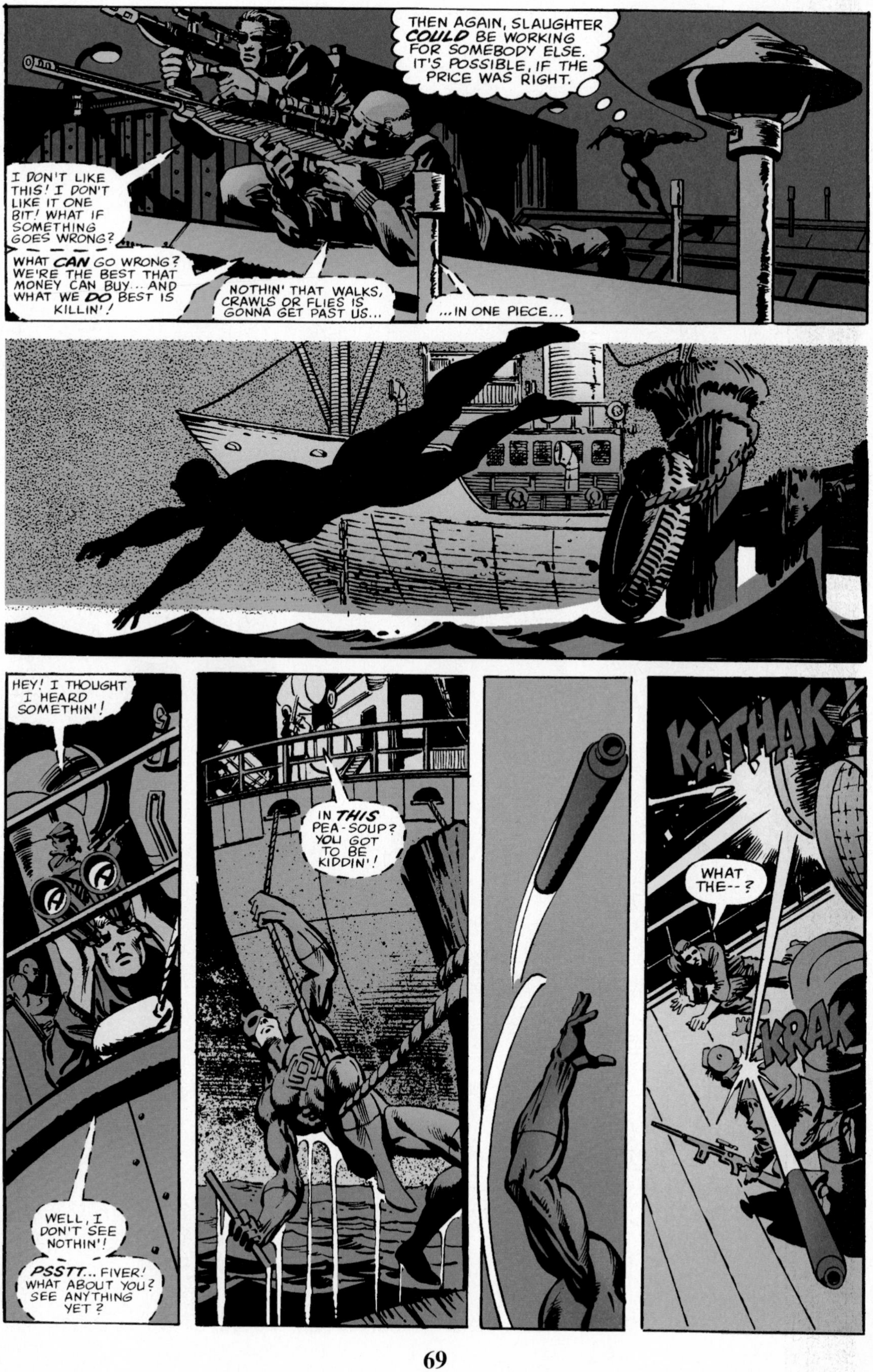
THEN AGAIN, SLAUGHTER COULD BE WORKING FOR SOMEBODY ELSE. IT'S POSSIBLE, IF THE PRICE WAS RIGHT.
I DON'T LIKE THIS! I DON'T LIKE IT ONE BIT! WHAT IF SOMETHING GOES WRONG?
WHAT CAN GO WRONG? WE'RE THE BEST THAT MONEY CAN BUY... AND WHAT WE DO BEST IS KILLIN'!
NOTHIN' THAT WALKS, CRAWLS OR FLIES IS GONNA GET PAST US...
...IN ONE PIECE...
HEY! I THOUGHT I HEARD SOMETHIN'!
WELL, I DON'T SEE NOTHIN'!
PSSTT... FIVER! WHAT ABOUT YOU? SEE ANYTHING YET?
IN THIS PEA-SOUP? YOU GOT TO BE KIDDIN'!
KATHAK
WHAT THE--?
KRAK

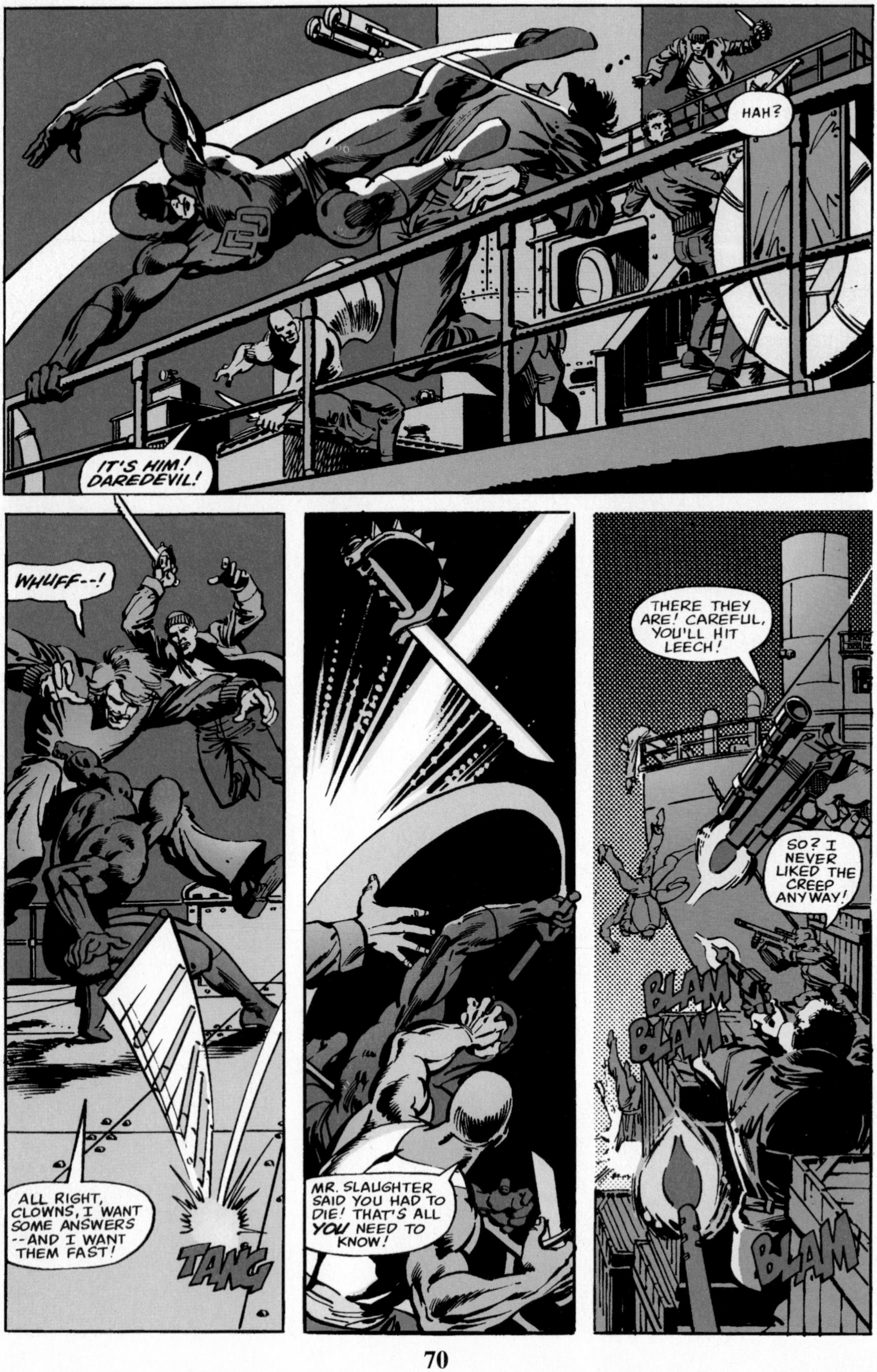
HAH?
IT'S HIM! DAREDEVIL!
WHUFF--!
ALL RIGHT, CLOWNS, I WANT SOME ANSWERS --AND I WANT THEM FAST!
TANG
MR. SLAUGHTER SAID YOU HAD TO DIE! THAT'S ALL YOU NEED TO KNOW!
THERE THEY ARE! CAREFUL, YOU'LL HIT LEECH!
SO? I NEVER LIKED THE CREEP ANYWAY!
BLAM
BLAM
BLAM

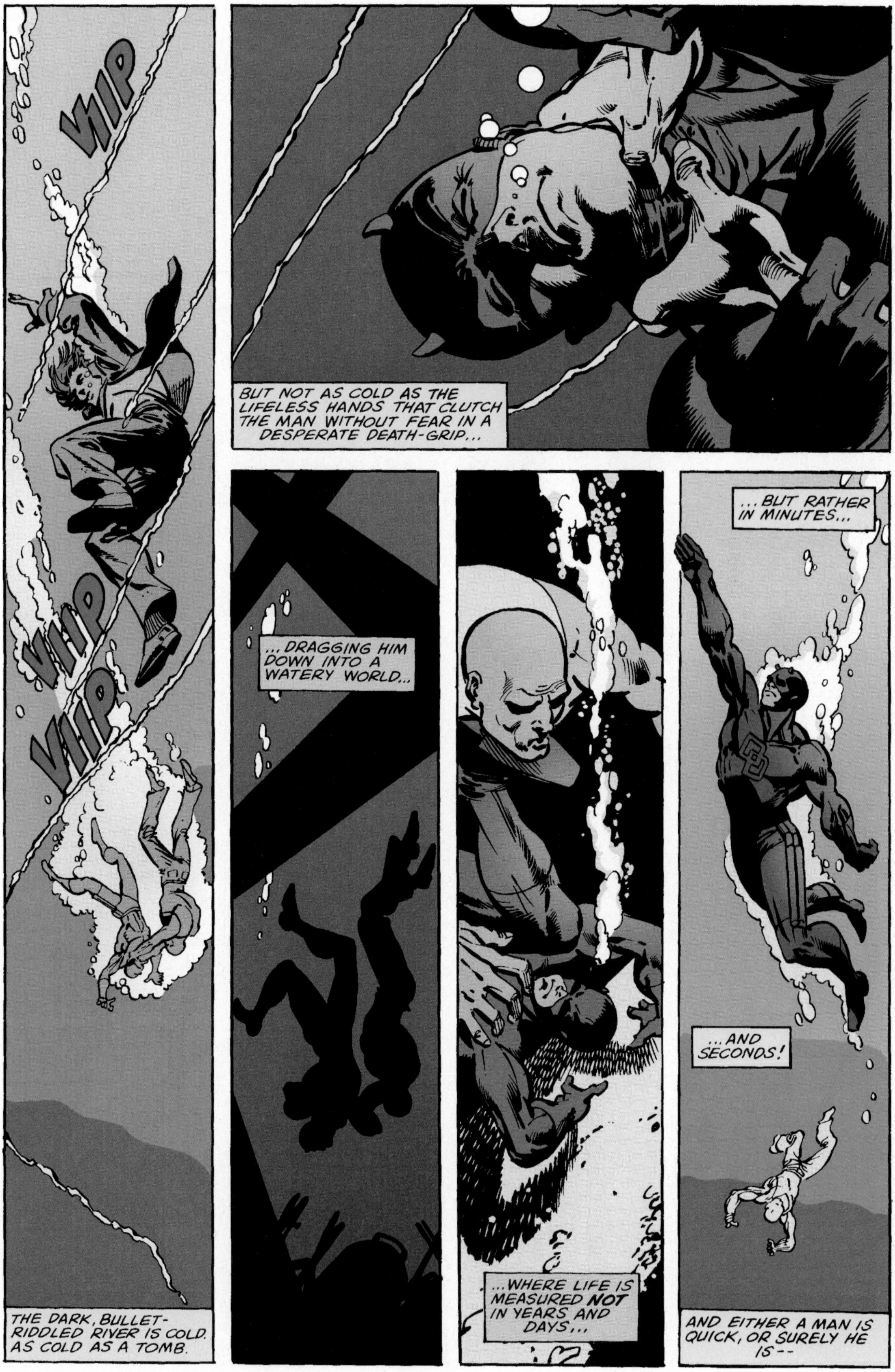
VIIP
VIIP
VIIP
THE DARK, BULLET-RIDDLED RIVER IS COLD. AS COLD AS A TOMB.
BUT NOT AS COLD AS THE LIFELESS HANDS THAT CLUTCH THE MAN WITHOUT FEAR IN A DESPERATE DEATH-GRIP...
...DRAGGING HIM DOWN INTO A WATERY WORLD...
...WHERE LIFE IS MEASURED NOT IN YEARS AND DAYS...
...BUT RATHER IN MINUTES...
...AND SECONDS!
AND EITHER A MAN IS QUICK, OR SURELY HE IS--

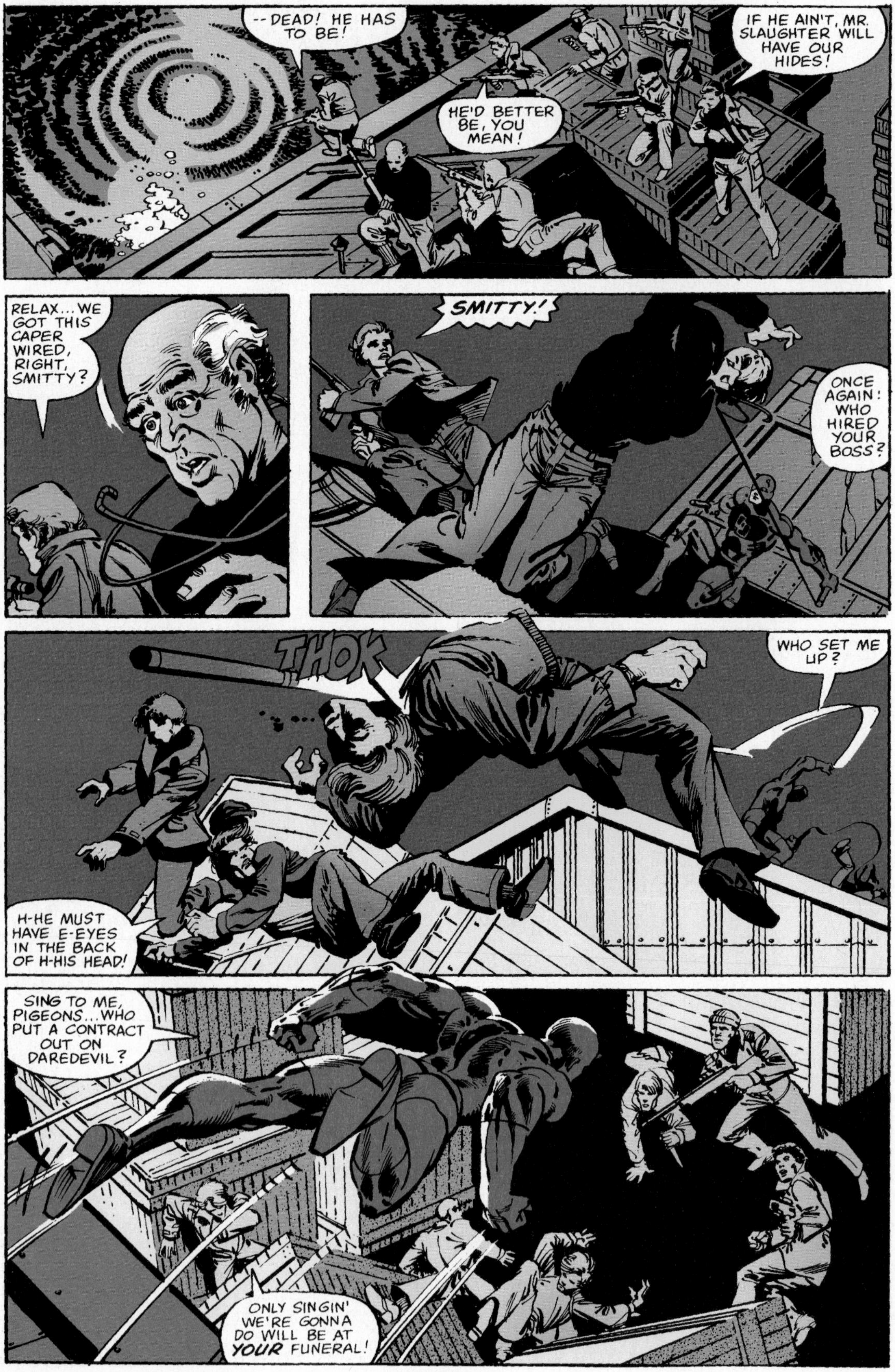

--DEAD! HE HAS TO BE!
HE'D BETTER BE, YOU MEAN!
IF HE AIN'T, MR. SLAUGHTER WILL HAVE OUR HIDES!
RELAX... WE GOT THIS CAPER WIRED, RIGHT, SMITTY?
SMITTY!
ONCE AGAIN: WHO HIRED YOUR BOSS?
THOK
WHO SET ME UP?
H-HE MUST HAVE E-EYES IN THE BACK OF H-HIS HEAD!
SING TO ME, PIGEONS... WHO PUT A CONTRACT OUT ON DAREDEVIL?
ONLY SINGIN' WE'RE GONNA DO WILL BE AT YOUR FUNERAL!

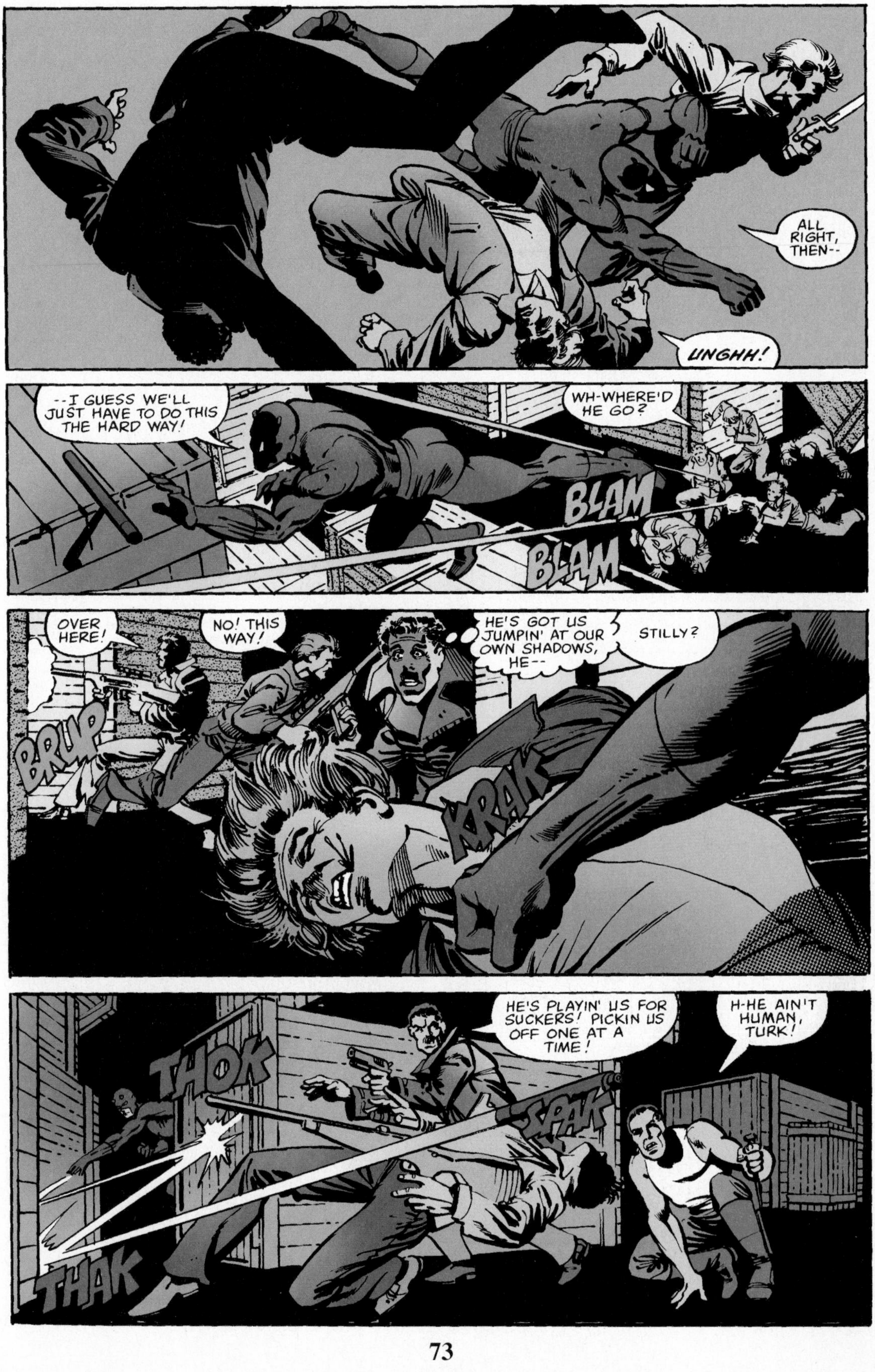
ALL RIGHT, THEN--
UNGHH!
--I GUESS WE'LL JUST HAVE TO DO THIS THE HARD WAY!
WH-WHERE'D HE GO?
BLAM
BLAM
OVER HERE!
NO! THIS WAY!
HE'S GOT US JUMPIN' AT OUR OWN SHADOWS, HE--
STILLY?
BRUP
KRAK
HE'S PLAYIN' US FOR SUCKERS! PICKIN US OFF ONE AT A TIME!
H-HE AIN'T HUMAN, TURK!
THOK
SPAK
THAK

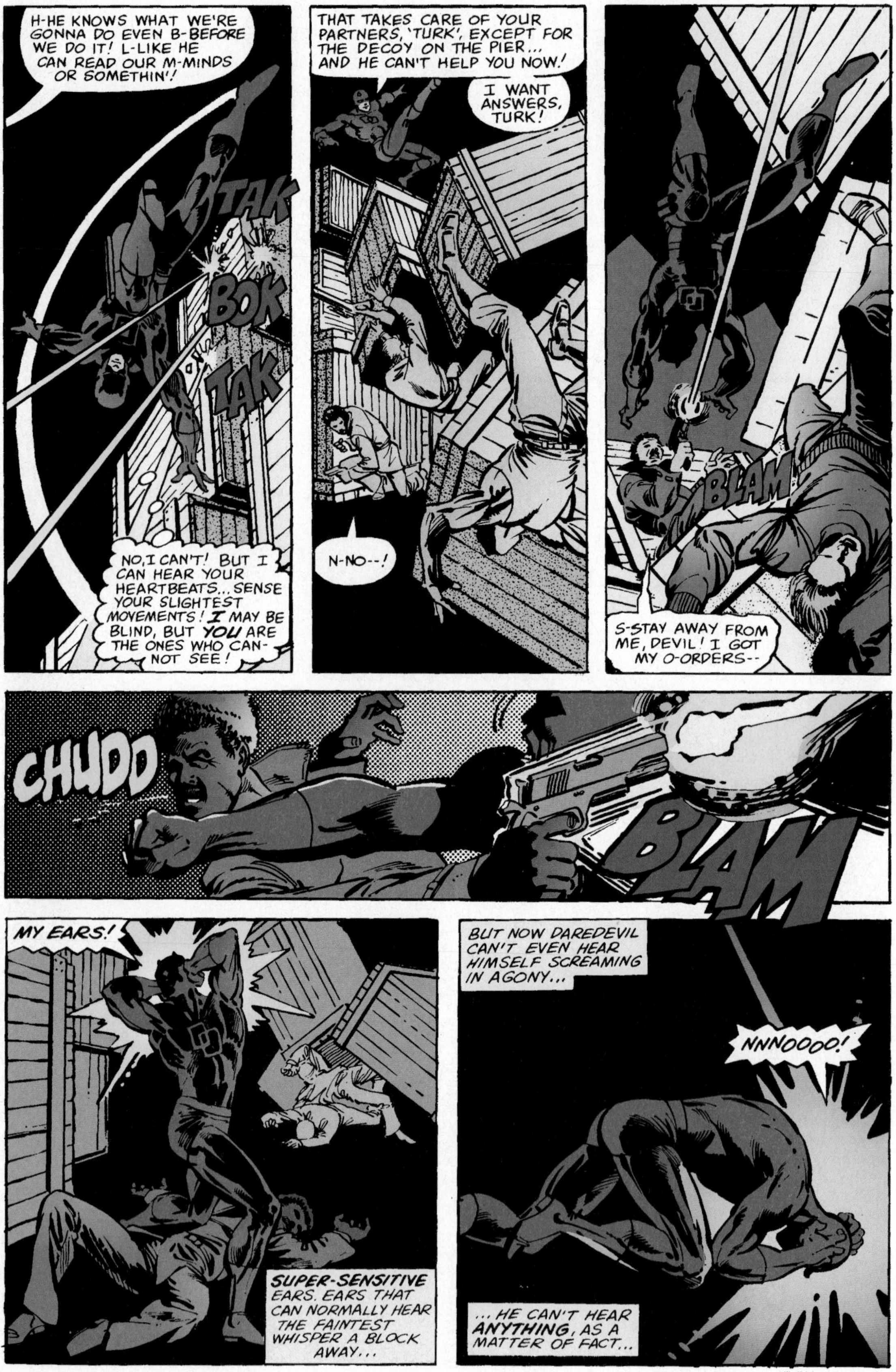

H-HE KNOWS WHAT WE'RE GONNA DO EVEN B-BEFORE WE DO IT! L-LIKE HE CAN READ OUR M-MINDS OR SOMETHIN'!
TAK
BOK
TAK
NO, I CAN'T! BUT I CAN HEAR YOUR HEARTBEATS... SENSE YOUR SLIGHTEST MOVEMENTS! I MAY BE BLIND, BUT YOU ARE THE ONES WHO CAN-NOT SEE!
THAT TAKES CARE OF YOUR PARTNERS, 'TURK', EXCEPT FOR THE DECOY ON THE PIER... AND HE CAN'T HELP YOU NOW!
I WANT ANSWERS, TURK!
N-NO--!
BLAM
S-STAY AWAY FROM ME, DEVIL! I GOT MY O-ORDERS--
CHUDD
BLAM
MY EARS!
SUPER-SENSITIVE EARS. EARS THAT CAN NORMALLY HEAR THE FAINTEST WHISPER A BLOCK AWAY...
BUT NOW DAREDEVIL CAN'T EVEN HEAR HIMSELF SCREAMING IN AGONY...
NNNOOOO!
... HE CAN'T HEAR ANYTHING, AS A MATTER OF FACT...

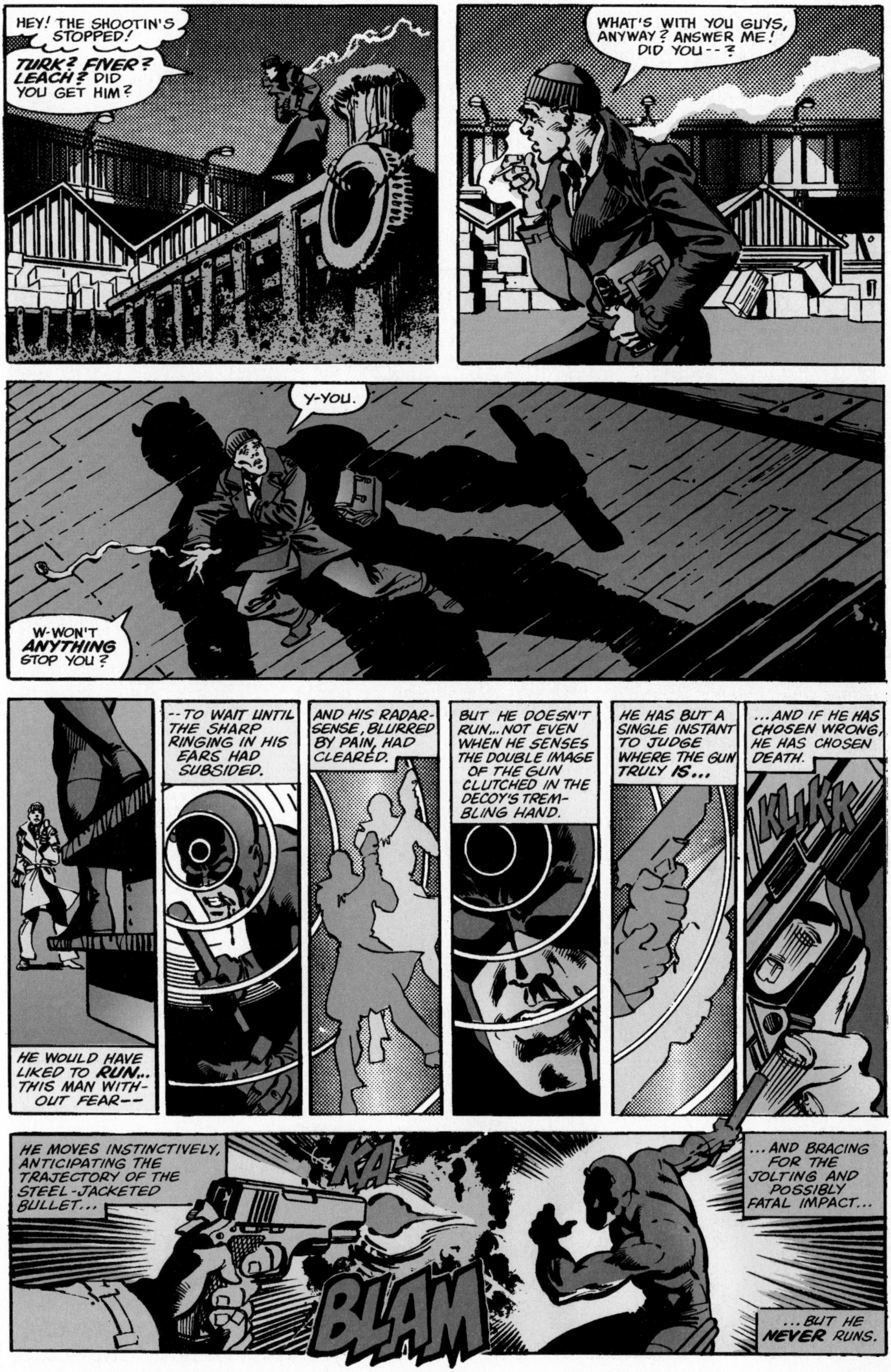

HEY! THE SHOOTIN'S STOPPED!
TURK? FIVER? LEACH? DID YOU GET HIM?
WHAT'S WITH YOU GUYS, ANYWAY? ANSWER ME! DID YOU--?
Y-YOU.
W-WON'T ANYTHING STOP YOU?
HE WOULD HAVE LIKED TO RUN... THIS MAN WITH-OUT FEAR--
--TO WAIT UNTIL THE SHARP RINGING IN HIS EARS HAD SUBSIDED.
AND HIS RADAR-SENSE, BLURRED BY PAIN, HAD CLEARED.
BUT HE DOESN'T RUN... NOT EVEN WHEN HE SENSES THE DOUBLE IMAGE OF THE GUN CLUTCHED IN THE DECOY'S TREM-BLING HAND.
HE HAS BUT A SINGLE INSTANT TO JUDGE WHERE THE GUN TRULY IS...
...AND IF HE HAS CHOSEN WRONG, HE HAS CHOSEN DEATH.
KLIKK
HE MOVES INSTINCTIVELY, ANTICIPATING THE TRAJECTORY OF THE STEEL-JACKETED BULLET...
KA-
BLAM
...AND BRACING FOR THE JOLTING AND POSSIBLY FATAL IMPACT...
...BUT HE NEVER RUNS.

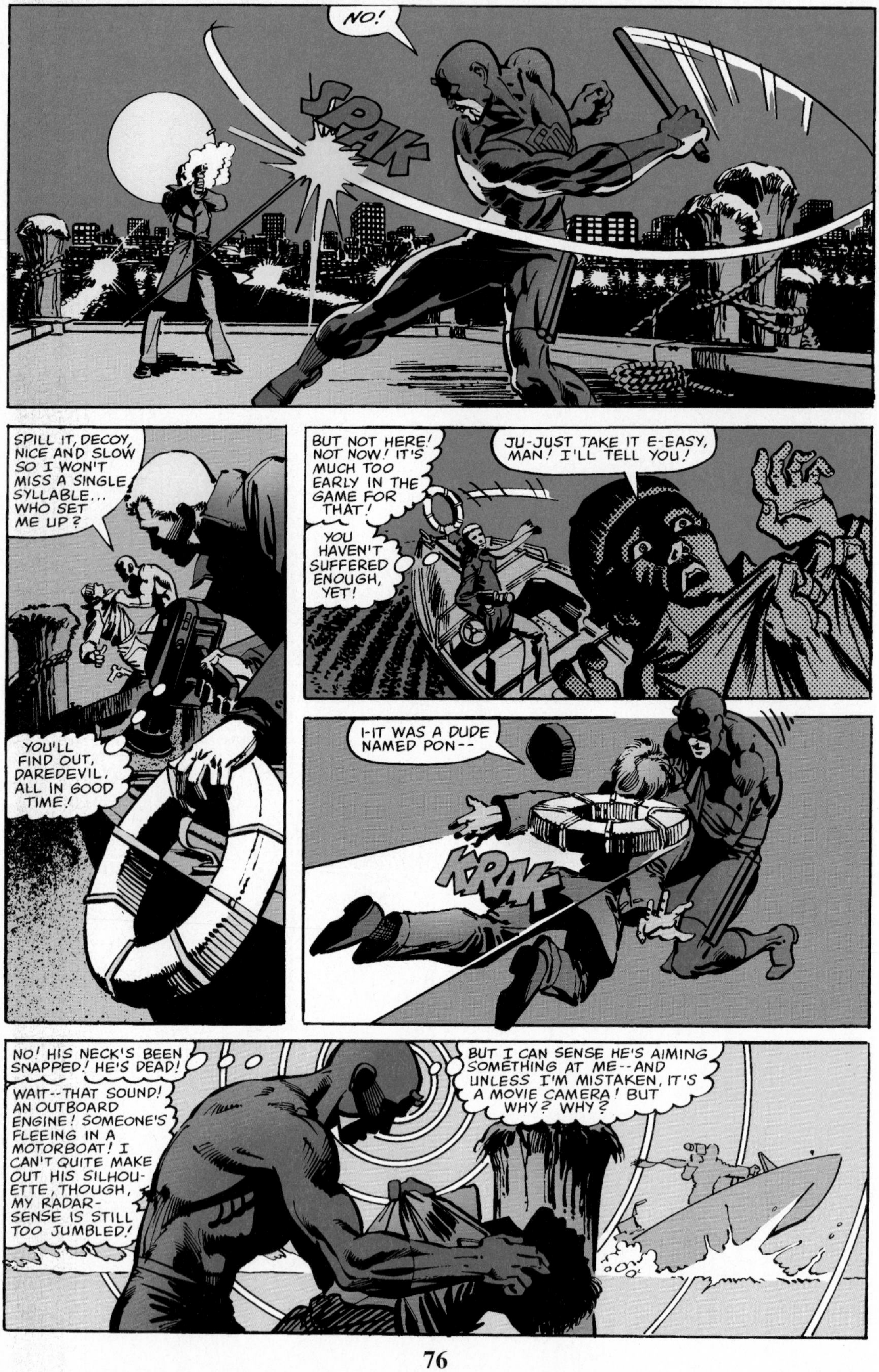

NO!
SPAK
SPILL IT, DECOY, NICE AND SLOW SO I WON'T MISS A SINGLE SYLLABLE... WHO SET ME UP?
YOU'LL FIND OUT, DAREDEVIL, ALL IN GOOD TIME!
BUT NOT HERE! NOT NOW! IT'S MUCH TOO EARLY IN THE GAME FOR THAT!
YOU HAVEN'T SUFFERED ENOUGH, YET!
JU-JUST TAKE IT E-EASY, MAN! I'LL TELL YOU!
I-IT WAS A DUDE NAMED PON--
KRAK
NO! HIS NECK'S BEEN SNAPPED! HE'S DEAD!
WAIT--THAT SOUND! AN OUTBOARD ENGINE! SOMEONE'S FLEEING IN A MOTORBOAT! I CAN'T QUITE MAKE OUT HIS SILHOUETTE, THOUGH, MY RADAR-SENSE IS STILL TOO JUMBLED!
BUT I CAN SENSE HE'S AIMING SOMETHING AT ME--AND UNLESS I'M MISTAKEN, IT'S A MOVIE CAMERA! BUT WHY? WHY?

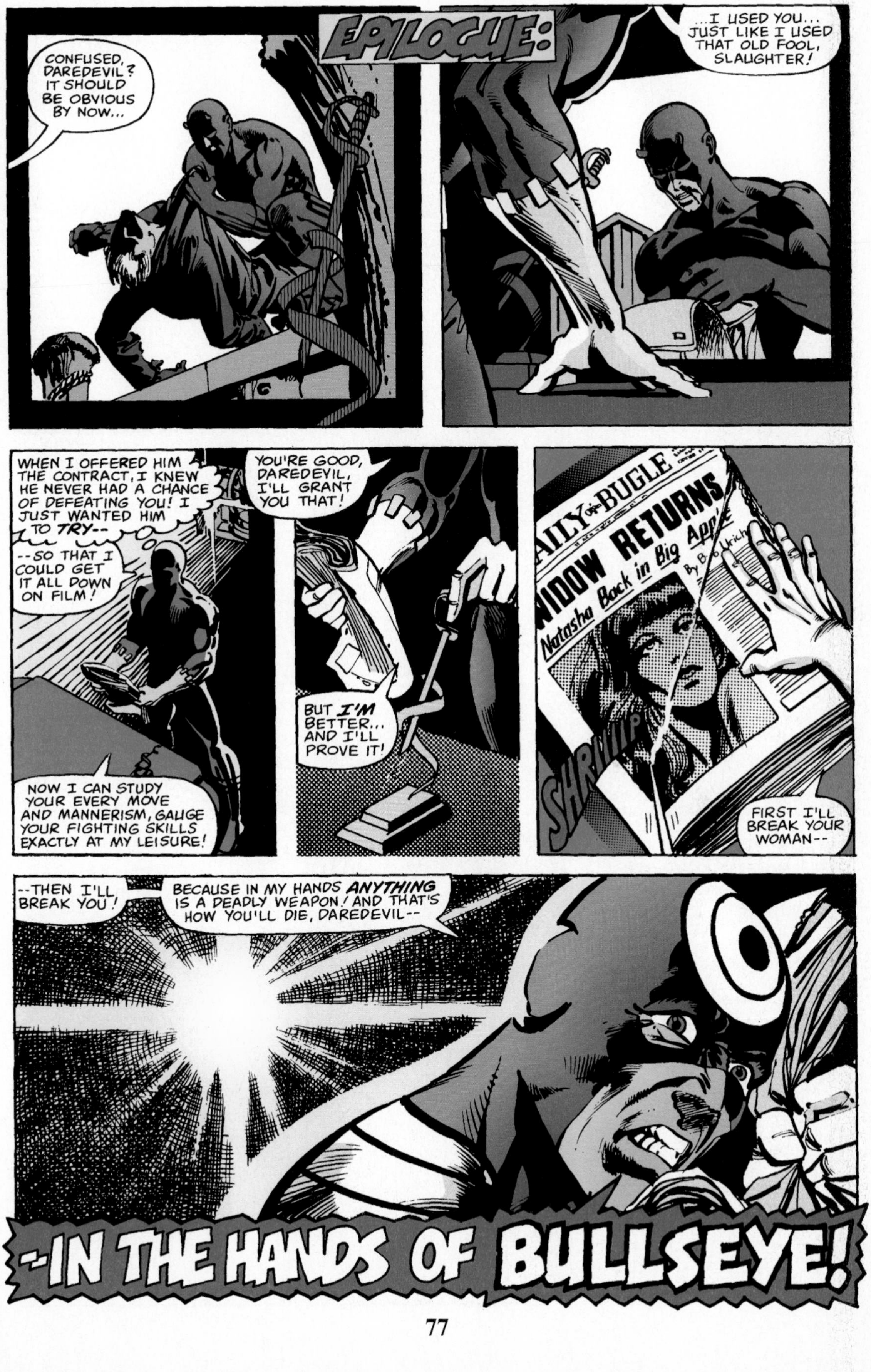
EPILOGUE:
CONFUSED, DAREDEVIL? IT SHOULD BE OBVIOUS BY NOW...
...I USED YOU... JUST LIKE I USED THAT OLD FOOL, SLAUGHTER!
WHEN I OFFERED HIM THE CONTRACT, I KNEW HE NEVER HAD A CHANCE OF DEFEATING YOU! I JUST WANTED HIM TO TRY--
--SO THAT I COULD GET IT ALL DOWN ON FILM!
NOW I CAN STUDY YOUR EVERY MOVE AND MANNERISM, GAUGE YOUR FIGHTING SKILLS EXACTLY AT MY LEISURE!
YOU'RE GOOD, DAREDEVIL, I'LL GRANT YOU THAT!
BUT I'M BETTER... AND I'LL PROVE IT!
DAILY BUGLE
WIDOW RETURNS
Natasha Back in Big Apple
SHRIIIP
FIRST I'LL BREAK YOUR WOMAN--
--THEN I'LL BREAK YOU!
BECAUSE IN MY HANDS ANYTHING IS A DEADLY WEAPON! AND THAT'S HOW YOU'LL DIE, DAREDEVIL--
--IN THE HANDS OF BULLSEYE!

PRESENTING A MIGHTY MARVEL BONUS PAGE-- THE *SECRETS* OF DAREDEVIL'S BILLY CLUB!

IN DAY TO DAY LIFE, D.D.'s FAMOUS BILLY CLUB IS DISGUISED AS A BLIND MAN'S CANE...

...BUT WHENEVER IT'S NEEDED, THE CANE CAN BE QUICKLY SNAPPED APART--

POK

--INTO TWO SECTIONS, EACH HAVING A SPECIFIC FUNCTION IN RELATION TO HIS DUTIES.

TAK

THE FIRST SECTION CONTAINS A SPRING-RELEASE MECHANISM, WHICH INSTANTLY STRAIGHTENS THE CURVED CANE HANDLE AT THE TOUCH OF A SINGLE STUD.

A SECOND TAP OF THE STUD EXTENDS A LENGTH OF CABLE FROM WITHIN THE HANDLE, TO FORM A RETRACTABLE, ROOF-CATCHING HOOK.

KDAK

THIS HOOK-AND-CABLE DEVICE ENABLES D.D. TO SWING ACROSS DISTANCES TOO GREAT FOR HIM TO LEAP.

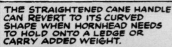

THE STRAIGHTENED CANE HANDLE CAN REVERT TO ITS CURVED SHAPE WHEN HORNHEAD NEEDS TO HOLD ONTO A LEDGE OR CARRY ADDED WEIGHT.

THOK!

THE REMAINING SECTION OF THE BILLY CLUB/CANE IS A SUPERBLY BALANCED PIECE OF STEEL-REINFORCED WOOD THAT D.D. THROWS WITH CONSUMMATE SKILL.

D.D.'s COSTUME FEATURES A LEG-HOLSTER, IN WHICH HE STORES BOTH SECTIONS OF THIS ELEGANT WEAPON.

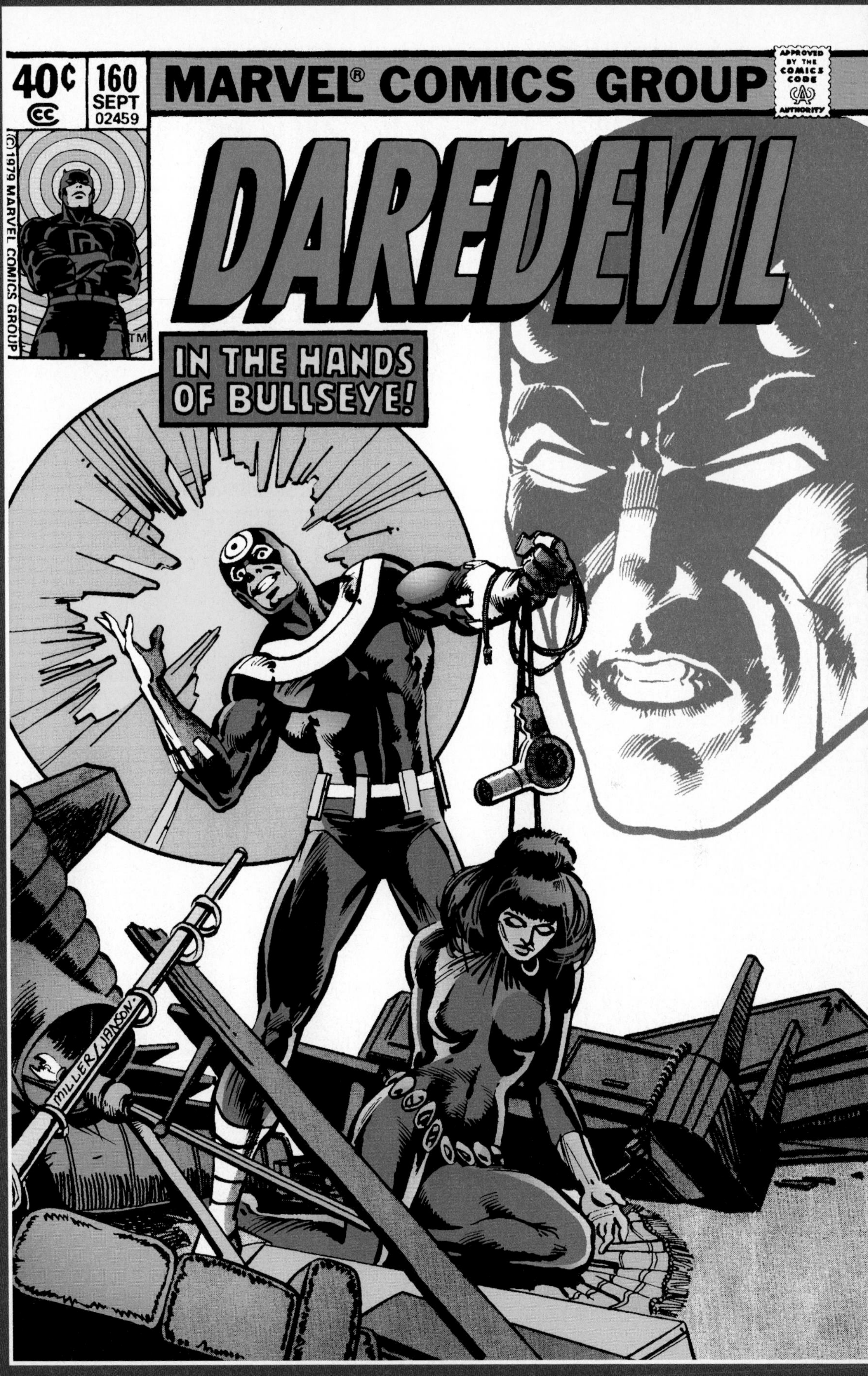
40¢
CC
160
SEPT
02459
MARVEL® COMICS GROUP
APPROVED BY THE COMICS CODE AUTHORITY
(C) 1979 MARVEL COMICS GROUP
TM
DAREDEVIL
IN THE HANDS OF BULLSEYE!
MILLER/JANSON

He dwells in eternal night—but the blackness is filled with sounds and scents other men cannot perceive. Though attorney MATT MURDOCK is *blind*, his other senses function with *superhuman sharpness*—his *radar sense* guides him over every obstacle! He stalks the streets by night, a red-garbed foe of evil!

Stan Lee PRESENTS: DAREDEVIL, THE MAN WITHOUT FEAR!®

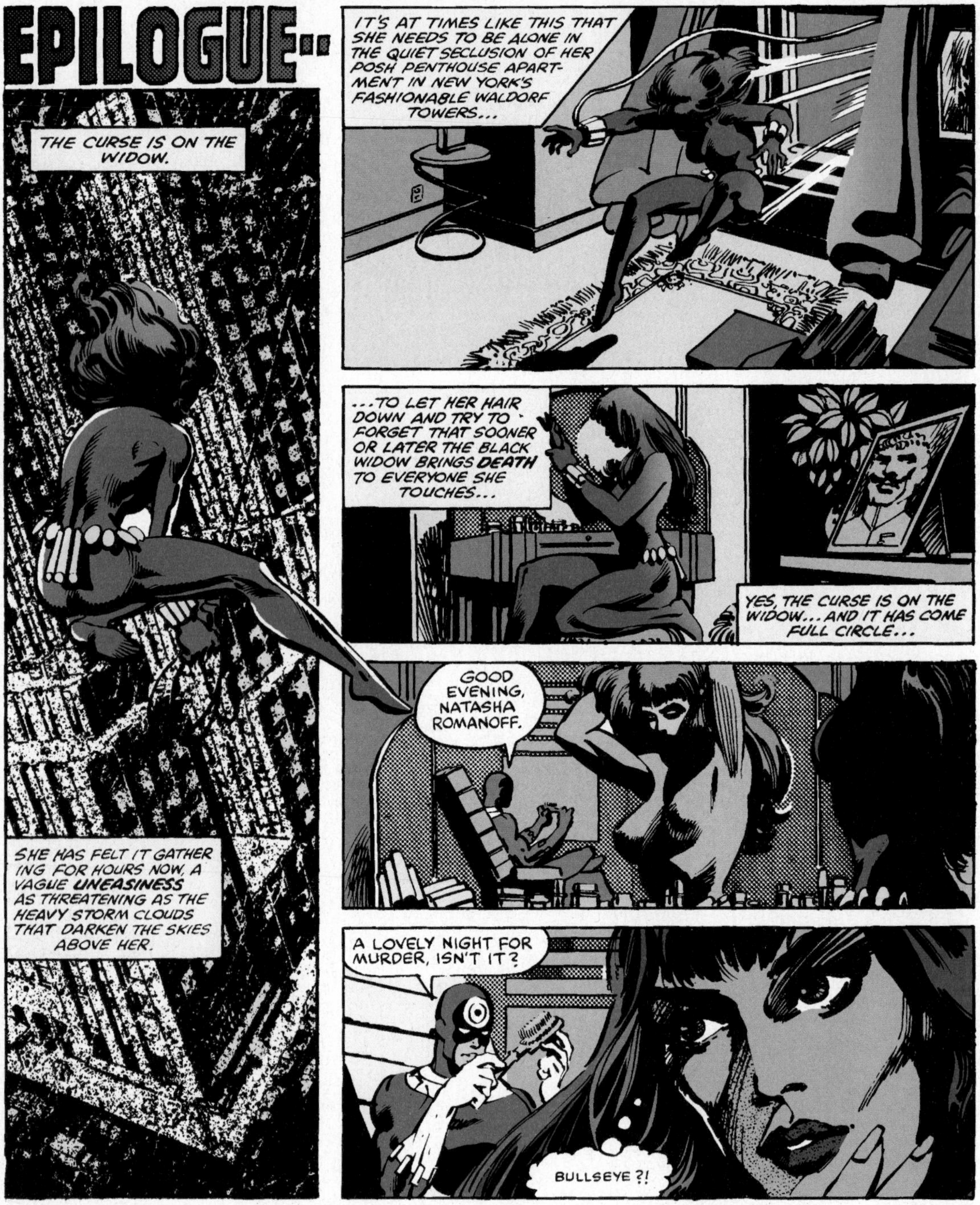
EPILOGUE--
THE CURSE IS ON THE WIDOW.
SHE HAS FELT IT GATHERING FOR HOURS NOW, A VAGUE UNEASINESS AS THREATENING AS THE HEAVY STORM CLOUDS THAT DARKEN THE SKIES ABOVE HER.
IT'S AT TIMES LIKE THIS THAT SHE NEEDS TO BE ALONE IN THE QUIET SECLUSION OF HER POSH PENTHOUSE APARTMENT IN NEW YORK'S FASHIONABLE WALDORF TOWERS...
...TO LET HER HAIR DOWN AND TRY TO FORGET THAT SOONER OR LATER THE BLACK WIDOW BRINGS DEATH TO EVERYONE SHE TOUCHES...
YES, THE CURSE IS ON THE WIDOW... AND IT HAS COME FULL CIRCLE...
GOOD EVENING, NATASHA ROMANOFF.
A LOVELY NIGHT FOR MURDER, ISN'T IT?
BULLSEYE ?!

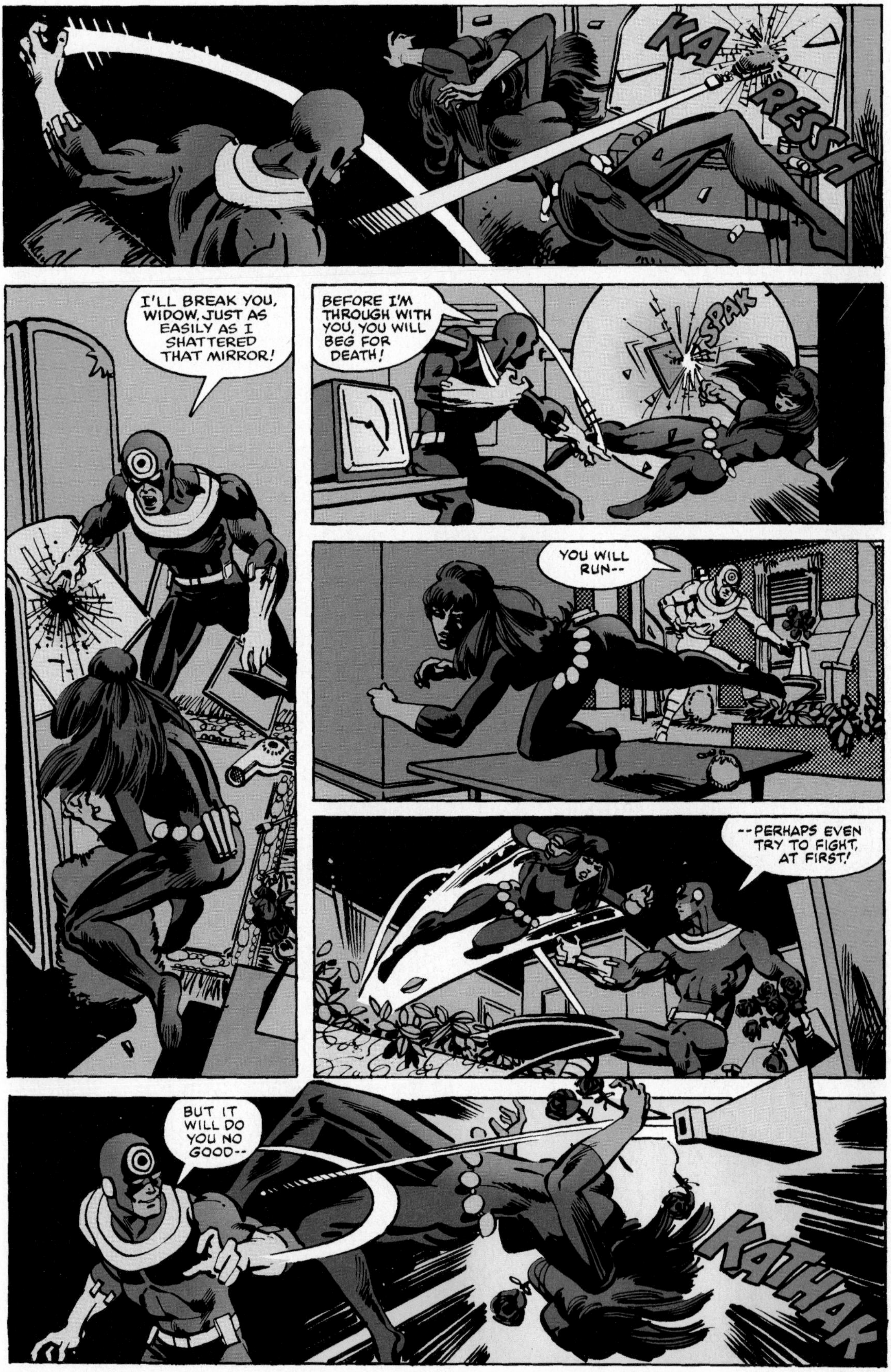
KA
RESSH
I'LL BREAK YOU, WIDOW, JUST AS EASILY AS I SHATTERED THAT MIRROR!
BEFORE I'M THROUGH WITH YOU, YOU WILL BEG FOR DEATH!
SPAK
YOU WILL RUN--
--PERHAPS EVEN TRY TO FIGHT, AT FIRST!
BUT IT WILL DO YOU NO GOOD--
KATHAK

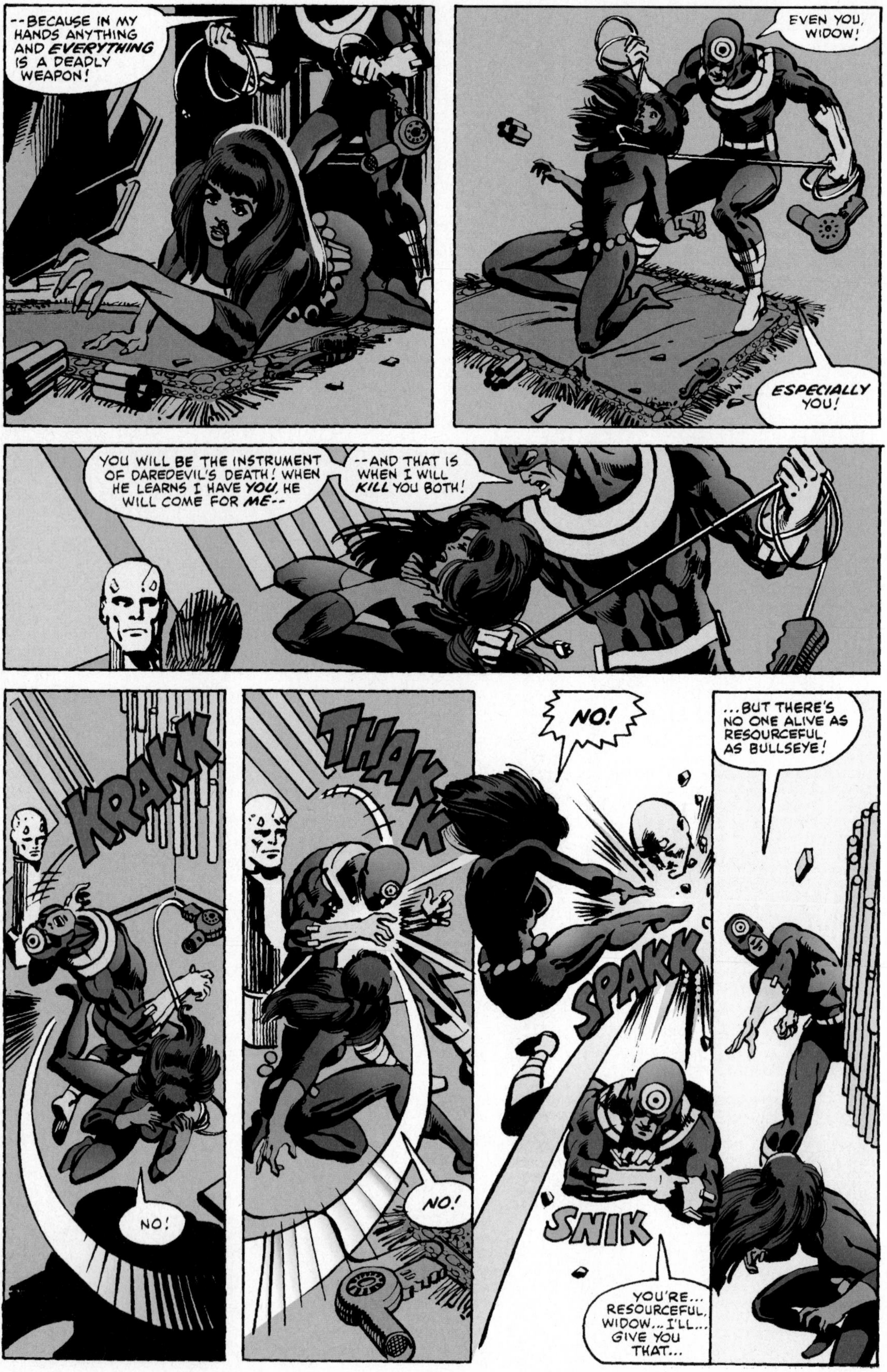
--BECAUSE IN MY HANDS ANYTHING AND EVERYTHING IS A DEADLY WEAPON!
EVEN YOU, WIDOW!
ESPECIALLY YOU!
YOU WILL BE THE INSTRUMENT OF DAREDEVIL'S DEATH! WHEN HE LEARNS I HAVE YOU, HE WILL COME FOR ME--
--AND THAT IS WHEN I WILL KILL YOU BOTH!
KRAKK
NO!
THAKK
NO!
NO!
SPAKK
SNIK
YOU'RE... RESOURCEFUL, WIDOW... I'LL... GIVE YOU THAT...
...BUT THERE'S NO ONE ALIVE AS RESOURCEFUL AS BULLSEYE!

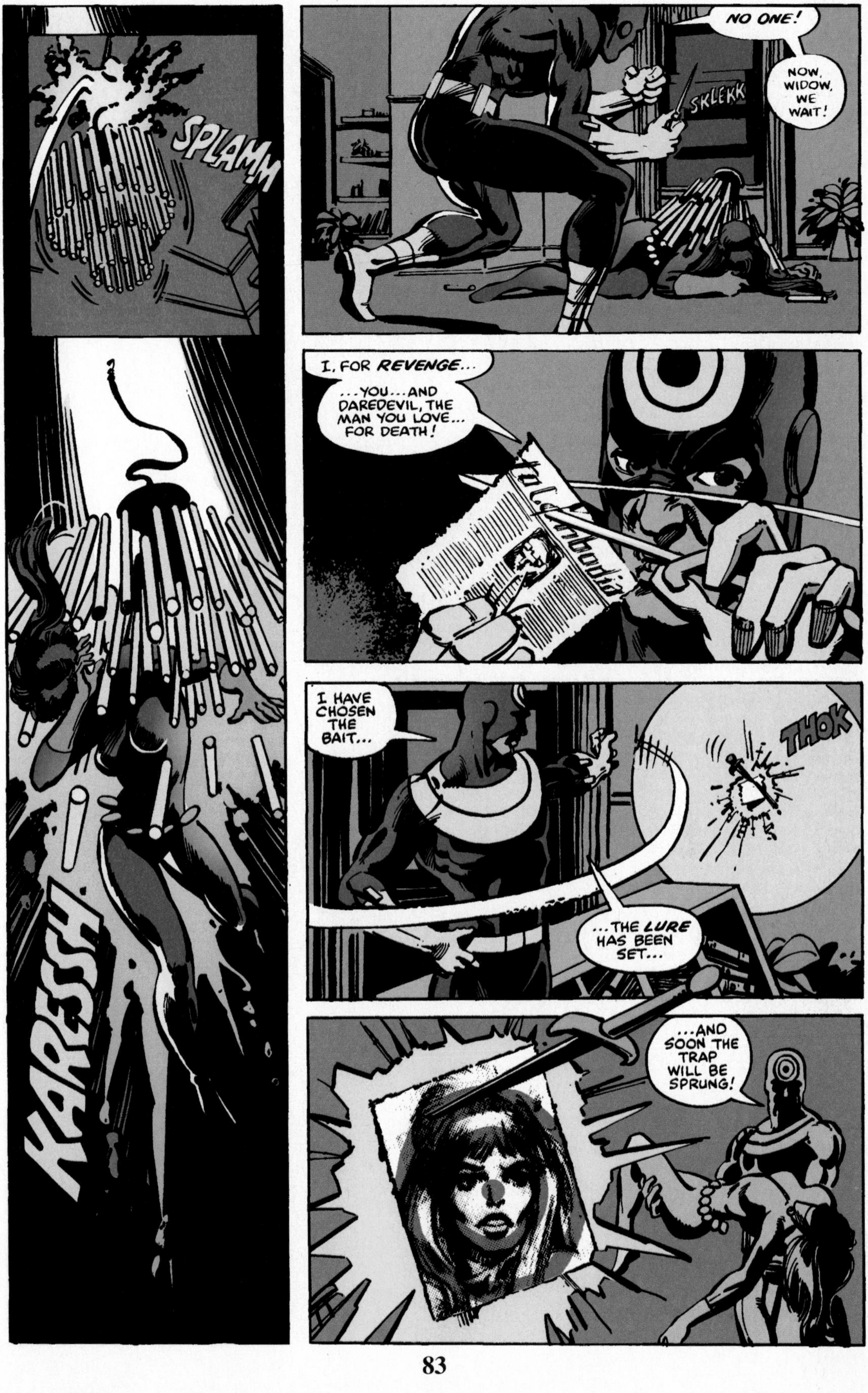
SPLAMM
KARESSH
NO ONE!
NOW, WIDOW, WE WAIT!
SKLEKK
I, FOR REVENGE...
...YOU...AND DAREDEVIL, THE MAN YOU LOVE... FOR DEATH!
I HAVE CHOSEN THE BAIT...
THOK
...THE LURE HAS BEEN SET...
...AND SOON THE TRAP WILL BE SPRUNG!

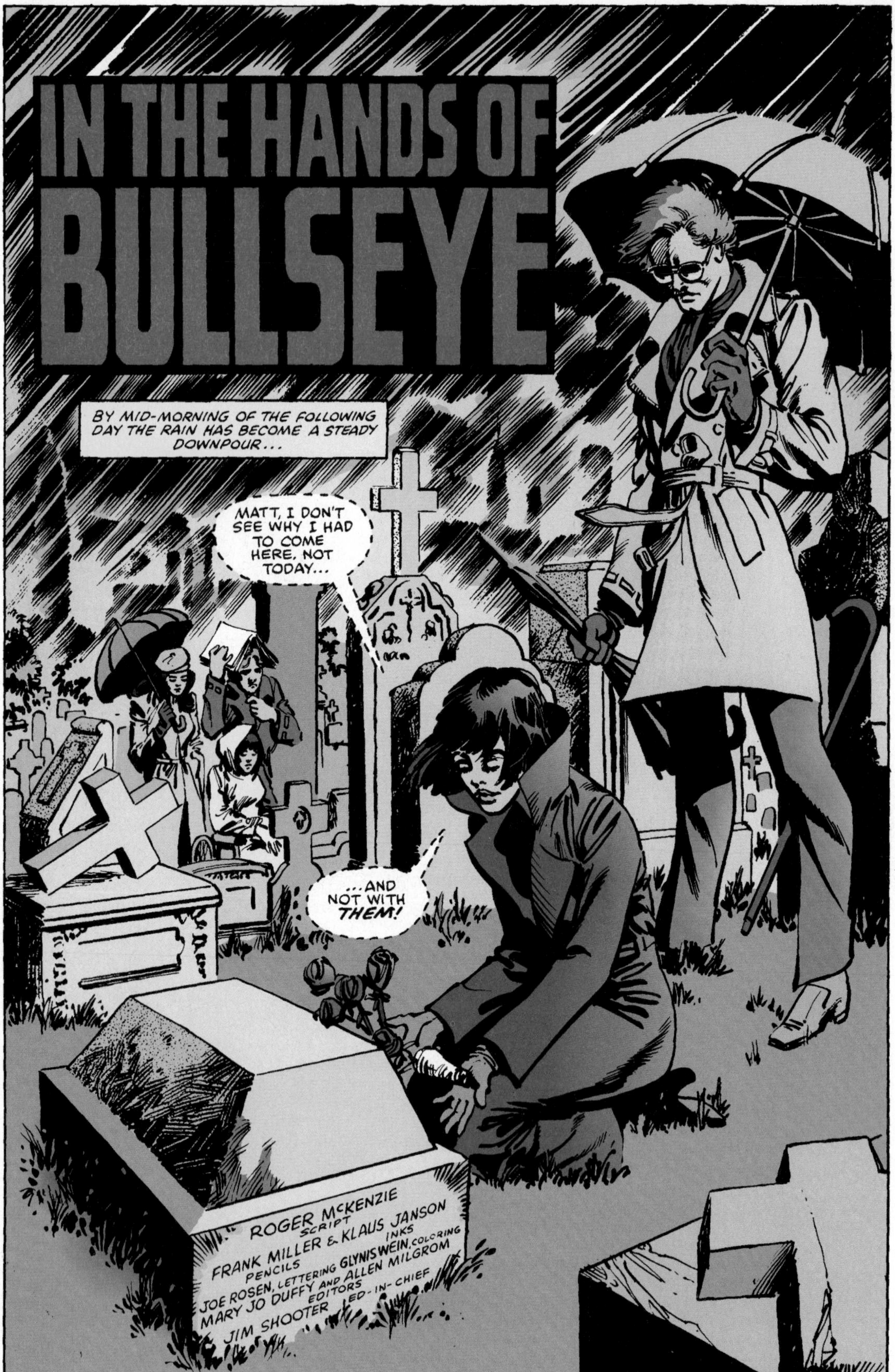
IN THE HANDS OF BULLSEYE
BY MID-MORNING OF THE FOLLOWING DAY THE RAIN HAS BECOME A STEADY DOWNPOUR...
MATT, I DON'T SEE WHY I HAD TO COME HERE, NOT TODAY...
...AND NOT WITH THEM!
ROGER McKENZIE SCRIPT
FRANK MILLER & KLAUS JANSON PENCILS INKS
JOE ROSEN, LETTERING GLYNIS WEIN, COLORING
MARY JO DUFFY AND ALLEN MILGROM EDITORS
JIM SHOOTER ED-IN-CHIEF

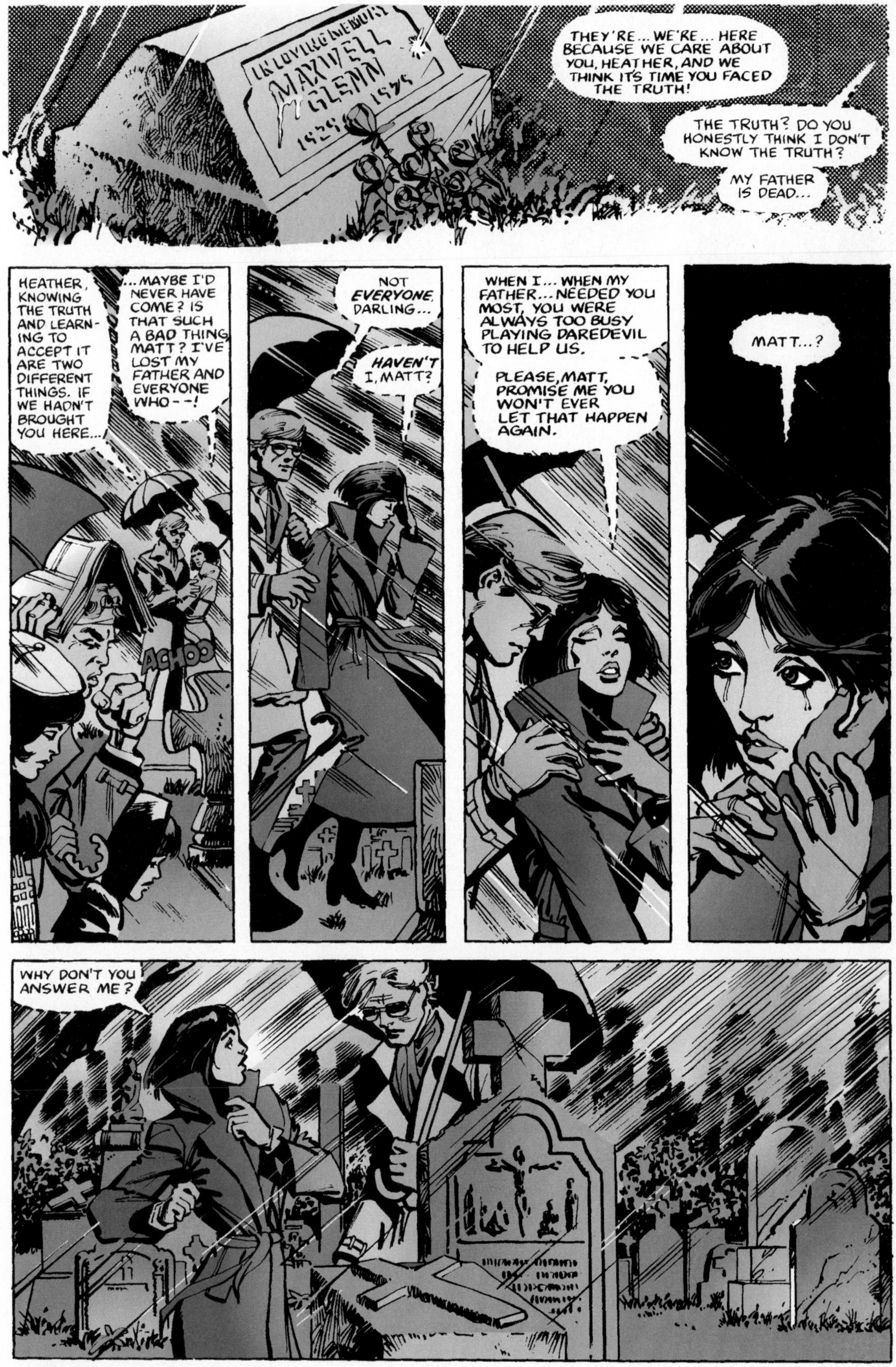
IN LOVING MEMORY
MAXWELL GLENN
1929 1979
THEY'RE... WE'RE... HERE BECAUSE WE CARE ABOUT YOU, HEATHER, AND WE THINK IT'S TIME YOU FACED THE TRUTH!
THE TRUTH? DO YOU HONESTLY THINK I DON'T KNOW THE TRUTH?
MY FATHER IS DEAD...
HEATHER, KNOWING THE TRUTH AND LEARNING TO ACCEPT IT ARE TWO DIFFERENT THINGS. IF WE HADN'T BROUGHT YOU HERE...
...MAYBE I'D NEVER HAVE COME? IS THAT SUCH A BAD THING MATT? I'VE LOST MY FATHER AND EVERYONE WHO--!
ACHOO
NOT EVERYONE, DARLING...
HAVEN'T I, MATT?
WHEN I... WHEN MY FATHER... NEEDED YOU MOST, YOU WERE ALWAYS TOO BUSY PLAYING DAREDEVIL TO HELP US.
PLEASE, MATT, PROMISE ME YOU WON'T EVER LET THAT HAPPEN AGAIN.
MATT...?
WHY DON'T YOU ANSWER ME?

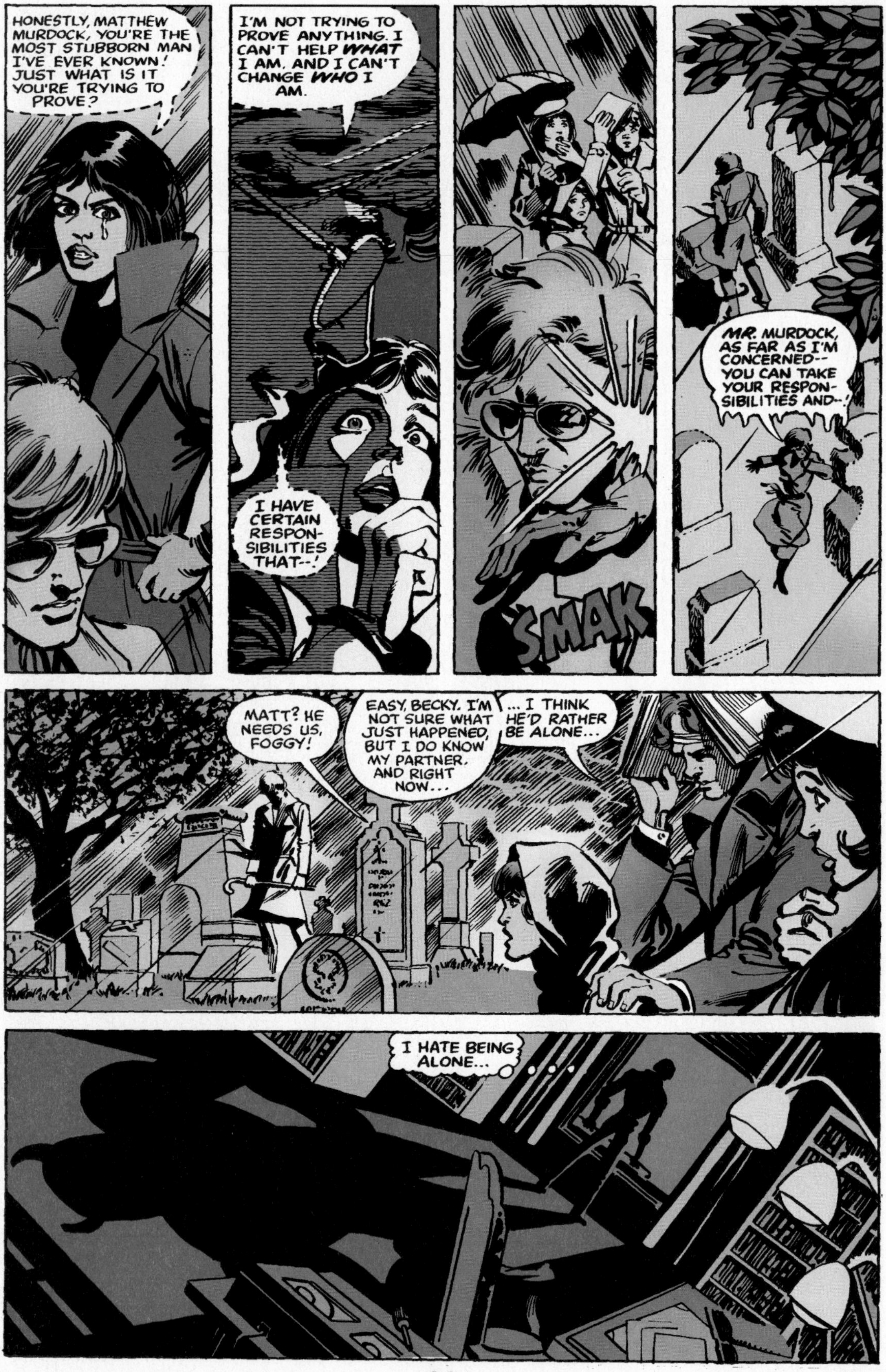
HONESTLY, MATTHEW MURDOCK, YOU'RE THE MOST STUBBORN MAN I'VE EVER KNOWN! JUST WHAT IS IT YOU'RE TRYING TO PROVE?
I'M NOT TRYING TO PROVE ANYTHING. I CAN'T HELP WHAT I AM. AND I CAN'T CHANGE WHO I AM.
I HAVE CERTAIN RESPONSIBILITIES THAT--!
SMAK
MR. MURDOCK, AS FAR AS I'M CONCERNED--YOU CAN TAKE YOUR RESPONSIBILITIES AND--!
MATT? HE NEEDS US, FOGGY!
EASY, BECKY. I'M NOT SURE WHAT JUST HAPPENED, BUT I DO KNOW MY PARTNER. AND RIGHT NOW...
... I THINK HE'D RATHER BE ALONE...
I HATE BEING ALONE...

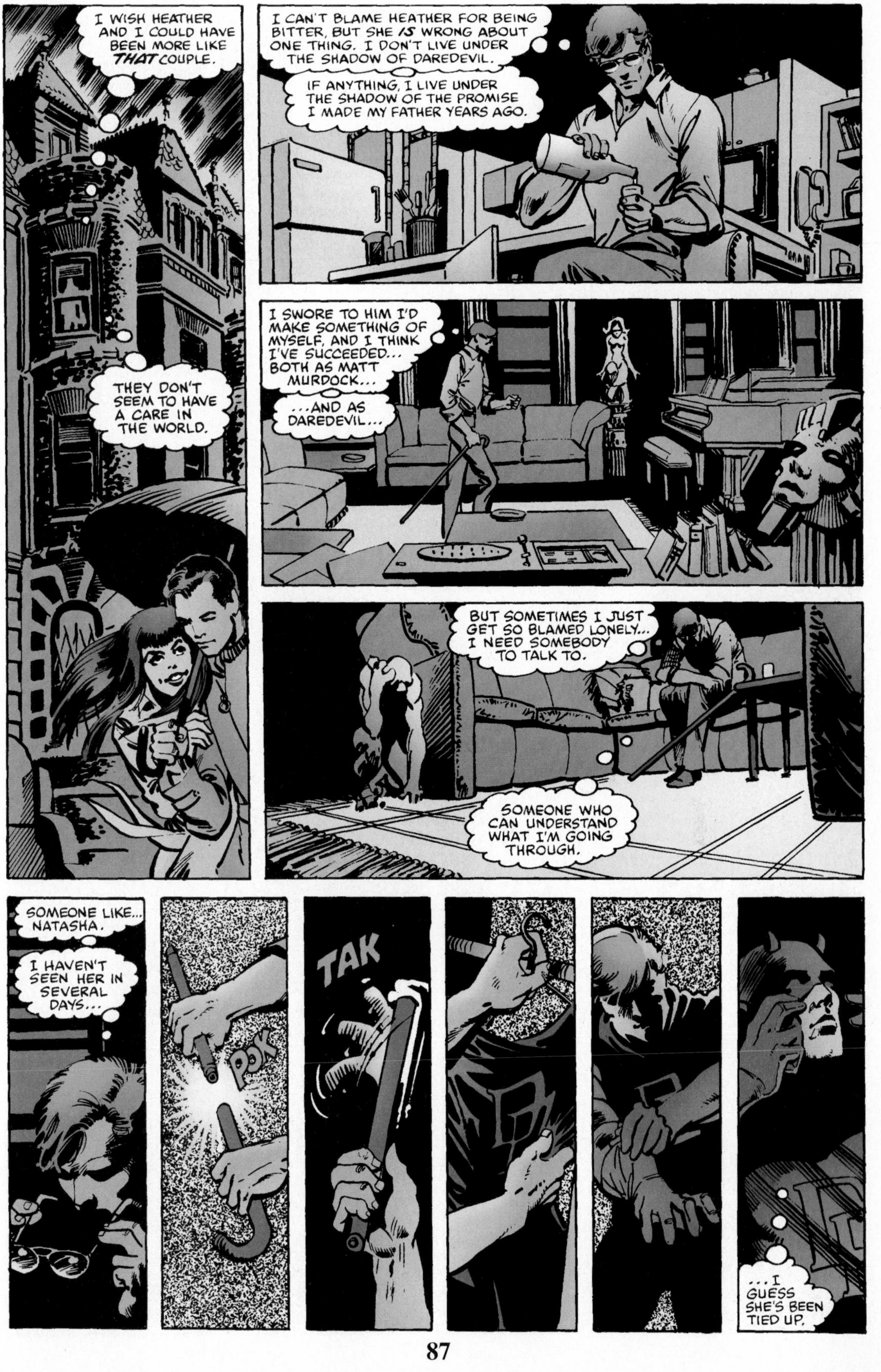
I WISH HEATHER AND I COULD HAVE BEEN MORE LIKE THAT COUPLE.
THEY DON'T SEEM TO HAVE A CARE IN THE WORLD.
I CAN'T BLAME HEATHER FOR BEING BITTER, BUT SHE IS WRONG ABOUT ONE THING. I DON'T LIVE UNDER THE SHADOW OF DAREDEVIL.
IF ANYTHING, I LIVE UNDER THE SHADOW OF THE PROMISE I MADE MY FATHER YEARS AGO.
I SWORE TO HIM I'D MAKE SOMETHING OF MYSELF, AND I THINK I'VE SUCCEEDED... BOTH AS MATT MURDOCK...
...AND AS DAREDEVIL...
BUT SOMETIMES I JUST GET SO BLAMED LONELY... I NEED SOMEBODY TO TALK TO.
SOMEONE WHO CAN UNDERSTAND WHAT I'M GOING THROUGH.
SOMEONE LIKE... NATASHA.
I HAVEN'T SEEN HER IN SEVERAL DAYS...
POK
TAK
...I GUESS SHE'S BEEN TIED UP.

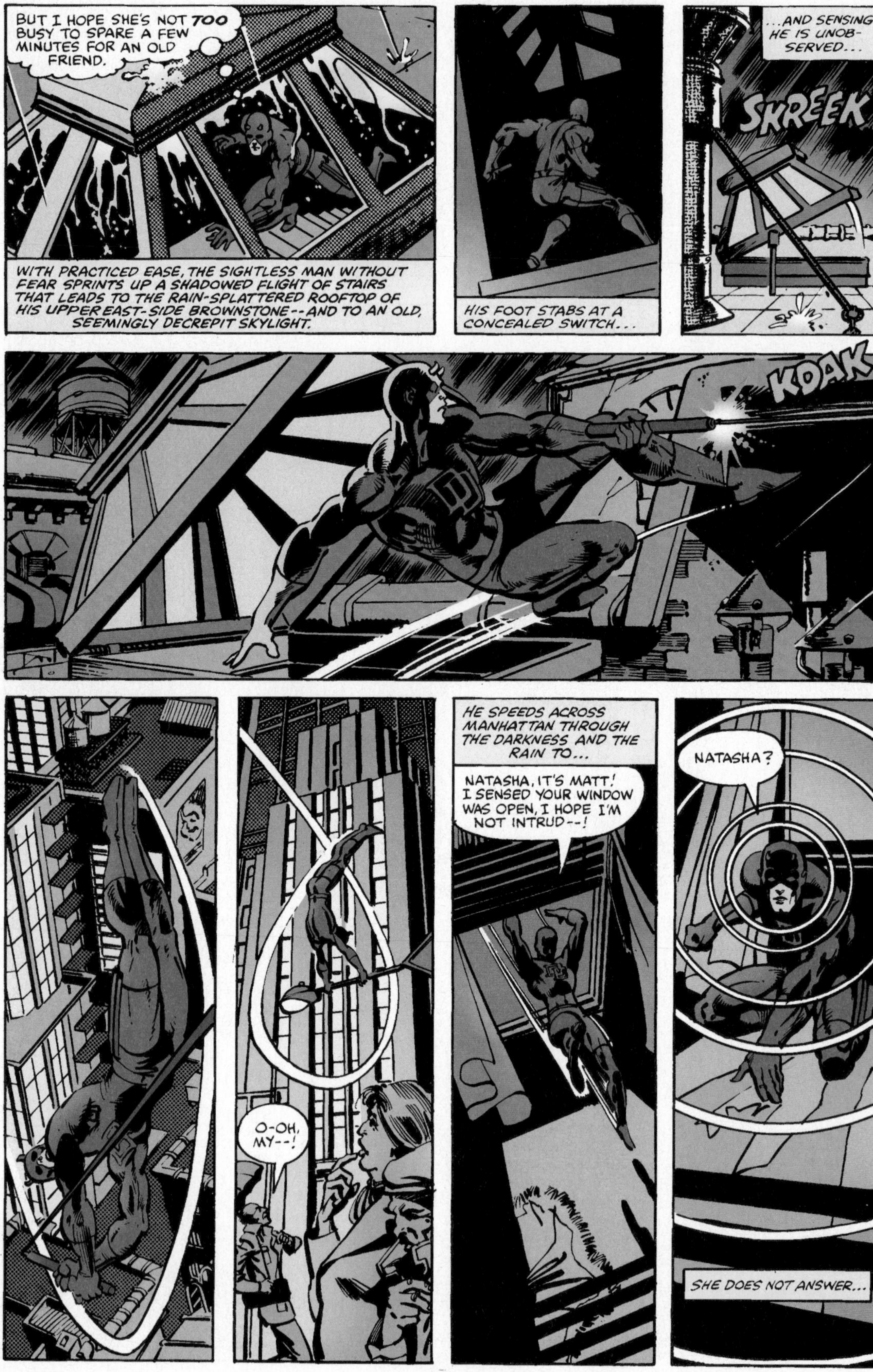

BUT I HOPE SHE'S NOT TOO BUSY TO SPARE A FEW MINUTES FOR AN OLD FRIEND.
WITH PRACTICED EASE, THE SIGHTLESS MAN WITHOUT FEAR SPRINTS UP A SHADOWED FLIGHT OF STAIRS THAT LEADS TO THE RAIN-SPLATTERED ROOFTOP OF HIS UPPER EAST-SIDE BROWNSTONE--AND TO AN OLD, SEEMINGLY DECREPIT SKYLIGHT.
HIS FOOT STABS AT A CONCEALED SWITCH...
...AND SENSING HE IS UNOBSERVED...
SKREEK
KDAK
O-OH, MY--!
HE SPEEDS ACROSS MANHATTAN THROUGH THE DARKNESS AND THE RAIN TO...
NATASHA, IT'S MATT! I SENSED YOUR WINDOW WAS OPEN. I HOPE I'M NOT INTRUD--!
NATASHA?
SHE DOES NOT ANSWER...

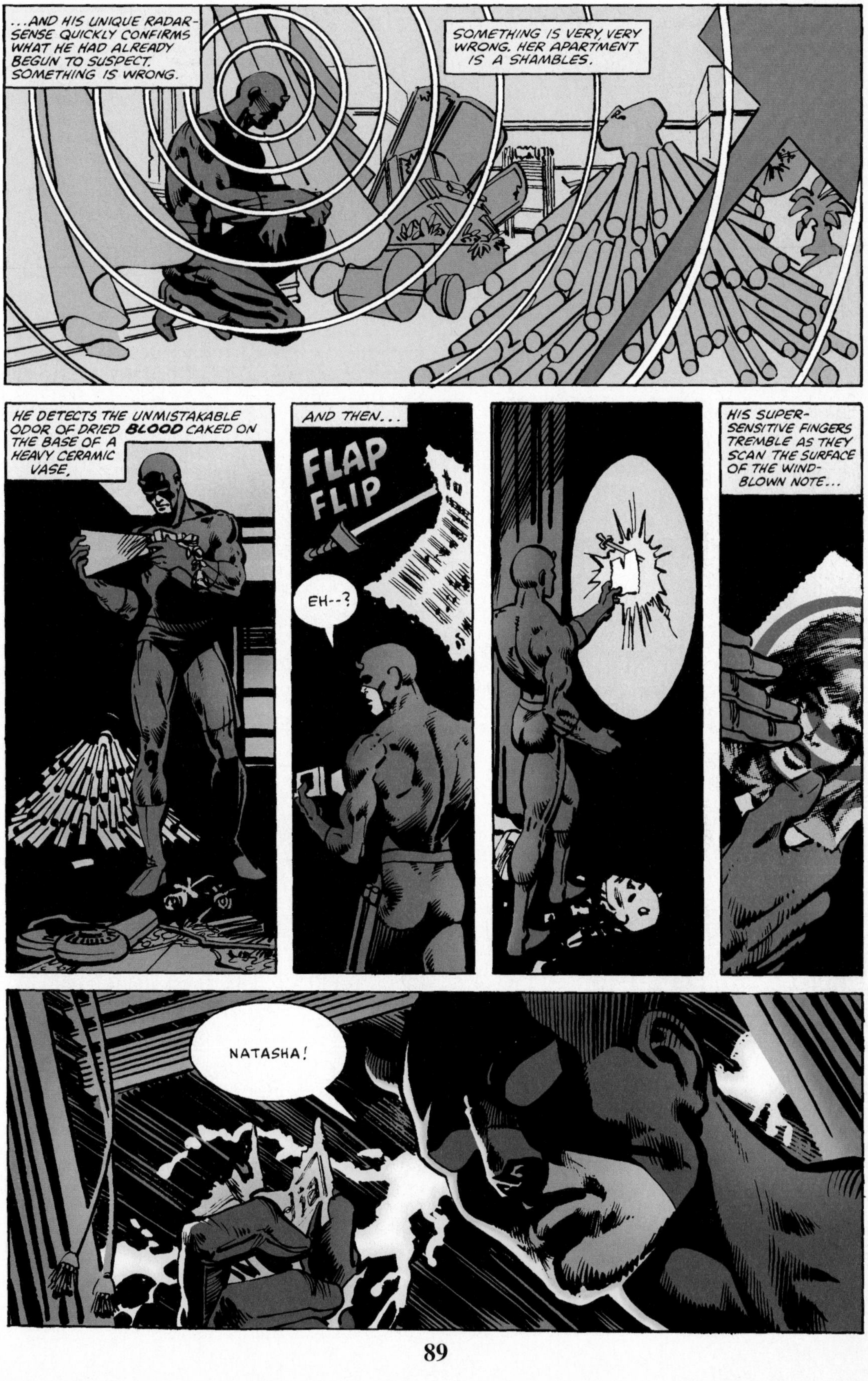
...AND HIS UNIQUE RADAR-SENSE QUICKLY CONFIRMS WHAT HE HAD ALREADY BEGUN TO SUSPECT. SOMETHING IS WRONG.
SOMETHING IS VERY, VERY WRONG. HER APARTMENT IS A SHAMBLES.
HE DETECTS THE UNMISTAKABLE ODOR OF DRIED BLOOD CAKED ON THE BASE OF A HEAVY CERAMIC VASE,
AND THEN...
FLAP FLIP
EH--?
HIS SUPER-SENSITIVE FINGERS TREMBLE AS THEY SCAN THE SURFACE OF THE WIND-BLOWN NOTE...
NATASHA!

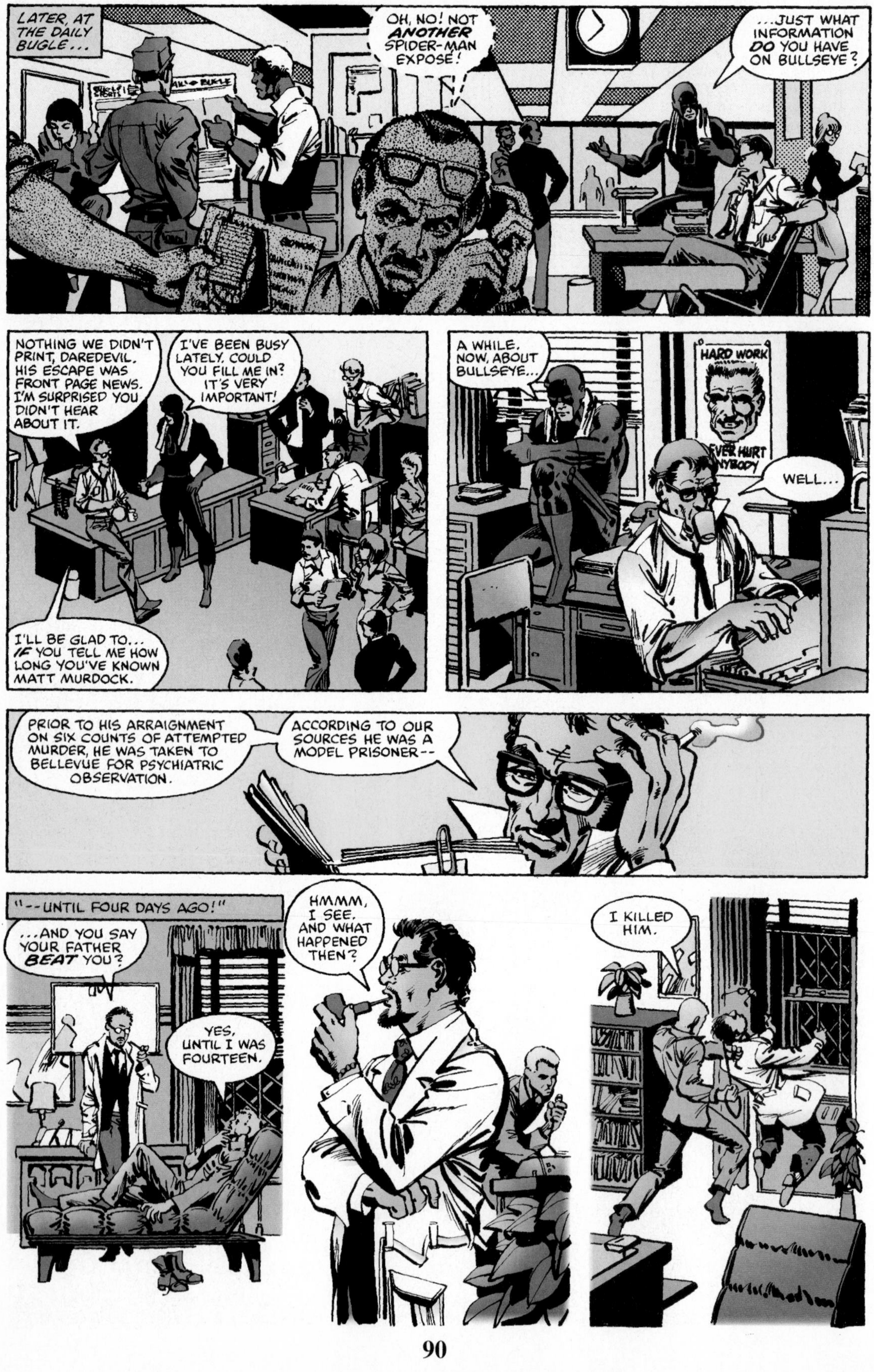
LATER, AT THE DAILY BUGLE...
OH, NO! NOT ANOTHER SPIDER-MAN EXPOSE!
...JUST WHAT INFORMATION DO YOU HAVE ON BULLSEYE?
NOTHING WE DIDN'T PRINT, DAREDEVIL. HIS ESCAPE WAS FRONT PAGE NEWS. I'M SURPRISED YOU DIDN'T HEAR ABOUT IT.
I'VE BEEN BUSY LATELY. COULD YOU FILL ME IN? IT'S VERY IMPORTANT!
I'LL BE GLAD TO... IF YOU TELL ME HOW LONG YOU'VE KNOWN MATT MURDOCK.
A WHILE. NOW, ABOUT BULLSEYE...
HARD WORK
WELL...
PRIOR TO HIS ARRAIGNMENT ON SIX COUNTS OF ATTEMPTED MURDER, HE WAS TAKEN TO BELLEVUE FOR PSYCHIATRIC OBSERVATION.
ACCORDING TO OUR SOURCES HE WAS A MODEL PRISONER--
"--UNTIL FOUR DAYS AGO!"
...AND YOU SAY YOUR FATHER BEAT YOU?
YES, UNTIL I WAS FOURTEEN.
HMMM, I SEE. AND WHAT HAPPENED THEN?
I KILLED HIM.

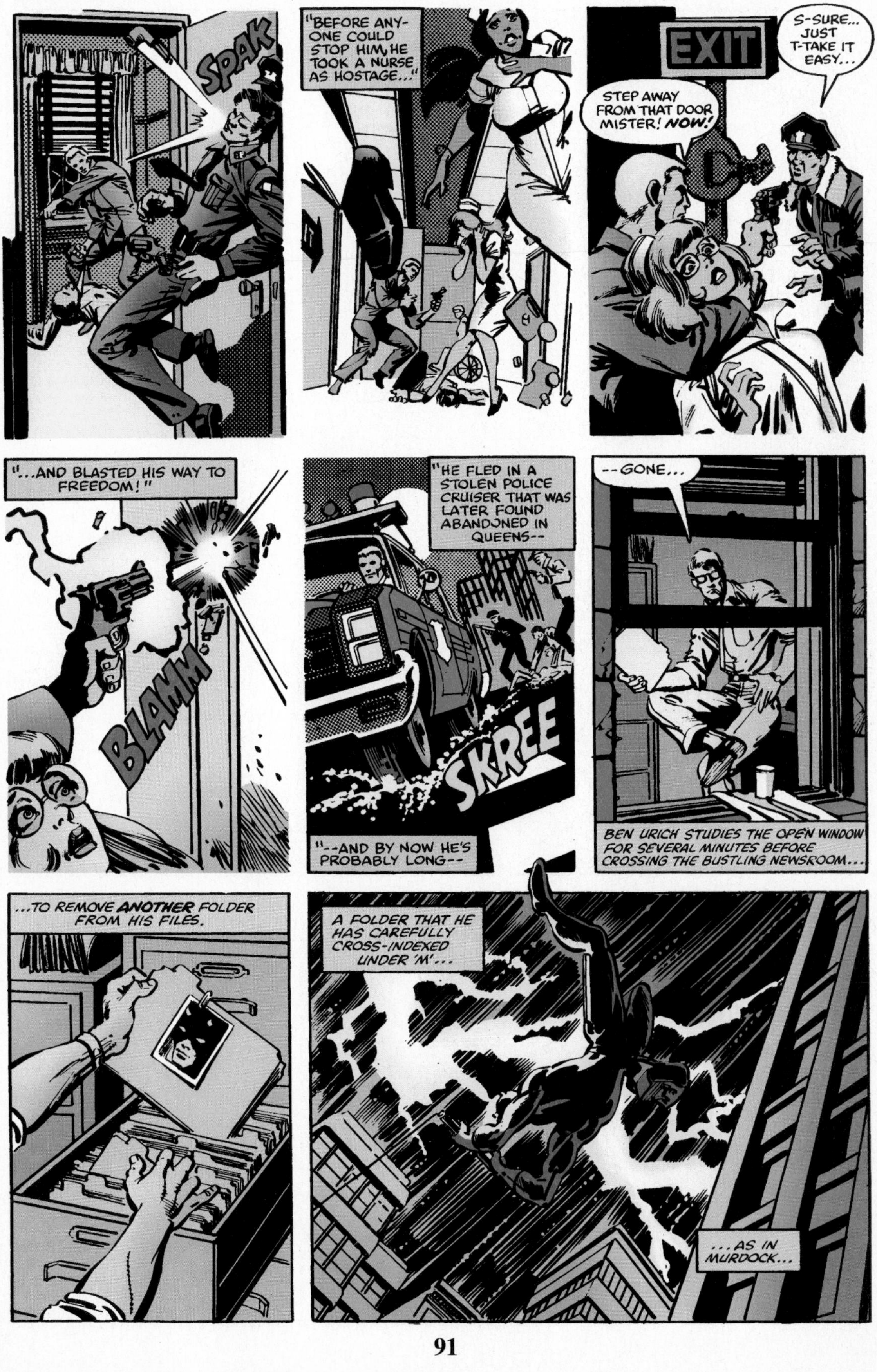
SPAK
"BEFORE ANYONE COULD STOP HIM, HE TOOK A NURSE AS HOSTAGE..."
EXIT
S-SURE... JUST T-TAKE IT EASY...
STEP AWAY FROM THAT DOOR MISTER! NOW!
"...AND BLASTED HIS WAY TO FREEDOM!"
BLAMM
"HE FLED IN A STOLEN POLICE CRUISER THAT WAS LATER FOUND ABANDONED IN QUEENS--
SKREE
"--AND BY NOW HE'S PROBABLY LONG--
--GONE...
BEN URICH STUDIES THE OPEN WINDOW FOR SEVERAL MINUTES BEFORE CROSSING THE BUSTLING NEWSROOM...
...TO REMOVE ANOTHER FOLDER FROM HIS FILES.
A FOLDER THAT HE HAS CAREFULLY CROSS-INDEXED UNDER 'M'...
...AS IN MURDOCK...

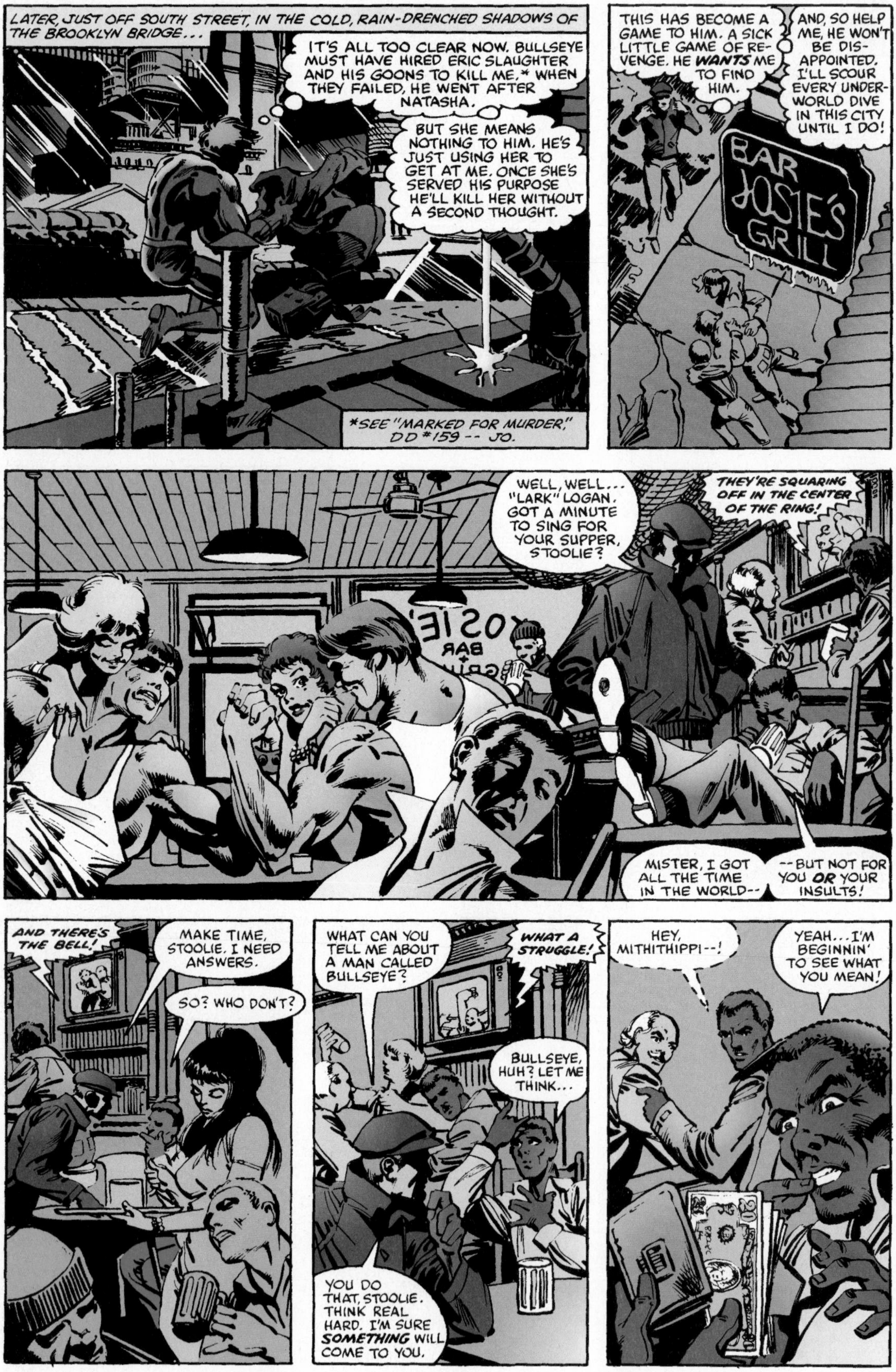
LATER, JUST OFF SOUTH STREET, IN THE COLD, RAIN-DRENCHED SHADOWS OF THE BROOKLYN BRIDGE...
IT'S ALL TOO CLEAR NOW. BULLSEYE MUST HAVE HIRED ERIC SLAUGHTER AND HIS GOONS TO KILL ME.* WHEN THEY FAILED, HE WENT AFTER NATASHA.
BUT SHE MEANS NOTHING TO HIM. HE'S JUST USING HER TO GET AT ME. ONCE SHE'S SERVED HIS PURPOSE HE'LL KILL HER WITHOUT A SECOND THOUGHT.
*SEE "MARKED FOR MURDER," DD #159 -- JO.
THIS HAS BECOME A GAME TO HIM. A SICK LITTLE GAME OF RE-VENGE. HE WANTS ME TO FIND HIM.
AND, SO HELP ME, HE WON'T BE DIS-APPOINTED. I'LL SCOUR EVERY UNDER-WORLD DIVE IN THIS CITY UNTIL I DO!
BAR JOSIE'S GRILL
WELL, WELL... "LARK" LOGAN. GOT A MINUTE TO SING FOR YOUR SUPPER, STOOLIE?
THEY'RE SQUARING OFF IN THE CENTER OF THE RING!
MISTER, I GOT ALL THE TIME IN THE WORLD--
--BUT NOT FOR YOU OR YOUR INSULTS!
AND THERE'S THE BELL!
MAKE TIME, STOOLIE. I NEED ANSWERS.
SO? WHO DON'T?
WHAT CAN YOU TELL ME ABOUT A MAN CALLED BULLSEYE?
WHAT A STRUGGLE!
BULLSEYE, HUH? LET ME THINK...
YOU DO THAT, STOOLIE. THINK REAL HARD. I'M SURE SOMETHING WILL COME TO YOU.
HEY, MITHITHIPPI--!
YEAH... I'M BEGINNIN' TO SEE WHAT YOU MEAN!

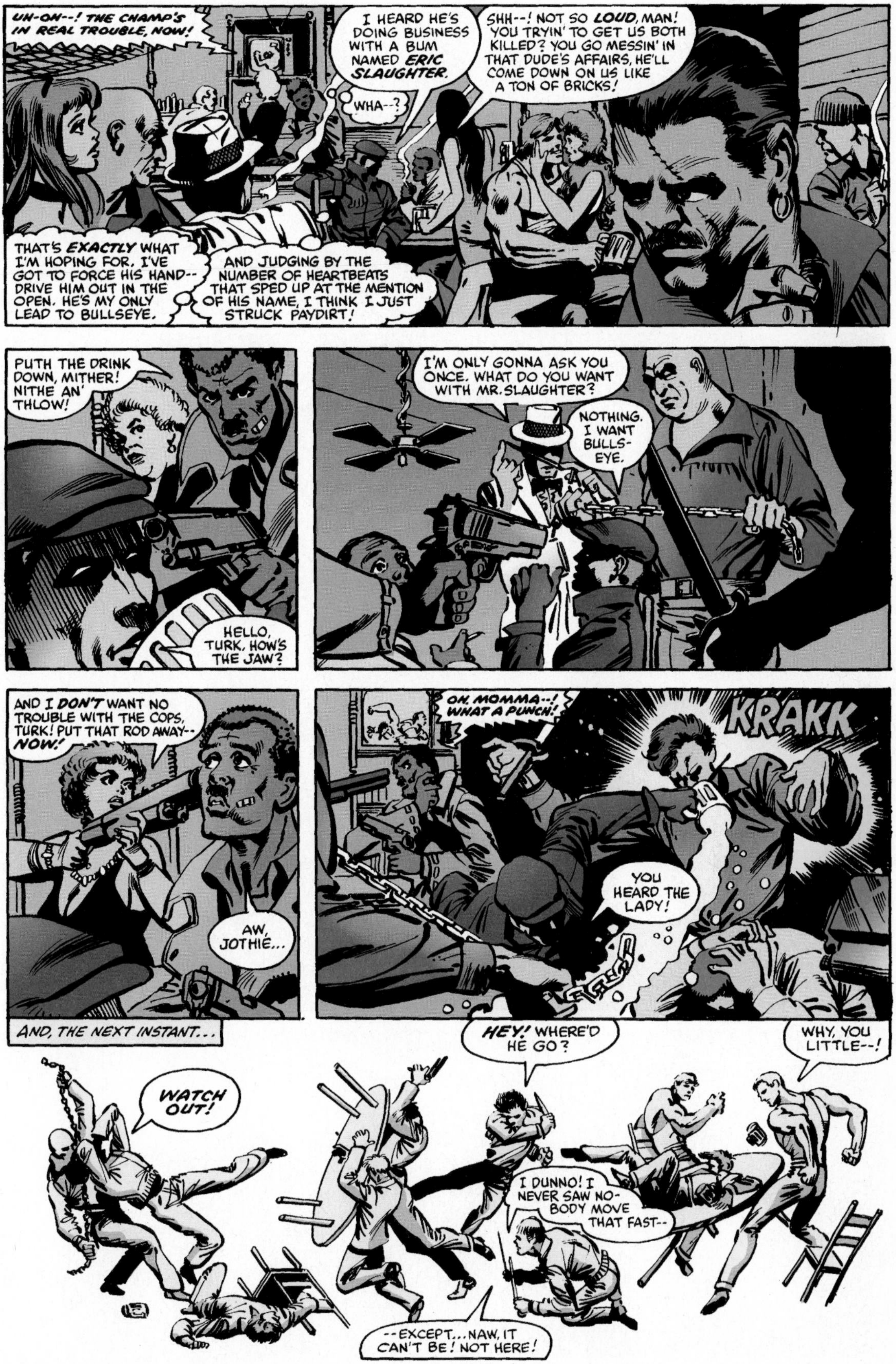

UH-OH--! THE CHAMP'S IN REAL TROUBLE, NOW!
I HEARD HE'S DOING BUSINESS WITH A BUM NAMED ERIC SLAUGHTER.
WHA--?
SHH--! NOT SO LOUD, MAN! YOU TRYIN' TO GET US BOTH KILLED? YOU GO MESSIN' IN THAT DUDE'S AFFAIRS, HE'LL COME DOWN ON US LIKE A TON OF BRICKS!
THAT'S EXACTLY WHAT I'M HOPING FOR. I'VE GOT TO FORCE HIS HAND-- DRIVE HIM OUT IN THE OPEN. HE'S MY ONLY LEAD TO BULLSEYE.
AND JUDGING BY THE NUMBER OF HEARTBEATS THAT SPED UP AT THE MENTION OF HIS NAME, I THINK I JUST STRUCK PAYDIRT!
PUTH THE DRINK DOWN, MITHER! NITHE AN' THLOW!
HELLO, TURK. HOW'S THE JAW?
I'M ONLY GONNA ASK YOU ONCE. WHAT DO YOU WANT WITH MR. SLAUGHTER?
NOTHING. I WANT BULLS-EYE.
AND I DON'T WANT NO TROUBLE WITH THE COPS, TURK! PUT THAT ROD AWAY-- NOW!
AW, JOTHIE...
OH, MOMMA--! WHAT A PUNCH!
KRAKK
YOU HEARD THE LADY!
AND, THE NEXT INSTANT...
WATCH OUT!
HEY! WHERE'D HE GO?
WHY, YOU LITTLE--!
I DUNNO! I NEVER SAW NO-BODY MOVE THAT FAST--
--EXCEPT...NAW, IT CAN'T BE! NOT HERE!

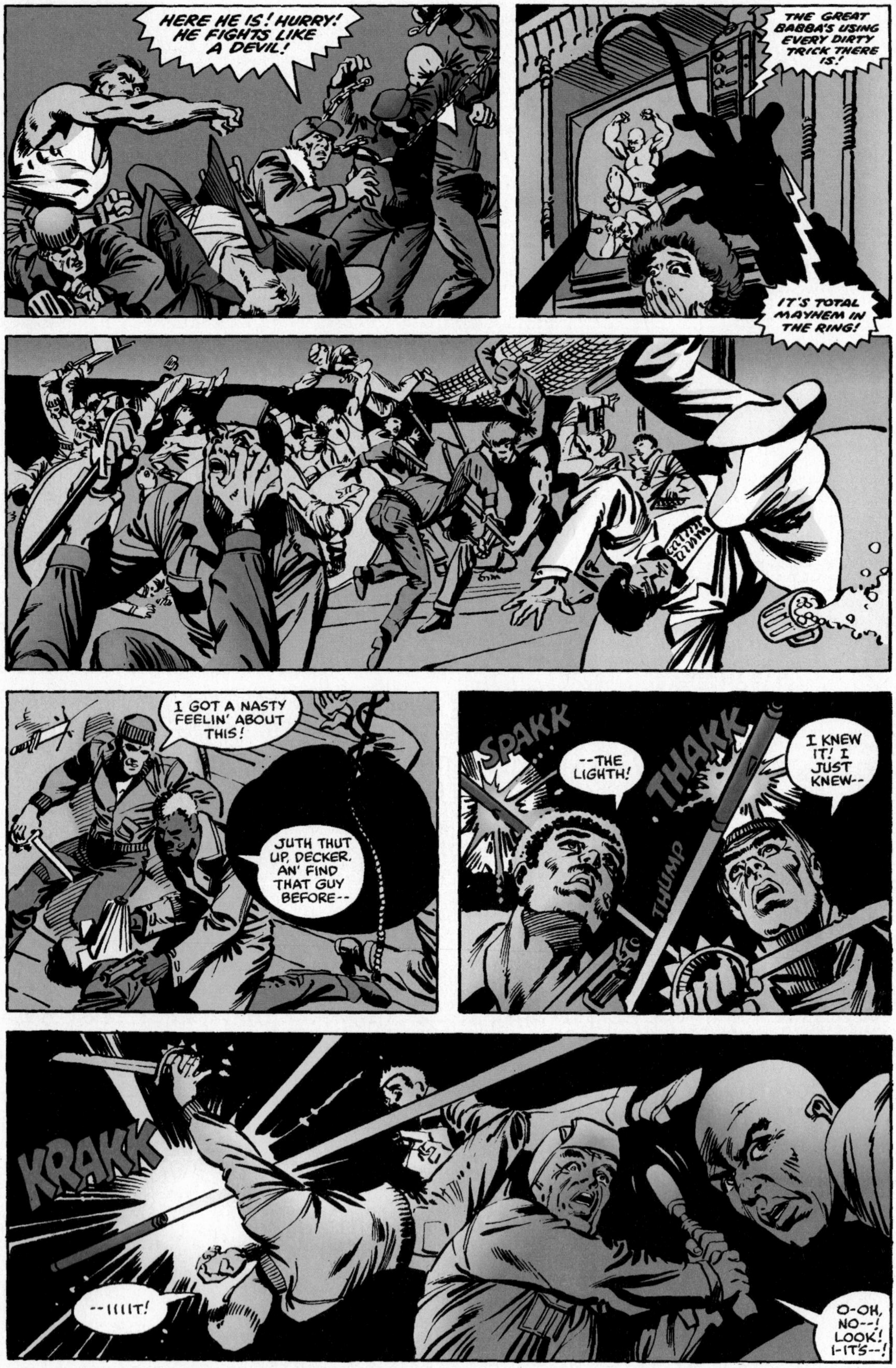
HERE HE IS! HURRY! HE FIGHTS LIKE A DEVIL!
THE GREAT BABBA'S USING EVERY DIRTY TRICK THERE IS!
IT'S TOTAL MAYHEM IN THE RING!
I GOT A NASTY FEELIN' ABOUT THIS!
JUTH THUT UP, DECKER. AN' FIND THAT GUY BEFORE--
SPAKK
--THE LIGHTH!
THAKK
THUMP
I KNEW IT! I JUST KNEW--
KRAKK
--IIIIT!
O-OH, NO--! LOOK! I-IT'S--!

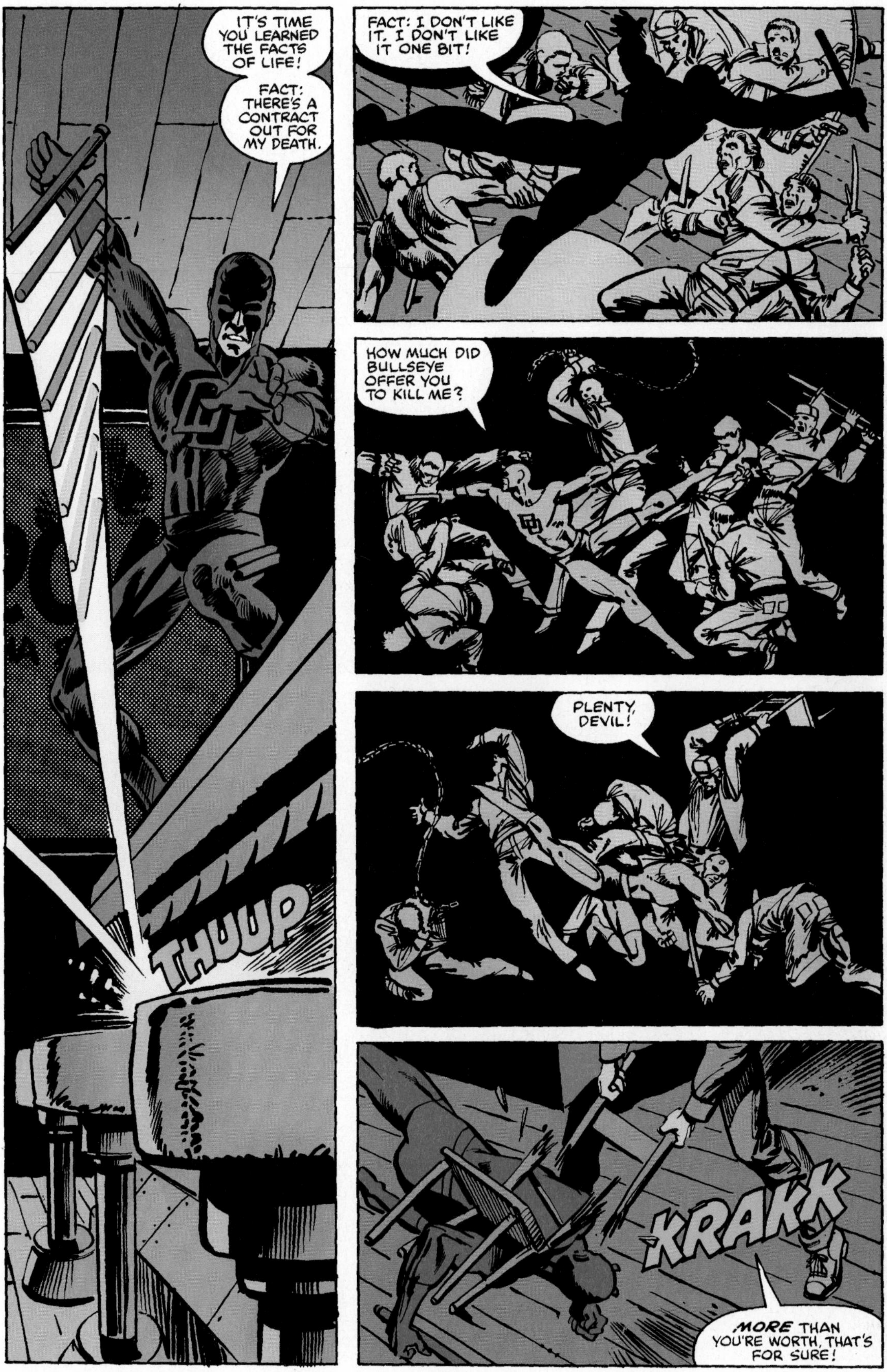
IT'S TIME YOU LEARNED THE FACTS OF LIFE!
FACT: THERE'S A CONTRACT OUT FOR MY DEATH.
THUUP
FACT: I DON'T LIKE IT. I DON'T LIKE IT ONE BIT!
HOW MUCH DID BULLSEYE OFFER YOU TO KILL ME?
PLENTY, DEVIL!
KRAKK
MORE THAN YOU'RE WORTH, THAT'S FOR SURE!

NOW'S OUR CHANCE!

STICK 'IM!

NO, YOU DON'T HAVE A CHANCE.

YOU NEVER DID.

O-OH, DEAR--!

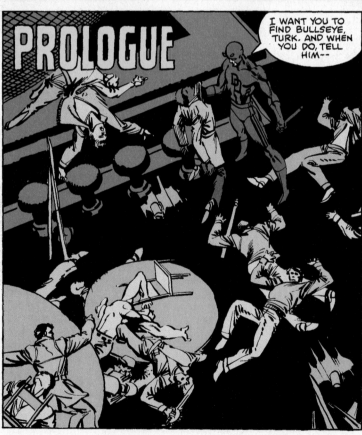

PROLOGUE

I WANT YOU TO FIND BULLSEYE, TURK. AND WHEN YOU DO, TELL HIM--

--DAREDEVIL IS COMING!

NEXT: FOR THE *LIFE* OF THE WIDOW, DAREDEVIL STALKS AN--

ISLAND OF DEATH!

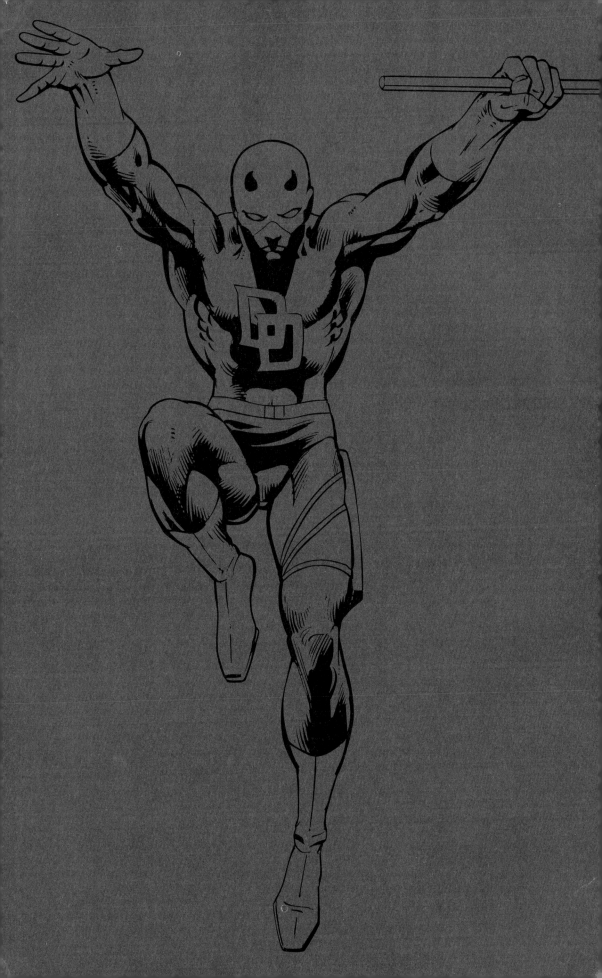

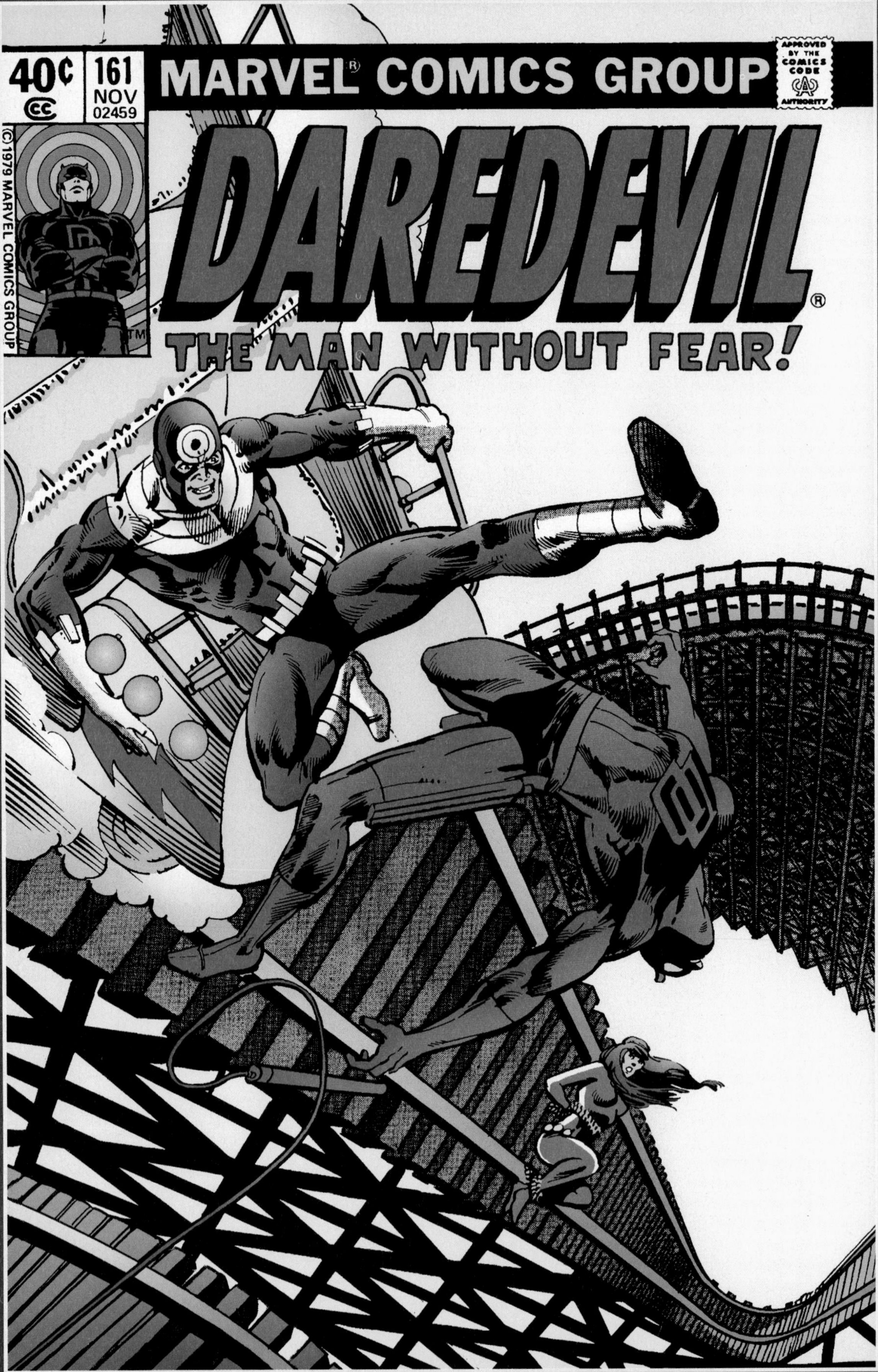
40¢
CC
161
NOV
02459
MARVEL® COMICS GROUP
APPROVED BY THE COMICS CODE AUTHORITY
(C) 1979 MARVEL COMICS GROUP
TM
DAREDEVIL®
THE MAN WITHOUT FEAR!

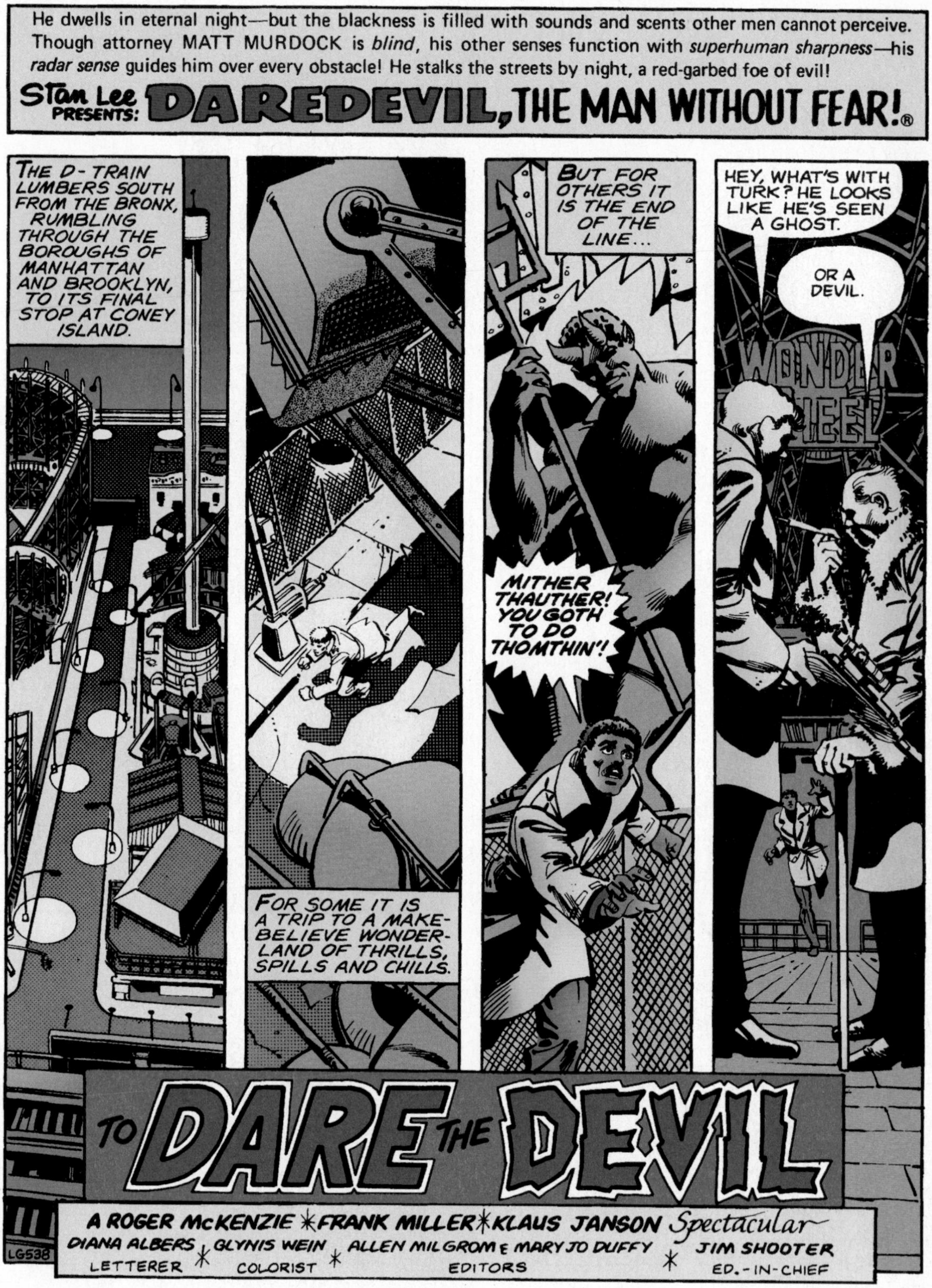
He dwells in eternal night—but the blackness is filled with sounds and scents other men cannot perceive. Though attorney MATT MURDOCK is blind, his other senses function with superhuman sharpness—his radar sense guides him over every obstacle! He stalks the streets by night, a red-garbed foe of evil!
Stan Lee PRESENTS: DAREDEVIL, THE MAN WITHOUT FEAR!®
THE D-TRAIN LUMBERS SOUTH FROM THE BRONX, RUMBLING THROUGH THE BOROUGHS OF MANHATTAN AND BROOKLYN, TO ITS FINAL STOP AT CONEY ISLAND.
FOR SOME IT IS A TRIP TO A MAKE-BELIEVE WONDER-LAND OF THRILLS, SPILLS AND CHILLS.
BUT FOR OTHERS IT IS THE END OF THE LINE...
MITHER THAUTHER! YOU GOTH TO DO THOMTHIN'!
HEY, WHAT'S WITH TURK? HE LOOKS LIKE HE'S SEEN A GHOST.
OR A DEVIL.
WONDER WHEEL
TO DARE THE DEVIL
A ROGER McKENZIE * FRANK MILLER * KLAUS JANSON Spectacular
DIANA ALBERS LETTERER * GLYNIS WEIN COLORIST * ALLEN MILGROM & MARY JO DUFFY EDITORS * JIM SHOOTER ED.-IN-CHIEF
LG538

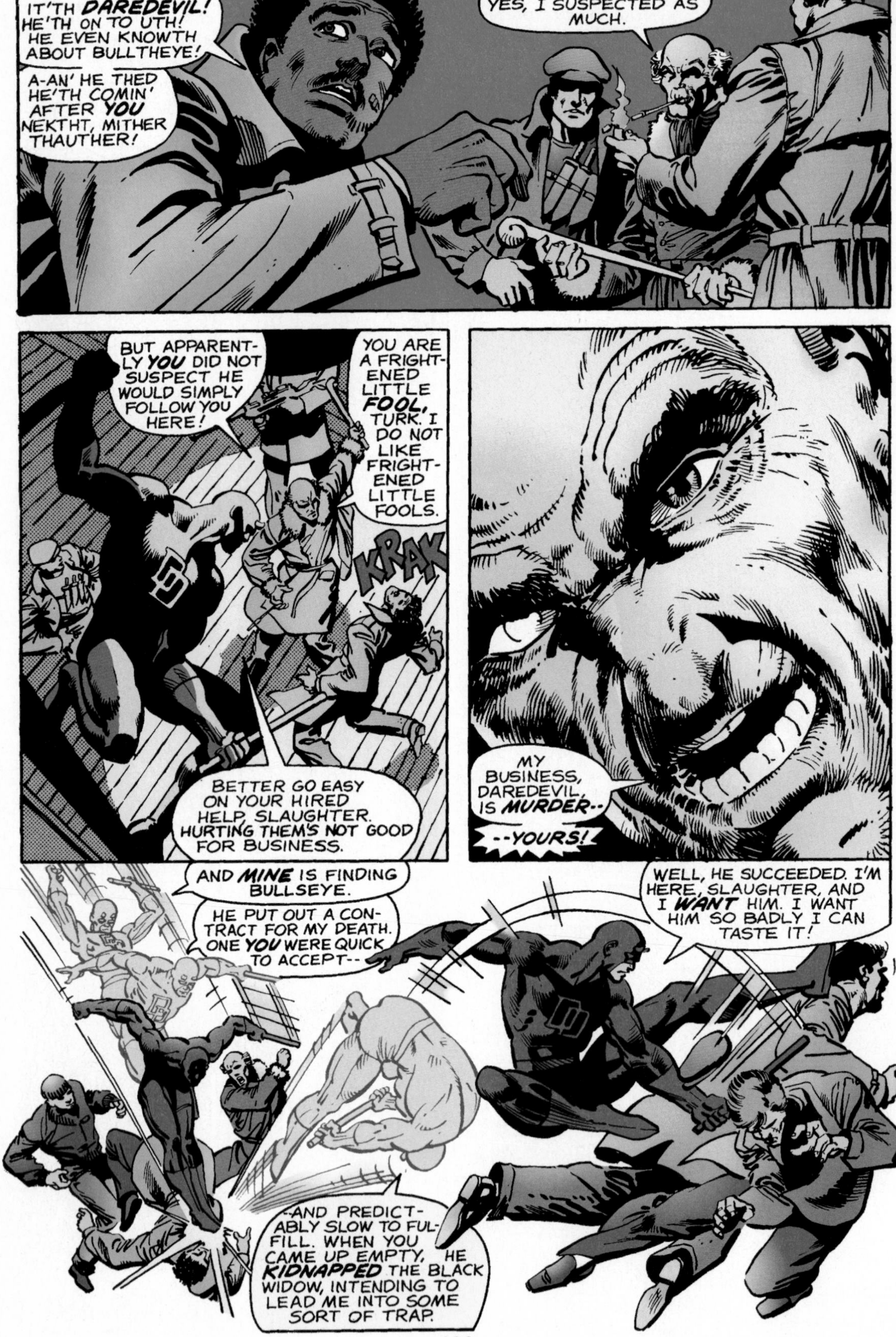

IT'TH DAREDEVIL! HE'TH ON TO UTH! HE EVEN KNOWTH ABOUT BULLTHEYE!
A-AN' HE THED HE'TH COMIN' AFTER YOU NEKTHT, MITHER THAUTHER!
YES, I SUSPECTED AS MUCH.
BUT APPARENTLY YOU DID NOT SUSPECT HE WOULD SIMPLY FOLLOW YOU HERE!
YOU ARE A FRIGHTENED LITTLE FOOL, TURK. I DO NOT LIKE FRIGHTENED LITTLE FOOLS.
KRAK
BETTER GO EASY ON YOUR HIRED HELP, SLAUGHTER. HURTING THEM'S NOT GOOD FOR BUSINESS.
MY BUSINESS, DAREDEVIL, IS MURDER--
--YOURS!
AND MINE IS FINDING BULLSEYE.
HE PUT OUT A CONTRACT FOR MY DEATH. ONE YOU WERE QUICK TO ACCEPT--
--AND PREDICTABLY SLOW TO FULFILL. WHEN YOU CAME UP EMPTY, HE KIDNAPPED THE BLACK WIDOW, INTENDING TO LEAD ME INTO SOME SORT OF TRAP.
WELL, HE SUCCEEDED. I'M HERE, SLAUGHTER, AND I WANT HIM. I WANT HIM SO BADLY I CAN TASTE IT!

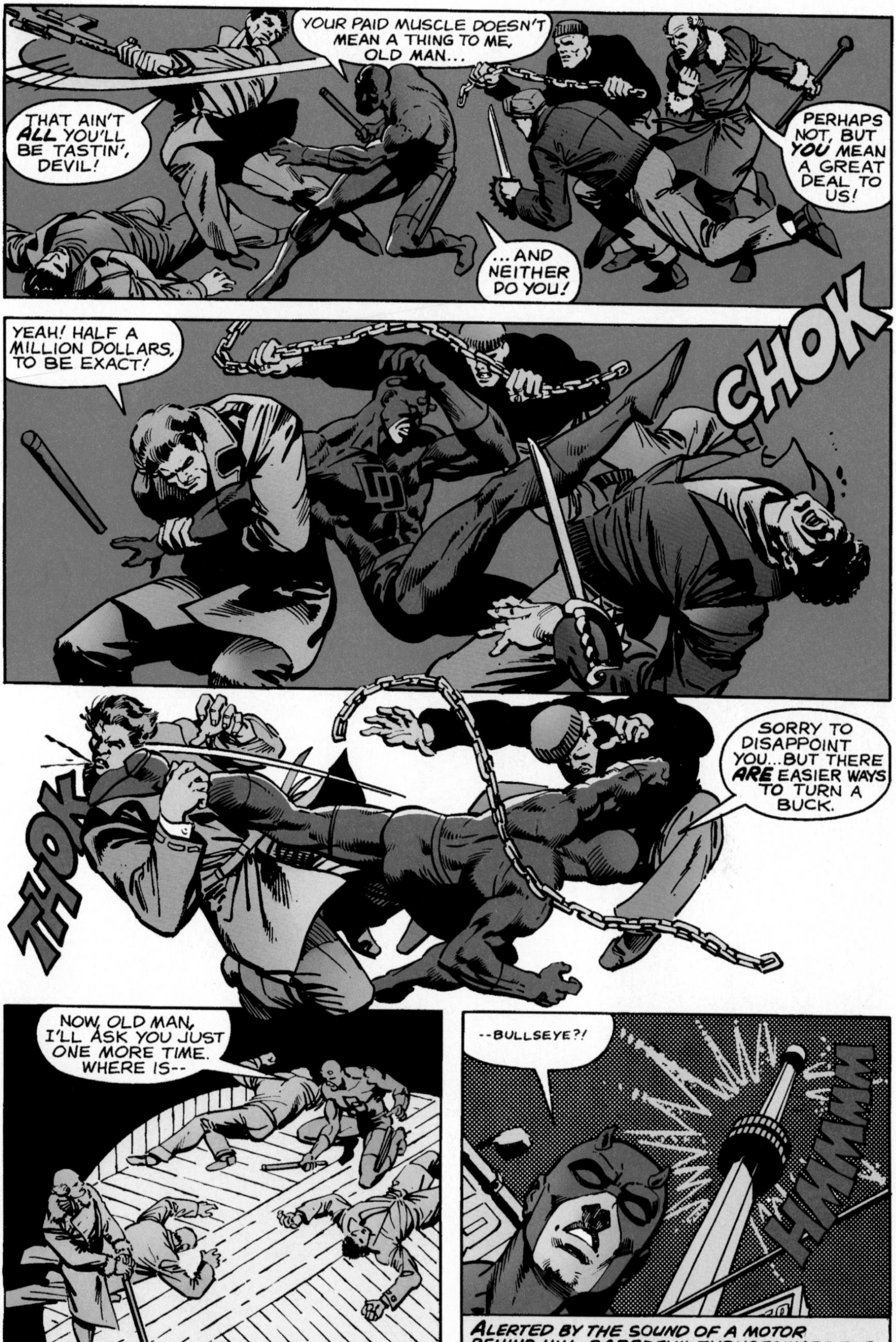
YOUR PAID MUSCLE DOESN'T MEAN A THING TO ME, OLD MAN...
THAT AIN'T ALL YOU'LL BE TASTIN', DEVIL!
PERHAPS NOT, BUT YOU MEAN A GREAT DEAL TO US!
...AND NEITHER DO YOU!
YEAH! HALF A MILLION DOLLARS, TO BE EXACT!
CHOK
THOK
SORRY TO DISAPPOINT YOU...BUT THERE ARE EASIER WAYS TO TURN A BUCK.
NOW, OLD MAN, I'LL ASK YOU JUST ONE MORE TIME. WHERE IS--
--BULLSEYE?!
HMMMM
ALERTED BY THE SOUND OF A MOTOR BEHIND HIM, DAREDEVIL TURNS TOWARD THE ASTROTOWER, WHICH HAS BEGUN TO RISE...

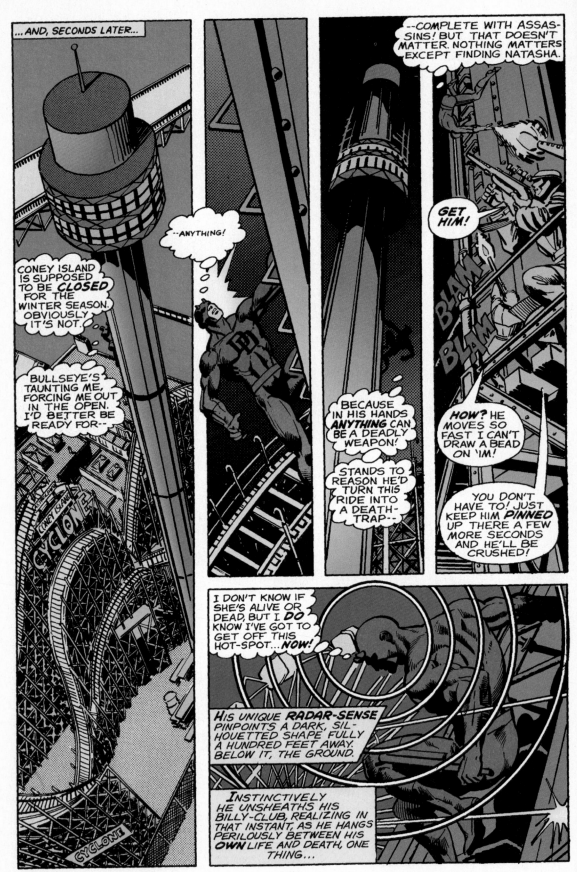

...AND, SECONDS LATER...

CONEY ISLAND IS SUPPOSED TO BE *CLOSED* FOR THE WINTER SEASON. OBVIOUSLY IT'S NOT.

BULLSEYE'S TAUNTING ME, FORCING ME OUT IN THE OPEN. I'D BETTER BE READY FOR--

--ANYTHING!

BECAUSE IN HIS HANDS *ANYTHING* CAN BE A DEADLY WEAPON!

STANDS TO REASON HE'D TURN THIS RIDE INTO A DEATH-TRAP--

--COMPLETE WITH ASSASSINS! BUT THAT DOESN'T MATTER. NOTHING MATTERS EXCEPT FINDING NATASHA.

GET HIM!

HOW? HE MOVES SO FAST I CAN'T DRAW A BEAD ON 'IM!

YOU DON'T HAVE TO! JUST KEEP HIM *PINNED* UP THERE A FEW MORE SECONDS AND HE'LL BE CRUSHED!

BLAM BLAM BLAM

I DON'T KNOW IF SHE'S ALIVE OR DEAD, BUT I *DO* KNOW I'VE GOT TO GET OFF THIS HOT-SPOT...*NOW!*

HIS UNIQUE *RADAR-SENSE* PINPOINTS A DARK, SILHOUETTED SHAPE FULLY A HUNDRED FEET AWAY. BELOW IT, THE GROUND.

INSTINCTIVELY HE UNSHEATHS HIS BILLY-CLUB, REALIZING IN THAT INSTANT, AS HE HANGS PERILOUSLY BETWEEN HIS *OWN* LIFE AND DEATH, ONE THING...

102

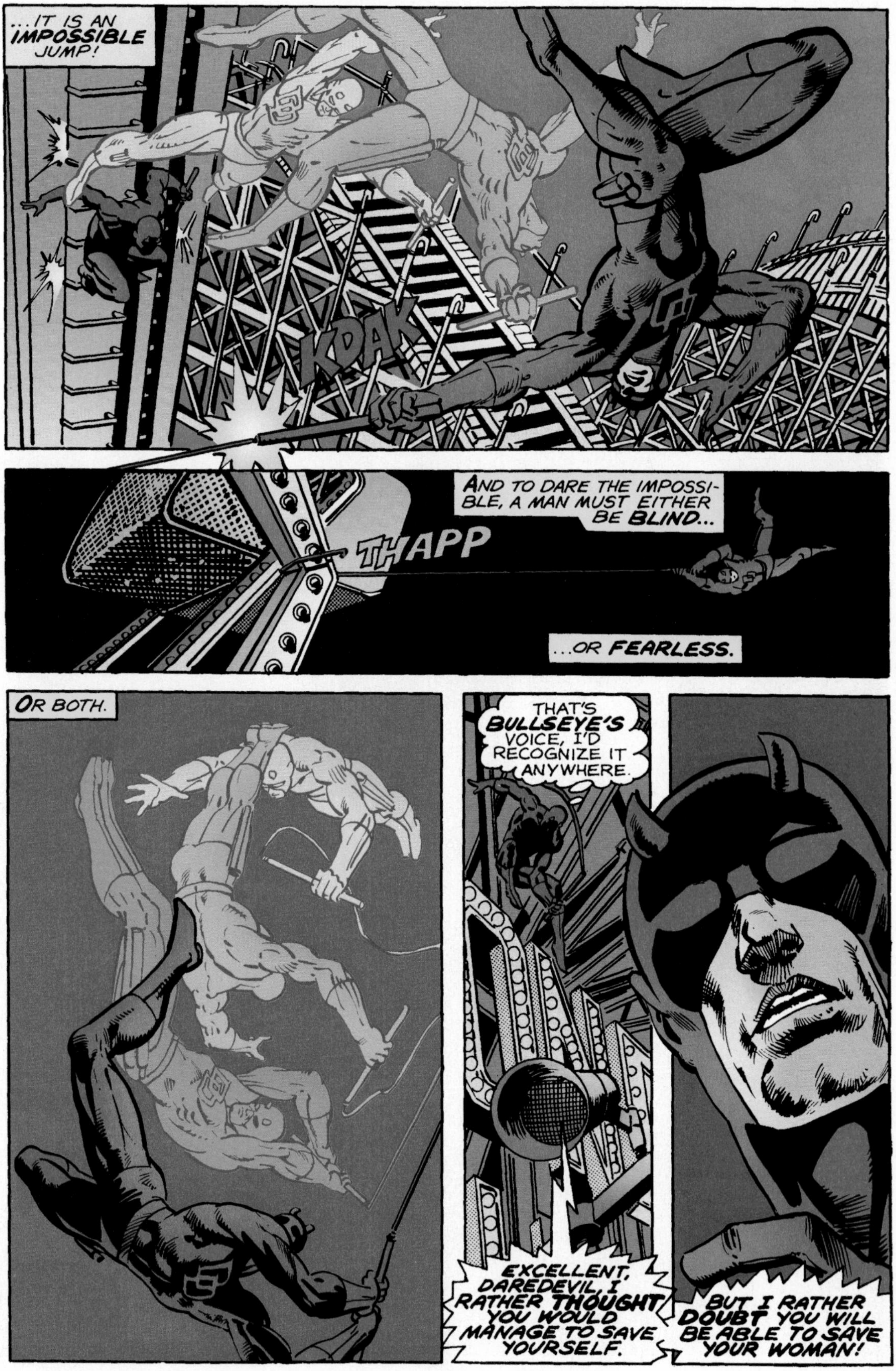
...IT IS AN IMPOSSIBLE JUMP!
KDAK
AND TO DARE THE IMPOSSIBLE, A MAN MUST EITHER BE BLIND...
THAPP
...OR FEARLESS.
OR BOTH.
THAT'S BULLSEYE'S VOICE, I'D RECOGNIZE IT ANYWHERE.
EXCELLENT, DAREDEVIL. I RATHER THOUGHT YOU WOULD MANAGE TO SAVE YOURSELF.
BUT I RATHER DOUBT YOU WILL BE ABLE TO SAVE YOUR WOMAN!

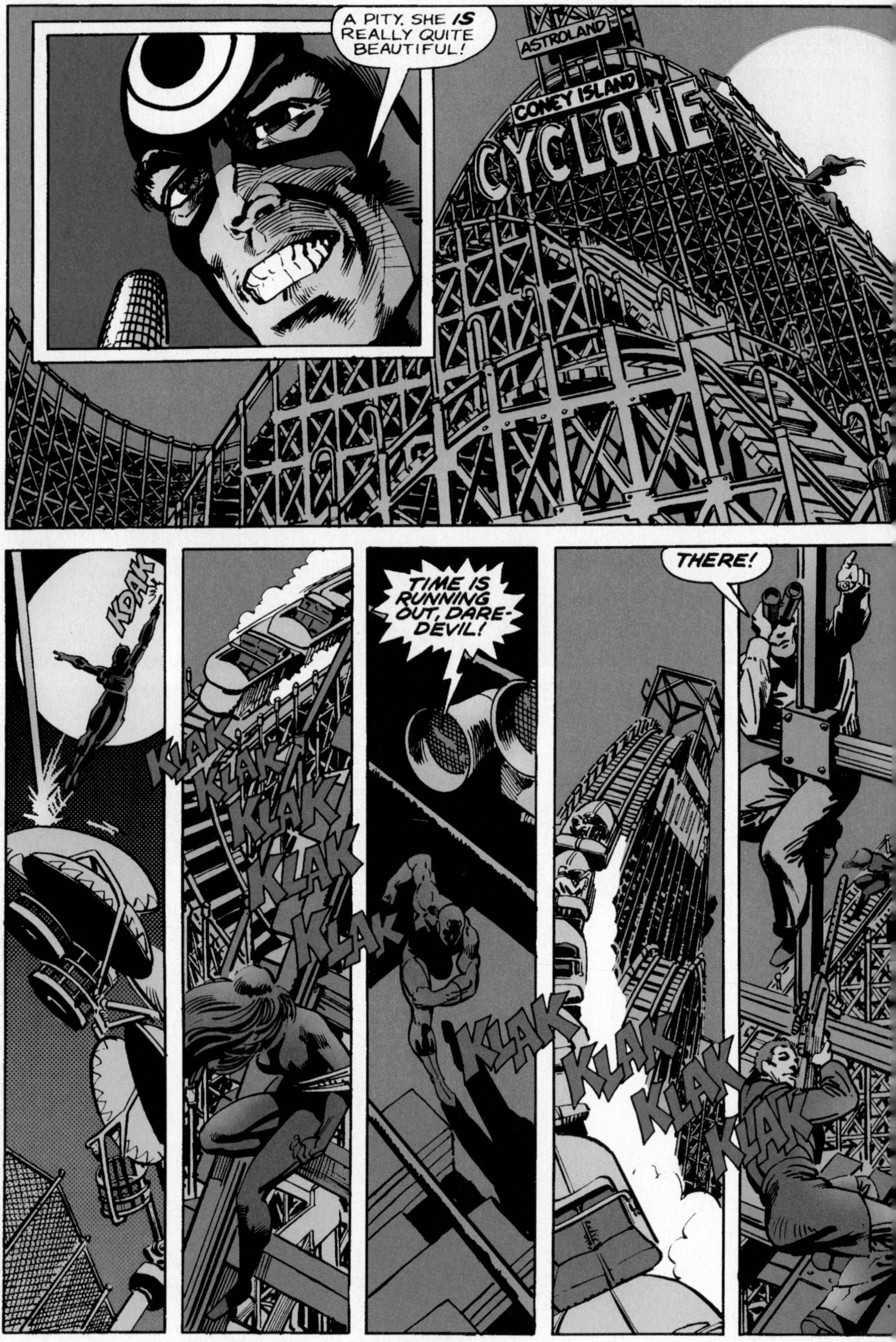
A PITY. SHE IS REALLY QUITE BEAUTIFUL!
ASTROLAND
CONEY ISLAND
CYCLONE
KDAK
KLAK KLAK KLAK KLAK KLAK KLAK
TIME IS RUNNING OUT, DARE-DEVIL!
KLAK KLAK KLAK KLAK
THERE!

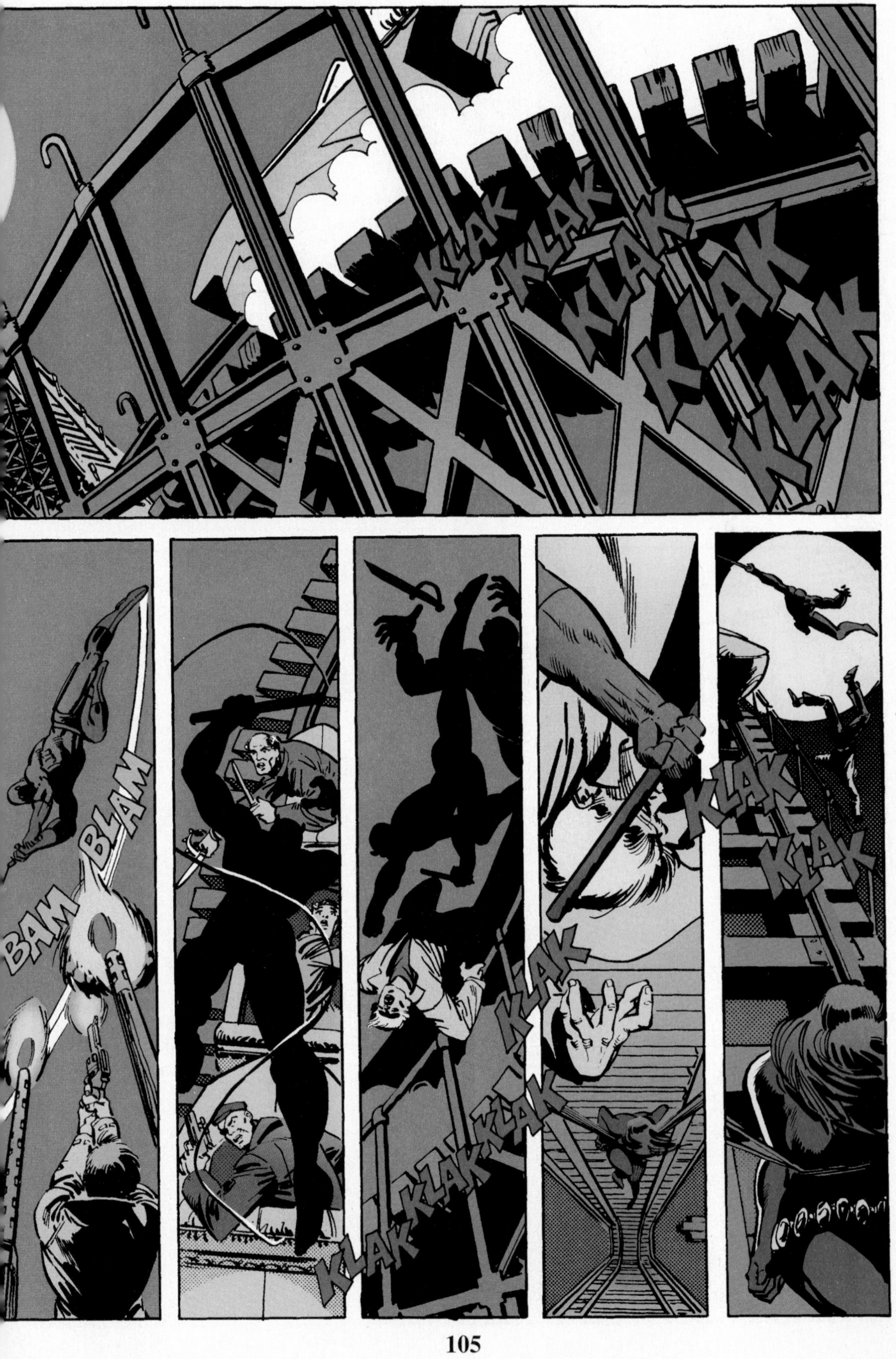
KLAK
KLAK
KLAK
KLAK
KLAK
BLAM
BAM
KLAK
KLAK
KLAK
KLAK
KLAK
KLAK
KLAK

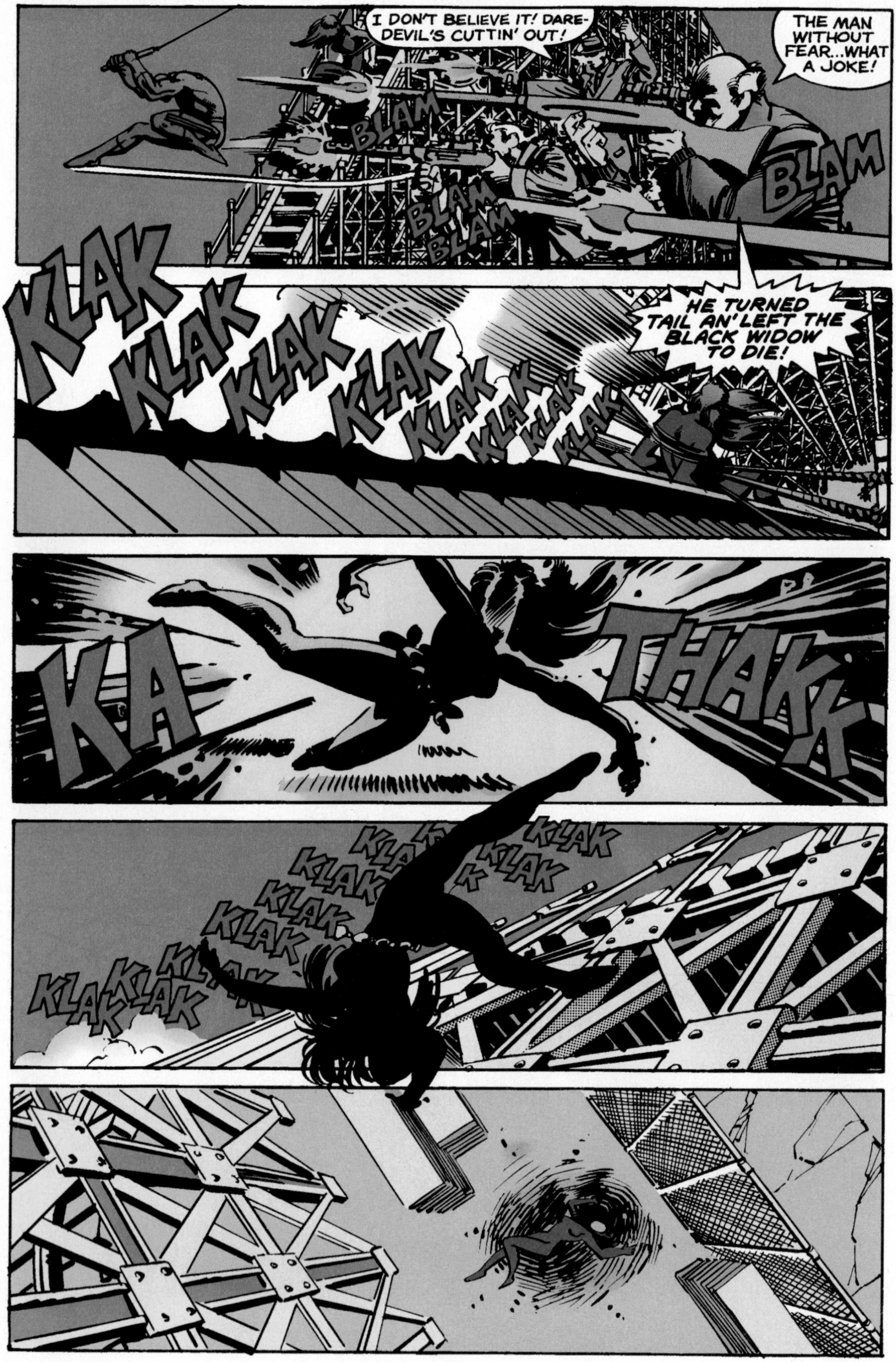
I DON'T BELIEVE IT! DAREDEVIL'S CUTTIN' OUT!
THE MAN WITHOUT FEAR...WHAT A JOKE!
BLAM
BLAM
BLAM BLAM
HE TURNED TAIL AN' LEFT THE BLACK WIDOW TO DIE!
KLAK KLAK KLAK KLAK KLAK KLAK KLAK KLAK
KA THAKK
KLAK KLAK KLAK KLAK KLAK KLAK KLAK KLAK

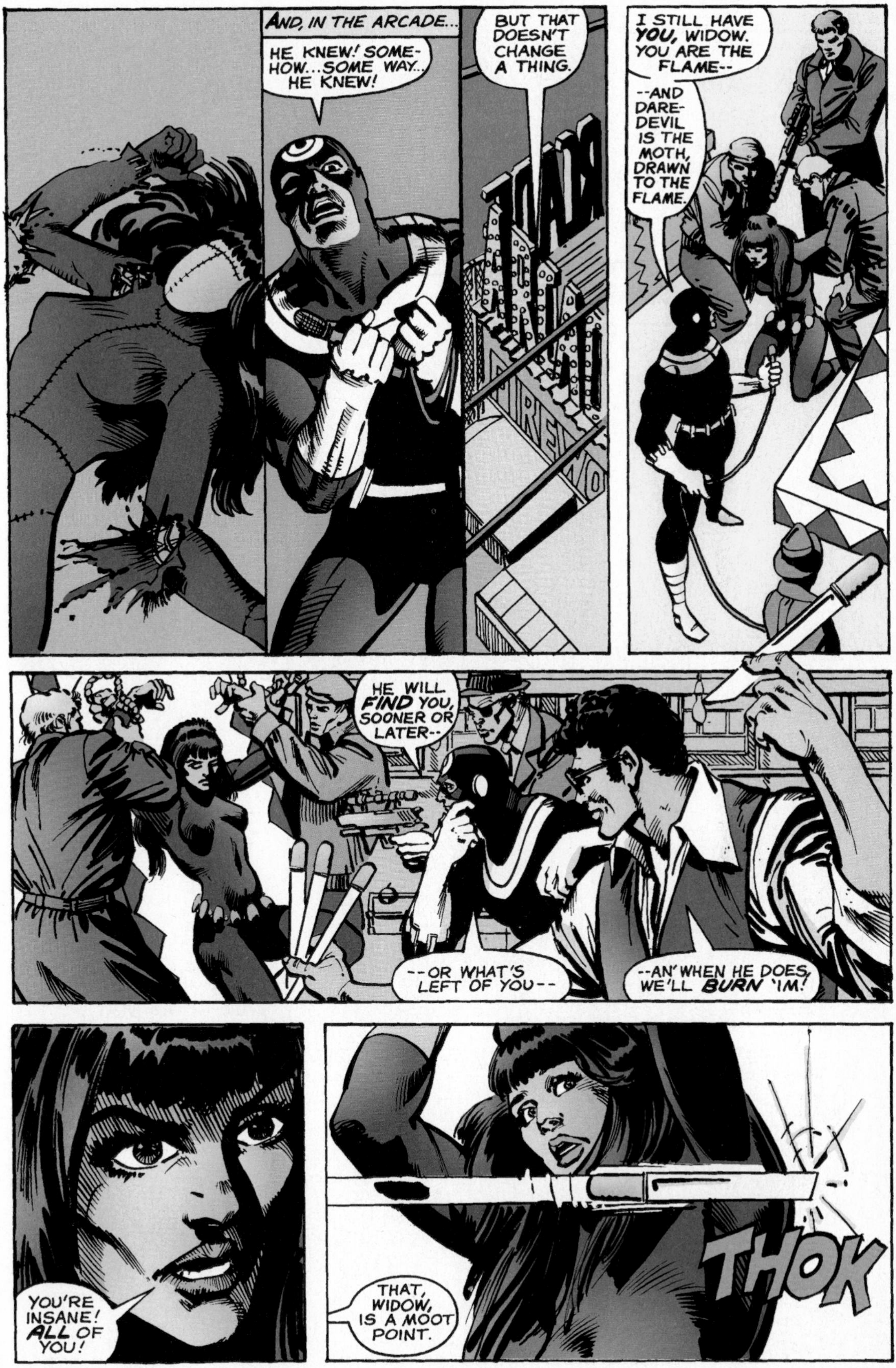
AND, IN THE ARCADE...
HE KNEW! SOME-HOW...SOME WAY... HE KNEW!
BUT THAT DOESN'T CHANGE A THING.
I STILL HAVE YOU, WIDOW. YOU ARE THE FLAME--
--AND DARE-DEVIL IS THE MOTH, DRAWN TO THE FLAME.
HE WILL FIND YOU, SOONER OR LATER--
--OR WHAT'S LEFT OF YOU--
--AN' WHEN HE DOES, WE'LL BURN 'IM!
YOU'RE INSANE! ALL OF YOU!
THAT, WIDOW, IS A MOOT POINT.
THOK

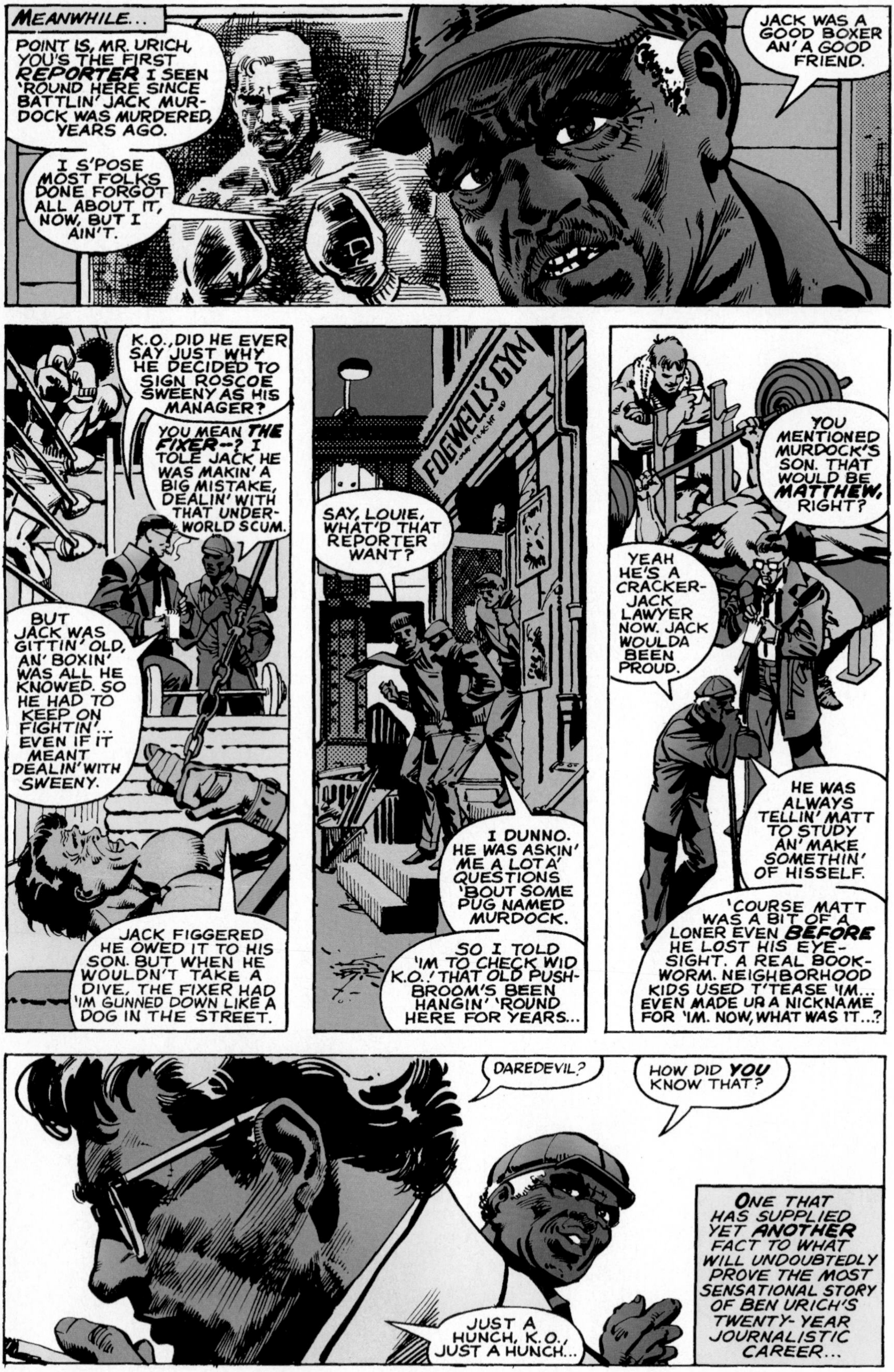
MEANWHILE...
POINT IS, MR. URICH, YOU'S THE FIRST REPORTER I SEEN 'ROUND HERE SINCE BATTLIN' JACK MURDOCK WAS MURDERED, YEARS AGO.
I S'POSE MOST FOLKS DONE FORGOT ALL ABOUT IT, NOW, BUT I AIN'T.
JACK WAS A GOOD BOXER AN' A GOOD FRIEND.
K.O., DID HE EVER SAY JUST WHY HE DECIDED TO SIGN ROSCOE SWEENY AS HIS MANAGER?
YOU MEAN THE FIXER--? I TOLE JACK HE WAS MAKIN' A BIG MISTAKE, DEALIN' WITH THAT UNDER-WORLD SCUM.
BUT JACK WAS GITTIN' OLD, AN' BOXIN' WAS ALL HE KNOWED. SO HE HAD TO KEEP ON FIGHTIN'... EVEN IF IT MEANT DEALIN' WITH SWEENY.
JACK FIGGERED HE OWED IT TO HIS SON. BUT WHEN HE WOULDN'T TAKE A DIVE, THE FIXER HAD 'IM GUNNED DOWN LIKE A DOG IN THE STREET.
FOGWELL'S GYM
SAY, LOUIE, WHAT'D THAT REPORTER WANT?
I DUNNO. HE WAS ASKIN' ME A LOTA' QUESTIONS 'BOUT SOME PUG NAMED MURDOCK.
SO I TOLD 'IM TO CHECK WID K.O.! THAT OLD PUSH-BROOM'S BEEN HANGIN' 'ROUND HERE FOR YEARS...
YOU MENTIONED MURDOCK'S SON. THAT WOULD BE MATTHEW, RIGHT?
YEAH HE'S A CRACKER-JACK LAWYER NOW. JACK WOULDA BEEN PROUD.
HE WAS ALWAYS TELLIN' MATT TO STUDY AN' MAKE SOMETHIN' OF HISSELF.
'COURSE MATT WAS A BIT OF A LONER EVEN BEFORE HE LOST HIS EYE-SIGHT. A REAL BOOK-WORM. NEIGHBORHOOD KIDS USED T'TEASE 'IM... EVEN MADE UP A NICKNAME FOR 'IM. NOW, WHAT WAS IT...?
DAREDEVIL?
HOW DID YOU KNOW THAT?
JUST A HUNCH, K.O., JUST A HUNCH...
ONE THAT HAS SUPPLIED YET ANOTHER FACT TO WHAT WILL UNDOUBTEDLY PROVE THE MOST SENSATIONAL STORY OF BEN URICH'S TWENTY-YEAR JOURNALISTIC CAREER...

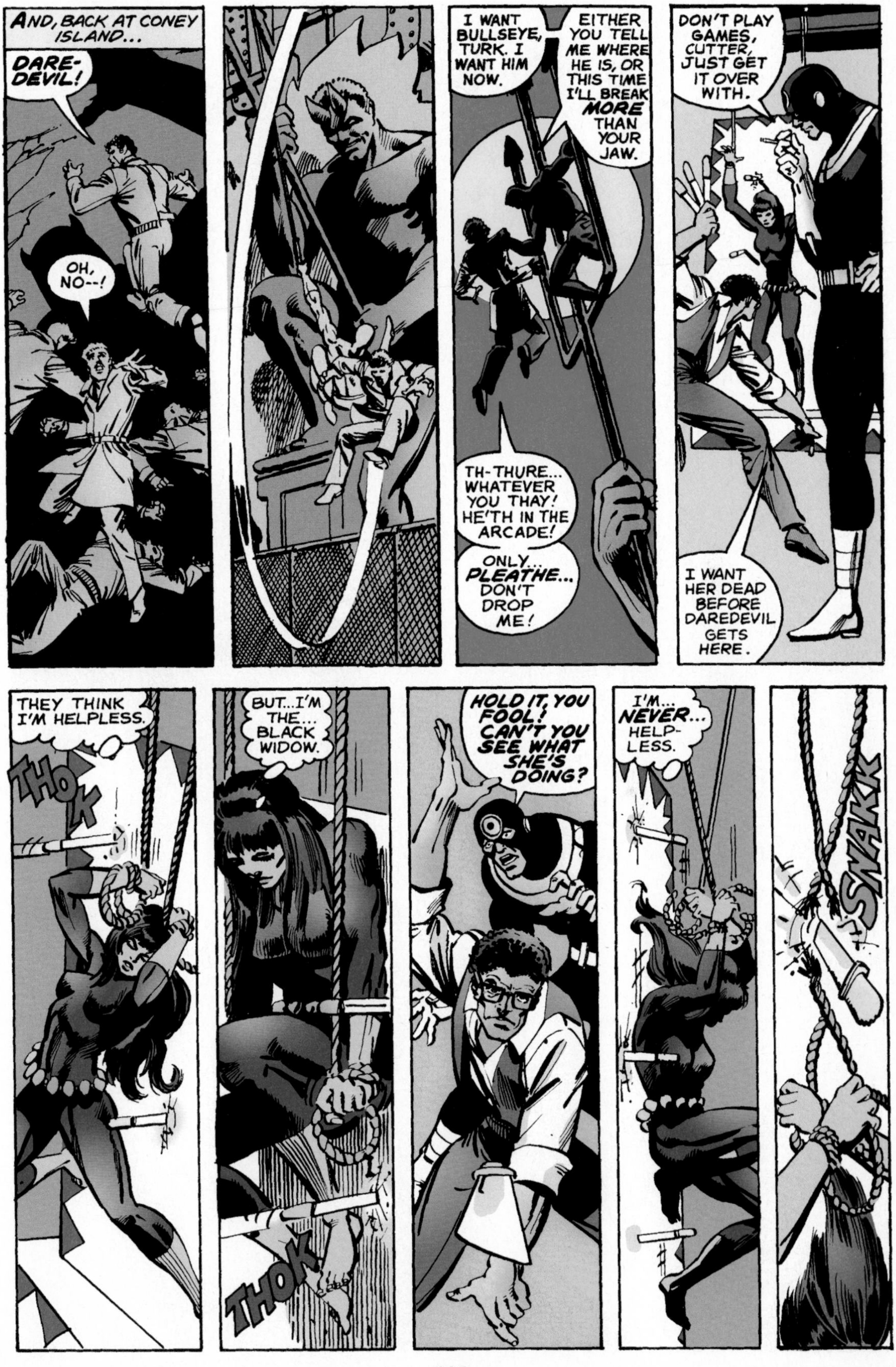
AND, BACK AT CONEY ISLAND...
DARE-DEVIL!
OH, NO--!
I WANT BULLSEYE, TURK. I WANT HIM NOW.
EITHER YOU TELL ME WHERE HE IS, OR THIS TIME I'LL BREAK MORE THAN YOUR JAW.
TH-THURE... WHATEVER YOU THAY! HE'TH IN THE ARCADE!
ONLY... PLEATHE... DON'T DROP ME!
DON'T PLAY GAMES, CUTTER, JUST GET IT OVER WITH.
I WANT HER DEAD BEFORE DAREDEVIL GETS HERE.
THEY THINK I'M HELPLESS.
THOK
BUT...I'M THE... BLACK WIDOW.
THOK
HOLD IT, YOU FOOL! CAN'T YOU SEE WHAT SHE'S DOING?
I'M... NEVER... HELP-LESS.
SNAKK

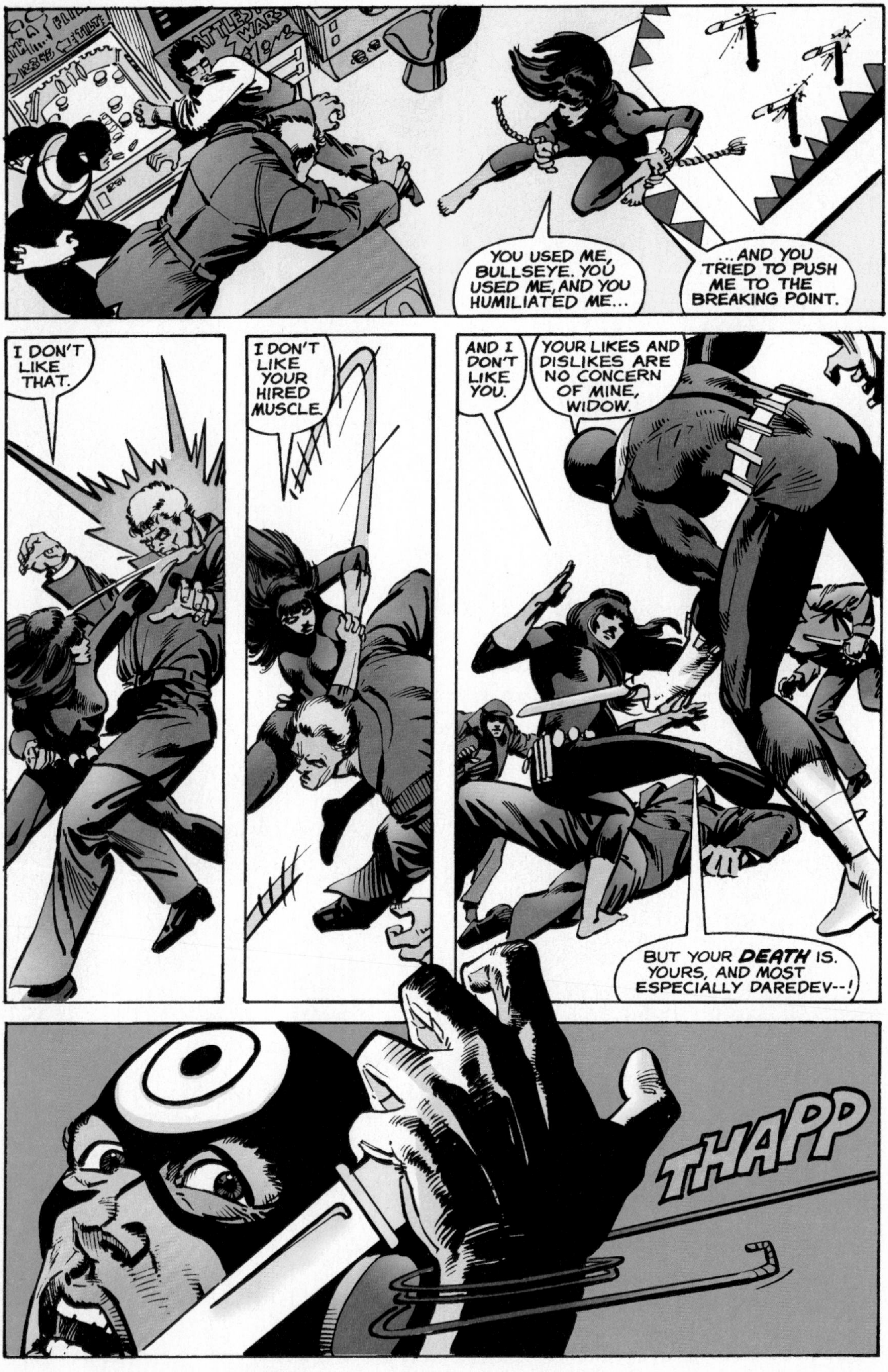
YOU USED ME, BULLSEYE. YOU USED ME, AND YOU HUMILIATED ME...
...AND YOU TRIED TO PUSH ME TO THE BREAKING POINT.
I DON'T LIKE THAT.
I DON'T LIKE YOUR HIRED MUSCLE.
AND I DON'T LIKE YOU.
YOUR LIKES AND DISLIKES ARE NO CONCERN OF MINE, WIDOW.
BUT YOUR DEATH IS. YOURS, AND MOST ESPECIALLY DAREDEV--!
THAPP

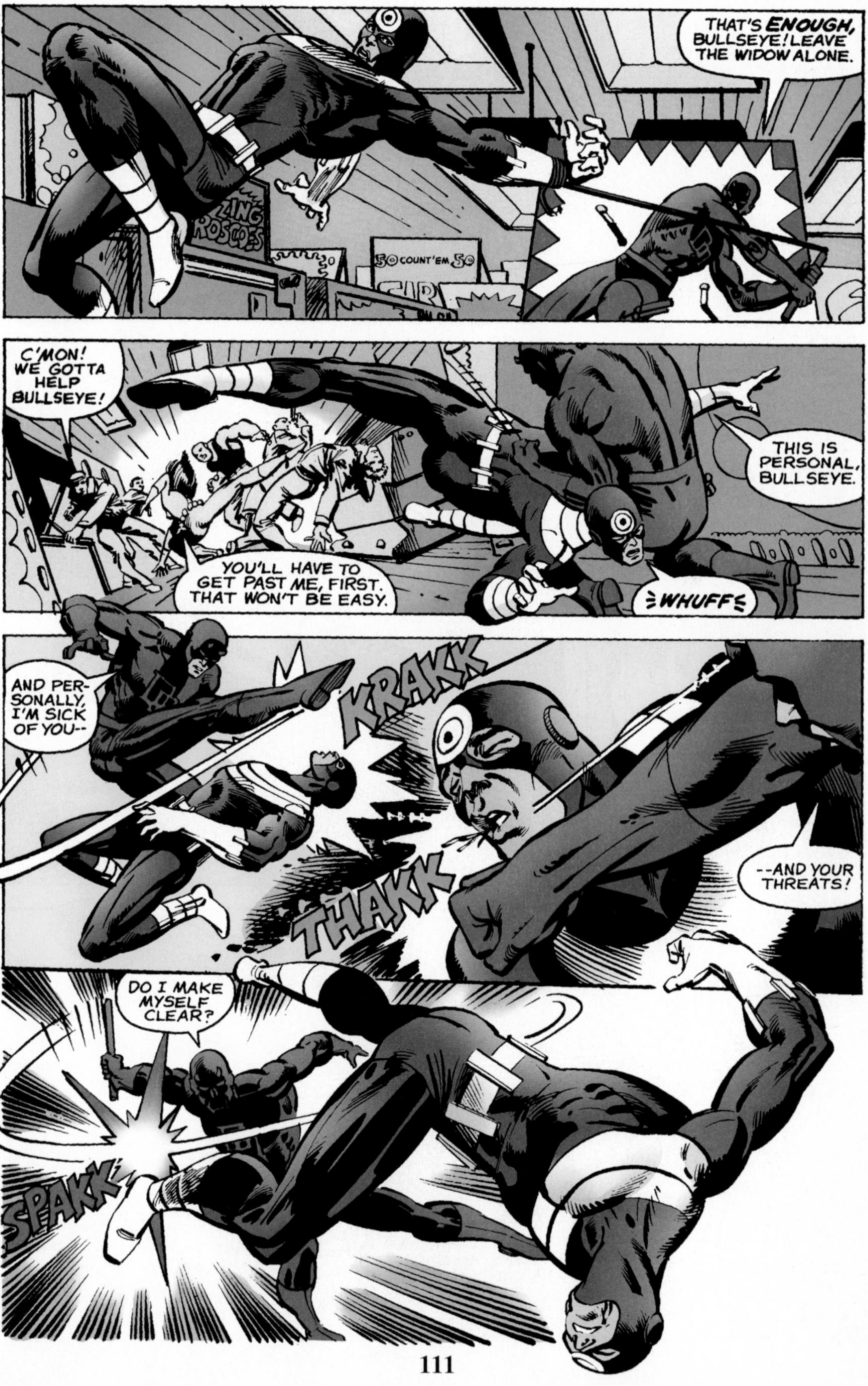
THAT'S ENOUGH, BULLSEYE! LEAVE THE WIDOW ALONE.
ZING
ROSCOES
50 COUNT'EM 50
C'MON! WE GOTTA HELP BULLSEYE!
THIS IS PERSONAL, BULLSEYE.
YOU'LL HAVE TO GET PAST ME, FIRST. THAT WON'T BE EASY.
WHUFF
AND PERSONALLY, I'M SICK OF YOU--
KRAKK
THAKK
--AND YOUR THREATS!
DO I MAKE MYSELF CLEAR?
SPAKK

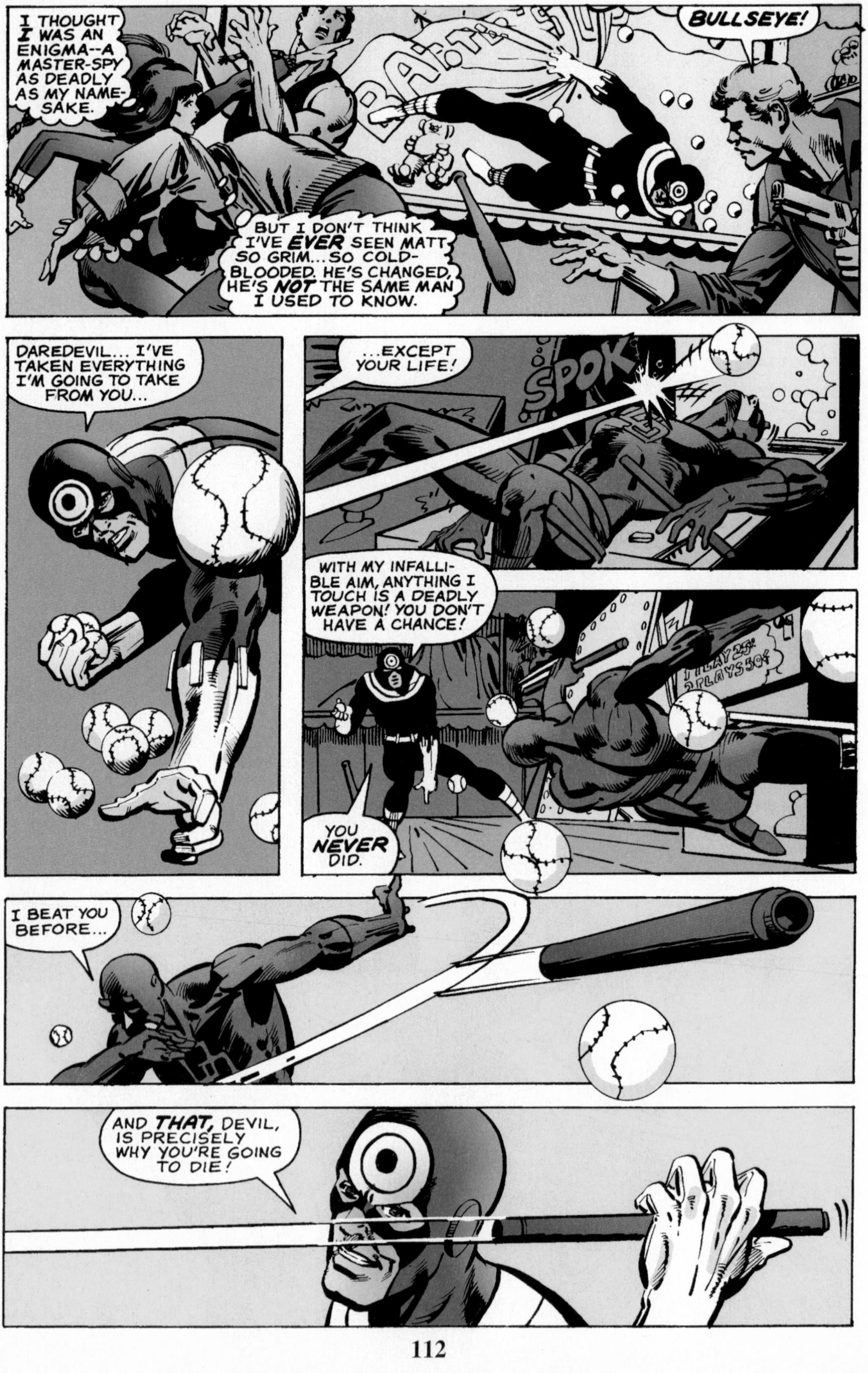
I THOUGHT I WAS AN ENIGMA--A MASTER-SPY AS DEADLY AS MY NAME-SAKE.
BULLSEYE!
BUT I DON'T THINK I'VE EVER SEEN MATT SO GRIM... SO COLD-BLOODED. HE'S CHANGED, HE'S NOT THE SAME MAN I USED TO KNOW.
DAREDEVIL... I'VE TAKEN EVERYTHING I'M GOING TO TAKE FROM YOU...
...EXCEPT YOUR LIFE!
SPOK
WITH MY INFALLI-BLE AIM, ANYTHING I TOUCH IS A DEADLY WEAPON! YOU DON'T HAVE A CHANCE!
YOU NEVER DID.
I BEAT YOU BEFORE...
AND THAT, DEVIL, IS PRECISELY WHY YOU'RE GOING TO DIE!

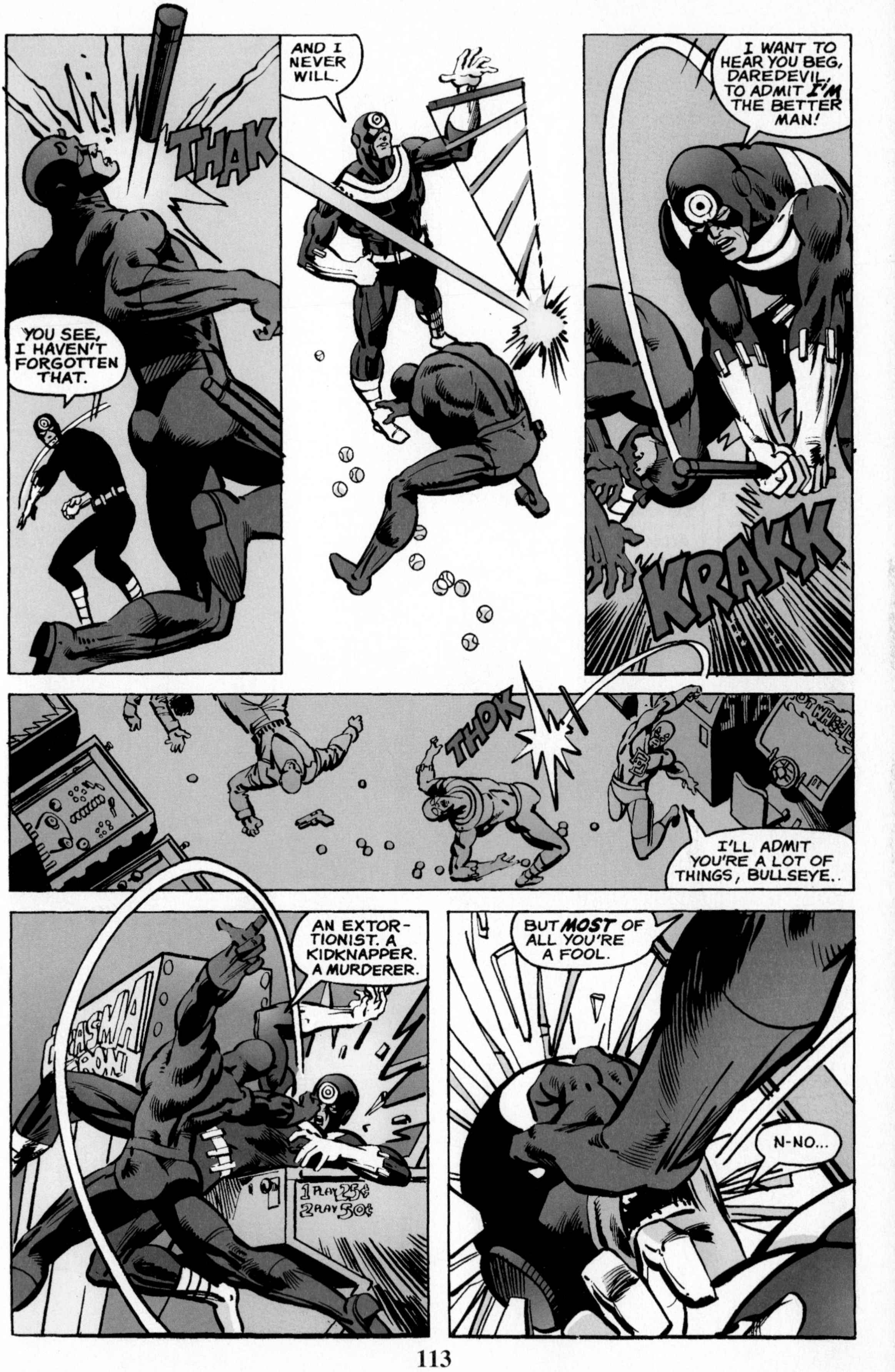
THAK
YOU SEE, I HAVEN'T FORGOTTEN THAT.
AND I NEVER WILL.
I WANT TO HEAR YOU BEG, DAREDEVIL, TO ADMIT I'M THE BETTER MAN!
KRAKK
THOK
I'LL ADMIT YOU'RE A LOT OF THINGS, BULLSEYE..
AN EXTOR-TIONIST. A KIDNAPPER. A MURDERER.
1 PLAY 25¢
2 PLAY 50¢
BUT MOST OF ALL YOU'RE A FOOL.
N-NO...

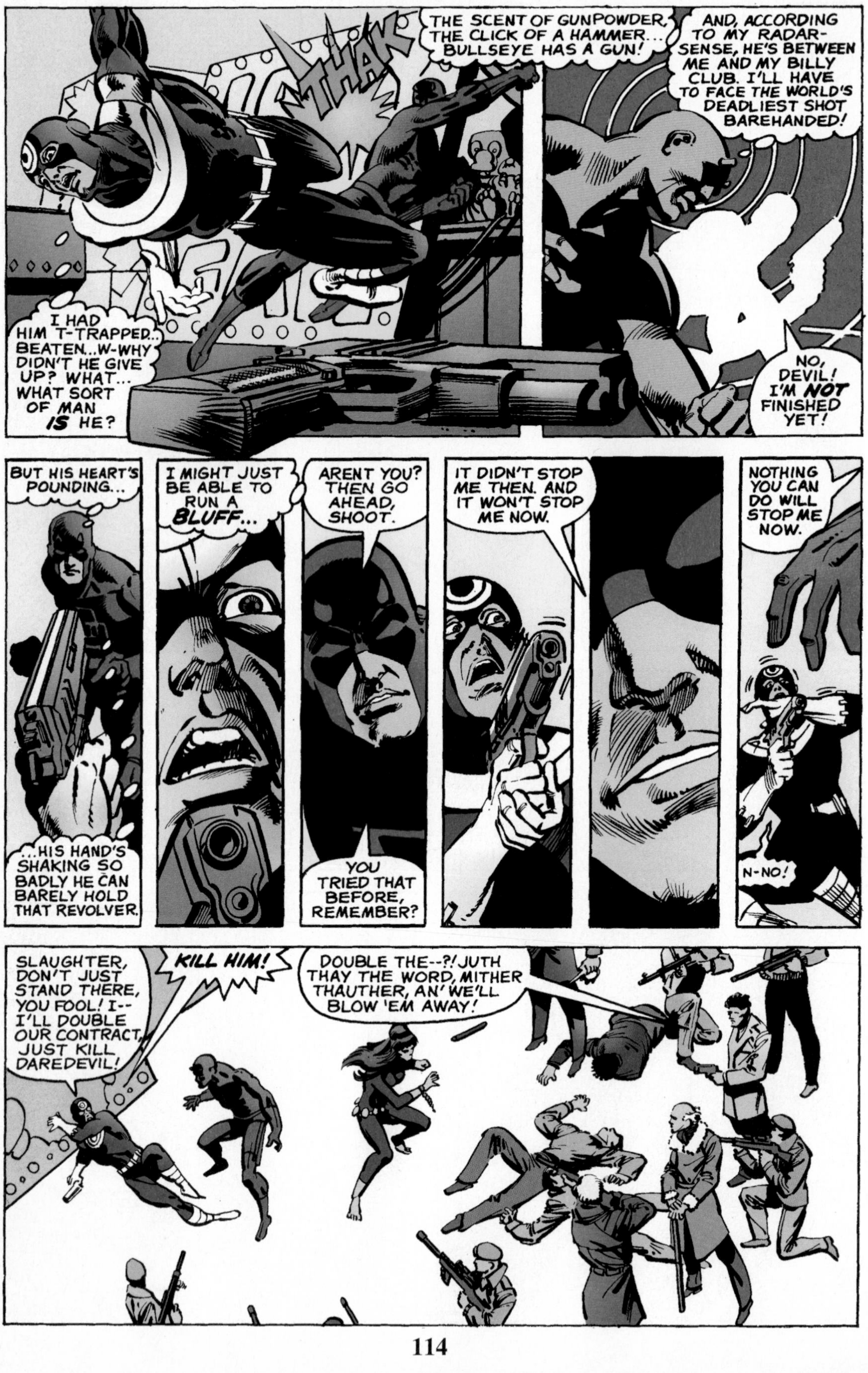
THAK
THE SCENT OF GUNPOWDER, THE CLICK OF A HAMMER... BULLSEYE HAS A GUN!
AND, ACCORDING TO MY RADAR-SENSE, HE'S BETWEEN ME AND MY BILLY CLUB. I'LL HAVE TO FACE THE WORLD'S DEADLIEST SHOT BAREHANDED!
I HAD HIM T-TRAPPED... BEATEN... W-WHY DIDN'T HE GIVE UP? WHAT... WHAT SORT OF MAN IS HE?
NO, DEVIL! I'M NOT FINISHED YET!
BUT HIS HEART'S POUNDING...
...HIS HAND'S SHAKING SO BADLY HE CAN BARELY HOLD THAT REVOLVER.
I MIGHT JUST BE ABLE TO RUN A BLUFF...
ARENT YOU? THEN GO AHEAD, SHOOT.
YOU TRIED THAT BEFORE, REMEMBER?
IT DIDN'T STOP ME THEN. AND IT WON'T STOP ME NOW.
NOTHING YOU CAN DO WILL STOP ME NOW.
N-NO!
SLAUGHTER, DON'T JUST STAND THERE, YOU FOOL! I-- I'LL DOUBLE OUR CONTRACT, JUST KILL DAREDEVIL!
KILL HIM!
DOUBLE THE--?! JUTH THAY THE WORD, MITHER THAUTHER, AN' WE'LL BLOW 'EM AWAY!

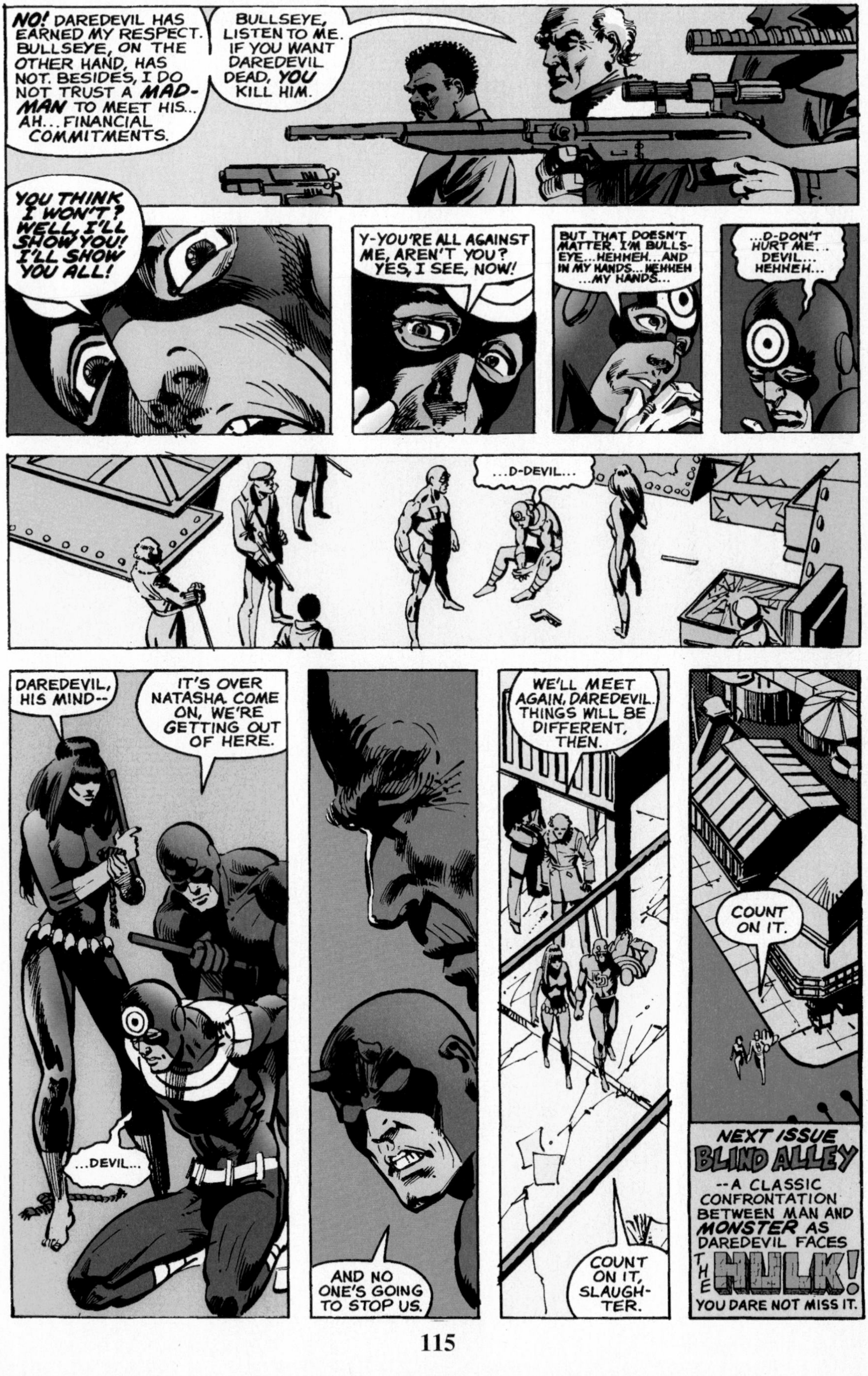
NO! DAREDEVIL HAS EARNED MY RESPECT. BULLSEYE, ON THE OTHER HAND, HAS NOT. BESIDES, I DO NOT TRUST A MAD-MAN TO MEET HIS... AH... FINANCIAL COMMITMENTS.
BULLSEYE, LISTEN TO ME. IF YOU WANT DAREDEVIL DEAD, YOU KILL HIM.
YOU THINK I WON'T? WELL, I'LL SHOW YOU! I'LL SHOW YOU ALL!
Y-YOU'RE ALL AGAINST ME, AREN'T YOU? YES, I SEE, NOW!
BUT THAT DOESN'T MATTER. I'M BULLS-EYE...HEHHEH...AND IN MY HANDS...HEHHEH ...MY HANDS...
...D-DON'T HURT ME... DEVIL... HEHHEH...
...D-DEVIL...
DAREDEVIL, HIS MIND--
IT'S OVER NATASHA. COME ON, WE'RE GETTING OUT OF HERE.
...DEVIL...
AND NO ONE'S GOING TO STOP US.
WE'LL MEET AGAIN, DAREDEVIL. THINGS WILL BE DIFFERENT, THEN.
COUNT ON IT, SLAUGH-TER.
COUNT ON IT.
NEXT ISSUE
BLIND ALLEY
--A CLASSIC CONFRONTATION BETWEEN MAN AND MONSTER AS DAREDEVIL FACES THE HULK!
YOU DARE NOT MISS IT.

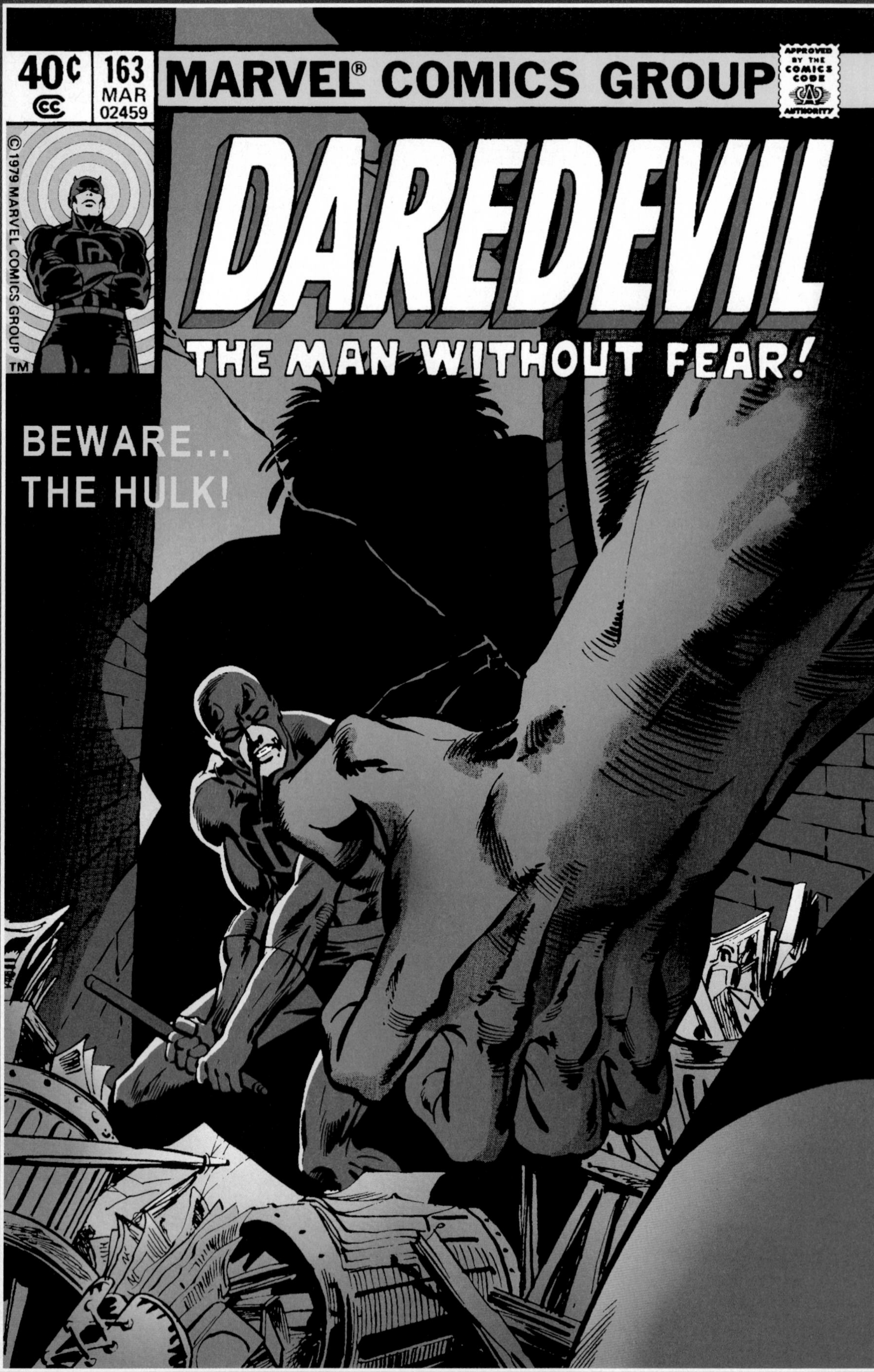
40¢
CC
163
MAR
02459
MARVEL® COMICS GROUP
APPROVED BY THE COMICS CODE AUTHORITY
© 1979 MARVEL COMICS GROUP
TM
DAREDEVIL
THE MAN WITHOUT FEAR!
BEWARE...
THE HULK!

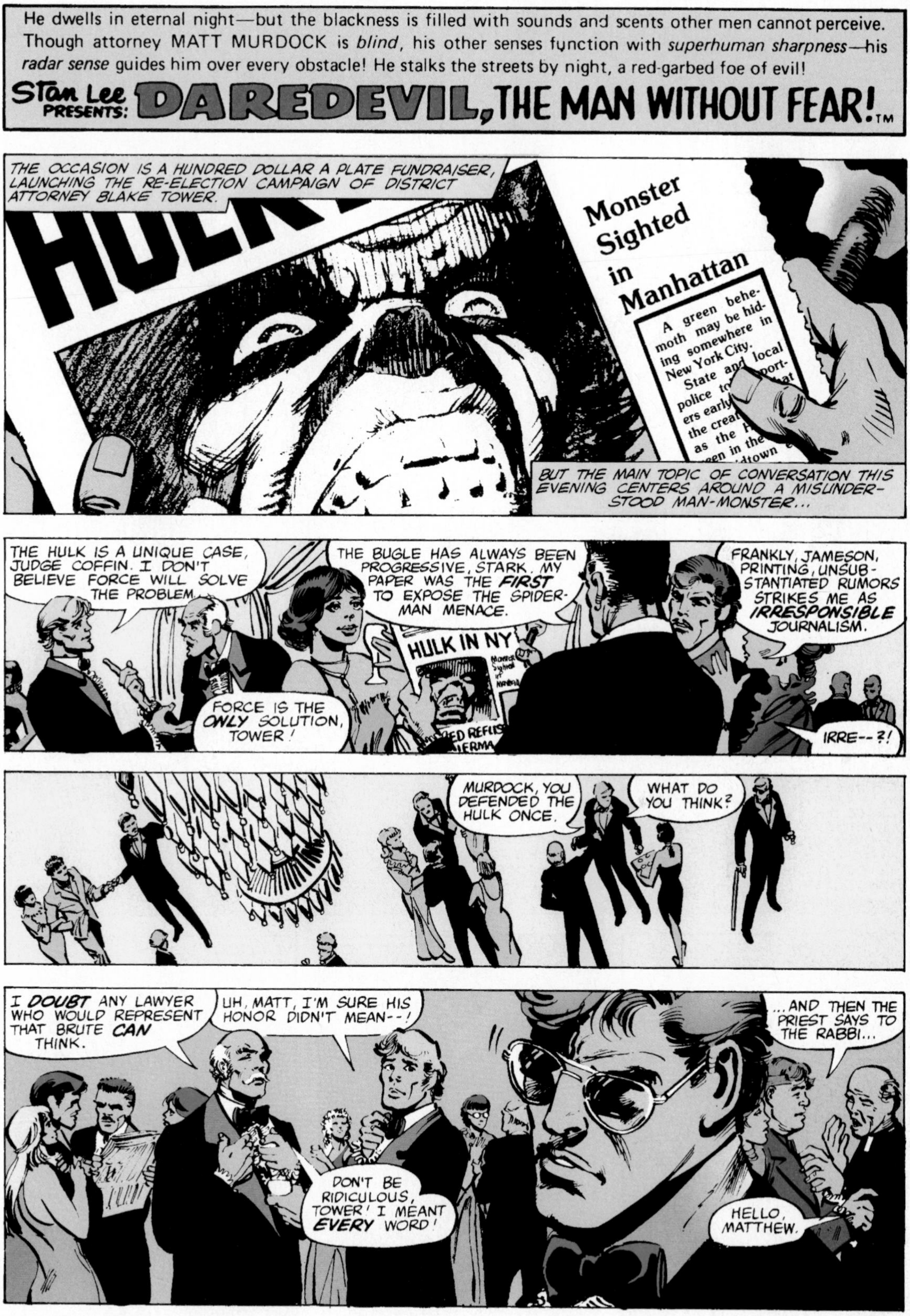
He dwells in eternal night—but the blackness is filled with sounds and scents other men cannot perceive. Though attorney MATT MURDOCK is *blind*, his other senses function with *superhuman sharpness*—his *radar sense* guides him over every obstacle! He stalks the streets by night, a red-garbed foe of evil!
Stan Lee PRESENTS: DAREDEVIL, THE MAN WITHOUT FEAR!™
THE OCCASION IS A HUNDRED DOLLAR A PLATE FUNDRAISER, LAUNCHING THE RE-ELECTION CAMPAIGN OF DISTRICT ATTORNEY BLAKE TOWER.
Monster Sighted in Manhattan
A green behemoth may be hiding somewhere in New York City.
BUT THE MAIN TOPIC OF CONVERSATION THIS EVENING CENTERS AROUND A MISUNDERSTOOD MAN-MONSTER...
THE HULK IS A UNIQUE CASE, JUDGE COFFIN. I DON'T BELIEVE FORCE WILL SOLVE THE PROBLEM.
FORCE IS THE *ONLY* SOLUTION, TOWER!
THE BUGLE HAS ALWAYS BEEN PROGRESSIVE, STARK. MY PAPER WAS THE *FIRST* TO EXPOSE THE SPIDER-MAN MENACE.
HULK IN NY
FRANKLY, JAMESON, PRINTING UNSUBSTANTIATED RUMORS STRIKES ME AS *IRRESPONSIBLE* JOURNALISM.
IRRE--?!
MURDOCK, YOU DEFENDED THE HULK ONCE.
WHAT DO YOU THINK?
I *DOUBT* ANY LAWYER WHO WOULD REPRESENT THAT BRUTE *CAN* THINK.
UH, MATT, I'M SURE HIS HONOR DIDN'T MEAN--!
DON'T BE RIDICULOUS, TOWER! I MEANT *EVERY* WORD!
...AND THEN THE PRIEST SAYS TO THE RABBI...
HELLO, MATTHEW.

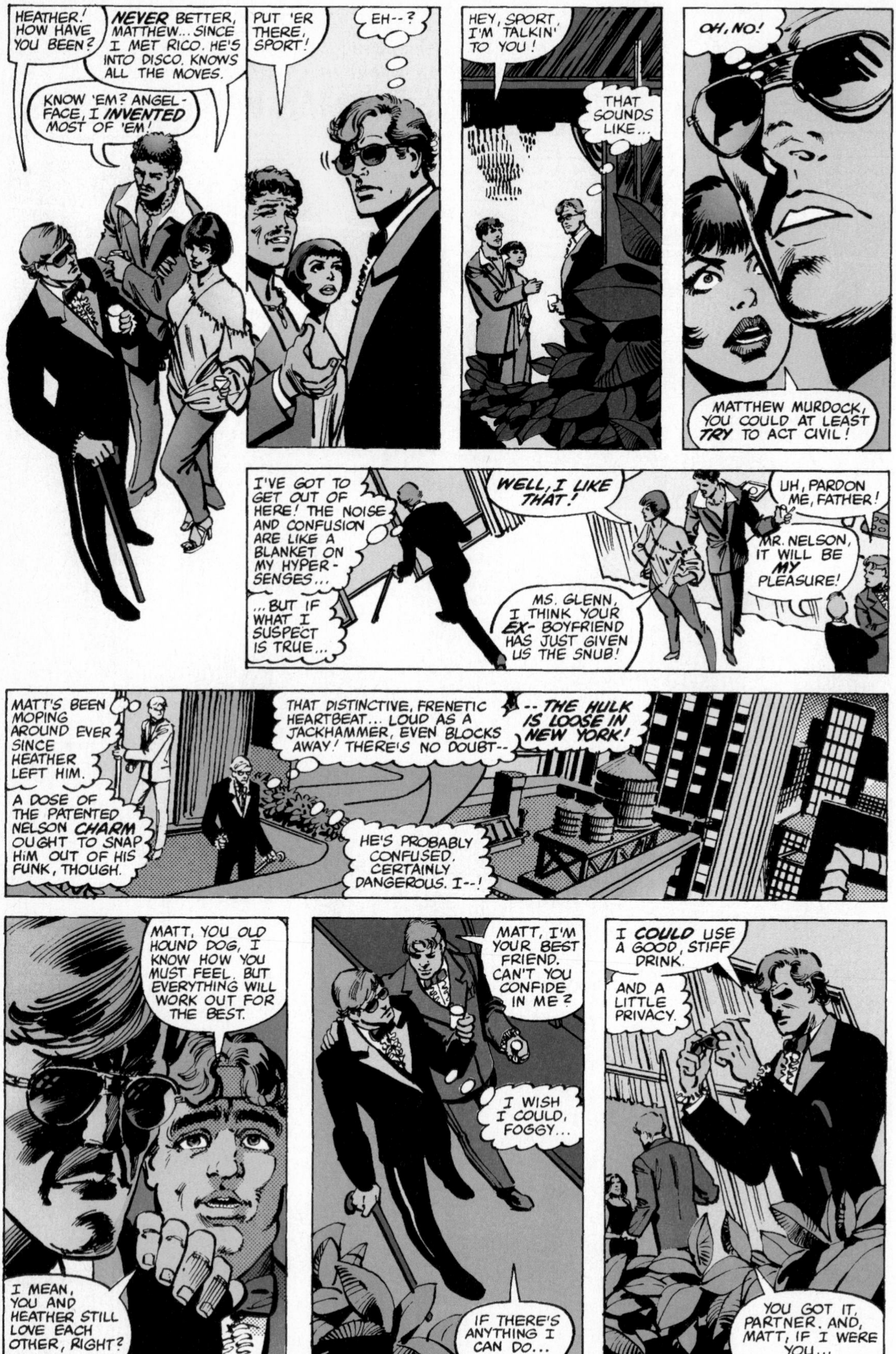

HEATHER! HOW HAVE YOU BEEN?
NEVER BETTER, MATTHEW... SINCE I MET RICO. HE'S INTO DISCO. KNOWS ALL THE MOVES.
KNOW 'EM? ANGEL-FACE, I INVENTED MOST OF 'EM!
PUT 'ER THERE, SPORT!
EH--?
HEY, SPORT, I'M TALKIN' TO YOU!
THAT SOUNDS LIKE...
OH, NO!
MATTHEW MURDOCK, YOU COULD AT LEAST TRY TO ACT CIVIL!
I'VE GOT TO GET OUT OF HERE! THE NOISE AND CONFUSION ARE LIKE A BLANKET ON MY HYPER-SENSES...
...BUT IF WHAT I SUSPECT IS TRUE...
WELL, I LIKE THAT!
MS. GLENN, I THINK YOUR EX-BOYFRIEND HAS JUST GIVEN US THE SNUB!
UH, PARDON ME, FATHER!
MR. NELSON, IT WILL BE MY PLEASURE!
MATT'S BEEN MOPING AROUND EVER SINCE HEATHER LEFT HIM.
A DOSE OF THE PATENTED NELSON CHARM OUGHT TO SNAP HIM OUT OF HIS FUNK, THOUGH.
THAT DISTINCTIVE, FRENETIC HEARTBEAT... LOUD AS A JACKHAMMER, EVEN BLOCKS AWAY! THERE'S NO DOUBT--
--THE HULK IS LOOSE IN NEW YORK!
HE'S PROBABLY CONFUSED. CERTAINLY DANGEROUS. I--!
MATT, YOU OLD HOUND DOG, I KNOW HOW YOU MUST FEEL. BUT EVERYTHING WILL WORK OUT FOR THE BEST.
I MEAN, YOU AND HEATHER STILL LOVE EACH OTHER, RIGHT?
MATT, I'M YOUR BEST FRIEND. CAN'T YOU CONFIDE IN ME?
I WISH I COULD, FOGGY...
IF THERE'S ANYTHING I CAN DO...
I COULD USE A GOOD, STIFF DRINK.
AND A LITTLE PRIVACY.
YOU GOT IT, PARTNER. AND, MATT, IF I WERE YOU...

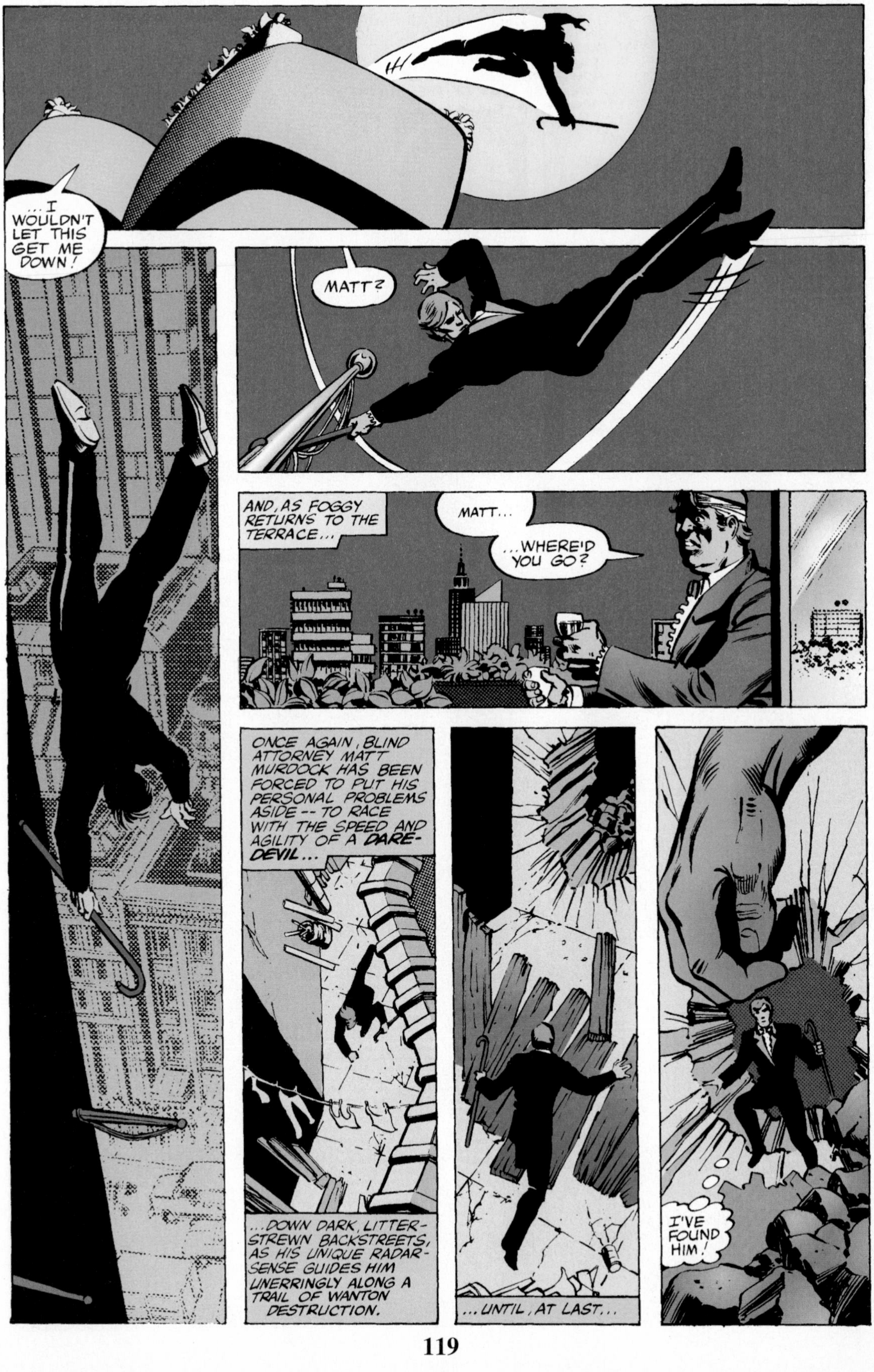
...I WOULDN'T LET THIS GET ME DOWN!
MATT?
AND, AS FOGGY RETURNS TO THE TERRACE...
MATT...
...WHERE'D YOU GO?
ONCE AGAIN, BLIND ATTORNEY MATT MURDOCK HAS BEEN FORCED TO PUT HIS PERSONAL PROBLEMS ASIDE -- TO RACE WITH THE SPEED AND AGILITY OF A DAREDEVIL...
...DOWN DARK, LITTER-STREWN BACKSTREETS, AS HIS UNIQUE RADAR-SENSE GUIDES HIM UNERRINGLY ALONG A TRAIL OF WANTON DESTRUCTION.
...UNTIL, AT LAST...
I'VE FOUND HIM!

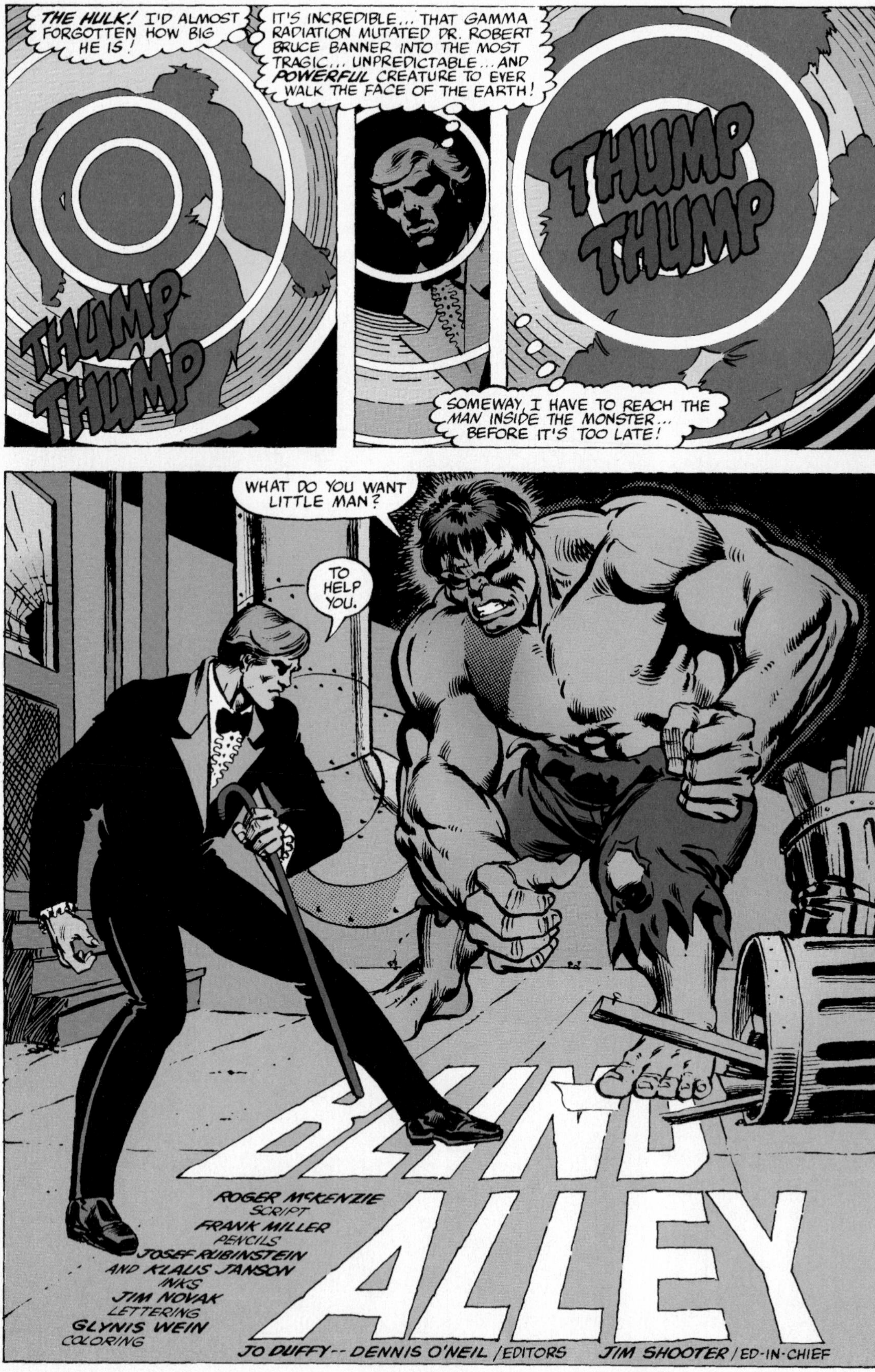
THE HULK! I'D ALMOST FORGOTTEN HOW BIG HE IS!
IT'S INCREDIBLE... THAT GAMMA RADIATION MUTATED DR. ROBERT BRUCE BANNER INTO THE MOST TRAGIC... UNPREDICTABLE... AND POWERFUL CREATURE TO EVER WALK THE FACE OF THE EARTH!
THUMP THUMP
THUMP THUMP
SOMEWAY, I HAVE TO REACH THE MAN INSIDE THE MONSTER... BEFORE IT'S TOO LATE!
WHAT DO YOU WANT LITTLE MAN?
TO HELP YOU.
BLIND ALLEY
ROGER MCKENZIE SCRIPT
FRANK MILLER PENCILS
JOSEF RUBINSTEIN AND KLAUS JANSON INKS
JIM NOVAK LETTERING
GLYNIS WEIN COLORING
JO DUFFY -- DENNIS O'NEIL / EDITORS
JIM SHOOTER / ED-IN-CHIEF

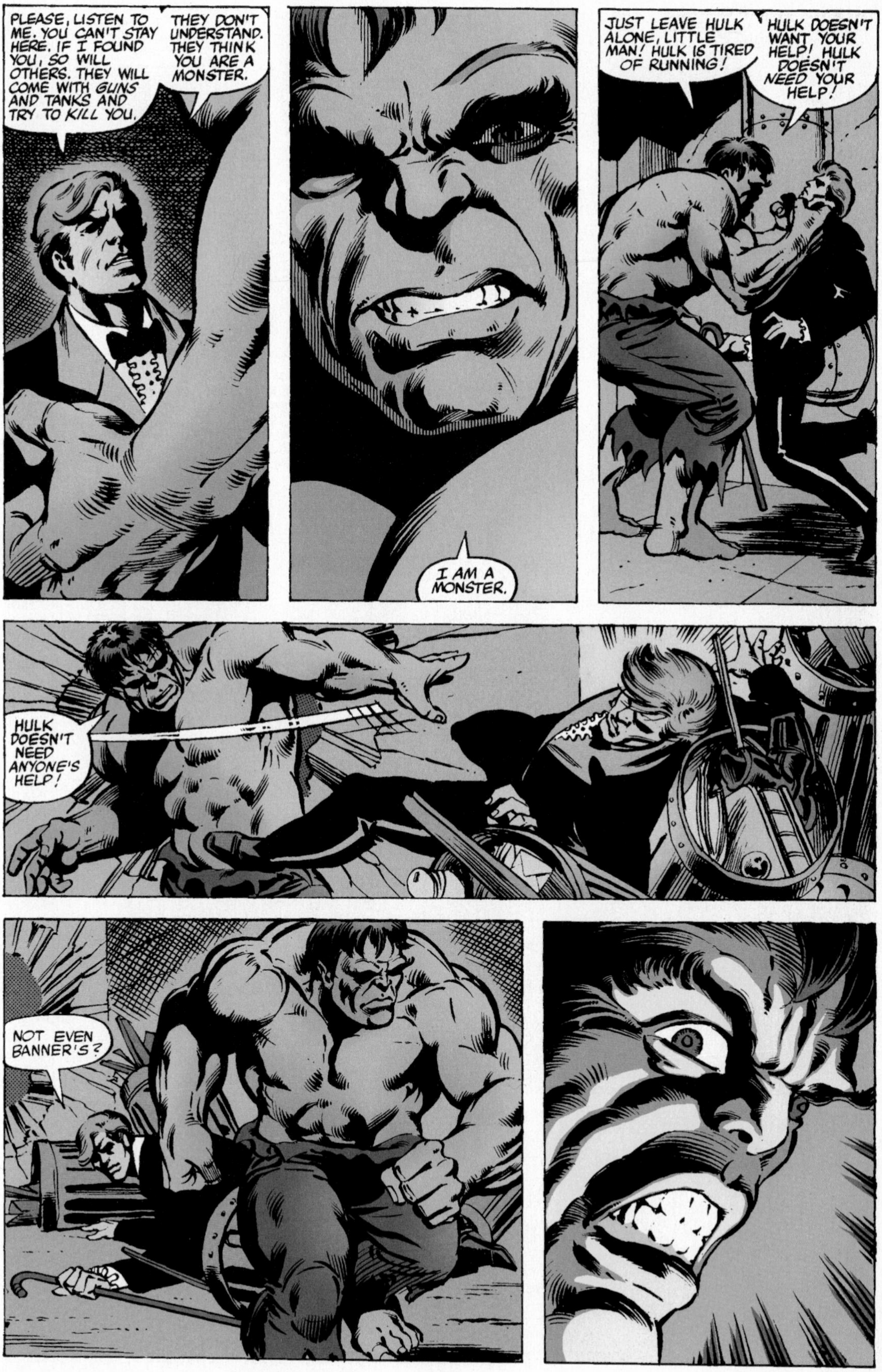
PLEASE, LISTEN TO ME. YOU CAN'T STAY HERE. IF I FOUND YOU, SO WILL OTHERS. THEY WILL COME WITH GUNS AND TANKS AND TRY TO KILL YOU.
THEY DON'T UNDERSTAND. THEY THINK YOU ARE A MONSTER.
I AM A MONSTER.
JUST LEAVE HULK ALONE, LITTLE MAN! HULK IS TIRED OF RUNNING!
HULK DOESN'T WANT YOUR HELP! HULK DOESN'T NEED YOUR HELP!
HULK DOESN'T NEED ANYONE'S HELP!
NOT EVEN BANNER'S?

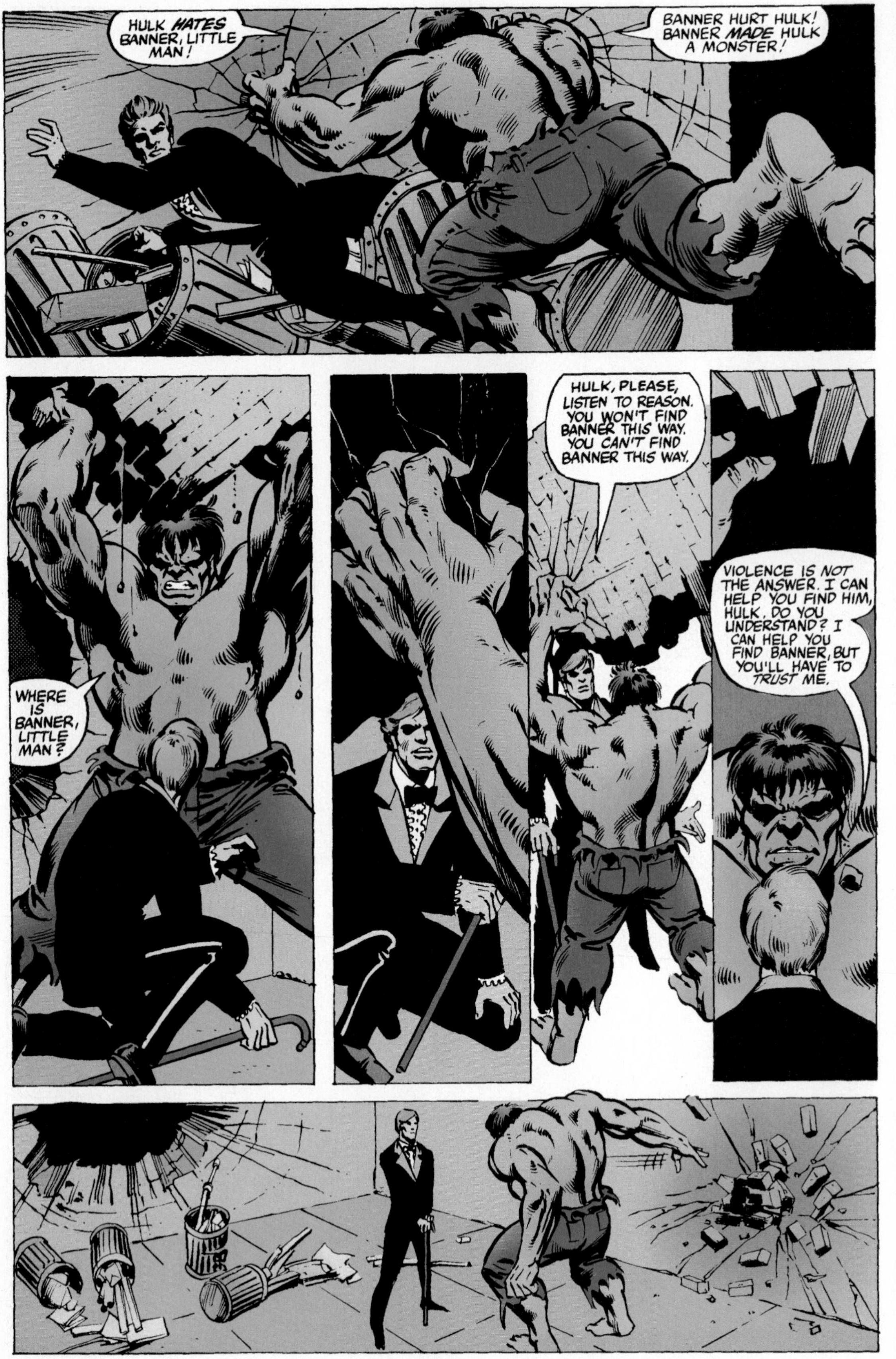
HULK *HATES* BANNER, LITTLE MAN!
BANNER HURT HULK! BANNER *MADE* HULK A MONSTER!
WHERE IS BANNER, LITTLE MAN?
HULK, PLEASE, LISTEN TO REASON. YOU WON'T FIND BANNER THIS WAY. YOU CAN'T FIND BANNER THIS WAY.
VIOLENCE IS *NOT* THE ANSWER. I CAN HELP YOU FIND HIM, HULK. DO YOU UNDERSTAND? I CAN HELP YOU FIND BANNER, BUT YOU'LL HAVE TO *TRUST* ME.

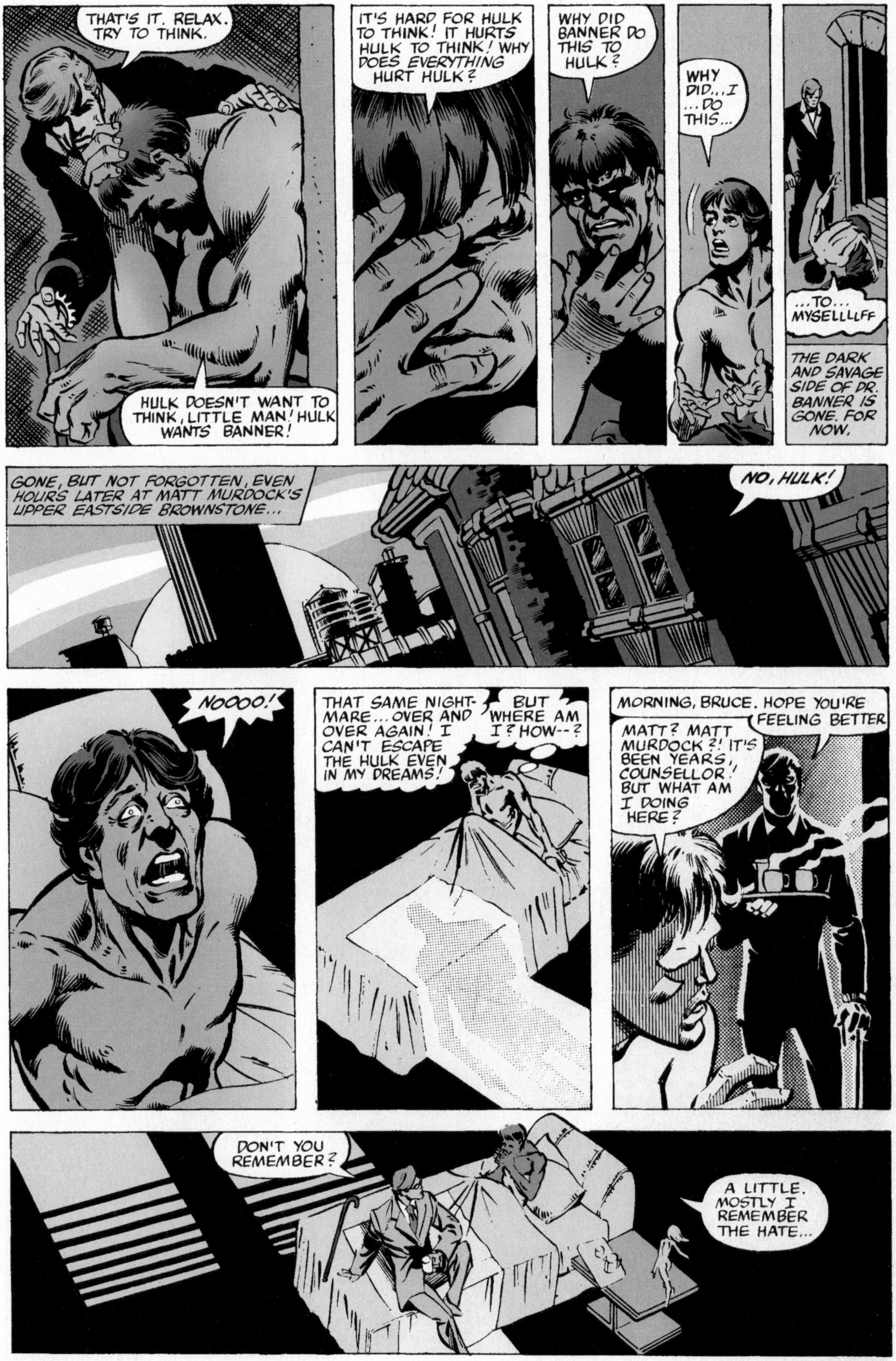
THAT'S IT. RELAX. TRY TO THINK.
HULK DOESN'T WANT TO THINK, LITTLE MAN! HULK WANTS BANNER!
IT'S HARD FOR HULK TO THINK! IT HURTS HULK TO THINK! WHY DOES EVERYTHING HURT HULK?
WHY DID BANNER DO THIS TO HULK?
WHY DID... I ...DO THIS...
...TO... MYSELLLLLFF
THE DARK AND SAVAGE SIDE OF DR. BANNER IS GONE. FOR NOW.
GONE, BUT NOT FORGOTTEN, EVEN HOURS LATER AT MATT MURDOCK'S UPPER EASTSIDE BROWNSTONE...
NO, HULK!
NOOOO!
THAT SAME NIGHT-MARE... OVER AND OVER AGAIN! I CAN'T ESCAPE THE HULK EVEN IN MY DREAMS!
BUT WHERE AM I? HOW--?
MORNING, BRUCE. HOPE YOU'RE FEELING BETTER
MATT? MATT MURDOCK?! IT'S BEEN YEARS, COUNSELLOR! BUT WHAT AM I DOING HERE?
DON'T YOU REMEMBER?
A LITTLE. MOSTLY I REMEMBER THE HATE...

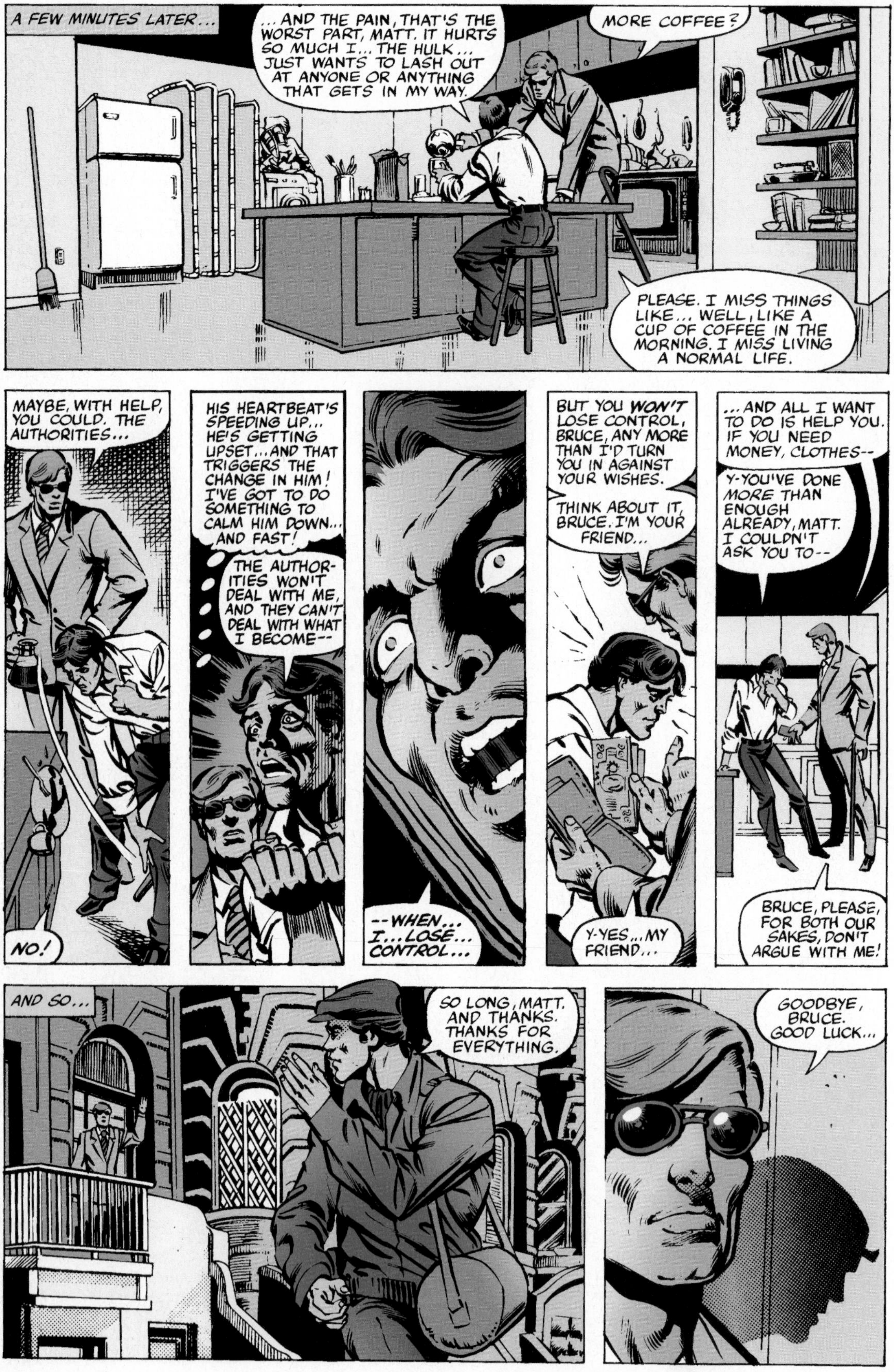
A FEW MINUTES LATER...
...AND THE PAIN, THAT'S THE WORST PART, MATT. IT HURTS SO MUCH I... THE HULK... JUST WANTS TO LASH OUT AT ANYONE OR ANYTHING THAT GETS IN MY WAY.
MORE COFFEE?
PLEASE. I MISS THINGS LIKE... WELL, LIKE A CUP OF COFFEE IN THE MORNING. I MISS LIVING A NORMAL LIFE.
MAYBE, WITH HELP, YOU COULD. THE AUTHORITIES...
NO!
HIS HEARTBEAT'S SPEEDING UP... HE'S GETTING UPSET... AND THAT TRIGGERS THE CHANGE IN HIM! I'VE GOT TO DO SOMETHING TO CALM HIM DOWN... AND FAST!
THE AUTHORITIES WON'T DEAL WITH ME, AND THEY CAN'T DEAL WITH WHAT I BECOME--
--WHEN... I... LOSE... CONTROL...
BUT YOU WON'T LOSE CONTROL, BRUCE, ANY MORE THAN I'D TURN YOU IN AGAINST YOUR WISHES.
THINK ABOUT IT, BRUCE. I'M YOUR FRIEND...
Y-YES... MY FRIEND...
...AND ALL I WANT TO DO IS HELP YOU. IF YOU NEED MONEY, CLOTHES--
Y-YOU'VE DONE MORE THAN ENOUGH ALREADY, MATT. I COULDN'T ASK YOU TO--
BRUCE, PLEASE, FOR BOTH OUR SAKES, DON'T ARGUE WITH ME!
AND SO...
SO LONG, MATT. AND THANKS. THANKS FOR EVERYTHING.
GOODBYE, BRUCE. GOOD LUCK...

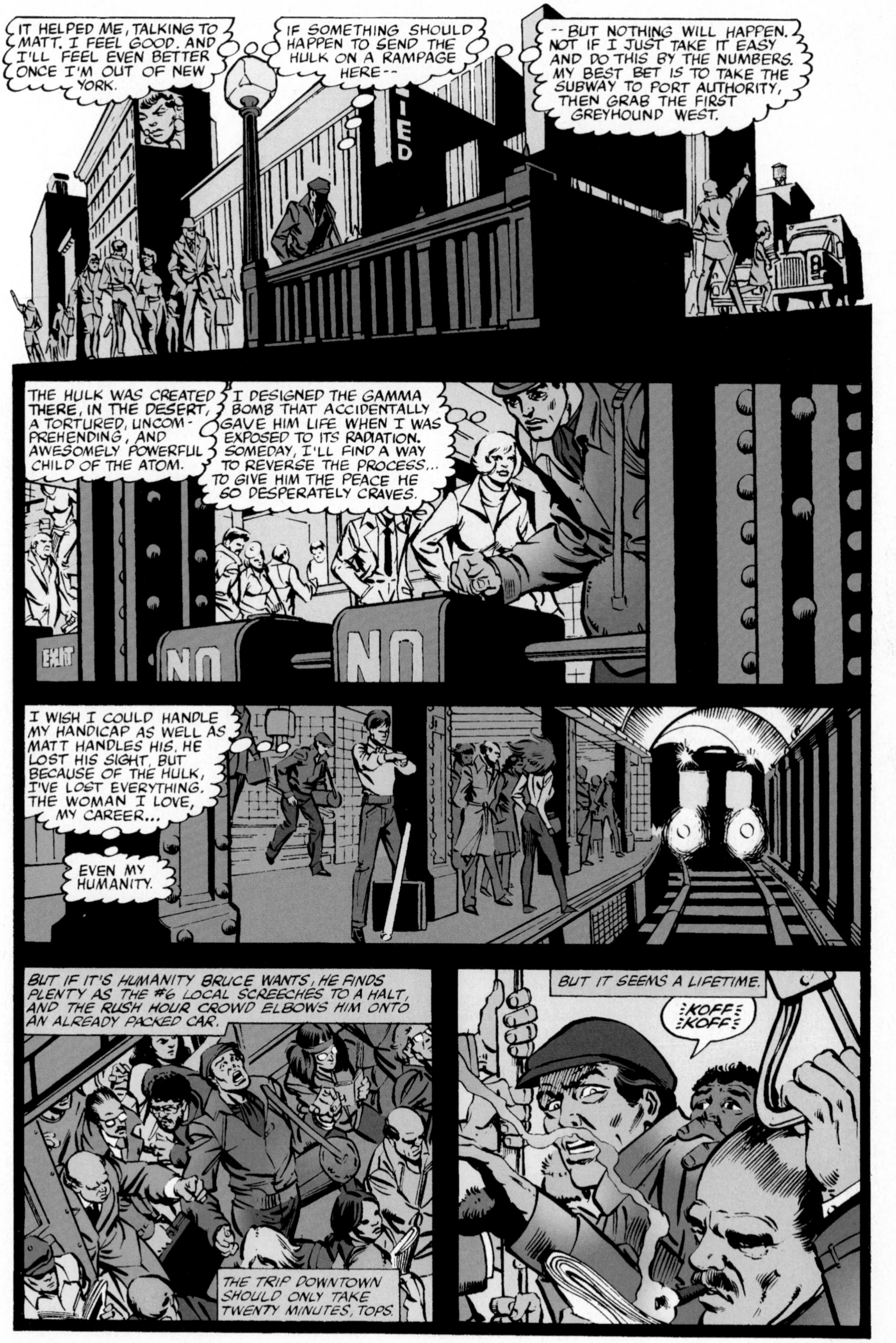
IT HELPED ME, TALKING TO MATT. I FEEL GOOD. AND I'LL FEEL EVEN BETTER ONCE I'M OUT OF NEW YORK.
IF SOMETHING SHOULD HAPPEN TO SEND THE HULK ON A RAMPAGE HERE--
-- BUT NOTHING WILL HAPPEN. NOT IF I JUST TAKE IT EASY AND DO THIS BY THE NUMBERS. MY BEST BET IS TO TAKE THE SUBWAY TO PORT AUTHORITY, THEN GRAB THE FIRST GREYHOUND WEST.
THE HULK WAS CREATED THERE, IN THE DESERT, A TORTURED, UNCOMPREHENDING, AND AWESOMELY POWERFUL CHILD OF THE ATOM.
I DESIGNED THE GAMMA BOMB THAT ACCIDENTALLY GAVE HIM LIFE WHEN I WAS EXPOSED TO ITS RADIATION. SOMEDAY, I'LL FIND A WAY TO REVERSE THE PROCESS... TO GIVE HIM THE PEACE HE SO DESPERATELY CRAVES.
EXIT
NO
NO
I WISH I COULD HANDLE MY HANDICAP AS WELL AS MATT HANDLES HIS. HE LOST HIS SIGHT, BUT BECAUSE OF THE HULK, I'VE LOST EVERYTHING. THE WOMAN I LOVE, MY CAREER...
EVEN MY HUMANITY.
BUT IF IT'S HUMANITY BRUCE WANTS, HE FINDS PLENTY AS THE #6 LOCAL SCREECHES TO A HALT, AND THE RUSH HOUR CROWD ELBOWS HIM ONTO AN ALREADY PACKED CAR.
THE TRIP DOWNTOWN SHOULD ONLY TAKE TWENTY MINUTES, TOPS.
BUT IT SEEMS A LIFETIME.
KOFF KOFF

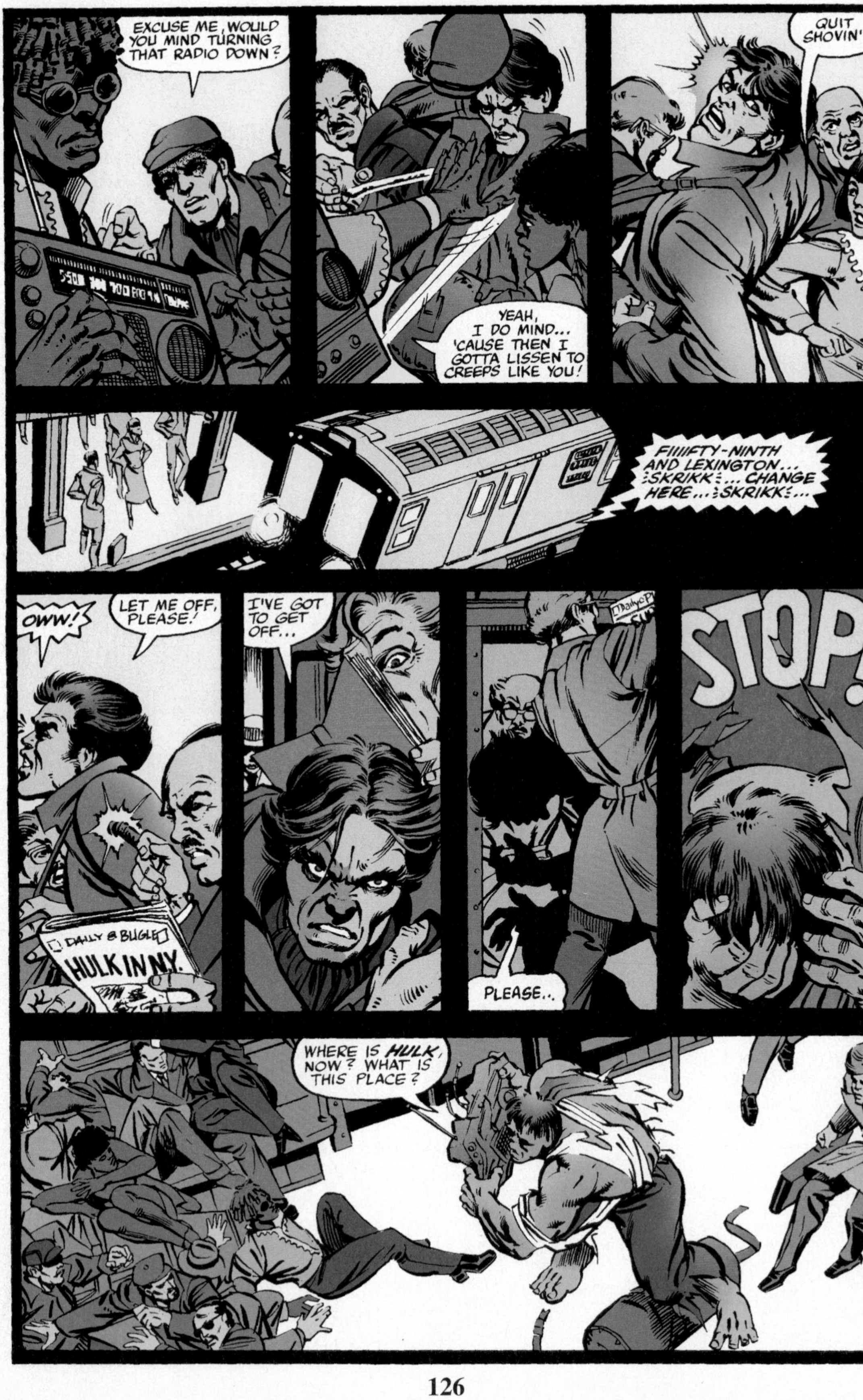
EXCUSE ME, WOULD YOU MIND TURNING THAT RADIO DOWN?
YEAH, I DO MIND... 'CAUSE THEN I GOTTA LISSEN TO CREEPS LIKE YOU!
QUIT SHOVIN'!
FIIIIFTY-NINTH AND LEXINGTON... SKRIKK... CHANGE HERE... SKRIKK...
OWW!
LET ME OFF, PLEASE!
DAILY BUGLE
HULK IN N.Y.
I'VE GOT TO GET OFF...
PLEASE..
STOP!
WHERE IS HULK, NOW? WHAT IS THIS PLACE?

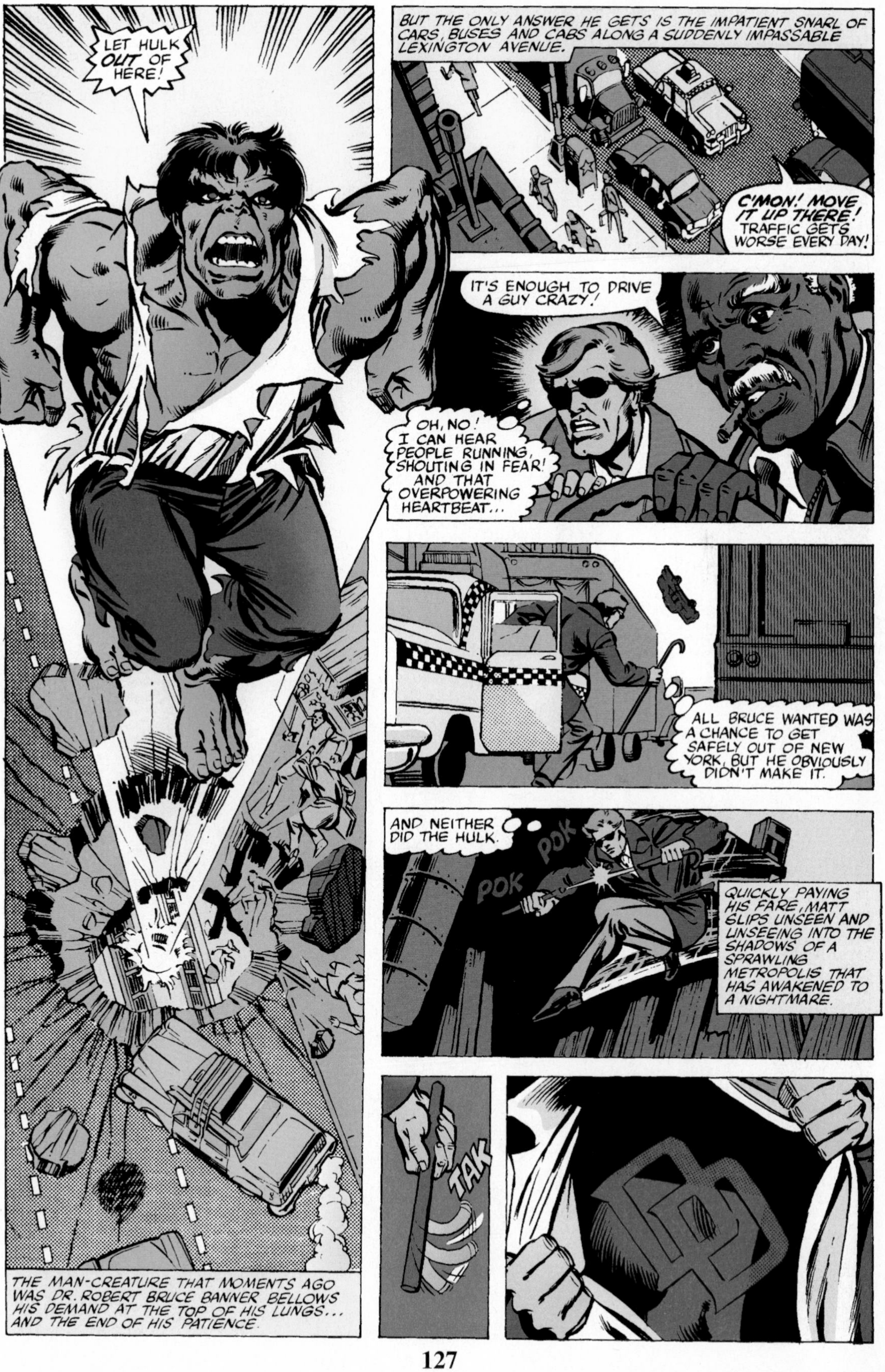
LET HULK OUT OF HERE!
BUT THE ONLY ANSWER HE GETS IS THE IMPATIENT SNARL OF CARS, BUSES AND CABS ALONG A SUDDENLY IMPASSABLE LEXINGTON AVENUE.
C'MON! MOVE IT UP THERE! TRAFFIC GETS WORSE EVERY DAY!
IT'S ENOUGH TO DRIVE A GUY CRAZY!
OH, NO! I CAN HEAR PEOPLE RUNNING, SHOUTING IN FEAR! AND THAT OVERPOWERING HEARTBEAT...
ALL BRUCE WANTED WAS A CHANCE TO GET SAFELY OUT OF NEW YORK, BUT HE OBVIOUSLY DIDN'T MAKE IT.
AND NEITHER DID THE HULK.
POK
POK
QUICKLY PAYING HIS FARE, MATT SLIPS UNSEEN AND UNSEEING INTO THE SHADOWS OF A SPRAWLING METROPOLIS THAT HAS AWAKENED TO A NIGHTMARE.
TAK
THE MAN-CREATURE THAT MOMENTS AGO WAS DR. ROBERT BRUCE BANNER BELLOWS HIS DEMAND AT THE TOP OF HIS LUNGS... AND THE END OF HIS PATIENCE.

A RAMPAGING NIGHT-MARE CALLED--

THE HULK!

RUN!

WHAT DO YOU WANT, HULK?

BANNER! HULK WILL NOT LEAVE THE CITY UNTIL HULK FINDS BANNER!

...EVACUATE THE AREA! WE'LL NEED RIOT SQUADS, FIRETRUCKS, AND AMBULANCES!

YEAH, DARE-DEVIL'S HERE, BUT YOU'D BETTER CONTACT THE AVENGERS. WHAT?! YOU CAN'T? THEY AREN'T? AND THE FANTASTIC FOUR'S OUTTA TOWN, TOO?

YEAH, RIGHT. I'LL DO WHAT I CAN...

BANNER TORMENTS HULK, LITTLE MAN!

NO, YOU TORMENT YOURSELF. PLEASE, CALM DOWN BEFORE SOMEONE GETS HURT.

BLAMMM

SO, LITTLE MAN, YOU TRIED TO TRICK HULK! ALL YOU KNOW IS HOW TO HURT!

BUT HULK CAN HURT, TOO! YOU TAUGHT HULK HOW! BANNER TAUGHT HULK HOW, TOO! AND NOW HULK IS THROUGH RUNNING!

BLAM

BLAM

BLAMM

BLAM

BLAM

KLIK KLIK KLIK

128

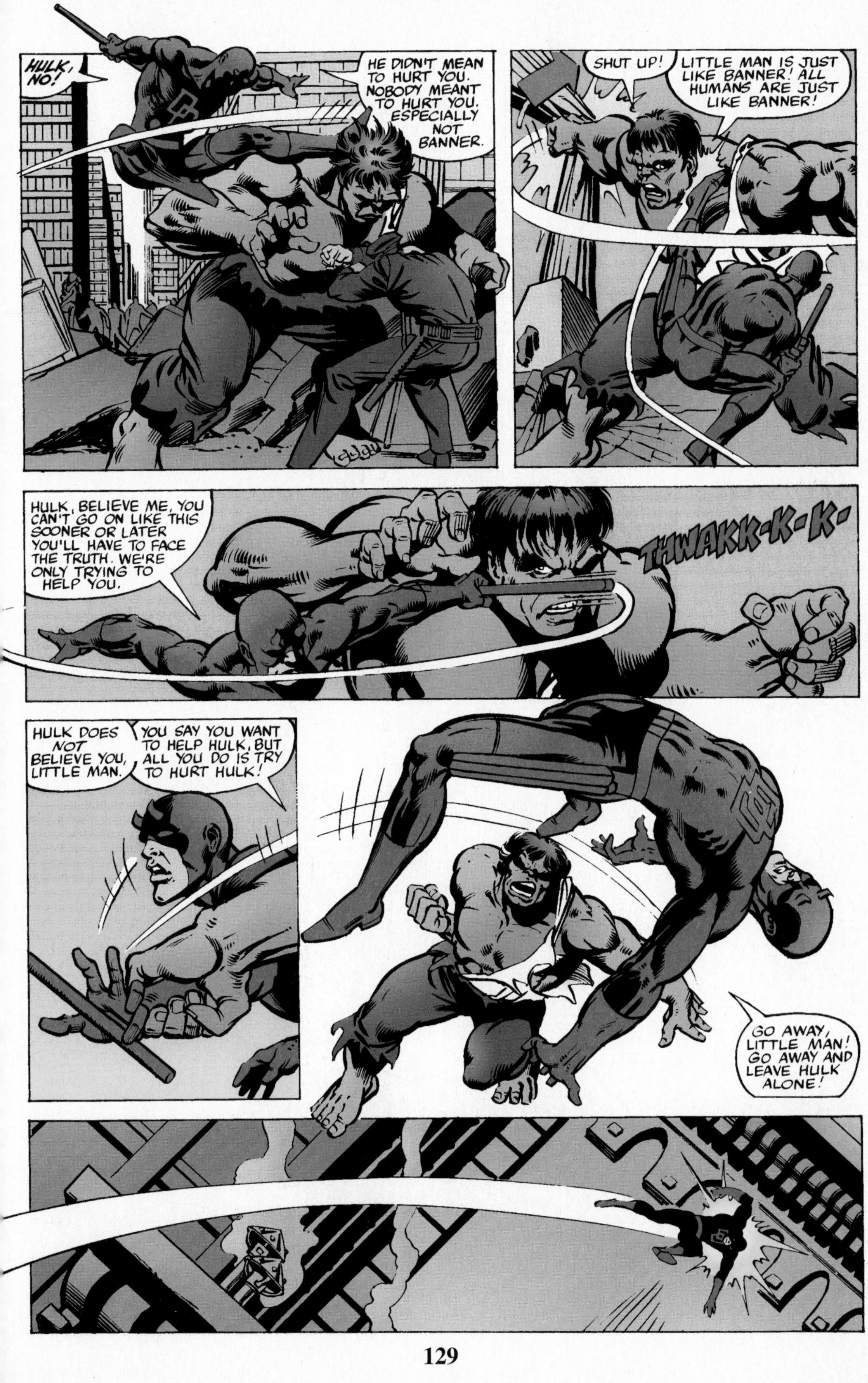
HULK, NO!
HE DIDN'T MEAN TO HURT YOU. NOBODY MEANT TO HURT YOU. ESPECIALLY NOT BANNER.
SHUT UP!
LITTLE MAN IS JUST LIKE BANNER! ALL HUMANS ARE JUST LIKE BANNER!
HULK, BELIEVE ME, YOU CAN'T GO ON LIKE THIS SOONER OR LATER YOU'LL HAVE TO FACE THE TRUTH. WE'RE ONLY TRYING TO HELP YOU.
THWAKK-K-K-
HULK DOES NOT BELIEVE YOU, LITTLE MAN.
YOU SAY YOU WANT TO HELP HULK, BUT ALL YOU DO IS TRY TO HURT HULK!
GO AWAY, LITTLE MAN! GO AWAY AND LEAVE HULK ALONE!

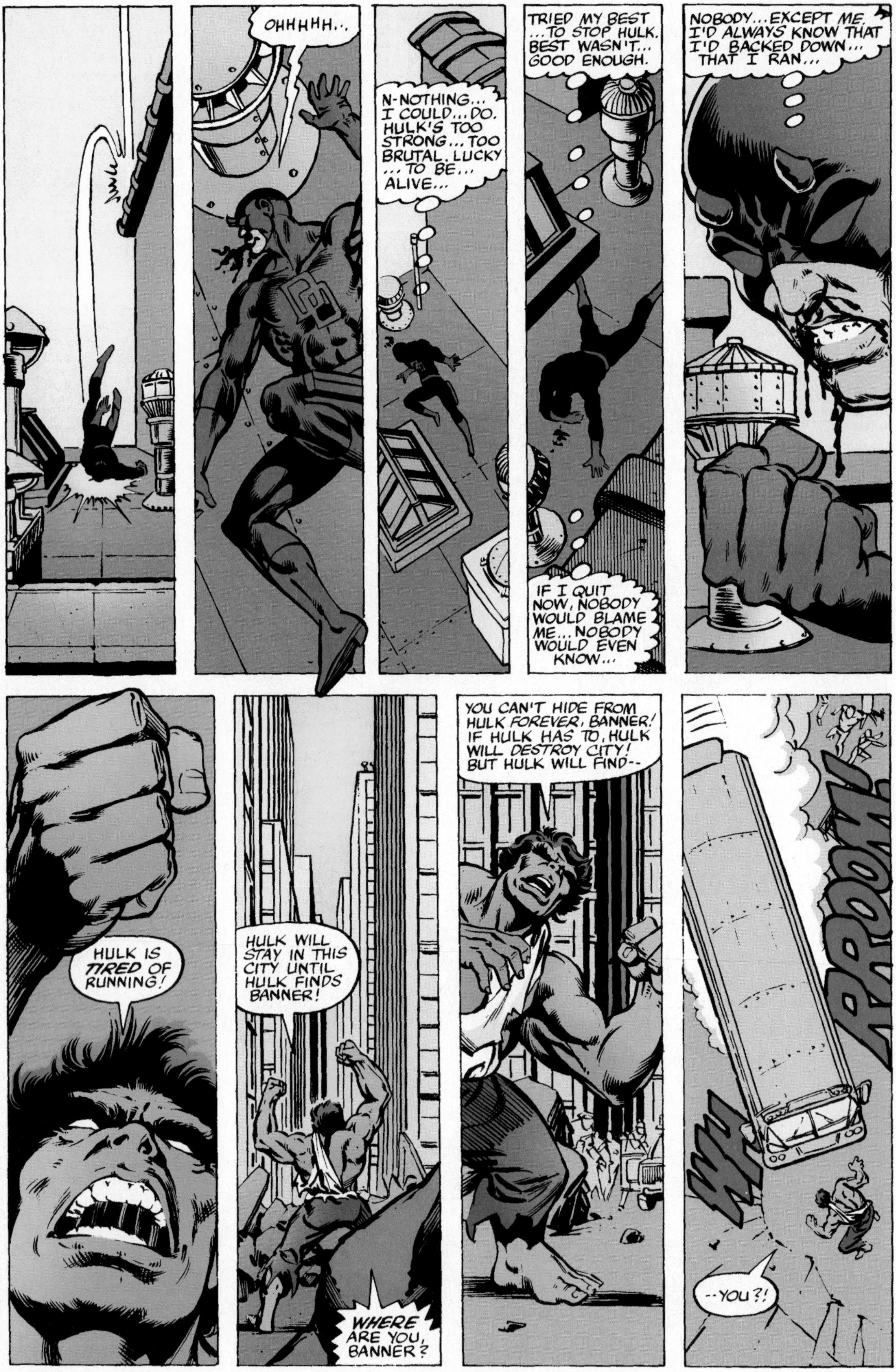
OHHHHH...
N-NOTHING... I COULD... DO. HULK'S TOO STRONG... TOO BRUTAL. LUCKY ... TO BE... ALIVE...
TRIED MY BEST ...TO STOP HULK. BEST WASN'T... GOOD ENOUGH.
IF I QUIT NOW, NOBODY WOULD BLAME ME... NOBODY WOULD EVEN KNOW...
NOBODY... EXCEPT ME. I'D ALWAYS KNOW THAT I'D BACKED DOWN... THAT I RAN...
HULK IS TIRED OF RUNNING!
HULK WILL STAY IN THIS CITY UNTIL HULK FINDS BANNER!
WHERE ARE YOU, BANNER?
YOU CAN'T HIDE FROM HULK FOREVER, BANNER! IF HULK HAS TO, HULK WILL DESTROY CITY! BUT HULK WILL FIND--
KRROOM!
WH
--YOU?!

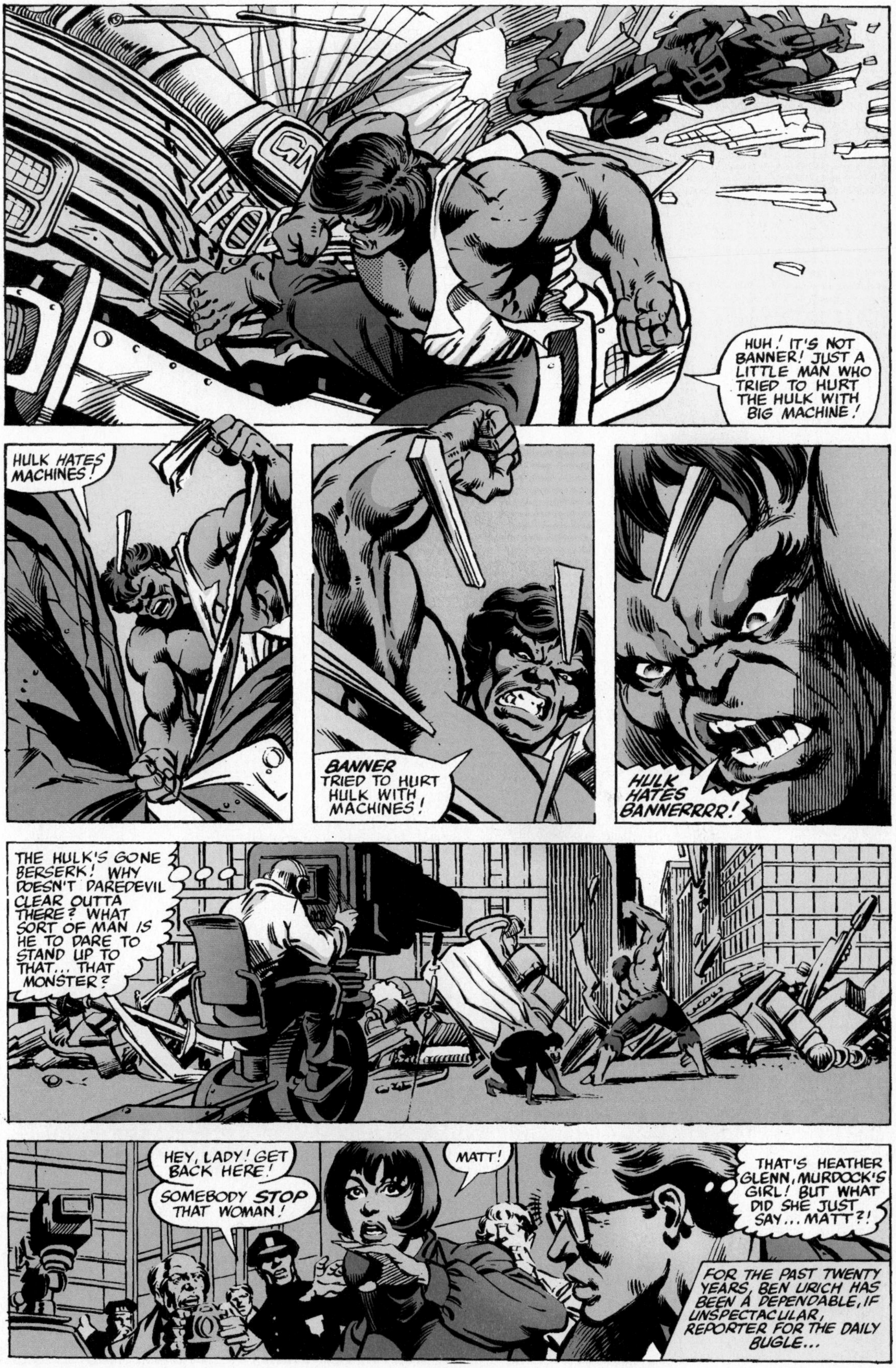
HUH! IT'S NOT BANNER! JUST A LITTLE MAN WHO TRIED TO HURT THE HULK WITH BIG MACHINE!
HULK HATES MACHINES!
BANNER TRIED TO HURT HULK WITH MACHINES!
HULK HATES BANNERRRR!
THE HULK'S GONE BERSERK! WHY DOESN'T DAREDEVIL CLEAR OUTTA THERE? WHAT SORT OF MAN IS HE TO DARE TO STAND UP TO THAT... THAT MONSTER?
HEY, LADY! GET BACK HERE!
SOMEBODY STOP THAT WOMAN!
MATT!
THAT'S HEATHER GLENN, MURDOCK'S GIRL! BUT WHAT DID SHE JUST SAY... MATT?!
FOR THE PAST TWENTY YEARS, BEN URICH HAS BEEN A DEPENDABLE, IF UNSPECTACULAR, REPORTER FOR THE DAILY BUGLE...

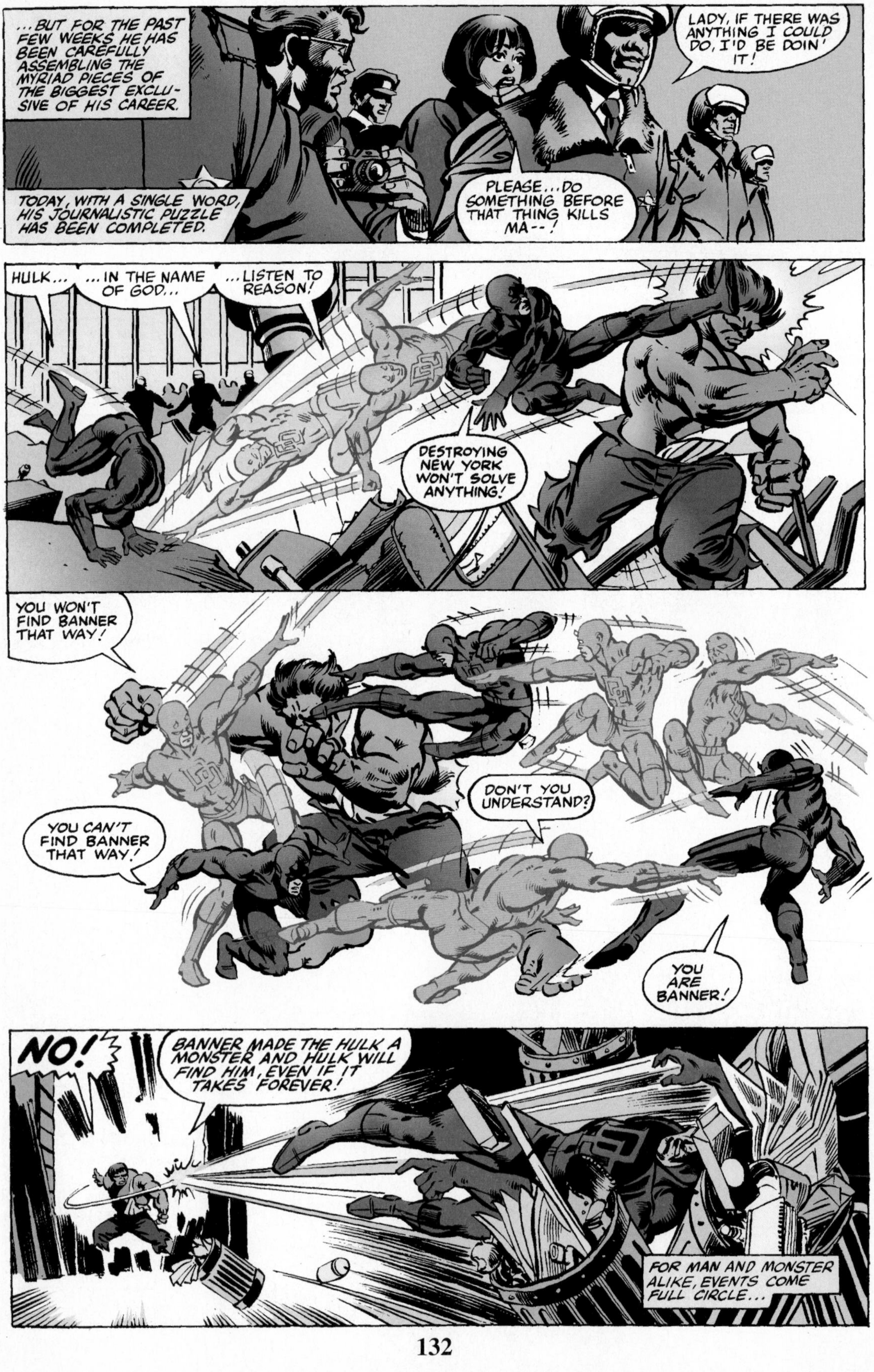
...BUT FOR THE PAST FEW WEEKS HE HAS BEEN CAREFULLY ASSEMBLING THE MYRIAD PIECES OF THE BIGGEST EXCLUSIVE OF HIS CAREER.
TODAY, WITH A SINGLE WORD, HIS JOURNALISTIC PUZZLE HAS BEEN COMPLETED.
LADY, IF THERE WAS ANYTHING I COULD DO, I'D BE DOIN' IT!
PLEASE...DO SOMETHING BEFORE THAT THING KILLS MA--!
HULK...
...IN THE NAME OF GOD...
...LISTEN TO REASON!
DESTROYING NEW YORK WON'T SOLVE ANYTHING!
YOU WON'T FIND BANNER THAT WAY!
DON'T YOU UNDERSTAND?
YOU CAN'T FIND BANNER THAT WAY!
YOU ARE BANNER!
NO!
BANNER MADE THE HULK A MONSTER AND HULK WILL FIND HIM, EVEN IF IT TAKES FOREVER!
FOR MAN AND MONSTER ALIKE, EVENTS COME FULL CIRCLE...

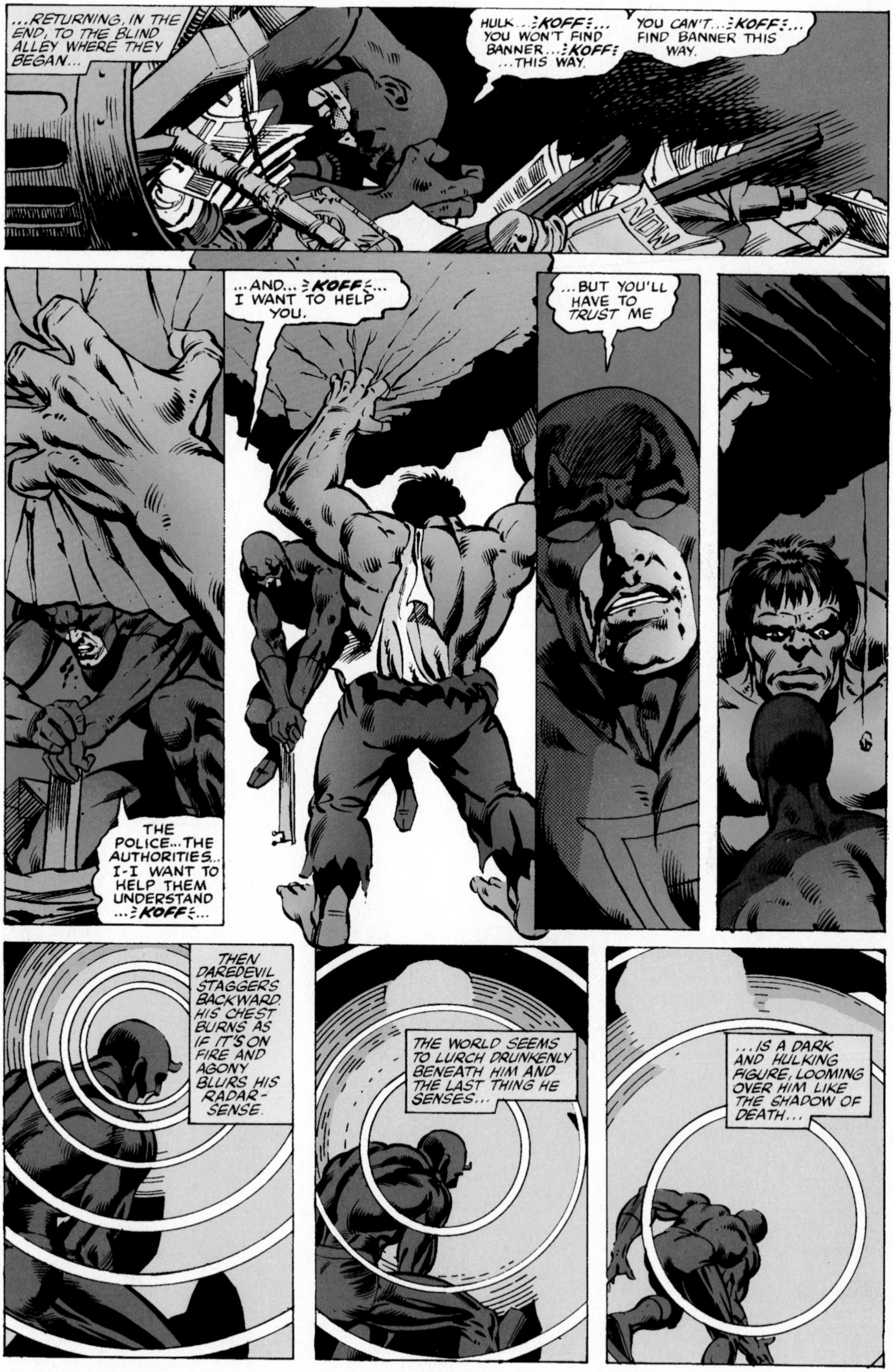
...RETURNING, IN THE END, TO THE BLIND ALLEY WHERE THEY BEGAN...
HULK...KOFF... YOU WON'T FIND BANNER...KOFF ...THIS WAY.
YOU CAN'T...KOFF... FIND BANNER THIS WAY.
NOW
...AND...KOFF... I WANT TO HELP YOU.
THE POLICE...THE AUTHORITIES... I-I WANT TO HELP THEM UNDERSTAND ...KOFF...
...BUT YOU'LL HAVE TO TRUST ME
THEN DAREDEVIL STAGGERS BACKWARD. HIS CHEST BURNS AS IF IT'S ON FIRE AND AGONY BLURS HIS RADAR-SENSE.
THE WORLD SEEMS TO LURCH DRUNKENLY BENEATH HIM AND THE LAST THING HE SENSES...
...IS A DARK AND HULKING FIGURE, LOOMING OVER HIM LIKE THE SHADOW OF DEATH...

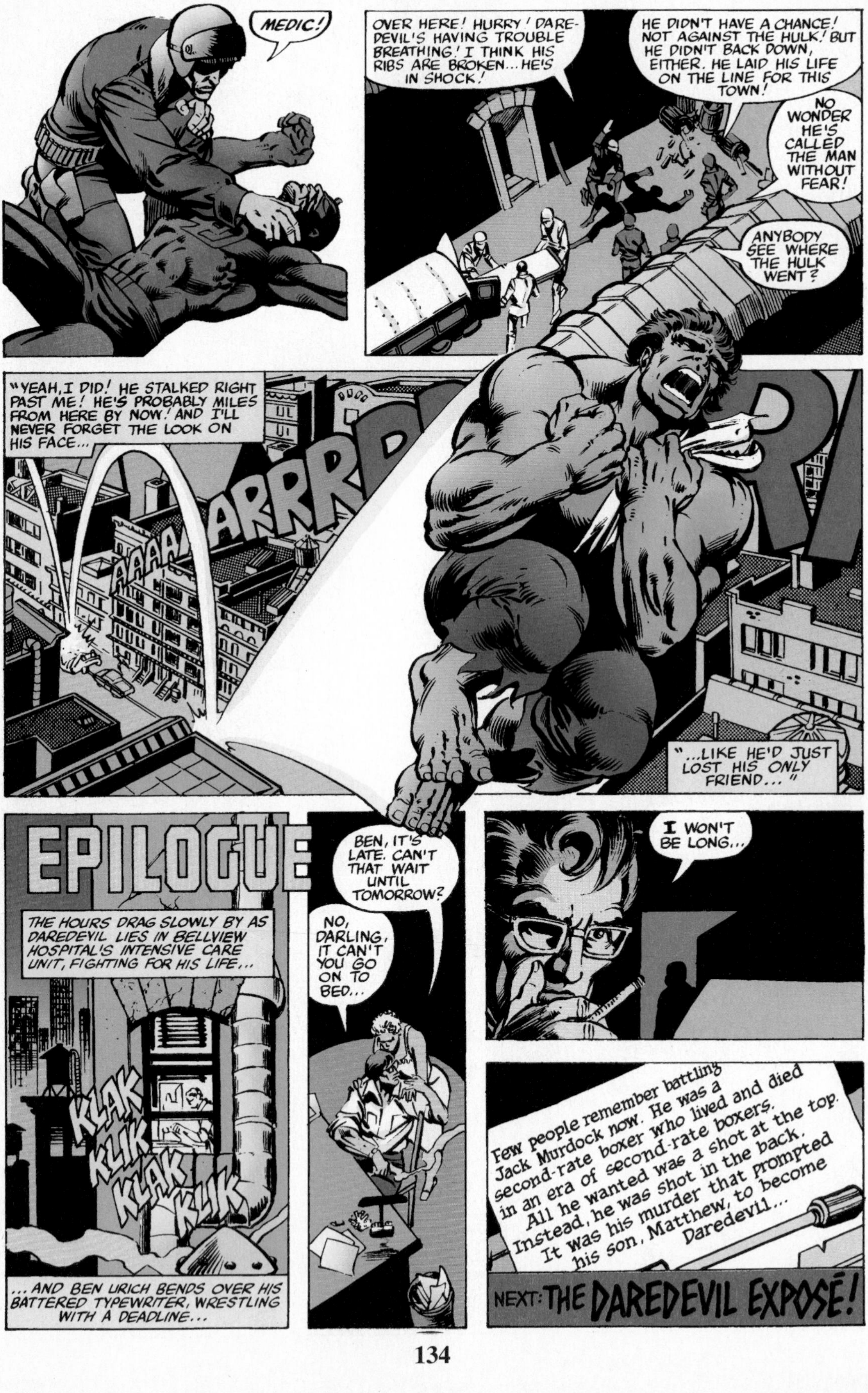
MEDIC!
OVER HERE! HURRY! DAREDEVIL'S HAVING TROUBLE BREATHING! I THINK HIS RIBS ARE BROKEN... HE'S IN SHOCK!
HE DIDN'T HAVE A CHANCE! NOT AGAINST THE HULK! BUT HE DIDN'T BACK DOWN, EITHER. HE LAID HIS LIFE ON THE LINE FOR THIS TOWN!
NO WONDER HE'S CALLED THE MAN WITHOUT FEAR!
ANYBODY SEE WHERE THE HULK WENT?
"YEAH, I DID! HE STALKED RIGHT PAST ME! HE'S PROBABLY MILES FROM HERE BY NOW! AND I'LL NEVER FORGET THE LOOK ON HIS FACE...
AAAAARRRR
"...LIKE HE'D JUST LOST HIS ONLY FRIEND..."
EPILOGUE
THE HOURS DRAG SLOWLY BY AS DAREDEVIL LIES IN BELLVIEW HOSPITAL'S INTENSIVE CARE UNIT, FIGHTING FOR HIS LIFE...
KLAK KLIK KLAK KLIK
...AND BEN URICH BENDS OVER HIS BATTERED TYPEWRITER, WRESTLING WITH A DEADLINE...
BEN, IT'S LATE. CAN'T THAT WAIT UNTIL TOMORROW?
NO, DARLING, IT CAN'T. YOU GO ON TO BED...
I WON'T BE LONG...
Few people remember battling Jack Murdock now. He was a second-rate boxer who lived and died in an era of second-rate boxers. All he wanted was a shot at the top. Instead, he was shot in the back. It was his murder that prompted his son, Matthew, to become Daredevil...
NEXT: THE DAREDEVIL EXPOSÉ!

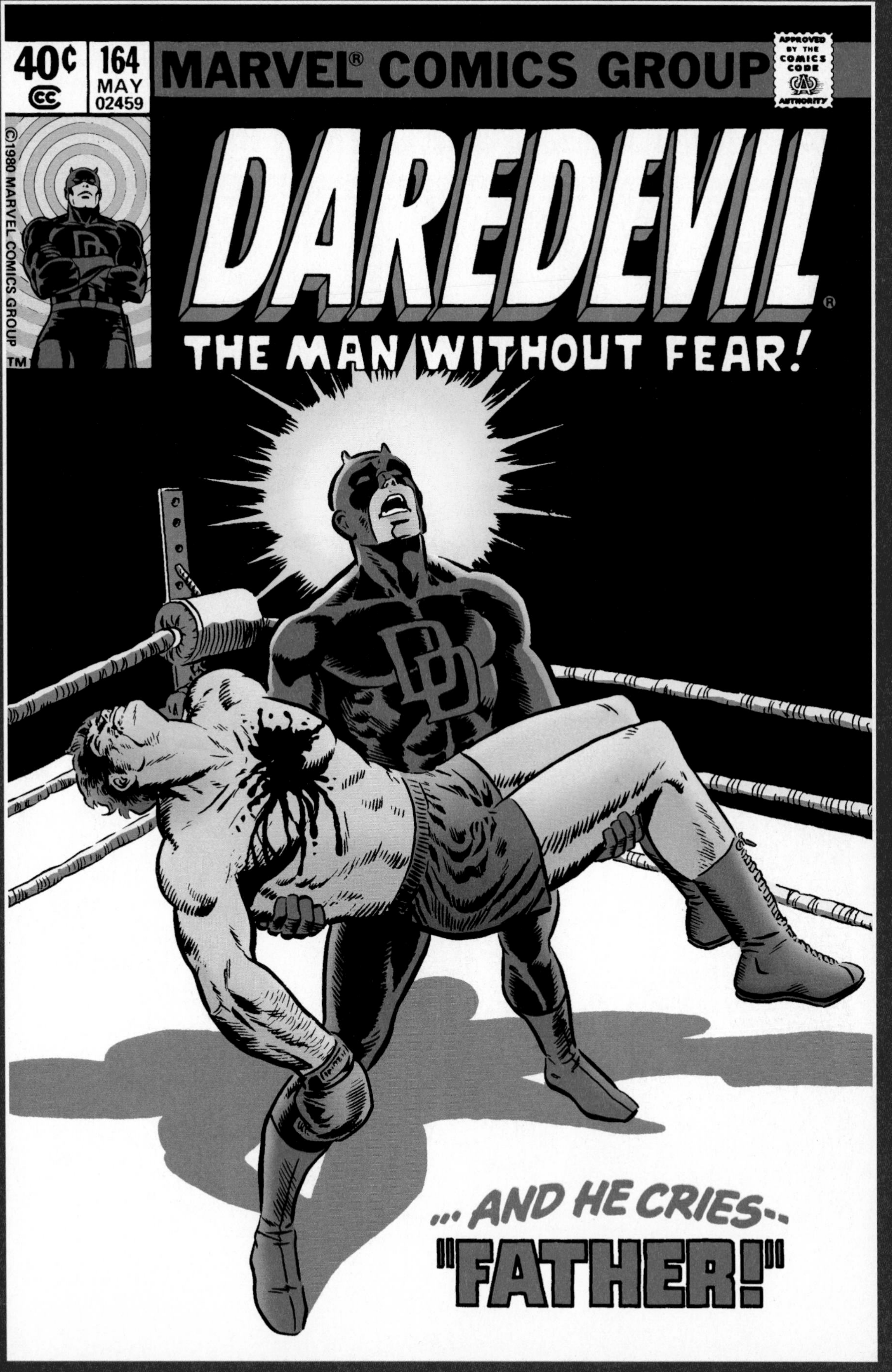
40¢
CC
164
MAY
02459
MARVEL® COMICS GROUP
APPROVED BY THE COMICS CODE AUTHORITY
©1980 MARVEL COMICS GROUP
TM
DAREDEVIL®
THE MAN WITHOUT FEAR!
...AND HE CRIES--
"FATHER!"

He dwells in eternal night—but the blackness is filled with sounds and scents other men cannot perceive. Though attorney MATT MURDOCK is *blind*, his other senses function with *superhuman sharpness*—his *radar sense* guides him over every obstacle! He stalks the streets by night, a red-garbed foe of evil!
STAN LEE PRESENTS: DAREDEVIL, THE MAN WITHOUT FEAR!®
EXPOSÉ
NATASHA, IF THERE'S ANYTHING WE CAN DO...
DAILY BUGLE
DAREDEVIL BATTLES HULK
Man Without Fear Hospitalized — Condition
The mysterious, red-clad figure known as Daredevil was
to City Hospital early to-
a battle with the
street.
According to witnesses
Hulk escaped by bou
over rooftops in the di
of the Jersey shore.
The incident begar
sources say, when
encountered the H
in the mi
Roger McKenzie
WRITER
Frank Miller
ARTIST
Klaus Janson
INKER
John Costanza
LETTERER
Glynis Wein
COLORIST
Denny O'Neil
EDITOR
Jim Shooter - EDITOR-IN-CHIEF

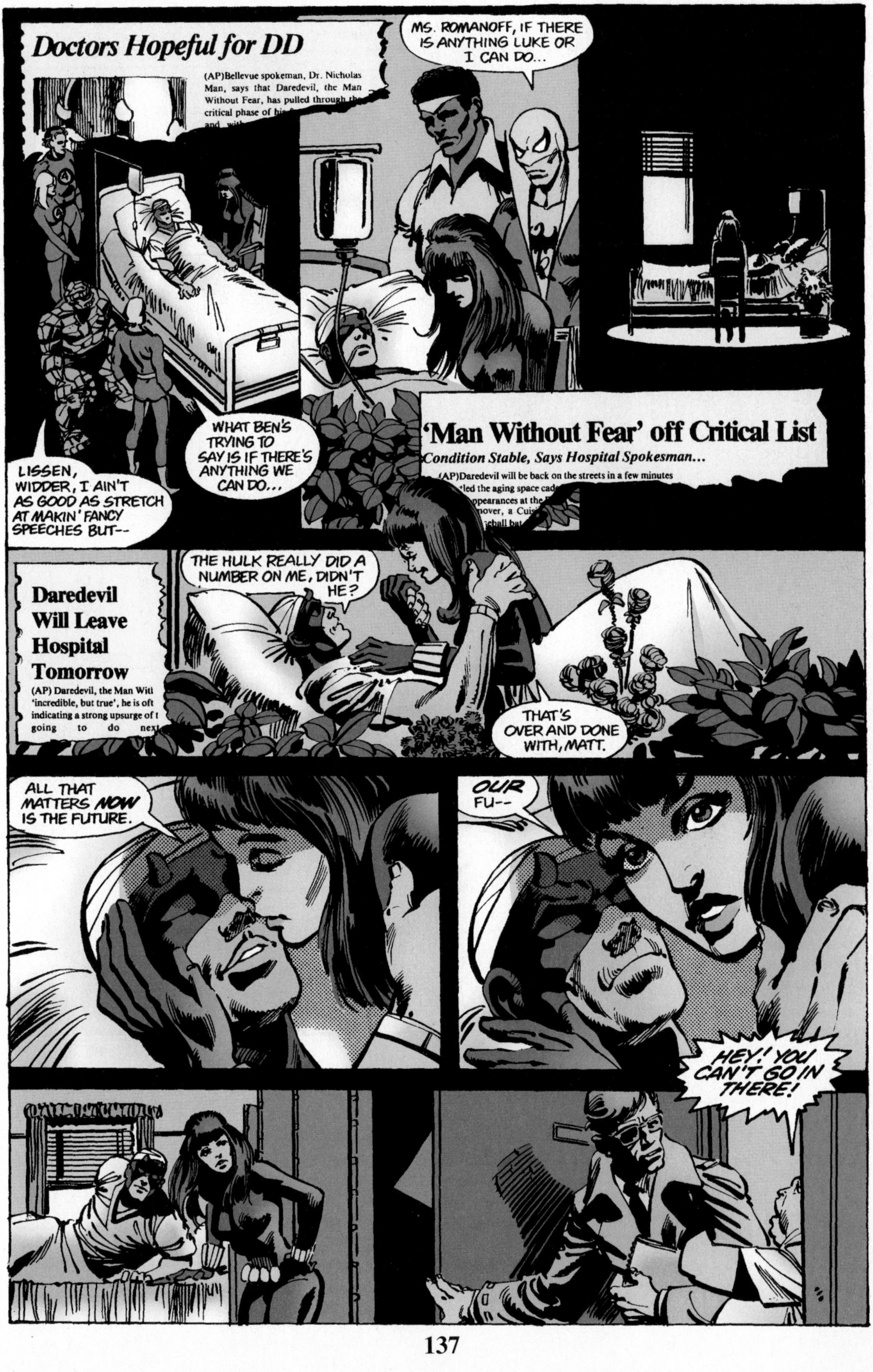

Doctors Hopeful for DD
(AP)Bellevue spokeman, Dr. Nicholas
Man, says that Daredevil, the Man
Without Fear, has pulled through the
LISSEN, WIDDER, I AIN'T AS GOOD AS STRETCH AT MAKIN' FANCY SPEECHES BUT--
WHAT BEN'S TRYING TO SAY IS IF THERE'S ANYTHING WE CAN DO...
MS. ROMANOFF, IF THERE IS ANYTHING LUKE OR I CAN DO...
'Man Without Fear' off Critical List
Condition Stable, Says Hospital Spokesman...
(AP)Daredevil will be back on the streets in a few minutes
Daredevil Will Leave Hospital Tomorrow
(AP) Daredevil, the Man Witl
'incredible, but true', he is oft
indicating a strong upsurge of t
THE HULK REALLY DID A NUMBER ON ME, DIDN'T HE?
THAT'S OVER AND DONE WITH, MATT.
ALL THAT MATTERS NOW IS THE FUTURE.
OUR FU--
HEY! YOU CAN'T GO IN THERE!

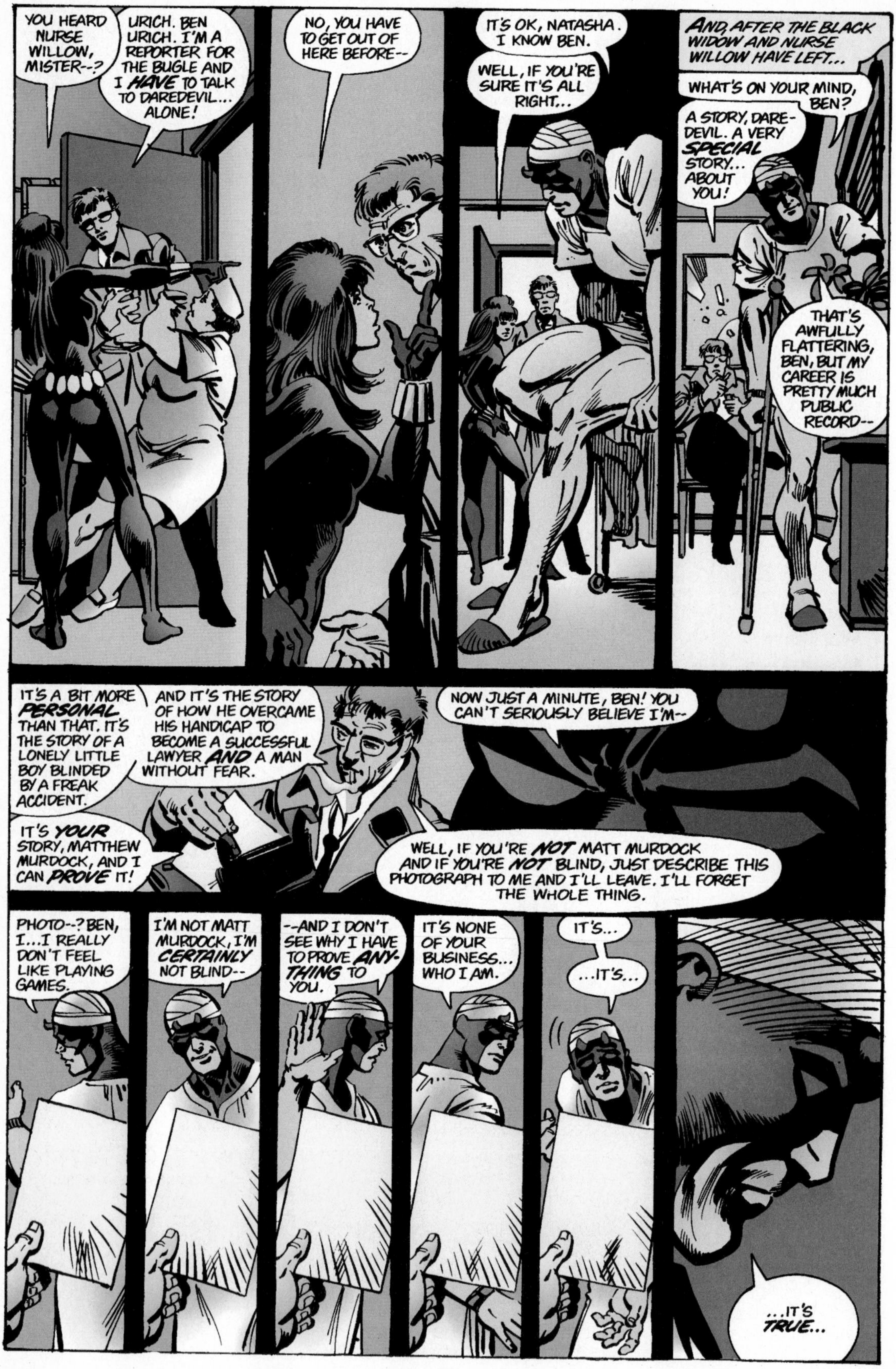
YOU HEARD NURSE WILLOW, MISTER--?
URICH. BEN URICH. I'M A REPORTER FOR THE BUGLE AND I HAVE TO TALK TO DAREDEVIL... ALONE!
NO, YOU HAVE TO GET OUT OF HERE BEFORE--
IT'S OK, NATASHA. I KNOW BEN.
WELL, IF YOU'RE SURE IT'S ALL RIGHT...
AND, AFTER THE BLACK WIDOW AND NURSE WILLOW HAVE LEFT...
WHAT'S ON YOUR MIND, BEN?
A STORY, DAREDEVIL. A VERY SPECIAL STORY... ABOUT YOU!
THAT'S AWFULLY FLATTERING, BEN, BUT MY CAREER IS PRETTY MUCH PUBLIC RECORD--
IT'S A BIT MORE PERSONAL THAN THAT. IT'S THE STORY OF A LONELY LITTLE BOY BLINDED BY A FREAK ACCIDENT.
AND IT'S THE STORY OF HOW HE OVERCAME HIS HANDICAP TO BECOME A SUCCESSFUL LAWYER AND A MAN WITHOUT FEAR.
IT'S YOUR STORY, MATTHEW MURDOCK, AND I CAN PROVE IT!
NOW JUST A MINUTE, BEN! YOU CAN'T SERIOUSLY BELIEVE I'M--
WELL, IF YOU'RE NOT MATT MURDOCK AND IF YOU'RE NOT BLIND, JUST DESCRIBE THIS PHOTOGRAPH TO ME AND I'LL LEAVE. I'LL FORGET THE WHOLE THING.
PHOTO--? BEN, I...I REALLY DON'T FEEL LIKE PLAYING GAMES.
I'M NOT MATT MURDOCK, I'M CERTAINLY NOT BLIND--
--AND I DON'T SEE WHY I HAVE TO PROVE ANYTHING TO YOU.
IT'S NONE OF YOUR BUSINESS... WHO I AM.
IT'S...
...IT'S...
...IT'S TRUE...

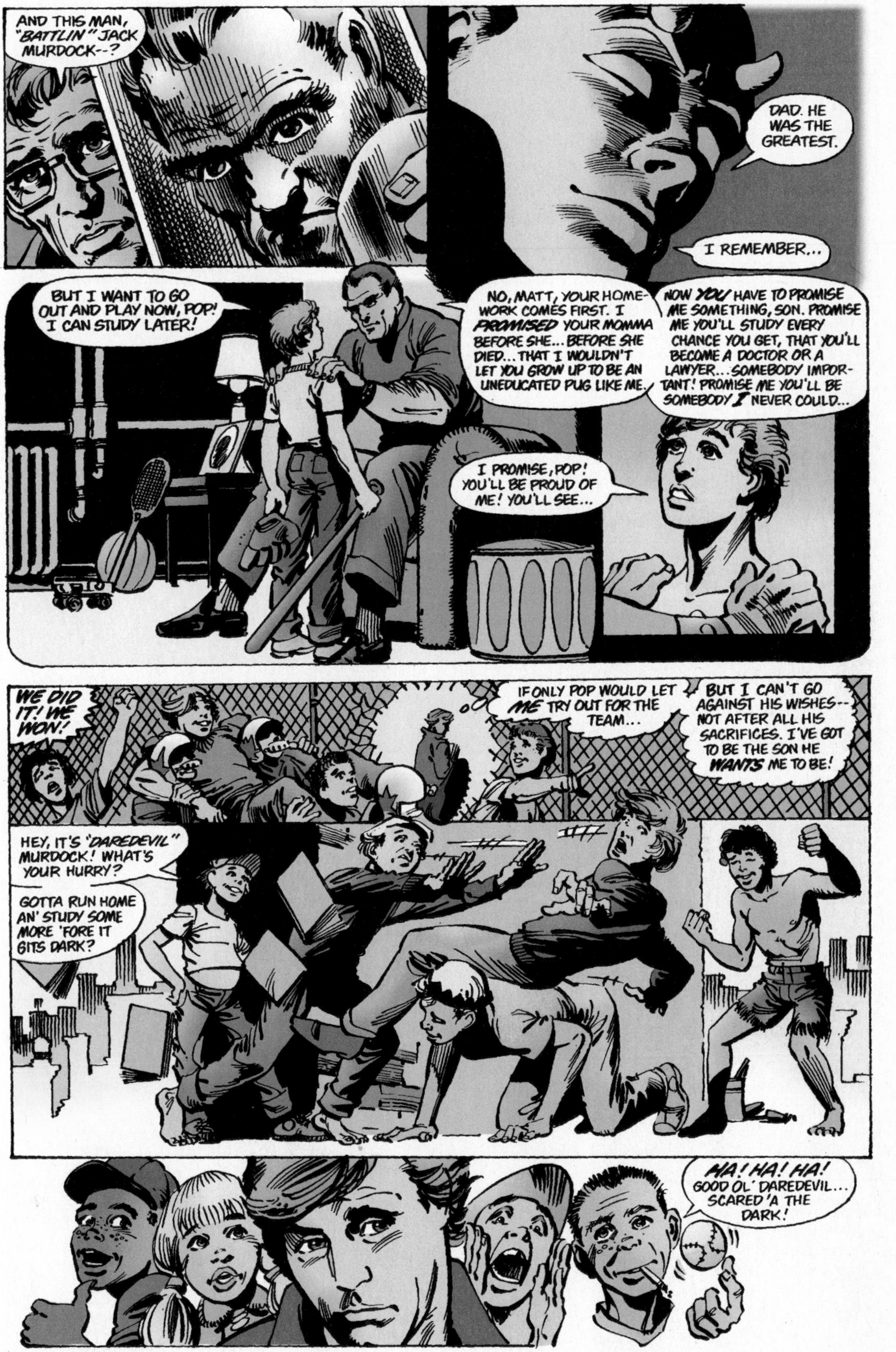
AND THIS MAN, "BATTLIN'" JACK MURDOCK--?
DAD. HE WAS THE GREATEST.
I REMEMBER...
BUT I WANT TO GO OUT AND PLAY NOW, POP! I CAN STUDY LATER!
NO, MATT, YOUR HOMEWORK COMES FIRST. I PROMISED YOUR MOMMA BEFORE SHE... BEFORE SHE DIED... THAT I WOULDN'T LET YOU GROW UP TO BE AN UNEDUCATED PUG LIKE ME.
NOW YOU HAVE TO PROMISE ME SOMETHING, SON. PROMISE ME YOU'LL STUDY EVERY CHANCE YOU GET, THAT YOU'LL BECOME A DOCTOR OR A LAWYER... SOMEBODY IMPORTANT! PROMISE ME YOU'LL BE SOMEBODY I NEVER COULD...
I PROMISE, POP! YOU'LL BE PROUD OF ME! YOU'LL SEE...
WE DID IT! WE WON!
IF ONLY POP WOULD LET ME TRY OUT FOR THE TEAM...
BUT I CAN'T GO AGAINST HIS WISHES-- NOT AFTER ALL HIS SACRIFICES. I'VE GOT TO BE THE SON HE WANTS ME TO BE!
HEY, IT'S "DAREDEVIL" MURDOCK! WHAT'S YOUR HURRY?
GOTTA RUN HOME AN' STUDY SOME MORE 'FORE IT GITS DARK?
HA! HA! HA! GOOD OL' DAREDEVIL... SCARED 'A THE DARK!

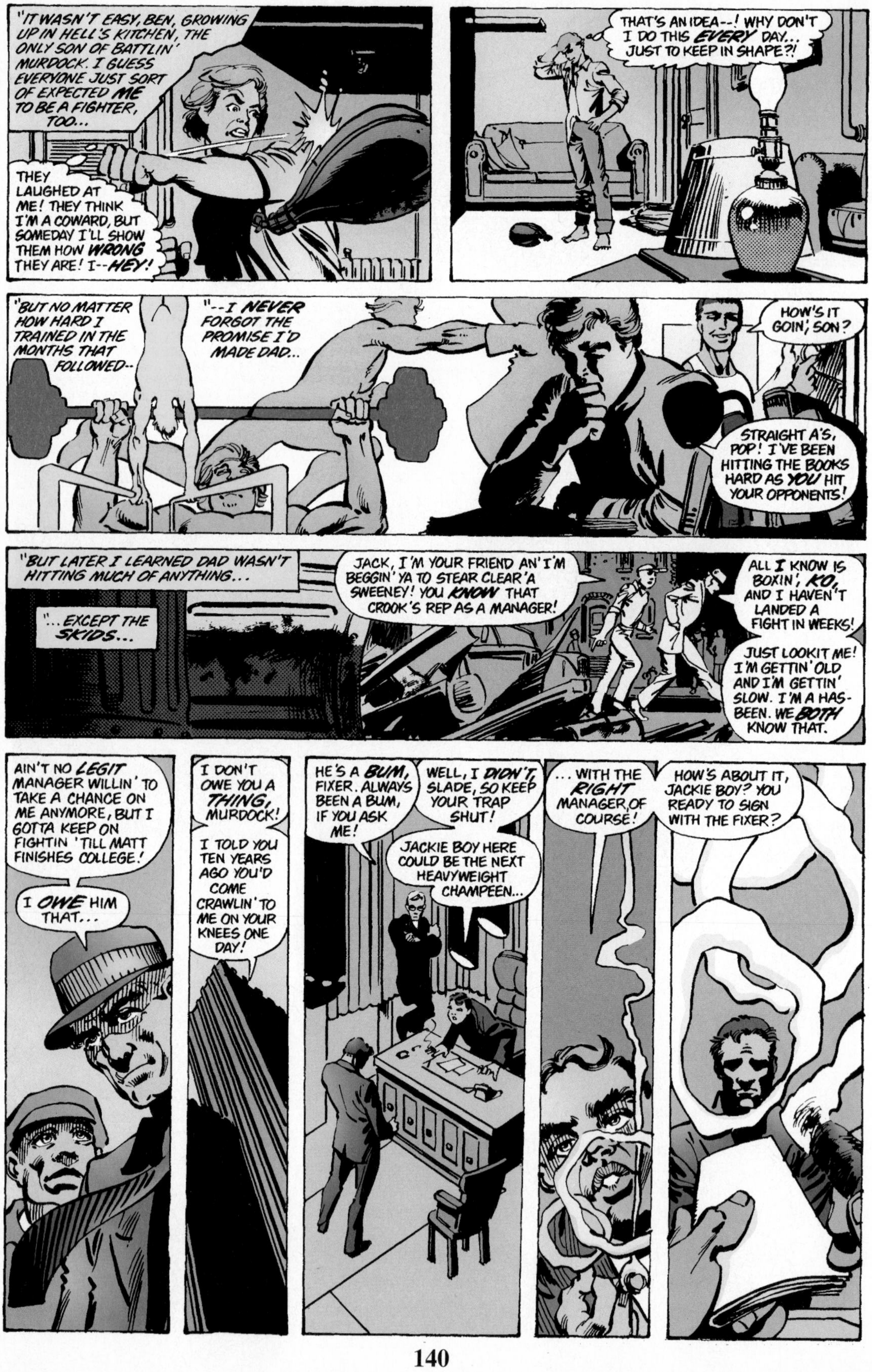
"IT WASN'T EASY, BEN, GROWING UP IN HELL'S KITCHEN, THE ONLY SON OF BATTLIN' MURDOCK. I GUESS EVERYONE JUST SORT OF EXPECTED ME TO BE A FIGHTER, TOO...
THEY LAUGHED AT ME! THEY THINK I'M A COWARD, BUT SOMEDAY I'LL SHOW THEM HOW WRONG THEY ARE! I--HEY!
THAT'S AN IDEA--! WHY DON'T I DO THIS EVERY DAY... JUST TO KEEP IN SHAPE?!
"BUT NO MATTER HOW HARD I TRAINED IN THE MONTHS THAT FOLLOWED--
"--I NEVER FORGOT THE PROMISE I'D MADE DAD...
HOW'S IT GOIN', SON?
STRAIGHT A'S, POP! I'VE BEEN HITTING THE BOOKS HARD AS YOU HIT YOUR OPPONENTS!
"BUT LATER I LEARNED DAD WASN'T HITTING MUCH OF ANYTHING...
"...EXCEPT THE SKIDS...
JACK, I'M YOUR FRIEND AN' I'M BEGGIN' YA TO STEAR CLEAR 'A SWEENEY! YOU KNOW THAT CROOK'S REP AS A MANAGER!
ALL I KNOW IS BOXIN', KO, AND I HAVEN'T LANDED A FIGHT IN WEEKS!
JUST LOOKIT ME! I'M GETTIN' OLD AND I'M GETTIN' SLOW. I'M A HAS-BEEN. WE BOTH KNOW THAT.
AIN'T NO LEGIT MANAGER WILLIN' TO TAKE A CHANCE ON ME ANYMORE, BUT I GOTTA KEEP ON FIGHTIN 'TILL MATT FINISHES COLLEGE!
I OWE HIM THAT...
I DON'T OWE YOU A THING, MURDOCK!
I TOLD YOU TEN YEARS AGO YOU'D COME CRAWLIN' TO ME ON YOUR KNEES ONE DAY!
HE'S A BUM, FIXER. ALWAYS BEEN A BUM, IF YOU ASK ME!
WELL, I DIDN'T, SLADE, SO KEEP YOUR TRAP SHUT!
JACKIE BOY HERE COULD BE THE NEXT HEAVYWEIGHT CHAMPEEN...
...WITH THE RIGHT MANAGER, OF COURSE!
HOW'S ABOUT IT, JACKIE BOY? YOU READY TO SIGN WITH THE FIXER?

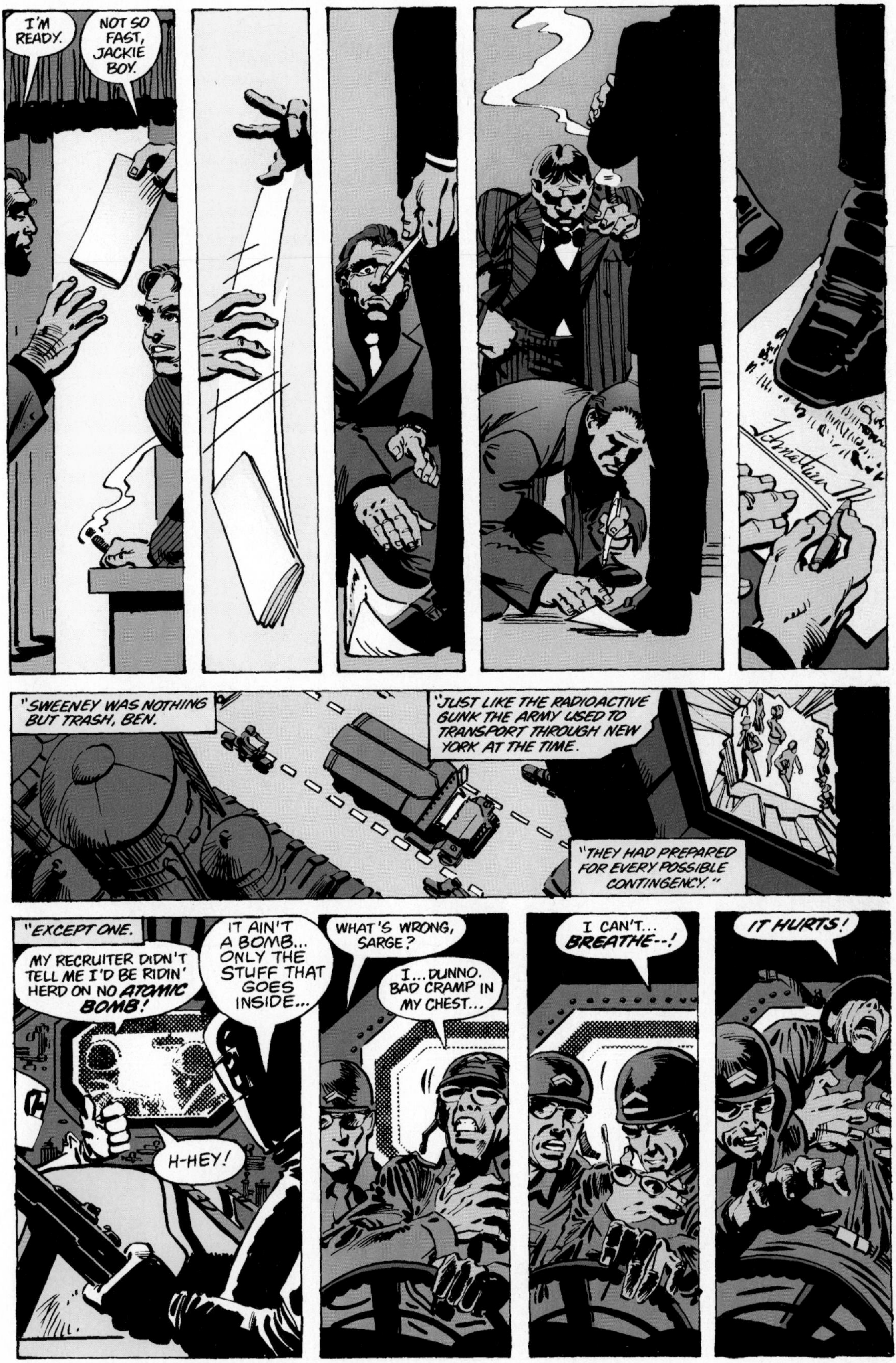
I'M READY.
NOT SO FAST, JACKIE BOY.
"SWEENEY WAS NOTHING BUT TRASH, BEN.
"JUST LIKE THE RADIOACTIVE GUNK THE ARMY USED TO TRANSPORT THROUGH NEW YORK AT THE TIME.
"THEY HAD PREPARED FOR EVERY POSSIBLE CONTINGENCY."
"EXCEPT ONE.
MY RECRUITER DIDN'T TELL ME I'D BE RIDIN' HERD ON NO ATOMIC BOMB!
IT AIN'T A BOMB... ONLY THE STUFF THAT GOES INSIDE...
H-HEY!
WHAT'S WRONG, SARGE?
I...DUNNO. BAD CRAMP IN MY CHEST...
I CAN'T... BREATHE--!
IT HURTS!

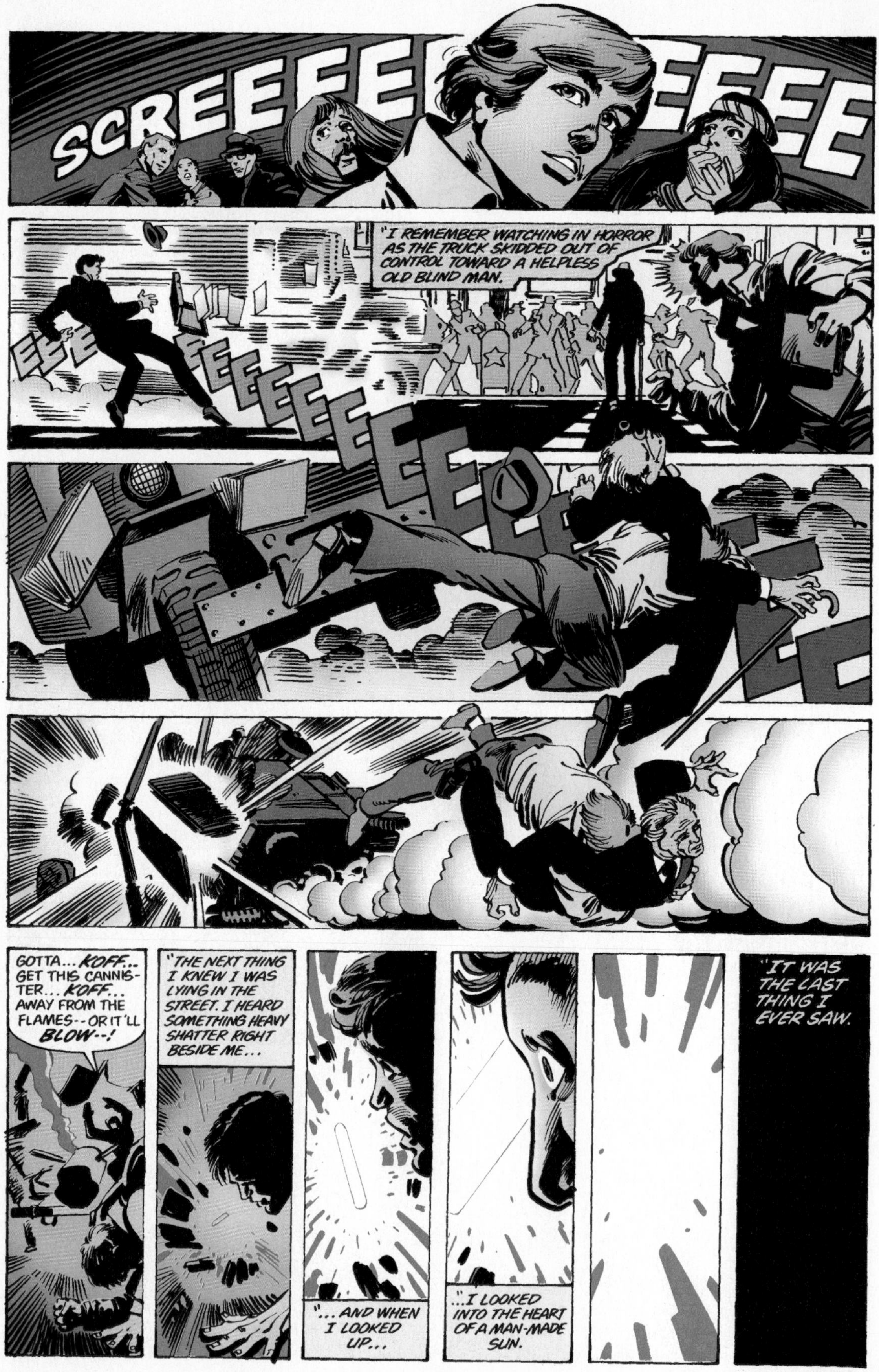
SCREEEEEEEEEE
"I REMEMBER WATCHING IN HORROR AS THE TRUCK SKIDDED OUT OF CONTROL TOWARD A HELPLESS OLD BLIND MAN.
EEEEEEEEEEEE
GOTTA... KOFF... GET THIS CANNISTER... KOFF... AWAY FROM THE FLAMES--OR IT'LL BLOW--!
"THE NEXT THING I KNEW I WAS LYING IN THE STREET. I HEARD SOMETHING HEAVY SHATTER RIGHT BESIDE ME...
"...AND WHEN I LOOKED UP...
...I LOOKED INTO THE HEART OF A MAN-MADE SUN.
"IT WAS THE LAST THING I EVER SAW.

"I WOKE TO A HOSPITAL... AND DAD--

SON, THAT WAS A BRAVE THING YOU DID. I JUST HOPE... SOMEDAY... I CAN MAKE YOU AS PROUD OF ME AS I AM OF YOU...

"MY REHABILITATION WAS A SLOW, PAINFUL, AND AT TIMES FRUSTRATING ORDEAL. I DON'T THINK I COULD HAVE MADE IT WITHOUT THE LOVE AND SUPPORT OF PEOPLE LIKE DAD--

"--OR MY COLLEGE ROOMIE, FOGGY NELSON. THEY NEVER LET ME DOWN. NOT ONCE.

MATT, YOU OL' HOUND DOG, HOW DO YOU DO IT? I STUDY LIKE A DEMON, BUT YOU JUST BREEZE ALONG WITH TOP GRADES!

"AND, BEN, BECAUSE OF THE ACCIDENT, I WAS MORE DETERMINED THEN EVER TO GET MY LAW DEGREE. TO PROVE I COULD STILL BE A HUMAN BEING... DESPITE MY HANDICAP.

POP DESERVES THE CREDIT, FOGGY. HE HAD ME STUDY SO HARD WHEN I WAS YOUNGER THAT IT ALL SEEMS TO COME EASY FOR ME NOW.

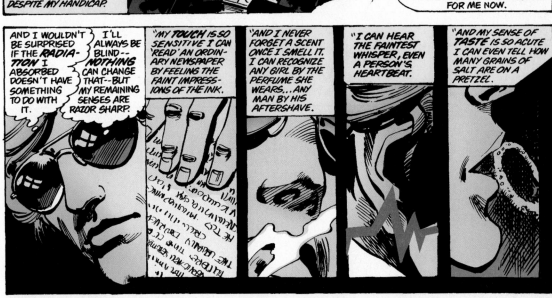

AND I WOULDN'T BE SURPRISED IF THE RADIATION I ABSORBED DOESN'T HAVE SOMETHING TO DO WITH IT.

I'LL ALWAYS BE BLIND-- NOTHING CAN CHANGE THAT--BUT MY REMAINING SENSES ARE RAZOR SHARP.

"MY TOUCH IS SO SENSITIVE I CAN 'READ' AN ORDINARY NEWSPAPER BY FEELING THE FAINT IMPRESSIONS OF THE INK.

"AND I NEVER FORGET A SCENT ONCE I SMELL IT. I CAN RECOGNIZE ANY GIRL BY THE PERFUME SHE WEARS... ANY MAN BY HIS AFTERSHAVE.

"I CAN HEAR THE FAINTEST WHISPER, EVEN A PERSON'S HEARTBEAT.

"AND MY SENSE OF TASTE IS SO ACUTE I CAN EVEN TELL HOW MANY GRAINS OF SALT ARE ON A PRETZEL.

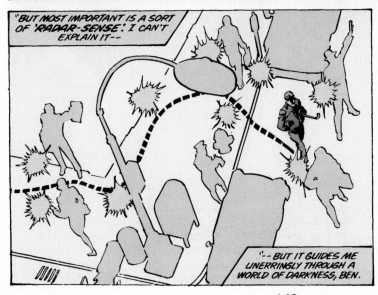

"BUT MOST IMPORTANT IS A SORT OF 'RADAR-SENSE': I CAN'T EXPLAIN IT--

"-- BUT IT GUIDES ME UNERRINGLY THROUGH A WORLD OF DARKNESS, BEN.

SAY, SON... WANT ANY HELP CROSSING THE STREET?

NO THANKS, I CAN MAKE IT.

143

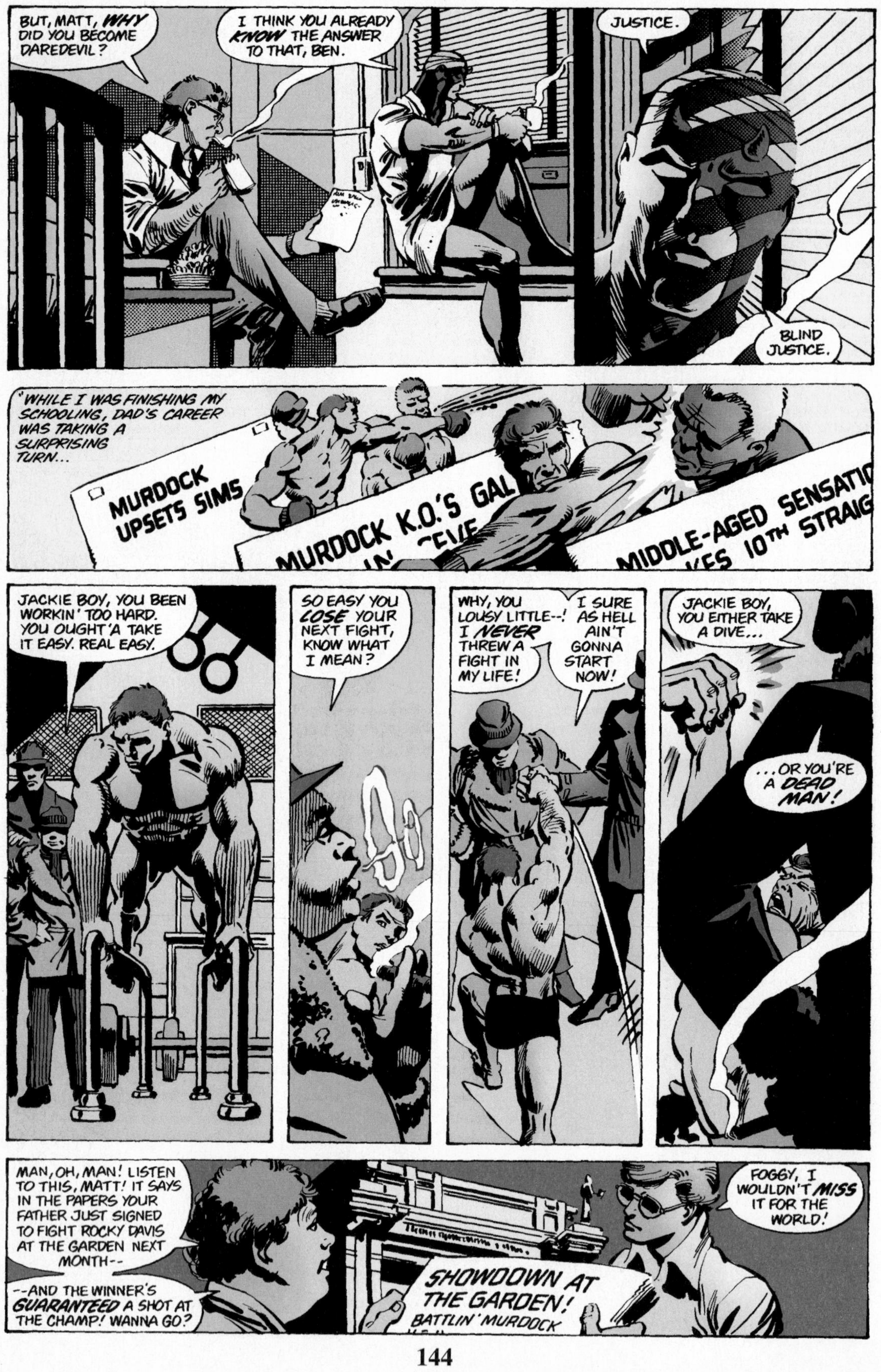
BUT, MATT, WHY DID YOU BECOME DAREDEVIL?
I THINK YOU ALREADY KNOW THE ANSWER TO THAT, BEN.
JUSTICE.
BLIND JUSTICE.
"WHILE I WAS FINISHING MY SCHOOLING, DAD'S CAREER WAS TAKING A SURPRISING TURN...
MURDOCK UPSETS SIMS
MURDOCK K.O.'S GAL
MIDDLE-AGED SENSATIO
JACKIE BOY, YOU BEEN WORKIN' TOO HARD. YOU OUGHT'A TAKE IT EASY. REAL EASY.
SO EASY YOU LOSE YOUR NEXT FIGHT, KNOW WHAT I MEAN?
WHY, YOU LOUSY LITTLE--! I NEVER THREW A FIGHT IN MY LIFE!
I SURE AS HELL AIN'T GONNA START NOW!
JACKIE BOY, YOU EITHER TAKE A DIVE...
...OR YOU'RE A DEAD MAN!
MAN, OH, MAN! LISTEN TO THIS, MATT! IT SAYS IN THE PAPERS YOUR FATHER JUST SIGNED TO FIGHT ROCKY DAVIS AT THE GARDEN NEXT MONTH--
--AND THE WINNER'S GUARANTEED A SHOT AT THE CHAMP! WANNA GO?
FOGGY, I WOULDN'T MISS IT FOR THE WORLD!
SHOWDOWN AT THE GARDEN!
BATTLIN' MURDOCK

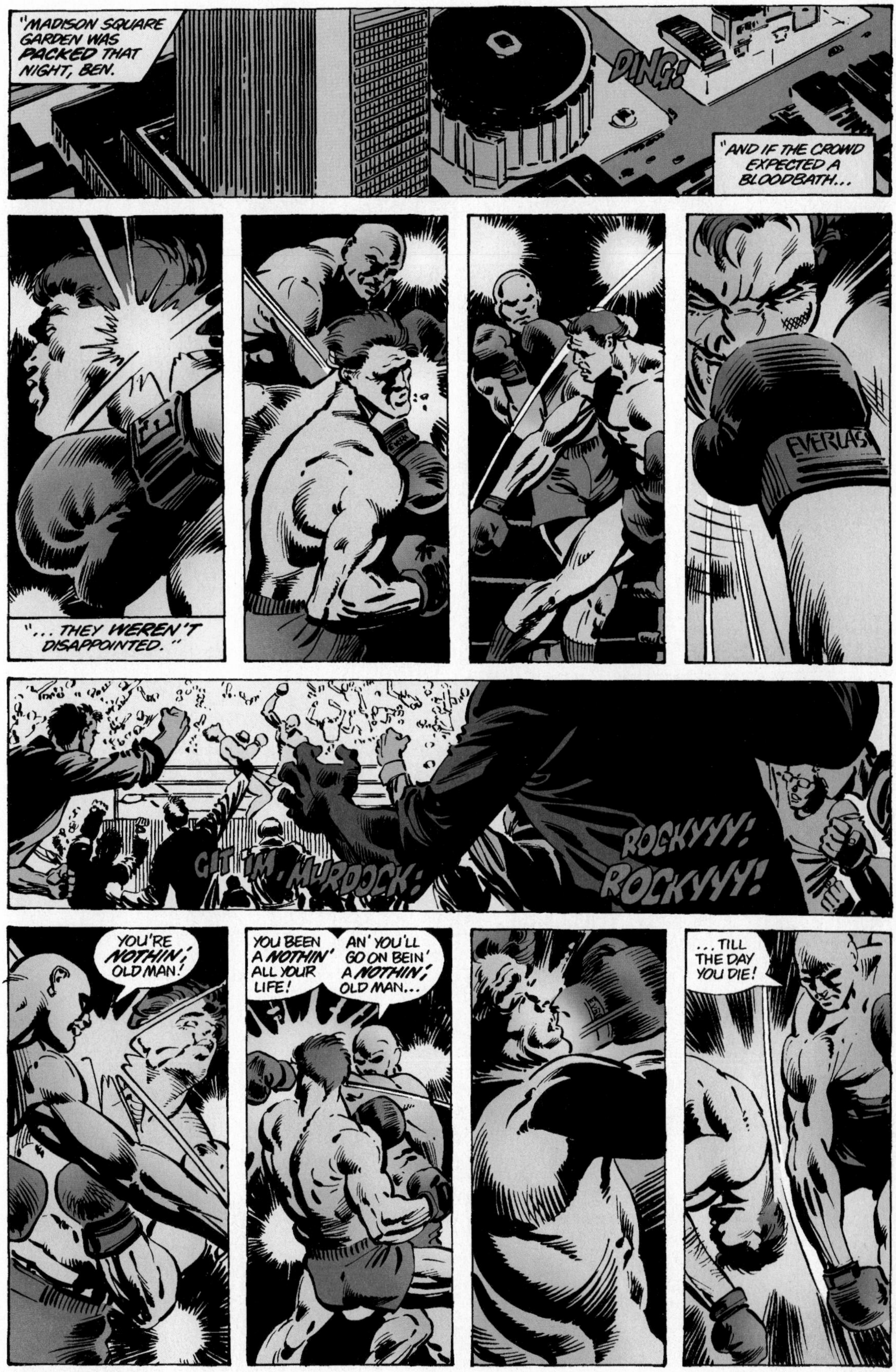
"MADISON SQUARE GARDEN WAS PACKED THAT NIGHT, BEN.
DING!
"AND IF THE CROWD EXPECTED A BLOODBATH...
"...THEY WEREN'T DISAPPOINTED."
EVERLAST
GIT 'IM, MURDOCK!
ROCKYYY! ROCKYYY!
YOU'RE NOTHIN', OLD MAN!
YOU BEEN A NOTHIN' ALL YOUR LIFE!
AN' YOU'LL GO ON BEIN' A NOTHIN', OLD MAN...
...TILL THE DAY YOU DIE!

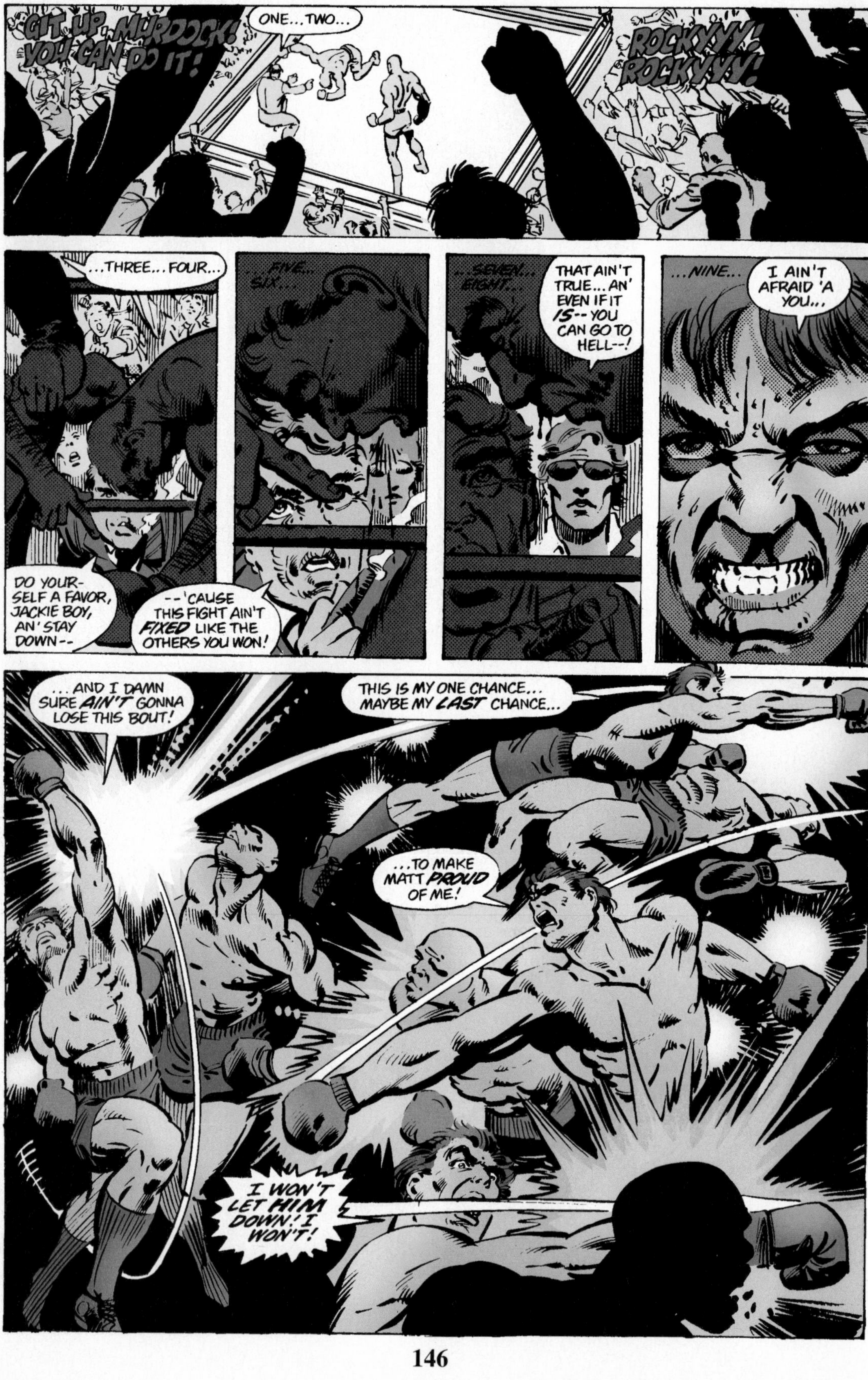
GIT UP, MURDOCK! YOU CAN DO IT!
ONE... TWO...
ROCKYYY! ROCKYYY!
...THREE... FOUR...
DO YOURSELF A FAVOR, JACKIE BOY, AN' STAY DOWN--
...FIVE... SIX...
--'CAUSE THIS FIGHT AIN'T FIXED LIKE THE OTHERS YOU WON!
...SEVEN... EIGHT...
THAT AIN'T TRUE... AN' EVEN IF IT IS-- YOU CAN GO TO HELL--!
...NINE...
I AIN'T AFRAID 'A YOU...
...AND I DAMN SURE AIN'T GONNA LOSE THIS BOUT!
THIS IS MY ONE CHANCE... MAYBE MY LAST CHANCE...
...TO MAKE MATT PROUD OF ME!
I WON'T LET HIM DOWN! I WON'T!

THIS ONE'S FOR *YOU*, MATT!

"DAD *WON* THE FIGHT.

BLAM

"BUT HE *LOST* HIS LIFE...

THIS ONE'S FOR *YOU*, BUM!

EASY, SON--

--THERE'S NOTHIN' YOU CAN DO, MATT. CAN'T *NOBODY* DO NOTHIN'!

HELL, MATT, YOU THINK I DON'T KNOW HOW YOU FEEL? YOU THINK *I* DON'T HURT, TOO?

JACK AN' ME, WE WENT BACK A LONG WAYS.

I *TOLD* 'IM NOT TO MESS WITH SWEENEY.

I'M TELLIN' *YOU* THE SAME THING. SWEENEY'S A *KILLER*, MATT.

JUST GIVE IT UP.

POP *NEVER* GAVE UP, K.O.

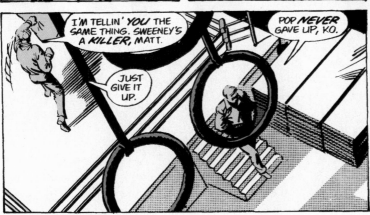

NEITHER WILL I.

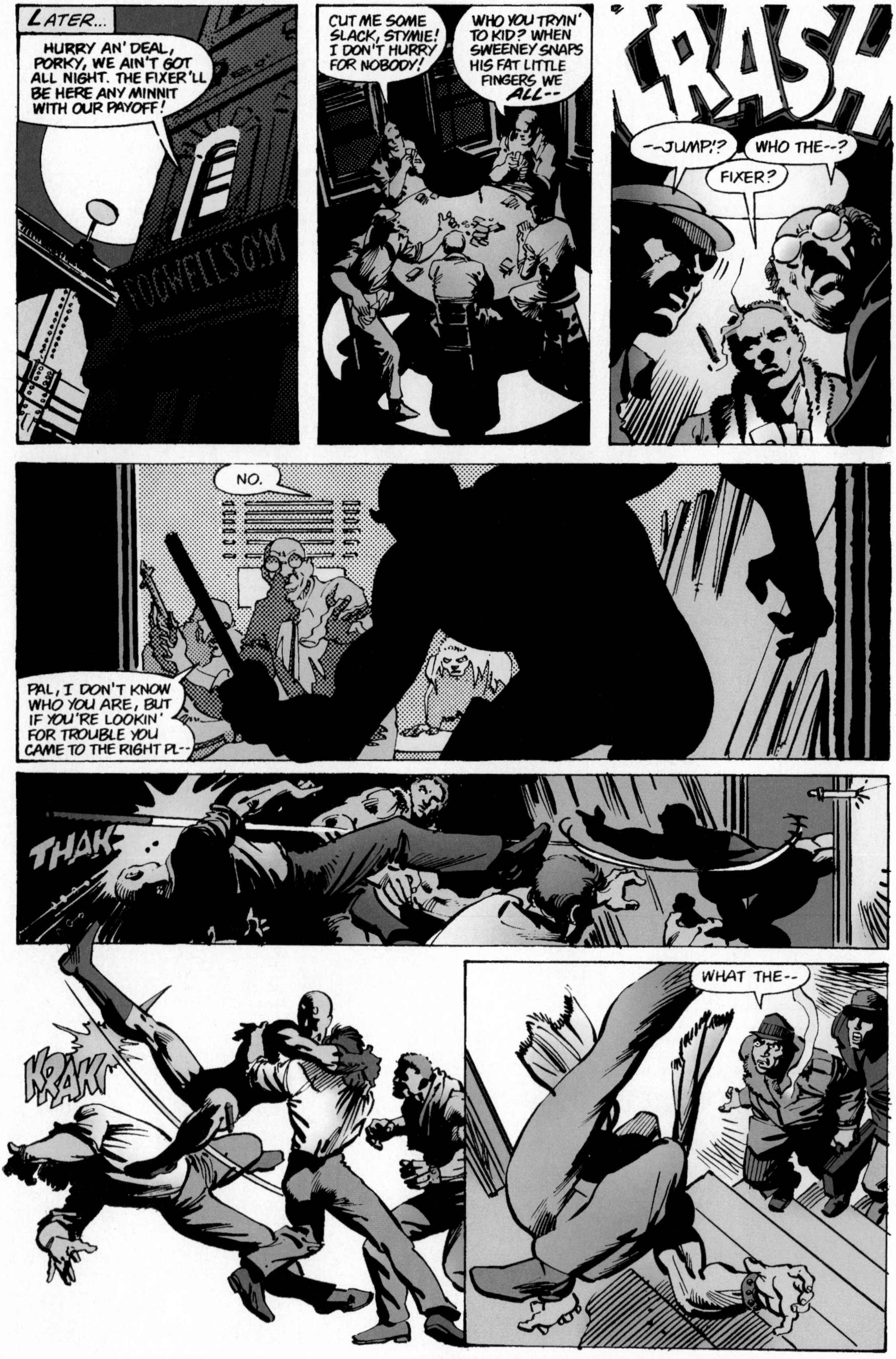
LATER...
HURRY AN' DEAL, PORKY, WE AIN'T GOT ALL NIGHT. THE FIXER'LL BE HERE ANY MINNIT WITH OUR PAYOFF!
CUT ME SOME SLACK, STYMIE! I DON'T HURRY FOR NOBODY!
WHO YOU TRYIN' TO KID? WHEN SWEENEY SNAPS HIS FAT LITTLE FINGERS WE ALL--
CRASH!
--JUMP!?
WHO THE--?
FIXER?
NO.
PAL, I DON'T KNOW WHO YOU ARE, BUT IF YOU'RE LOOKIN' FOR TROUBLE YOU CAME TO THE RIGHT PL--
THAK
KRAK
WHAT THE--

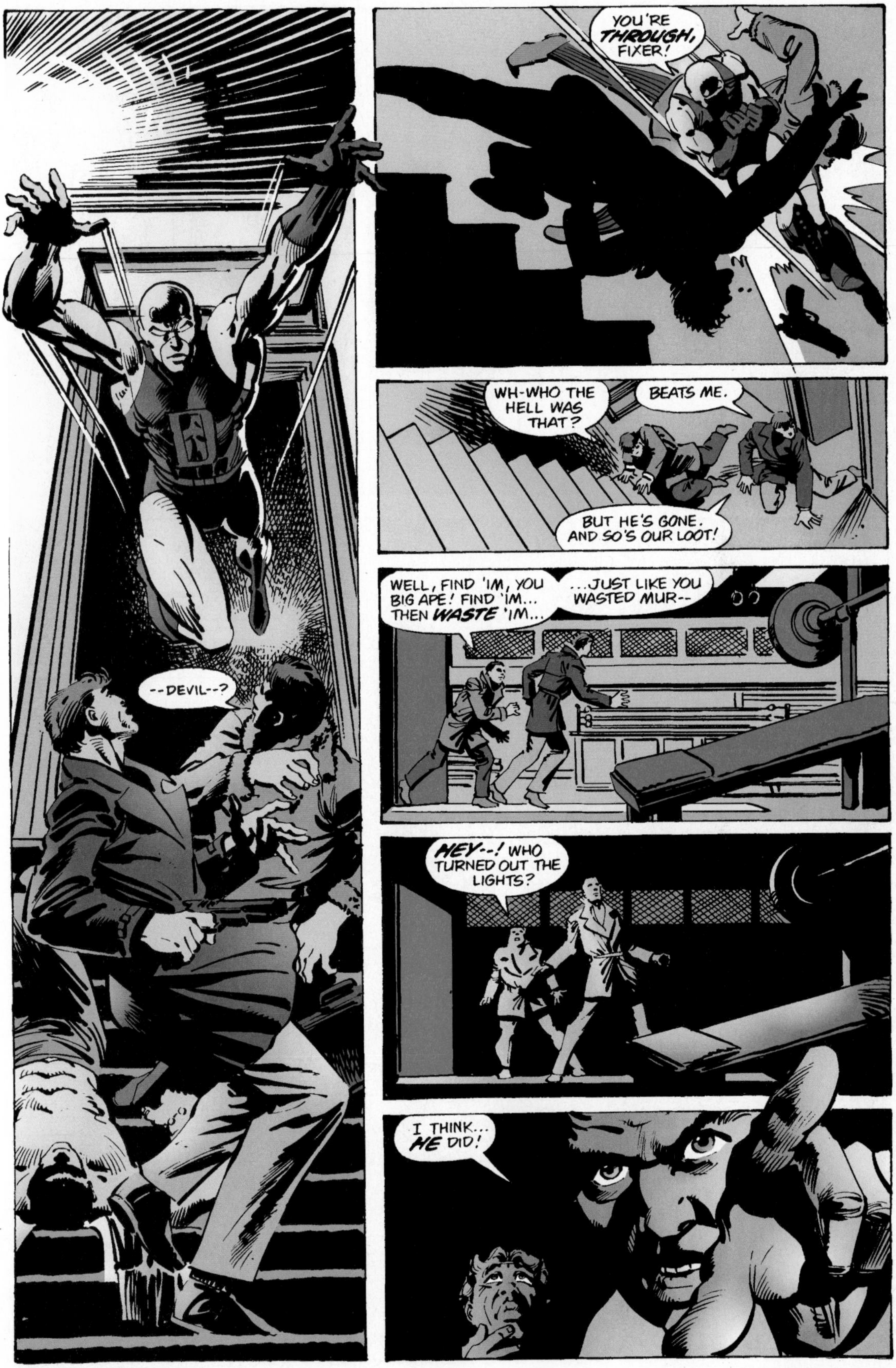
YOU'RE THROUGH, FIXER!
--DEVIL--?
WH-WHO THE HELL WAS THAT?
BEATS ME.
BUT HE'S GONE. AND SO'S OUR LOOT!
WELL, FIND 'IM, YOU BIG APE! FIND 'IM... THEN WASTE 'IM...
...JUST LIKE YOU WASTED MUR--
HEY--! WHO TURNED OUT THE LIGHTS?
I THINK... HE DID!

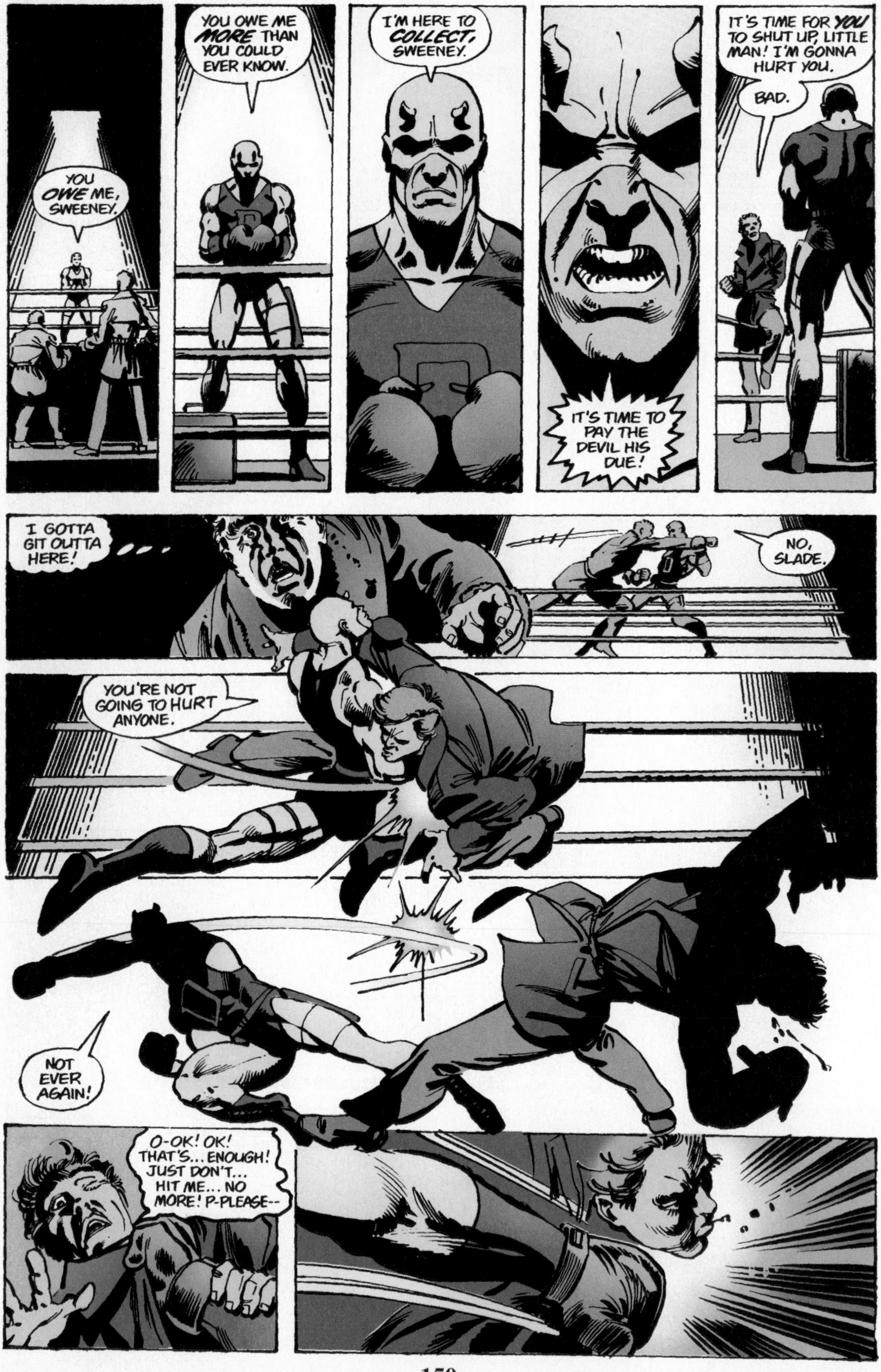
YOU OWE ME, SWEENEY.
YOU OWE ME MORE THAN YOU COULD EVER KNOW.
I'M HERE TO COLLECT, SWEENEY.
IT'S TIME TO PAY THE DEVIL HIS DUE!
IT'S TIME FOR YOU TO SHUT UP, LITTLE MAN! I'M GONNA HURT YOU.
BAD.
I GOTTA GIT OUTTA HERE!
NO, SLADE.
YOU'RE NOT GOING TO HURT ANYONE.
NOT EVER AGAIN!
O-OK! OK! THAT'S... ENOUGH! JUST DON'T... HIT ME... NO MORE! P-PLEASE--

GOD...MY *HEART* FEELS LIKE...IT'S GONNA BUST! I GOTTA STOP... GOTTA REST!

I NEED... TIME TO THINK!

I SHOULD BE... SAFE... IN THE SUBWAY!

N-NOBODY... COULD 'A FOLLOWED ME...

END OF THE LINE, SWEENEY.

NO...

...NO...

...NO...

...NO...

Y-YOU AIN'T HUMAN!

YOU'RE A... DEVIL...

A...A...

...DEVIL...

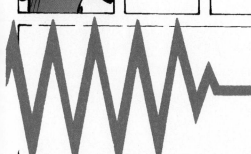

THIS ONE'S FOR *YOU,* DAD...

151

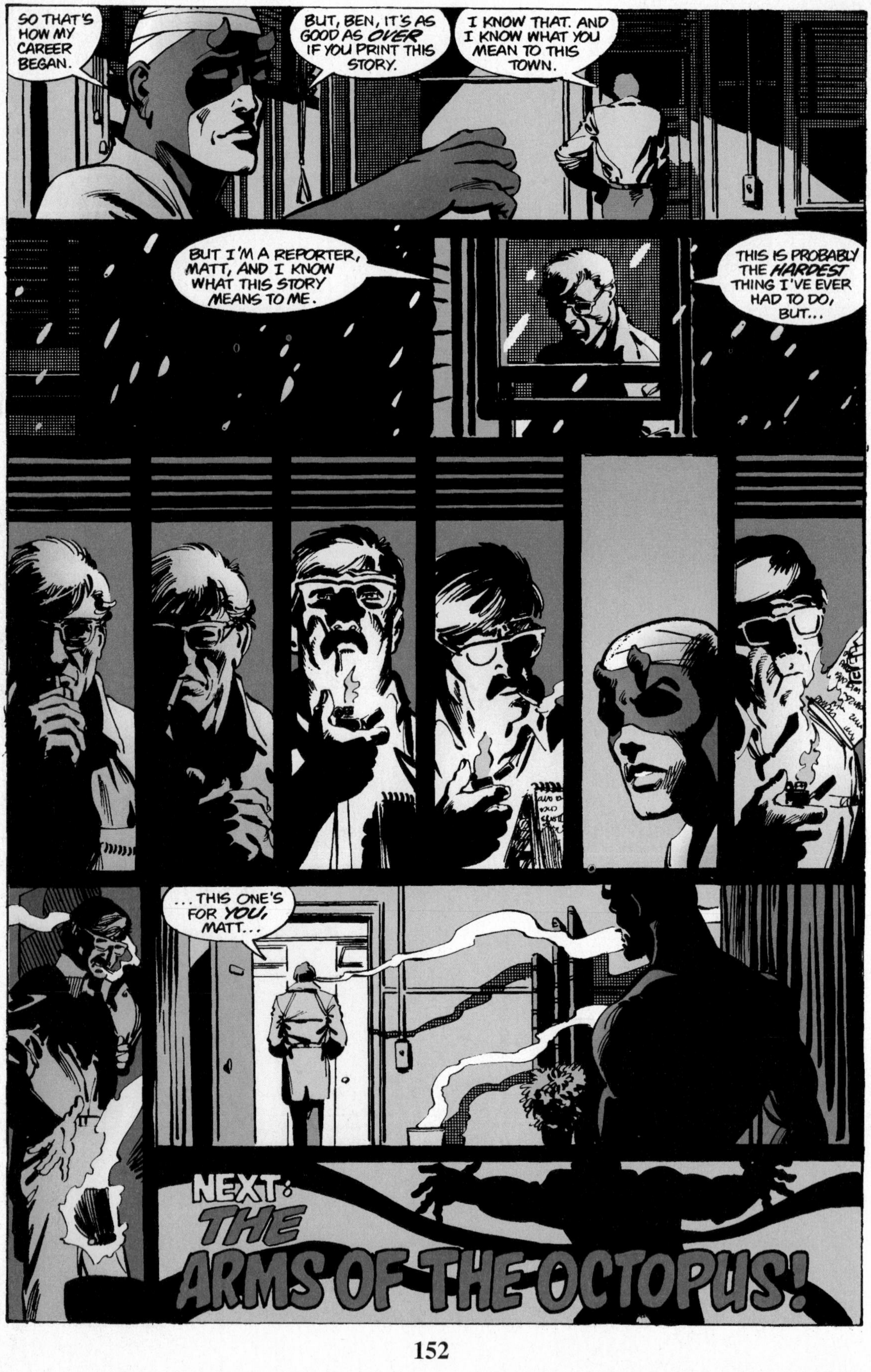

SO THAT'S HOW MY CAREER BEGAN.
BUT, BEN, IT'S AS GOOD AS OVER IF YOU PRINT THIS STORY.
I KNOW THAT. AND I KNOW WHAT YOU MEAN TO THIS TOWN.
BUT I'M A REPORTER, MATT, AND I KNOW WHAT THIS STORY MEANS TO ME.
THIS IS PROBABLY THE HARDEST THING I'VE EVER HAD TO DO, BUT...
...THIS ONE'S FOR YOU, MATT...
NEXT: THE ARMS OF THE OCTOPUS!

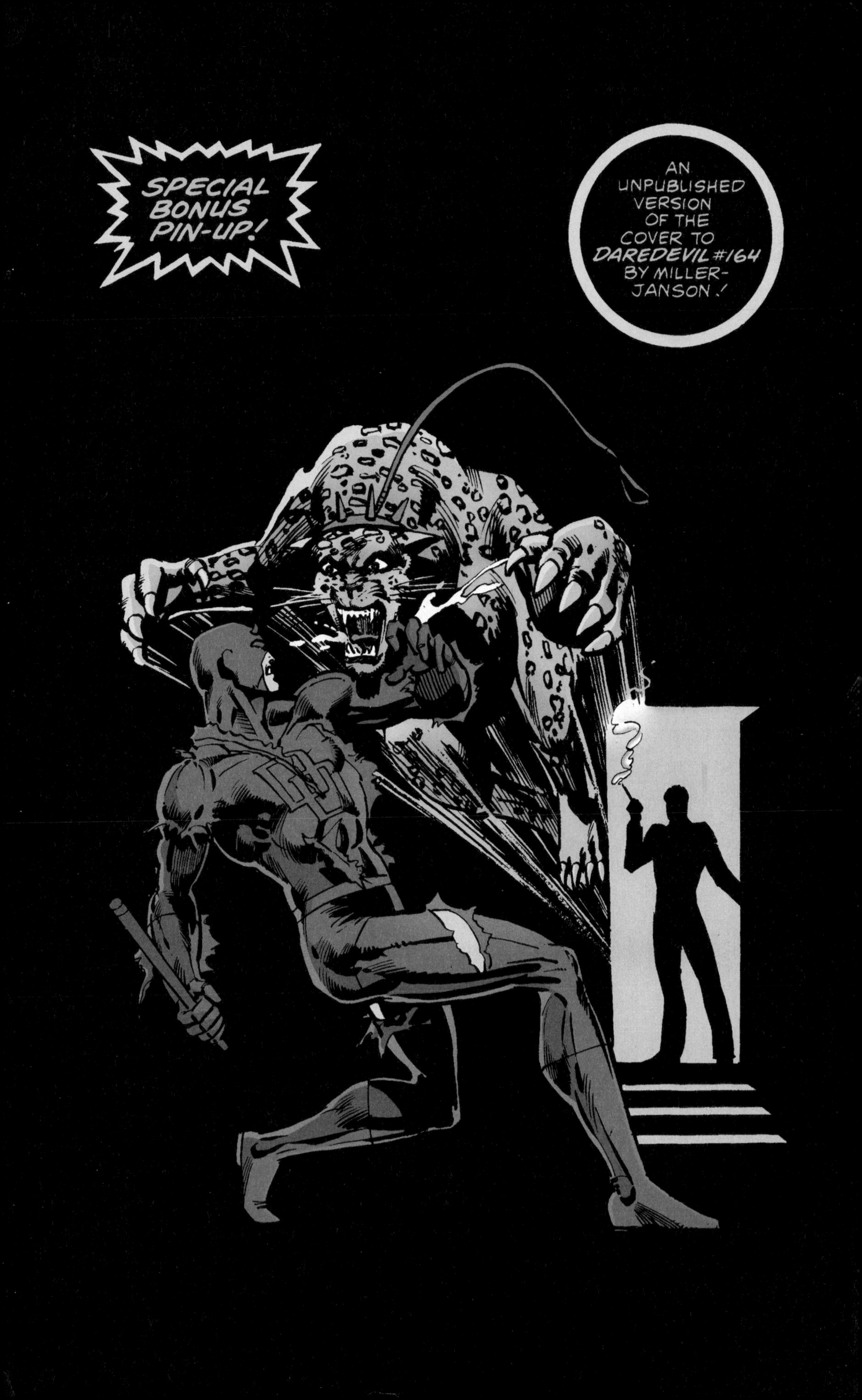
SPECIAL BONUS PIN-UP!
AN UNPUBLISHED VERSION OF THE COVER TO DAREDEVIL #164 BY MILLER-JANSON!

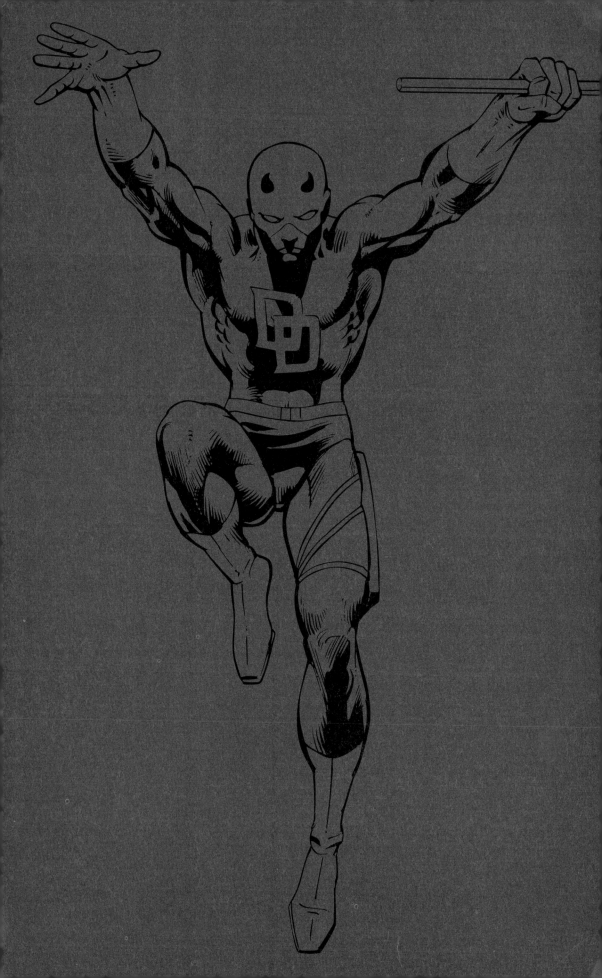

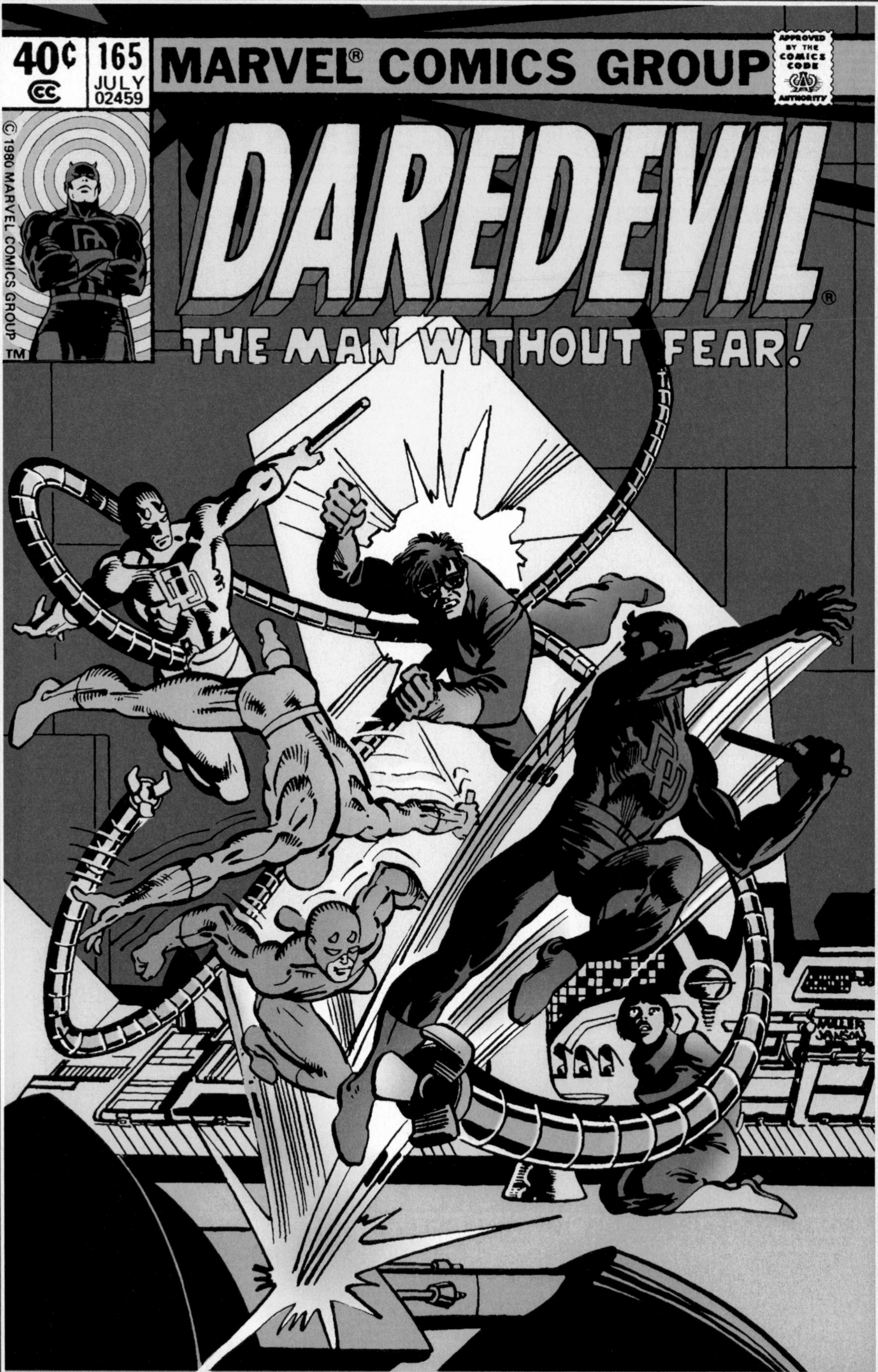

40¢
165
JULY
02459
MARVEL® COMICS GROUP
APPROVED BY THE COMICS CODE AUTHORITY
© 1980 MARVEL COMICS GROUP
DAREDEVIL®
THE MAN WITHOUT FEAR!
MILLER
JANSON

He dwells in eternal night—but the blackness is filled with sounds and scents other men cannot perceive. Though attorney MATT MURDOCK is *blind*, his other senses function with *superhuman sharpness*—his *radar sense* guides him over every obstacle! He stalks the streets by night, a red-garbed foe of evil!

Stan Lee PRESENTS: DAREDEVIL, THE MAN WITHOUT FEAR!®

HIGH ABOVE THE BUSTLING CANYONS OF MANHATTAN THIS COOL MARCH EVENING, THE NOISE OF RUSH-HOUR TRAFFIC IS ONLY A DISTANT ECHO...

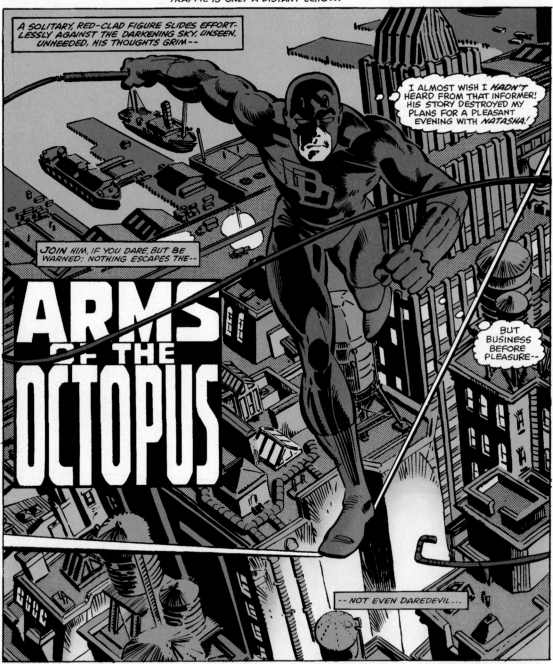

A SOLITARY, RED-CLAD FIGURE SLIDES EFFORT-LESSLY AGAINST THE DARKENING SKY, UNSEEN, UNHEEDED, HIS THOUGHTS GRIM--

I ALMOST WISH I *HADN'T* HEARD FROM THAT INFORMER! HIS STORY DESTROYED MY PLANS FOR A PLEASANT EVENING WITH *NATASHA!*

JOIN HIM, IF YOU DARE, BUT BE WARNED: NOTHING ESCAPES THE--

ARMS OF THE OCTOPUS

BUT BUSINESS BEFORE PLEASURE--

-- NOT EVEN DAREDEVIL...

ROGER McKENZIE & FRANK MILLER
SCRIPT / CO-PLOTTERS / PENCILS

KLAUS JANSON
INKS

JOE ROSEN
LETTERING

BOB SHAREN
COLORING

DENNY O'NEIL
EDITOR

JIM SHOOTER
EDITOR IN CHIEF

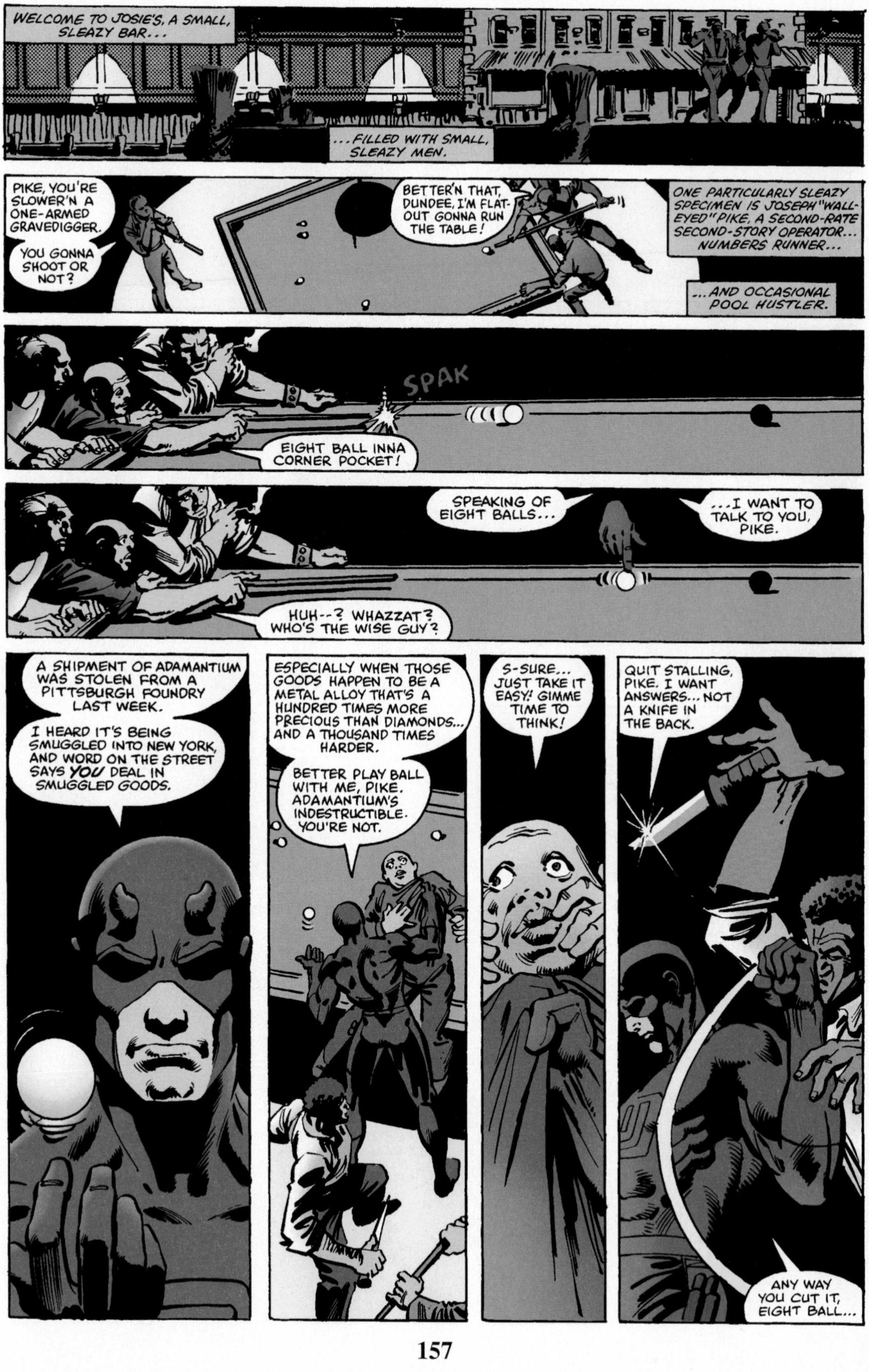

WELCOME TO JOSIE'S, A SMALL, SLEAZY BAR...
...FILLED WITH SMALL, SLEAZY MEN.
PIKE, YOU'RE SLOWER'N A ONE-ARMED GRAVEDIGGER.
YOU GONNA SHOOT OR NOT?
BETTER'N THAT, DUNDEE, I'M FLAT-OUT GONNA RUN THE TABLE!
ONE PARTICULARLY SLEAZY SPECIMEN IS JOSEPH "WALL-EYED" PIKE, A SECOND-RATE SECOND-STORY OPERATOR... NUMBERS RUNNER...
...AND OCCASIONAL POOL HUSTLER.
SPAK
EIGHT BALL INNA CORNER POCKET!
SPEAKING OF EIGHT BALLS...
...I WANT TO TALK TO YOU, PIKE.
HUH--? WHAZZAT? WHO'S THE WISE GUY?
A SHIPMENT OF ADAMANTIUM WAS STOLEN FROM A PITTSBURGH FOUNDRY LAST WEEK.
I HEARD IT'S BEING SMUGGLED INTO NEW YORK, AND WORD ON THE STREET SAYS YOU DEAL IN SMUGGLED GOODS.
ESPECIALLY WHEN THOSE GOODS HAPPEN TO BE A METAL ALLOY THAT'S A HUNDRED TIMES MORE PRECIOUS THAN DIAMONDS... AND A THOUSAND TIMES HARDER.
BETTER PLAY BALL WITH ME, PIKE. ADAMANTIUM'S INDESTRUCTIBLE. YOU'RE NOT.
S-SURE... JUST TAKE IT EASY! GIMME TIME TO THINK!
QUIT STALLING, PIKE. I WANT ANSWERS... NOT A KNIFE IN THE BACK.
ANY WAY YOU CUT IT, EIGHT BALL...

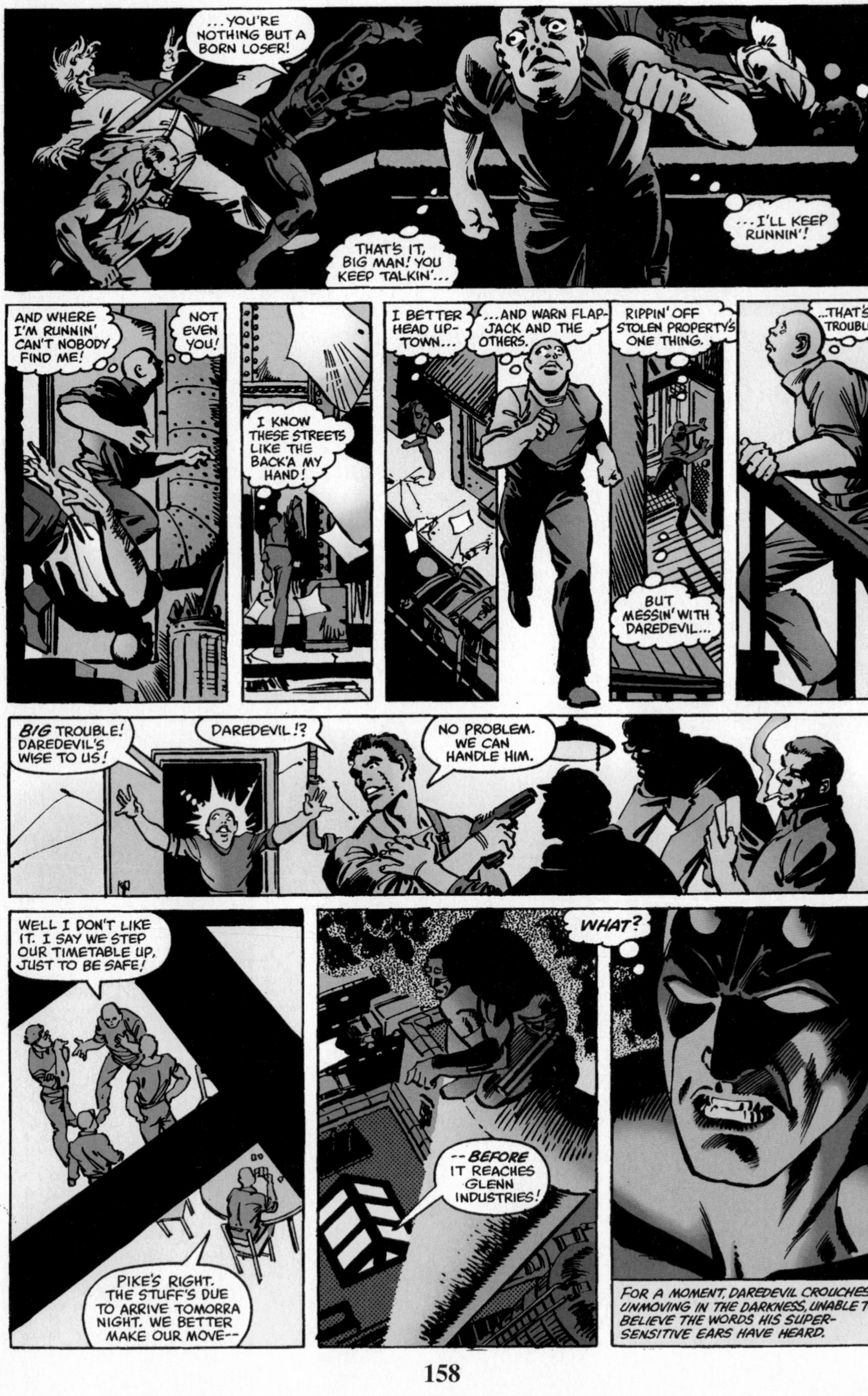
...YOU'RE NOTHING BUT A BORN LOSER!
THAT'S IT, BIG MAN! YOU KEEP TALKIN'...
...I'LL KEEP RUNNIN'!
AND WHERE I'M RUNNIN' CAN'T NOBODY FIND ME!
NOT EVEN YOU!
I KNOW THESE STREETS LIKE THE BACK'A MY HAND!
I BETTER HEAD UP-TOWN...
...AND WARN FLAP-JACK AND THE OTHERS.
RIPPIN' OFF STOLEN PROPERTY'S ONE THING.
BUT MESSIN' WITH DAREDEVIL...
...THAT'S TROUBLE!
BIG TROUBLE! DAREDEVIL'S WISE TO US!
DAREDEVIL!?
NO PROBLEM. WE CAN HANDLE HIM.
WELL I DON'T LIKE IT. I SAY WE STEP OUR TIMETABLE UP, JUST TO BE SAFE!
PIKE'S RIGHT. THE STUFF'S DUE TO ARRIVE TOMORRA NIGHT. WE BETTER MAKE OUR MOVE--
--BEFORE IT REACHES GLENN INDUSTRIES!
WHAT?
FOR A MOMENT, DAREDEVIL CROUCHES UNMOVING IN THE DARKNESS, UNABLE TO BELIEVE THE WORDS HIS SUPER-SENSITIVE EARS HAVE HEARD.

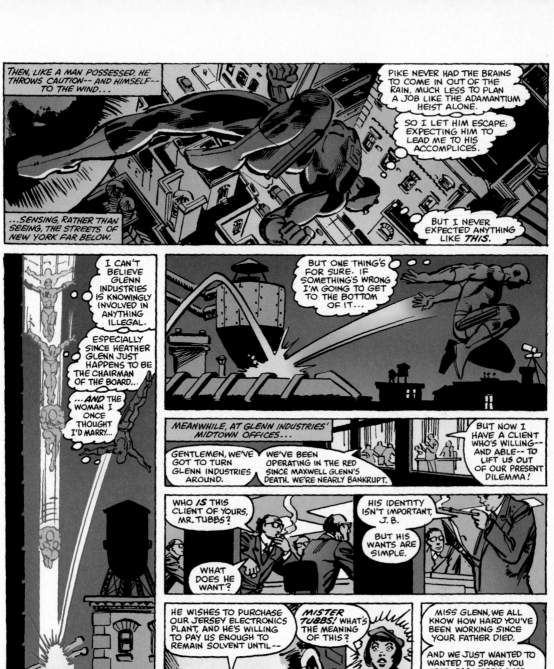

THEN, LIKE A MAN POSSESSED, HE THROWS CAUTION-- AND HIMSELF-- TO THE WIND...

PIKE NEVER HAD THE BRAINS TO COME IN OUT OF THE RAIN, MUCH LESS TO PLAN A JOB LIKE THE ADAMANTIUM HEIST ALONE.

SO I LET HIM ESCAPE, EXPECTING HIM TO LEAD ME TO HIS ACCOMPLICES.

...SENSING, RATHER THAN SEEING, THE STREETS OF NEW YORK FAR BELOW.

BUT I NEVER EXPECTED ANYTHING LIKE THIS.

I CAN'T BELIEVE GLENN INDUSTRIES IS KNOWINGLY INVOLVED IN ANYTHING ILLEGAL.

ESPECIALLY SINCE HEATHER GLENN JUST HAPPENS TO BE THE CHAIRMAN OF THE BOARD...

...AND THE WOMAN I ONCE THOUGHT I'D MARRY...

BUT ONE THING'S FOR SURE. IF SOMETHING'S WRONG I'M GOING TO GET TO THE BOTTOM OF IT...

MEANWHILE, AT GLENN INDUSTRIES' MIDTOWN OFFICES...

GENTLEMEN, WE'VE GOT TO TURN GLENN INDUSTRIES AROUND.

WE'VE BEEN OPERATING IN THE RED SINCE MAXWELL GLENN'S DEATH. WE'RE NEARLY BANKRUPT.

BUT NOW I HAVE A CLIENT WHO'S WILLING-- AND ABLE-- TO LIFT US OUT OF OUR PRESENT DILEMMA!

WHO IS THIS CLIENT OF YOURS, MR. TUBBS?

HIS IDENTITY ISN'T IMPORTANT, J.B. BUT HIS WANTS ARE SIMPLE.

WHAT DOES HE WANT?

HE WISHES TO PURCHASE OUR JERSEY ELECTRONICS PLANT, AND HE'S WILLING TO PAY US ENOUGH TO REMAIN SOLVENT UNTIL--

MISTER TUBBS! WHAT'S THE MEANING OF THIS?

MISS GLENN, WE ALL KNOW HOW HARD YOU'VE BEEN WORKING SINCE YOUR FATHER DIED.

AND WE JUST WANTED TO WANTED TO SPARE YOU NEEDLESS WORRY OVER ROUTINE BUSINESS MATTERS.

WHY WASN'T I INFORMED OF THIS BOARD MEETING?

KTANG

159

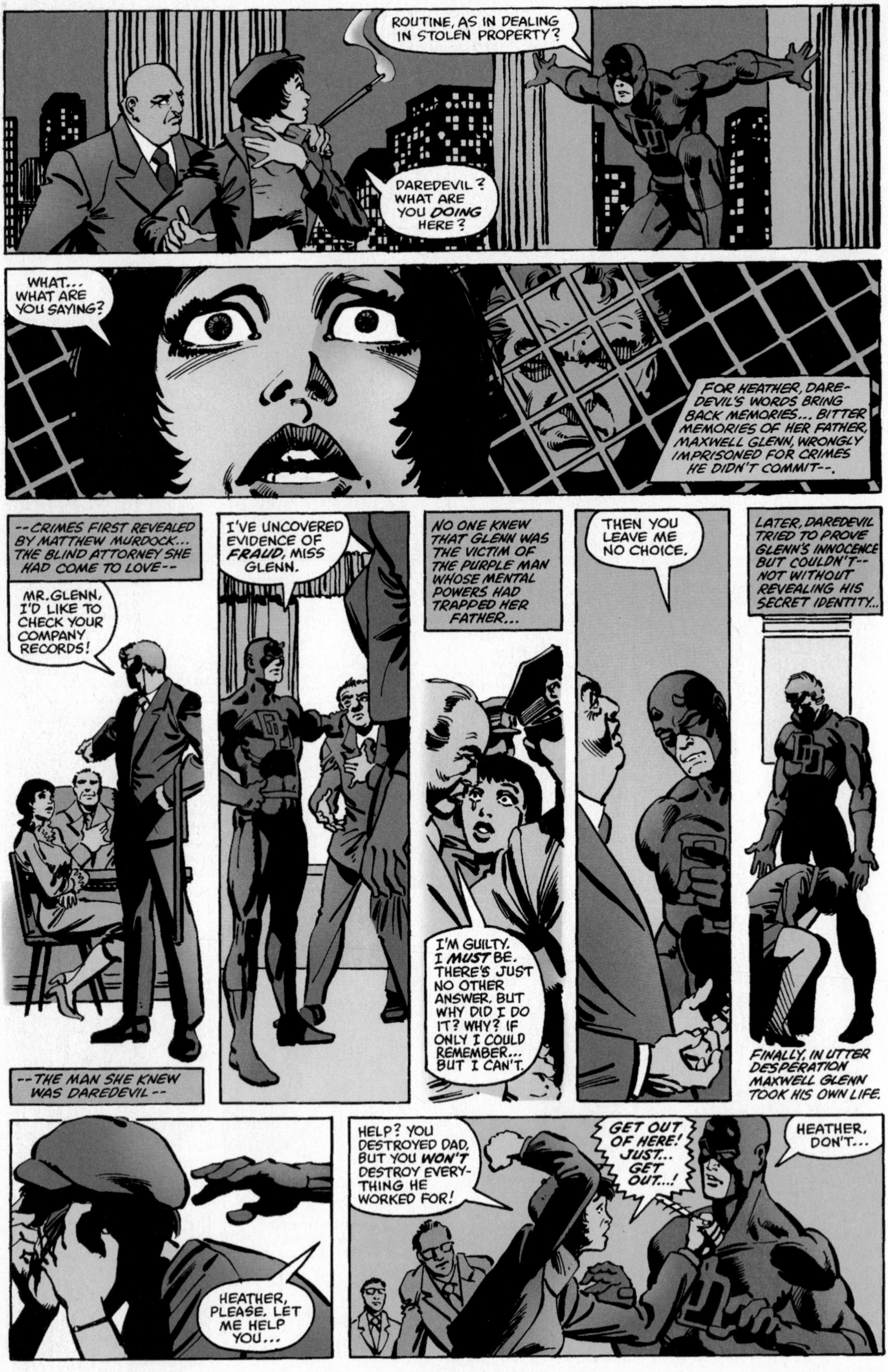

ROUTINE, AS IN DEALING IN STOLEN PROPERTY?
DAREDEVIL? WHAT ARE YOU DOING HERE?
WHAT... WHAT ARE YOU SAYING?
FOR HEATHER, DAREDEVIL'S WORDS BRING BACK MEMORIES... BITTER MEMORIES OF HER FATHER, MAXWELL GLENN, WRONGLY IMPRISONED FOR CRIMES HE DIDN'T COMMIT--.
--CRIMES FIRST REVEALED BY MATTHEW MURDOCK... THE BLIND ATTORNEY SHE HAD COME TO LOVE--
MR. GLENN, I'D LIKE TO CHECK YOUR COMPANY RECORDS!
--THE MAN SHE KNEW WAS DAREDEVIL--
I'VE UNCOVERED EVIDENCE OF FRAUD, MISS GLENN.
NO ONE KNEW THAT GLENN WAS THE VICTIM OF THE PURPLE MAN WHOSE MENTAL POWERS HAD TRAPPED HER FATHER...
I'M GUILTY. I MUST BE. THERE'S JUST NO OTHER ANSWER. BUT WHY DID I DO IT? WHY? IF ONLY I COULD REMEMBER... BUT I CAN'T.
THEN YOU LEAVE ME NO CHOICE.
LATER, DAREDEVIL TRIED TO PROVE GLENN'S INNOCENCE BUT COULDN'T--NOT WITHOUT REVEALING HIS SECRET IDENTITY...
FINALLY, IN UTTER DESPERATION MAXWELL GLENN TOOK HIS OWN LIFE.
HEATHER, PLEASE. LET ME HELP YOU...
HELP? YOU DESTROYED DAD, BUT YOU WON'T DESTROY EVERYTHING HE WORKED FOR!
GET OUT OF HERE! JUST... GET OUT...!
HEATHER, DON'T...

CAN'T YOU SEE WHAT'S HAPPENING? THESE MEN ARE USING YOU.

THERE, THERE, MY CHILD. NO NEED TO CRY. I'LL TAKE CARE OF EVERYTHING.

IT'S WHAT YOUR FATHER WOULD HAVE WANTED.

GENTLEMEN, IF YOU'LL BE SO KIND AS TO ESCORT THIS... DEVIL...TO THE DOOR...

DON'T BOTHER.

AND THE FOLLOWING MORNING FINDS MATT'S BEST FRIEND AND LAW PARTNER, FRANKLIN "FOGGY" NELSON, HURRYING TO THEIR DOWNTOWN STOREFRONT OFFICES...

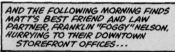

FREE LEGAL CL

ZIPPITY DO-DA! ZIPPITY YAY! MY, OH MY, WHAT A WONDERFUL DAY... ♪

...HIS MIND'S ON ANYTHING BUT WORK...

MATT, YOU OL' HOUND DOG, I WISH YOU COULD SEE WHAT I'M HOLDING IN MY HOT LITTLE HANDS!

GOT IT JUST FOR MY WEDDING NEXT WEEK.

THE LATEST IN TUXEDOES.

...SHE'S A REAL BEAUT!

HEY, DID I SAY SOMETHING WRONG?

I'M BUSY! SO JUST GET OFF MY BACK, OK?

BECKY, YOU GET ME THOSE GLENN INDUSTRIES TRANSCRIPTS.

MATT'S BEEN SNAPPING AT EVERYONE ALL MORNING. I WONDER WHAT'S WRONG?

MEANWHILE, AT GLENN INDUSTRIES...

SO THAT'S WHAT'S WRONG--!

I'M GLAD I COOLED OFF AND DECIDED TO GO OVER THESE RECORDS LIKE MATT SUGGESTED.

THE PROPOSED SALE OF OUR JERSEY BRANCH IS NOTHING BUT A FRONT FOR--

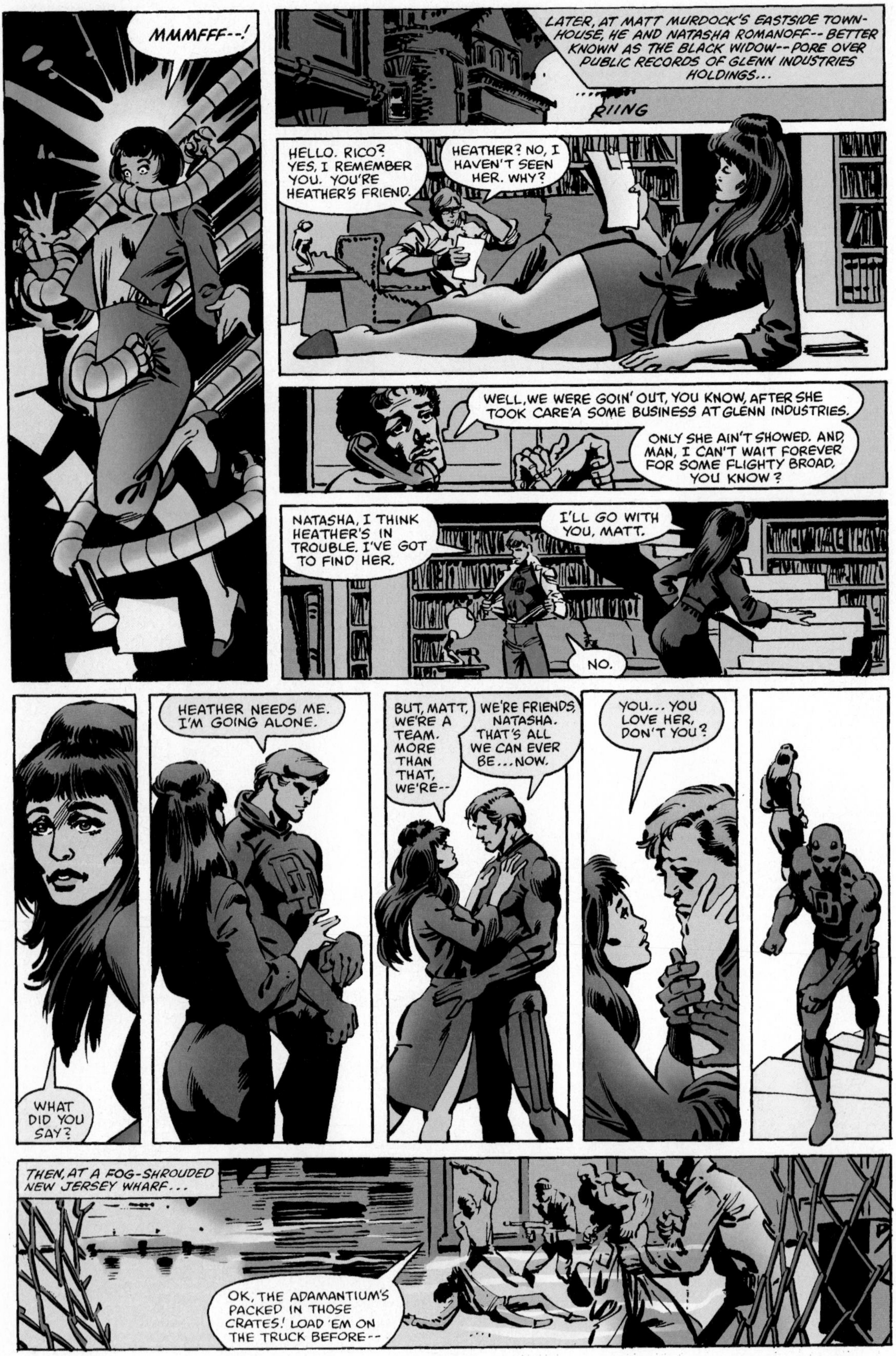
MMMFFF--!
LATER, AT MATT MURDOCK'S EASTSIDE TOWN-HOUSE, HE AND NATASHA ROMANOFF--BETTER KNOWN AS THE BLACK WIDOW--PORE OVER PUBLIC RECORDS OF GLENN INDUSTRIES HOLDINGS...
...RIING
HELLO. RICO? YES, I REMEMBER YOU. YOU'RE HEATHER'S FRIEND.
HEATHER? NO, I HAVEN'T SEEN HER. WHY?
WELL, WE WERE GOIN' OUT, YOU KNOW, AFTER SHE TOOK CARE'A SOME BUSINESS AT GLENN INDUSTRIES.
ONLY SHE AIN'T SHOWED. AND, MAN, I CAN'T WAIT FOREVER FOR SOME FLIGHTY BROAD, YOU KNOW?
NATASHA, I THINK HEATHER'S IN TROUBLE. I'VE GOT TO FIND HER.
I'LL GO WITH YOU, MATT.
NO.
WHAT DID YOU SAY?
HEATHER NEEDS ME. I'M GOING ALONE.
BUT, MATT, WE'RE A TEAM. MORE THAN THAT, WE'RE--
WE'RE FRIENDS, NATASHA. THAT'S ALL WE CAN EVER BE...NOW.
YOU... YOU LOVE HER, DON'T YOU?
THEN, AT A FOG-SHROUDED NEW JERSEY WHARF...
OK, THE ADAMANTIUM'S PACKED IN THOSE CRATES! LOAD 'EM ON THE TRUCK BEFORE--

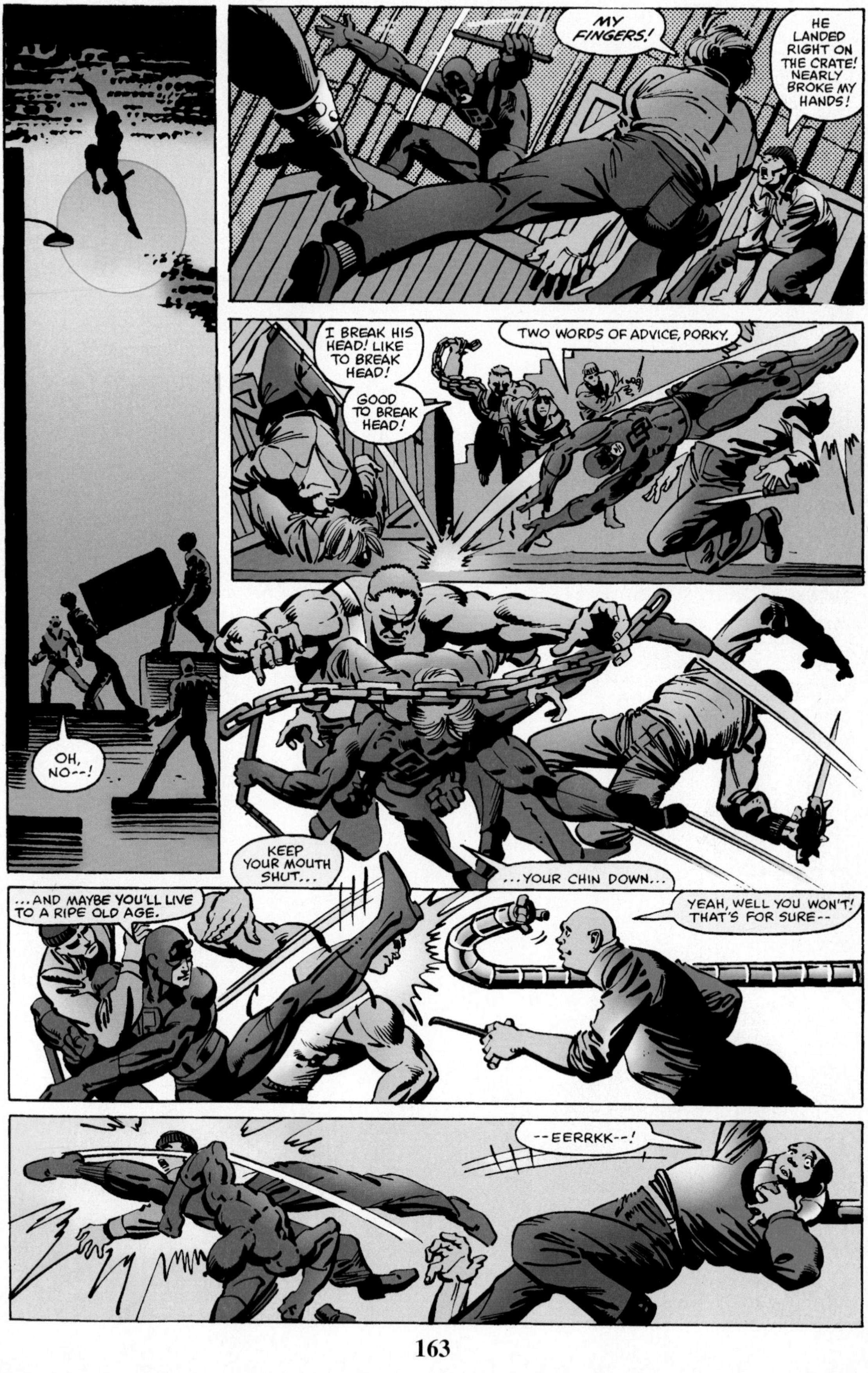
MY FINGERS!
HE LANDED RIGHT ON THE CRATE! NEARLY BROKE MY HANDS!
OH, NO--!
I BREAK HIS HEAD! LIKE TO BREAK HEAD!
GOOD TO BREAK HEAD!
TWO WORDS OF ADVICE, PORKY.
KEEP YOUR MOUTH SHUT...
...YOUR CHIN DOWN...
...AND MAYBE YOU'LL LIVE TO A RIPE OLD AGE.
YEAH, WELL YOU WON'T! THAT'S FOR SURE--
--EERRKK--!

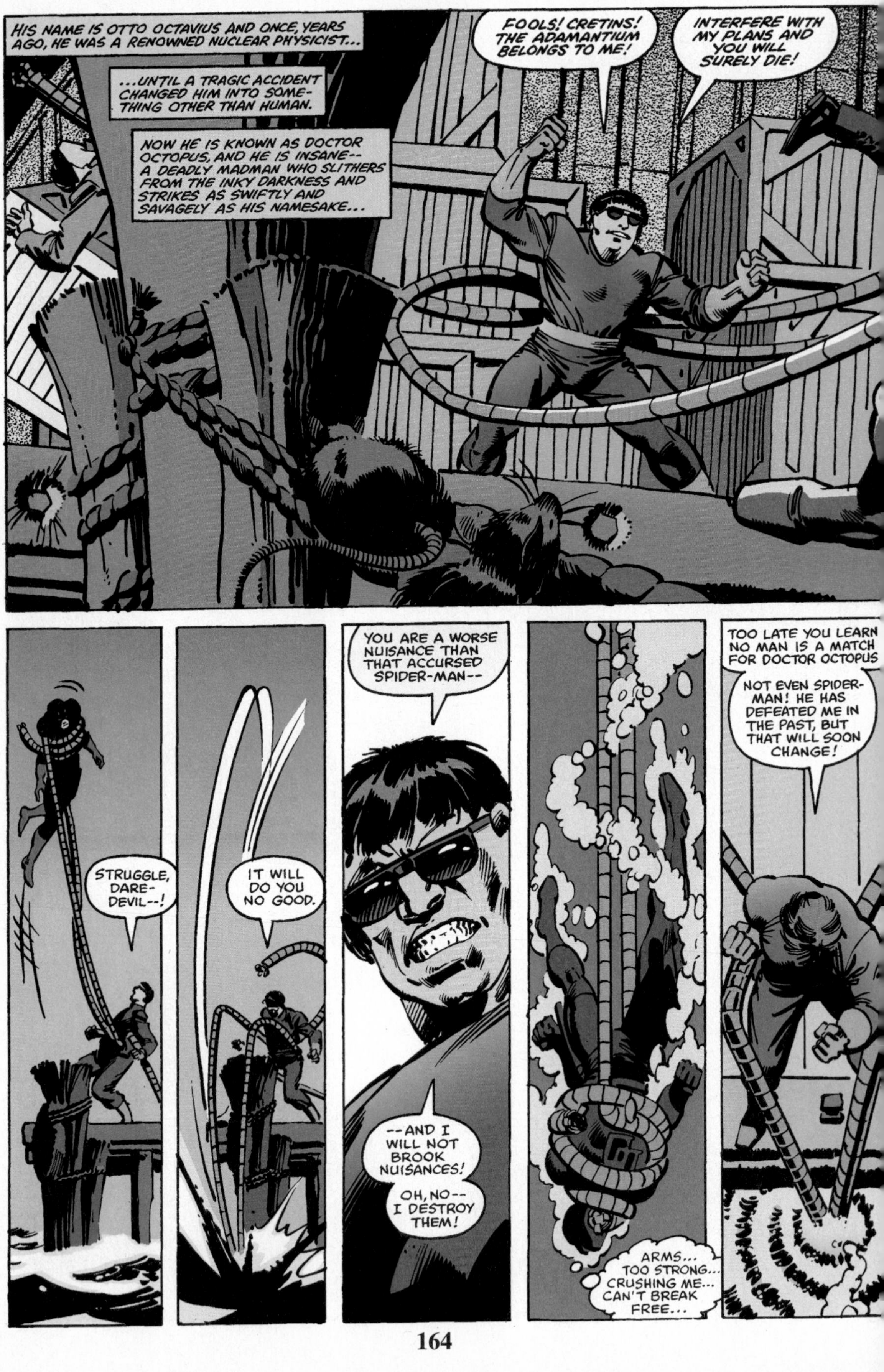
HIS NAME IS OTTO OCTAVIUS AND ONCE, YEARS AGO, HE WAS A RENOWNED NUCLEAR PHYSICIST...
...UNTIL A TRAGIC ACCIDENT CHANGED HIM INTO SOMETHING OTHER THAN HUMAN.
NOW HE IS KNOWN AS DOCTOR OCTOPUS, AND HE IS INSANE-- A DEADLY MADMAN WHO SLITHERS FROM THE INKY DARKNESS AND STRIKES AS SWIFTLY AND SAVAGELY AS HIS NAMESAKE...
FOOLS! CRETINS! THE ADAMANTIUM BELONGS TO ME!
INTERFERE WITH MY PLANS AND YOU WILL SURELY DIE!
STRUGGLE, DAREDEVIL--!
IT WILL DO YOU NO GOOD.
YOU ARE A WORSE NUISANCE THAN THAT ACCURSED SPIDER-MAN--
--AND I WILL NOT BROOK NUISANCES!
OH, NO-- I DESTROY THEM!
ARMS... TOO STRONG... CRUSHING ME... CAN'T BREAK FREE...
TOO LATE YOU LEARN NO MAN IS A MATCH FOR DOCTOR OCTOPUS
NOT EVEN SPIDER-MAN! HE HAS DEFEATED ME IN THE PAST, BUT THAT WILL SOON CHANGE!

DOCTOR OCTOPUS! I WASN'T EXPECTING-- *UNGHH--!*

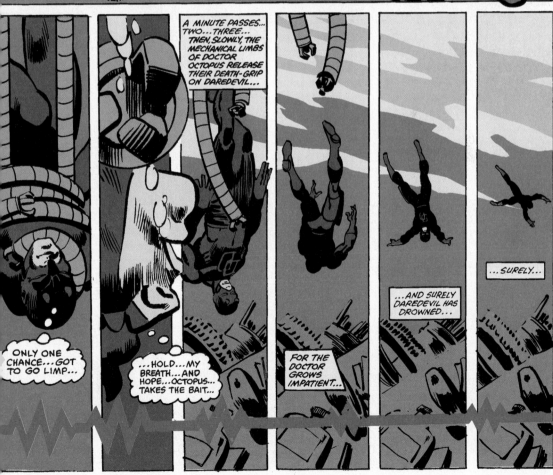

A MINUTE PASSES... TWO... THREE... THEN, SLOWLY, THE MECHANICAL LIMBS OF DOCTOR OCTOPUS RELEASE THEIR DEATH-GRIP ON DAREDEVIL...

ONLY ONE CHANCE...GOT TO GO LIMP...

...HOLD...MY BREATH...AND HOPE...OCTOPUS... TAKES THE BAIT...

FOR THE DOCTOR GROWS IMPATIENT...

...AND SURELY DAREDEVIL HAS DROWNED...

...SURELY...

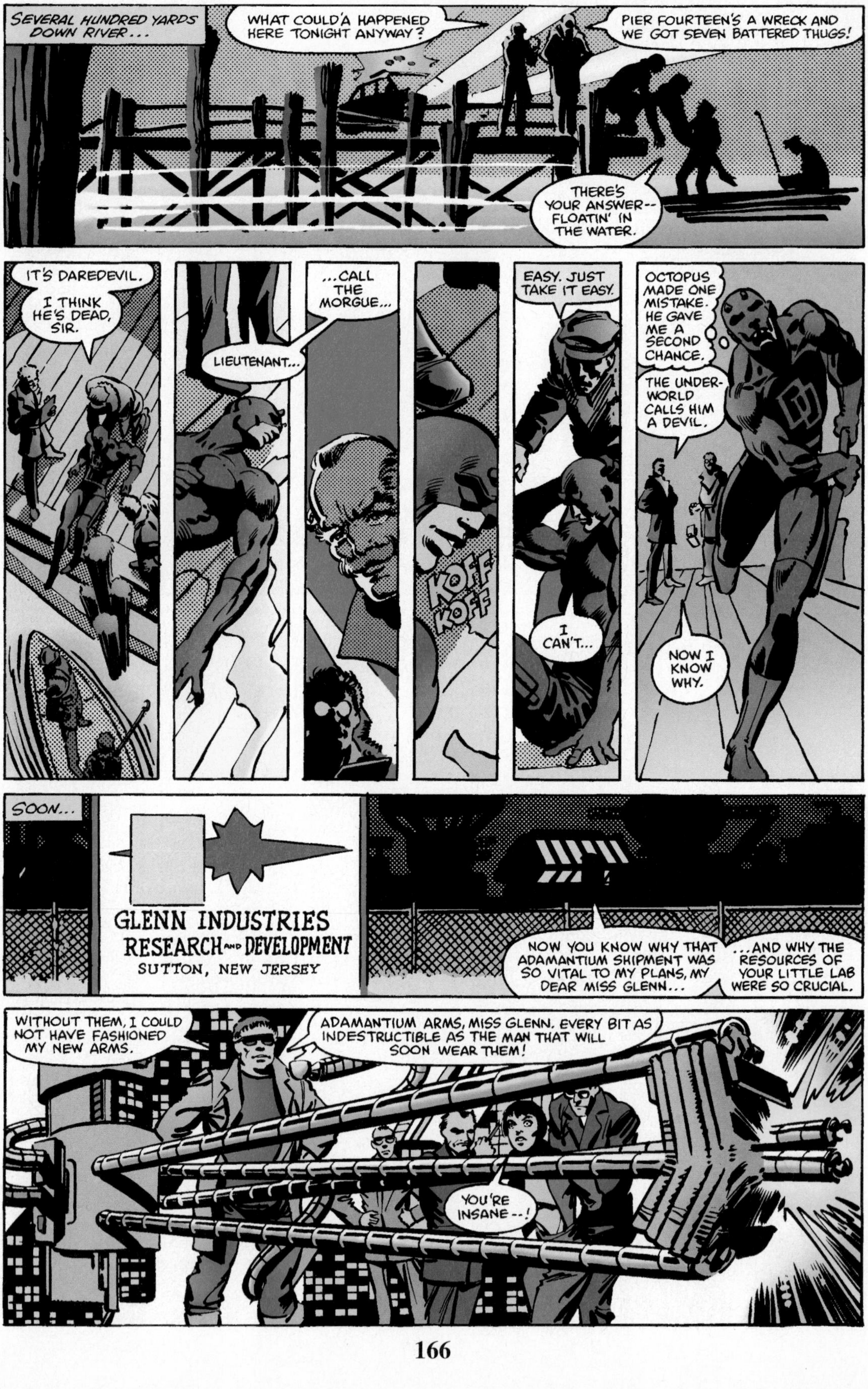
SEVERAL HUNDRED YARDS DOWN RIVER...
WHAT COULD'A HAPPENED HERE TONIGHT ANYWAY?
PIER FOURTEEN'S A WRECK AND WE GOT SEVEN BATTERED THUGS!
THERE'S YOUR ANSWER-- FLOATIN' IN THE WATER.
IT'S DAREDEVIL.
I THINK HE'S DEAD, SIR.
LIEUTENANT...
...CALL THE MORGUE...
KOFF KOFF
EASY. JUST TAKE IT EASY.
I CAN'T...
OCTOPUS MADE ONE MISTAKE. HE GAVE ME A SECOND CHANCE.
THE UNDER-WORLD CALLS HIM A DEVIL.
NOW I KNOW WHY.
SOON...
GLENN INDUSTRIES
RESEARCH AND DEVELOPMENT
SUTTON, NEW JERSEY
NOW YOU KNOW WHY THAT ADAMANTIUM SHIPMENT WAS SO VITAL TO MY PLANS, MY DEAR MISS GLENN...
...AND WHY THE RESOURCES OF YOUR LITTLE LAB WERE SO CRUCIAL.
WITHOUT THEM, I COULD NOT HAVE FASHIONED MY NEW ARMS.
ADAMANTIUM ARMS, MISS GLENN. EVERY BIT AS INDESTRUCTIBLE AS THE MAN THAT WILL SOON WEAR THEM!
YOU'RE INSANE--!

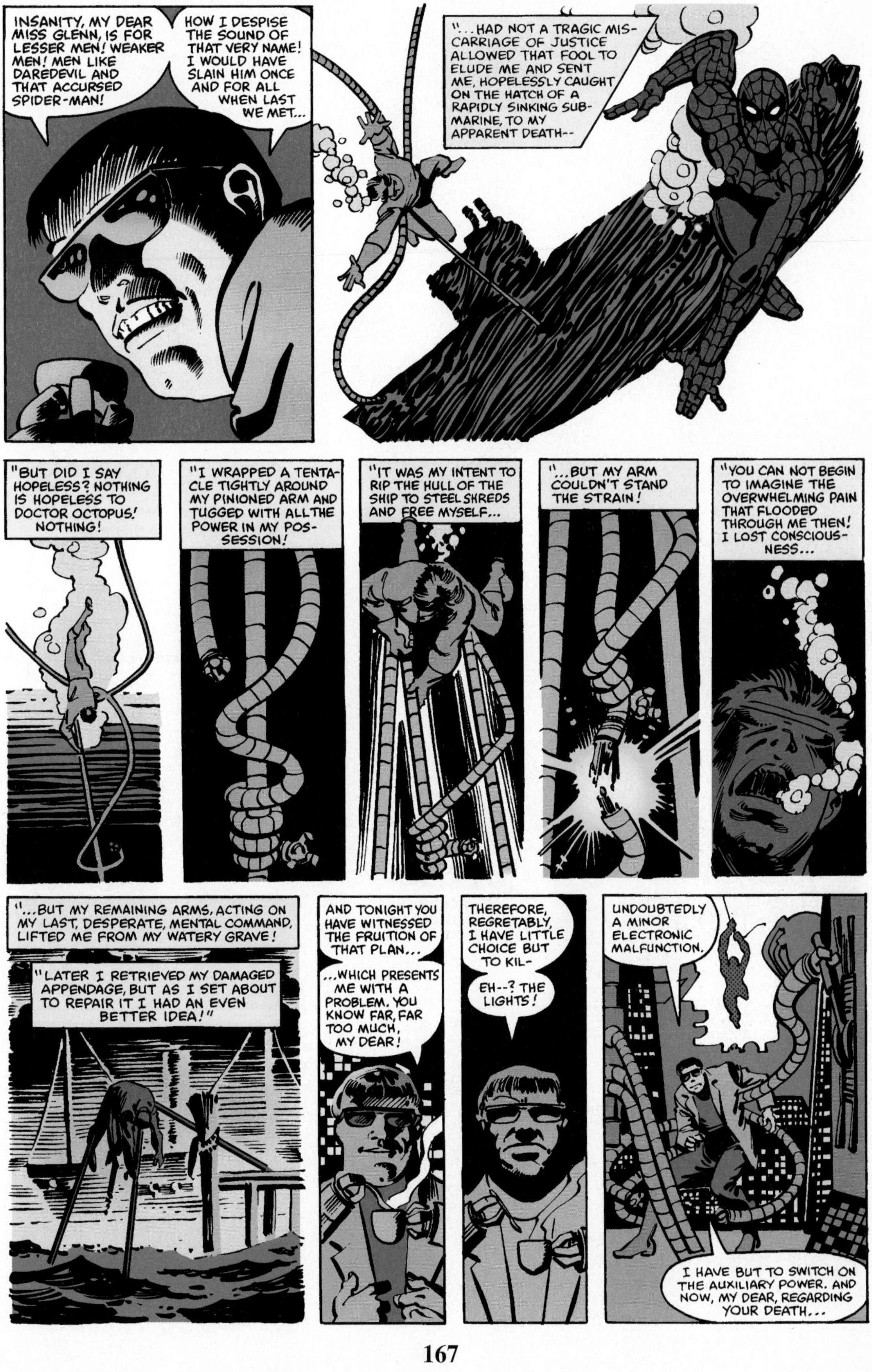
INSANITY, MY DEAR MISS GLENN, IS FOR LESSER MEN! WEAKER MEN! MEN LIKE DAREDEVIL AND THAT ACCURSED SPIDER-MAN!
HOW I DESPISE THE SOUND OF THAT VERY NAME! I WOULD HAVE SLAIN HIM ONCE AND FOR ALL WHEN LAST WE MET...
"...HAD NOT A TRAGIC MIS-CARRIAGE OF JUSTICE ALLOWED THAT FOOL TO ELUDE ME AND SENT ME, HOPELESSLY CAUGHT ON THE HATCH OF A RAPIDLY SINKING SUB-MARINE, TO MY APPARENT DEATH--
"BUT DID I SAY HOPELESS? NOTHING IS HOPELESS TO DOCTOR OCTOPUS! NOTHING!
"I WRAPPED A TENTA-CLE TIGHTLY AROUND MY PINIONED ARM AND TUGGED WITH ALL THE POWER IN MY POS-SESSION!
"IT WAS MY INTENT TO RIP THE HULL OF THE SHIP TO STEEL SHREDS AND FREE MYSELF...
"...BUT MY ARM COULDN'T STAND THE STRAIN!
"YOU CAN NOT BEGIN TO IMAGINE THE OVERWHELMING PAIN THAT FLOODED THROUGH ME THEN! I LOST CONSCIOUS-NESS...
"...BUT MY REMAINING ARMS, ACTING ON MY LAST, DESPERATE, MENTAL COMMAND, LIFTED ME FROM MY WATERY GRAVE!
"LATER I RETRIEVED MY DAMAGED APPENDAGE, BUT AS I SET ABOUT TO REPAIR IT I HAD AN EVEN BETTER IDEA!"
AND TONIGHT YOU HAVE WITNESSED THE FRUITION OF THAT PLAN...
...WHICH PRESENTS ME WITH A PROBLEM. YOU KNOW FAR, FAR TOO MUCH, MY DEAR!
THEREFORE, REGRETABLY, I HAVE LITTLE CHOICE BUT TO KIL-
EH--? THE LIGHTS!
UNDOUBTEDLY A MINOR ELECTRONIC MALFUNCTION.
I HAVE BUT TO SWITCH ON THE AUXILIARY POWER. AND NOW, MY DEAR, REGARDING YOUR DEATH...

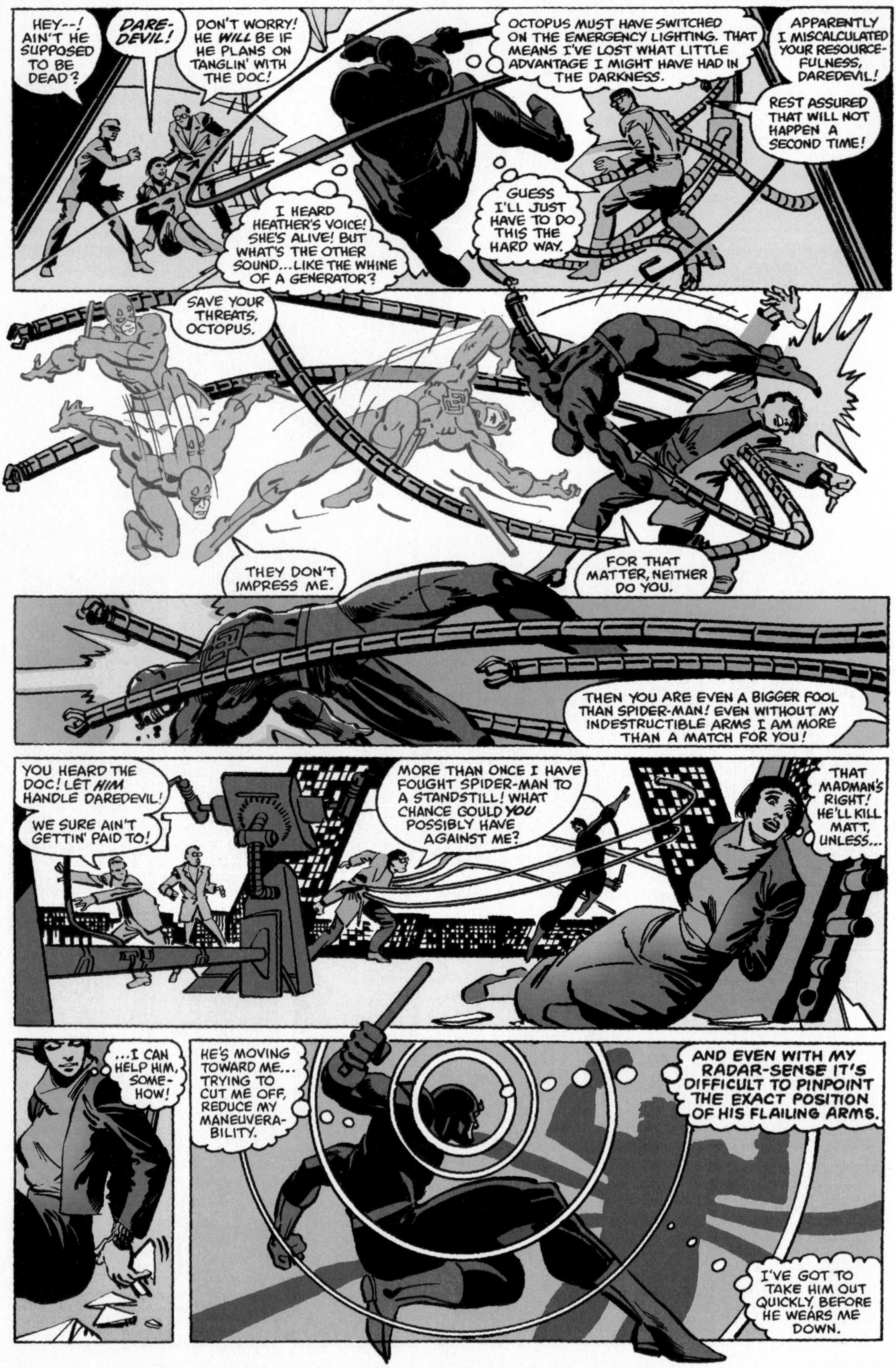
HEY--! AIN'T HE SUPPOSED TO BE DEAD?
DARE-DEVIL!
DON'T WORRY! HE WILL BE IF HE PLANS ON TANGLIN' WITH THE DOC!
OCTOPUS MUST HAVE SWITCHED ON THE EMERGENCY LIGHTING. THAT MEANS I'VE LOST WHAT LITTLE ADVANTAGE I MIGHT HAVE HAD IN THE DARKNESS.
APPARENTLY I MISCALCULATED YOUR RESOURCE-FULNESS, DAREDEVIL!
REST ASSURED THAT WILL NOT HAPPEN A SECOND TIME!
I HEARD HEATHER'S VOICE! SHE'S ALIVE! BUT WHAT'S THE OTHER SOUND...LIKE THE WHINE OF A GENERATOR?
GUESS I'LL JUST HAVE TO DO THIS THE HARD WAY.
SAVE YOUR THREATS, OCTOPUS.
THEY DON'T IMPRESS ME.
FOR THAT MATTER, NEITHER DO YOU.
THEN YOU ARE EVEN A BIGGER FOOL THAN SPIDER-MAN! EVEN WITHOUT MY INDESTRUCTIBLE ARMS I AM MORE THAN A MATCH FOR YOU!
YOU HEARD THE DOC! LET HIM HANDLE DAREDEVIL!
WE SURE AIN'T GETTIN' PAID TO!
MORE THAN ONCE I HAVE FOUGHT SPIDER-MAN TO A STANDSTILL! WHAT CHANCE COULD YOU POSSIBLY HAVE AGAINST ME?
THAT MADMAN'S RIGHT! HE'LL KILL MATT, UNLESS...
...I CAN HELP HIM, SOME-HOW!
HE'S MOVING TOWARD ME... TRYING TO CUT ME OFF, REDUCE MY MANEUVERA-BILITY.
AND EVEN WITH MY RADAR-SENSE IT'S DIFFICULT TO PINPOINT THE EXACT POSITION OF HIS FLAILING ARMS.
I'VE GOT TO TAKE HIM OUT QUICKLY, BEFORE HE WEARS ME DOWN.

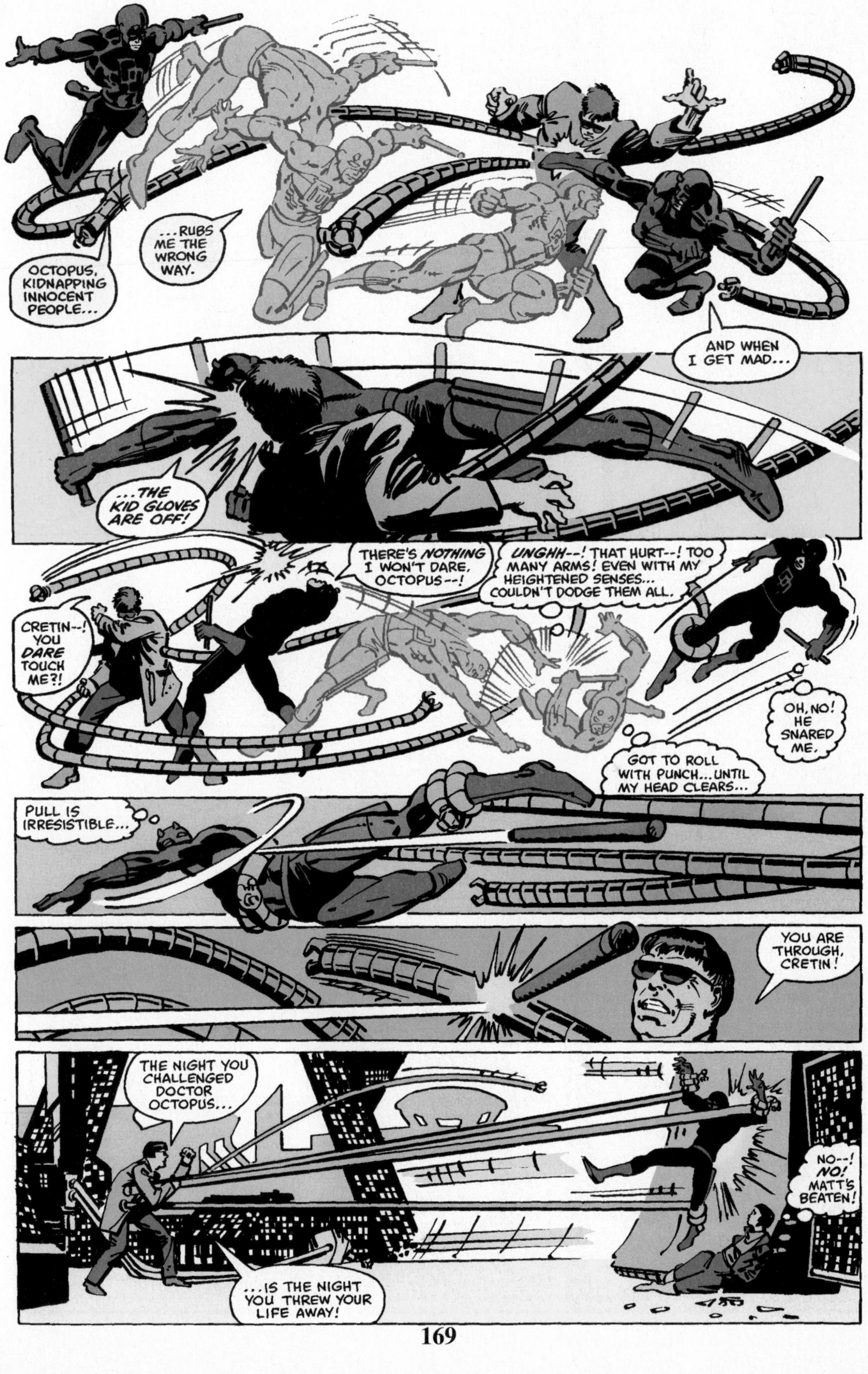
OCTOPUS, KIDNAPPING INNOCENT PEOPLE...
...RUBS ME THE WRONG WAY.
AND WHEN I GET MAD...
...THE KID GLOVES ARE OFF!
THERE'S NOTHING I WON'T DARE, OCTOPUS--!
CRETIN--! YOU DARE TOUCH ME?!
UNGHH--! THAT HURT--! TOO MANY ARMS! EVEN WITH MY HEIGHTENED SENSES... COULDN'T DODGE THEM ALL.
GOT TO ROLL WITH PUNCH...UNTIL MY HEAD CLEARS...
OH, NO! HE SNARED ME.
PULL IS IRRESISTIBLE...
YOU ARE THROUGH, CRETIN!
THE NIGHT YOU CHALLENGED DOCTOR OCTOPUS...
...IS THE NIGHT YOU THREW YOUR LIFE AWAY!
NO--! NO! MATT'S BEATEN!

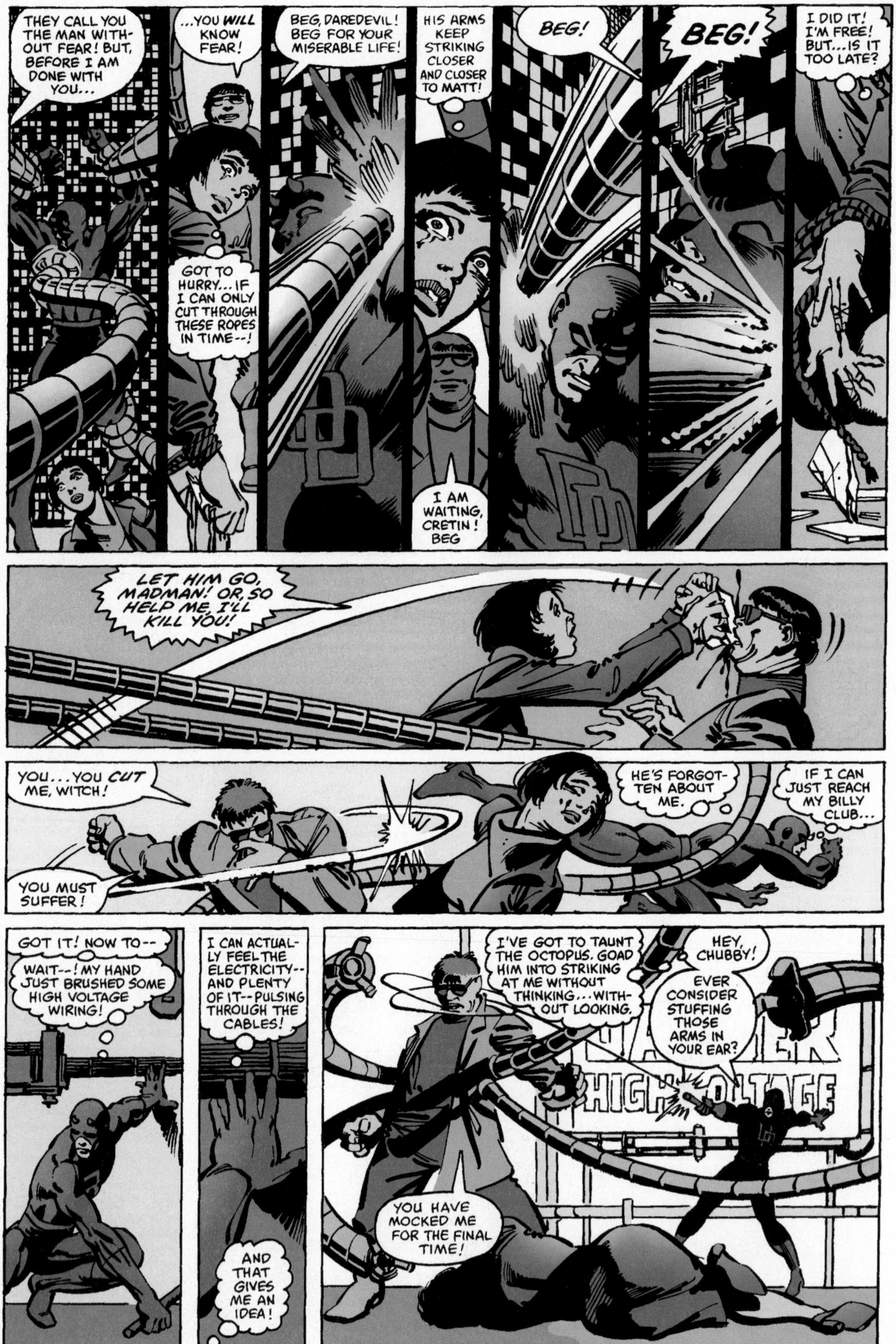
THEY CALL YOU THE MAN WITH-OUT FEAR! BUT, BEFORE I AM DONE WITH YOU...
...YOU WILL KNOW FEAR!
GOT TO HURRY... IF I CAN ONLY CUT THROUGH THESE ROPES IN TIME--!
BEG, DAREDEVIL! BEG FOR YOUR MISERABLE LIFE!
HIS ARMS KEEP STRIKING CLOSER AND CLOSER TO MATT!
I AM WAITING, CRETIN! BEG
BEG!
BEG!
I DID IT! I'M FREE! BUT... IS IT TOO LATE?
LET HIM GO, MADMAN! OR, SO HELP ME, I'LL KILL YOU!
YOU... YOU CUT ME, WITCH!
YOU MUST SUFFER!
HE'S FORGOT-TEN ABOUT ME.
IF I CAN JUST REACH MY BILLY CLUB...
GOT IT! NOW TO--
WAIT--! MY HAND JUST BRUSHED SOME HIGH VOLTAGE WIRING!
I CAN ACTUAL-LY FEEL THE ELECTRICITY-- AND PLENTY OF IT--PULSING THROUGH THE CABLES!
AND THAT GIVES ME AN IDEA!
I'VE GOT TO TAUNT THE OCTOPUS. GOAD HIM INTO STRIKING AT ME WITHOUT THINKING... WITH-OUT LOOKING.
HEY, CHUBBY!
EVER CONSIDER STUFFING THOSE ARMS IN YOUR EAR?
YOU HAVE MOCKED ME FOR THE FINAL TIME!

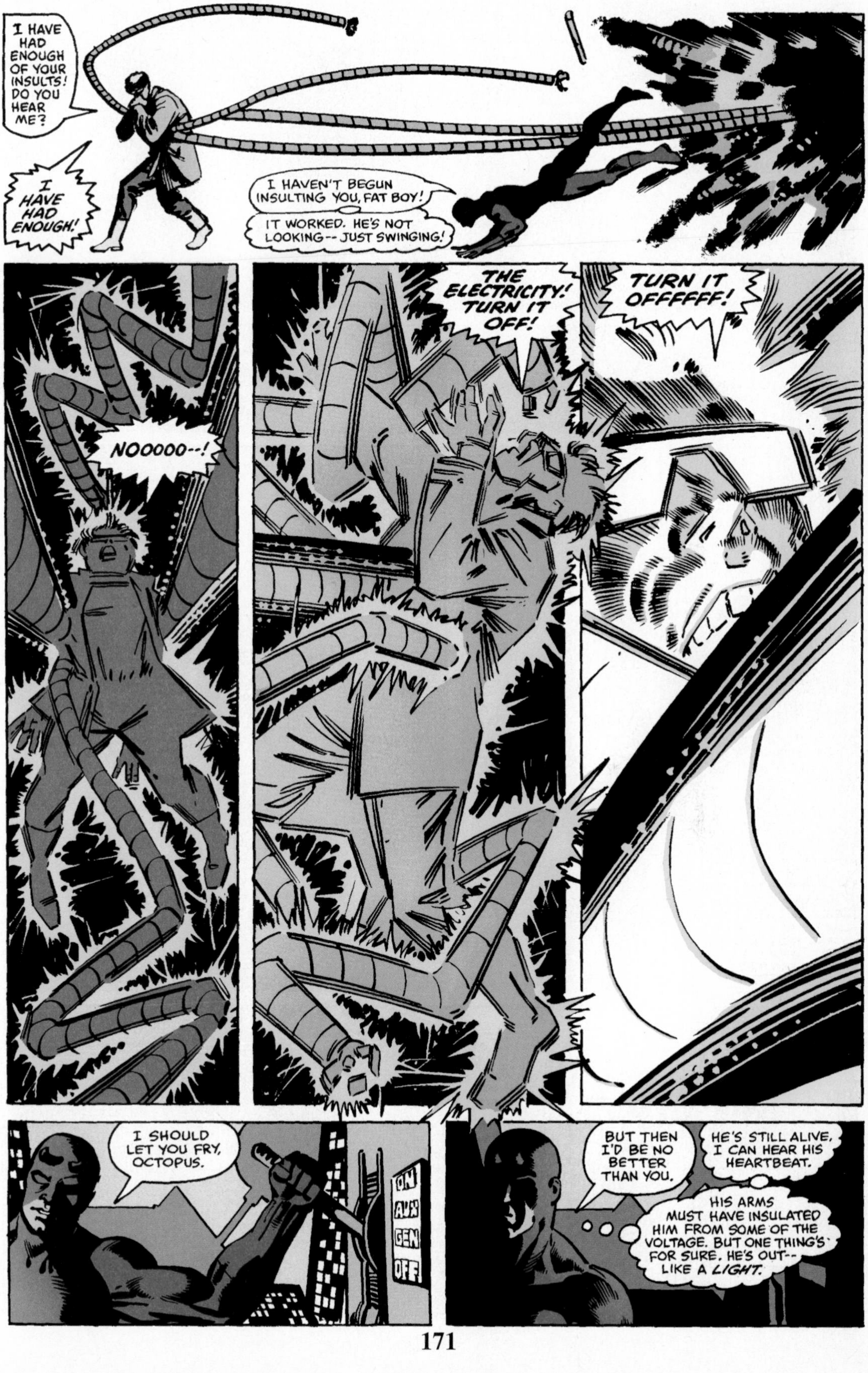
I HAVE HAD ENOUGH OF YOUR INSULTS! DO YOU HEAR ME?
I HAVE HAD ENOUGH!
I HAVEN'T BEGUN INSULTING YOU, FAT BOY!
IT WORKED. HE'S NOT LOOKING -- JUST SWINGING!
NOOOOO--!
THE ELECTRICITY! TURN IT OFF!
TURN IT OFFFFFF!
I SHOULD LET YOU FRY, OCTOPUS.
ON
AUX
GEN
OFF
BUT THEN I'D BE NO BETTER THAN YOU.
HE'S STILL ALIVE. I CAN HEAR HIS HEARTBEAT.
HIS ARMS MUST HAVE INSULATED HIM FROM SOME OF THE VOLTAGE. BUT ONE THING'S FOR SURE. HE'S OUT-- LIKE A LIGHT.

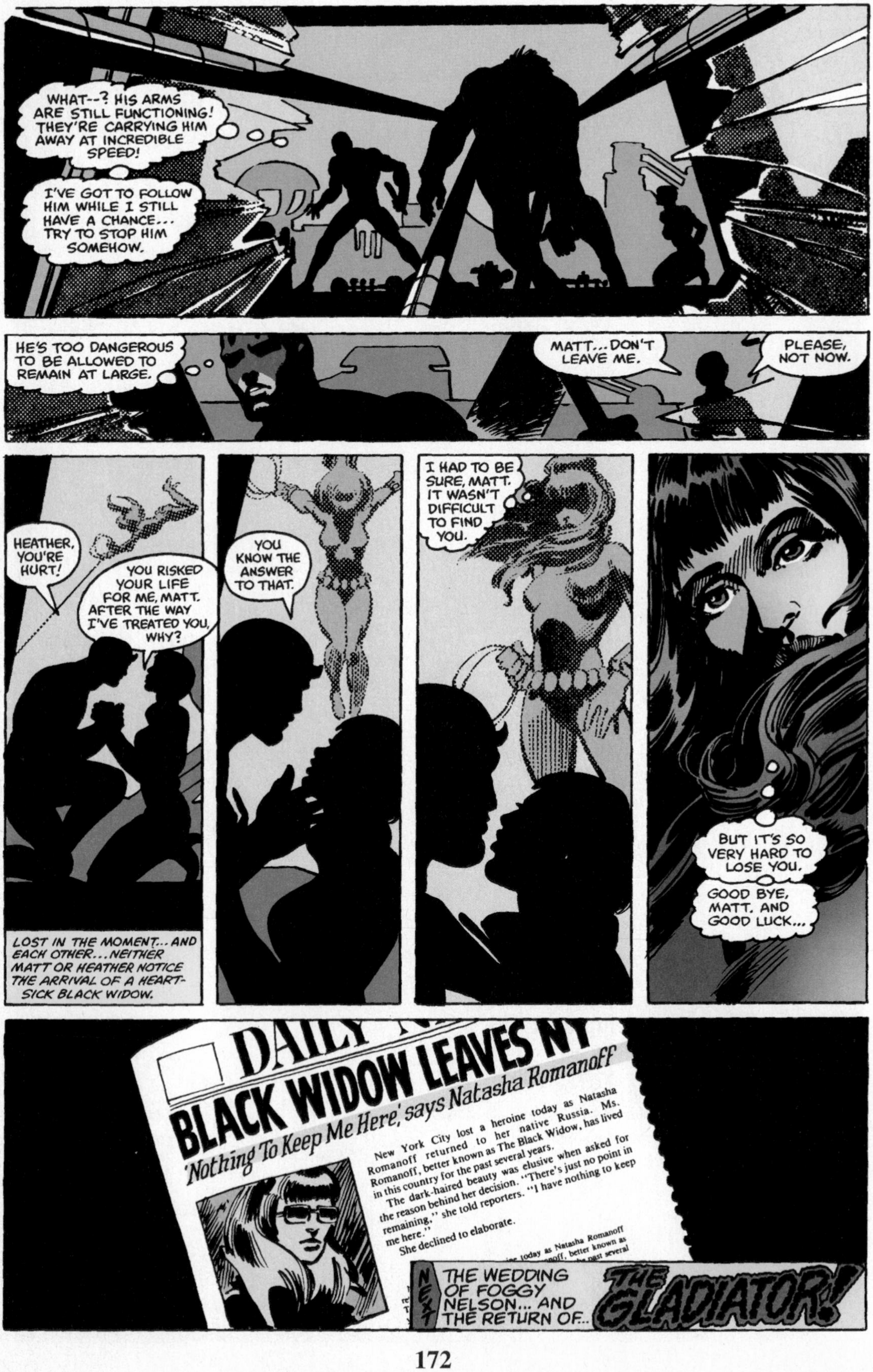
WHAT--? HIS ARMS ARE STILL FUNCTIONING! THEY'RE CARRYING HIM AWAY AT INCREDIBLE SPEED!
I'VE GOT TO FOLLOW HIM WHILE I STILL HAVE A CHANCE... TRY TO STOP HIM SOMEHOW.
HE'S TOO DANGEROUS TO BE ALLOWED TO REMAIN AT LARGE.
MATT... DON'T LEAVE ME.
PLEASE, NOT NOW.
HEATHER, YOU'RE HURT!
YOU RISKED YOUR LIFE FOR ME, MATT. AFTER THE WAY I'VE TREATED YOU, WHY?
LOST IN THE MOMENT... AND EACH OTHER... NEITHER MATT OR HEATHER NOTICE THE ARRIVAL OF A HEART-SICK BLACK WIDOW.
YOU KNOW THE ANSWER TO THAT.
I HAD TO BE SURE, MATT. IT WASN'T DIFFICULT TO FIND YOU.
BUT IT'S SO VERY HARD TO LOSE YOU.
GOOD BYE, MATT. AND GOOD LUCK...
DAILY
BLACK WIDOW LEAVES NY
'Nothing To Keep Me Here,' says Natasha Romanoff
New York City lost a heroine today as Natasha Romanoff returned to her native Russia. Ms. Romanoff, better known as The Black Widow, has lived in this country for the past several years.
The dark-haired beauty was elusive when asked for the reason behind her decision. "There's just no point in remaining," she told reporters. "I have nothing to keep me here."
She declined to elaborate.
NEXT
THE WEDDING OF FOGGY NELSON... AND THE RETURN OF... THE GLADIATOR!

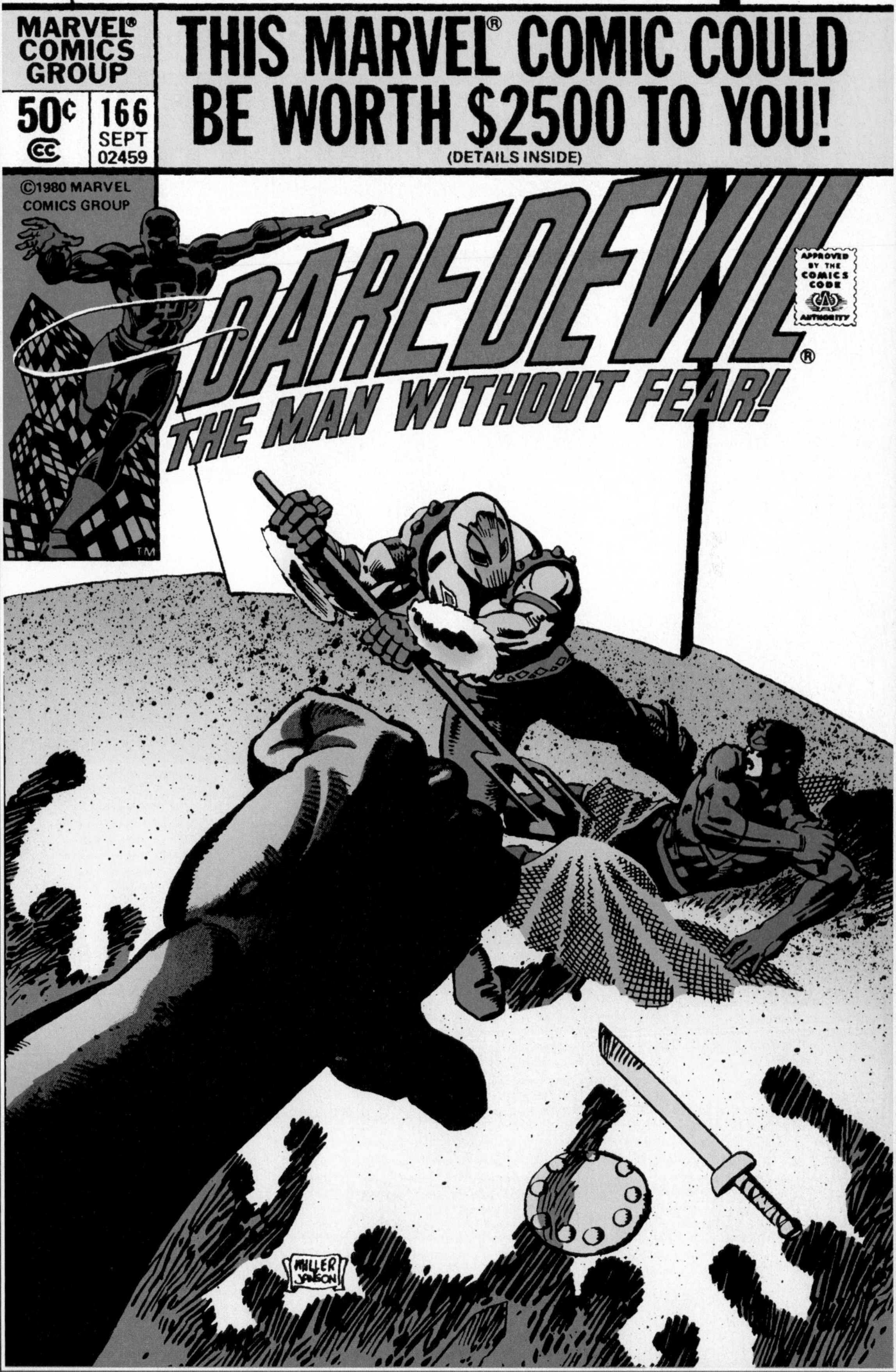
MARVEL® COMICS GROUP
50¢
166
SEPT
02459
THIS MARVEL® COMIC COULD BE WORTH $2500 TO YOU!
(DETAILS INSIDE)
©1980 MARVEL COMICS GROUP
DAREDEVIL®
THE MAN WITHOUT FEAR!
APPROVED BY THE COMICS CODE AUTHORITY
MILLER JANSON

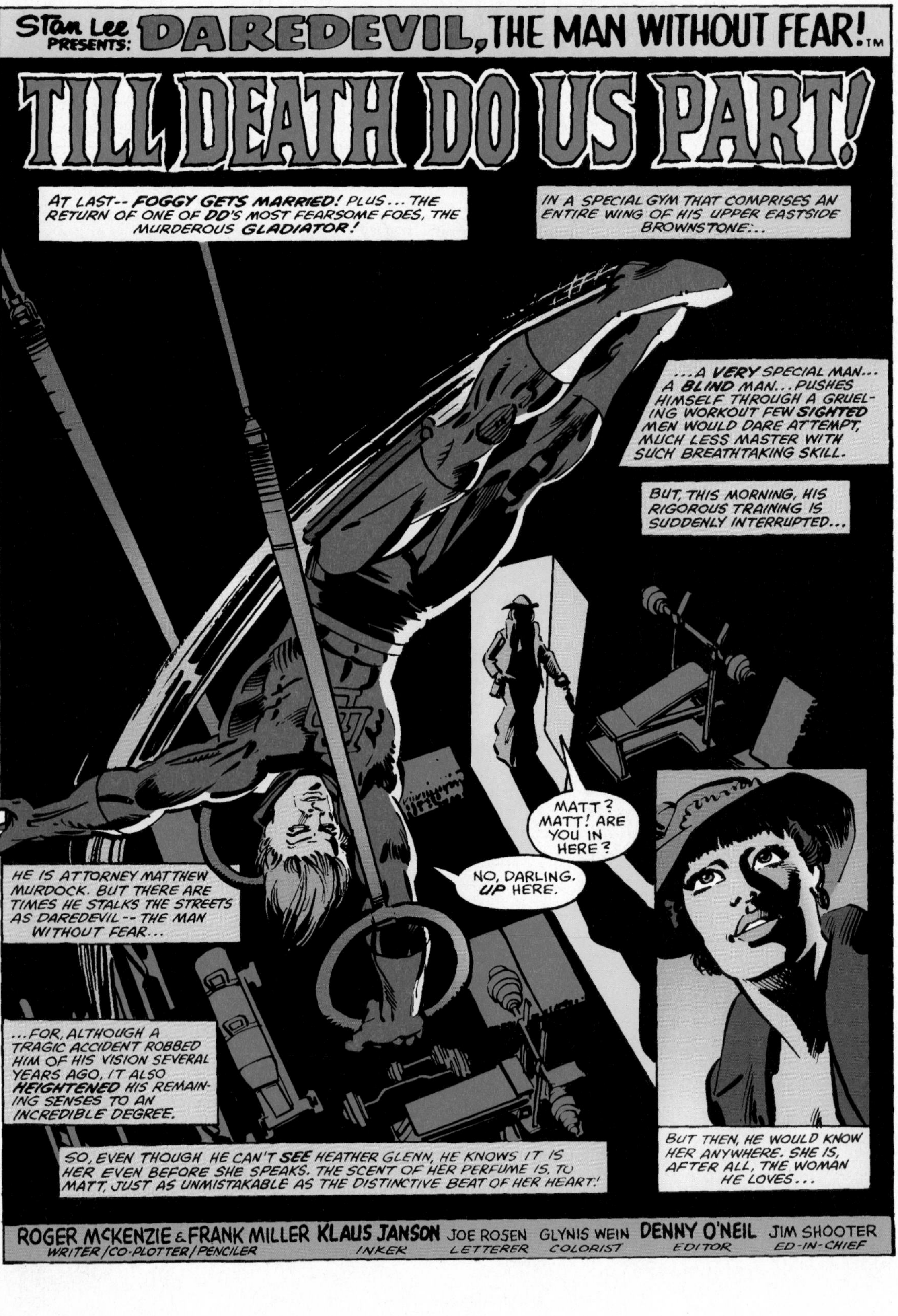

Stan Lee PRESENTS: DAREDEVIL, THE MAN WITHOUT FEAR! TM
TILL DEATH DO US PART!
AT LAST-- FOGGY GETS MARRIED! PLUS... THE RETURN OF ONE OF DD'S MOST FEARSOME FOES, THE MURDEROUS GLADIATOR!
IN A SPECIAL GYM THAT COMPRISES AN ENTIRE WING OF HIS UPPER EASTSIDE BROWNSTONE...
...A VERY SPECIAL MAN... A BLIND MAN... PUSHES HIMSELF THROUGH A GRUELING WORKOUT FEW SIGHTED MEN WOULD DARE ATTEMPT, MUCH LESS MASTER WITH SUCH BREATHTAKING SKILL.
BUT, THIS MORNING, HIS RIGOROUS TRAINING IS SUDDENLY INTERRUPTED...
MATT? MATT! ARE YOU IN HERE?
NO, DARLING. UP HERE.
HE IS ATTORNEY MATTHEW MURDOCK. BUT THERE ARE TIMES HE STALKS THE STREETS AS DAREDEVIL -- THE MAN WITHOUT FEAR...
...FOR, ALTHOUGH A TRAGIC ACCIDENT ROBBED HIM OF HIS VISION SEVERAL YEARS AGO, IT ALSO HEIGHTENED HIS REMAINING SENSES TO AN INCREDIBLE DEGREE.
SO, EVEN THOUGH HE CAN'T SEE HEATHER GLENN, HE KNOWS IT IS HER EVEN BEFORE SHE SPEAKS. THE SCENT OF HER PERFUME IS, TO MATT, JUST AS UNMISTAKABLE AS THE DISTINCTIVE BEAT OF HER HEART!
BUT THEN, HE WOULD KNOW HER ANYWHERE. SHE IS, AFTER ALL, THE WOMAN HE LOVES...
ROGER McKENZIE & FRANK MILLER WRITER/CO-PLOTTER/PENCILER
KLAUS JANSON INKER
JOE ROSEN LETTERER
GLYNIS WEIN COLORIST
DENNY O'NEIL EDITOR
JIM SHOOTER ED-IN-CHIEF

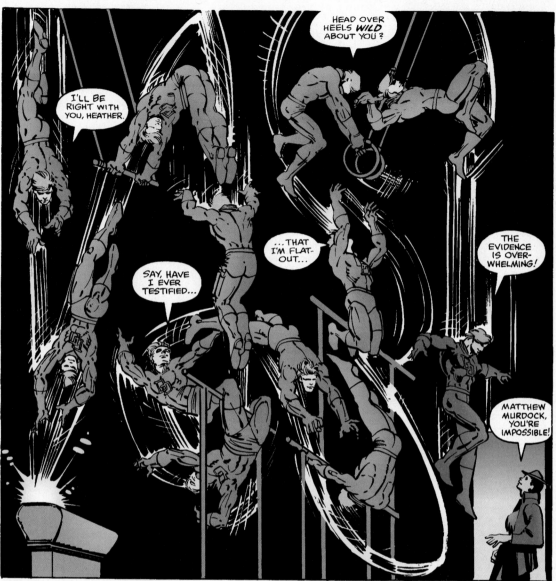

HEAD OVER HEELS *WILD* ABOUT YOU?

I'LL BE RIGHT WITH YOU, HEATHER.

...THAT I'M FLAT-OUT...

SAY, HAVE I EVER TESTIFIED...

THE EVIDENCE IS OVERWHELMING!

MATTHEW MURDOCK, YOU'RE IMPOSSIBLE!

NOLO CONTENDRE, M'LADY! I'M AFRAID I'VE NO CHOICE BUT TO THROW MYSELF TO THE MERCY OF THE COURT!

YOUR WISH IS MY COMMAND!

WELL, IN *THAT* CASE, M'LORD...

...I WISH YOU'D GET *OUT* OF THAT SMELLY COSTUME AND *INTO* YOUR TUX!

BUT...BUT...

WE'RE RUNNING *LATE* AS IT IS, COUNSELLOR --

--OR HAVE YOU *FORGOTTEN* YOUR BEST FRIEND'S GETTING MARRIED TODAY?

THEN, IMPATIENTLY, HEATHER PULLS A RELUCTANT MATT MURDOCK FROM HIS TRAINING...

175

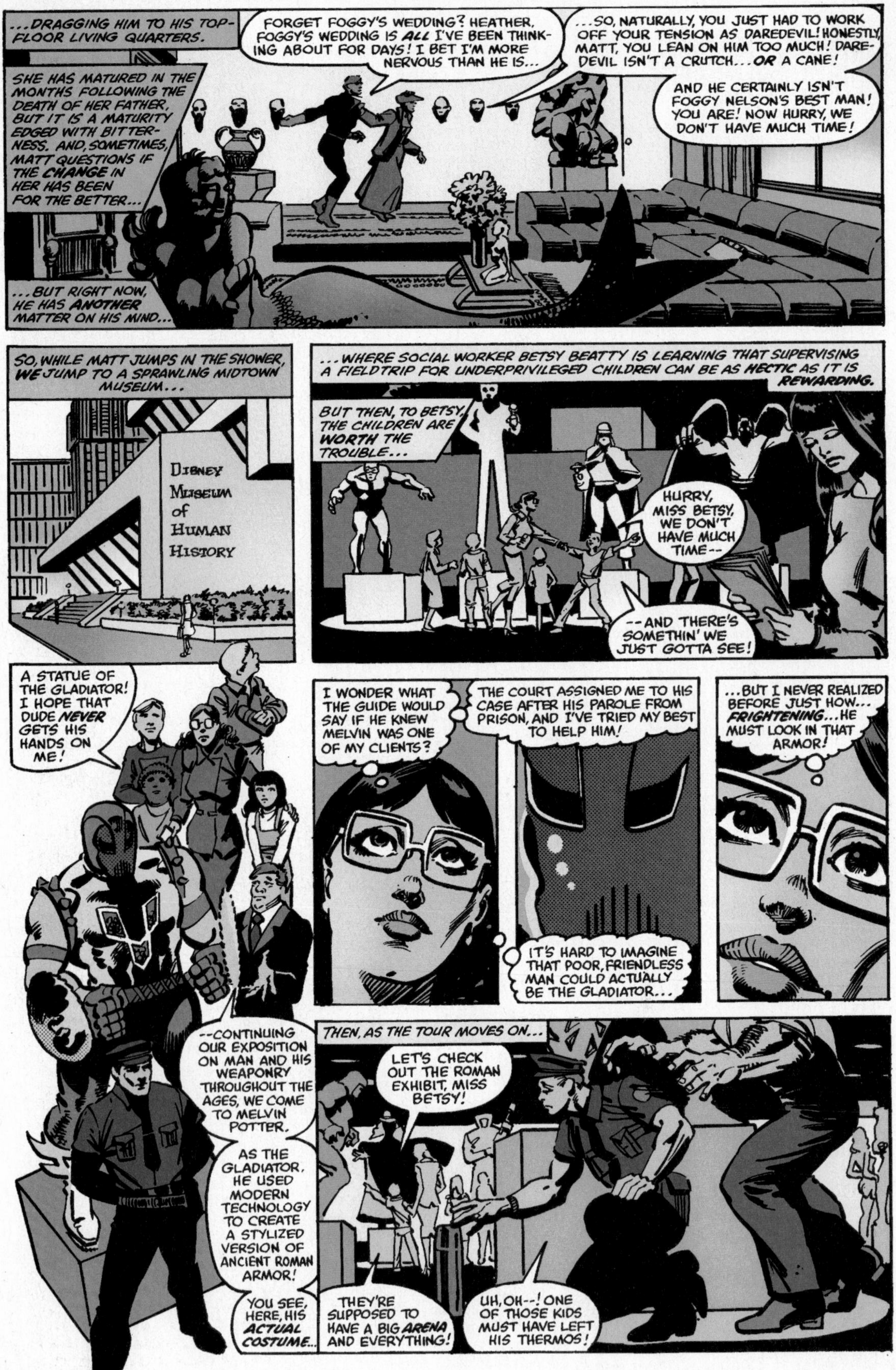
...DRAGGING HIM TO HIS TOP-FLOOR LIVING QUARTERS.
SHE HAS MATURED IN THE MONTHS FOLLOWING THE DEATH OF HER FATHER, BUT IT IS A MATURITY EDGED WITH BITTERNESS. AND, SOMETIMES, MATT QUESTIONS IF THE CHANGE IN HER HAS BEEN FOR THE BETTER...
FORGET FOGGY'S WEDDING? HEATHER, FOGGY'S WEDDING IS ALL I'VE BEEN THINKING ABOUT FOR DAYS! I BET I'M MORE NERVOUS THAN HE IS...
...SO, NATURALLY, YOU JUST HAD TO WORK OFF YOUR TENSION AS DAREDEVIL! HONESTLY, MATT, YOU LEAN ON HIM TOO MUCH! DAREDEVIL ISN'T A CRUTCH... OR A CANE!
AND HE CERTAINLY ISN'T FOGGY NELSON'S BEST MAN! YOU ARE! NOW HURRY, WE DON'T HAVE MUCH TIME!
...BUT RIGHT NOW, HE HAS ANOTHER MATTER ON HIS MIND...
SO, WHILE MATT JUMPS IN THE SHOWER, WE JUMP TO A SPRAWLING MIDTOWN MUSEUM...
DISNEY MUSEUM of HUMAN HISTORY
...WHERE SOCIAL WORKER BETSY BEATTY IS LEARNING THAT SUPERVISING A FIELDTRIP FOR UNDERPRIVILEGED CHILDREN CAN BE AS HECTIC AS IT IS REWARDING.
BUT THEN, TO BETSY, THE CHILDREN ARE WORTH THE TROUBLE...
HURRY, MISS BETSY, WE DON'T HAVE MUCH TIME--
--AND THERE'S SOMETHIN' WE JUST GOTTA SEE!
A STATUE OF THE GLADIATOR! I HOPE THAT DUDE NEVER GETS HIS HANDS ON ME!
I WONDER WHAT THE GUIDE WOULD SAY IF HE KNEW MELVIN WAS ONE OF MY CLIENTS?
THE COURT ASSIGNED ME TO HIS CASE AFTER HIS PAROLE FROM PRISON, AND I'VE TRIED MY BEST TO HELP HIM!
IT'S HARD TO IMAGINE THAT POOR, FRIENDLESS MAN COULD ACTUALLY BE THE GLADIATOR...
...BUT I NEVER REALIZED BEFORE JUST HOW... FRIGHTENING... HE MUST LOOK IN THAT ARMOR!
--CONTINUING OUR EXPOSITION ON MAN AND HIS WEAPONRY THROUGHOUT THE AGES, WE COME TO MELVIN POTTER.
AS THE GLADIATOR, HE USED MODERN TECHNOLOGY TO CREATE A STYLIZED VERSION OF ANCIENT ROMAN ARMOR!
YOU SEE, HERE, HIS ACTUAL COSTUME...
THEN, AS THE TOUR MOVES ON...
LET'S CHECK OUT THE ROMAN EXHIBIT, MISS BETSY!
THEY'RE SUPPOSED TO HAVE A BIG ARENA AND EVERYTHING!
UH, OH--! ONE OF THOSE KIDS MUST HAVE LEFT HIS THERMOS!

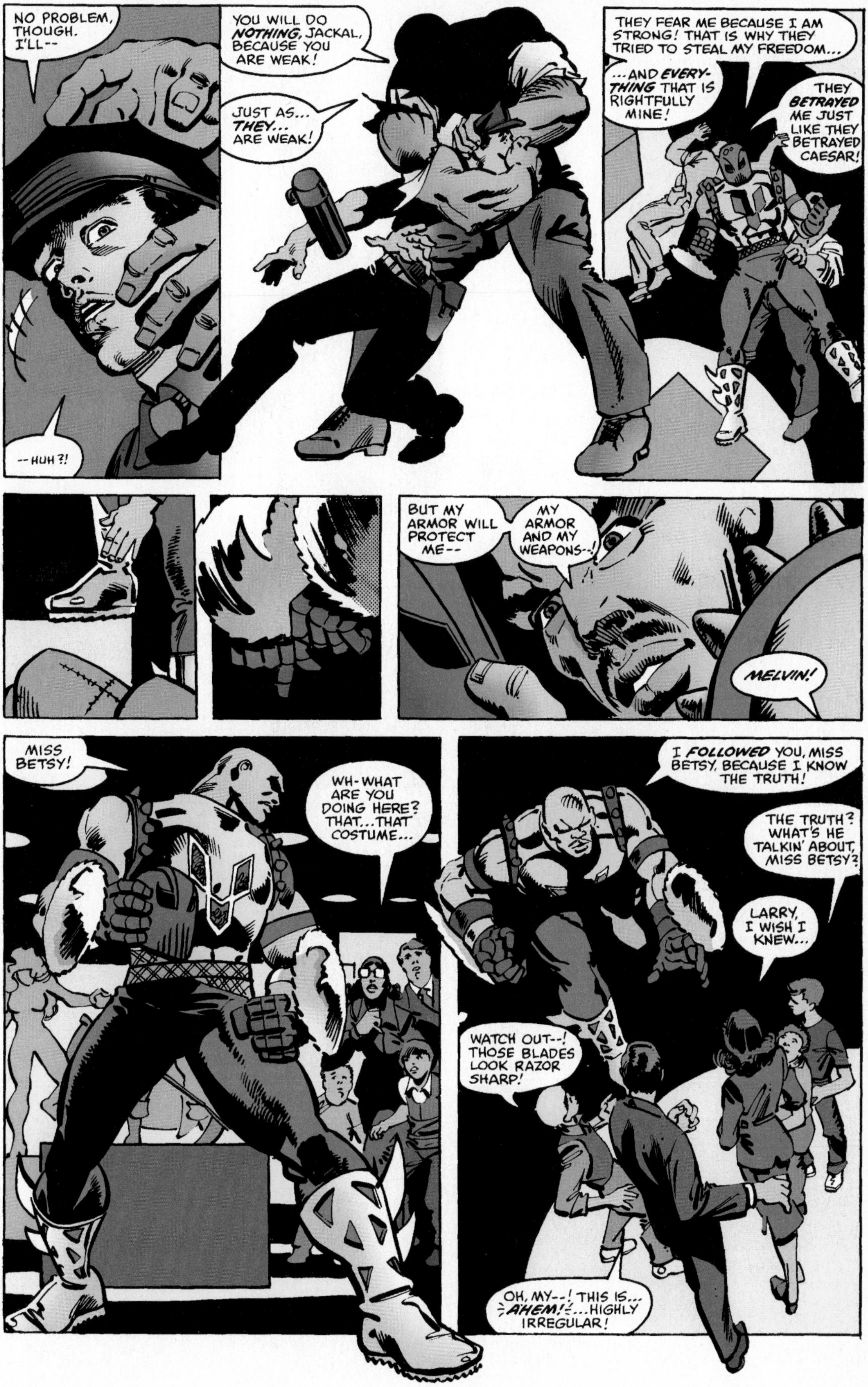

NO PROBLEM, THOUGH. I'LL--
--HUH?!
YOU WILL DO NOTHING, JACKAL, BECAUSE YOU ARE WEAK!
JUST AS... THEY... ARE WEAK!
THEY FEAR ME BECAUSE I AM STRONG! THAT IS WHY THEY TRIED TO STEAL MY FREEDOM...
...AND EVERYTHING THAT IS RIGHTFULLY MINE!
THEY BETRAYED ME JUST LIKE THEY BETRAYED CAESAR!
BUT MY ARMOR WILL PROTECT ME--
MY ARMOR AND MY WEAPONS--!
MELVIN!
MISS BETSY!
WH-WHAT ARE YOU DOING HERE? THAT...THAT COSTUME...
I FOLLOWED YOU, MISS BETSY, BECAUSE I KNOW THE TRUTH!
THE TRUTH? WHAT'S HE TALKIN' ABOUT, MISS BETSY?
LARRY, I WISH I KNEW...
WATCH OUT--! THOSE BLADES LOOK RAZOR SHARP!
OH, MY--! THIS IS... AHEM!... HIGHLY IRREGULAR!

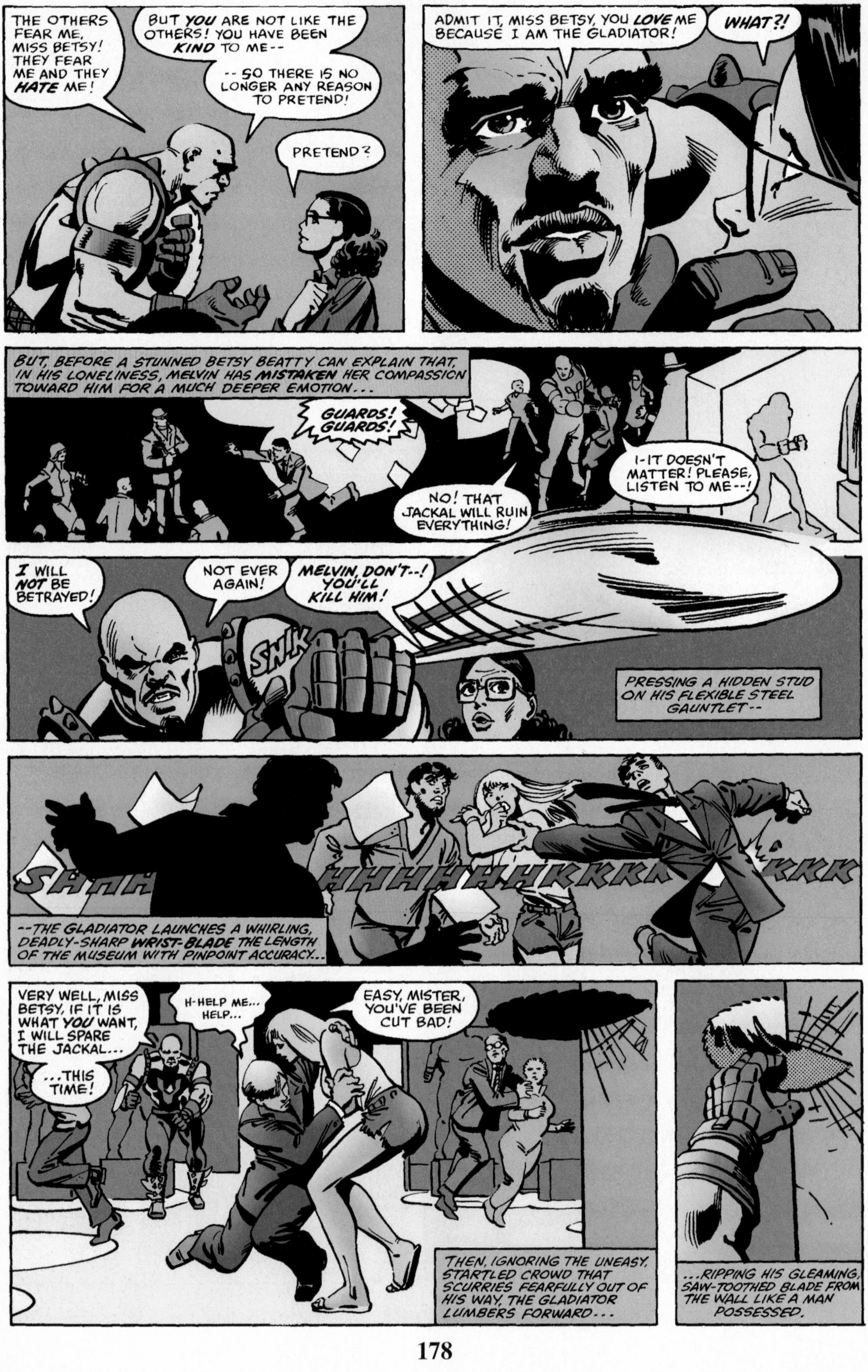
THE OTHERS FEAR ME, MISS BETSY! THEY FEAR ME AND THEY HATE ME!
BUT YOU ARE NOT LIKE THE OTHERS! YOU HAVE BEEN KIND TO ME--
-- SO THERE IS NO LONGER ANY REASON TO PRETEND!
PRETEND?
ADMIT IT, MISS BETSY, YOU LOVE ME BECAUSE I AM THE GLADIATOR!
WHAT?!
BUT, BEFORE A STUNNED BETSY BEATTY CAN EXPLAIN THAT, IN HIS LONELINESS, MELVIN HAS MISTAKEN HER COMPASSION TOWARD HIM FOR A MUCH DEEPER EMOTION...
GUARDS! GUARDS!
I-IT DOESN'T MATTER! PLEASE, LISTEN TO ME--!
NO! THAT JACKAL WILL RUIN EVERYTHING!
I WILL NOT BE BETRAYED!
NOT EVER AGAIN!
MELVIN, DON'T--! YOU'LL KILL HIM!
SNIK
PRESSING A HIDDEN STUD ON HIS FLEXIBLE STEEL GAUNTLET--
SHHHHHHHHHKKKKKKK
--THE GLADIATOR LAUNCHES A WHIRLING, DEADLY-SHARP WRIST-BLADE THE LENGTH OF THE MUSEUM WITH PINPOINT ACCURACY...
VERY WELL, MISS BETSY, IF IT IS WHAT YOU WANT, I WILL SPARE THE JACKAL...
...THIS TIME!
H-HELP ME... HELP...
EASY, MISTER, YOU'VE BEEN CUT BAD!
THEN, IGNORING THE UNEASY, STARTLED CROWD THAT SCURRIES FEARFULLY OUT OF HIS WAY, THE GLADIATOR LUMBERS FORWARD...
...RIPPING HIS GLEAMING, SAW-TOOTHED BLADE FROM THE WALL LIKE A MAN POSSESSED.

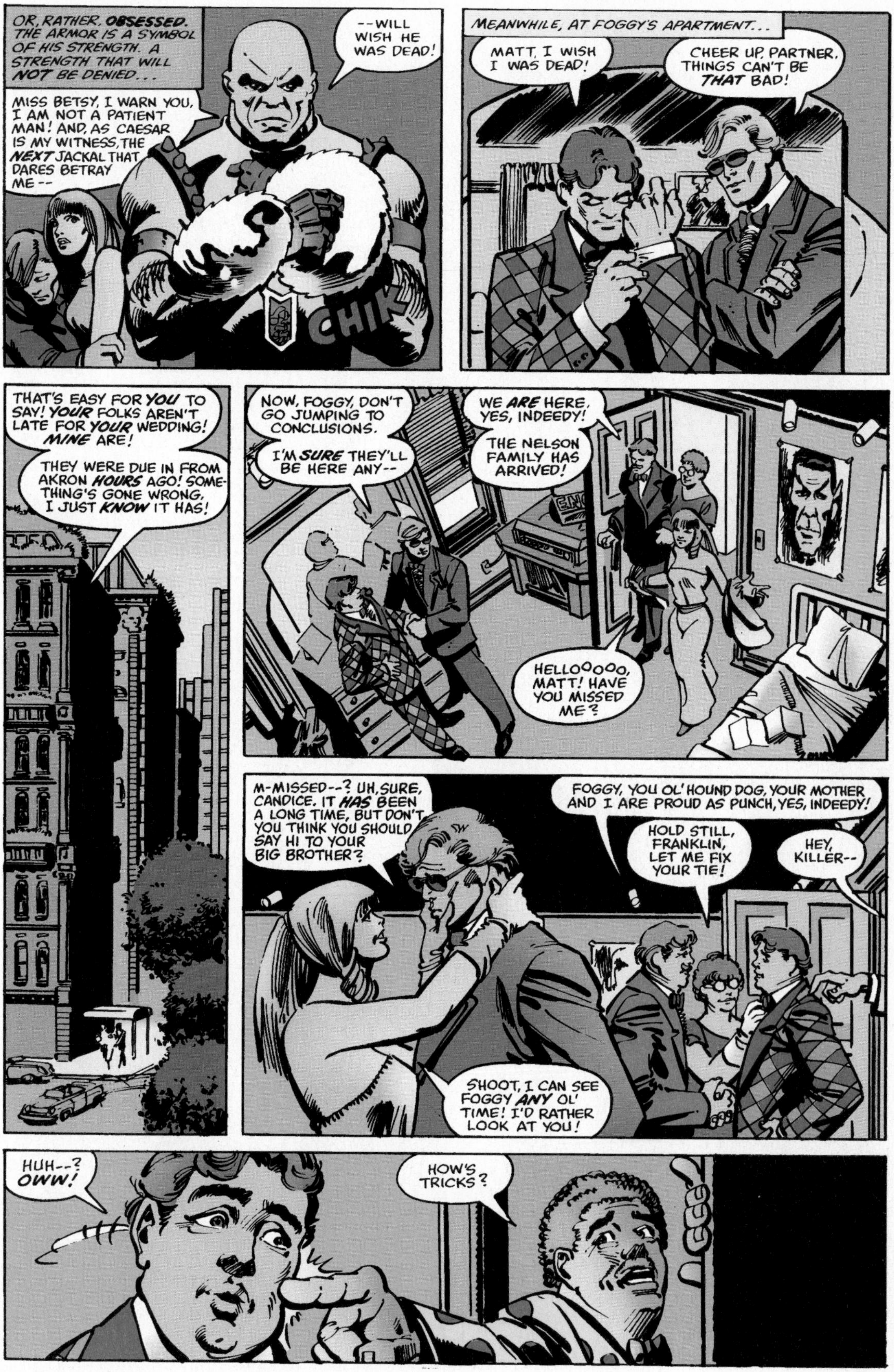
OR, RATHER, OBSESSED. THE ARMOR IS A SYMBOL OF HIS STRENGTH. A STRENGTH THAT WILL NOT BE DENIED...
MISS BETSY, I WARN YOU, I AM NOT A PATIENT MAN! AND, AS CAESAR IS MY WITNESS, THE NEXT JACKAL THAT DARES BETRAY ME--
--WILL WISH HE WAS DEAD!
CHIK
MEANWHILE, AT FOGGY'S APARTMENT...
MATT, I WISH I WAS DEAD!
CHEER UP, PARTNER, THINGS CAN'T BE THAT BAD!
THAT'S EASY FOR YOU TO SAY! YOUR FOLKS AREN'T LATE FOR YOUR WEDDING! MINE ARE!
THEY WERE DUE IN FROM AKRON HOURS AGO! SOMETHING'S GONE WRONG, I JUST KNOW IT HAS!
NOW, FOGGY, DON'T GO JUMPING TO CONCLUSIONS.
I'M SURE THEY'LL BE HERE ANY--
WE ARE HERE, YES, INDEEDY!
THE NELSON FAMILY HAS ARRIVED!
HELLOOOOO, MATT! HAVE YOU MISSED ME?
M-MISSED--? UH, SURE, CANDICE. IT HAS BEEN A LONG TIME, BUT DON'T YOU THINK YOU SHOULD SAY HI TO YOUR BIG BROTHER?
SHOOT, I CAN SEE FOGGY ANY OL' TIME! I'D RATHER LOOK AT YOU!
FOGGY, YOU OL' HOUND DOG, YOUR MOTHER AND I ARE PROUD AS PUNCH, YES, INDEEDY!
HOLD STILL, FRANKLIN, LET ME FIX YOUR TIE!
HEY, KILLER--
HUH--? OWW!
HOW'S TRICKS?

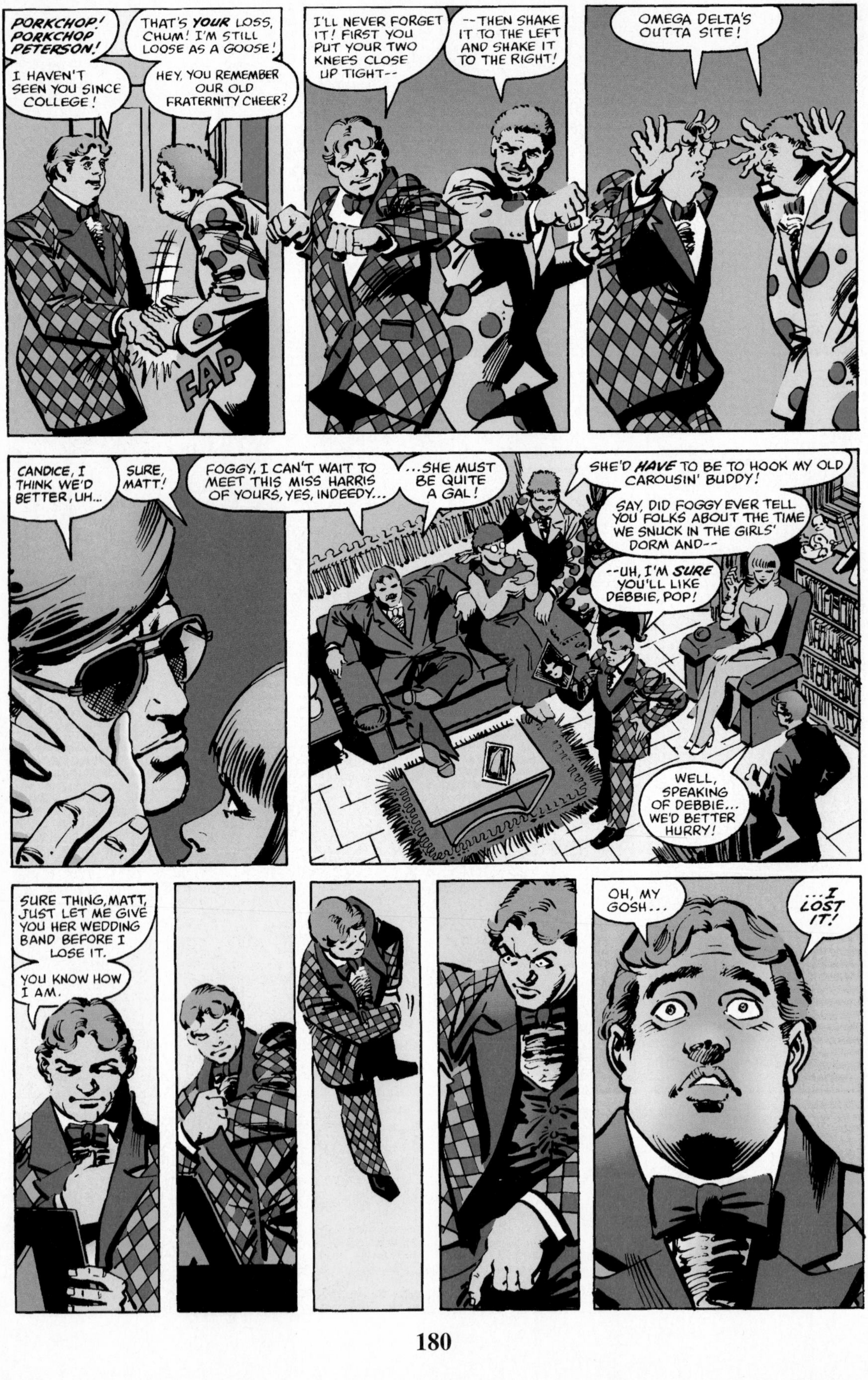
PORKCHOP! PORKCHOP PETERSON!
I HAVEN'T SEEN YOU SINCE COLLEGE!
THAT'S YOUR LOSS, CHUM! I'M STILL LOOSE AS A GOOSE!
HEY, YOU REMEMBER OUR OLD FRATERNITY CHEER?
FAP
I'LL NEVER FORGET IT! FIRST YOU PUT YOUR TWO KNEES CLOSE UP TIGHT--
--THEN SHAKE IT TO THE LEFT AND SHAKE IT TO THE RIGHT!
OMEGA DELTA'S OUTTA SITE!
CANDICE, I THINK WE'D BETTER, UH...
SURE, MATT!
FOGGY, I CAN'T WAIT TO MEET THIS MISS HARRIS OF YOURS, YES, INDEEDY...
...SHE MUST BE QUITE A GAL!
SHE'D HAVE TO BE TO HOOK MY OLD CAROUSIN' BUDDY!
SAY, DID FOGGY EVER TELL YOU FOLKS ABOUT THE TIME WE SNUCK IN THE GIRLS' DORM AND--
--UH, I'M SURE YOU'LL LIKE DEBBIE, POP!
WELL, SPEAKING OF DEBBIE... WE'D BETTER HURRY!
SURE THING, MATT, JUST LET ME GIVE YOU HER WEDDING BAND BEFORE I LOSE IT.
YOU KNOW HOW I AM.
OH, MY GOSH...
...I LOST IT!

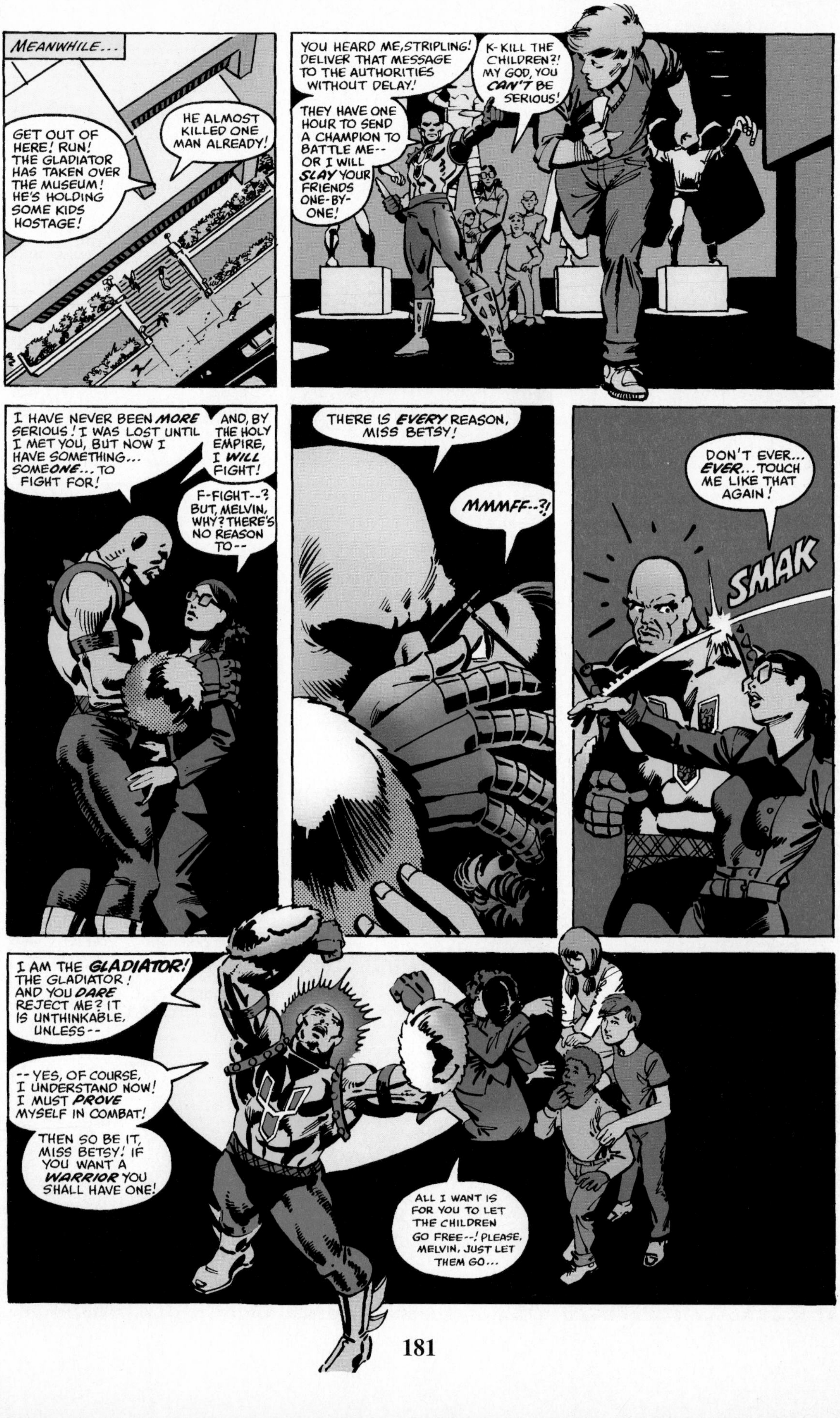
MEANWHILE...
GET OUT OF HERE! RUN! THE GLADIATOR HAS TAKEN OVER THE MUSEUM! HE'S HOLDING SOME KIDS HOSTAGE!
HE ALMOST KILLED ONE MAN ALREADY!
YOU HEARD ME, STRIPLING! DELIVER THAT MESSAGE TO THE AUTHORITIES WITHOUT DELAY!
THEY HAVE ONE HOUR TO SEND A CHAMPION TO BATTLE ME-- OR I WILL SLAY YOUR FRIENDS ONE-BY-ONE!
K-KILL THE CHILDREN?! MY GOD, YOU CAN'T BE SERIOUS!
I HAVE NEVER BEEN MORE SERIOUS! I WAS LOST UNTIL I MET YOU, BUT NOW I HAVE SOMETHING... SOMEONE... TO FIGHT FOR!
AND, BY THE HOLY EMPIRE, I WILL FIGHT!
F-FIGHT--? BUT, MELVIN, WHY? THERE'S NO REASON TO--
THERE IS EVERY REASON, MISS BETSY!
MMMFF--?!
DON'T EVER... EVER... TOUCH ME LIKE THAT AGAIN!
SMAK
I AM THE GLADIATOR! THE GLADIATOR! AND YOU DARE REJECT ME? IT IS UNTHINKABLE, UNLESS--
--YES, OF COURSE, I UNDERSTAND NOW! I MUST PROVE MYSELF IN COMBAT!
THEN SO BE IT, MISS BETSY! IF YOU WANT A WARRIOR YOU SHALL HAVE ONE!
ALL I WANT IS FOR YOU TO LET THE CHILDREN GO FREE--! PLEASE, MELVIN, JUST LET THEM GO...

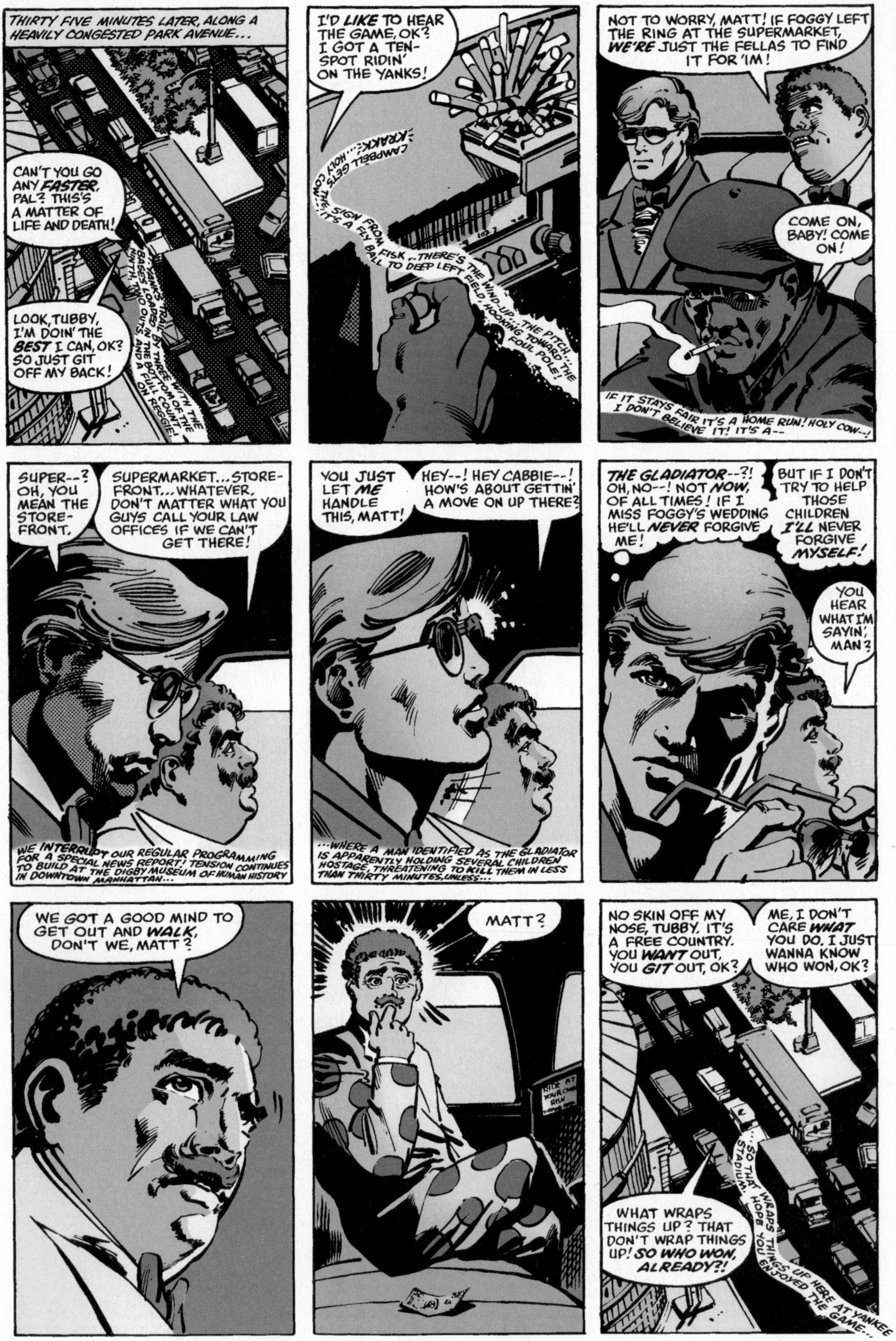
THIRTY FIVE MINUTES LATER, ALONG A HEAVILY CONGESTED PARK AVENUE...
CAN'T YOU GO ANY FASTER, PAL? THIS'S A MATTER OF LIFE AND DEATH!
...YANKS TRAIL BY THREE WITH THE BASES LOADED IN THE BOTTOM OF THE NINTH, TWO OUTS, AND A FULL COUNT ON REGGIE!
LOOK, TUBBY, I'M DOIN' THE BEST I CAN, OK? SO JUST GIT OFF MY BACK!
I'D LIKE TO HEAR THE GAME, OK? I GOT A TEN-SPOT RIDIN' ON THE YANKS!
CAMPBELL GETS THE SIGN FROM FISK...THERE'S THE WIND-UP...THE PITCH...THE
KRAKK!... HOLY COW--! IT'S A FLY BALL TO DEEP LEFT FIELD, HOOKING TOWARD THE FOUL POLE!
NOT TO WORRY, MATT! IF FOGGY LEFT THE RING AT THE SUPERMARKET, WE'RE JUST THE FELLAS TO FIND IT FOR 'IM!
COME ON, BABY! COME ON!
IF IT STAYS FAIR IT'S A HOME RUN! HOLY COW--! I DON'T BELIEVE IT! IT'S A--
SUPER--? OH, YOU MEAN THE STORE-FRONT.
SUPERMARKET...STORE-FRONT...WHATEVER. DON'T MATTER WHAT YOU GUYS CALL YOUR LAW OFFICES IF WE CAN'T GET THERE!
WE INTERRUPT OUR REGULAR PROGRAMMING FOR A SPECIAL NEWS REPORT! TENSION CONTINUES TO BUILD AT THE DIGBY MUSEUM OF HUMAN HISTORY IN DOWNTOWN MANHATTAN...
YOU JUST LET ME HANDLE THIS, MATT!
HEY--! HEY CABBIE--! HOW'S ABOUT GETTIN' A MOVE ON UP THERE?
...WHERE A MAN IDENTIFIED AS THE GLADIATOR IS APPARENTLY HOLDING SEVERAL CHILDREN HOSTAGE, THREATENING TO KILL THEM IN LESS THAN THIRTY MINUTES, UNLESS...
THE GLADIATOR--?! OH, NO--! NOT NOW, OF ALL TIMES! IF I MISS FOGGY'S WEDDING HE'LL NEVER FORGIVE ME!
BUT IF I DON'T TRY TO HELP THOSE CHILDREN I'LL NEVER FORGIVE MYSELF!
YOU HEAR WHAT I'M SAYIN', MAN?
WE GOT A GOOD MIND TO GET OUT AND WALK, DON'T WE, MATT?
MATT?
RIDE AT YOUR OWN RISK
NO SKIN OFF MY NOSE, TUBBY. IT'S A FREE COUNTRY. YOU WANT OUT, YOU GIT OUT, OK?
ME, I DON'T CARE WHAT YOU DO. I JUST WANNA KNOW WHO WON, OK?
...SO THAT WRAPS THINGS UP HERE AT YANKEE STADIUM. HOPE YOU ENJOYED THE GAME...
WHAT WRAPS THINGS UP? THAT DON'T WRAP THINGS UP! SO WHO WON, ALREADY?!

SOME TWENTY MINUTES LATER, A GRIM AND SIGHTLESS *DEVIL* PAUSES IN THE SHADOWS SURROUNDING THE BESIEGED MUSEUM.

BUT, IF HE FEELS THE GROWING *RESTLESSNESS* OF THE CROWD ALREADY GATHERED SO VERY FAR BELOW HIM--AN UNEASY, MILLING THRONG HE CAN ONLY *SENSE*, RATHER THAN SEE--

--HE DOESN'T LET IT SHOW AS HE SEEMS TO GLIDE ALMOST *EFFORTLESSLY* ACROSS THE CITY'S DARKENING SKYLINE.

AND THEN, USING HIS CANE-- A CANE HE DESIGNED TO DOUBLE AS AN ALL-PURPOSE BILLY CLUB--

--HE SWINGS QUICKLY TO THE ROOFTOP OF THE SLEEK CONCRETE AND STEEL GALLERY THAT HAS BECOME A CHAMBER OF FEAR FOR BETSY BEATTY AND THE CHILDREN HELD CAPTIVE WITHIN.

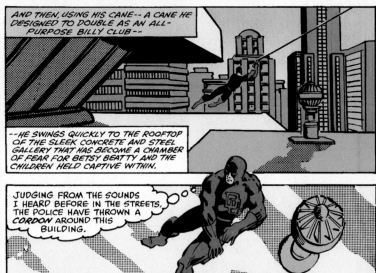

JUDGING FROM THE SOUNDS I HEARD BEFORE IN THE STREETS, THE POLICE HAVE THROWN A *CORDON* AROUND THIS BUILDING.

BUT IT'S A STAND-OFF, AT BEST. THEY CAN'T ATTACK THE GLADIATOR WITHOUT JEOPARDIZING THE LIVES OF THE KIDS.

IF ANYTHING'S TO BE DONE, *I'LL* HAVE TO BE THE ONE TO DO IT.

AND SOON.

I CAN PINPOINT THE GLADIATOR'S EXACT POSITION THANKS TO MY SUPER-SENSITIVE HEARING AND RADAR-SENSE, BUT THAT'S THE *LEAST* OF MY PROBLEMS.

SOMEHOW I'VE GOT TO LURE HIM *AWAY* FROM THE KIDS TO GIVE THEM A CHANCE TO ESCAPE.

THE HOUR HAS PASSED! THEY HAVE SENT NO CHAMPION!

HOW CAN I WIN YOUR HEART, MISS BETSY, IF THEY WILL NOT LET ME *FIGHT* FOR IT?

THEY DENY ME EVERYTHING, MISS BETSY! THEY WILL NOT DENY ME YOU AS WELL!

THE DEATHS OF THE STRIPLINGS ARE ON *THEIR* HANDS, NOW!

MELVIN, *PLEASE,* I-- I'LL DO WHATEVER YOU SAY! JUST DON'T HARM THE CHILDREN!

THEN, THE NEXT INSTANT...

YOU HEARD THE LADY!

WHO'S THAT?

AN OLD FOE!

I KNOW HIS VOICE!

IT IS THE VOICE OF A DEVIL!

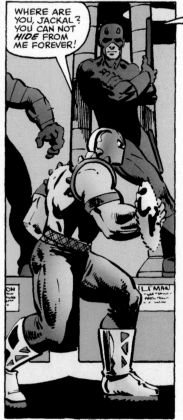

WHERE ARE YOU, JACKAL? YOU CAN NOT *HIDE* FROM ME FOREVER!

WHO'S HIDING?

ZZZRRR

184

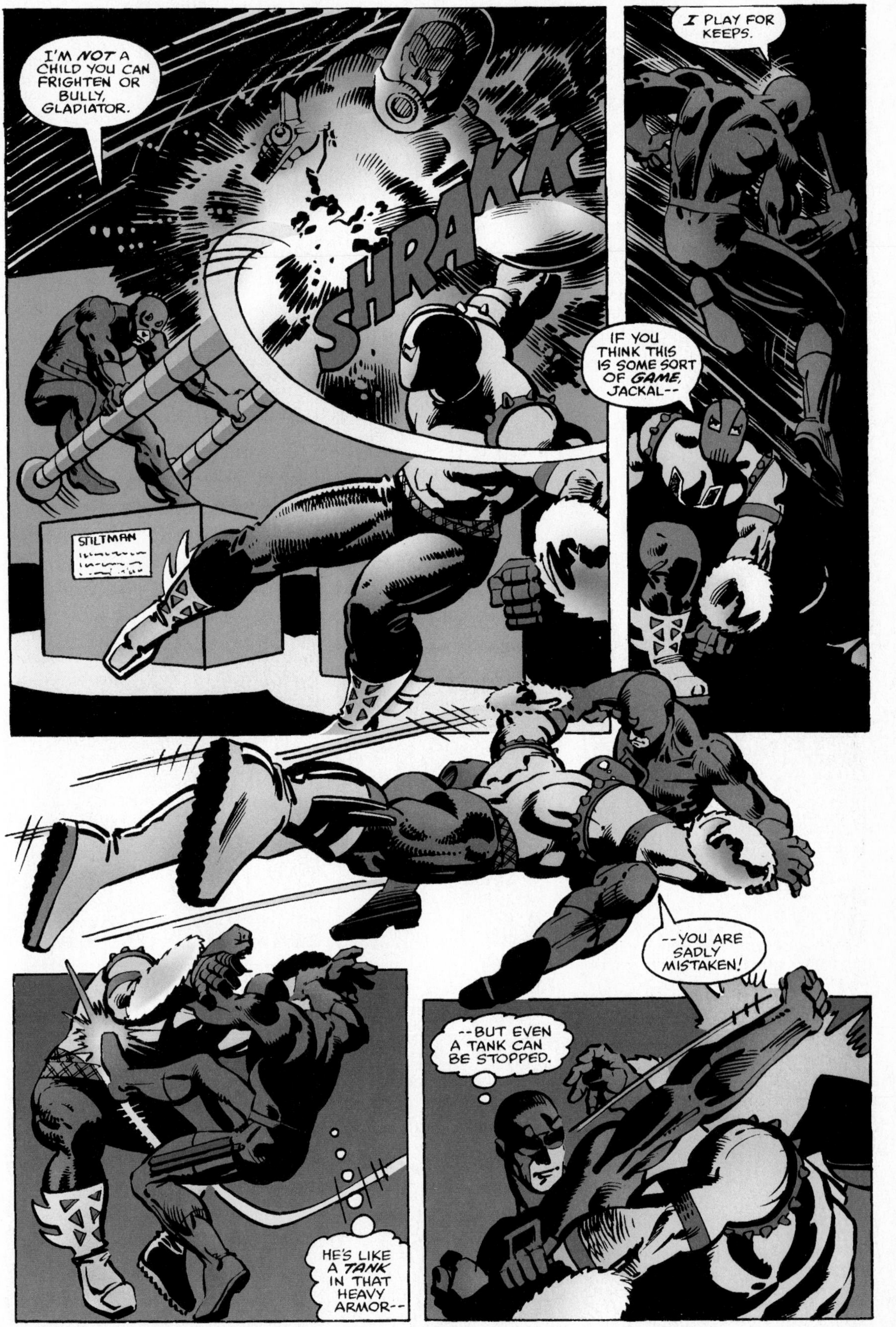
I'M NOT A CHILD YOU CAN FRIGHTEN OR BULLY, GLADIATOR.
SHRAKK
STILTMAN
I PLAY FOR KEEPS.
IF YOU THINK THIS IS SOME SORT OF GAME, JACKAL--
--YOU ARE SADLY MISTAKEN!
HE'S LIKE A TANK IN THAT HEAVY ARMOR--
--BUT EVEN A TANK CAN BE STOPPED.

THAT BLOW WOULD HAVE *KILLED* AN ORDINARY MAN, IT DIDN'T EVEN *STUN* THE GLADIATOR.

I'VE GOT TO GET OUT OF HIS REACH BEFORE *UNGHH*

YOU ARE SWIFT, JACKAL! MY SLASHING BLADE MERELY *GRAZED* YOU!

BUT THE LION IS SWIFTER-- AND *FAR* MORE DEADLY!

IN COMBAT THE LION *ALWAYS* SLAYS THE JACKAL!

AND YOU, DEVIL, *YOU* ARE THE JACKAL!

HURRY, CHILDREN! RUN!

YOU HAVE *NEVER* BEEN ANYTHING ELSE!

ARENA

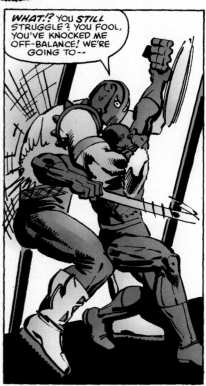

WHAT!? YOU *STILL* STRUGGLE? YOU FOOL, YOU'VE KNOCKED ME OFF-BALANCE! WE'RE GOING TO--

CAESAR'S BLOOD!

LOCKED IN A DEATHGRIP, THEY TOPPLE BACKWARD... AND IT IS AS IF TIME ITSELF SHATTERS THEN, LIKE A PANE OF GLASS...

186

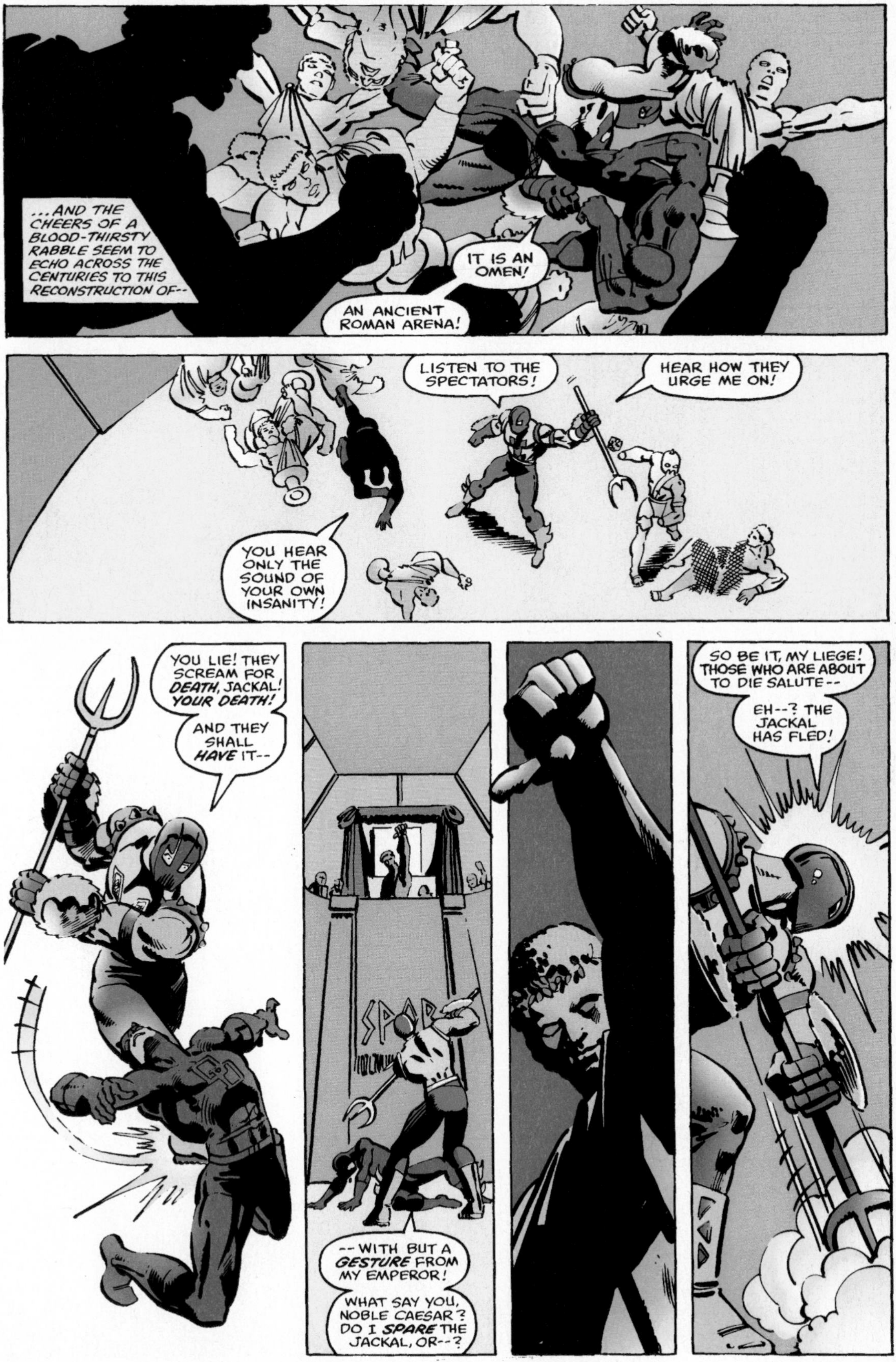
...AND THE CHEERS OF A BLOOD-THIRSTY RABBLE SEEM TO ECHO ACROSS THE CENTURIES TO THIS RECONSTRUCTION OF--
IT IS AN OMEN!
AN ANCIENT ROMAN ARENA!
LISTEN TO THE SPECTATORS!
HEAR HOW THEY URGE ME ON!
YOU HEAR ONLY THE SOUND OF YOUR OWN INSANITY!
YOU LIE! THEY SCREAM FOR DEATH, JACKAL! YOUR DEATH!
AND THEY SHALL HAVE IT--
--WITH BUT A GESTURE FROM MY EMPEROR!
WHAT SAY YOU, NOBLE CAESAR? DO I SPARE THE JACKAL, OR--?
SO BE IT, MY LIEGE! THOSE WHO ARE ABOUT TO DIE SALUTE--
EH--? THE JACKAL HAS FLED!

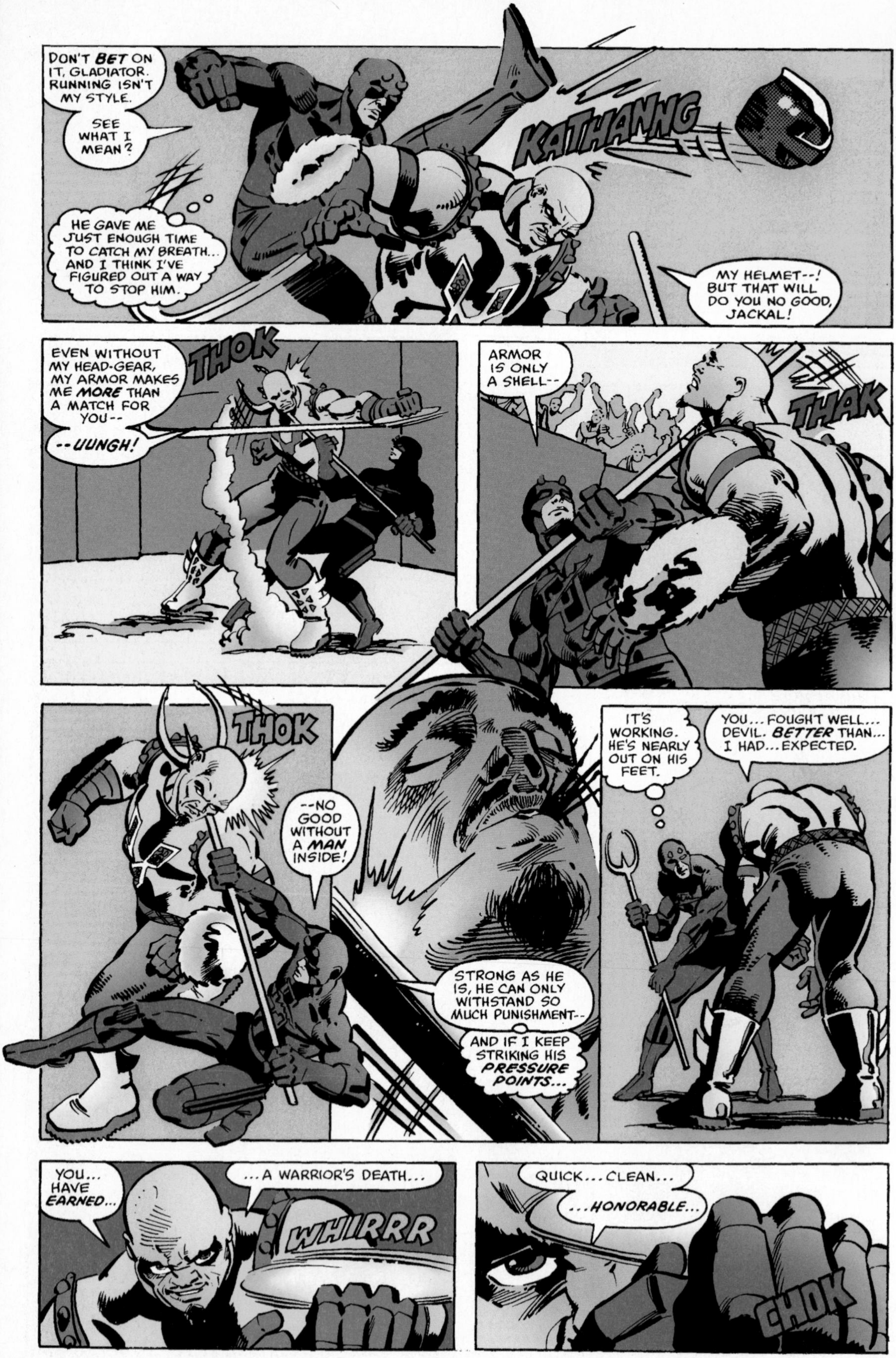
DON'T BET ON IT, GLADIATOR. RUNNING ISN'T MY STYLE.
SEE WHAT I MEAN?
KATHANNG
HE GAVE ME JUST ENOUGH TIME TO CATCH MY BREATH... AND I THINK I'VE FIGURED OUT A WAY TO STOP HIM.
MY HELMET--! BUT THAT WILL DO YOU NO GOOD, JACKAL!
EVEN WITHOUT MY HEAD-GEAR, MY ARMOR MAKES ME MORE THAN A MATCH FOR YOU--
--UUNGH!
THOK
ARMOR IS ONLY A SHELL--
THAK
THOK
--NO GOOD WITHOUT A MAN INSIDE!
STRONG AS HE IS, HE CAN ONLY WITHSTAND SO MUCH PUNISHMENT--
AND IF I KEEP STRIKING HIS PRESSURE POINTS...
IT'S WORKING. HE'S NEARLY OUT ON HIS FEET.
YOU... FOUGHT WELL... DEVIL. BETTER THAN... I HAD... EXPECTED.
YOU... HAVE EARNED...
...A WARRIOR'S DEATH...
WHIRRR
QUICK... CLEAN...
...HONORABLE...
CHOK

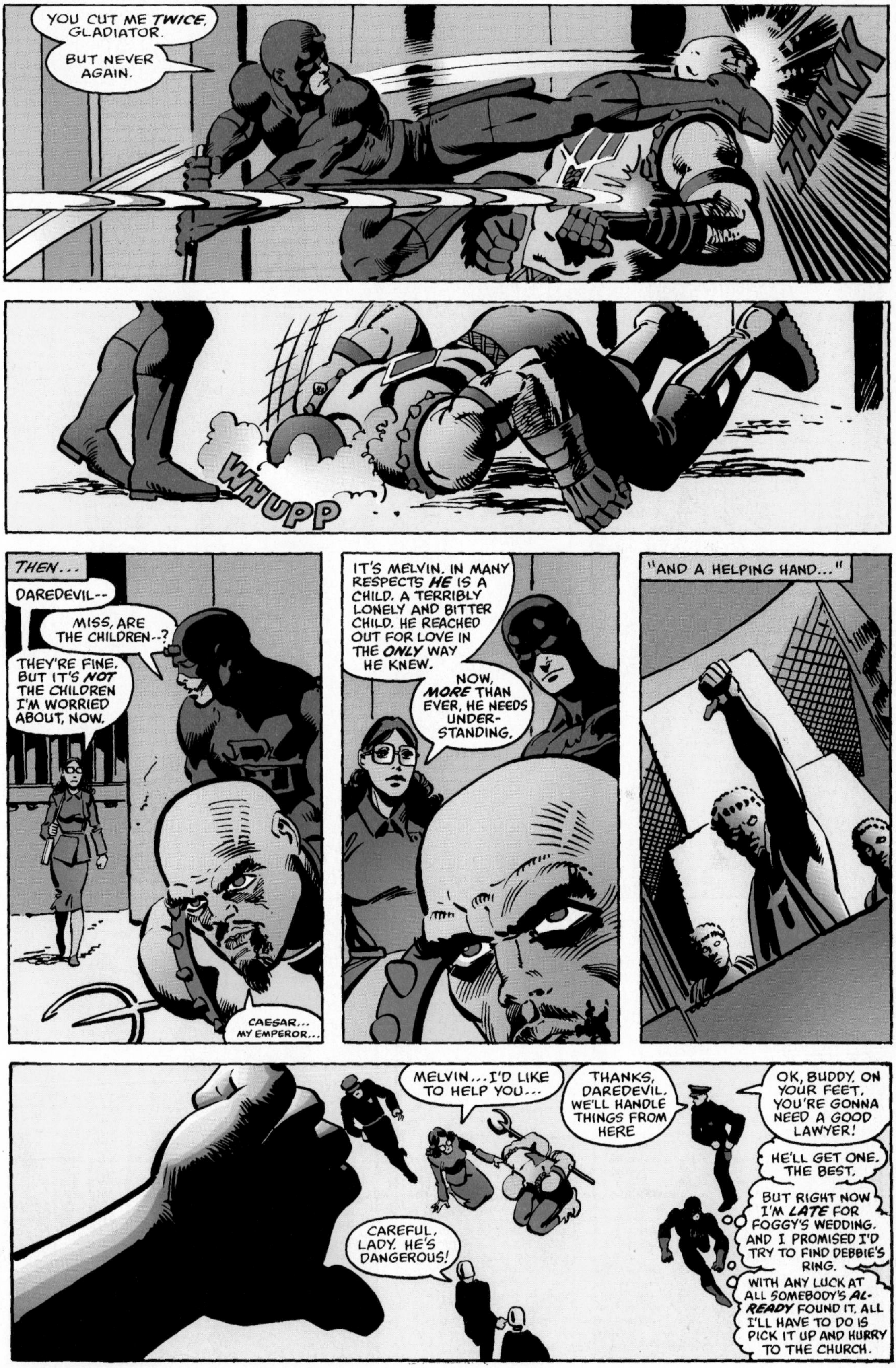
YOU CUT ME TWICE, GLADIATOR.
BUT NEVER AGAIN.
THAKK
WHUPP
THEN...
DAREDEVIL--
MISS, ARE THE CHILDREN--?
THEY'RE FINE. BUT IT'S NOT THE CHILDREN I'M WORRIED ABOUT, NOW.
CAESAR... MY EMPEROR...
IT'S MELVIN. IN MANY RESPECTS HE IS A CHILD. A TERRIBLY LONELY AND BITTER CHILD. HE REACHED OUT FOR LOVE IN THE ONLY WAY HE KNEW.
NOW, MORE THAN EVER, HE NEEDS UNDER-STANDING.
"AND A HELPING HAND..."
MELVIN... I'D LIKE TO HELP YOU...
CAREFUL, LADY. HE'S DANGEROUS!
THANKS, DAREDEVIL. WE'LL HANDLE THINGS FROM HERE
OK, BUDDY. ON YOUR FEET. YOU'RE GONNA NEED A GOOD LAWYER!
HE'LL GET ONE. THE BEST.
BUT RIGHT NOW I'M LATE FOR FOGGY'S WEDDING. AND I PROMISED I'D TRY TO FIND DEBBIE'S RING.
WITH ANY LUCK AT ALL SOMEBODY'S AL-READY FOUND IT. ALL I'LL HAVE TO DO IS PICK IT UP AND HURRY TO THE CHURCH.

AND SO...

...IF THERE IS ANYONE WITH *GOOD REASON* WHY THESE TWO SHOULD *NOT* BE WED IN HOLY MATRIMONY, LET HIM SPEAK NOW OR--

FOGGY! AM I TOO LATE?

NEARLY, MATT, NEARLY! I *STALLED* AS LONG AS I COULD.

JUST GIVE ME THE RING AND--

THAT'S JUST IT, FOGGY,

BECKY AND I TURNED THE STOREFRONT UP-SIDE DOWN BUT WE COULDN'T FIND IT! I'M SORRY...

OH, NO--! WHAT AM I GOING TO DO NOW?

IF I COULD ONLY *REMEMBER* WHERE I --

--PUT IT--!?

UH, GUESS WHAT, MATT...

MISS HARRIS, ARE YOU *SURE* YOU WANT TO GO THROUGH WITH THIS?

FOR BETTER OR WORSE, REVEREND!

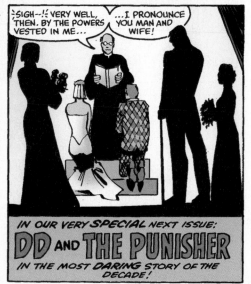

SIGH--!: VERY WELL, THEN, BY THE POWERS VESTED IN ME...

...I PRONOUNCE YOU MAN AND WIFE!

IN OUR VERY *SPECIAL* NEXT ISSUE:

DD AND THE PUNISHER

IN THE MOST *DARING* STORY OF THE DECADE!

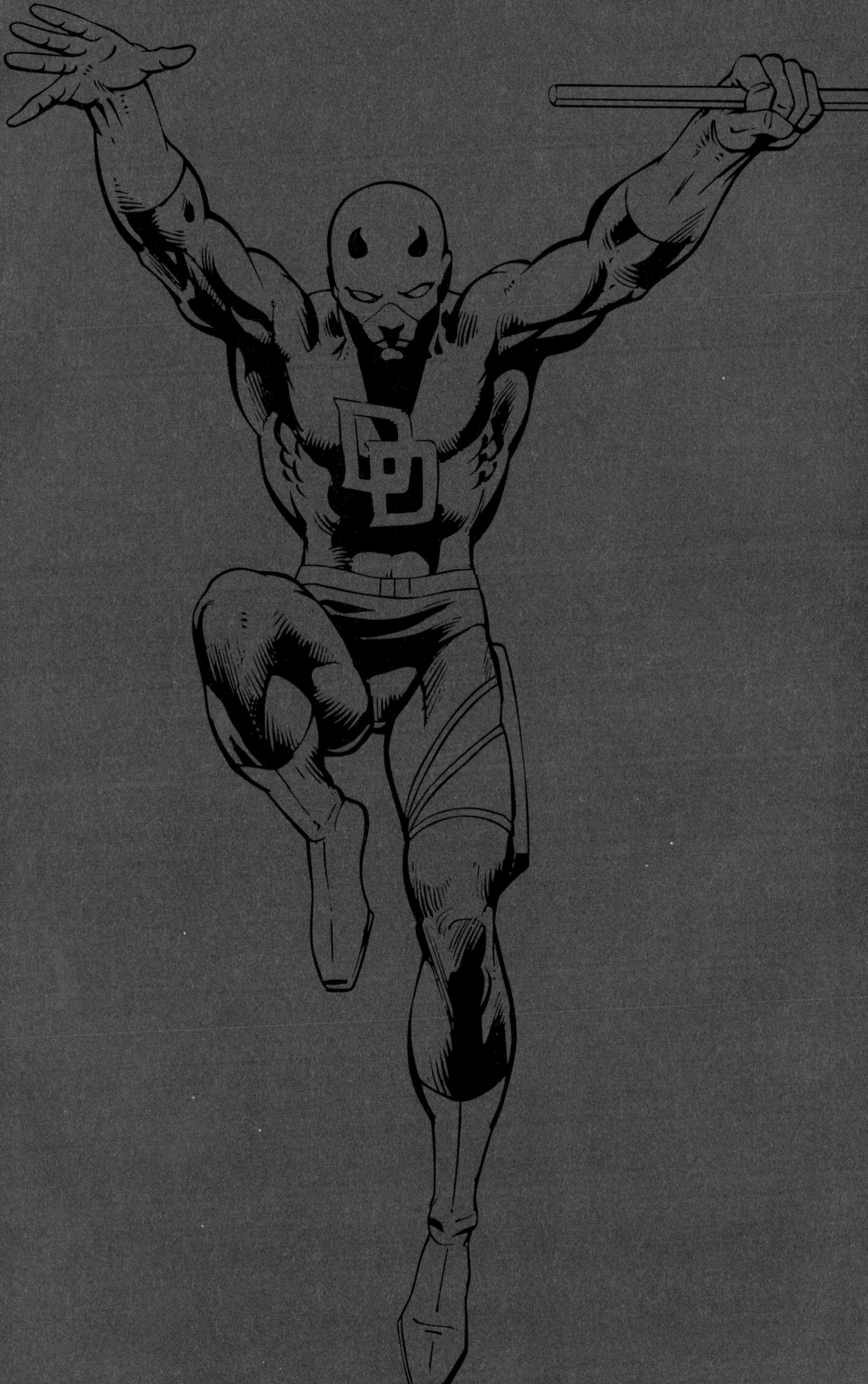

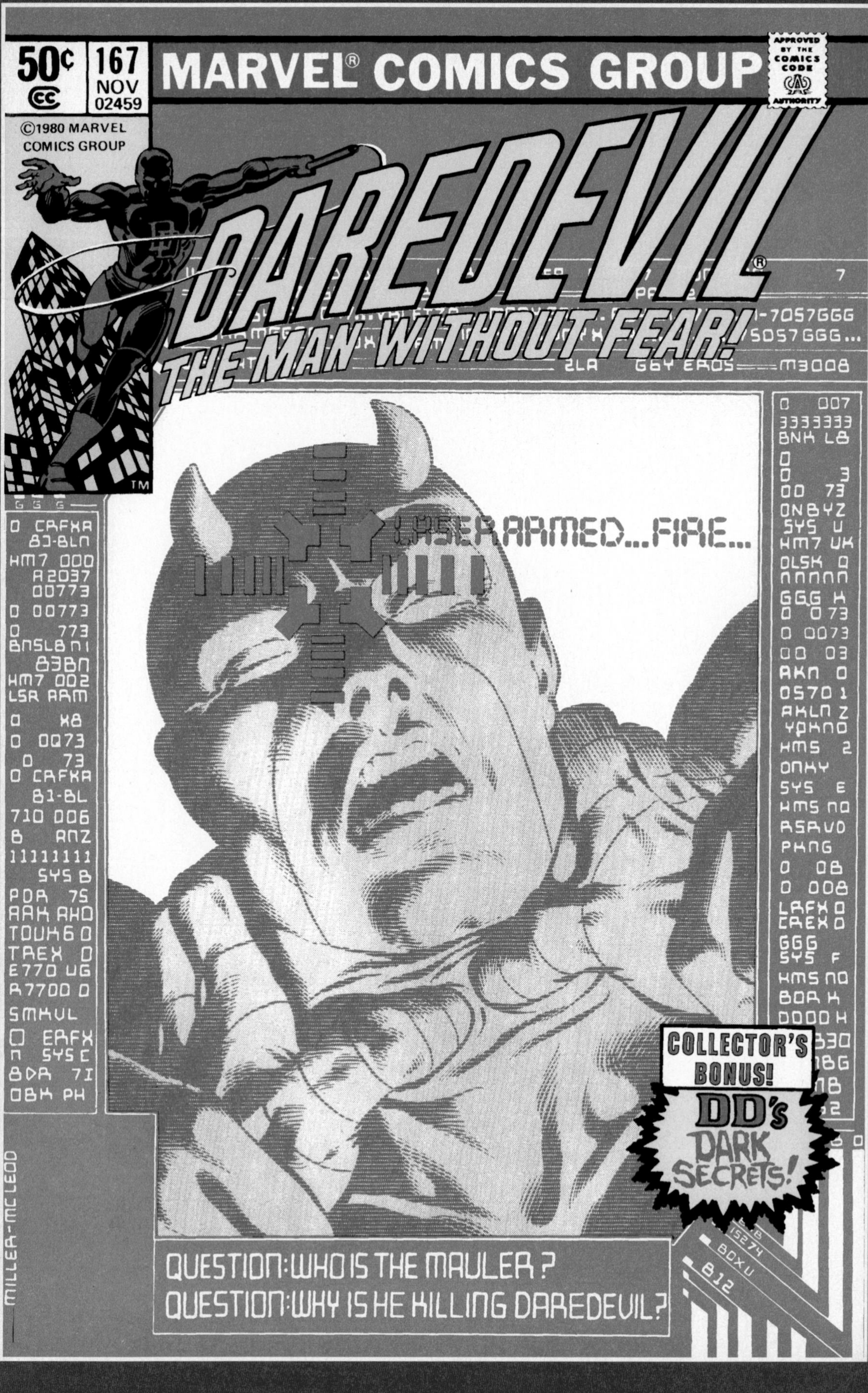

50¢
167
NOV
02459
MARVEL® COMICS GROUP
APPROVED BY THE COMICS CODE AUTHORITY
©1980 MARVEL COMICS GROUP
DAREDEVIL®
THE MAN WITHOUT FEAR!
LASER ARMED...FIRE...
COLLECTOR'S BONUS!
DD's DARK SECRETS!
QUESTION: WHO IS THE MAULER ?
QUESTION: WHY IS HE KILLING DAREDEVIL?
MILLER-MC LEOD

He dwells in eternal night—but the blackness is filled with sounds and scents other men cannot perceive. Though attorney MATT MURDOCK is *blind*, his other senses function with *superhuman sharpness*—his *radar sense* guides him over every obstacle! He stalks the streets by night, a red-garbed foe of evil!

Stan Lee PRESENTS: DAREDEVIL, THE MAN WITHOUT FEAR!®

DAVID MICHELINIE	FRANK MILLER	KLAUS JANSON	JOE ROSEN	GLYNIS WEIN	DENNY O'NEIL	JIM SHOOTER
WRITER	PENCILER	INKER	LETTERER	COLORIST	EDITOR	EDITOR-IN-CHIEF

TIME WAS WHEN MOST HIGH-LEVEL COMMERCE WAS CONDUCTED BEHIND CLOSED DOORS, CLOAKED IN BUSINESS-SUIT FORMALITY AND CLOUDS OF THICK, STALE SMOKE.

PERIMETER SECURITY NEUTRALIZED. BEGIN VISUAL SCAN FOR ENEMY.

BUT NOWADAYS, MANY MASTERS OF HIGH ENTERPRISE CHOOSE TO ABANDON STUFFY TRADITION, PREFERRING INSTEAD THE ILLUSORY OPENNESS OF COUNTRY CLUB COCKTAIL PARTIES--

...LIKE THE ONE THAT HAS BROUGHT BLIND ATTORNEY MATTHEW MURDOCK AND HIS LADYFRIEND, HEATHER GLENN, TO FOREST HILLS GARDENS THIS SUNNY AFTERNOON...

ENEMY OBSERVED AND IDENTIFIED; INSTIGATE TARGETING SEQUENCE.

...WHERE THEY WILL SOON FIND THAT CLOSED DOORS-- PREFERABLY OF THICK, SOLID CONSTRUCTION WITH STURDY DEADBOLT LOCKS--DO HAVE THEIR ADVANTAGES!

BLAZE CANNON LOCKED ON AND PRIMED. DESTRUCTION OF EDWIN CORD...IMMINENT!

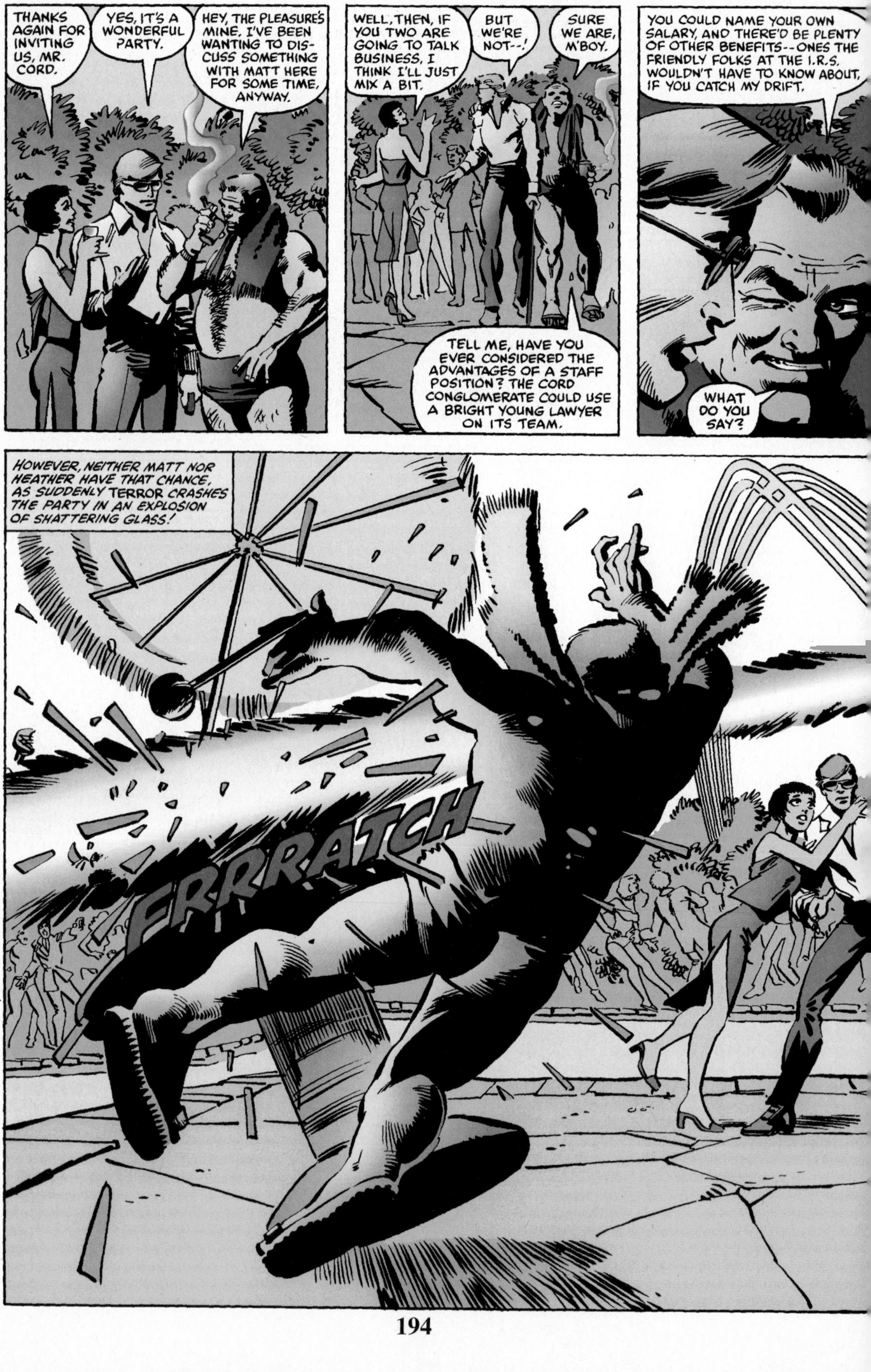
THANKS AGAIN FOR INVITING US, MR. CORD.
YES, IT'S A WONDERFUL PARTY.
HEY, THE PLEASURE'S MINE. I'VE BEEN WANTING TO DISCUSS SOMETHING WITH MATT HERE FOR SOME TIME, ANYWAY.
WELL, THEN, IF YOU TWO ARE GOING TO TALK BUSINESS, I THINK I'LL JUST MIX A BIT.
BUT WE'RE NOT--!
SURE WE ARE, M'BOY.
TELL ME, HAVE YOU EVER CONSIDERED THE ADVANTAGES OF A STAFF POSITION? THE CORD CONGLOMERATE COULD USE A BRIGHT YOUNG LAWYER ON ITS TEAM.
YOU COULD NAME YOUR OWN SALARY, AND THERE'D BE PLENTY OF OTHER BENEFITS--ONES THE FRIENDLY FOLKS AT THE I.R.S. WOULDN'T HAVE TO KNOW ABOUT, IF YOU CATCH MY DRIFT.
WHAT DO YOU SAY?
HOWEVER, NEITHER MATT NOR HEATHER HAVE THAT CHANCE, AS SUDDENLY TERROR CRASHES THE PARTY IN AN EXPLOSION OF SHATTERING GLASS!
FRRRATCH

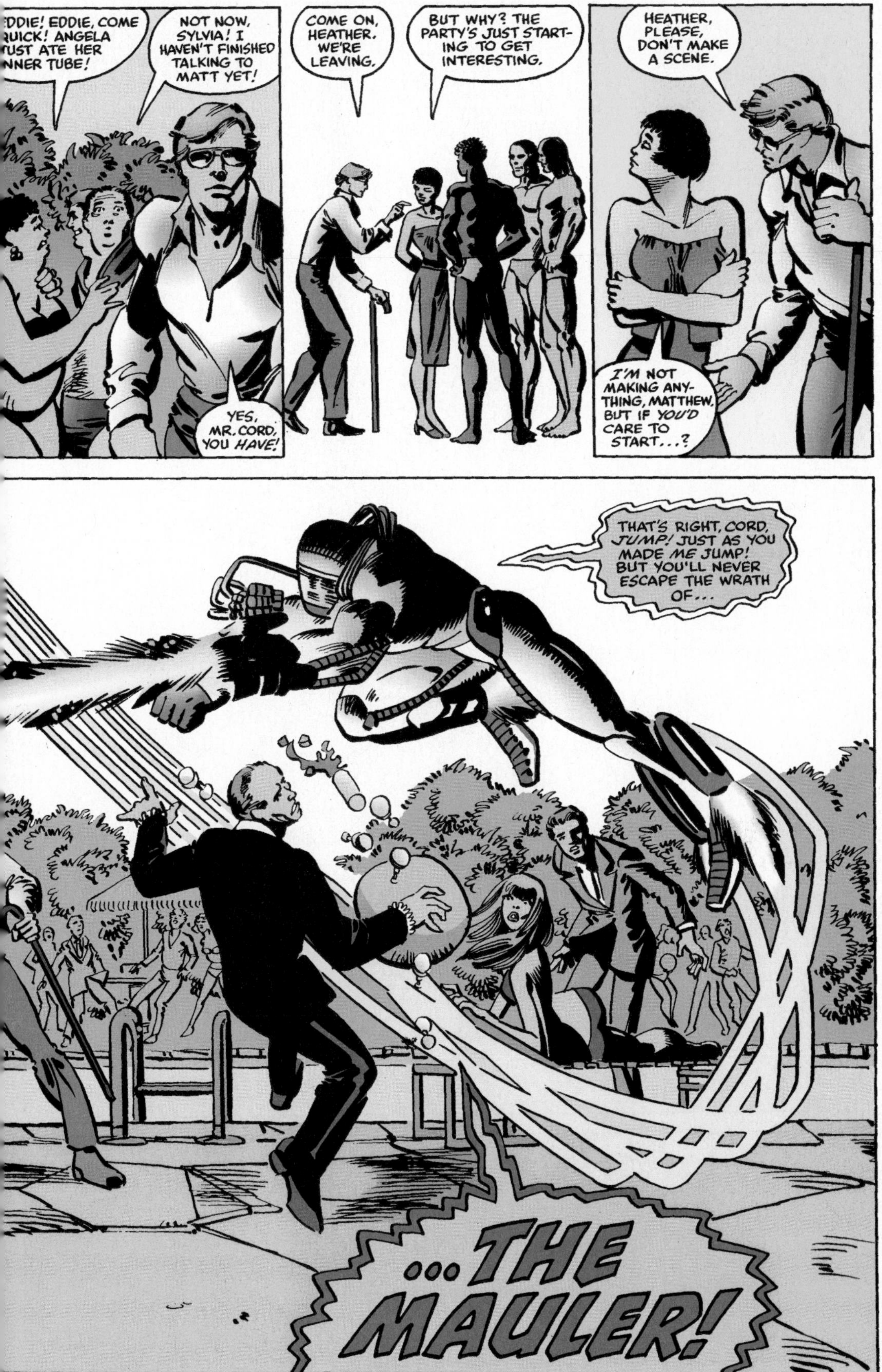
EDDIE! EDDIE, COME QUICK! ANGELA JUST ATE HER INNER TUBE!
NOT NOW, SYLVIA! I HAVEN'T FINISHED TALKING TO MATT YET!
YES, MR. CORD, YOU HAVE!
COME ON, HEATHER. WE'RE LEAVING.
BUT WHY? THE PARTY'S JUST STARTING TO GET INTERESTING.
HEATHER, PLEASE, DON'T MAKE A SCENE.
I'M NOT MAKING ANYTHING, MATTHEW, BUT IF YOU'D CARE TO START...?
THAT'S RIGHT, CORD, JUMP! JUST AS YOU MADE ME JUMP! BUT YOU'LL NEVER ESCAPE THE WRATH OF...
...THE MAULER!

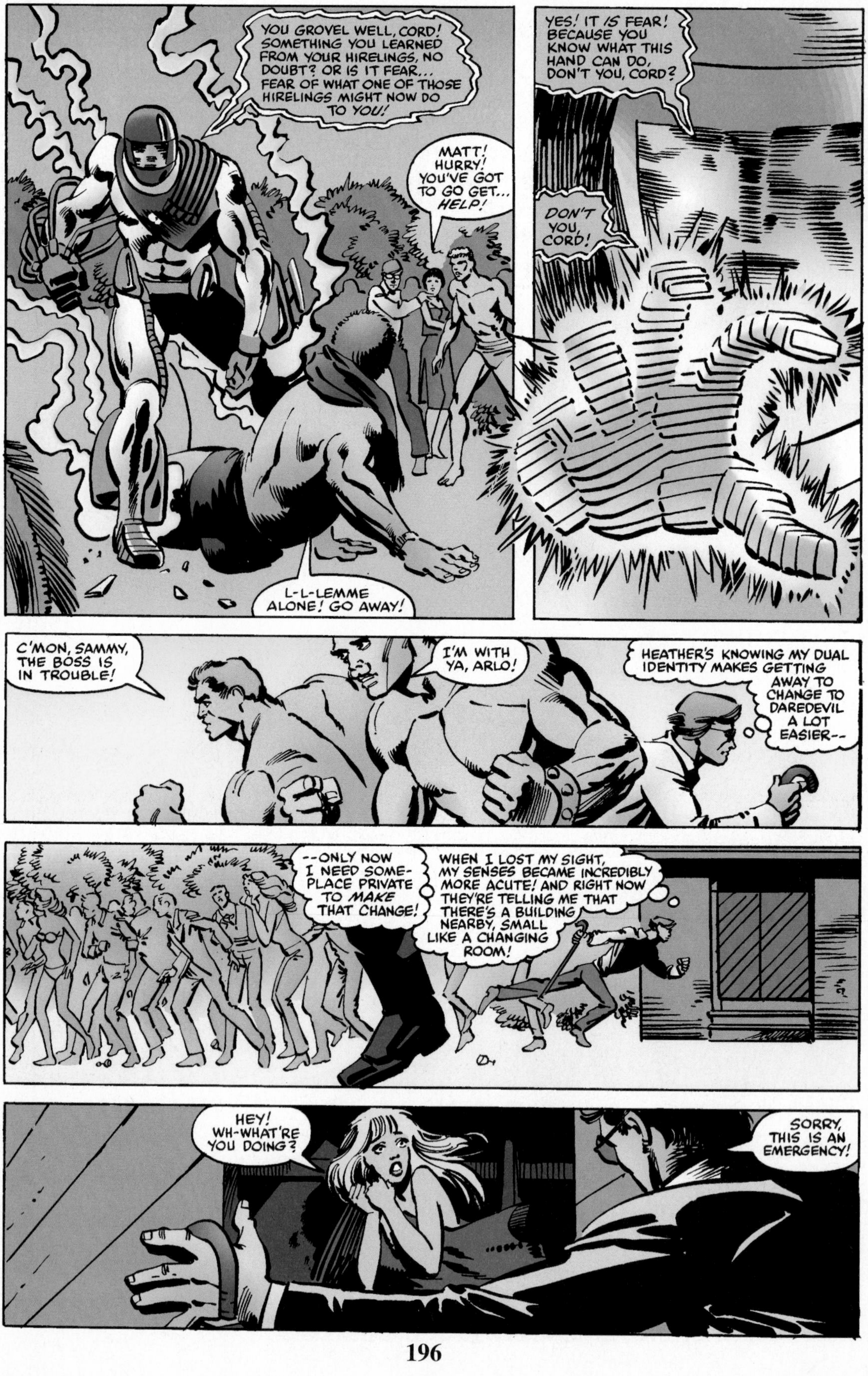

YOU GROVEL WELL, CORD! SOMETHING YOU LEARNED FROM YOUR HIRELINGS, NO DOUBT? OR IS IT FEAR... FEAR OF WHAT ONE OF THOSE HIRELINGS MIGHT NOW DO TO YOU!
MATT! HURRY! YOU'VE GOT TO GO GET... HELP!
L-L-LEMME ALONE! GO AWAY!
YES! IT IS FEAR! BECAUSE YOU KNOW WHAT THIS HAND CAN DO, DON'T YOU, CORD?
DON'T YOU, CORD!
C'MON, SAMMY, THE BOSS IS IN TROUBLE!
I'M WITH YA, ARLO!
HEATHER'S KNOWING MY DUAL IDENTITY MAKES GETTING AWAY TO CHANGE TO DAREDEVIL A LOT EASIER--
--ONLY NOW I NEED SOME-PLACE PRIVATE TO MAKE THAT CHANGE!
WHEN I LOST MY SIGHT, MY SENSES BECAME INCREDIBLY MORE ACUTE! AND RIGHT NOW THEY'RE TELLING ME THAT THERE'S A BUILDING NEARBY, SMALL LIKE A CHANGING ROOM!
HEY! WH-WHAT'RE YOU DOING?
SORRY, THIS IS AN EMERGENCY!

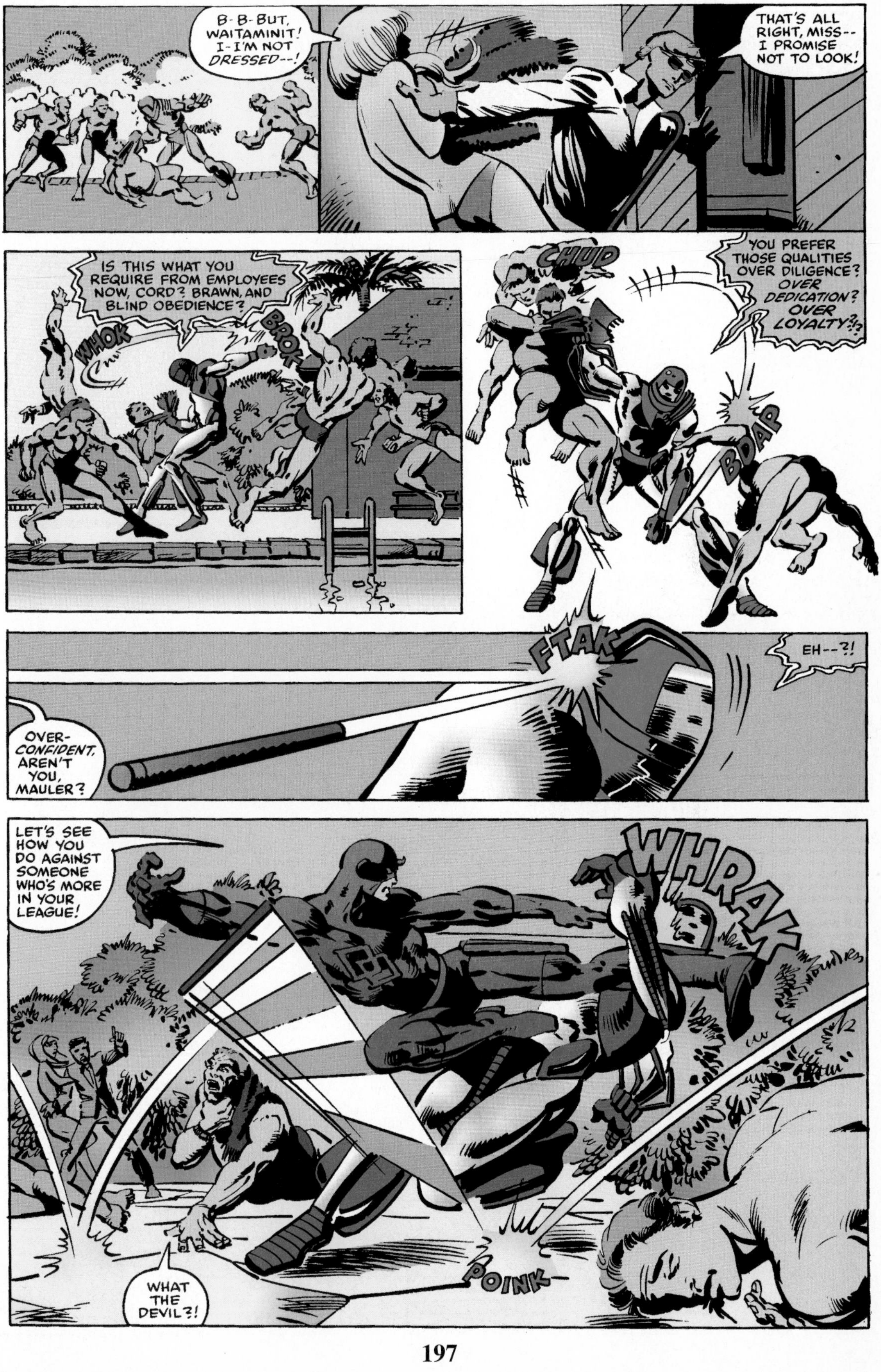
B-B-BUT, WAITAMINIT! I-I'M NOT DRESSED--!
THAT'S ALL RIGHT, MISS-- I PROMISE NOT TO LOOK!
IS THIS WHAT YOU REQUIRE FROM EMPLOYEES NOW, CORD? BRAWN, AND BLIND OBEDIENCE?
WHOK
BROK
CHUD
YOU PREFER THOSE QUALITIES OVER DILIGENCE? OVER DEDICATION? OVER LOYALTY?!?
BDAP
FTAK
EH--?!
OVER-CONFIDENT, AREN'T YOU, MAULER?
LET'S SEE HOW YOU DO AGAINST SOMEONE WHO'S MORE IN YOUR LEAGUE!
WHRAK
POINK
WHAT THE DEVIL?!

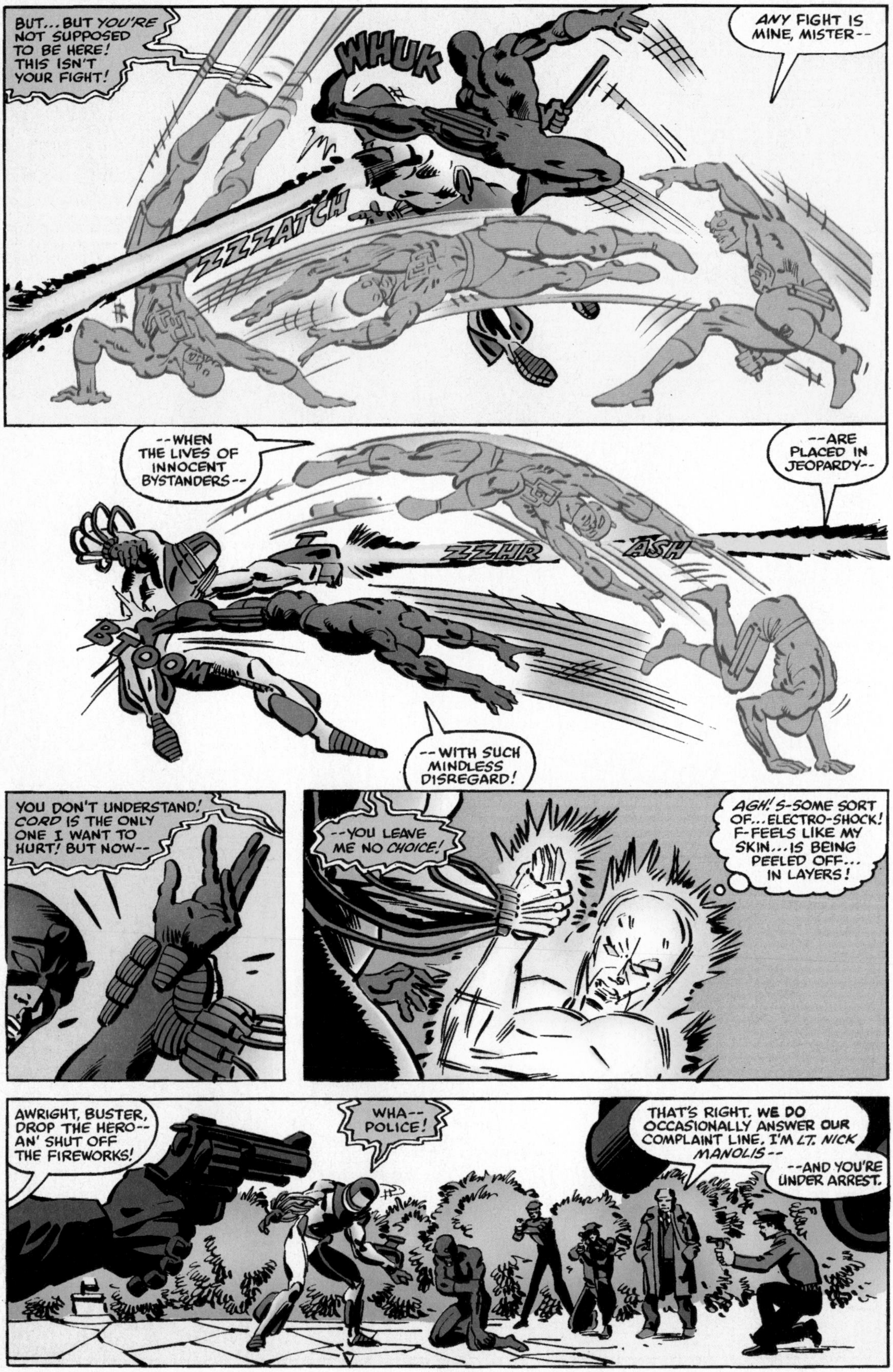
BUT... BUT YOU'RE NOT SUPPOSED TO BE HERE! THIS ISN'T YOUR FIGHT!
WHUK
ANY FIGHT IS MINE, MISTER--
ZZZATCH
--WHEN THE LIVES OF INNOCENT BYSTANDERS--
--ARE PLACED IN JEOPARDY--
ZZZHR
ASH
BTOOM
--WITH SUCH MINDLESS DISREGARD!
YOU DON'T UNDERSTAND! CORD IS THE ONLY ONE I WANT TO HURT! BUT NOW--
--YOU LEAVE ME NO CHOICE!
AGH! S-SOME SORT OF... ELECTRO-SHOCK! F-FEELS LIKE MY SKIN... IS BEING PEELED OFF... IN LAYERS!
AWRIGHT, BUSTER, DROP THE HERO-- AN' SHUT OFF THE FIREWORKS!
WHA-- POLICE!
THAT'S RIGHT. WE DO OCCASIONALLY ANSWER OUR COMPLAINT LINE. I'M LT. NICK MANOLIS--
--AND YOU'RE UNDER ARREST.

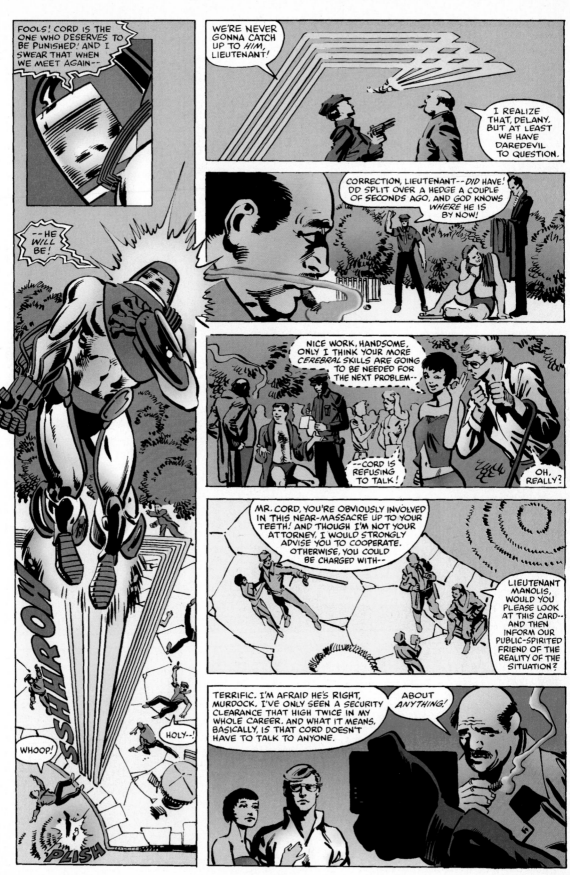

FOOLS! CORD IS THE ONE WHO DESERVES TO BE PUNISHED! AND I SWEAR THAT WHEN WE MEET AGAIN--

--HE WILL BE!

SSSHROW

WHOOP!

HOLY--!

PLISH

WE'RE NEVER GONNA CATCH UP TO HIM, LIEUTENANT!

I REALIZE THAT, DELANY, BUT AT LEAST WE HAVE DAREDEVIL TO QUESTION.

CORRECTION, LIEUTENANT--DID HAVE! DD SPLIT OVER A HEDGE A COUPLE OF SECONDS AGO, AND GOD KNOWS WHERE HE IS BY NOW!

NICE WORK, HANDSOME, ONLY I THINK YOUR MORE CEREBRAL SKILLS ARE GOING TO BE NEEDED FOR THE NEXT PROBLEM--

--CORD IS REFUSING TO TALK!

OH, REALLY?

MR. CORD, YOU'RE OBVIOUSLY INVOLVED IN THIS NEAR-MASSACRE UP TO YOUR TEETH! AND THOUGH I'M NOT YOUR ATTORNEY, I WOULD STRONGLY ADVISE YOU TO COOPERATE. OTHERWISE, YOU COULD BE CHARGED WITH--

LIEUTENANT MANOLIS, WOULD YOU PLEASE LOOK AT THIS CARD-- AND THEN INFORM OUR PUBLIC-SPIRITED FRIEND OF THE REALITY OF THE SITUATION?

TERRIFIC. I'M AFRAID HE'S RIGHT, MURDOCK. I'VE ONLY SEEN A SECURITY CLEARANCE THAT HIGH TWICE IN MY WHOLE CAREER. AND WHAT IT MEANS, BASICALLY, IS THAT CORD DOESN'T HAVE TO TALK TO ANYONE.

ABOUT ANYTHING!

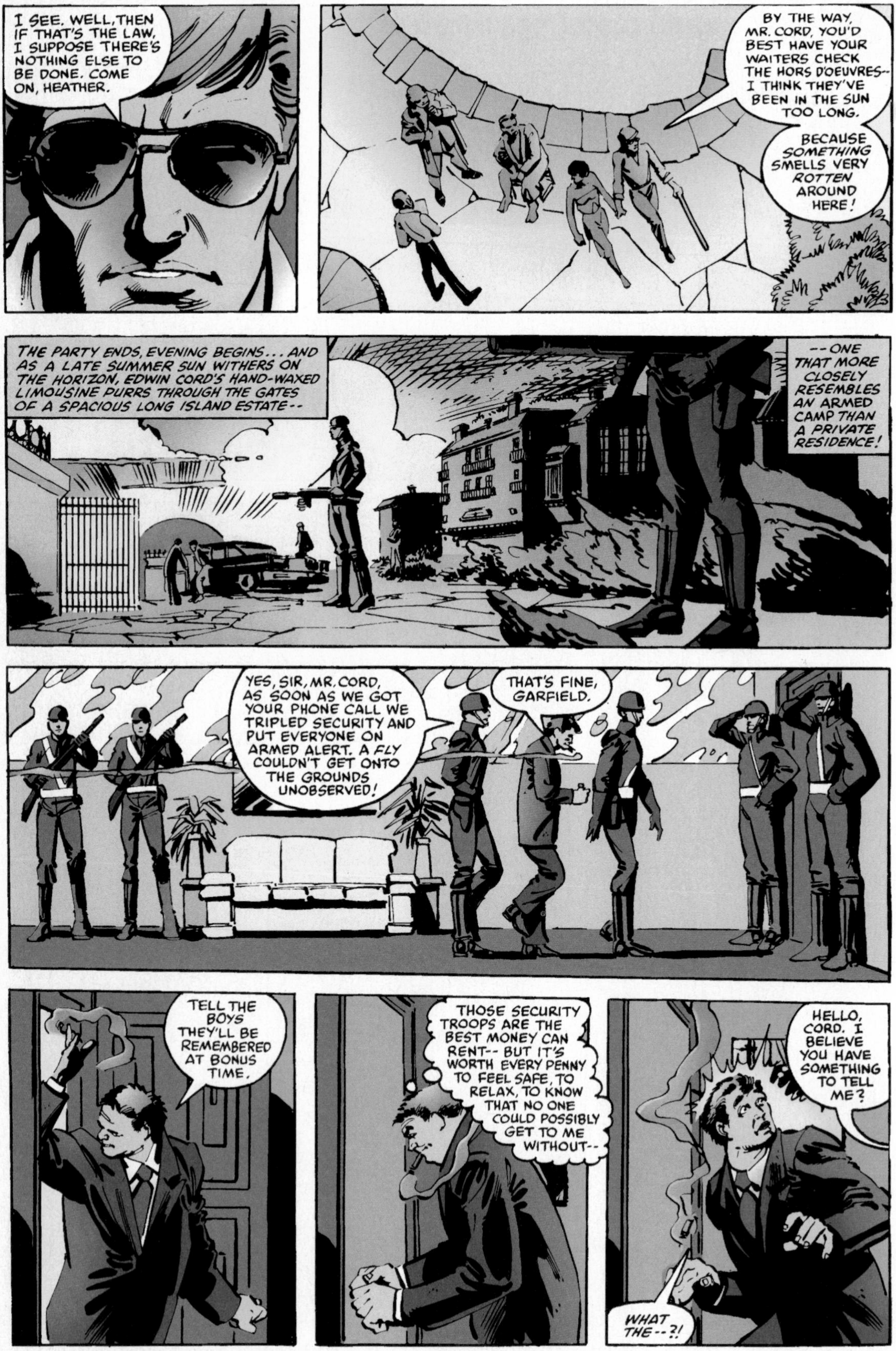

I SEE. WELL, THEN IF THAT'S THE LAW, I SUPPOSE THERE'S NOTHING ELSE TO BE DONE. COME ON, HEATHER.
BY THE WAY, MR. CORD, YOU'D BEST HAVE YOUR WAITERS CHECK THE HORS D'OEUVRES-- I THINK THEY'VE BEEN IN THE SUN TOO LONG.
BECAUSE SOMETHING SMELLS VERY ROTTEN AROUND HERE!
THE PARTY ENDS, EVENING BEGINS... AND AS A LATE SUMMER SUN WITHERS ON THE HORIZON, EDWIN CORD'S HAND-WAXED LIMOUSINE PURRS THROUGH THE GATES OF A SPACIOUS LONG ISLAND ESTATE--
--ONE THAT MORE CLOSELY RESEMBLES AN ARMED CAMP THAN A PRIVATE RESIDENCE!
YES, SIR, MR. CORD, AS SOON AS WE GOT YOUR PHONE CALL WE TRIPLED SECURITY AND PUT EVERYONE ON ARMED ALERT. A FLY COULDN'T GET ONTO THE GROUNDS UNOBSERVED!
THAT'S FINE, GARFIELD.
TELL THE BOYS THEY'LL BE REMEMBERED AT BONUS TIME.
THOSE SECURITY TROOPS ARE THE BEST MONEY CAN RENT-- BUT IT'S WORTH EVERY PENNY TO FEEL SAFE, TO RELAX, TO KNOW THAT NO ONE COULD POSSIBLY GET TO ME WITHOUT--
HELLO, CORD. I BELIEVE YOU HAVE SOMETHING TO TELL ME?
WHAT THE--?!

DAREDEVIL! B-BUT, HOW DID YOU--I-I MEAN, I DIDN'T EXPECT SUCH AN ILLUSTRIOUS VISITOR!

PLEASE, FORGIVE MY POOR MANNERS. WOULD YOU LIKE SOMETHING TO DRINK?

I'LL JUST RING FOR THE BUTLER AND--

GET YOUR FINGER OFF THAT BUTTON, CORD-- IF YOU WANT TO KEEP IT ON YOUR HAND!

BUT, WH-WHAT DO YOU WANT FROM ME? WHAT?

INFORMATION, CORD, THERE WAS SOME RATHER SEVERE UNPLEASANT-NESS AT YOUR COUNTRY CLUB TODAY--

--AND YOU'RE GOING TO TELL ME WHY.

PAK

PAK

PAK

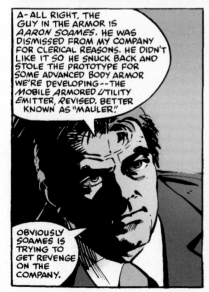

A-ALL RIGHT, THE GUY IN THE ARMOR IS AARON SOAMES. HE WAS DISMISSED FROM MY COMPANY FOR CLERICAL REASONS. HE DIDN'T LIKE IT SO HE SNUCK BACK AND STOLE THE PROTOTYPE FOR SOME ADVANCED BODY ARMOR WE'RE DEVELOPING--THE MOBILE ARMORED UTILITY EMITTER, REVISED, BETTER KNOWN AS "MAULER."

OBVIOUSLY SOAMES IS TRYING TO GET REVENGE ON THE COMPANY.

I DON'T THINK YOU'RE TELLING ME EVERYTHING, CORD, BUT AT LEAST YOU'VE GIVEN ME SOMETHING TO THINK ABOUT. NOW I'LL GIVE YOU SOMETHING TO THINK ABOUT: IF I FIND YOU'VE LIED TO ME--

--I'LL BE BACK.

KLIK

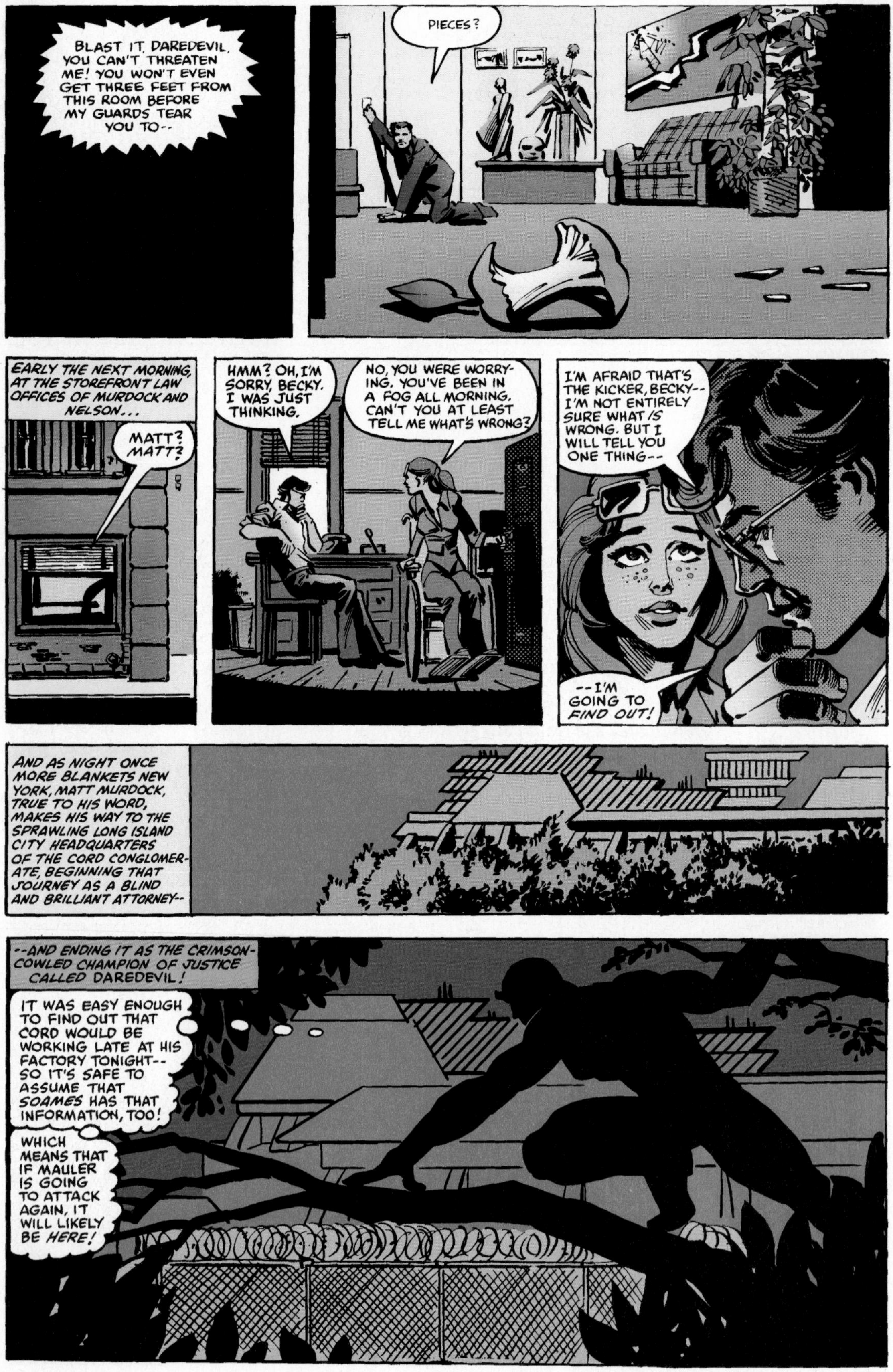

BLAST IT, DAREDEVIL, YOU CAN'T THREATEN ME! YOU WON'T EVEN GET THREE FEET FROM THIS ROOM BEFORE MY GUARDS TEAR YOU TO--
PIECES?
EARLY THE NEXT MORNING, AT THE STOREFRONT LAW OFFICES OF MURDOCK AND NELSON...
MATT? MATT?
HMM? OH, I'M SORRY, BECKY. I WAS JUST THINKING.
NO, YOU WERE WORRYING. YOU'VE BEEN IN A FOG ALL MORNING. CAN'T YOU AT LEAST TELL ME WHAT'S WRONG?
I'M AFRAID THAT'S THE KICKER, BECKY-- I'M NOT ENTIRELY SURE WHAT IS WRONG. BUT I WILL TELL YOU ONE THING--
--I'M GOING TO FIND OUT!
AND AS NIGHT ONCE MORE BLANKETS NEW YORK, MATT MURDOCK, TRUE TO HIS WORD, MAKES HIS WAY TO THE SPRAWLING LONG ISLAND CITY HEADQUARTERS OF THE CORD CONGLOMERATE, BEGINNING THAT JOURNEY AS A BLIND AND BRILLIANT ATTORNEY--
--AND ENDING IT AS THE CRIMSON-COWLED CHAMPION OF JUSTICE CALLED DAREDEVIL!
IT WAS EASY ENOUGH TO FIND OUT THAT CORD WOULD BE WORKING LATE AT HIS FACTORY TONIGHT-- SO IT'S SAFE TO ASSUME THAT SOAMES HAS THAT INFORMATION, TOO!
WHICH MEANS THAT IF MAULER IS GOING TO ATTACK AGAIN, IT WILL LIKELY BE HERE!

AND THUS THE MAN WITHOUT FEAR CROUCHES, MUSCLES AS LITHE AND LEAN AS THOSE OF SOME PREDATORY CAT, WILLING TO WAIT FOR THE PROPER PREY.

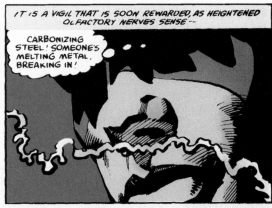

IT IS A VIGIL THAT IS SOON REWARDED, AS HEIGHTENED OLFACTORY NERVES SENSE--

CARBONIZING STEEL! SOMEONE'S MELTING METAL, BREAKING IN!

ALMOST WITHOUT CONSCIOUS THOUGHT HE UNSHEATHES THE BILLY CLUB AT HIS SIDE, PRESSING A HIDDEN STUD TO SEND A HIGH-TENSILE GRAPPLING WIRE UNREELING--

...ALLOWING HIM TO ARC THROUGH THE NIGHT LIKE A SILENT, SOARING SHADOW!

I'M PICKING UP HEARTBEATS FROM SEVERAL MEN, TOO SLOW-- UNCONSCIOUS!

AND MORE FROM INSIDE THE BUILDING! ONE EXCITED, SCARED! THE OTHER MASKED BY SOME SORT OF ENERGY FIELD! IT'S GOT TO BE--

--MAULER! LEAVE HIM ALONE!

YOU?! STAY OUT OF THIS!

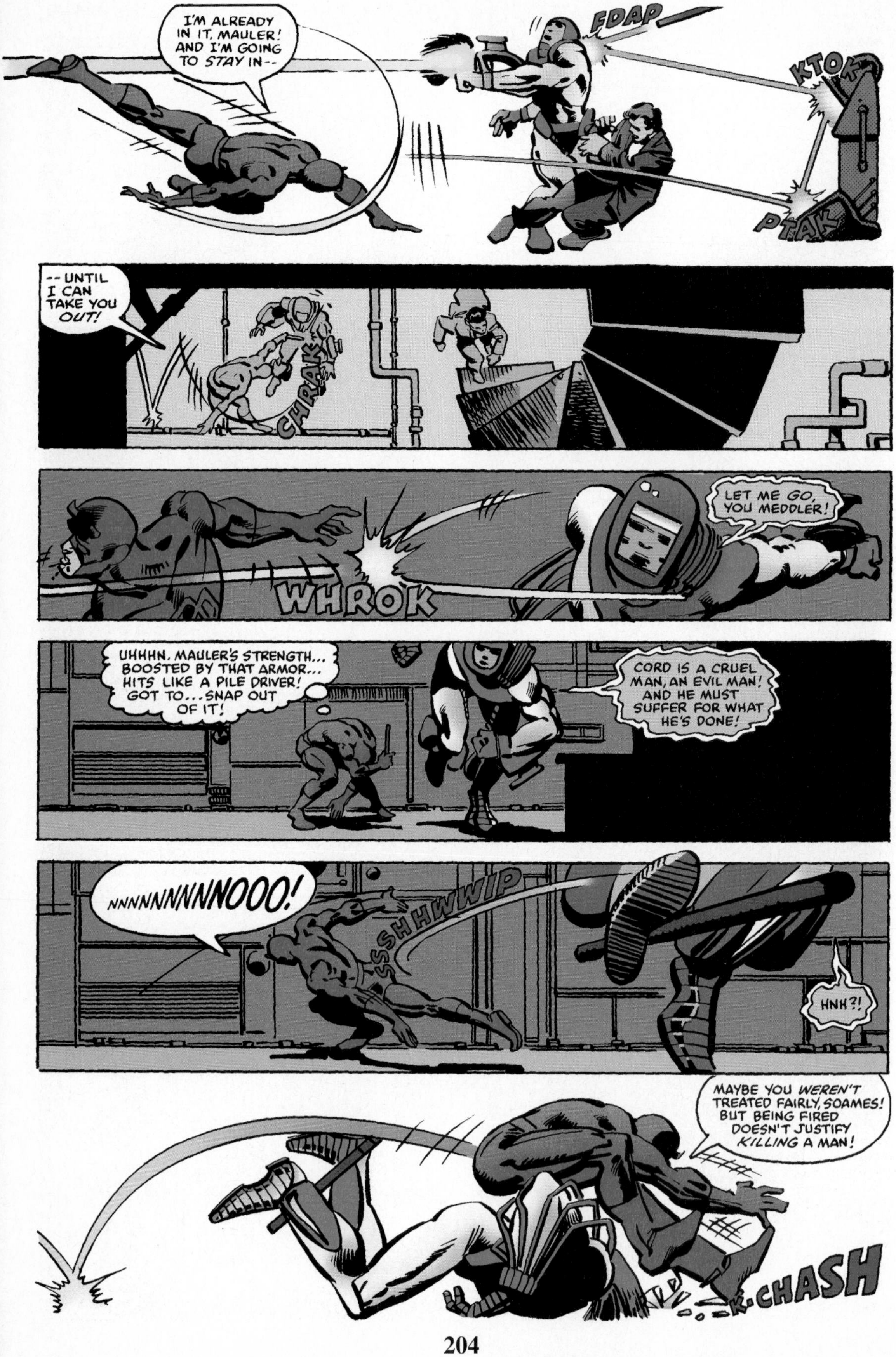
I'M ALREADY IN IT, MAULER! AND I'M GOING TO STAY IN--
FDAP
KTOK
PTAK
--UNTIL I CAN TAKE YOU OUT!
CHRAK
LET ME GO, YOU MEDDLER!
WHROK
UHHHN. MAULER'S STRENGTH... BOOSTED BY THAT ARMOR... HITS LIKE A PILE DRIVER! GOT TO... SNAP OUT OF IT!
CORD IS A CRUEL MAN, AN EVIL MAN! AND HE MUST SUFFER FOR WHAT HE'S DONE!
NNNNNNNNNOOO!
SSSHHWWIP
HNH?!
MAYBE YOU WEREN'T TREATED FAIRLY, SOAMES! BUT BEING FIRED DOESN'T JUSTIFY KILLING A MAN!
K-CHASH

"FIRED"? IS THAT WHAT HE TOLD YOU?

"FIRED"?!

LOOK AT THIS FACE, MAN! DO I LOOK LIKE THE KIND OF PERSON WHO'D GET HIMSELF *FIRED*?

YOUR *VOICE*! WITHOUT THE MASK TO MUFFLE IT, IT SOUNDS--

--*OLD*? THAT'S BECAUSE I *AM* OLD! SIXTY-THREE YEARS OLD! THIRTY-FIVE OF THEM SPENT AS A FILE CLERK FOR EDWIN CORD--

--UNTIL HE BROUGHT IN A COMPUTER TO DO MY JOB QUICKER AND CHEAPER.

BUT THE BIG SURPRISE CAME WHEN I TRIED TO COLLECT MY PENSION. SEEMS THE YOUNG HOT-SHOT WHO PROGRAMMED THE NEW COMPUTER HIT THE WRONG KEY--AND WIPED OUT MY ENTIRE 35-YEAR WORK RECORD!

I WENT TO MR. CORD ABOUT IT, AND YOU KNOW WHAT HE DID?

HE SMILED. HE SAID, "SORRY, SOAMES--NO RECORD, NO PENSION."

AND HE SMILED.

I APPLIED FOR SOCIAL SECURITY-- BUT THE INTERVIEWER DOZED OFF WHILE I WAS TRYING TO EXPLAIN!

SO I SPENT THE LAST OF MY SAVINGS ON A FANCY LAWYER, AND SURE ENOUGH, HE GOT ME A COURT DATE--

--A YEAR FROM NEXT THURSDAY!

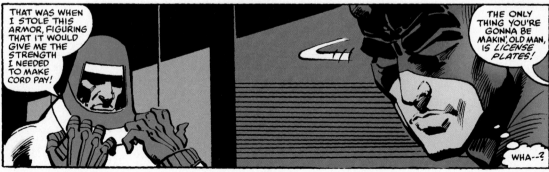

THAT WAS WHEN I STOLE THIS ARMOR, FIGURING THAT IT WOULD GIVE ME THE STRENGTH I NEEDED TO MAKE CORD PAY!

THE ONLY THING YOU'RE GONNA BE MAKIN', OLD MAN, IS *LICENSE PLATES*!

WHA--?

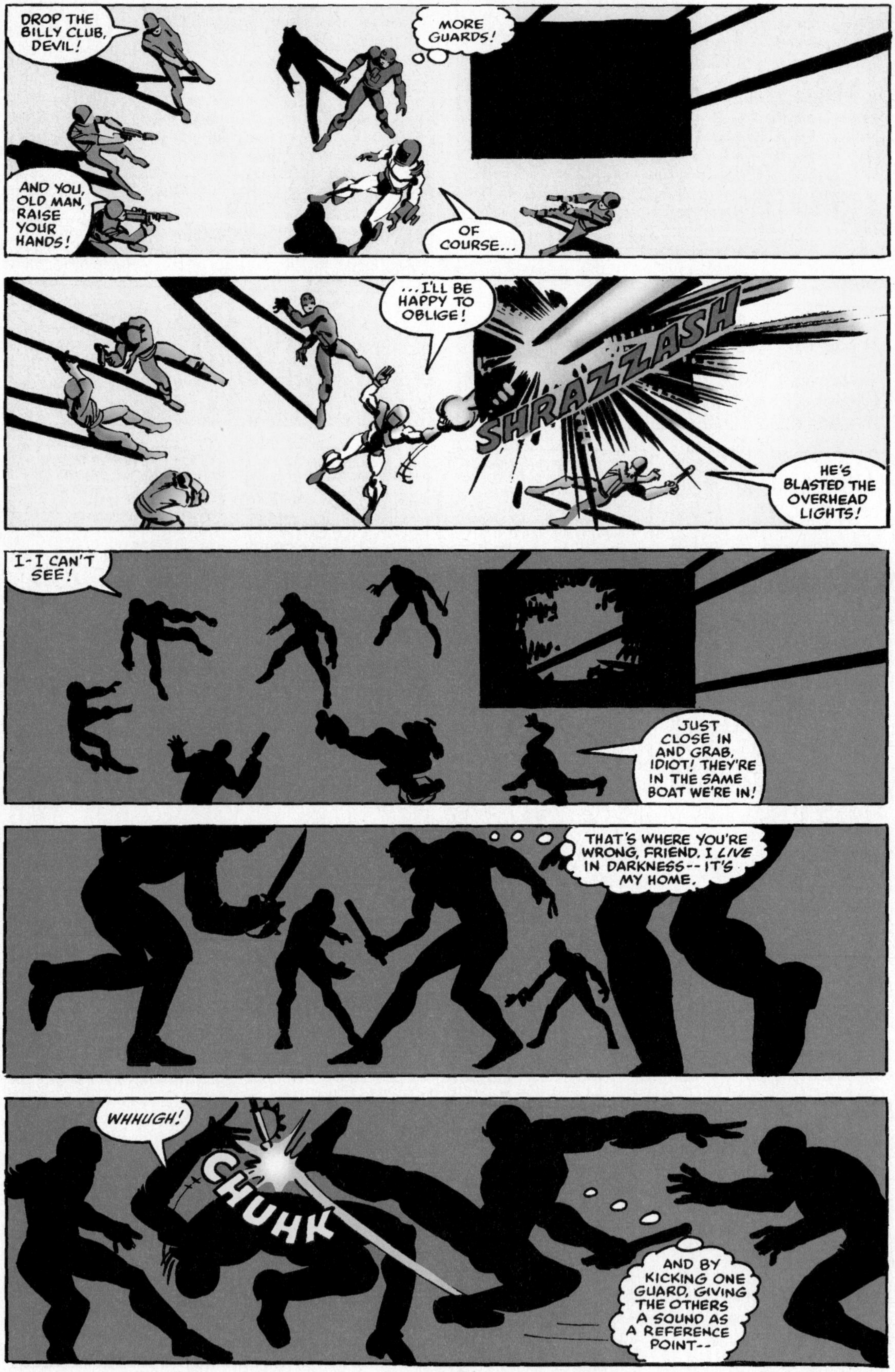
DROP THE BILLY CLUB, DEVIL!
MORE GUARDS!
AND YOU, OLD MAN, RAISE YOUR HANDS!
OF COURSE...
...I'LL BE HAPPY TO OBLIGE!
SHRAZZASH
HE'S BLASTED THE OVERHEAD LIGHTS!
I-I CAN'T SEE!
JUST CLOSE IN AND GRAB, IDIOT! THEY'RE IN THE SAME BOAT WE'RE IN!
THAT'S WHERE YOU'RE WRONG, FRIEND. I LIVE IN DARKNESS--IT'S MY HOME.
WHHUGH!
CHUHK
AND BY KICKING ONE GUARD, GIVING THE OTHERS A SOUND AS A REFERENCE POINT--

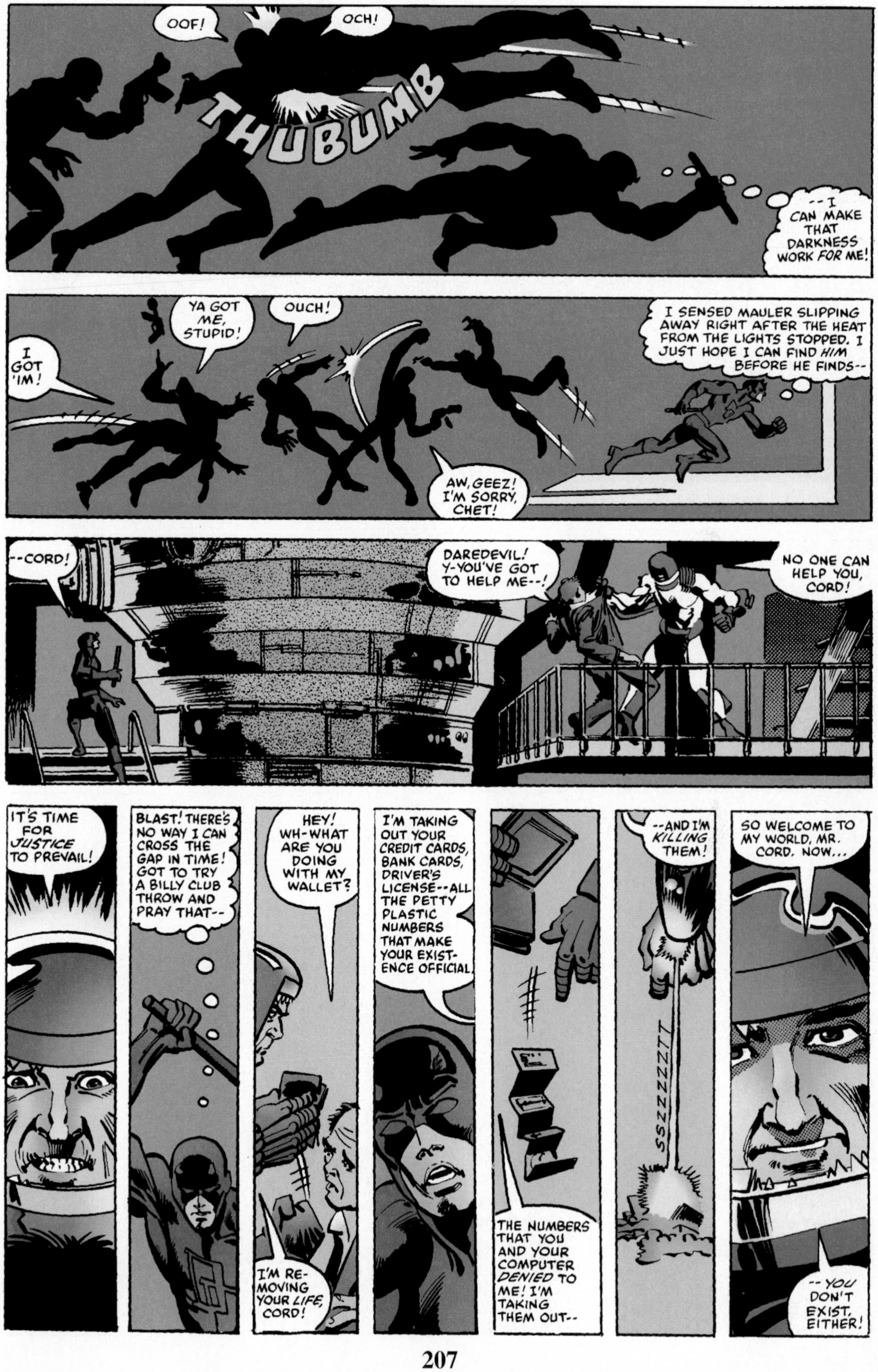
OOF!
OCH!
THUBUMB
--I CAN MAKE THAT DARKNESS WORK FOR ME!
I GOT 'IM!
YA GOT ME, STUPID!
OUCH!
AW, GEEZ! I'M SORRY, CHET!
I SENSED MAULER SLIPPING AWAY RIGHT AFTER THE HEAT FROM THE LIGHTS STOPPED. I JUST HOPE I CAN FIND HIM BEFORE HE FINDS--
--CORD!
DAREDEVIL! Y-YOU'VE GOT TO HELP ME--!
NO ONE CAN HELP YOU, CORD!
IT'S TIME FOR JUSTICE TO PREVAIL!
BLAST! THERE'S NO WAY I CAN CROSS THE GAP IN TIME! GOT TO TRY A BILLY CLUB THROW AND PRAY THAT--
HEY! WH-WHAT ARE YOU DOING WITH MY WALLET?
I'M REMOVING YOUR LIFE, CORD!
I'M TAKING OUT YOUR CREDIT CARDS, BANK CARDS, DRIVER'S LICENSE--ALL THE PETTY PLASTIC NUMBERS THAT MAKE YOUR EXISTENCE OFFICIAL.
THE NUMBERS THAT YOU AND YOUR COMPUTER DENIED TO ME! I'M TAKING THEM OUT--
--AND I'M KILLING THEM!
SSZZZZZT
SO WELCOME TO MY WORLD, MR. CORD. NOW...
--YOU DON'T EXIST, EITHER!

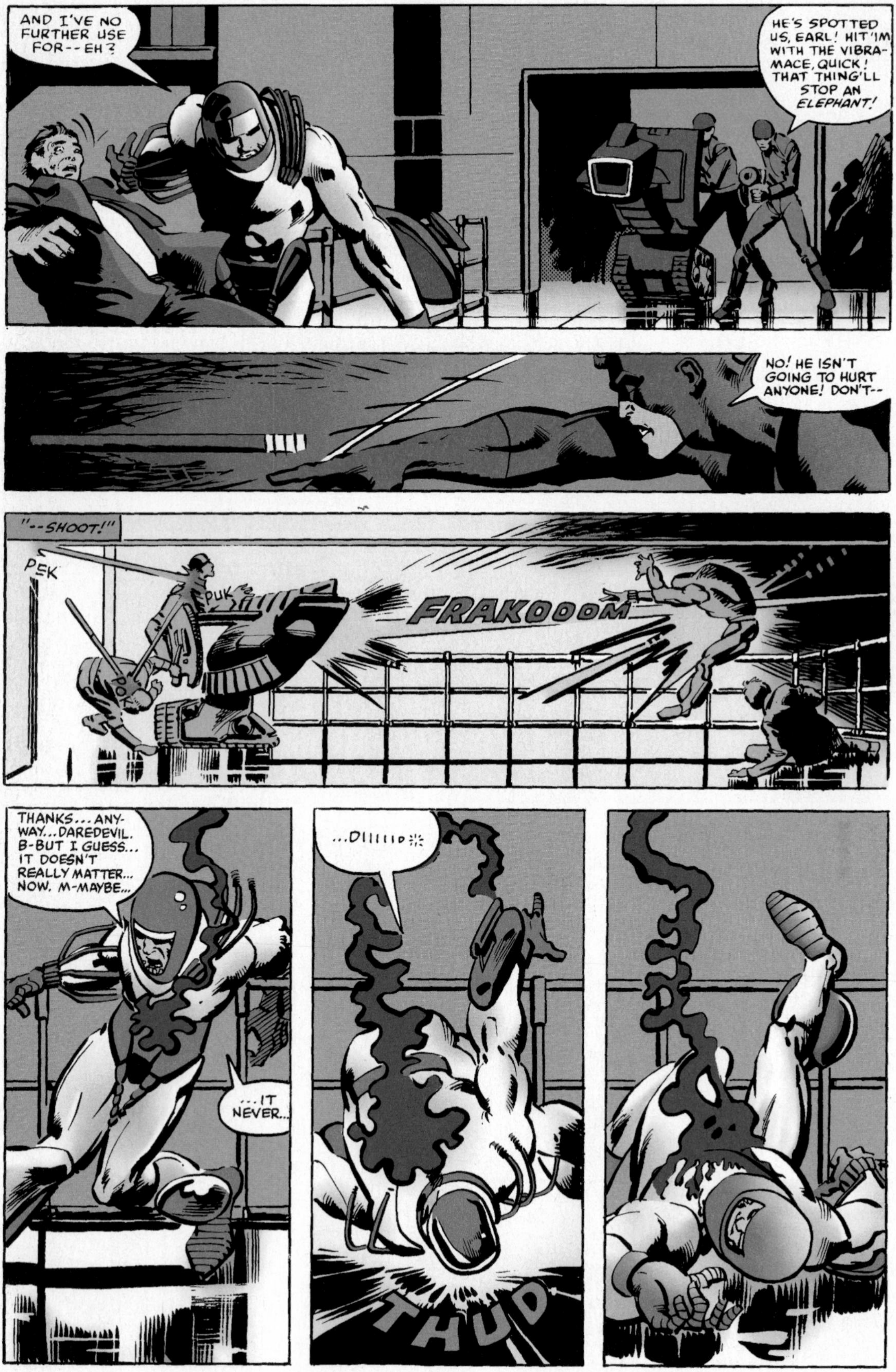
AND I'VE NO FURTHER USE FOR--EH?
HE'S SPOTTED US, EARL! HIT 'IM WITH THE VIBRA-MACE, QUICK! THAT THING'LL STOP AN ELEPHANT!
NO! HE ISN'T GOING TO HURT ANYONE! DON'T--
"--SHOOT!"
PEK
PUK
POK
FRAKOOOM
THANKS... ANY-WAY... DAREDEVIL. B-BUT I GUESS... IT DOESN'T REALLY MATTER... NOW. M-MAYBE...
...IT NEVER...
...DIIIIIP
THUD

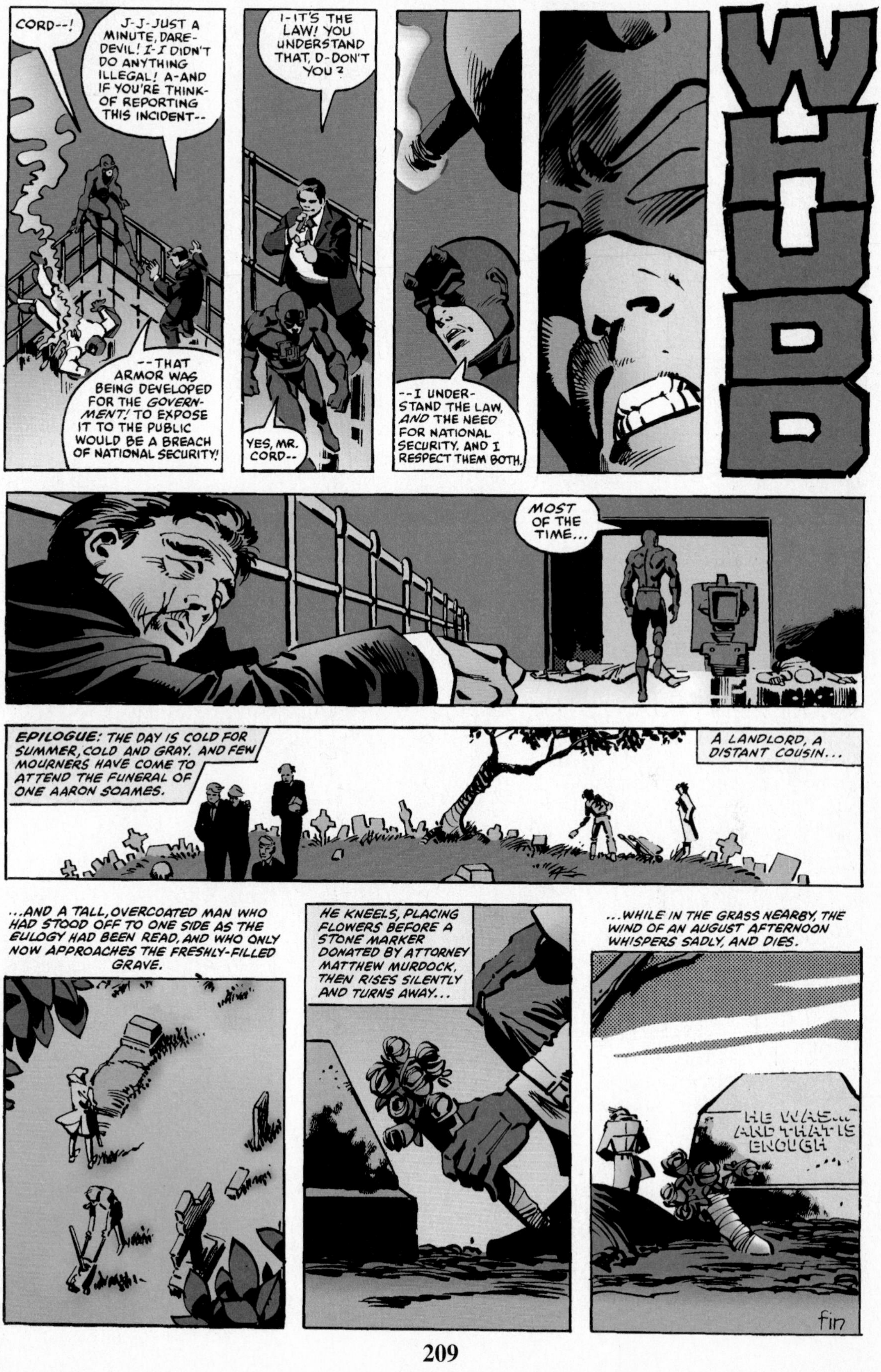

CORD--!
J-J-JUST A MINUTE, DAREDEVIL! I-I DIDN'T DO ANYTHING ILLEGAL! A-AND IF YOU'RE THINKING OF REPORTING THIS INCIDENT--
--THAT ARMOR WAS BEING DEVELOPED FOR THE GOVERNMENT! TO EXPOSE IT TO THE PUBLIC WOULD BE A BREACH OF NATIONAL SECURITY!
I-IT'S THE LAW! YOU UNDERSTAND THAT, D-DON'T YOU?
YES, MR. CORD--
--I UNDERSTAND THE LAW, AND THE NEED FOR NATIONAL SECURITY. AND I RESPECT THEM BOTH.
WHUDD
MOST OF THE TIME...
EPILOGUE: THE DAY IS COLD FOR SUMMER, COLD AND GRAY. AND FEW MOURNERS HAVE COME TO ATTEND THE FUNERAL OF ONE AARON SOAMES.
A LANDLORD, A DISTANT COUSIN...
...AND A TALL, OVERCOATED MAN WHO HAD STOOD OFF TO ONE SIDE AS THE EULOGY HAD BEEN READ, AND WHO ONLY NOW APPROACHES THE FRESHLY-FILLED GRAVE.
HE KNEELS, PLACING FLOWERS BEFORE A STONE MARKER DONATED BY ATTORNEY MATTHEW MURDOCK, THEN RISES SILENTLY AND TURNS AWAY...
...WHILE IN THE GRASS NEARBY, THE WIND OF AN AUGUST AFTERNOON WHISPERS SADLY, AND DIES.
HE WAS... AND THAT IS ENOUGH
fin

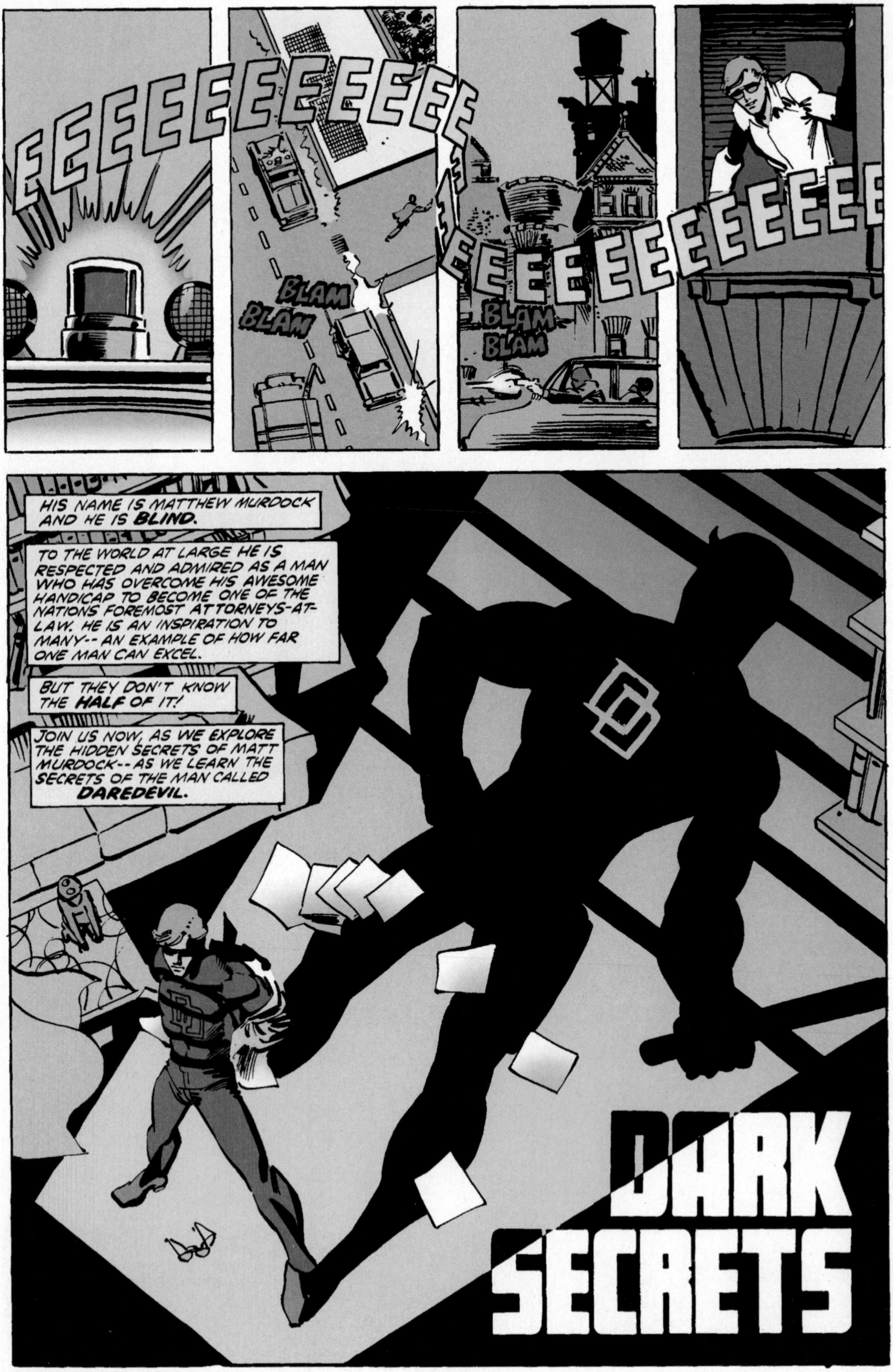
EEEEEEEEEEEE
BLAM
BLAM
EEEEEEEEEEEEEEEE
BLAM
BLAM
HIS NAME IS MATTHEW MURDOCK AND HE IS BLIND.
TO THE WORLD AT LARGE HE IS RESPECTED AND ADMIRED AS A MAN WHO HAS OVERCOME HIS AWESOME HANDICAP TO BECOME ONE OF THE NATIONS FOREMOST ATTORNEYS-AT-LAW. HE IS AN INSPIRATION TO MANY-- AN EXAMPLE OF HOW FAR ONE MAN CAN EXCEL.
BUT THEY DON'T KNOW THE HALF OF IT!
JOIN US NOW, AS WE EXPLORE THE HIDDEN SECRETS OF MATT MURDOCK--AS WE LEARN THE SECRETS OF THE MAN CALLED DAREDEVIL.
DARK SECRETS

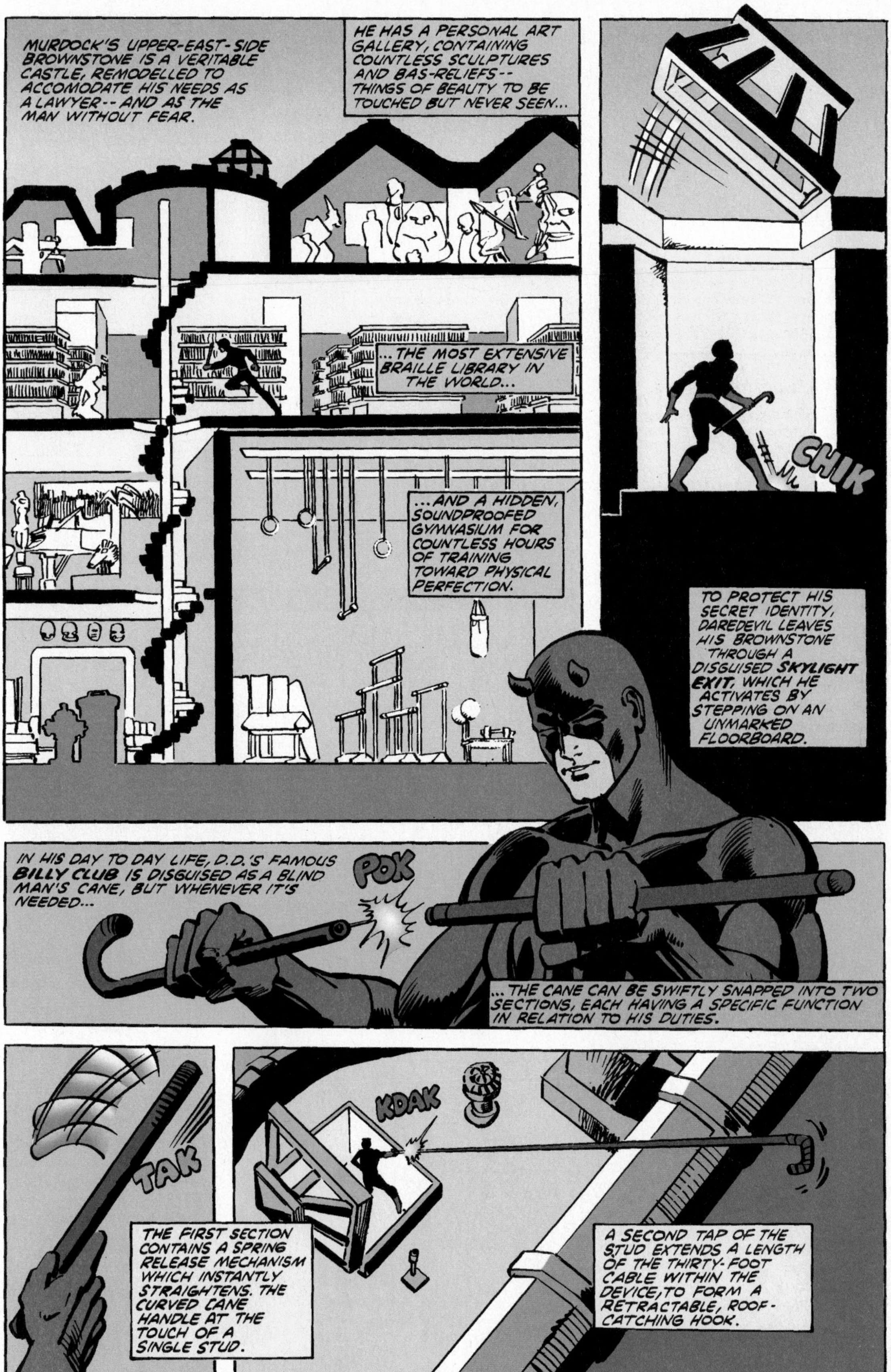
MURDOCK'S UPPER-EAST-SIDE BROWNSTONE IS A VERITABLE CASTLE, REMODELLED TO ACCOMODATE HIS NEEDS AS A LAWYER-- AND AS THE MAN WITHOUT FEAR.
HE HAS A PERSONAL ART GALLERY, CONTAINING COUNTLESS SCULPTURES AND BAS-RELIEFS-- THINGS OF BEAUTY TO BE TOUCHED BUT NEVER SEEN...
...THE MOST EXTENSIVE BRAILLE LIBRARY IN THE WORLD...
...AND A HIDDEN, SOUNDPROOFED GYMNASIUM FOR COUNTLESS HOURS OF TRAINING TOWARD PHYSICAL PERFECTION.
CHIK
TO PROTECT HIS SECRET IDENTITY, DAREDEVIL LEAVES HIS BROWNSTONE THROUGH A DISGUISED SKYLIGHT EXIT, WHICH HE ACTIVATES BY STEPPING ON AN UNMARKED FLOORBOARD.
IN HIS DAY TO DAY LIFE, D.D.'S FAMOUS BILLY CLUB IS DISGUISED AS A BLIND MAN'S CANE, BUT WHENEVER IT'S NEEDED...
POK
...THE CANE CAN BE SWIFTLY SNAPPED INTO TWO SECTIONS, EACH HAVING A SPECIFIC FUNCTION IN RELATION TO HIS DUTIES.
TAK
THE FIRST SECTION CONTAINS A SPRING RELEASE MECHANISM WHICH INSTANTLY STRAIGHTENS. THE CURVED CANE HANDLE AT THE TOUCH OF A SINGLE STUD.
KDAK
A SECOND TAP OF THE STUD EXTENDS A LENGTH OF THE THIRTY-FOOT CABLE WITHIN THE DEVICE, TO FORM A RETRACTABLE, ROOF-CATCHING HOOK.

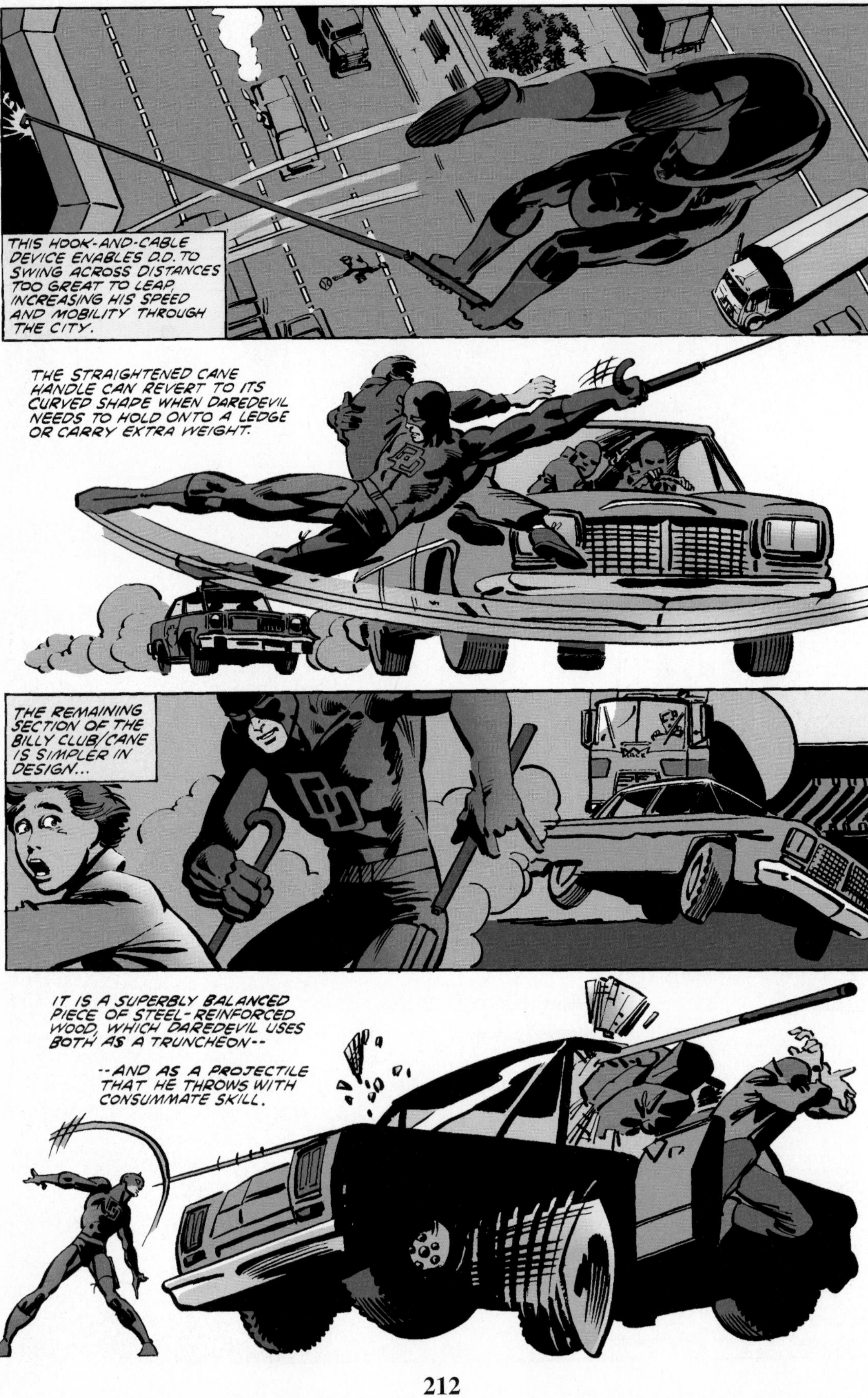
THIS HOOK-AND-CABLE DEVICE ENABLES D.D. TO SWING ACROSS DISTANCES TOO GREAT TO LEAP, INCREASING HIS SPEED AND MOBILITY THROUGH THE CITY.
THE STRAIGHTENED CANE HANDLE CAN REVERT TO ITS CURVED SHAPE WHEN DAREDEVIL NEEDS TO HOLD ONTO A LEDGE OR CARRY EXTRA WEIGHT.
THE REMAINING SECTION OF THE BILLY CLUB/CANE IS SIMPLER IN DESIGN...
IT IS A SUPERBLY BALANCED PIECE OF STEEL-REINFORCED WOOD, WHICH DAREDEVIL USES BOTH AS A TRUNCHEON--
--AND AS A PROJECTILE THAT HE THROWS WITH CONSUMMATE SKILL.

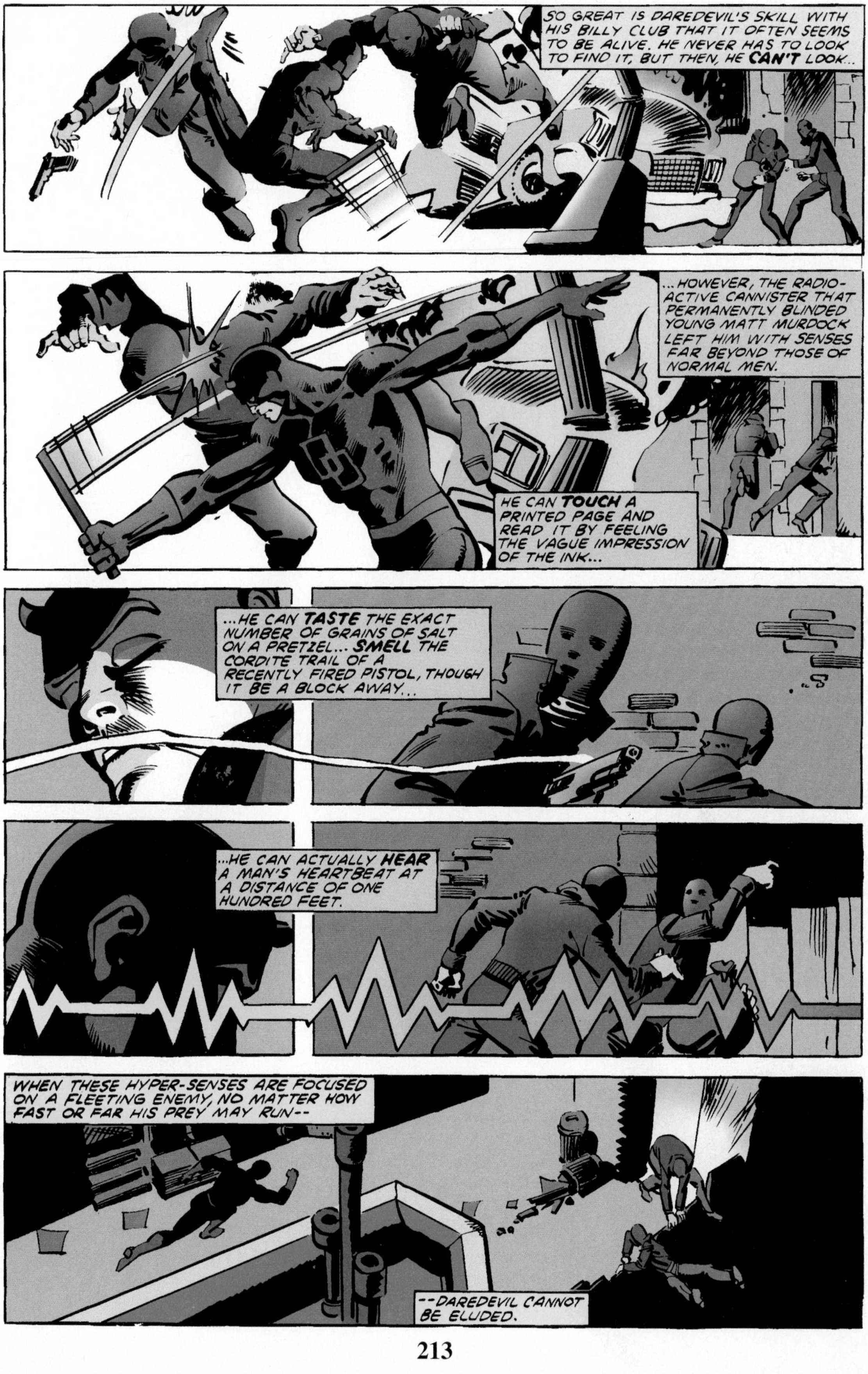
SO GREAT IS DAREDEVIL'S SKILL WITH HIS BILLY CLUB THAT IT OFTEN SEEMS TO BE ALIVE. HE NEVER HAS TO LOOK TO FIND IT, BUT THEN, HE CAN'T LOOK...
...HOWEVER, THE RADIO-ACTIVE CANNISTER THAT PERMANENTLY BLINDED YOUNG MATT MURDOCK LEFT HIM WITH SENSES FAR BEYOND THOSE OF NORMAL MEN.
HE CAN TOUCH A PRINTED PAGE AND READ IT BY FEELING THE VAGUE IMPRESSION OF THE INK...
...HE CAN TASTE THE EXACT NUMBER OF GRAINS OF SALT ON A PRETZEL... SMELL THE CORDITE TRAIL OF A RECENTLY FIRED PISTOL, THOUGH IT BE A BLOCK AWAY...
...HE CAN ACTUALLY HEAR A MAN'S HEARTBEAT AT A DISTANCE OF ONE HUNDRED FEET.
WHEN THESE HYPER-SENSES ARE FOCUSED ON A FLEETING ENEMY, NO MATTER HOW FAST OR FAR HIS PREY MAY RUN--
--DAREDEVIL CANNOT BE ELUDED.

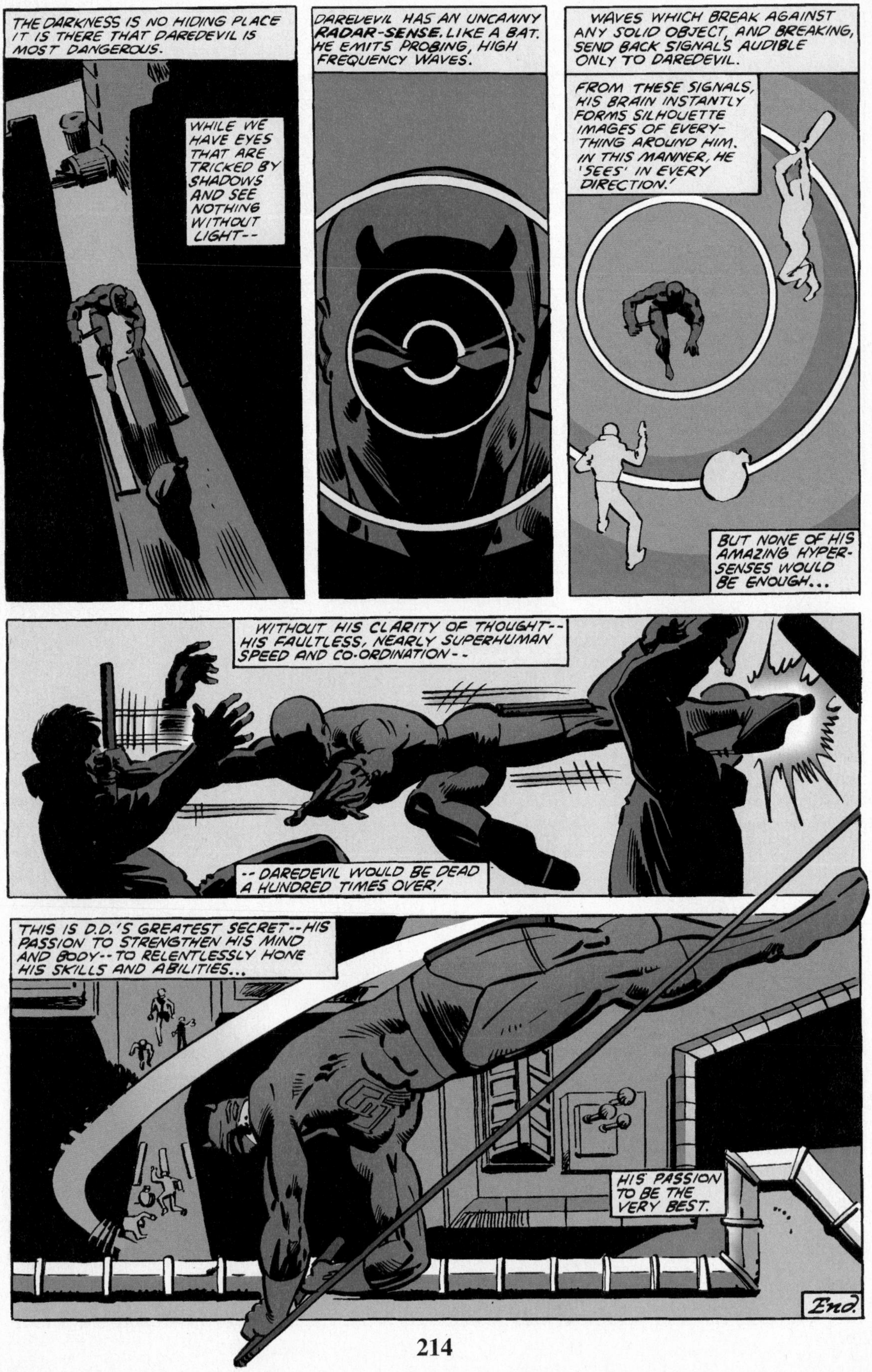
THE DARKNESS IS NO HIDING PLACE
IT IS THERE THAT DAREDEVIL IS MOST DANGEROUS.
WHILE WE HAVE EYES THAT ARE TRICKED BY SHADOWS AND SEE NOTHING WITHOUT LIGHT--
DAREDEVIL HAS AN UNCANNY RADAR-SENSE. LIKE A BAT, HE EMITS PROBING, HIGH FREQUENCY WAVES.
WAVES WHICH BREAK AGAINST ANY SOLID OBJECT, AND BREAKING, SEND BACK SIGNALS AUDIBLE ONLY TO DAREDEVIL.
FROM THESE SIGNALS, HIS BRAIN INSTANTLY FORMS SILHOUETTE IMAGES OF EVERY-THING AROUND HIM. IN THIS MANNER, HE 'SEES' IN EVERY DIRECTION.'
BUT NONE OF HIS AMAZING HYPER-SENSES WOULD BE ENOUGH...
WITHOUT HIS CLARITY OF THOUGHT--HIS FAULTLESS, NEARLY SUPERHUMAN SPEED AND CO-ORDINATION--
--DAREDEVIL WOULD BE DEAD A HUNDRED TIMES OVER!
THIS IS D.D.'S GREATEST SECRET--HIS PASSION TO STRENGTHEN HIS MIND AND BODY--TO RELENTLESSLY HONE HIS SKILLS AND ABILITIES...
HIS PASSION TO BE THE VERY BEST.
End.

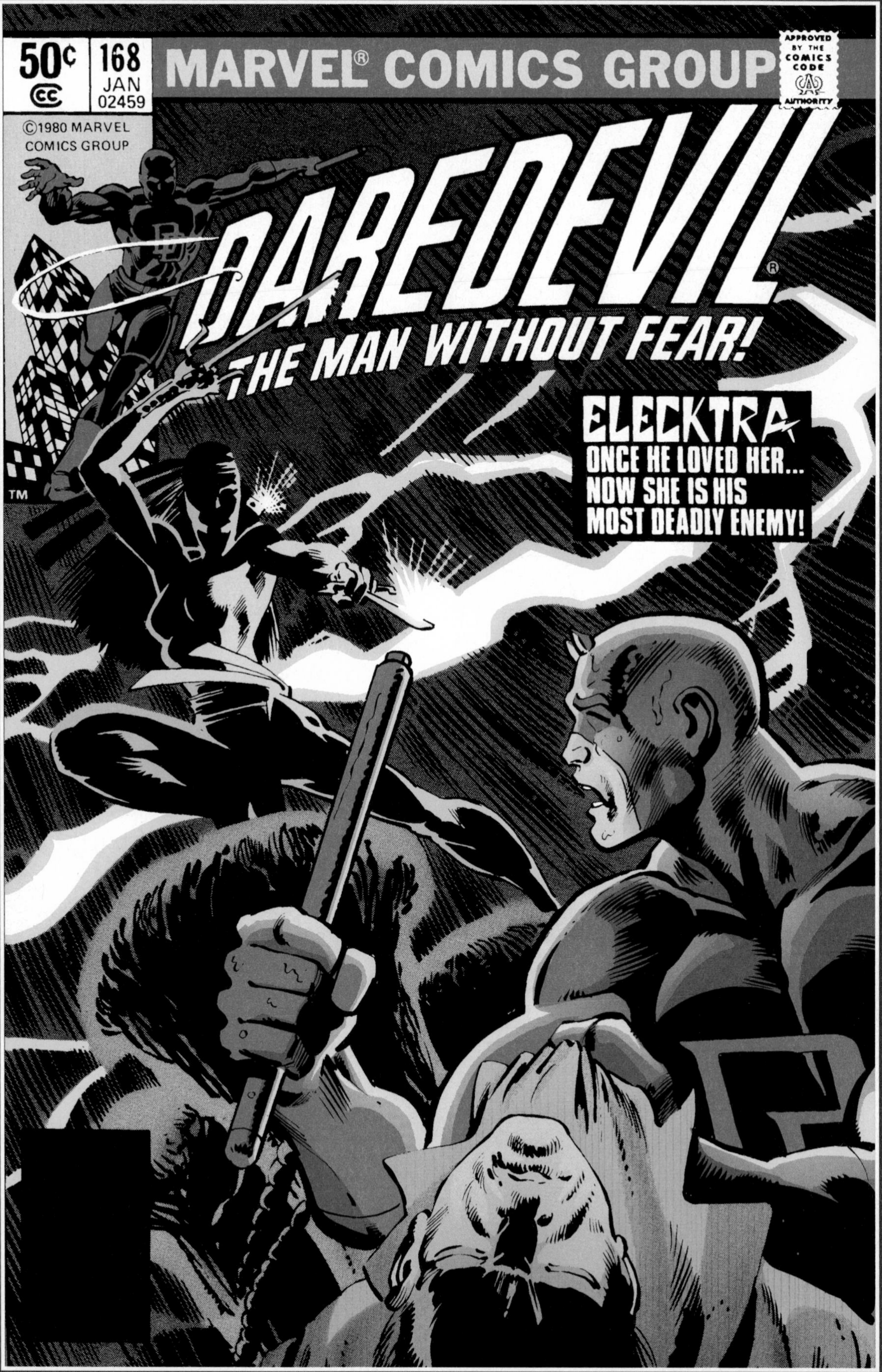
50¢
168
JAN
02459
MARVEL® COMICS GROUP
APPROVED BY THE COMICS CODE AUTHORITY
©1980 MARVEL COMICS GROUP
DAREDEVIL®
THE MAN WITHOUT FEAR!
ELECKTRA
ONCE HE LOVED HER...
NOW SHE IS HIS
MOST DEADLY ENEMY!
TM

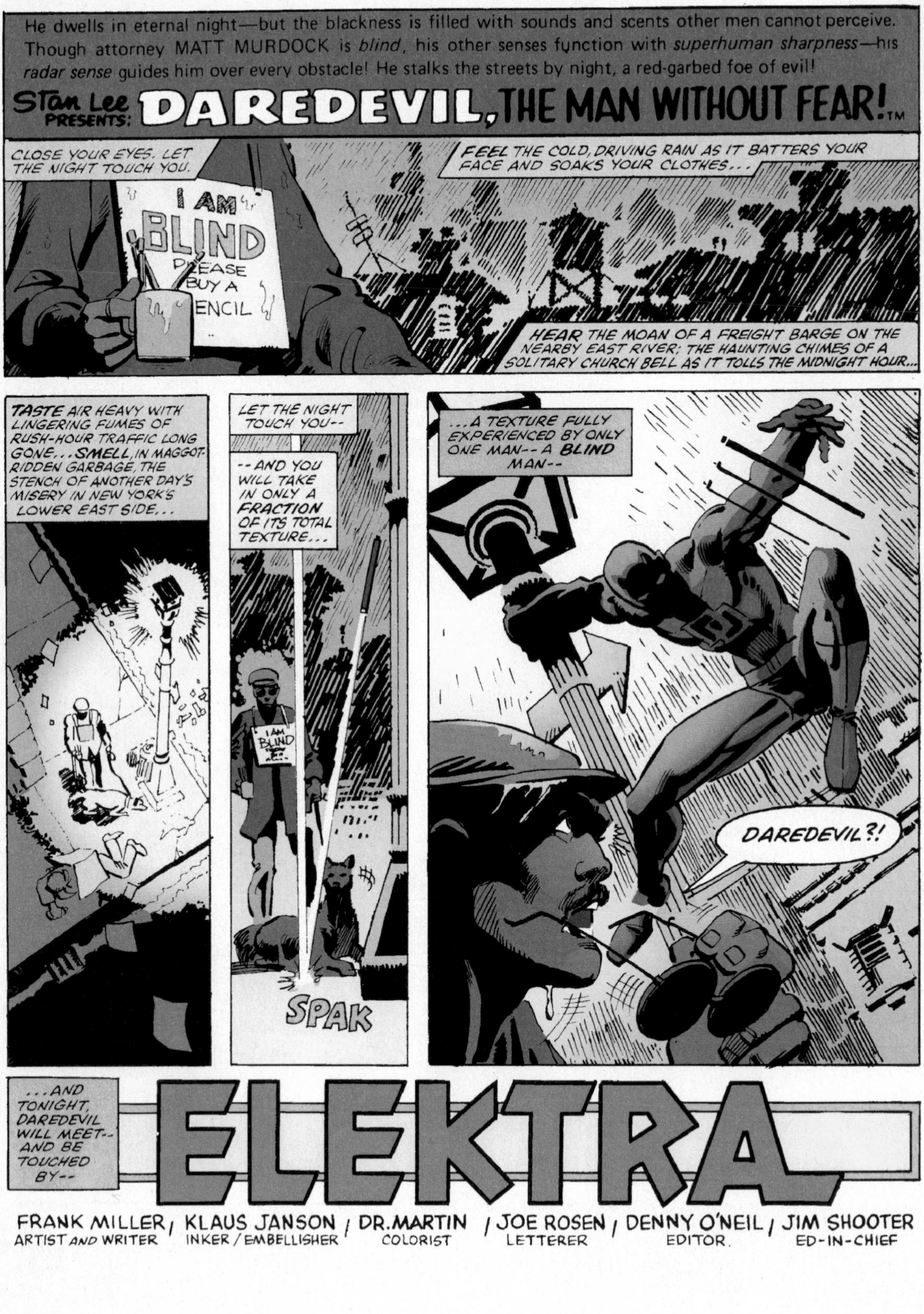
He dwells in eternal night—but the blackness is filled with sounds and scents other men cannot perceive. Though attorney MATT MURDOCK is *blind*, his other senses function with *superhuman sharpness*—his *radar sense* guides him over every obstacle! He stalks the streets by night, a red-garbed foe of evil!
STAN LEE PRESENTS: DAREDEVIL, THE MAN WITHOUT FEAR!™
CLOSE YOUR EYES. LET THE NIGHT TOUCH YOU.
I AM BLIND PLEASE BUY A PENCIL
FEEL THE COLD, DRIVING RAIN AS IT BATTERS YOUR FACE AND SOAKS YOUR CLOTHES...
HEAR THE MOAN OF A FREIGHT BARGE ON THE NEARBY EAST RIVER; THE HAUNTING CHIMES OF A SOLITARY CHURCH BELL AS IT TOLLS THE MIDNIGHT HOUR...
TASTE AIR HEAVY WITH LINGERING FUMES OF RUSH-HOUR TRAFFIC LONG GONE... SMELL, IN MAGGOT-RIDDEN GARBAGE, THE STENCH OF ANOTHER DAY'S MISERY IN NEW YORK'S LOWER EAST SIDE...
LET THE NIGHT TOUCH YOU--
--AND YOU WILL TAKE IN ONLY A FRACTION OF ITS TOTAL TEXTURE...
SPAK
...A TEXTURE FULLY EXPERIENCED BY ONLY ONE MAN-- A BLIND MAN--
DAREDEVIL?!
...AND TONIGHT, DAREDEVIL WILL MEET-- AND BE TOUCHED BY--
ELEKTRA
FRANK MILLER, ARTIST AND WRITER / KLAUS JANSON, INKER / EMBELLISHER / DR. MARTIN, COLORIST / JOE ROSEN, LETTERER / DENNY O'NEIL, EDITOR / JIM SHOOTER, ED-IN-CHIEF

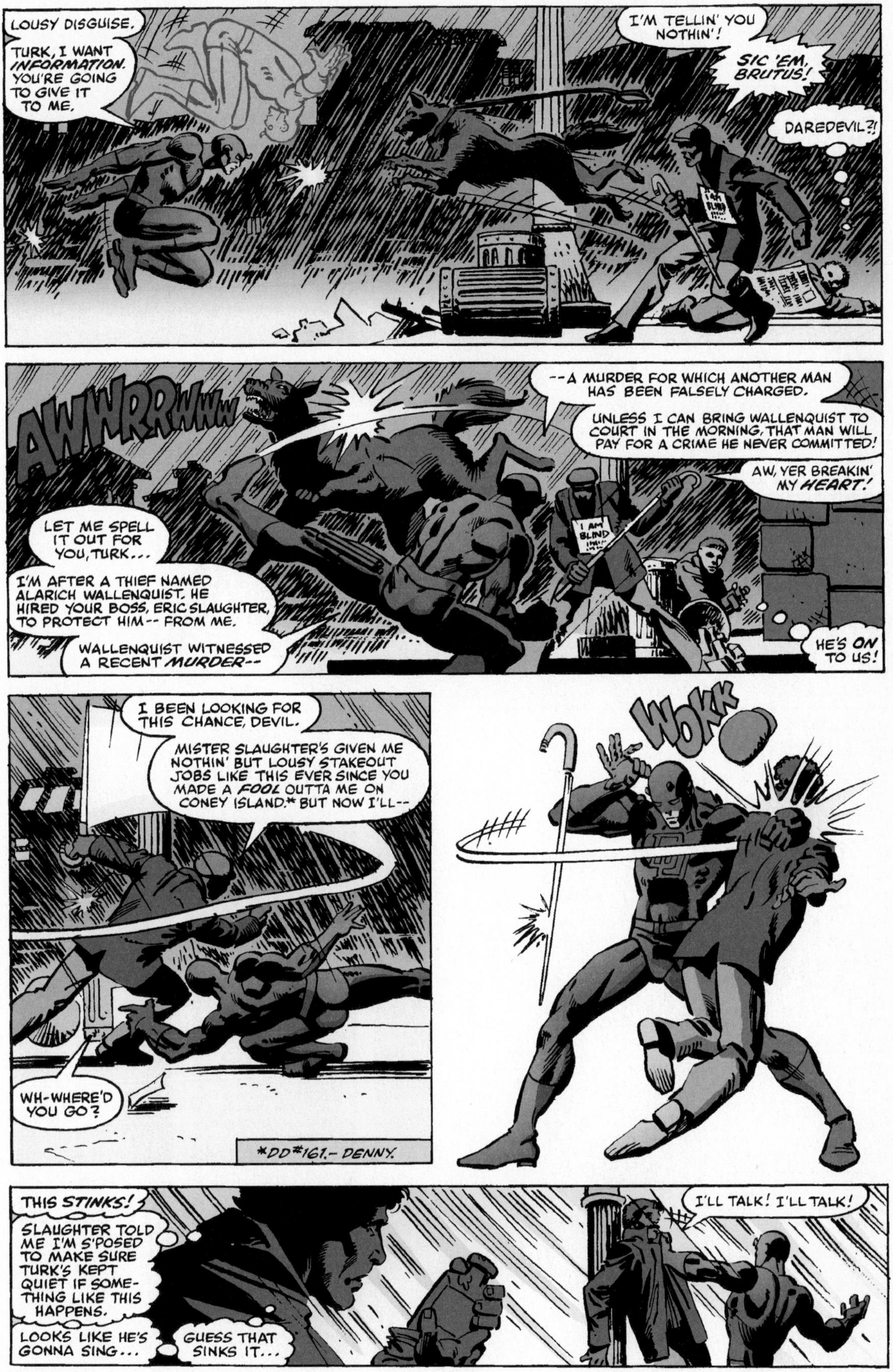
LOUSY DISGUISE.
TURK, I WANT INFORMATION. YOU'RE GOING TO GIVE IT TO ME.
I'M TELLIN' YOU NOTHIN'!
SIC 'EM, BRUTUS!
DAREDEVIL?!
I AM BLIND
AWWRRWWW
--A MURDER FOR WHICH ANOTHER MAN HAS BEEN FALSELY CHARGED.
UNLESS I CAN BRING WALLENQUIST TO COURT IN THE MORNING, THAT MAN WILL PAY FOR A CRIME HE NEVER COMMITTED!
AW, YER BREAKIN' MY HEART!
LET ME SPELL IT OUT FOR YOU, TURK...
I'M AFTER A THIEF NAMED ALARICH WALLENQUIST. HE HIRED YOUR BOSS, ERIC SLAUGHTER, TO PROTECT HIM-- FROM ME.
WALLENQUIST WITNESSED A RECENT MURDER--
I AM BLIND
HE'S ON TO US!
I BEEN LOOKING FOR THIS CHANCE, DEVIL.
MISTER SLAUGHTER'S GIVEN ME NOTHIN' BUT LOUSY STAKEOUT JOBS LIKE THIS EVER SINCE YOU MADE A FOOL OUTTA ME ON CONEY ISLAND.* BUT NOW I'LL--
WH-WHERE'D YOU GO?
*DD #161.- DENNY.
WOKK
THIS STINKS!
SLAUGHTER TOLD ME I'M S'POSED TO MAKE SURE TURK'S KEPT QUIET IF SOMETHING LIKE THIS HAPPENS.
LOOKS LIKE HE'S GONNA SING...
GUESS THAT SINKS IT...
I'LL TALK! I'LL TALK!

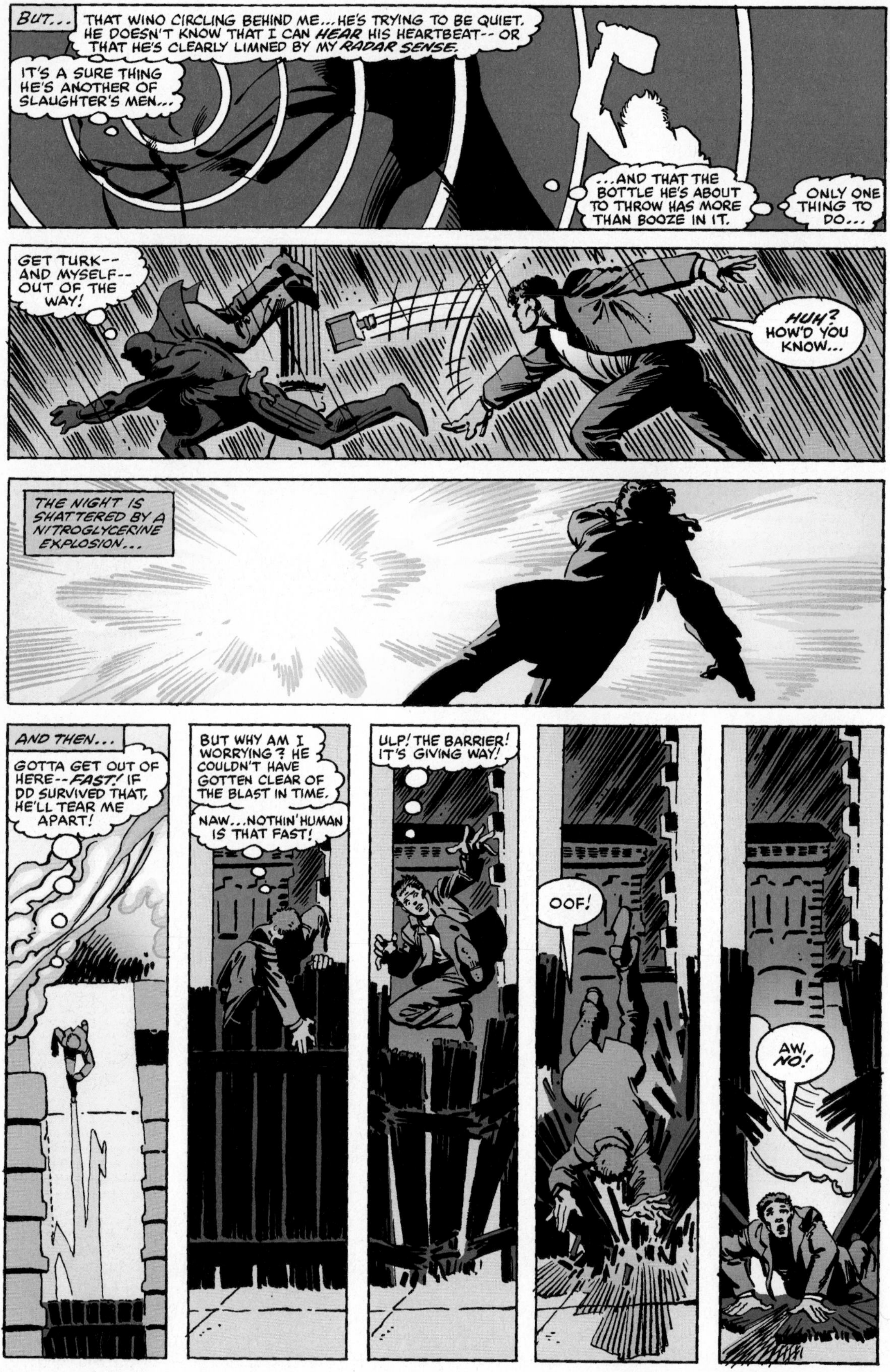

BUT...
THAT WINO CIRCLING BEHIND ME... HE'S TRYING TO BE QUIET. HE DOESN'T KNOW THAT I CAN HEAR HIS HEARTBEAT-- OR THAT HE'S CLEARLY LIMNED BY MY RADAR SENSE.
IT'S A SURE THING HE'S ANOTHER OF SLAUGHTER'S MEN...
...AND THAT THE BOTTLE HE'S ABOUT TO THROW HAS MORE THAN BOOZE IN IT.
ONLY ONE THING TO DO...
GET TURK-- AND MYSELF-- OUT OF THE WAY!
HUH? HOW'D YOU KNOW...
THE NIGHT IS SHATTERED BY A NITROGLYCERINE EXPLOSION...
AND THEN...
GOTTA GET OUT OF HERE--FAST! IF DD SURVIVED THAT, HE'LL TEAR ME APART!
BUT WHY AM I WORRYING? HE COULDN'T HAVE GOTTEN CLEAR OF THE BLAST IN TIME.
NAW... NOTHIN' HUMAN IS THAT FAST!
ULP! THE BARRIER! IT'S GIVING WAY!
OOF!
AW, NO!

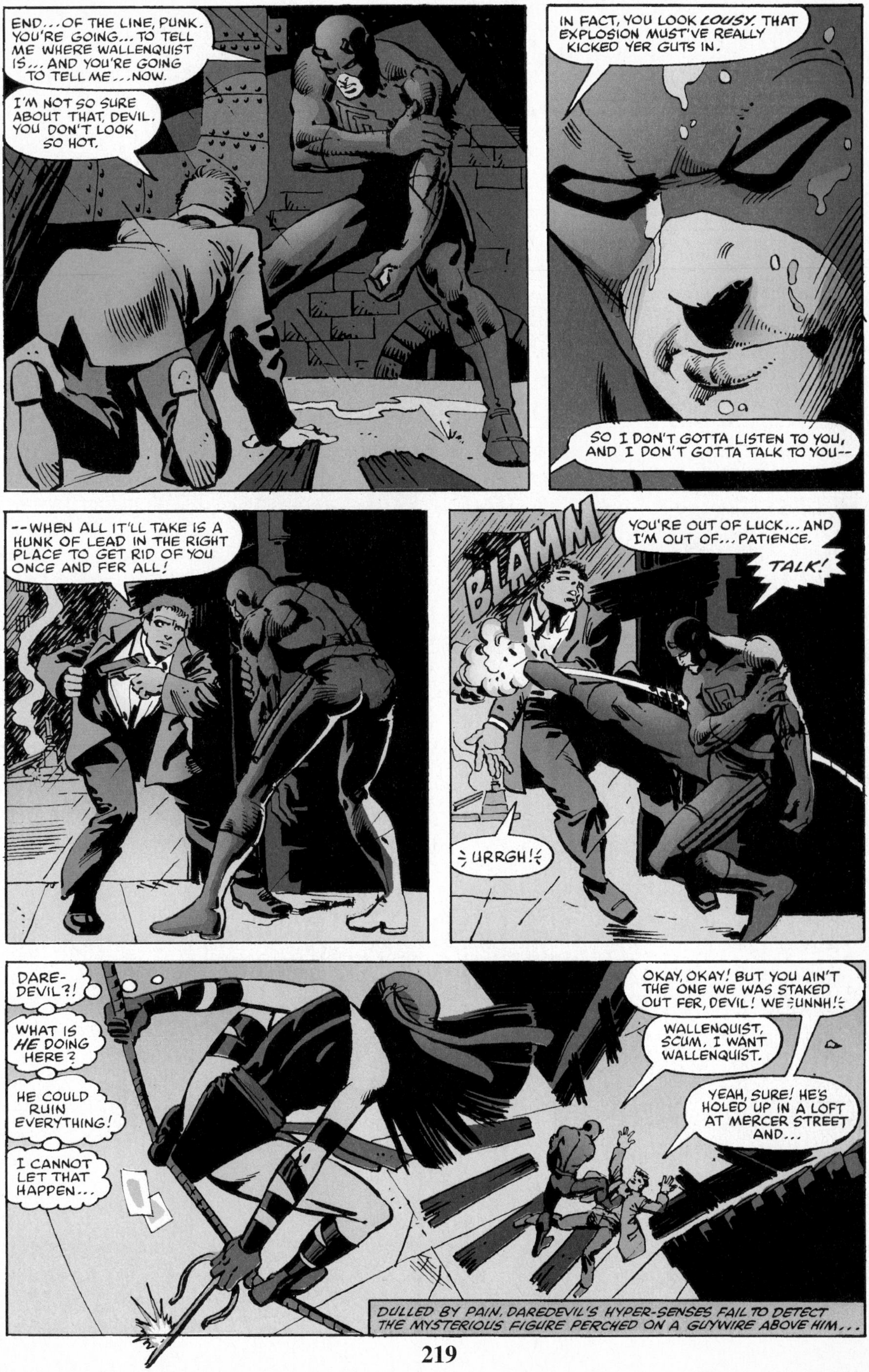
END... OF THE LINE, PUNK. YOU'RE GOING... TO TELL ME WHERE WALLENQUIST IS... AND YOU'RE GOING TO TELL ME... NOW.
I'M NOT SO SURE ABOUT THAT, DEVIL. YOU DON'T LOOK SO HOT.
IN FACT, YOU LOOK LOUSY. THAT EXPLOSION MUST'VE REALLY KICKED YER GUTS IN.
SO I DON'T GOTTA LISTEN TO YOU, AND I DON'T GOTTA TALK TO YOU--
--WHEN ALL IT'LL TAKE IS A HUNK OF LEAD IN THE RIGHT PLACE TO GET RID OF YOU ONCE AND FER ALL!
BLAMM
YOU'RE OUT OF LUCK... AND I'M OUT OF... PATIENCE.
TALK!
URRGH!
DARE-DEVIL?!
WHAT IS HE DOING HERE?
HE COULD RUIN EVERYTHING!
I CANNOT LET THAT HAPPEN...
OKAY, OKAY! BUT YOU AIN'T THE ONE WE WAS STAKED OUT FER, DEVIL! WE UNNH!
WALLENQUIST, SCUM. I WANT WALLENQUIST.
YEAH, SURE! HE'S HOLED UP IN A LOFT AT MERCER STREET AND...
DULLED BY PAIN, DAREDEVIL'S HYPER-SENSES FAIL TO DETECT THE MYSTERIOUS FIGURE PERCHED ON A GUYWIRE ABOVE HIM...

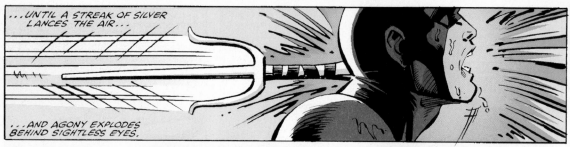

...UNTIL A STREAK OF SILVER LANCES THE AIR...

...AND AGONY EXPLODES BEHIND SIGHTLESS EYES.

HE REELS, DIMLY AWARE OF A WOMAN'S FORM--

--A MOMENT BEFORE SHE STRIKES HIM A BLOW THAT ROCKS HIS BRAIN AND STRETCHES THE CORDS IN HIS NECK.

HE FALLS. HE STRUGGLES TO REMAIN CONSCIOUS, SOME-HOW, HE HEARS FLEEING FOOTSTEPS...

...HEARS HIS ATTACKER WHIRL, AND THROW HER WEAPON...

...HEARS THE WEAPON STRIKE A WALL...

...HEARS THE SPLINTERING OF BONE AS IT SMASHES AN UNPROTECTED JAW.

THEN, HE HEARS HER SPEAK...

THERE IS A BOUNTY OUT IN EUROPE FOR ALARICH WALLENQUIST, BILGE--

--A BOUNTY I INTEND TO COLLECT.

YOU ARE GOING TO HELP ME CAPTURE HIM, OR I AM GOING TO KILL YOU.

IT IS AS SIMPLE AS THAT.

THAT VOICE--

ELEKTRA?!

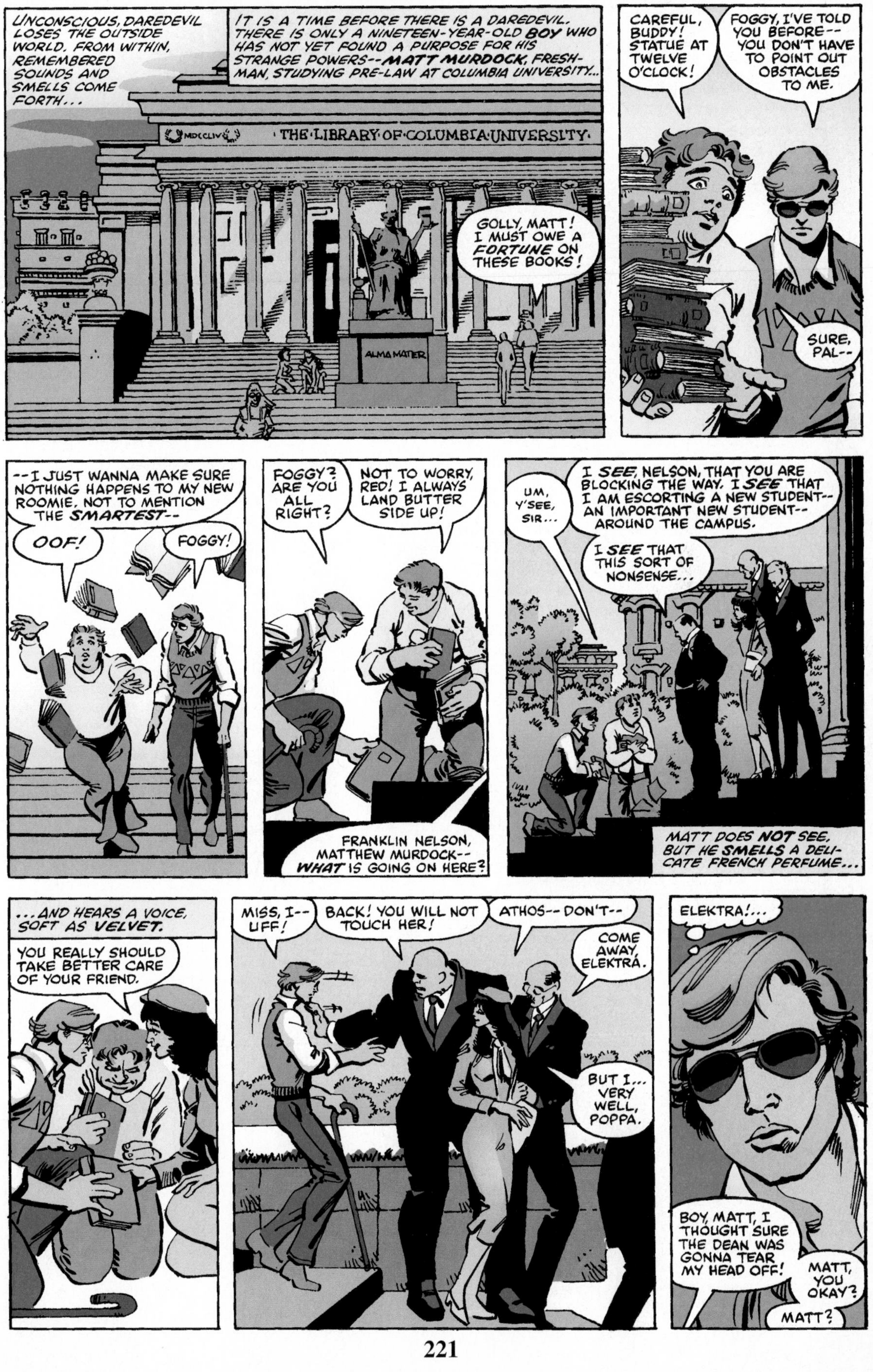
UNCONSCIOUS, DAREDEVIL LOSES THE OUTSIDE WORLD. FROM WITHIN, REMEMBERED SOUNDS AND SMELLS COME FORTH...
IT IS A TIME BEFORE THERE IS A DAREDEVIL. THERE IS ONLY A NINETEEN-YEAR-OLD BOY WHO HAS NOT YET FOUND A PURPOSE FOR HIS STRANGE POWERS--MATT MURDOCK, FRESHMAN, STUDYING PRE-LAW AT COLUMBIA UNIVERSITY...
MDCCLIV
THE LIBRARY OF COLUMBIA UNIVERSITY
ALMA MATER
GOLLY, MATT! I MUST OWE A FORTUNE ON THESE BOOKS!
CAREFUL, BUDDY! STATUE AT TWELVE O'CLOCK!
FOGGY, I'VE TOLD YOU BEFORE--YOU DON'T HAVE TO POINT OUT OBSTACLES TO ME.
SURE, PAL--
--I JUST WANNA MAKE SURE NOTHING HAPPENS TO MY NEW ROOMIE, NOT TO MENTION THE SMARTEST--
OOF!
FOGGY!
FOGGY? ARE YOU ALL RIGHT?
NOT TO WORRY, RED! I ALWAYS LAND BUTTER SIDE UP!
FRANKLIN NELSON, MATTHEW MURDOCK--WHAT IS GOING ON HERE?
UM, Y'SEE, SIR...
I SEE, NELSON, THAT YOU ARE BLOCKING THE WAY. I SEE THAT I AM ESCORTING A NEW STUDENT--AN IMPORTANT NEW STUDENT--AROUND THE CAMPUS.
I SEE THAT THIS SORT OF NONSENSE...
MATT DOES NOT SEE, BUT HE SMELLS A DELICATE FRENCH PERFUME...
...AND HEARS A VOICE, SOFT AS VELVET.
YOU REALLY SHOULD TAKE BETTER CARE OF YOUR FRIEND.
MISS, I--UFF!
BACK! YOU WILL NOT TOUCH HER!
ATHOS-- DON'T--
COME AWAY, ELEKTRA.
BUT I... VERY WELL, POPPA.
ELEKTRA!...
BOY, MATT, I THOUGHT SURE THE DEAN WAS GONNA TEAR MY HEAD OFF!
MATT, YOU OKAY?
MATT?

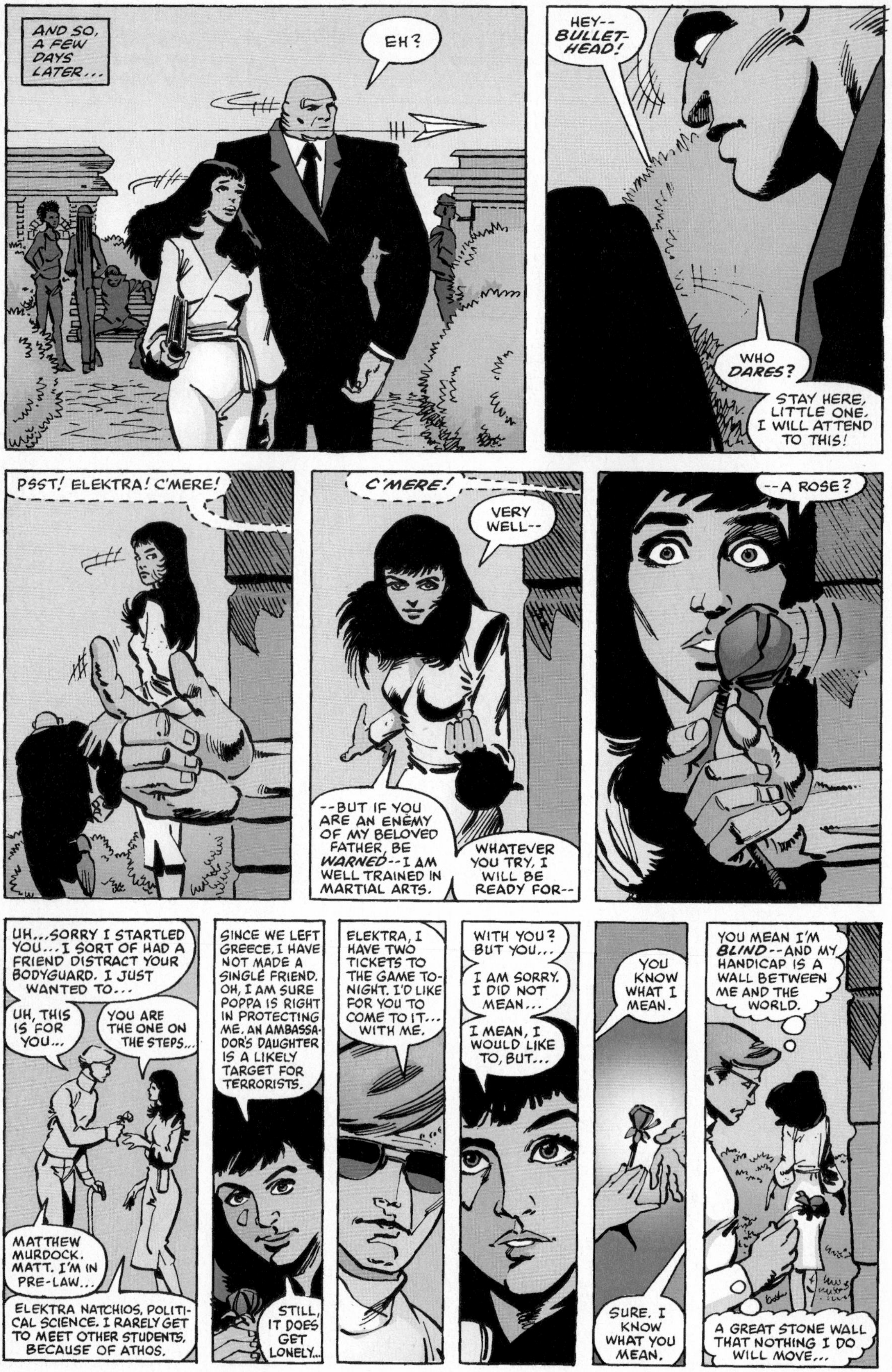

AND SO, A FEW DAYS LATER...
EH?
HEY-- BULLET-HEAD!
WHO DARES?
STAY HERE, LITTLE ONE. I WILL ATTEND TO THIS!
PSST! ELEKTRA! C'MERE!
C'MERE!
VERY WELL--
--BUT IF YOU ARE AN ENEMY OF MY BELOVED FATHER, BE WARNED--I AM WELL TRAINED IN MARTIAL ARTS.
WHATEVER YOU TRY, I WILL BE READY FOR--
--A ROSE?
UH...SORRY I STARTLED YOU...I SORT OF HAD A FRIEND DISTRACT YOUR BODYGUARD. I JUST WANTED TO...
UH, THIS IS FOR YOU...
YOU ARE THE ONE ON THE STEPS...
MATTHEW MURDOCK. MATT. I'M IN PRE-LAW...
ELEKTRA NATCHIOS, POLITICAL SCIENCE. I RARELY GET TO MEET OTHER STUDENTS, BECAUSE OF ATHOS.
SINCE WE LEFT GREECE, I HAVE NOT MADE A SINGLE FRIEND. OH, I AM SURE POPPA IS RIGHT IN PROTECTING ME. AN AMBASSADOR'S DAUGHTER IS A LIKELY TARGET FOR TERRORISTS.
STILL, IT DOES GET LONELY...
ELEKTRA, I HAVE TWO TICKETS TO THE GAME TONIGHT. I'D LIKE FOR YOU TO COME TO IT... WITH ME.
WITH YOU? BUT YOU...
I AM SORRY. I DID NOT MEAN...
I MEAN, I WOULD LIKE TO, BUT...
YOU KNOW WHAT I MEAN.
SURE. I KNOW WHAT YOU MEAN.
YOU MEAN I'M BLIND--AND MY HANDICAP IS A WALL BETWEEN ME AND THE WORLD.
A GREAT STONE WALL THAT NOTHING I DO WILL MOVE...

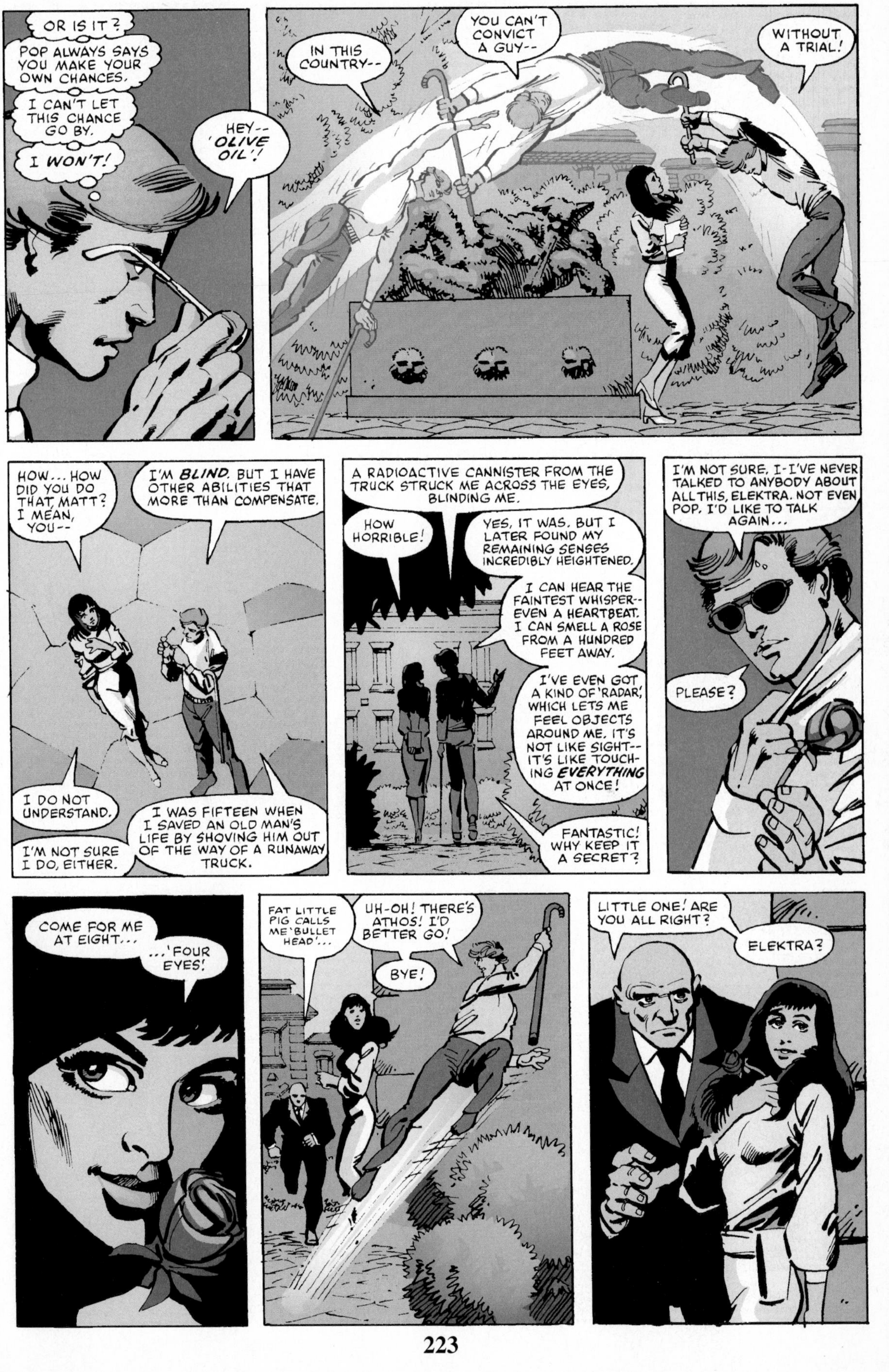
OR IS IT?
POP ALWAYS SAYS YOU MAKE YOUR OWN CHANCES.
I CAN'T LET THIS CHANCE GO BY.
I WON'T!
HEY-- 'OLIVE OIL'!
IN THIS COUNTRY--
YOU CAN'T CONVICT A GUY--
WITHOUT A TRIAL!
HOW... HOW DID YOU DO THAT, MATT? I MEAN, YOU--
I'M BLIND. BUT I HAVE OTHER ABILITIES THAT MORE THAN COMPENSATE.
I DO NOT UNDERSTAND.
I'M NOT SURE I DO, EITHER.
I WAS FIFTEEN WHEN I SAVED AN OLD MAN'S LIFE BY SHOVING HIM OUT OF THE WAY OF A RUNAWAY TRUCK.
A RADIOACTIVE CANNISTER FROM THE TRUCK STRUCK ME ACROSS THE EYES, BLINDING ME.
HOW HORRIBLE!
YES, IT WAS. BUT I LATER FOUND MY REMAINING SENSES INCREDIBLY HEIGHTENED.
I CAN HEAR THE FAINTEST WHISPER-- EVEN A HEARTBEAT. I CAN SMELL A ROSE FROM A HUNDRED FEET AWAY.
I'VE EVEN GOT A KIND OF 'RADAR,' WHICH LETS ME FEEL OBJECTS AROUND ME. IT'S NOT LIKE SIGHT-- IT'S LIKE TOUCHING EVERYTHING AT ONCE!
FANTASTIC! WHY KEEP IT A SECRET?
I'M NOT SURE. I-I'VE NEVER TALKED TO ANYBODY ABOUT ALL THIS, ELEKTRA. NOT EVEN POP. I'D LIKE TO TALK AGAIN...
PLEASE?
COME FOR ME AT EIGHT...
...'FOUR EYES'!
FAT LITTLE PIG CALLS ME 'BULLET HEAD'...
UH-OH! THERE'S ATHOS! I'D BETTER GO!
BYE!
LITTLE ONE! ARE YOU ALL RIGHT?
ELEKTRA?

THEY MEET THAT EVENING ...AND THE NEXT. VERY SOON, THEY FALL IN LOVE. IT IS A FIRST LOVE FOR BOTH...

...AND FOR A YEAR, THEY ARE EUPHORIC.

THEN... I'M NOT THE *ONLY* ONE THEY MADE WEAR THESE THINGS.

BUT, FOGGY-- MOOSE ANTLERS?

IT'S *INITIATION*, MATT.

I'M GONNA JOIN OMEGA DELTA IF IT KILLS ME. ANYBODY WHO'S EVERYBODY IS AT OMEGA DELTA!

GOSH, I'M HUNGRY AS A BEAR. WHAT SAY WE...

I CAN'T, FOGGY. TODAY'S ELEKTRA'S BIRTHDAY, AND WE'RE GOING TO...

WHAT'S THAT NOISE?

WHAT NOI-- OH, GOLLY! LOOK AT ALL THOSE COPS. WONDER WHAT'S GOING ON?

SOME-THING IS VERY WRONG HERE.

YOU COULD CUT THE TENSION IN THE AIR.

LIKE, THERE'S THIS RILLY INTENSE SCENE IN THERE, Y'KNOW? THERE'S THESE GUYS HOLDING HOSTAGES, LIKE IN THE ADMINI-STRATION BUILDING. INTENSE. RILLY INTENSE.

HEY-- I LIKE THE ANTLERS.

THANKS!

HOLD ON A SECOND... THE ADMINISTRATION BUILDING? ISN'T THAT WHERE YOU'RE MEET-ING ELEKTRA, MATT?

MATT?

HE'S GONE!

IN THE SHADOW OF A NEARBY BUILDING...

I MEANT TO GIVE THIS SCARF TO ELEKTRA AS A BIRTHDAY GIFT.

BUT NOW IT'S MY ONLY MEANS OF DISGUISE.

HAVE TO GAIN ALTITUDE-- SCAN THE SITUATION.

NOW I'LL SEE IF ALL THOSE HOURS OF SECRET TRAINING COUNT FOR ANYTHING!

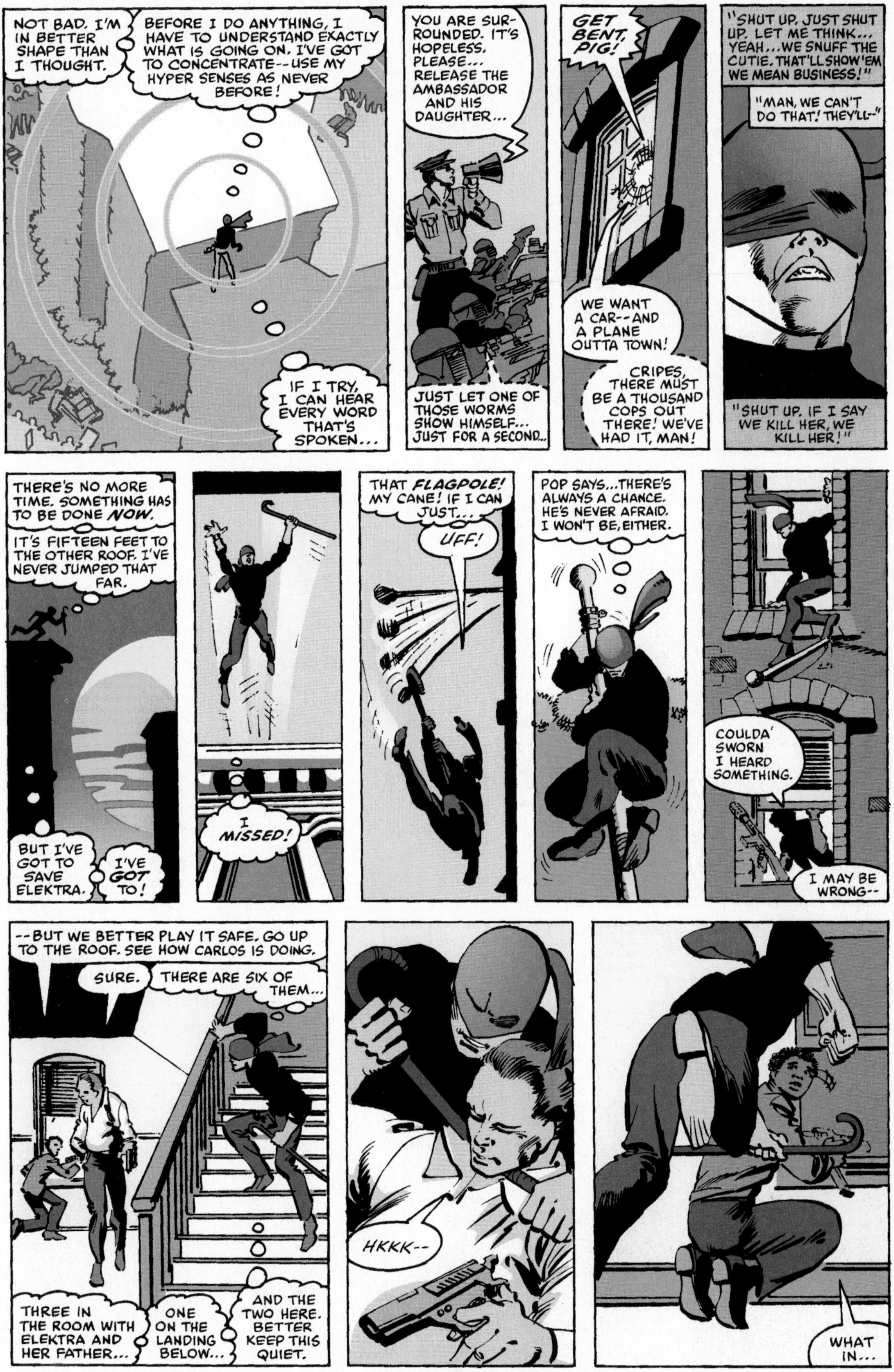

NOT BAD. I'M IN BETTER SHAPE THAN I THOUGHT.
BEFORE I DO ANYTHING, I HAVE TO UNDERSTAND EXACTLY WHAT IS GOING ON. I'VE GOT TO CONCENTRATE--USE MY HYPER SENSES AS NEVER BEFORE!
IF I TRY, I CAN HEAR EVERY WORD THAT'S SPOKEN...
YOU ARE SURROUNDED. IT'S HOPELESS. PLEASE... RELEASE THE AMBASSADOR AND HIS DAUGHTER...
JUST LET ONE OF THOSE WORMS SHOW HIMSELF... JUST FOR A SECOND...
GET BENT, PIG!
WE WANT A CAR--AND A PLANE OUTTA TOWN!
CRIPES, THERE MUST BE A THOUSAND COPS OUT THERE! WE'VE HAD IT, MAN!
"SHUT UP. JUST SHUT UP. LET ME THINK... YEAH... WE SNUFF THE CUTIE. THAT'LL SHOW 'EM WE MEAN BUSINESS!"
"MAN, WE CAN'T DO THAT! THEY'LL--"
"SHUT UP. IF I SAY WE KILL HER, WE KILL HER!"
THERE'S NO MORE TIME. SOMETHING HAS TO BE DONE NOW.
IT'S FIFTEEN FEET TO THE OTHER ROOF. I'VE NEVER JUMPED THAT FAR.
BUT I'VE GOT TO SAVE ELEKTRA.
I'VE GOT TO!
I MISSED!
THAT FLAGPOLE! MY CANE! IF I CAN JUST...
UFF!
POP SAYS... THERE'S ALWAYS A CHANCE. HE'S NEVER AFRAID. I WON'T BE, EITHER.
COULDA' SWORN I HEARD SOMETHING.
I MAY BE WRONG--
--BUT WE BETTER PLAY IT SAFE. GO UP TO THE ROOF. SEE HOW CARLOS IS DOING.
SURE.
THERE ARE SIX OF THEM...
THREE IN THE ROOM WITH ELEKTRA AND HER FATHER...
ONE ON THE LANDING BELOW...
AND THE TWO HERE. BETTER KEEP THIS QUIET.
HKKK--
WHAT IN...

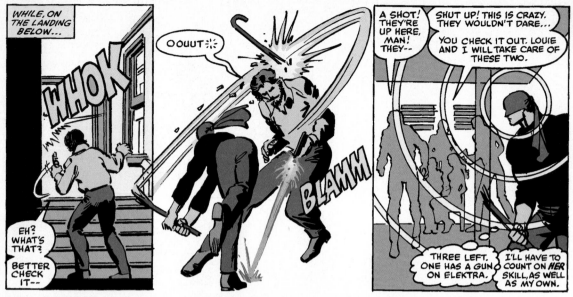

WHILE, ON THE LANDING BELOW...

WHOK

OOUUT ✳

EH? WHAT'S THAT? BETTER CHECK IT--

BLAMM

A SHOT! THEY'RE UP HERE, MAN! THEY--

SHUT UP! THIS IS CRAZY. THEY WOULDN'T DARE... YOU CHECK IT OUT. LOUIE AND I WILL TAKE CARE OF THESE TWO.

THREE LEFT. ONE HAS A GUN ON ELEKTRA.

I'LL HAVE TO COUNT ON HER SKILL, AS WELL AS MY OWN.

THOK

HIT 'EM LOW, OLIVE OIL!

THEY BOTH STRIKE SWIFTLY, EFFICIENTLY.

BUT THEN--

I MISCALCULATED. HE'S FALLING BACKWARD...

...AND THROUGH THE WINDOW!

THEY'RE KILLING THE HOSTAGES!

THOSE SLIMY... ALL I NEED IS A CLEAR SHOT, THAT'S ALL...

"...JUST A CLEAR SHOT AT ONE OF THEM, JUST FOR A SECOND...

"WAIT... WHAT'S THAT? I CAN SEE SOMETHING..."

OH, NO... STAY DOWN, SIR!

STAY DOWN!

BUT I...

URRGH!

FUP FUP FUP

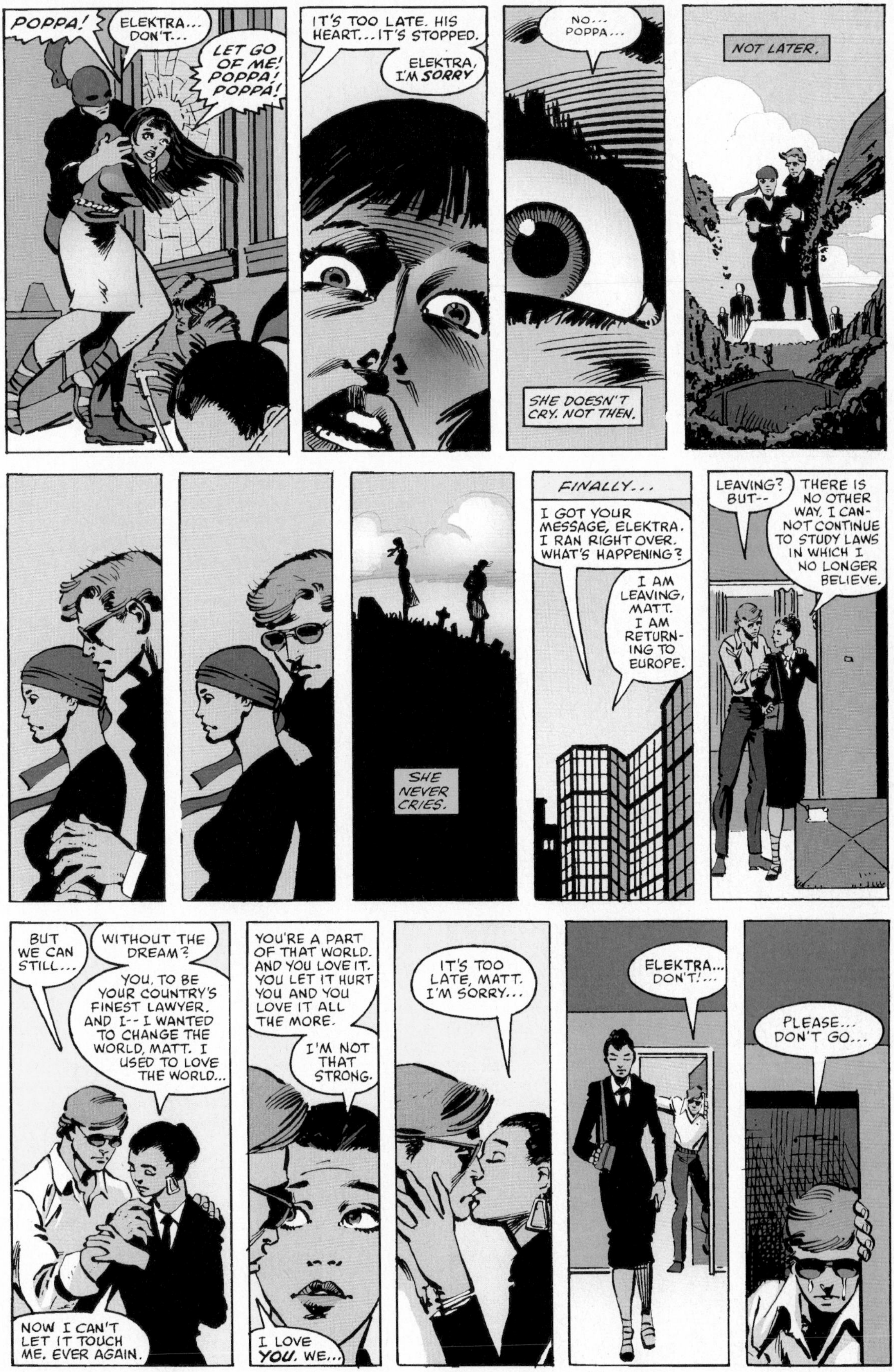
POPPA!
ELEKTRA... DON'T...
LET GO OF ME! POPPA! POPPA!
IT'S TOO LATE. HIS HEART... IT'S STOPPED.
ELEKTRA, I'M SORRY
NO... POPPA...
SHE DOESN'T CRY. NOT THEN.
NOT LATER.
SHE NEVER CRIES.
FINALLY...
I GOT YOUR MESSAGE, ELEKTRA. I RAN RIGHT OVER. WHAT'S HAPPENING?
I AM LEAVING, MATT. I AM RETURNING TO EUROPE.
LEAVING? BUT--
THERE IS NO OTHER WAY. I CANNOT CONTINUE TO STUDY LAWS IN WHICH I NO LONGER BELIEVE.
BUT WE CAN STILL...
WITHOUT THE DREAM?
YOU, TO BE YOUR COUNTRY'S FINEST LAWYER. AND I-- I WANTED TO CHANGE THE WORLD, MATT. I USED TO LOVE THE WORLD...
NOW I CAN'T LET IT TOUCH ME. EVER AGAIN.
YOU'RE A PART OF THAT WORLD. AND YOU LOVE IT. YOU LET IT HURT YOU AND YOU LOVE IT ALL THE MORE.
I'M NOT THAT STRONG.
I LOVE YOU. WE...
IT'S TOO LATE, MATT. I'M SORRY...
ELEKTRA... DON'T!...
PLEASE... DON'T GO...

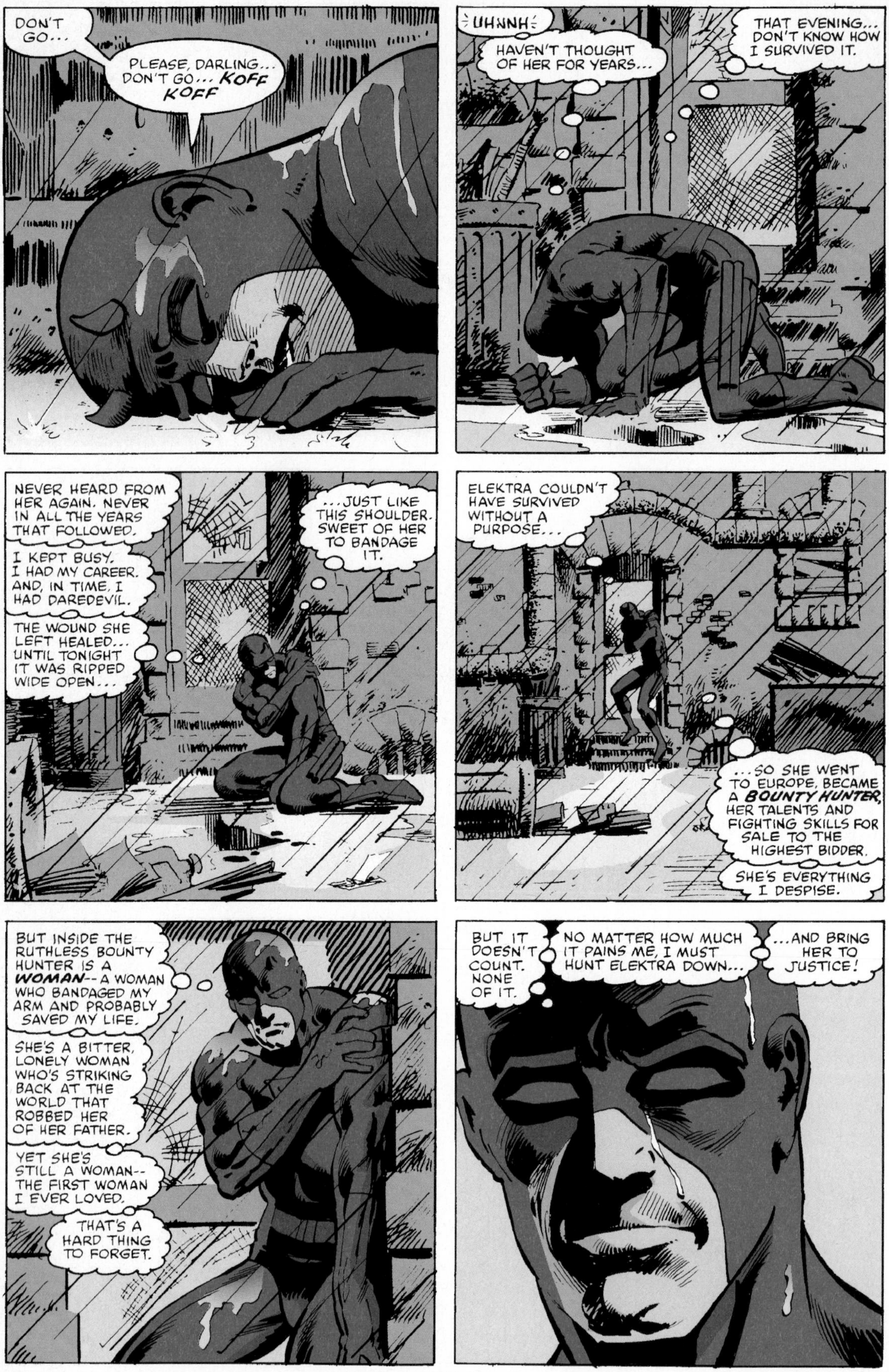
DON'T GO...
PLEASE, DARLING... DON'T GO... KOFF KOFF
UHHNH
HAVEN'T THOUGHT OF HER FOR YEARS...
THAT EVENING... DON'T KNOW HOW I SURVIVED IT.
NEVER HEARD FROM HER AGAIN. NEVER IN ALL THE YEARS THAT FOLLOWED.
I KEPT BUSY. I HAD MY CAREER. AND, IN TIME, I HAD DAREDEVIL.
THE WOUND SHE LEFT HEALED... UNTIL TONIGHT IT WAS RIPPED WIDE OPEN...
...JUST LIKE THIS SHOULDER. SWEET OF HER TO BANDAGE IT.
ELEKTRA COULDN'T HAVE SURVIVED WITHOUT A PURPOSE...
...SO SHE WENT TO EUROPE, BECAME A BOUNTY HUNTER, HER TALENTS AND FIGHTING SKILLS FOR SALE TO THE HIGHEST BIDDER.
SHE'S EVERYTHING I DESPISE.
BUT INSIDE THE RUTHLESS BOUNTY HUNTER IS A WOMAN-- A WOMAN WHO BANDAGED MY ARM AND PROBABLY SAVED MY LIFE.
SHE'S A BITTER, LONELY WOMAN WHO'S STRIKING BACK AT THE WORLD THAT ROBBED HER OF HER FATHER.
YET SHE'S STILL A WOMAN-- THE FIRST WOMAN I EVER LOVED.
THAT'S A HARD THING TO FORGET.
BUT IT DOESN'T COUNT. NONE OF IT.
NO MATTER HOW MUCH IT PAINS ME, I MUST HUNT ELEKTRA DOWN...
...AND BRING HER TO JUSTICE!

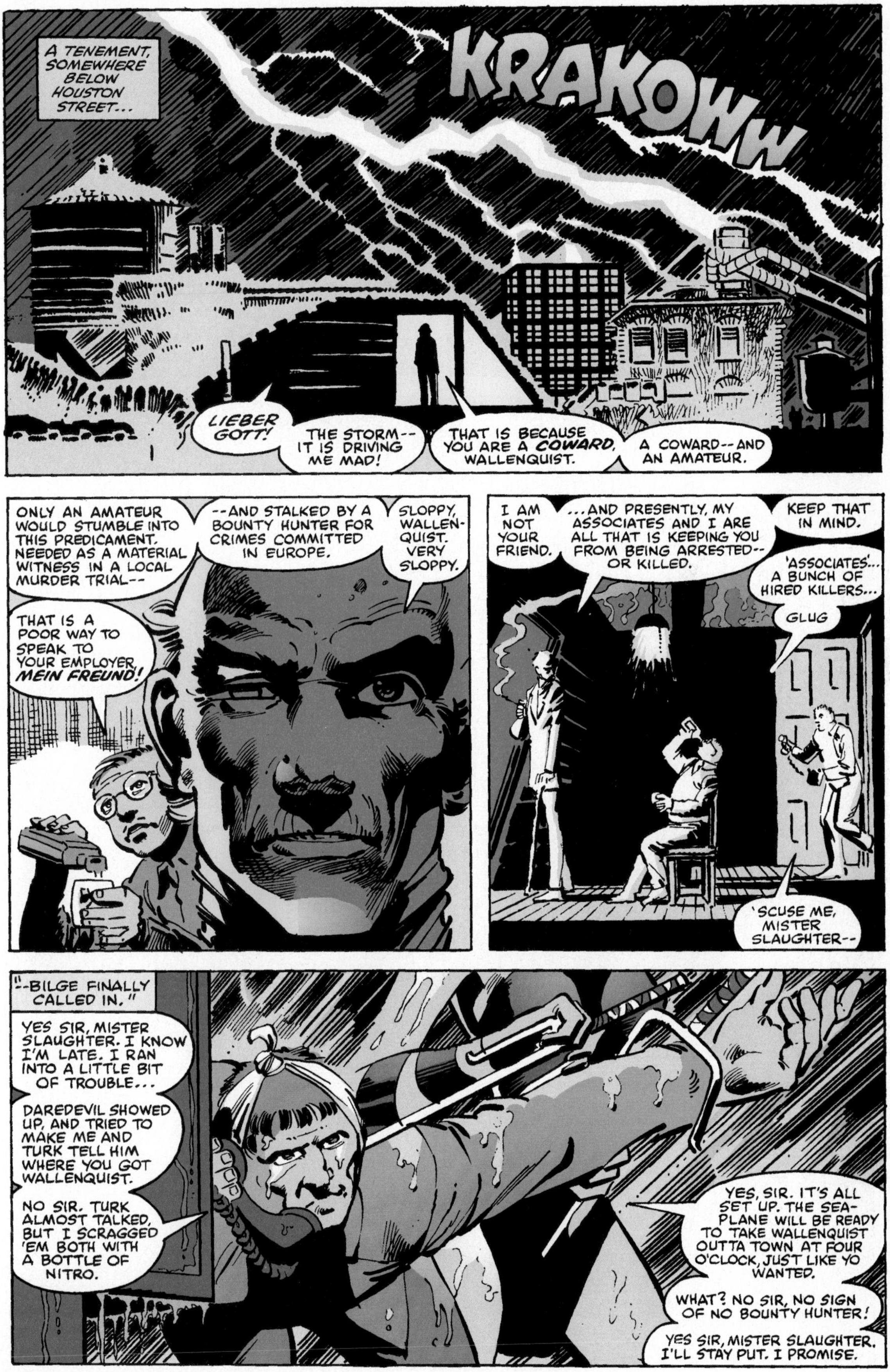
A TENEMENT, SOMEWHERE BELOW HOUSTON STREET...
KRAKOWW
LIEBER GOTT!
THE STORM-- IT IS DRIVING ME MAD!
THAT IS BECAUSE YOU ARE A COWARD, WALLENQUIST.
A COWARD--AND AN AMATEUR.
ONLY AN AMATEUR WOULD STUMBLE INTO THIS PREDICAMENT. NEEDED AS A MATERIAL WITNESS IN A LOCAL MURDER TRIAL--
--AND STALKED BY A BOUNTY HUNTER FOR CRIMES COMMITTED IN EUROPE.
SLOPPY, WALLENQUIST. VERY SLOPPY.
THAT IS A POOR WAY TO SPEAK TO YOUR EMPLOYER, MEIN FREUND!
I AM NOT YOUR FRIEND.
...AND PRESENTLY, MY ASSOCIATES AND I ARE ALL THAT IS KEEPING YOU FROM BEING ARRESTED-- OR KILLED.
KEEP THAT IN MIND.
'ASSOCIATES'... A BUNCH OF HIRED KILLERS...
GLUG
'SCUSE ME, MISTER SLAUGHTER--
"--BILGE FINALLY CALLED IN."
YES SIR, MISTER SLAUGHTER. I KNOW I'M LATE. I RAN INTO A LITTLE BIT OF TROUBLE...
DAREDEVIL SHOWED UP, AND TRIED TO MAKE ME AND TURK TELL HIM WHERE YOU GOT WALLENQUIST.
NO SIR. TURK ALMOST TALKED, BUT I SCRAGGED 'EM BOTH WITH A BOTTLE OF NITRO.
YES, SIR. IT'S ALL SET UP. THE SEA-PLANE WILL BE READY TO TAKE WALLENQUIST OUTTA TOWN AT FOUR O'CLOCK, JUST LIKE YO WANTED.
WHAT? NO SIR, NO SIGN OF NO BOUNTY HUNTER!
YES SIR, MISTER SLAUGHTER. I'LL STAY PUT. I PROMISE.

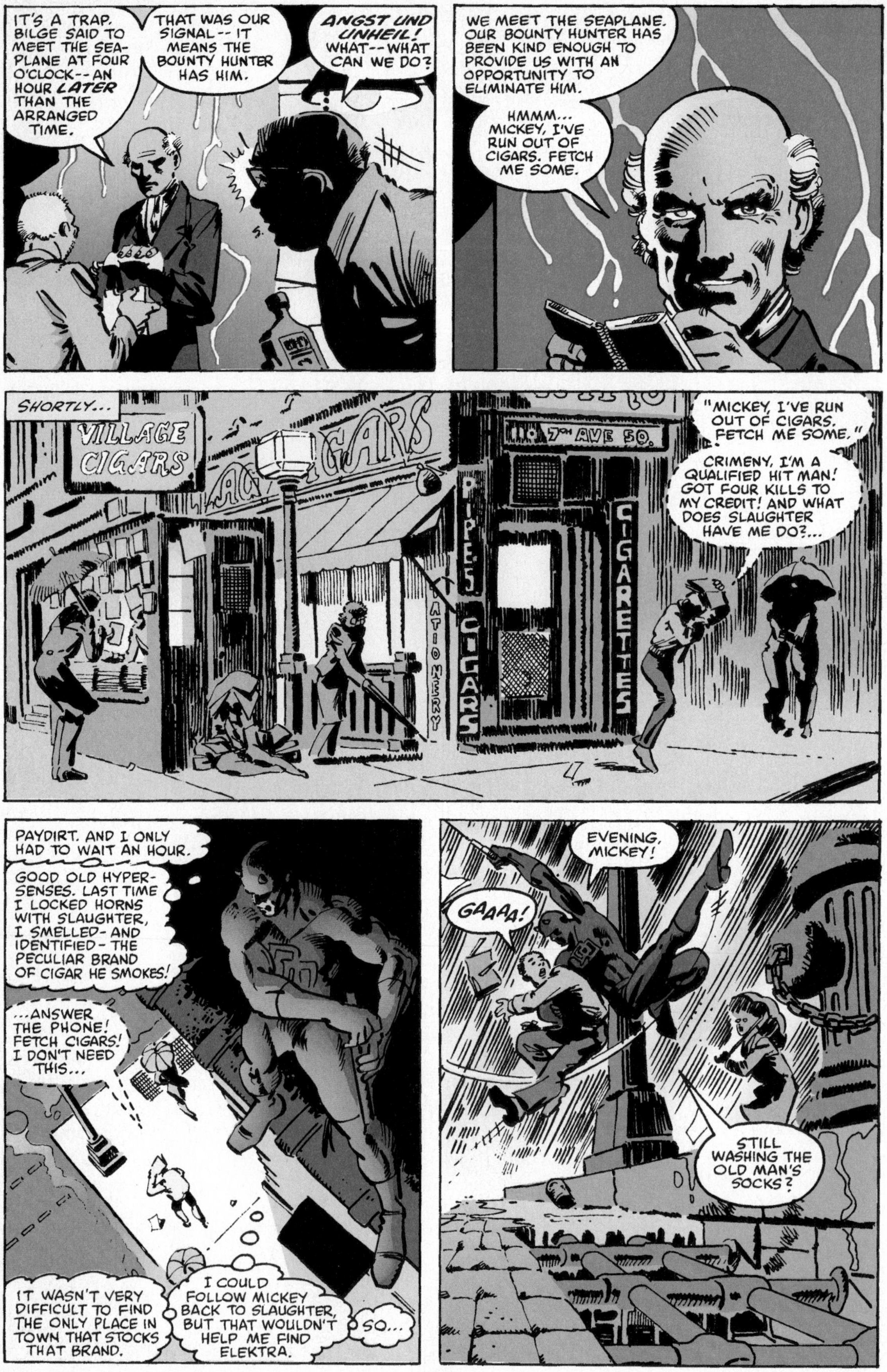
IT'S A TRAP. BILGE SAID TO MEET THE SEAPLANE AT FOUR O'CLOCK--AN HOUR **LATER** THAN THE ARRANGED TIME.
THAT WAS OUR SIGNAL-- IT MEANS THE BOUNTY HUNTER HAS HIM.
ANGST UND UNHEIL! WHAT--WHAT CAN WE DO?
WE MEET THE SEAPLANE. OUR BOUNTY HUNTER HAS BEEN KIND ENOUGH TO PROVIDE US WITH AN OPPORTUNITY TO ELIMINATE HIM.
HMMM... MICKEY, I'VE RUN OUT OF CIGARS. FETCH ME SOME.
SHORTLY...
VILLAGE CIGARS
PIPES
CIGARS
CIGARETTES
STATIONERY
"MICKEY, I'VE RUN OUT OF CIGARS. FETCH ME SOME."
CRIMENY, I'M A QUALIFIED HIT MAN! GOT FOUR KILLS TO MY CREDIT! AND WHAT DOES SLAUGHTER HAVE ME DO?...
PAYDIRT. AND I ONLY HAD TO WAIT AN HOUR.
GOOD OLD HYPER-SENSES. LAST TIME I LOCKED HORNS WITH SLAUGHTER, I SMELLED- AND IDENTIFIED- THE PECULIAR BRAND OF CIGAR HE SMOKES!
...ANSWER THE PHONE! FETCH CIGARS! I DON'T NEED THIS...
IT WASN'T VERY DIFFICULT TO FIND THE ONLY PLACE IN TOWN THAT STOCKS THAT BRAND.
I COULD FOLLOW MICKEY BACK TO SLAUGHTER, BUT THAT WOULDN'T HELP ME FIND ELEKTRA.
SO...
EVENING, MICKEY!
GAAAA!
STILL WASHING THE OLD MAN'S SOCKS?

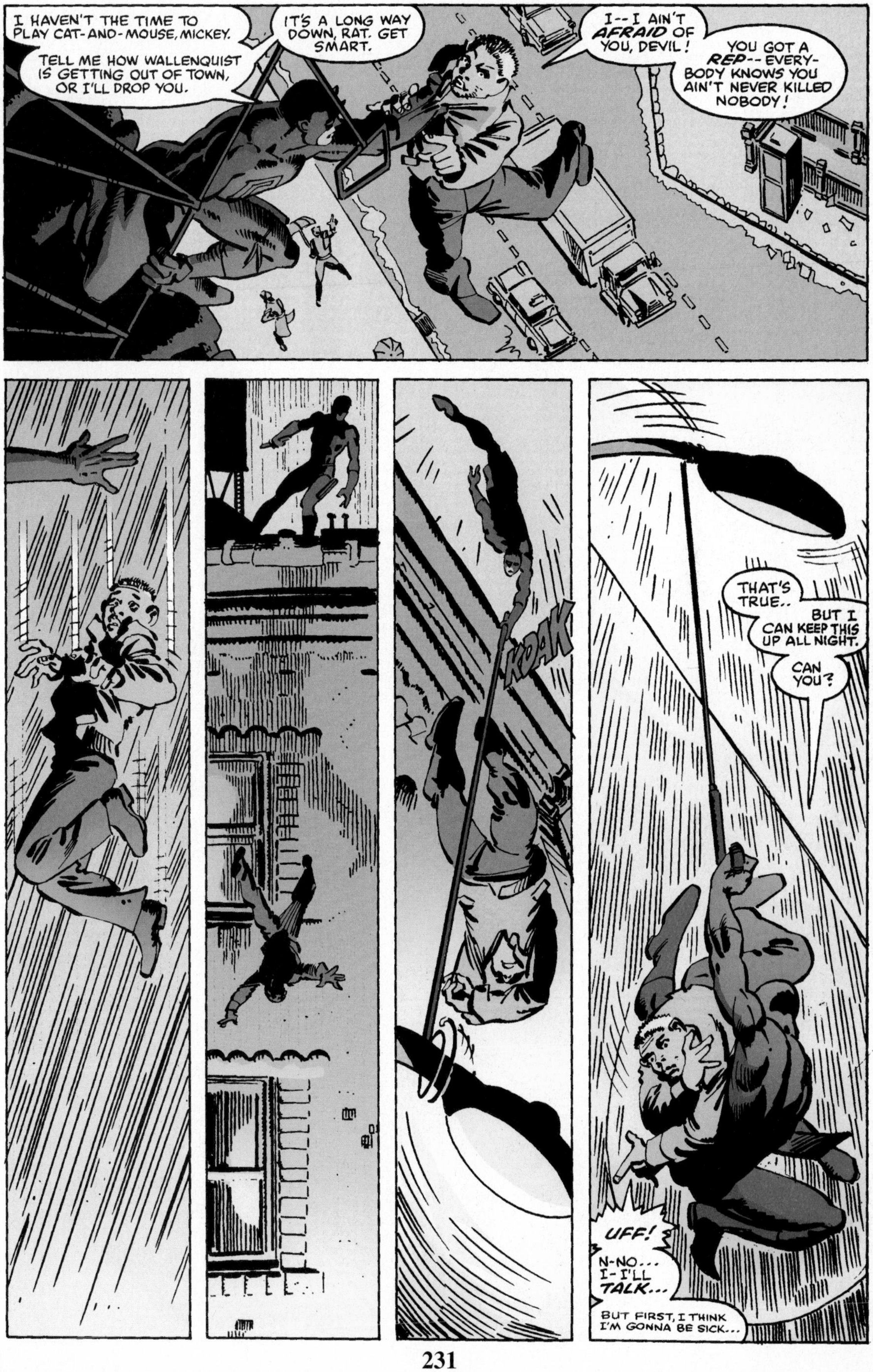
I HAVEN'T THE TIME TO PLAY CAT-AND-MOUSE, MICKEY.
TELL ME HOW WALLENQUIST IS GETTING OUT OF TOWN, OR I'LL DROP YOU.
IT'S A LONG WAY DOWN, RAT. GET SMART.
I-- I AIN'T AFRAID OF YOU, DEVIL!
YOU GOT A REP-- EVERYBODY KNOWS YOU AIN'T NEVER KILLED NOBODY!
KDAK
THAT'S TRUE..
BUT I CAN KEEP THIS UP ALL NIGHT.
CAN YOU?
UFF!
N-NO... I-I'LL TALK...
BUT FIRST, I THINK I'M GONNA BE SICK...

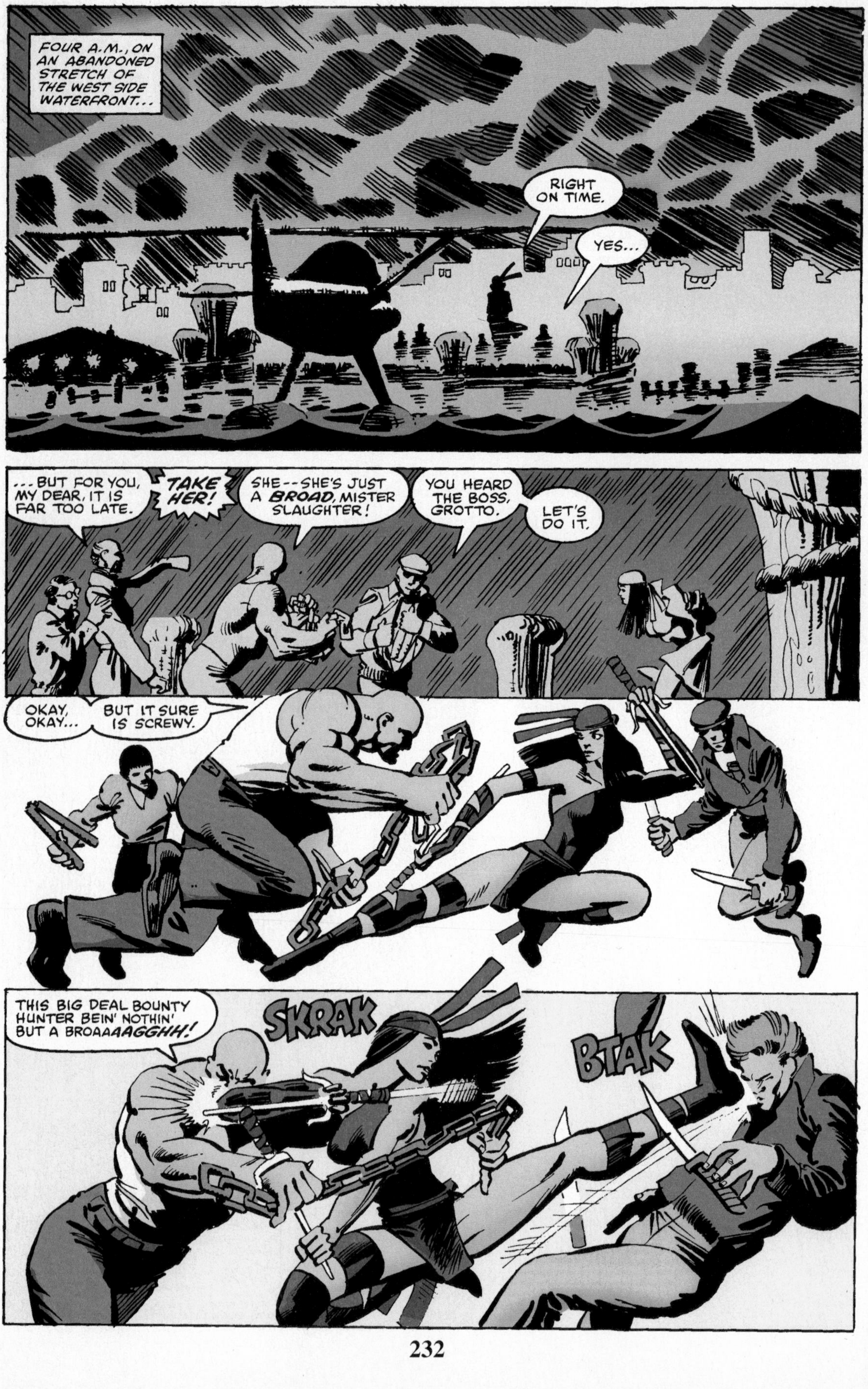
FOUR A.M., ON AN ABANDONED STRETCH OF THE WEST SIDE WATERFRONT...
RIGHT ON TIME.
YES...
...BUT FOR YOU, MY DEAR, IT IS FAR TOO LATE.
TAKE HER!
SHE--SHE'S JUST A BROAD, MISTER SLAUGHTER!
YOU HEARD THE BOSS, GROTTO.
LET'S DO IT.
OKAY, OKAY...
BUT IT SURE IS SCREWY.
THIS BIG DEAL BOUNTY HUNTER BEIN' NOTHIN' BUT A BROAAAAGGHH!
SKRAK
BTAK

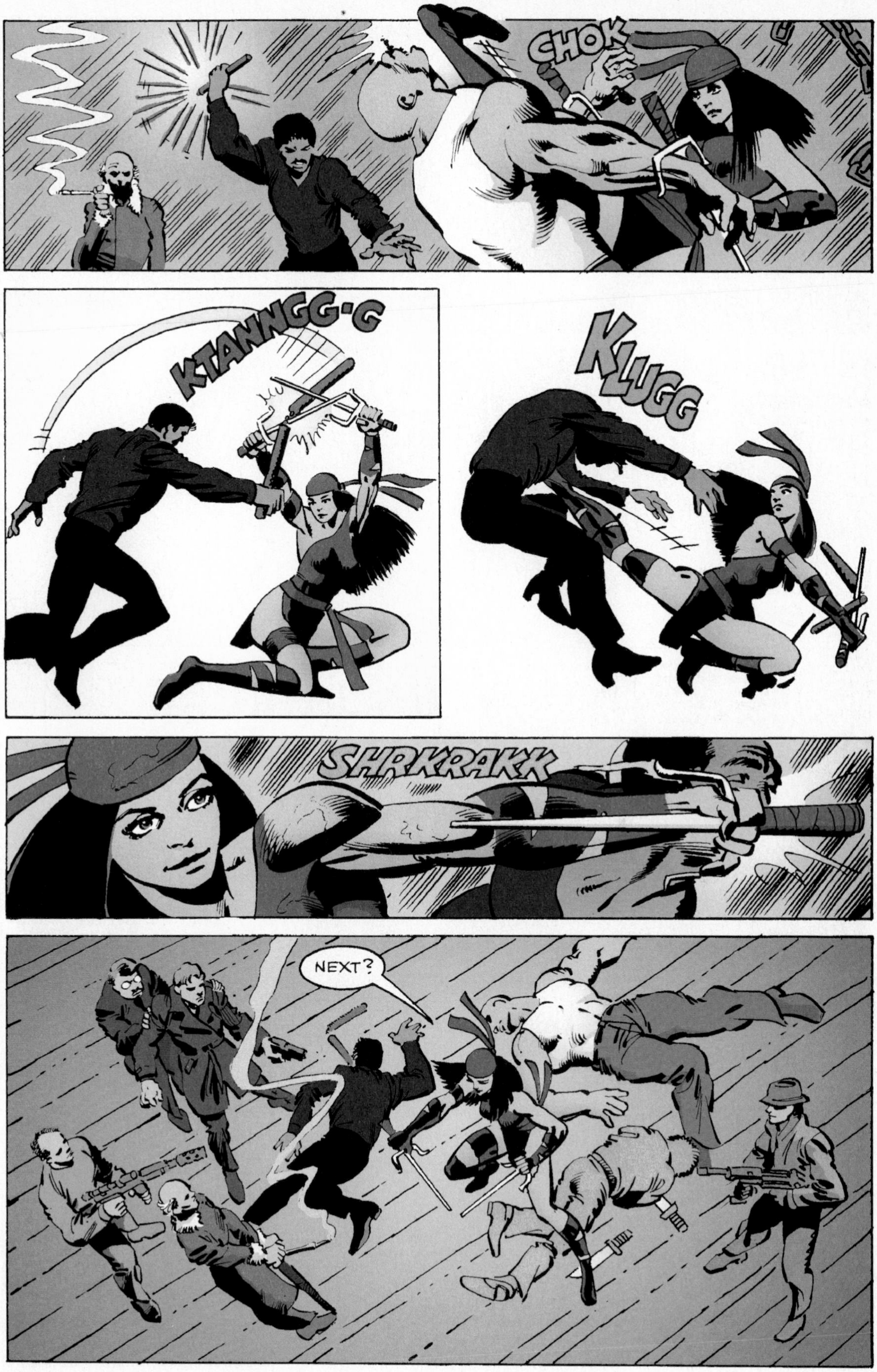
CHOK
KTANNGG-G
KLUGG
SHRKRAKK
NEXT?

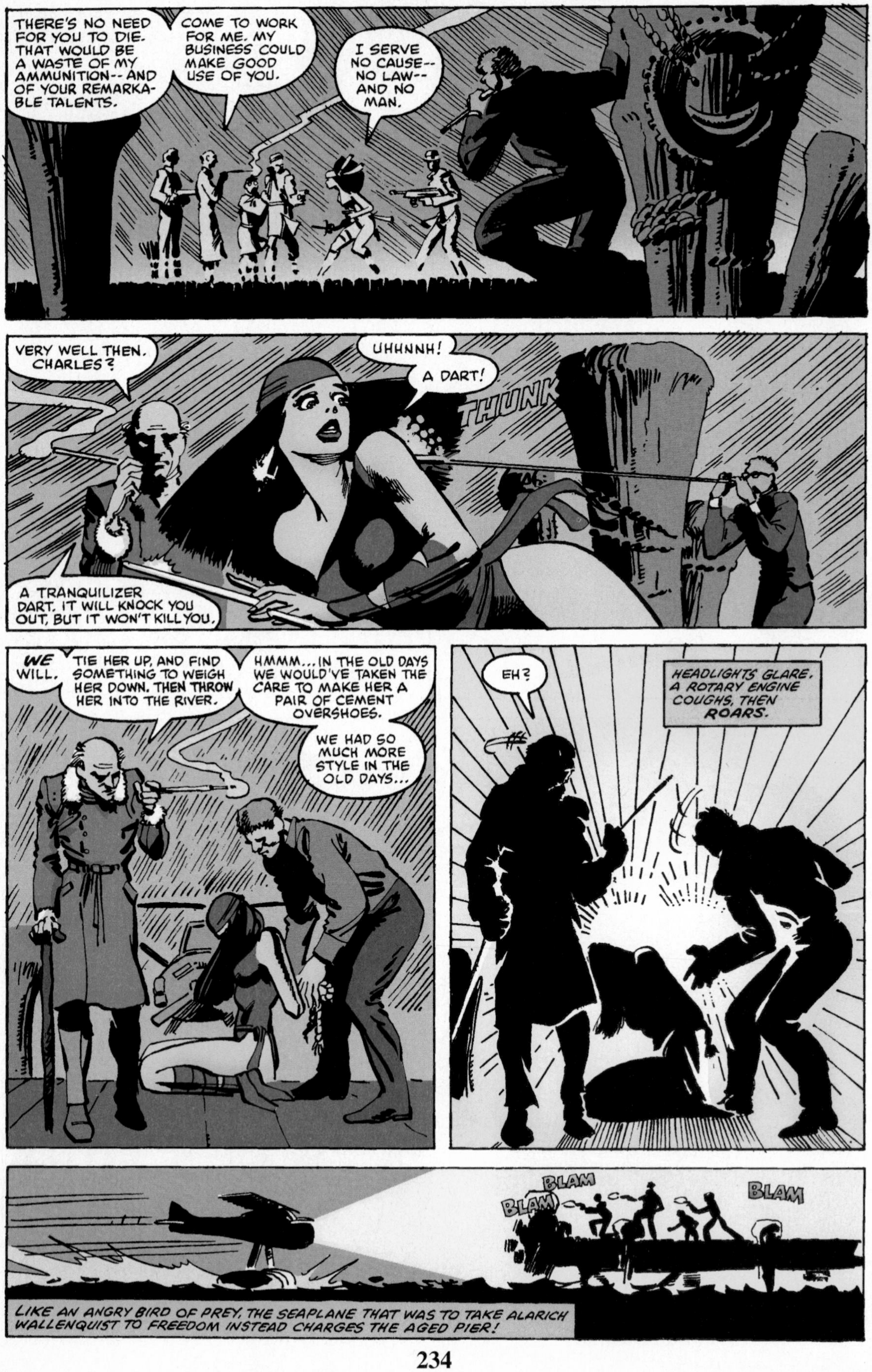
THERE'S NO NEED FOR YOU TO DIE. THAT WOULD BE A WASTE OF MY AMMUNITION-- AND OF YOUR REMARKABLE TALENTS.
COME TO WORK FOR ME. MY BUSINESS COULD MAKE GOOD USE OF YOU.
I SERVE NO CAUSE-- NO LAW-- AND NO MAN.
VERY WELL THEN. CHARLES?
UHHNNH!
A DART!
THUNK
A TRANQUILIZER DART. IT WILL KNOCK YOU OUT, BUT IT WON'T KILL YOU.
WE WILL.
TIE HER UP, AND FIND SOMETHING TO WEIGH HER DOWN. THEN THROW HER INTO THE RIVER.
HMMM... IN THE OLD DAYS WE WOULD'VE TAKEN THE CARE TO MAKE HER A PAIR OF CEMENT OVERSHOES.
WE HAD SO MUCH MORE STYLE IN THE OLD DAYS...
EH?
HEADLIGHTS GLARE. A ROTARY ENGINE COUGHS, THEN ROARS.
BLAM
BLAM
BLAM
LIKE AN ANGRY BIRD OF PREY, THE SEAPLANE THAT WAS TO TAKE ALARICH WALLENQUIST TO FREEDOM INSTEAD CHARGES THE AGED PIER!

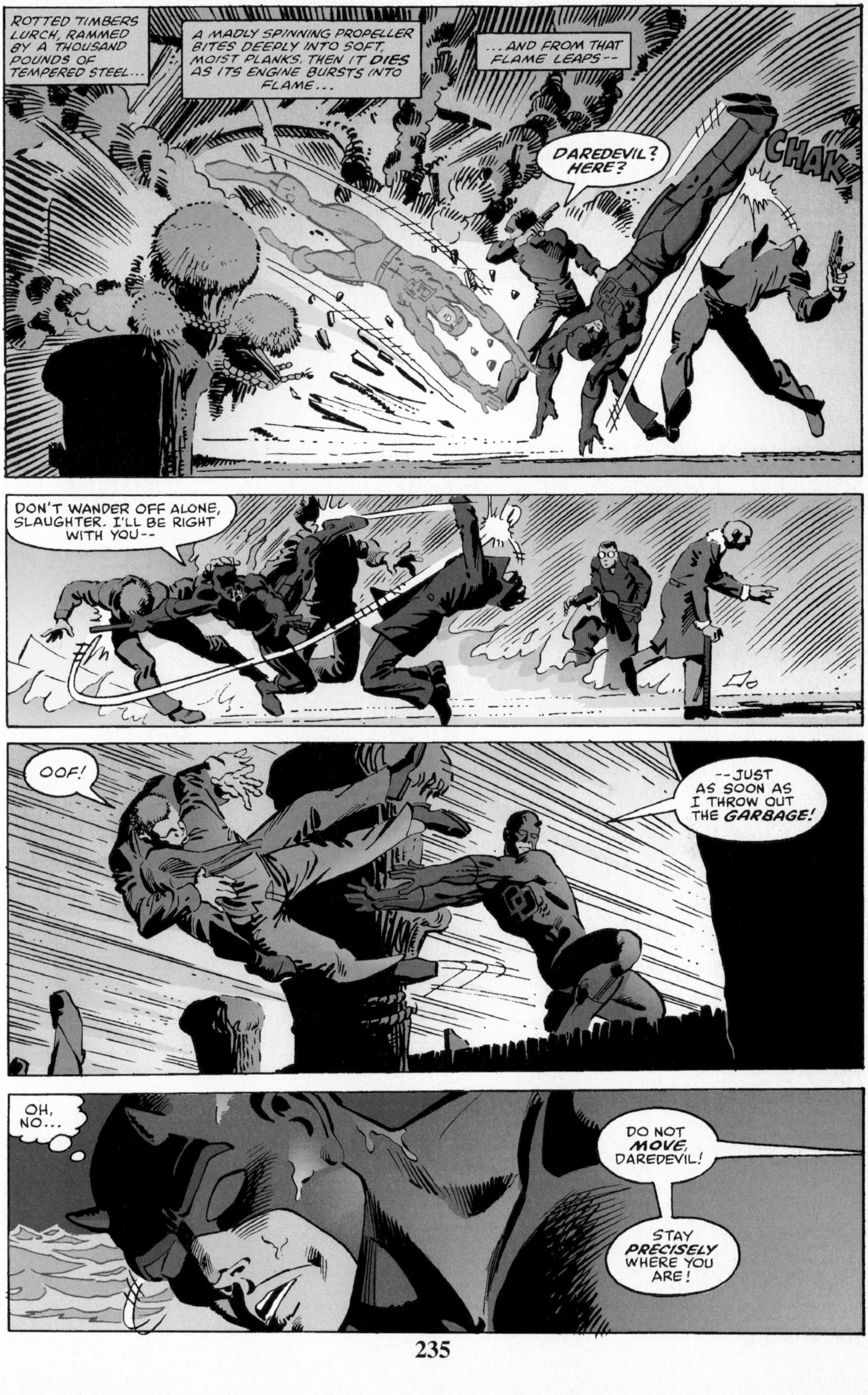
ROTTED TIMBERS LURCH, RAMMED BY A THOUSAND POUNDS OF TEMPERED STEEL...
A MADLY SPINNING PROPELLER BITES DEEPLY INTO SOFT, MOIST PLANKS, THEN IT DIES AS ITS ENGINE BURSTS INTO FLAME...
...AND FROM THAT FLAME LEAPS--
DAREDEVIL? HERE?
CHAK
DON'T WANDER OFF ALONE, SLAUGHTER. I'LL BE RIGHT WITH YOU--
OOF!
--JUST AS SOON AS I THROW OUT THE GARBAGE!
OH, NO...
DO NOT MOVE, DAREDEVIL!
STAY PRECISELY WHERE YOU ARE!

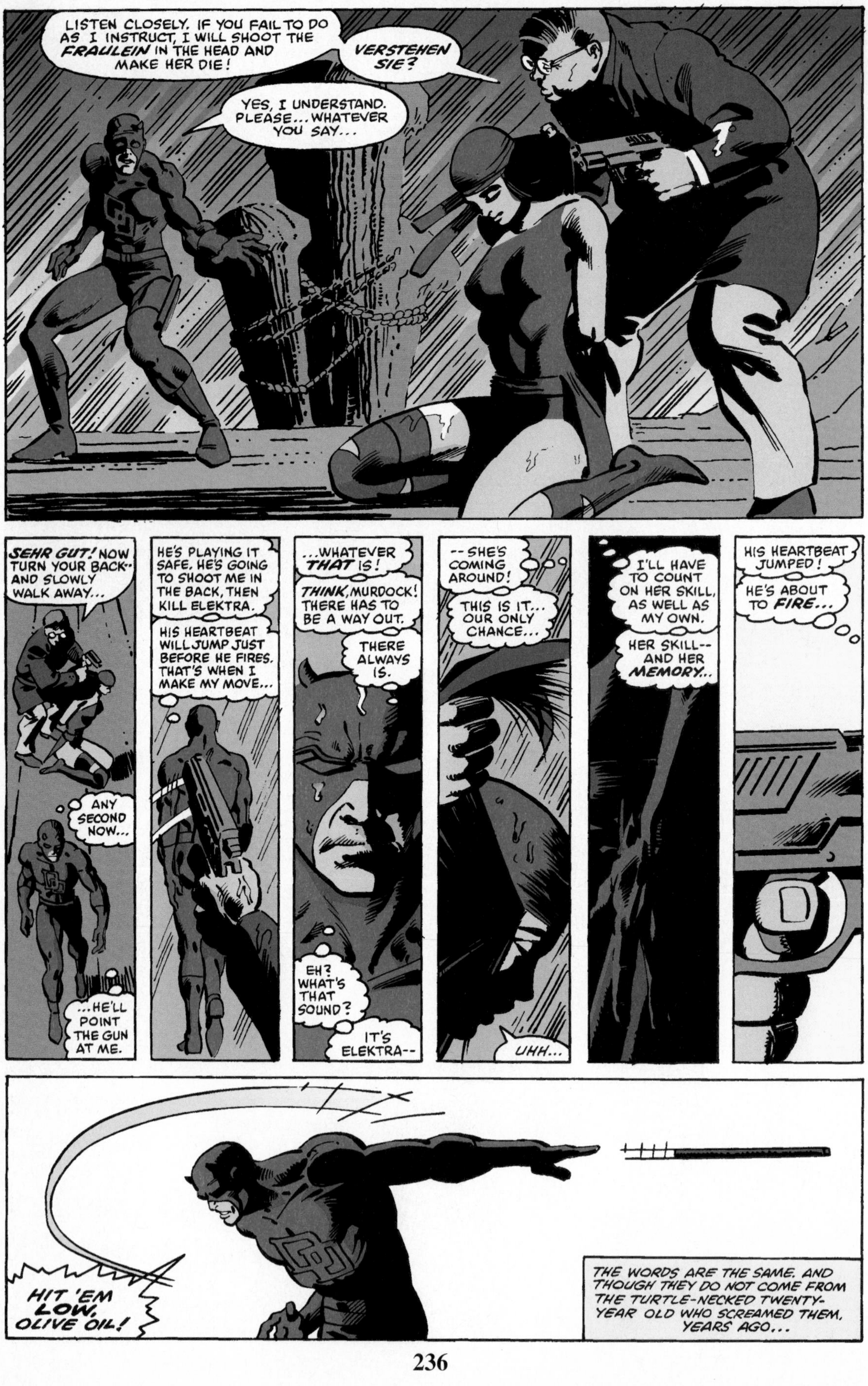
LISTEN CLOSELY. IF YOU FAIL TO DO AS I INSTRUCT, I WILL SHOOT THE FRAULEIN IN THE HEAD AND MAKE HER DIE!
VERSTEHEN SIE?
YES, I UNDERSTAND. PLEASE... WHATEVER YOU SAY...
SEHR GUT! NOW TURN YOUR BACK-- AND SLOWLY WALK AWAY...
ANY SECOND NOW...
...HE'LL POINT THE GUN AT ME.
HE'S PLAYING IT SAFE. HE'S GOING TO SHOOT ME IN THE BACK, THEN KILL ELEKTRA.
HIS HEARTBEAT WILL JUMP JUST BEFORE HE FIRES. THAT'S WHEN I MAKE MY MOVE...
...WHATEVER THAT IS!
THINK, MURDOCK! THERE HAS TO BE A WAY OUT.
THERE ALWAYS IS.
EH? WHAT'S THAT SOUND?
IT'S ELEKTRA--
--SHE'S COMING AROUND!
THIS IS IT... OUR ONLY CHANCE...
UHH...
I'LL HAVE TO COUNT ON HER SKILL, AS WELL AS MY OWN.
HER SKILL-- AND HER MEMORY...
HIS HEARTBEAT JUMPED!
HE'S ABOUT TO FIRE...
HIT 'EM LOW, OLIVE OIL!
THE WORDS ARE THE SAME. AND THOUGH THEY DO NOT COME FROM THE TURTLE-NECKED TWENTY-YEAR OLD WHO SCREAMED THEM, YEARS AGO...

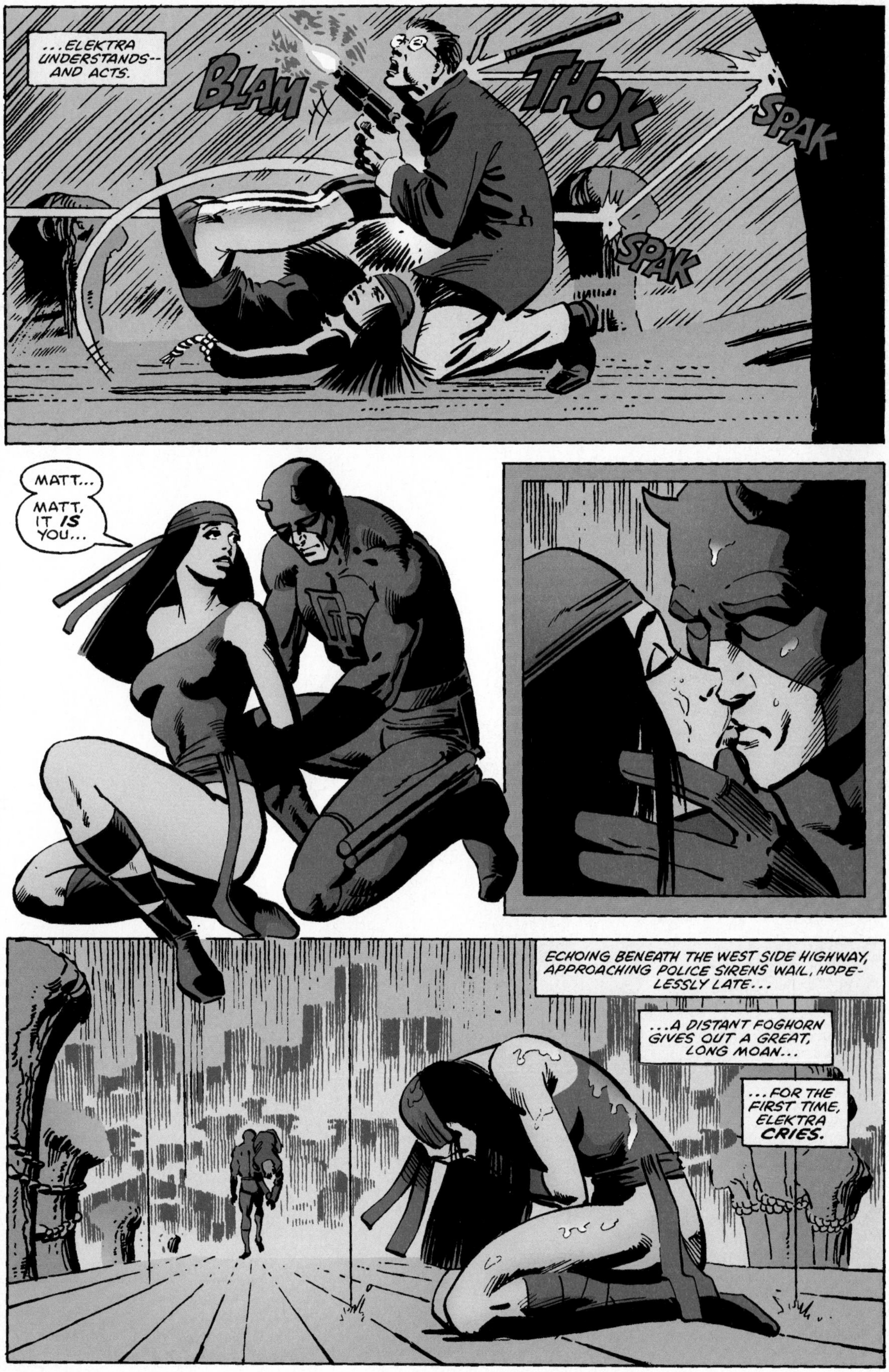
...ELEKTRA UNDERSTANDS-- AND ACTS.
BLAM
THOK
SPAK
SPAK
MATT...
MATT, IT IS YOU...
ECHOING BENEATH THE WEST SIDE HIGHWAY, APPROACHING POLICE SIRENS WAIL, HOPE-LESSLY LATE...
...A DISTANT FOGHORN GIVES OUT A GREAT, LONG MOAN...
...FOR THE FIRST TIME, ELEKTRA CRIES.

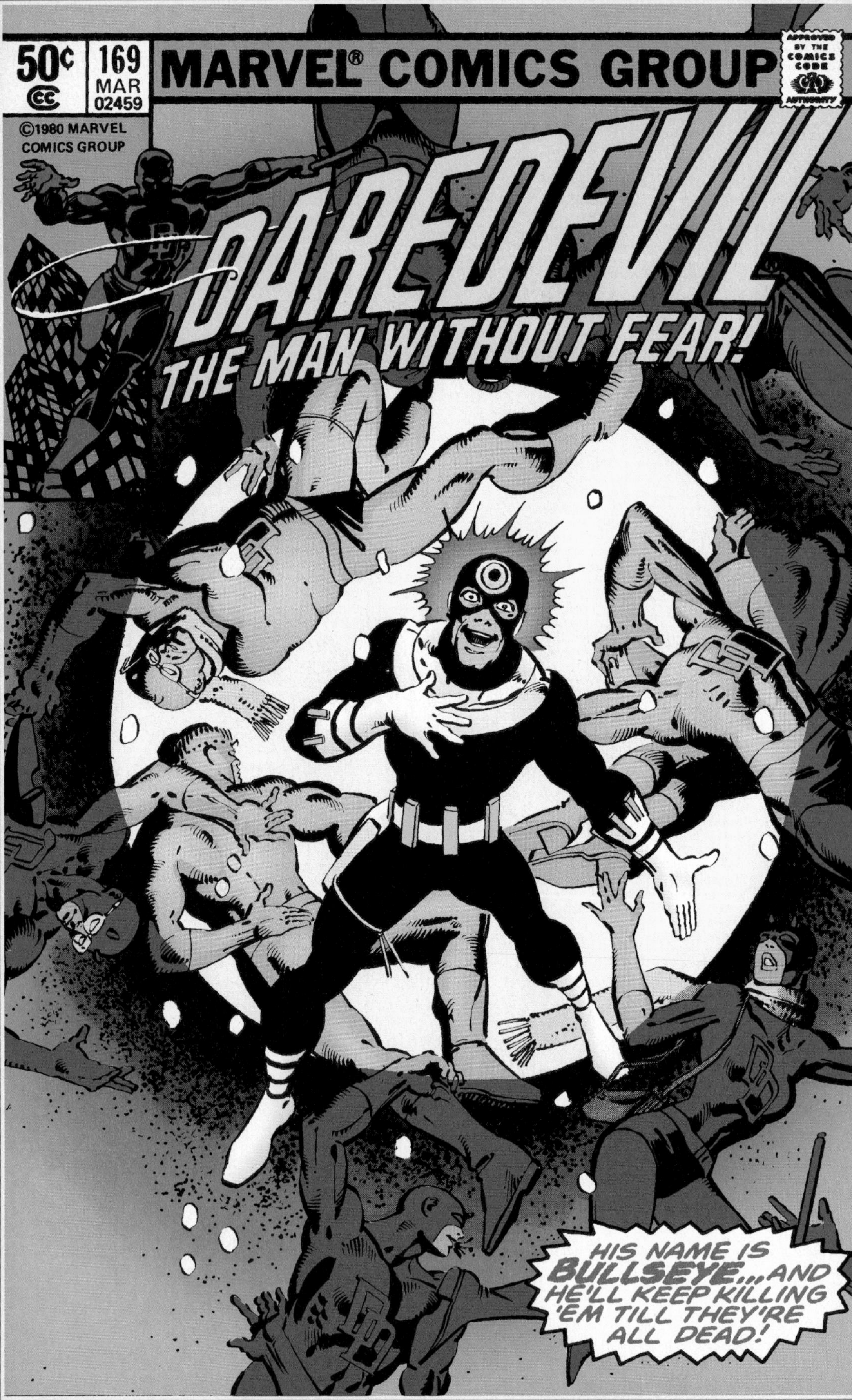
50¢
CC
169
MAR
02459
MARVEL® COMICS GROUP
APPROVED BY THE COMICS CODE AUTHORITY
©1980 MARVEL COMICS GROUP
DAREDEVIL
THE MAN WITHOUT FEAR!
HIS NAME IS BULLSEYE...AND HE'LL KEEP KILLING 'EM TILL THEY'RE ALL DEAD!

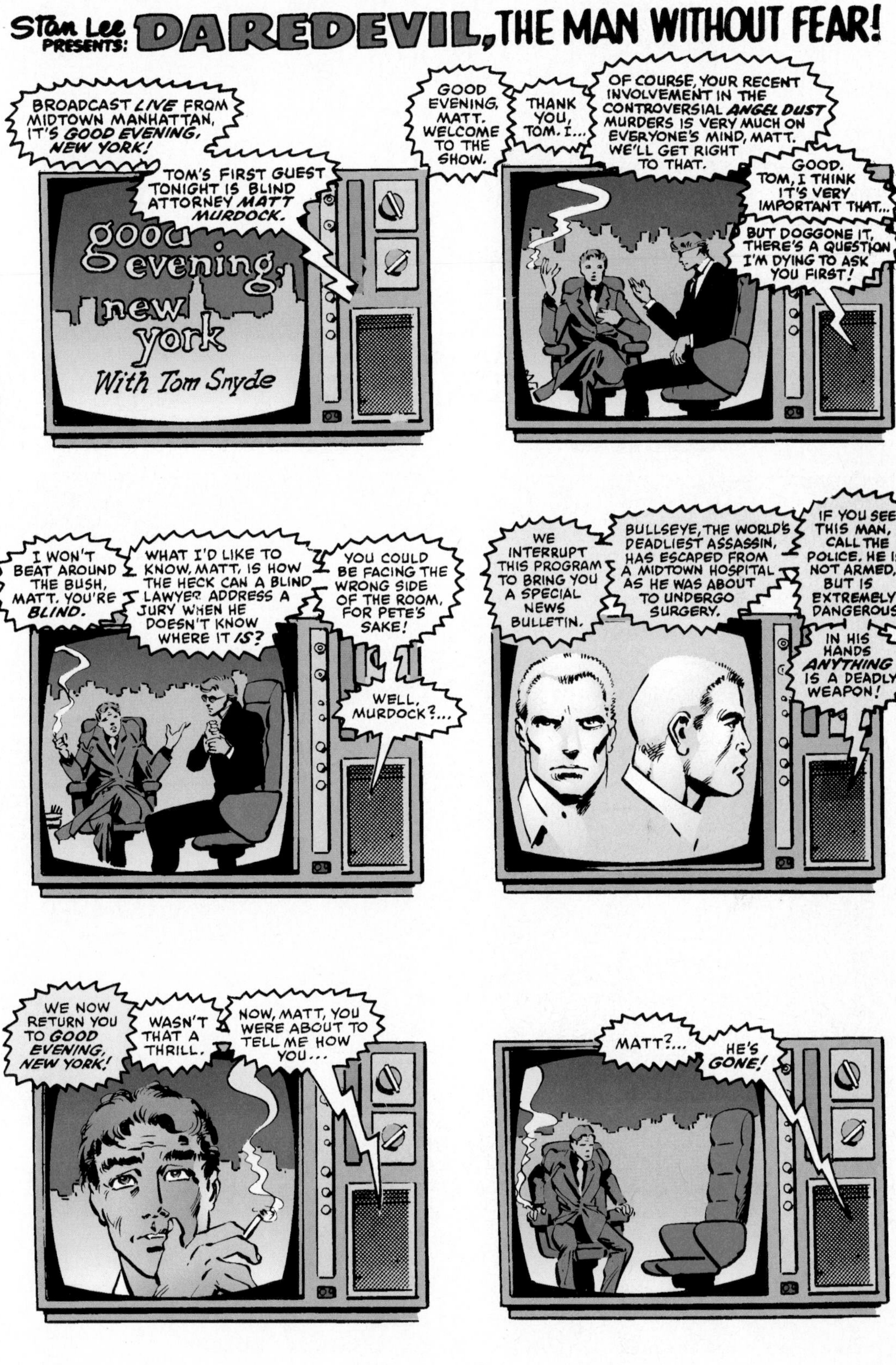

Stan Lee PRESENTS: DAREDEVIL, THE MAN WITHOUT FEAR!
BROADCAST LIVE FROM MIDTOWN MANHATTAN, IT'S GOOD EVENING, NEW YORK!
TOM'S FIRST GUEST TONIGHT IS BLIND ATTORNEY MATT MURDOCK.
good evening, new york
With Tom Snyde
GOOD EVENING, MATT. WELCOME TO THE SHOW.
THANK YOU, TOM. I...
OF COURSE, YOUR RECENT INVOLVEMENT IN THE CONTROVERSIAL ANGEL DUST MURDERS IS VERY MUCH ON EVERYONE'S MIND, MATT. WE'LL GET RIGHT TO THAT.
GOOD. TOM, I THINK IT'S VERY IMPORTANT THAT...
BUT DOGGONE IT, THERE'S A QUESTION I'M DYING TO ASK YOU FIRST!
I WON'T BEAT AROUND THE BUSH, MATT. YOU'RE BLIND.
WHAT I'D LIKE TO KNOW, MATT, IS HOW THE HECK CAN A BLIND LAWYER ADDRESS A JURY WHEN HE DOESN'T KNOW WHERE IT IS?
YOU COULD BE FACING THE WRONG SIDE OF THE ROOM, FOR PETE'S SAKE!
WELL, MURDOCK?...
WE INTERRUPT THIS PROGRAM TO BRING YOU A SPECIAL NEWS BULLETIN.
BULLSEYE, THE WORLD'S DEADLIEST ASSASSIN, HAS ESCAPED FROM A MIDTOWN HOSPITAL AS HE WAS ABOUT TO UNDERGO SURGERY.
IF YOU SEE THIS MAN, CALL THE POLICE. HE IS NOT ARMED, BUT IS EXTREMELY DANGEROUS.
IN HIS HANDS ANYTHING IS A DEADLY WEAPON!
WE NOW RETURN YOU TO GOOD EVENING, NEW YORK!
WASN'T THAT A THRILL.
NOW, MATT, YOU WERE ABOUT TO TELL ME HOW YOU...
MATT?...
HE'S GONE!

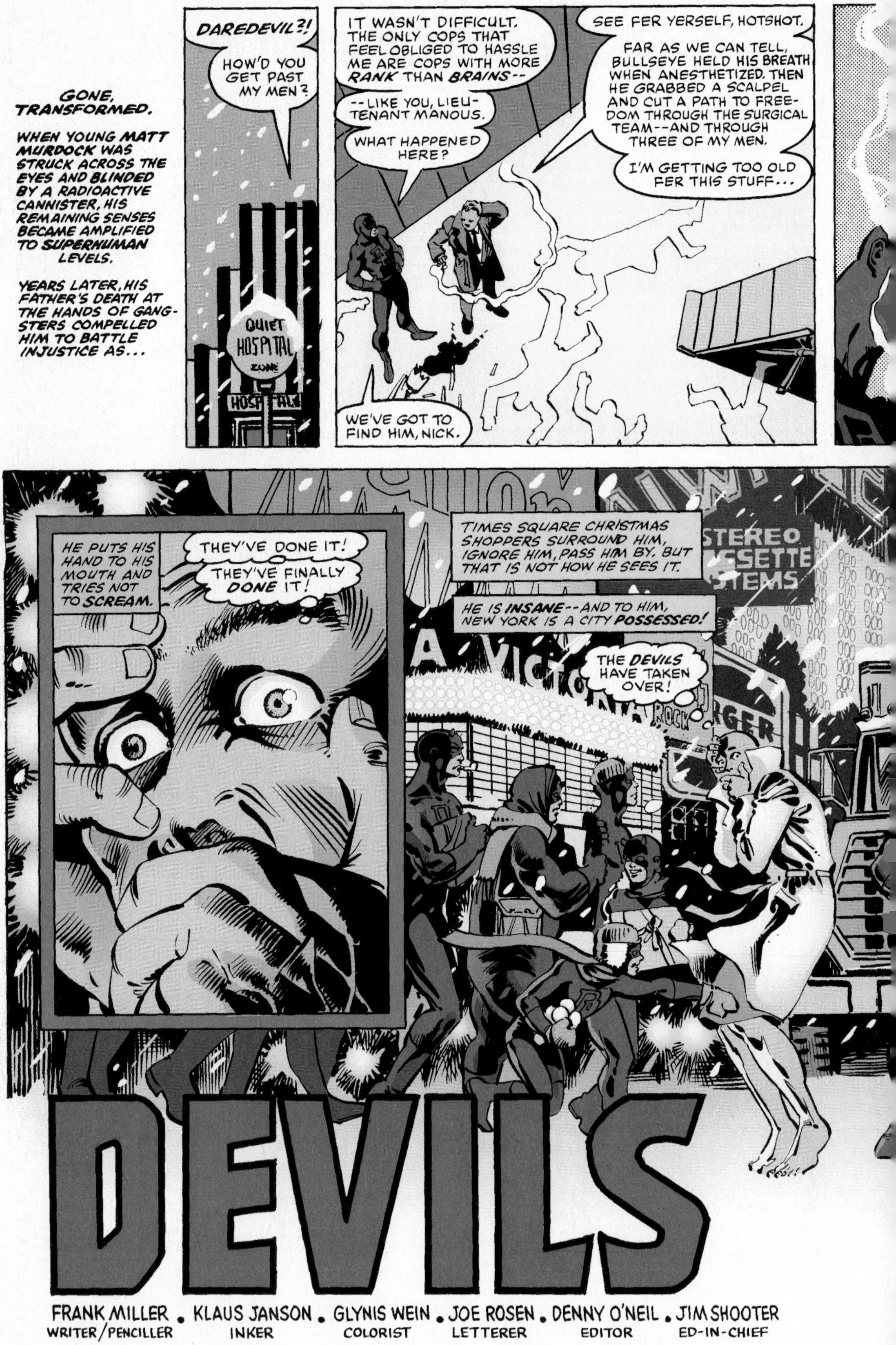
GONE, TRANSFORMED.
WHEN YOUNG MATT MURDOCK WAS STRUCK ACROSS THE EYES AND BLINDED BY A RADIOACTIVE CANNISTER, HIS REMAINING SENSES BECAME AMPLIFIED TO SUPERHUMAN LEVELS.
YEARS LATER, HIS FATHER'S DEATH AT THE HANDS OF GANGSTERS COMPELLED HIM TO BATTLE INJUSTICE AS...
DAREDEVIL?!
HOW'D YOU GET PAST MY MEN?
QUIET HOSPITAL ZONE
HOSPITAL
IT WASN'T DIFFICULT. THE ONLY COPS THAT FEEL OBLIGED TO HASSLE ME ARE COPS WITH MORE RANK THAN BRAINS--
--LIKE YOU, LIEUTENANT MANOUS.
WHAT HAPPENED HERE?
SEE FER YERSELF, HOTSHOT.
FAR AS WE CAN TELL, BULLSEYE HELD HIS BREATH WHEN ANESTHETIZED. THEN HE GRABBED A SCALPEL AND CUT A PATH TO FREEDOM THROUGH THE SURGICAL TEAM--AND THROUGH THREE OF MY MEN.
I'M GETTING TOO OLD FER THIS STUFF...
WE'VE GOT TO FIND HIM, NICK.
HE PUTS HIS HAND TO HIS MOUTH AND TRIES NOT TO SCREAM.
THEY'VE DONE IT!
THEY'VE FINALLY DONE IT!
TIMES SQUARE CHRISTMAS SHOPPERS SURROUND HIM, IGNORE HIM, PASS HIM BY. BUT THAT IS NOT HOW HE SEES IT.
HE IS INSANE--AND TO HIM, NEW YORK IS A CITY POSSESSED!
THE DEVILS HAVE TAKEN OVER!
STEREO CASSETTE SYSTEMS
DEVILS
FRANK MILLER WRITER/PENCILLER . KLAUS JANSON INKER . GLYNIS WEIN COLORIST . JOE ROSEN LETTERER . DENNY O'NEIL EDITOR . JIM SHOOTER ED-IN-CHIEF

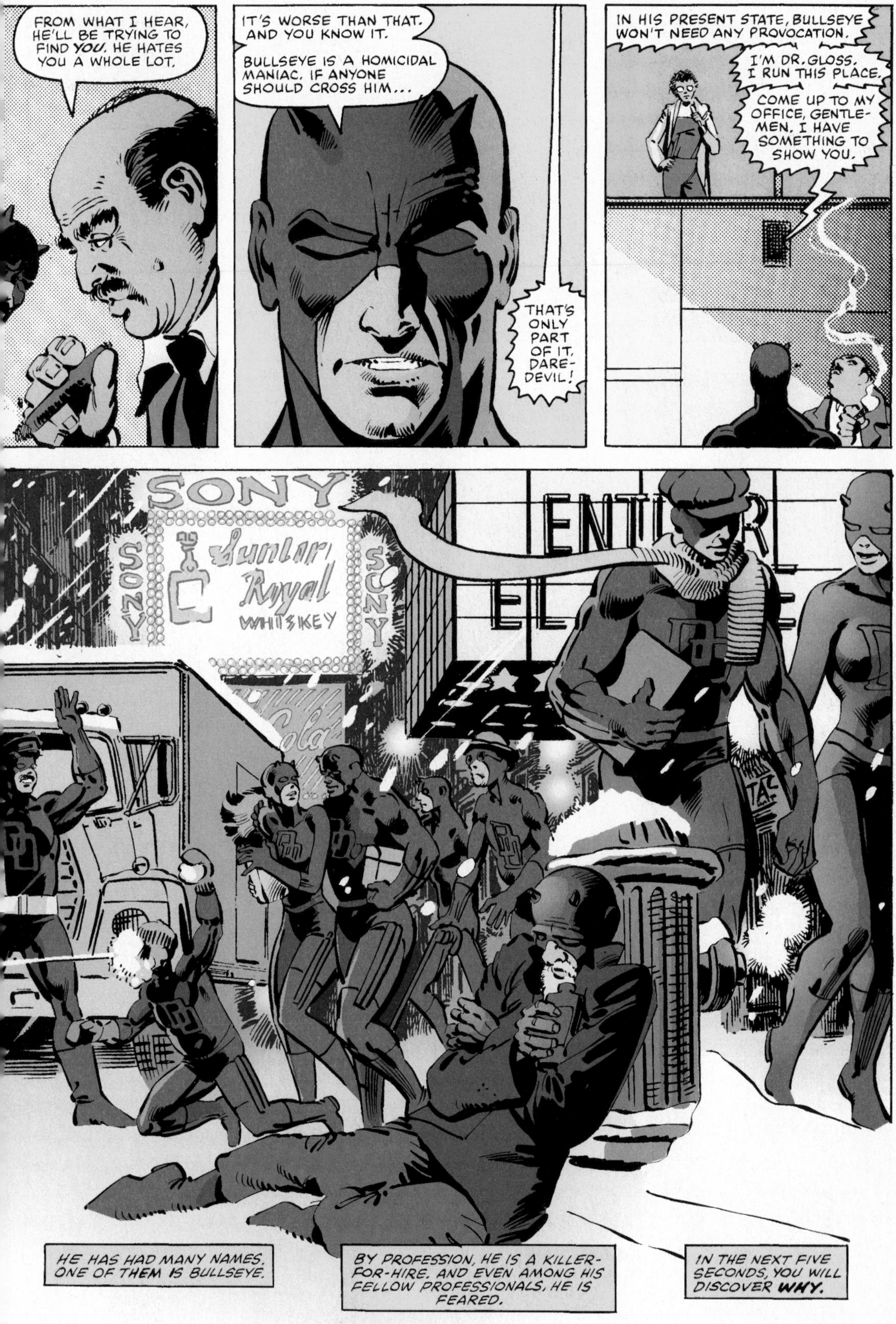
FROM WHAT I HEAR, HE'LL BE TRYING TO FIND *YOU*. HE HATES YOU A WHOLE LOT.
IT'S WORSE THAN THAT. AND YOU KNOW IT.
BULLSEYE IS A HOMICIDAL MANIAC. IF ANYONE SHOULD CROSS HIM...
THAT'S ONLY PART OF IT, DAREDEVIL!
IN HIS PRESENT STATE, BULLSEYE WON'T NEED ANY PROVOCATION.
I'M DR. GLOSS. I RUN THIS PLACE.
COME UP TO MY OFFICE, GENTLEMEN. I HAVE SOMETHING TO SHOW YOU.
SONY
HE HAS HAD MANY NAMES. ONE OF THEM IS BULLSEYE.
BY PROFESSION, HE IS A KILLER-FOR-HIRE. AND EVEN AMONG HIS FELLOW PROFESSIONALS, HE IS FEARED.
IN THE NEXT FIVE SECONDS, YOU WILL DISCOVER **WHY**.

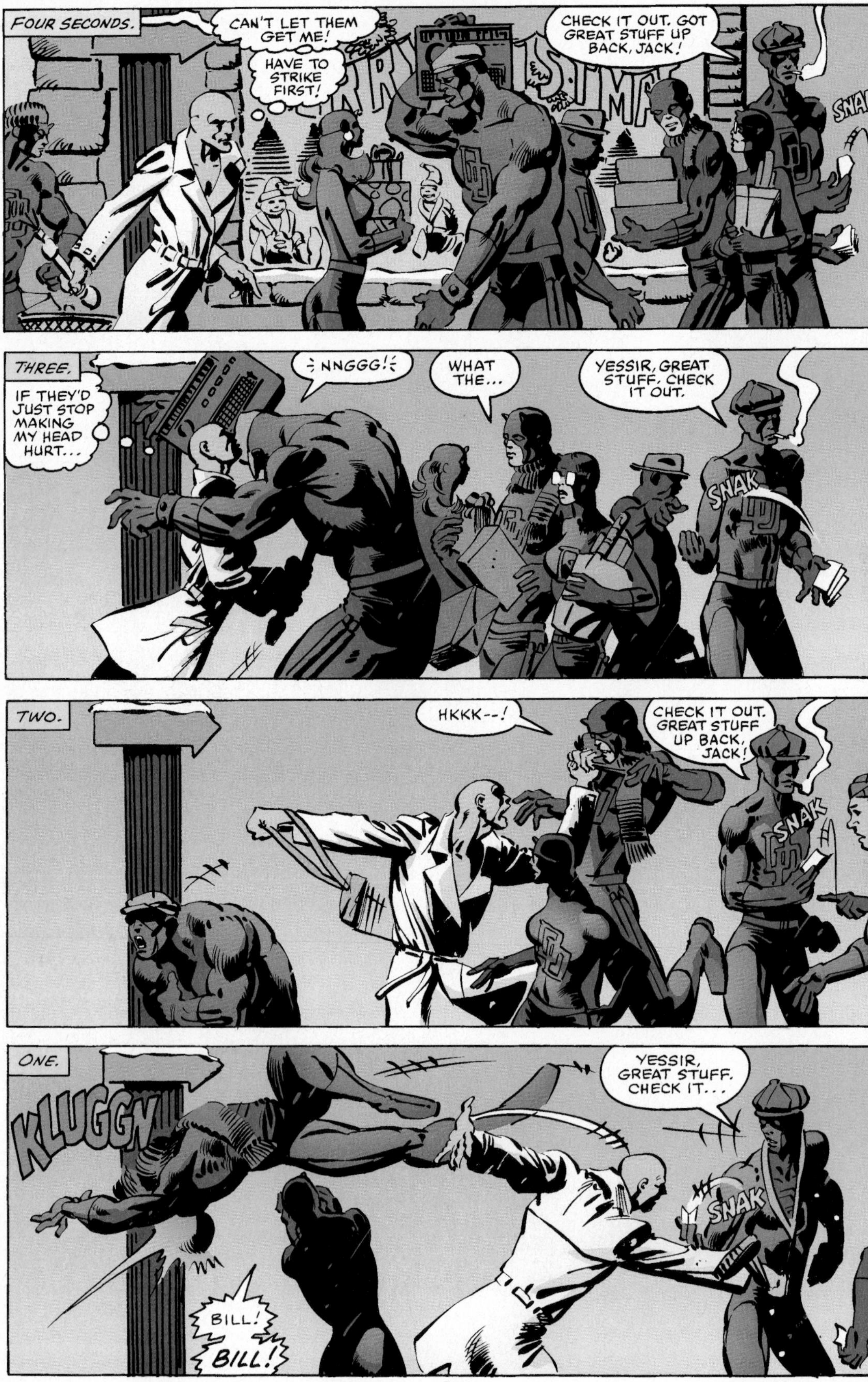
FOUR SECONDS.
CAN'T LET THEM GET ME!
HAVE TO STRIKE FIRST!
CHECK IT OUT. GOT GREAT STUFF UP BACK, JACK!
SNAK
THREE.
IF THEY'D JUST STOP MAKING MY HEAD HURT...
NNGGG!
WHAT THE...
YESSIR, GREAT STUFF, CHECK IT OUT.
SNAK
TWO.
HKKK--!
CHECK IT OUT. GREAT STUFF UP BACK, JACK!
SNAK
ONE.
KLUGGN
YESSIR, GREAT STUFF. CHECK IT...
SNAK
BILL!
BILL!

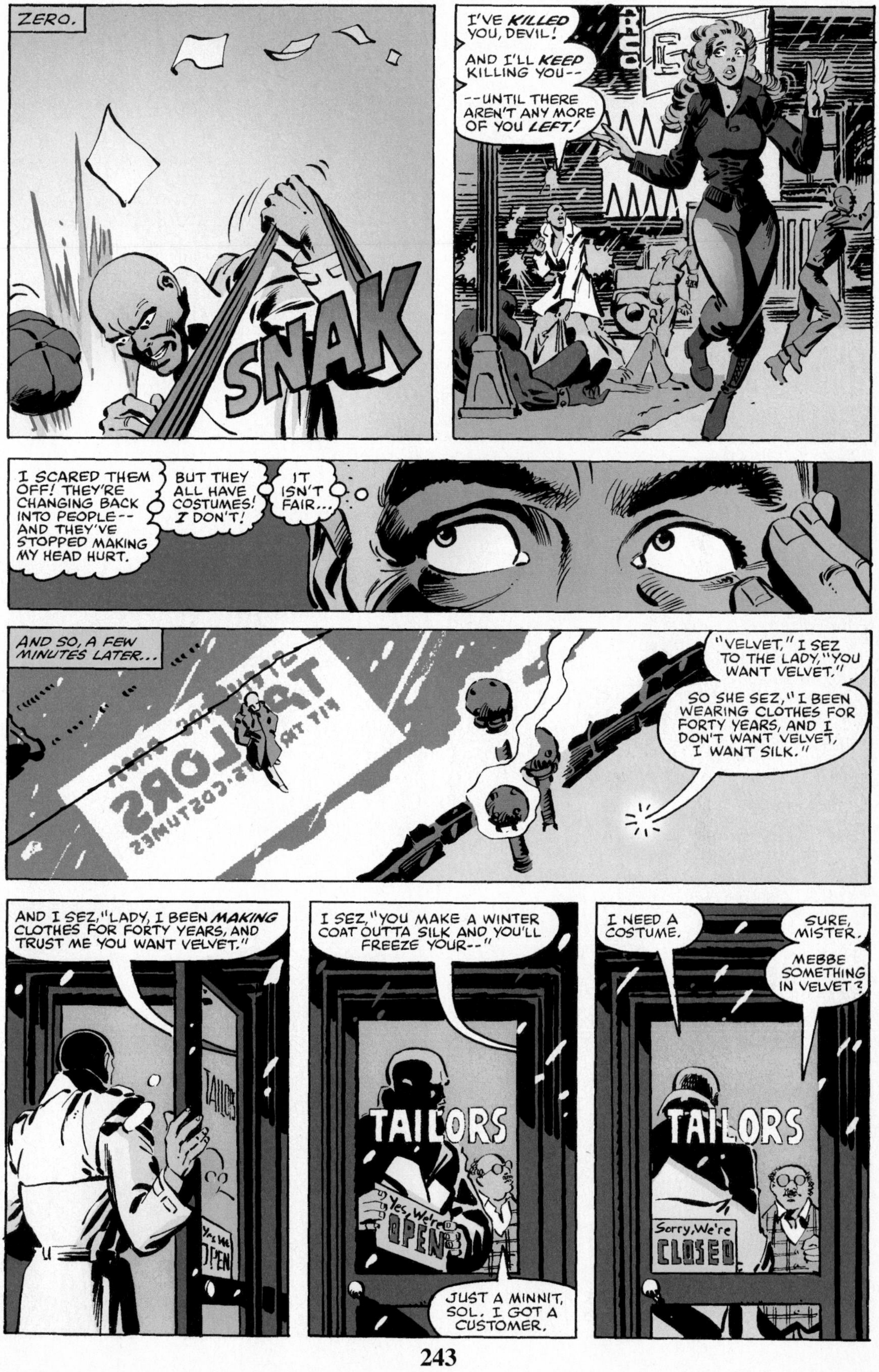
ZERO.
SNAK
I'VE KILLED YOU, DEVIL!
AND I'LL KEEP KILLING YOU--
--UNTIL THERE AREN'T ANY MORE OF YOU LEFT!
I SCARED THEM OFF! THEY'RE CHANGING BACK INTO PEOPLE-- AND THEY'VE STOPPED MAKING MY HEAD HURT.
BUT THEY ALL HAVE COSTUMES! I DON'T!
IT ISN'T FAIR...
AND SO, A FEW MINUTES LATER...
TAILORS
"VELVET," I SEZ TO THE LADY, "YOU WANT VELVET."
SO SHE SEZ, "I BEEN WEARING CLOTHES FOR FORTY YEARS, AND I DON'T WANT VELVET, I WANT SILK."
AND I SEZ, "LADY, I BEEN MAKING CLOTHES FOR FORTY YEARS, AND TRUST ME YOU WANT VELVET."
I SEZ, "YOU MAKE A WINTER COAT OUTTA SILK AND YOU'LL FREEZE YOUR--"
TAILORS
Yes, We're OPEN
JUST A MINNIT, SOL. I GOT A CUSTOMER.
I NEED A COSTUME.
SURE, MISTER.
MEBBE SOMETHING IN VELVET?
TAILORS
Sorry, We're CLOSED

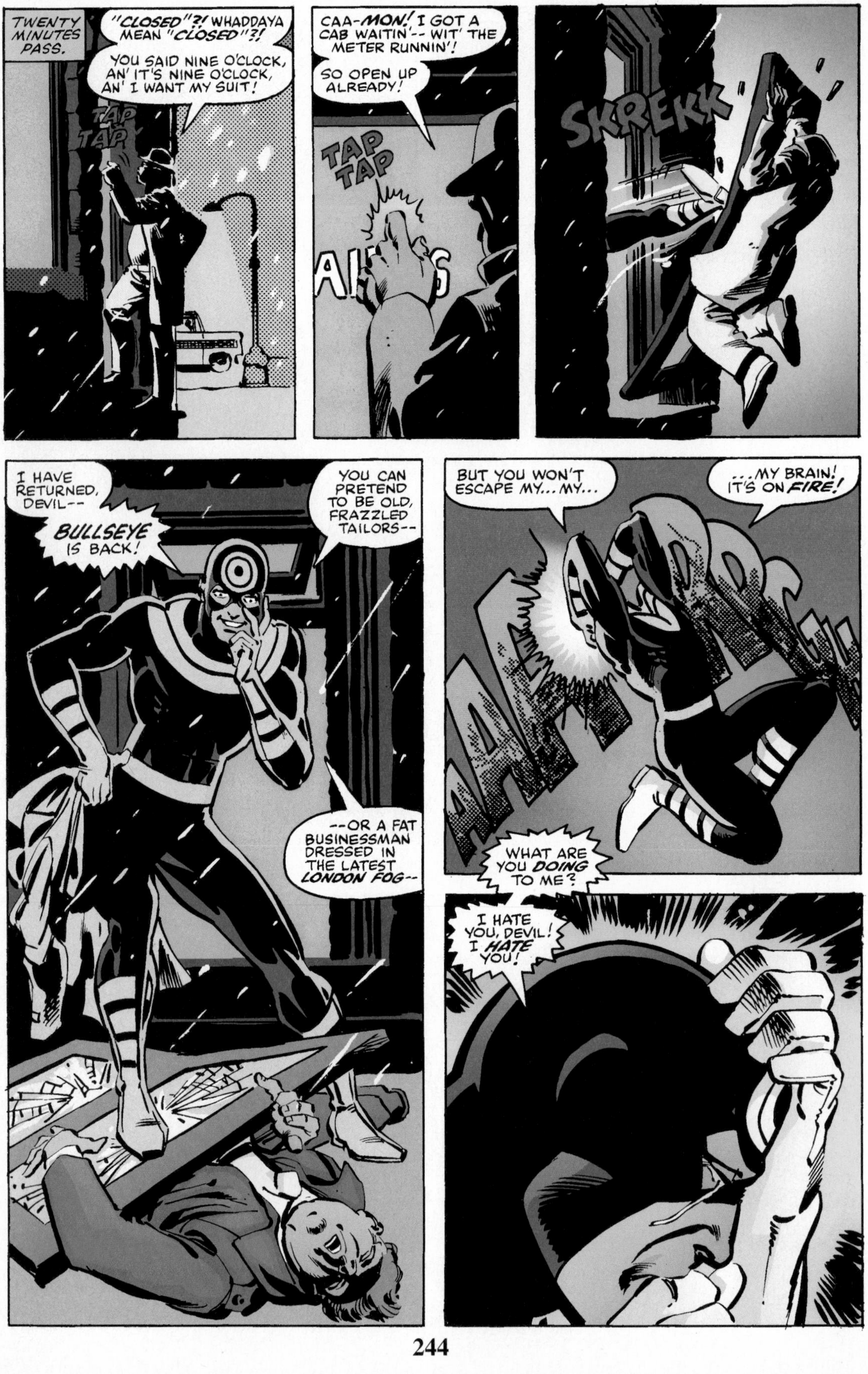
TWENTY MINUTES PASS.
"CLOSED"?! WHADDAYA MEAN "CLOSED"?!
YOU SAID NINE O'CLOCK, AN' IT'S NINE O'CLOCK, AN' I WANT MY SUIT!
TAP TAP
CAA-MON! I GOT A CAB WAITIN'-- WIT' THE METER RUNNIN'!
SO OPEN UP ALREADY!
TAP TAP
SKREKK
I HAVE RETURNED, DEVIL--
BULLSEYE IS BACK!
YOU CAN PRETEND TO BE OLD, FRAZZLED TAILORS--
--OR A FAT BUSINESSMAN DRESSED IN THE LATEST LONDON FOG--
BUT YOU WON'T ESCAPE MY... MY...
...MY BRAIN! IT'S ON FIRE!
WHAT ARE YOU DOING TO ME?
I HATE YOU, DEVIL! I HATE YOU!

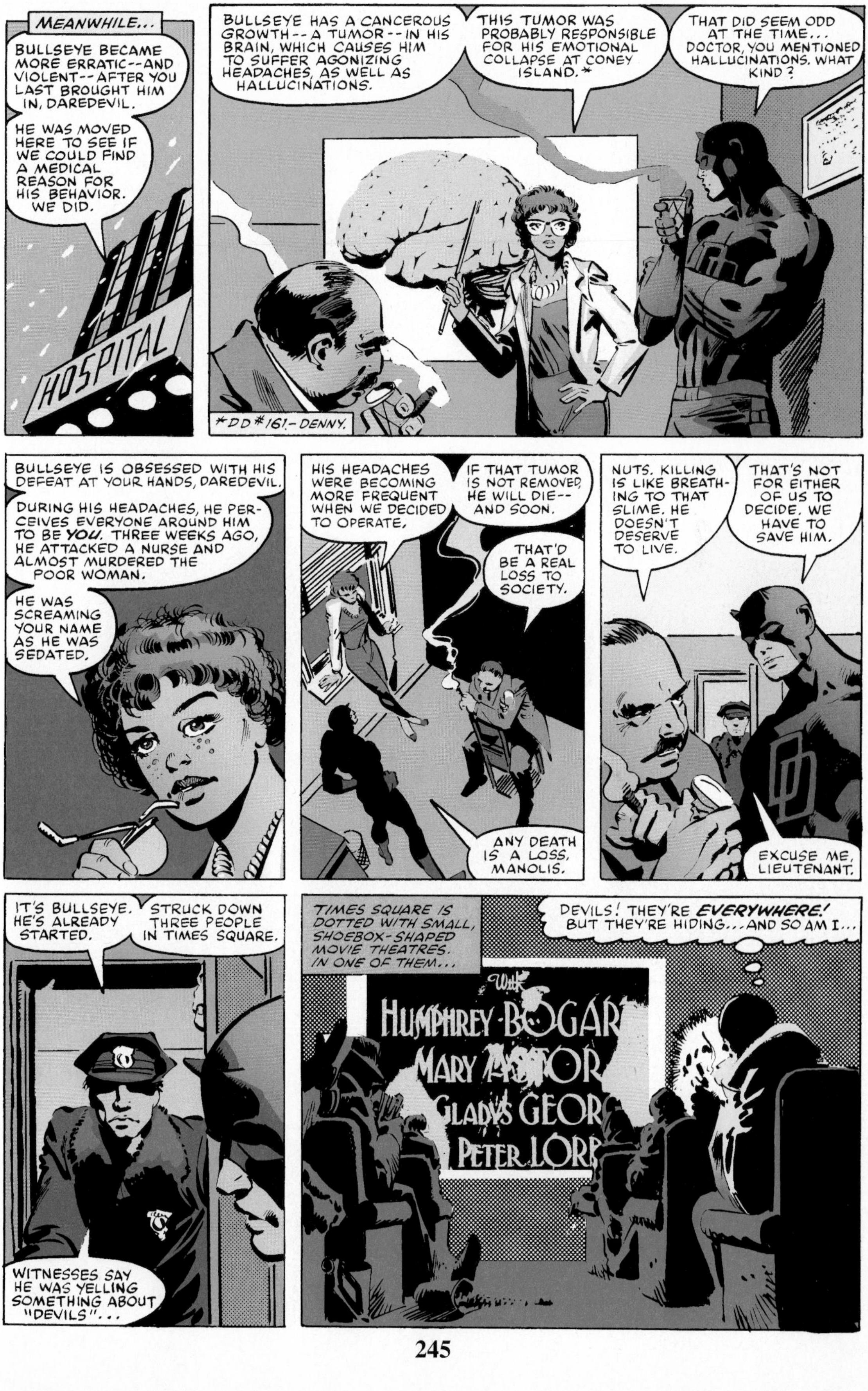
MEANWHILE...
BULLSEYE BECAME MORE ERRATIC--AND VIOLENT--AFTER YOU LAST BROUGHT HIM IN, DAREDEVIL.
HE WAS MOVED HERE TO SEE IF WE COULD FIND A MEDICAL REASON FOR HIS BEHAVIOR. WE DID.
HOSPITAL
BULLSEYE HAS A CANCEROUS GROWTH--A TUMOR--IN HIS BRAIN, WHICH CAUSES HIM TO SUFFER AGONIZING HEADACHES, AS WELL AS HALLUCINATIONS.
THIS TUMOR WAS PROBABLY RESPONSIBLE FOR HIS EMOTIONAL COLLAPSE AT CONEY ISLAND.*
THAT DID SEEM ODD AT THE TIME... DOCTOR, YOU MENTIONED HALLUCINATIONS. WHAT KIND?
*DD #161.-DENNY.
BULLSEYE IS OBSESSED WITH HIS DEFEAT AT YOUR HANDS, DAREDEVIL.
DURING HIS HEADACHES, HE PERCEIVES EVERYONE AROUND HIM TO BE YOU. THREE WEEKS AGO, HE ATTACKED A NURSE AND ALMOST MURDERED THE POOR WOMAN.
HE WAS SCREAMING YOUR NAME AS HE WAS SEDATED.
HIS HEADACHES WERE BECOMING MORE FREQUENT WHEN WE DECIDED TO OPERATE.
IF THAT TUMOR IS NOT REMOVED, HE WILL DIE--AND SOON.
THAT'D BE A REAL LOSS TO SOCIETY.
ANY DEATH IS A LOSS, MANOLIS.
NUTS. KILLING IS LIKE BREATHING TO THAT SLIME. HE DOESN'T DESERVE TO LIVE.
THAT'S NOT FOR EITHER OF US TO DECIDE. WE HAVE TO SAVE HIM.
EXCUSE ME, LIEUTENANT.
IT'S BULLSEYE. HE'S ALREADY STARTED.
STRUCK DOWN THREE PEOPLE IN TIMES SQUARE.
WITNESSES SAY HE WAS YELLING SOMETHING ABOUT "DEVILS"...
TIMES SQUARE IS DOTTED WITH SMALL, SHOEBOX-SHAPED MOVIE THEATRES. IN ONE OF THEM...
DEVILS! THEY'RE EVERYWHERE! BUT THEY'RE HIDING... AND SO AM I...
HUMPHREY BOGAR
MARY ASTOR
GLADYS GEOR
PETER LORR

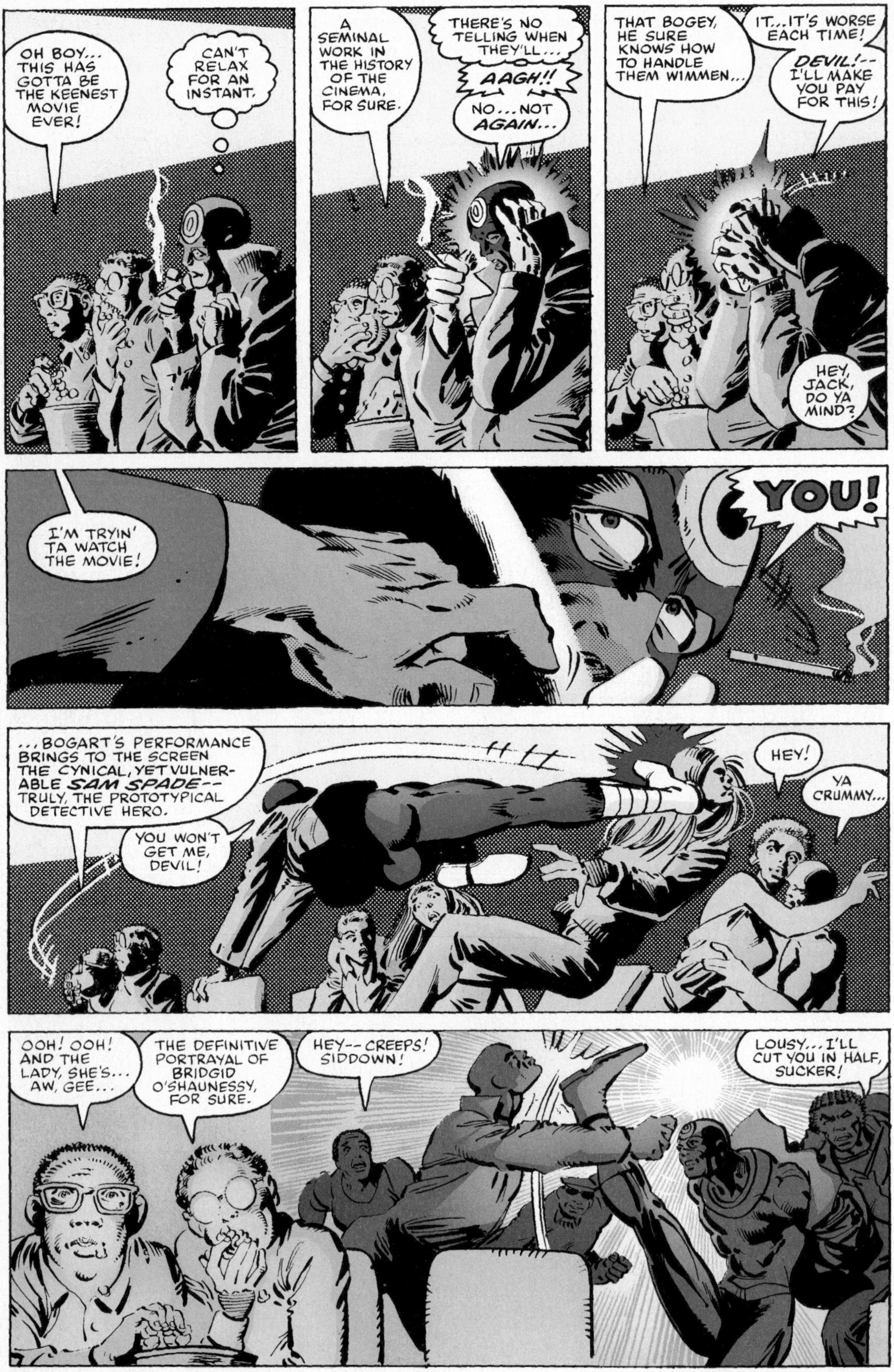

OH BOY... THIS HAS GOTTA BE THE KEENEST MOVIE EVER!
CAN'T RELAX FOR AN INSTANT.
A SEMINAL WORK IN THE HISTORY OF THE CINEMA, FOR SURE.
THERE'S NO TELLING WHEN THEY'LL...
AAGH!!
NO... NOT AGAIN...
THAT BOGEY, HE SURE KNOWS HOW TO HANDLE THEM WIMMEN...
IT...IT'S WORSE EACH TIME!
DEVIL!-- I'LL MAKE YOU PAY FOR THIS!
HEY, JACK, DO YA MIND?
I'M TRYIN' TA WATCH THE MOVIE!
YOU!
...BOGART'S PERFORMANCE BRINGS TO THE SCREEN THE CYNICAL, YET VULNERABLE SAM SPADE-- TRULY, THE PROTOTYPICAL DETECTIVE HERO.
YOU WON'T GET ME, DEVIL!
HEY!
YA CRUMMY...
OOH! OOH! AND THE LADY, SHE'S... AW, GEE...
THE DEFINITIVE PORTRAYAL OF BRIDGID O'SHAUNESSY, FOR SURE.
HEY-- CREEPS! SIDDOWN!
LOUSY... I'LL CUT YOU IN HALF, SUCKER!

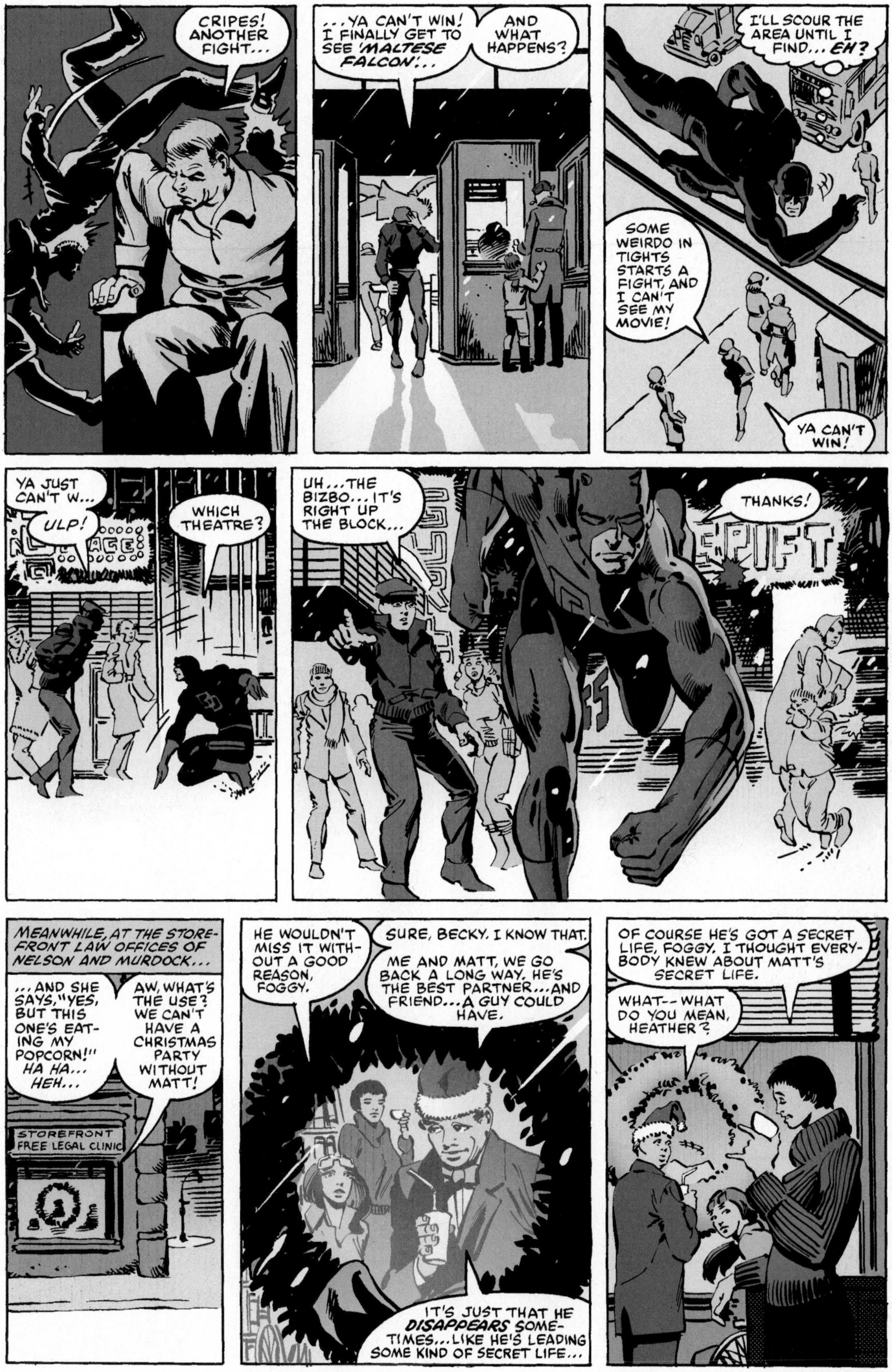
CRIPES! ANOTHER FIGHT...
...YA CAN'T WIN! I FINALLY GET TO SEE 'MALTESE FALCON'...
AND WHAT HAPPENS?
I'LL SCOUR THE AREA UNTIL I FIND... EH?
SOME WEIRDO IN TIGHTS STARTS A FIGHT, AND I CAN'T SEE MY MOVIE!
YA CAN'T WIN!
YA JUST CAN'T W...
ULP!
WHICH THEATRE?
UH... THE BIZBO... IT'S RIGHT UP THE BLOCK...
THANKS!
MEANWHILE, AT THE STOREFRONT LAW OFFICES OF NELSON AND MURDOCK...
...AND SHE SAYS, "YES, BUT THIS ONE'S EATING MY POPCORN!" HA HA... HEH...
AW, WHAT'S THE USE? WE CAN'T HAVE A CHRISTMAS PARTY WITHOUT MATT!
STOREFRONT FREE LEGAL CLINIC
HE WOULDN'T MISS IT WITHOUT A GOOD REASON, FOGGY.
SURE, BECKY. I KNOW THAT.
ME AND MATT, WE GO BACK A LONG WAY. HE'S THE BEST PARTNER... AND FRIEND... A GUY COULD HAVE.
IT'S JUST THAT HE DISAPPEARS SOMETIMES... LIKE HE'S LEADING SOME KIND OF SECRET LIFE...
OF COURSE HE'S GOT A SECRET LIFE, FOGGY. I THOUGHT EVERYBODY KNEW ABOUT MATT'S SECRET LIFE.
WHAT-- WHAT DO YOU MEAN, HEATHER?

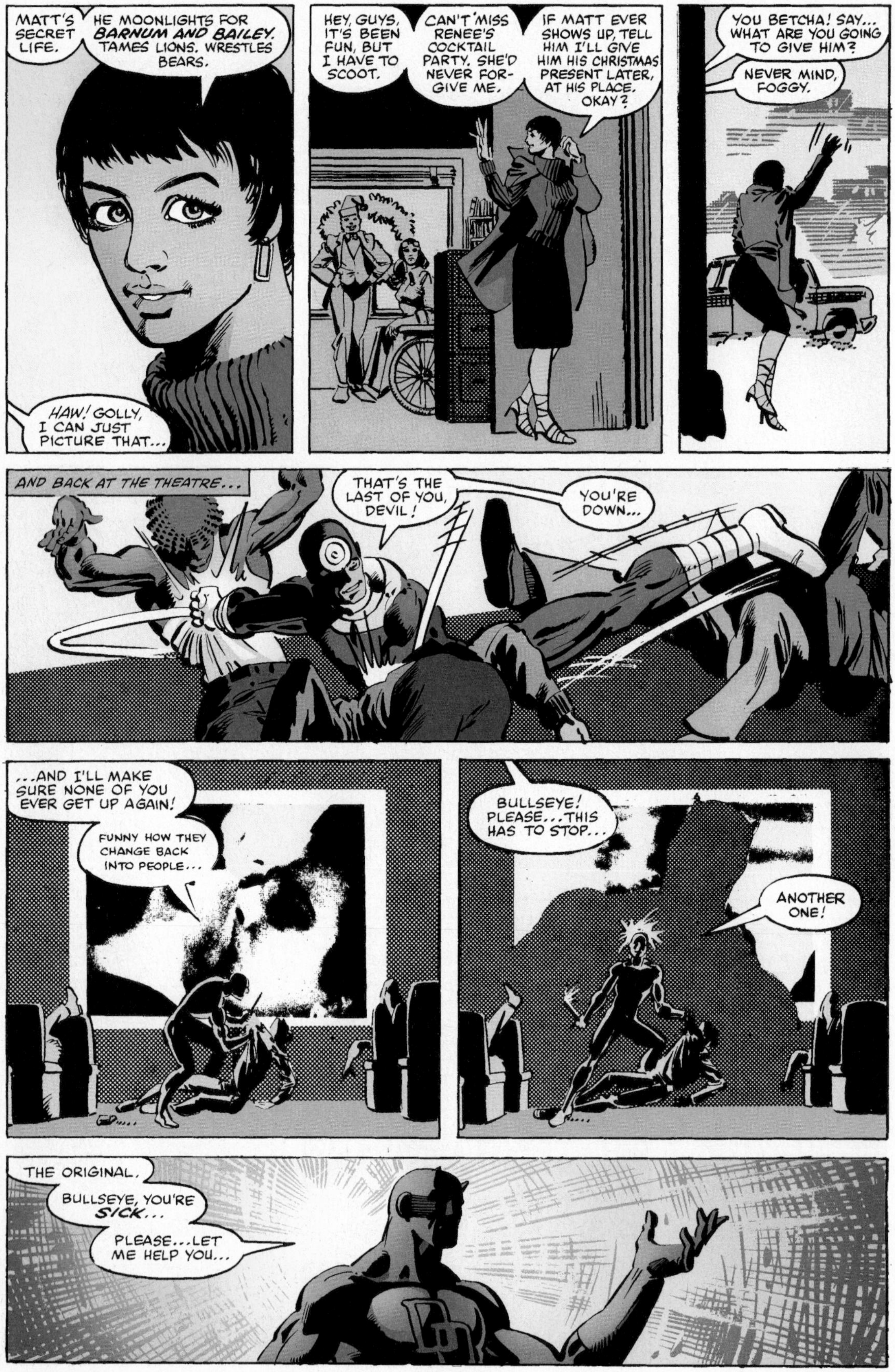
MATT'S SECRET LIFE.
HE MOONLIGHTS FOR BARNUM AND BAILEY. TAMES LIONS. WRESTLES BEARS.
HAW! GOLLY, I CAN JUST PICTURE THAT...
HEY, GUYS, IT'S BEEN FUN, BUT I HAVE TO SCOOT.
CAN'T MISS RENEE'S COCKTAIL PARTY. SHE'D NEVER FORGIVE ME.
IF MATT EVER SHOWS UP, TELL HIM I'LL GIVE HIM HIS CHRISTMAS PRESENT LATER, AT HIS PLACE. OKAY?
YOU BETCHA! SAY... WHAT ARE YOU GOING TO GIVE HIM?
NEVER MIND, FOGGY.
AND BACK AT THE THEATRE...
THAT'S THE LAST OF YOU, DEVIL!
YOU'RE DOWN...
...AND I'LL MAKE SURE NONE OF YOU EVER GET UP AGAIN!
FUNNY HOW THEY CHANGE BACK INTO PEOPLE...
BULLSEYE! PLEASE...THIS HAS TO STOP...
ANOTHER ONE!
THE ORIGINAL.
BULLSEYE, YOU'RE SICK...
PLEASE...LET ME HELP YOU...

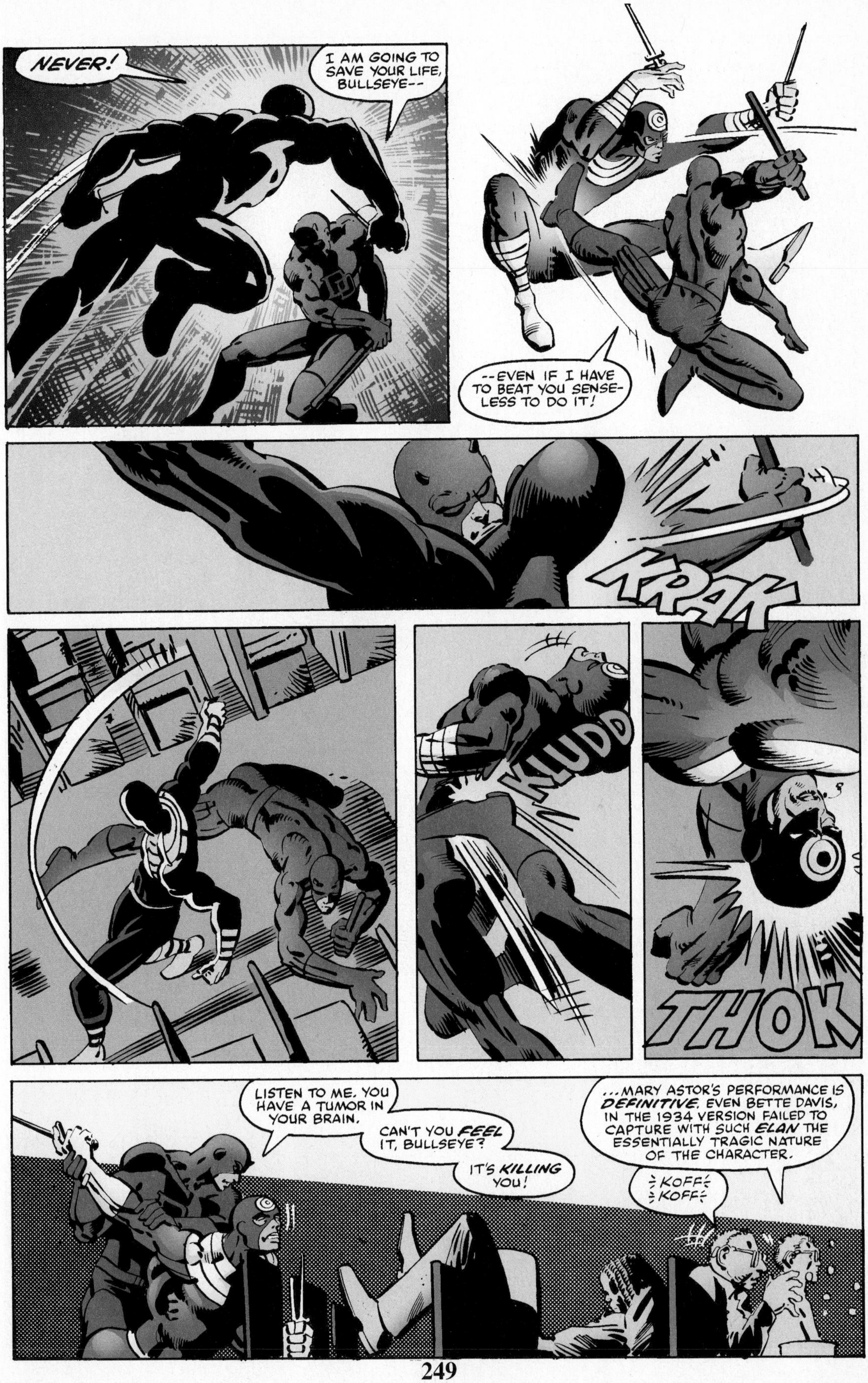
I AM GOING TO SAVE YOUR LIFE, BULLSEYE--
NEVER!
--EVEN IF I HAVE TO BEAT YOU SENSE-LESS TO DO IT!
KRAK
KLUDD
THOK
LISTEN TO ME. YOU HAVE A TUMOR IN YOUR BRAIN.
CAN'T YOU FEEL IT, BULLSEYE?
IT'S KILLING YOU!
...MARY ASTOR'S PERFORMANCE IS DEFINITIVE. EVEN BETTE DAVIS, IN THE 1934 VERSION FAILED TO CAPTURE WITH SUCH ELAN THE ESSENTIALLY TRAGIC NATURE OF THE CHARACTER.
KOFF KOFF

AW, GEE...HE'S GOT A BIG GUN... ≥KOFF≤ ≥KOFF≤

FOR SURE...

THE FRIGHTENING, YET ATTRACTIVE NATURE OF VIOLENCE IS THE QUINTESSENTIAL ELEMENT OF THE DETECTIVE GENRE...

THAT DICHOTOMY PERMEATES THE FILM, IT...

IT...

HOLD IT RIGHT THERE, DEVIL! I THINK YOU CAN GUESS WHAT COMES NEXT.

DROP YOUR BILLY CLUB-- STAND STOCK STILL AND LET ME KILL YOU--

--OR I'LL SKEWER THIS LITTLE CREEP!

IT'S YOUR CHOICE, DEVIL!

HIS LIFE--OR YOURS!

THUNK

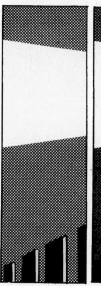

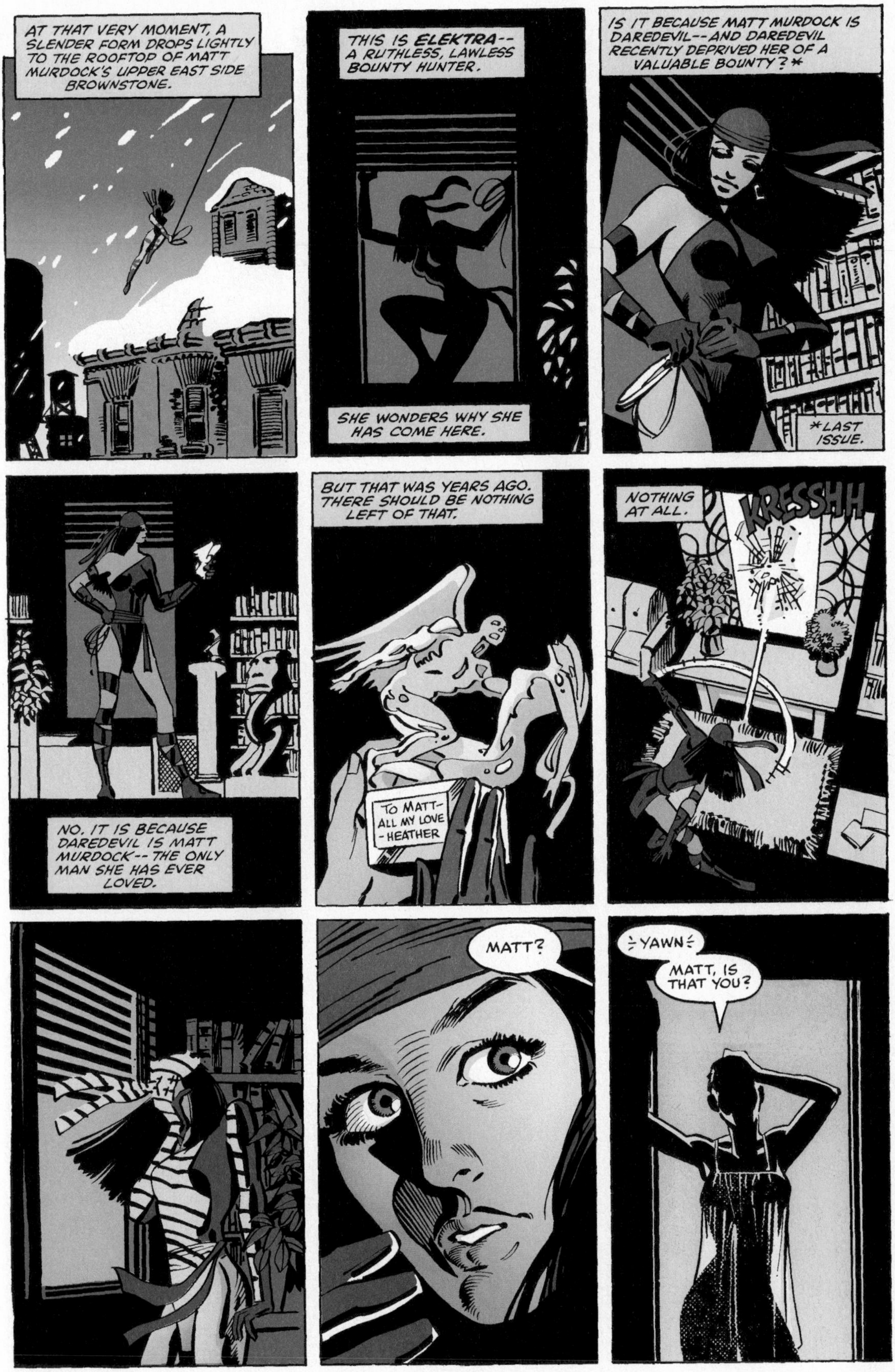
AT THAT VERY MOMENT, A SLENDER FORM DROPS LIGHTLY TO THE ROOFTOP OF MATT MURDOCK'S UPPER EAST SIDE BROWNSTONE.
THIS IS ELEKTRA-- A RUTHLESS, LAWLESS BOUNTY HUNTER.
SHE WONDERS WHY SHE HAS COME HERE.
IS IT BECAUSE MATT MURDOCK IS DAREDEVIL--AND DAREDEVIL RECENTLY DEPRIVED HER OF A VALUABLE BOUNTY?*
*LAST ISSUE.
NO. IT IS BECAUSE DAREDEVIL IS MATT MURDOCK--THE ONLY MAN SHE HAS EVER LOVED.
BUT THAT WAS YEARS AGO. THERE SHOULD BE NOTHING LEFT OF THAT.
TO MATT- ALL MY LOVE -HEATHER
NOTHING AT ALL.
KRESSHH
MATT?
YAWN
MATT, IS THAT YOU?

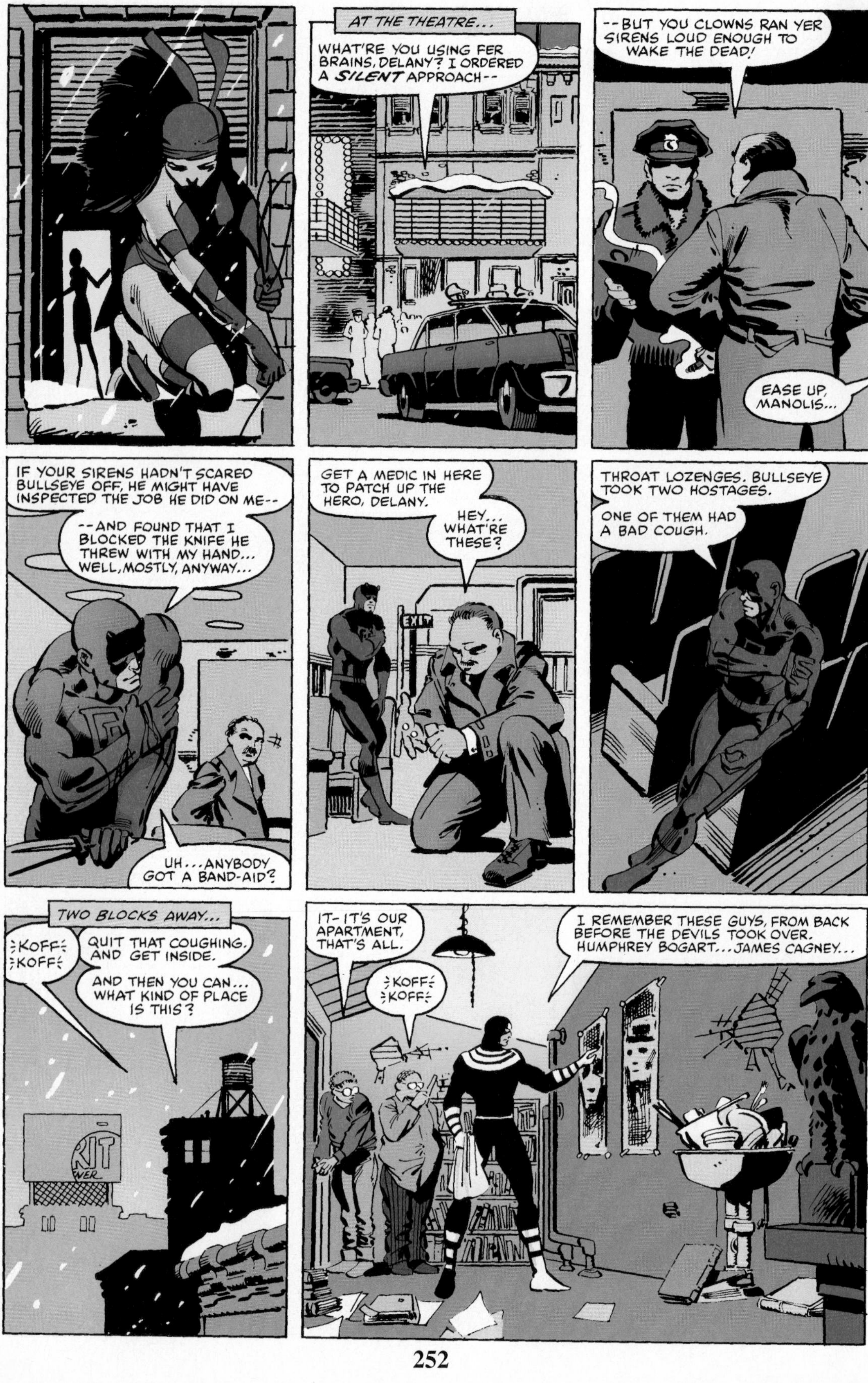
AT THE THEATRE...
WHAT'RE YOU USING FER BRAINS, DELANY? I ORDERED A SILENT APPROACH--
--BUT YOU CLOWNS RAN YER SIRENS LOUD ENOUGH TO WAKE THE DEAD!
EASE UP, MANOLIS...
IF YOUR SIRENS HADN'T SCARED BULLSEYE OFF, HE MIGHT HAVE INSPECTED THE JOB HE DID ON ME--
--AND FOUND THAT I BLOCKED THE KNIFE HE THREW WITH MY HAND... WELL, MOSTLY, ANYWAY...
UH... ANYBODY GOT A BAND-AID?
GET A MEDIC IN HERE TO PATCH UP THE HERO, DELANY.
HEY... WHAT'RE THESE?
EXIT
THROAT LOZENGES. BULLSEYE TOOK TWO HOSTAGES.
ONE OF THEM HAD A BAD COUGH.
TWO BLOCKS AWAY...
KOFF KOFF
QUIT THAT COUGHING. AND GET INSIDE.
AND THEN YOU CAN... WHAT KIND OF PLACE IS THIS?
IT- IT'S OUR APARTMENT, THAT'S ALL.
KOFF KOFF
I REMEMBER THESE GUYS, FROM BACK BEFORE THE DEVILS TOOK OVER. HUMPHREY BOGART... JAMES CAGNEY...

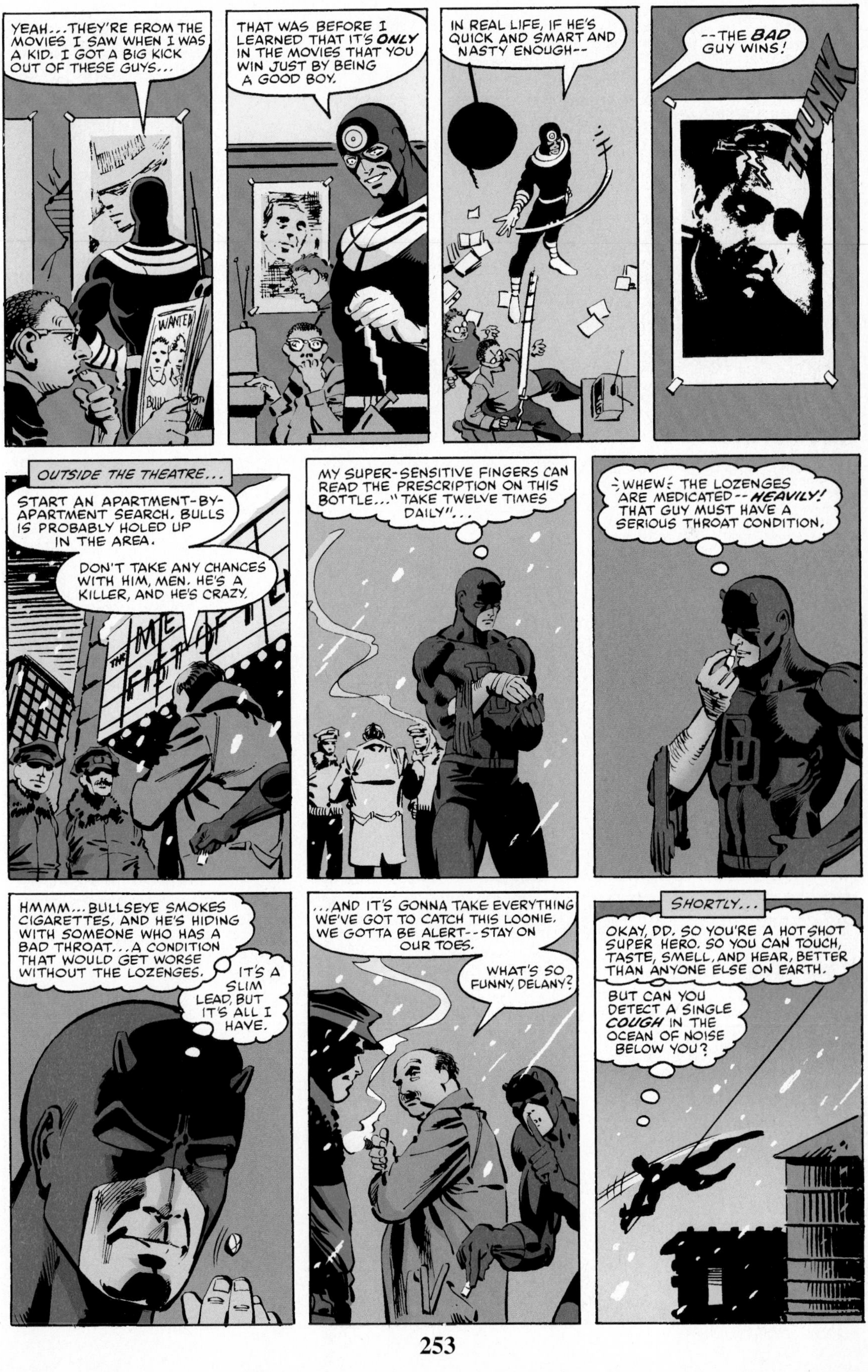
YEAH...THEY'RE FROM THE MOVIES I SAW WHEN I WAS A KID. I GOT A BIG KICK OUT OF THESE GUYS...
WANTED
THAT WAS BEFORE I LEARNED THAT IT'S ONLY IN THE MOVIES THAT YOU WIN JUST BY BEING A GOOD BOY.
IN REAL LIFE, IF HE'S QUICK AND SMART AND NASTY ENOUGH--
--THE BAD GUY WINS!
THUNK
OUTSIDE THE THEATRE...
START AN APARTMENT-BY-APARTMENT SEARCH. BULLS IS PROBABLY HOLED UP IN THE AREA.
DON'T TAKE ANY CHANCES WITH HIM, MEN. HE'S A KILLER, AND HE'S CRAZY.
MY SUPER-SENSITIVE FINGERS CAN READ THE PRESCRIPTION ON THIS BOTTLE..."TAKE TWELVE TIMES DAILY"...
WHEW! THE LOZENGES ARE MEDICATED--HEAVILY! THAT GUY MUST HAVE A SERIOUS THROAT CONDITION.
HMMM...BULLSEYE SMOKES CIGARETTES, AND HE'S HIDING WITH SOMEONE WHO HAS A BAD THROAT...A CONDITION THAT WOULD GET WORSE WITHOUT THE LOZENGES.
IT'S A SLIM LEAD, BUT IT'S ALL I HAVE.
...AND IT'S GONNA TAKE EVERYTHING WE'VE GOT TO CATCH THIS LOONIE. WE GOTTA BE ALERT--STAY ON OUR TOES.
WHAT'S SO FUNNY, DELANY?
SHORTLY...
OKAY, DD. SO YOU'RE A HOT SHOT SUPER HERO. SO YOU CAN TOUCH, TASTE, SMELL, AND HEAR, BETTER THAN ANYONE ELSE ON EARTH.
BUT CAN YOU DETECT A SINGLE COUGH IN THE OCEAN OF NOISE BELOW YOU?

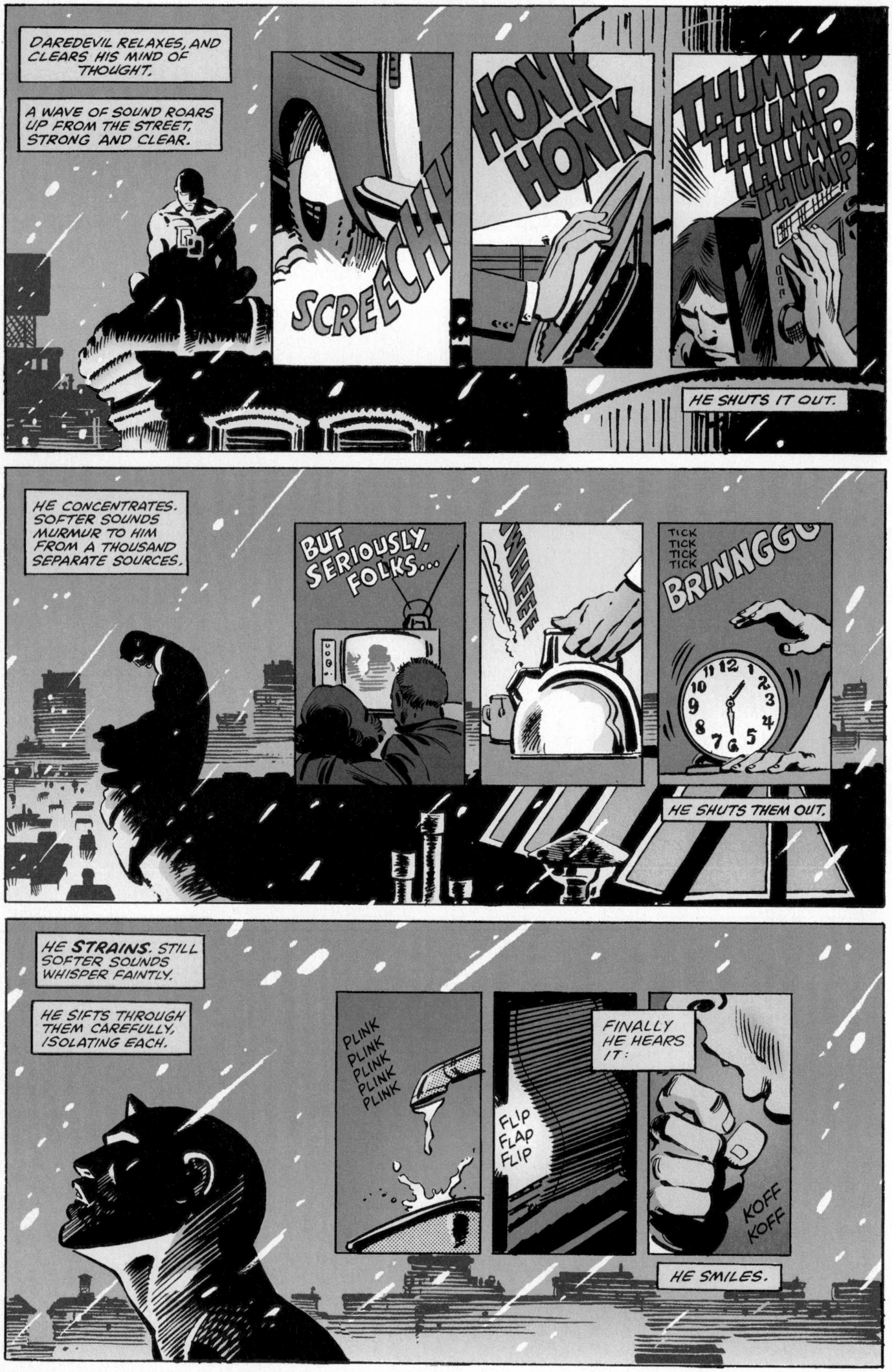
DAREDEVIL RELAXES, AND CLEARS HIS MIND OF THOUGHT.
A WAVE OF SOUND ROARS UP FROM THE STREET, STRONG AND CLEAR.
SCREECH
HONK HONK
THUMP THUMP THUMP THUMP
HE SHUTS IT OUT.
HE CONCENTRATES. SOFTER SOUNDS MURMUR TO HIM FROM A THOUSAND SEPARATE SOURCES.
BUT SERIOUSLY, FOLKS...
TICK TICK TICK TICK
BRINNGG
HE SHUTS THEM OUT.
HE STRAINS. STILL SOFTER SOUNDS WHISPER FAINTLY.
HE SIFTS THROUGH THEM CAREFULLY, ISOLATING EACH.
PLINK PLINK PLINK PLINK PLINK
FLIP FLAP FLIP
FINALLY HE HEARS IT:
KOFF KOFF
HE SMILES.

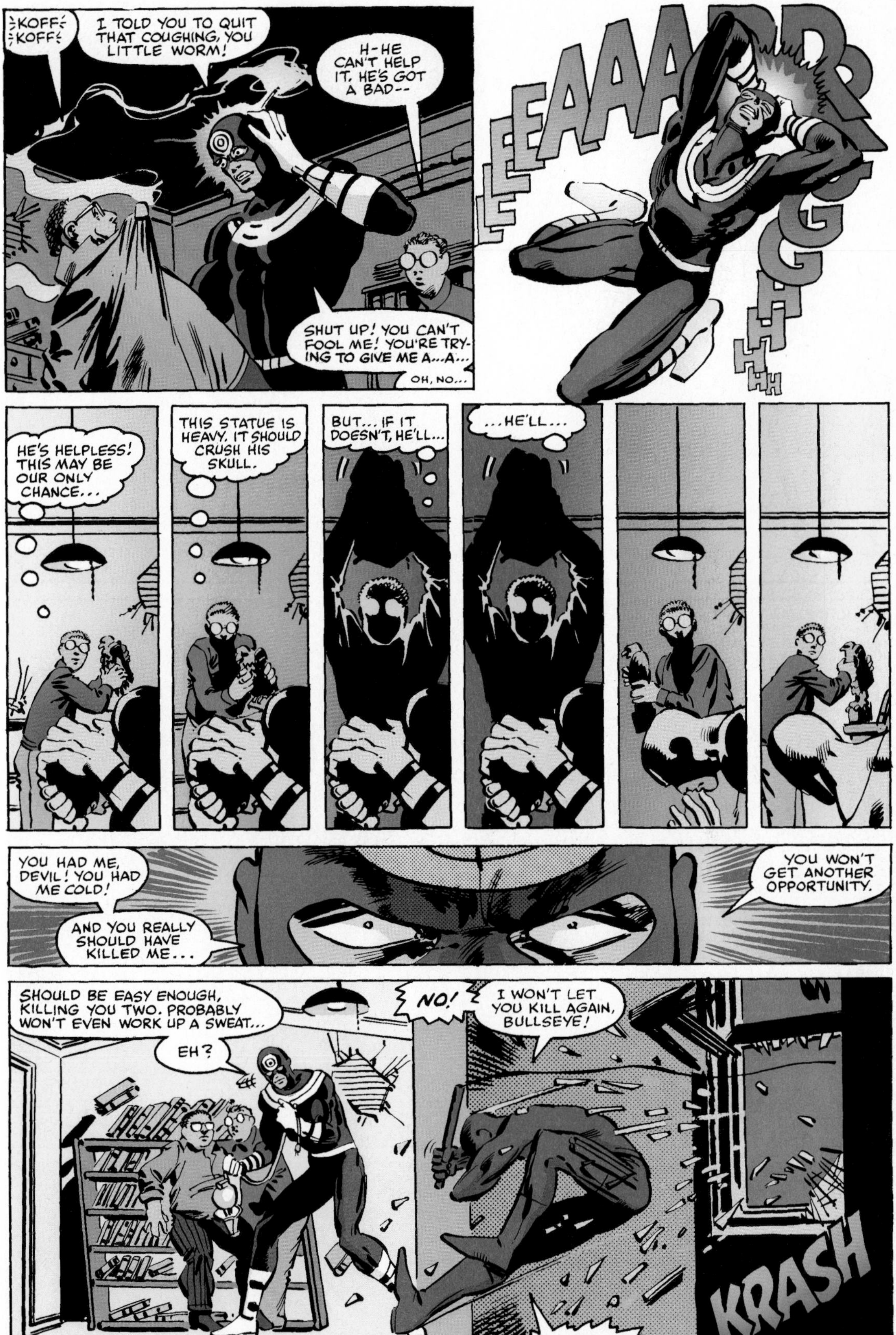
KOFF KOFF
I TOLD YOU TO QUIT THAT COUGHING, YOU LITTLE WORM!
H-HE CAN'T HELP IT. HE'S GOT A BAD--
SHUT UP! YOU CAN'T FOOL ME! YOU'RE TRYING TO GIVE ME A...A...
OH, NO...
LEEEAAAARRRGGGHHHHH
HE'S HELPLESS! THIS MAY BE OUR ONLY CHANCE...
THIS STATUE IS HEAVY. IT SHOULD CRUSH HIS SKULL.
BUT... IF IT DOESN'T, HE'LL...
...HE'LL...
YOU HAD ME, DEVIL! YOU HAD ME COLD!
AND YOU REALLY SHOULD HAVE KILLED ME...
YOU WON'T GET ANOTHER OPPORTUNITY.
SHOULD BE EASY ENOUGH, KILLING YOU TWO. PROBABLY WON'T EVEN WORK UP A SWEAT...
EH?
NO!
I WON'T LET YOU KILL AGAIN, BULLSEYE!
KRASH
I WON'T!

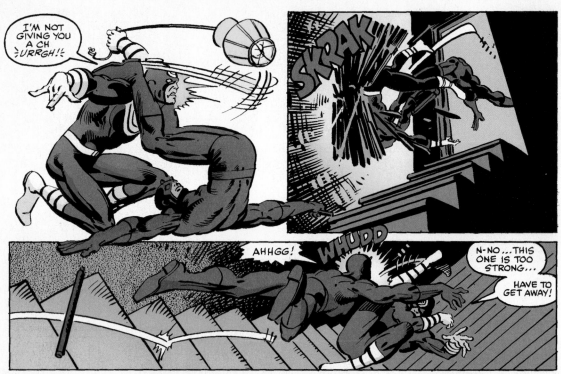

I'M NOT GIVING YOU A CH—*URRGH!*

SKRAK

AHHGG!

WHUDD

N-NO... THIS ONE IS TOO STRONG...

HAVE TO GET AWAY!

LUCKY MY JAW WASN'T BROKEN BY THAT KICK. JUST NEED A SECOND, TO CLEAR MY HEAD.

OH, NO! HE'S HEADED FOR THE SUBWAY!

I'VE ALMOST NO CHANCE OF WINNING—OR EVEN SURVIVING—IN COMBAT DOWN THERE. THE TRAINS ARE NOISY... FAR *TOO* NOISY—

I'D BE A *FOOL* TO FOLLOW HIM.

YET, FOLLOW HE DOES...

...INTO A MAN-MADE PURGATORY THAT *BRUTALIZES* HIS HYPER-SENSES.

ITS STENCH RISES TO MEET HIM, ON AIR DISPLACED BY A SEVENTY-FOOT, STEEL-AND-GLASS *MONSTER.*

THE MONSTER CHARGES DEEP INTO THE EARTH, AND CHARGING, IT *SCREAMS*—

--A SINGLE, SHATTERING HORN-BLAST THAT HAMMERS SUPERSENSITIVE EARDRUMS INTO NUMBNESS.

BLIND, NOW *DEAFENED*--

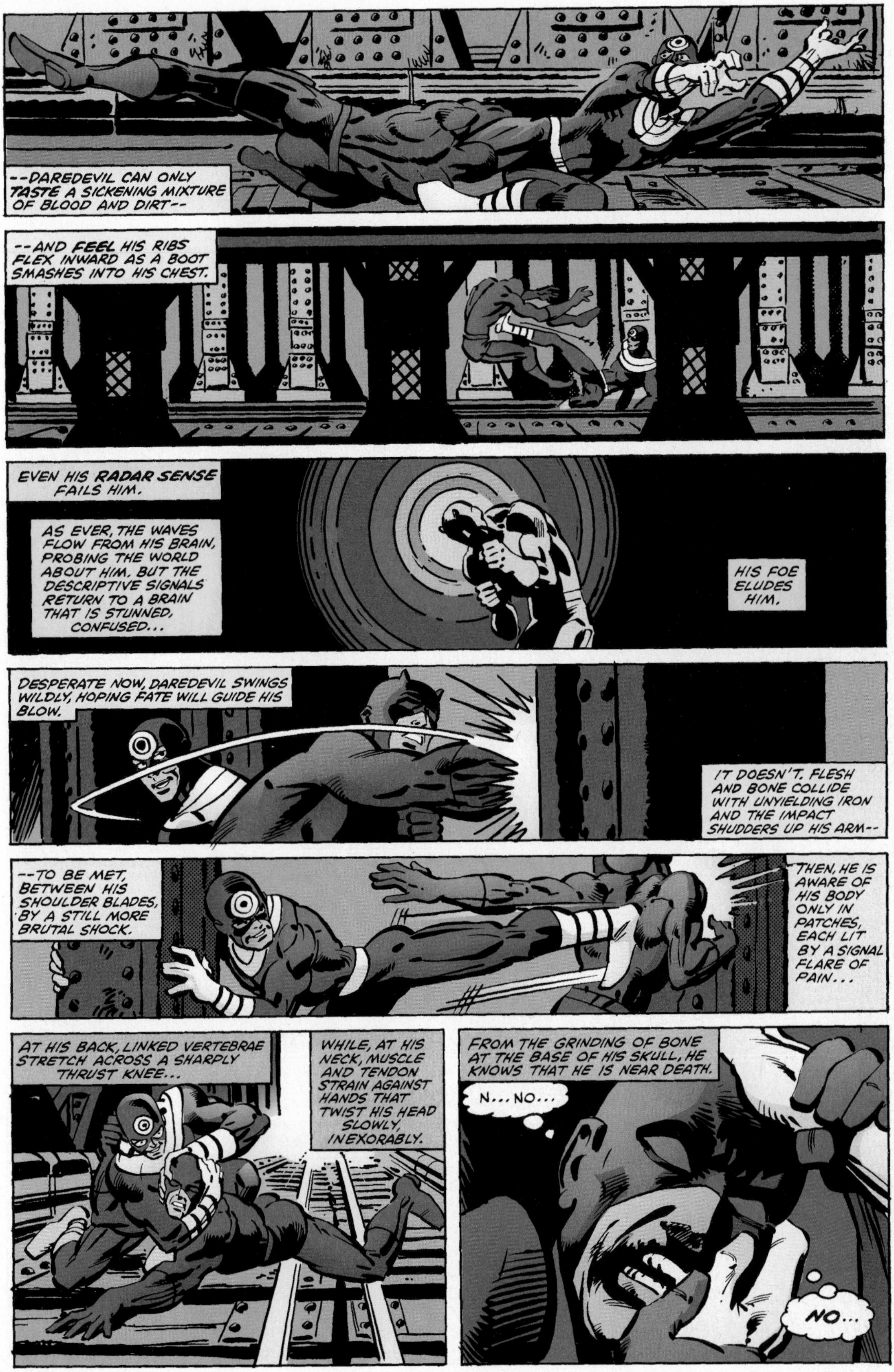
--DAREDEVIL CAN ONLY TASTE A SICKENING MIXTURE OF BLOOD AND DIRT--
--AND FEEL HIS RIBS FLEX INWARD AS A BOOT SMASHES INTO HIS CHEST.
EVEN HIS RADAR SENSE FAILS HIM.
AS EVER, THE WAVES FLOW FROM HIS BRAIN, PROBING THE WORLD ABOUT HIM. BUT THE DESCRIPTIVE SIGNALS RETURN TO A BRAIN THAT IS STUNNED, CONFUSED...
HIS FOE ELUDES HIM.
DESPERATE NOW, DAREDEVIL SWINGS WILDLY, HOPING FATE WILL GUIDE HIS BLOW.
IT DOESN'T. FLESH AND BONE COLLIDE WITH UNYIELDING IRON AND THE IMPACT SHUDDERS UP HIS ARM--
--TO BE MET, BETWEEN HIS SHOULDER BLADES, BY A STILL MORE BRUTAL SHOCK.
THEN, HE IS AWARE OF HIS BODY ONLY IN PATCHES, EACH LIT BY A SIGNAL FLARE OF PAIN...
AT HIS BACK, LINKED VERTEBRAE STRETCH ACROSS A SHARPLY THRUST KNEE...
WHILE, AT HIS NECK, MUSCLE AND TENDON STRAIN AGAINST HANDS THAT TWIST HIS HEAD SLOWLY, INEXORABLY.
FROM THE GRINDING OF BONE AT THE BASE OF HIS SKULL, HE KNOWS THAT HE IS NEAR DEATH.
N... NO...
NO...

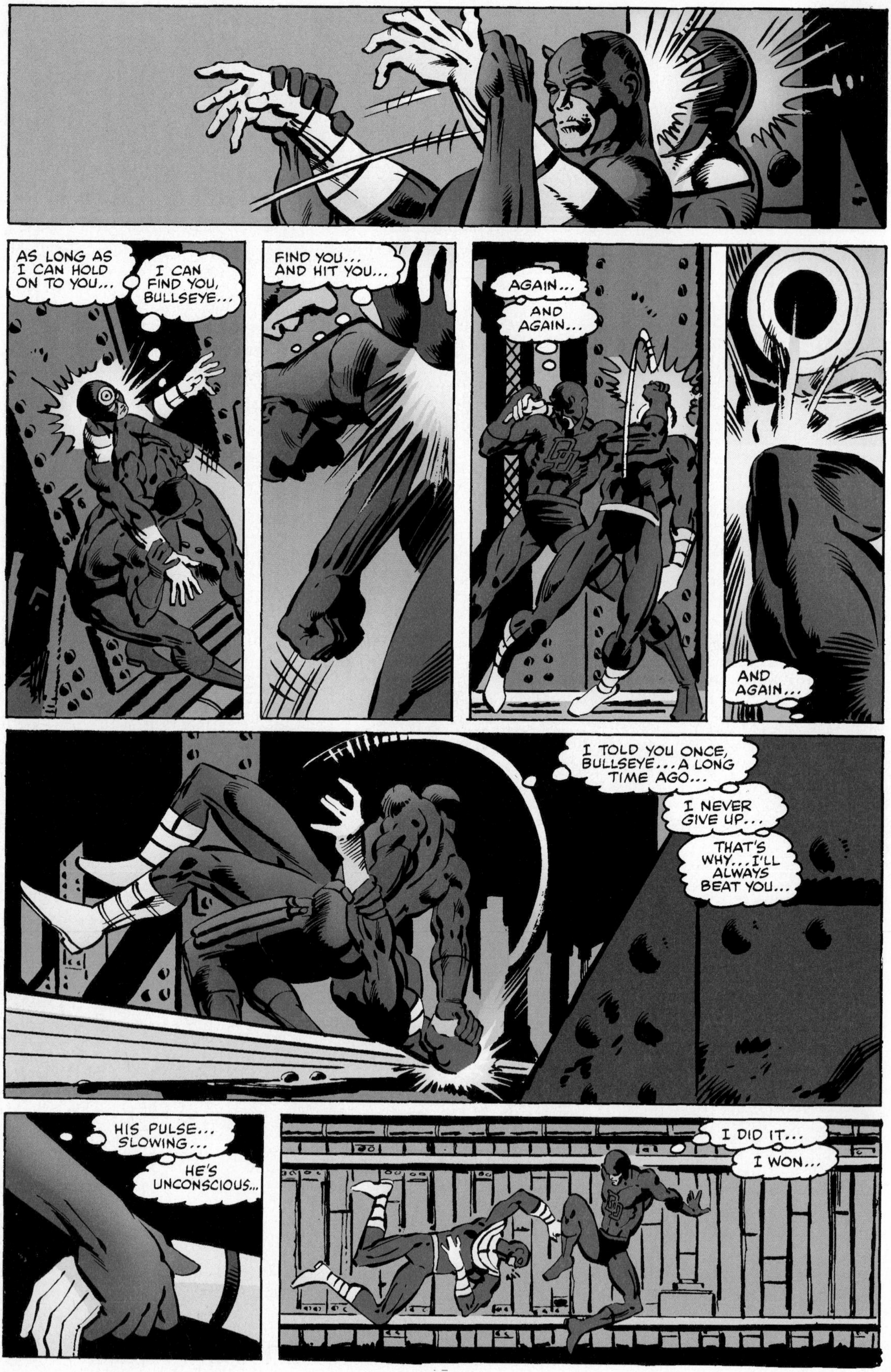
AS LONG AS I CAN HOLD ON TO YOU...
I CAN FIND YOU, BULLSEYE...
FIND YOU... AND HIT YOU...
AGAIN...
AND AGAIN...
AND AGAIN...
I TOLD YOU ONCE, BULLSEYE... A LONG TIME AGO...
I NEVER GIVE UP...
THAT'S WHY... I'LL ALWAYS BEAT YOU...
HIS PULSE... SLOWING...
HE'S UNCONSCIOUS...
I DID IT...
I WON...

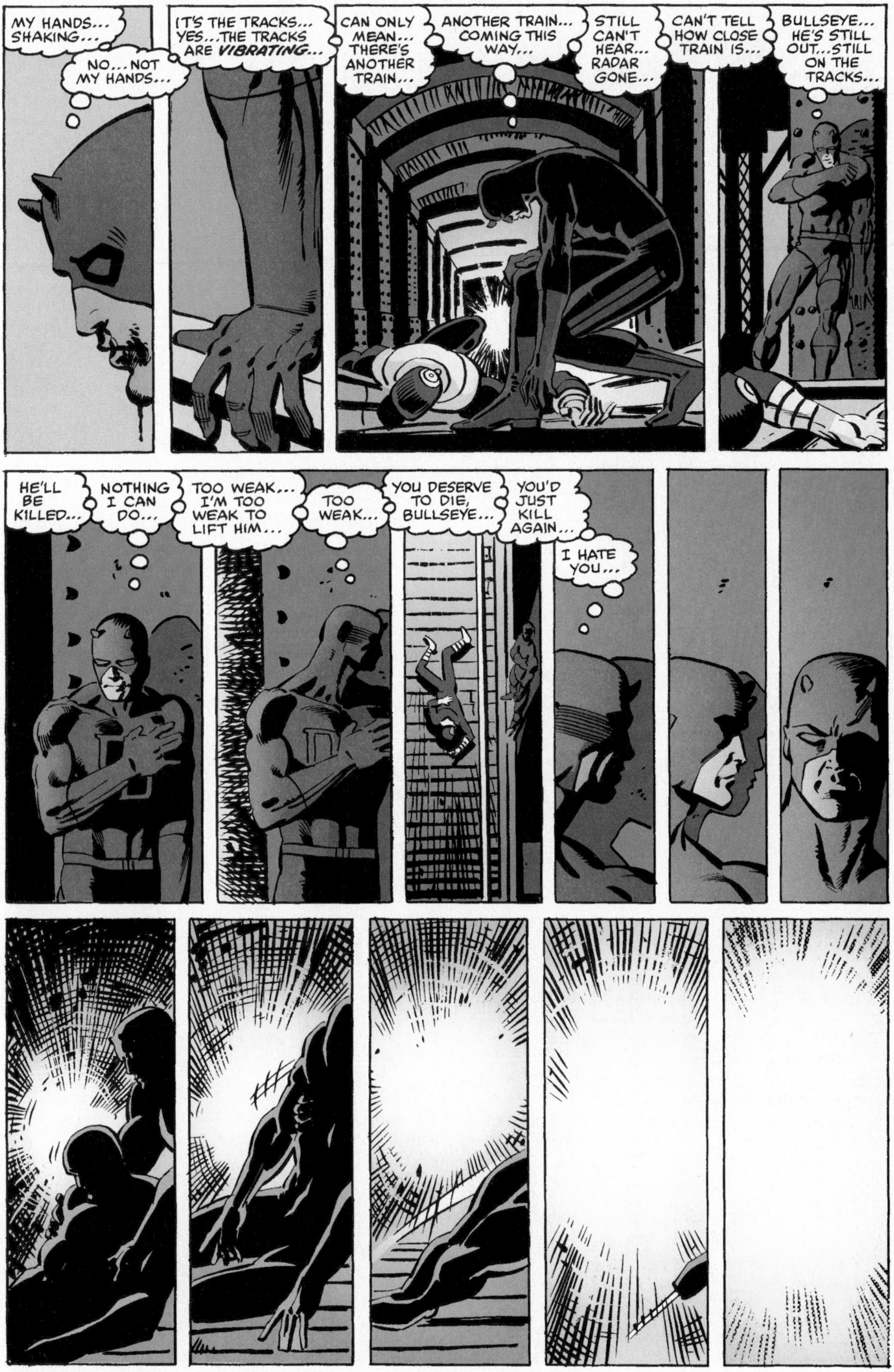
MY HANDS... SHAKING...
NO... NOT MY HANDS...
IT'S THE TRACKS... YES... THE TRACKS ARE VIBRATING...
CAN ONLY MEAN... THERE'S ANOTHER TRAIN...
ANOTHER TRAIN... COMING THIS WAY...
STILL CAN'T HEAR... RADAR GONE...
CAN'T TELL HOW CLOSE TRAIN IS...
BULLSEYE... HE'S STILL OUT... STILL ON THE TRACKS...
HE'LL BE KILLED...
NOTHING I CAN DO...
TOO WEAK... I'M TOO WEAK TO LIFT HIM...
TOO WEAK...
YOU DESERVE TO DIE, BULLSEYE...
YOU'D JUST KILL AGAIN...
I HATE YOU...

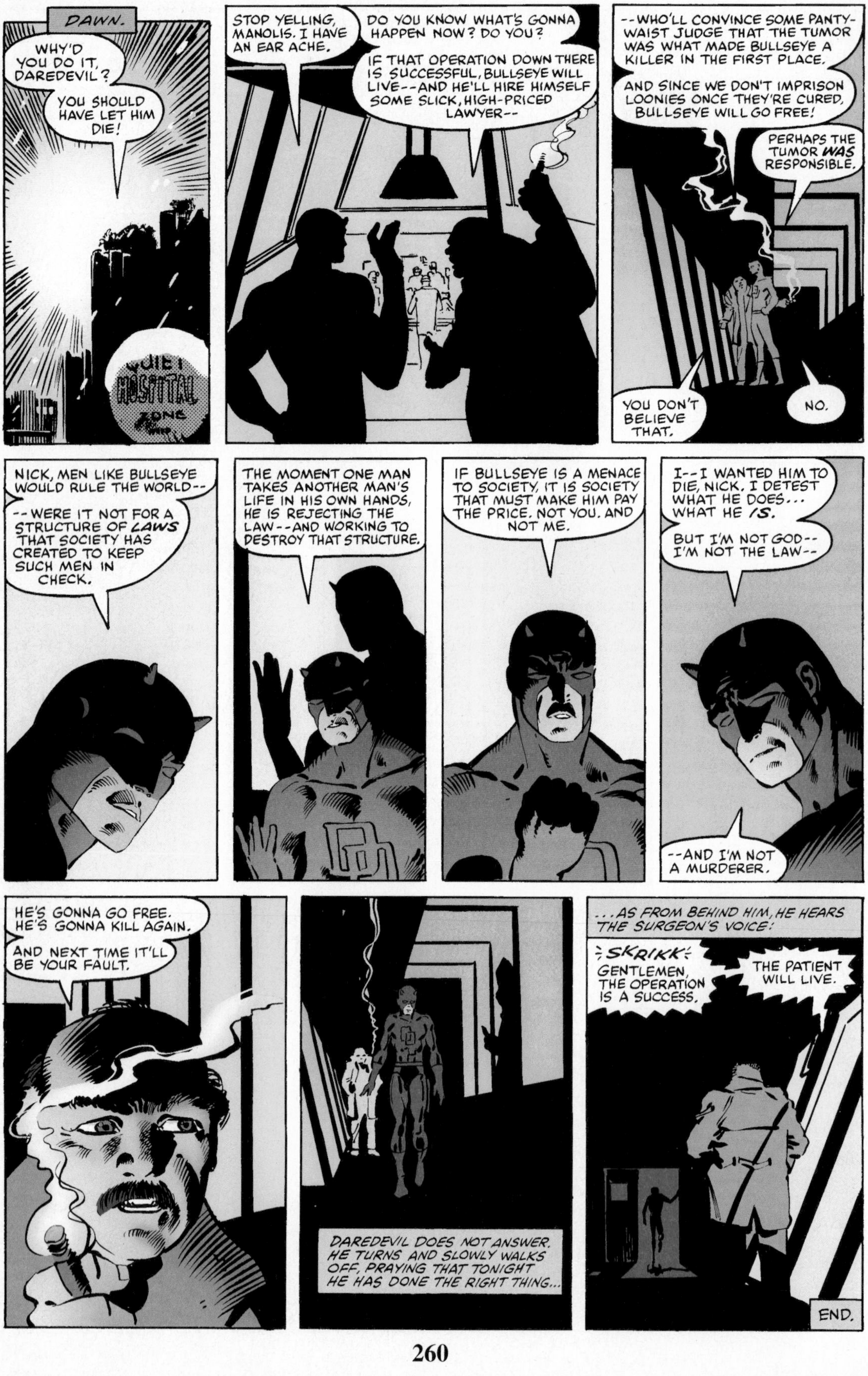
DAWN.
WHY'D YOU DO IT, DAREDEVIL?
YOU SHOULD HAVE LET HIM DIE!
QUIET HOSPITAL ZONE
STOP YELLING, MANOLIS. I HAVE AN EAR ACHE.
DO YOU KNOW WHAT'S GONNA HAPPEN NOW? DO YOU?
IF THAT OPERATION DOWN THERE IS SUCCESSFUL, BULLSEYE WILL LIVE--AND HE'LL HIRE HIMSELF SOME SLICK, HIGH-PRICED LAWYER--
--WHO'LL CONVINCE SOME PANTY-WAIST JUDGE THAT THE TUMOR WAS WHAT MADE BULLSEYE A KILLER IN THE FIRST PLACE.
AND SINCE WE DON'T IMPRISON LOONIES ONCE THEY'RE CURED, BULLSEYE WILL GO FREE!
PERHAPS THE TUMOR WAS RESPONSIBLE.
YOU DON'T BELIEVE THAT.
NO.
NICK, MEN LIKE BULLSEYE WOULD RULE THE WORLD--
--WERE IT NOT FOR A STRUCTURE OF LAWS THAT SOCIETY HAS CREATED TO KEEP SUCH MEN IN CHECK.
THE MOMENT ONE MAN TAKES ANOTHER MAN'S LIFE IN HIS OWN HANDS, HE IS REJECTING THE LAW--AND WORKING TO DESTROY THAT STRUCTURE.
IF BULLSEYE IS A MENACE TO SOCIETY, IT IS SOCIETY THAT MUST MAKE HIM PAY THE PRICE. NOT YOU. AND NOT ME.
I--I WANTED HIM TO DIE, NICK. I DETEST WHAT HE DOES... WHAT HE IS.
BUT I'M NOT GOD--I'M NOT THE LAW--
--AND I'M NOT A MURDERER.
HE'S GONNA GO FREE. HE'S GONNA KILL AGAIN.
AND NEXT TIME IT'LL BE YOUR FAULT.
DAREDEVIL DOES NOT ANSWER. HE TURNS AND SLOWLY WALKS OFF, PRAYING THAT TONIGHT HE HAS DONE THE RIGHT THING...
...AS FROM BEHIND HIM, HE HEARS THE SURGEON'S VOICE:
SKRIKK
GENTLEMEN, THE OPERATION IS A SUCCESS.
THE PATIENT WILL LIVE.
END.

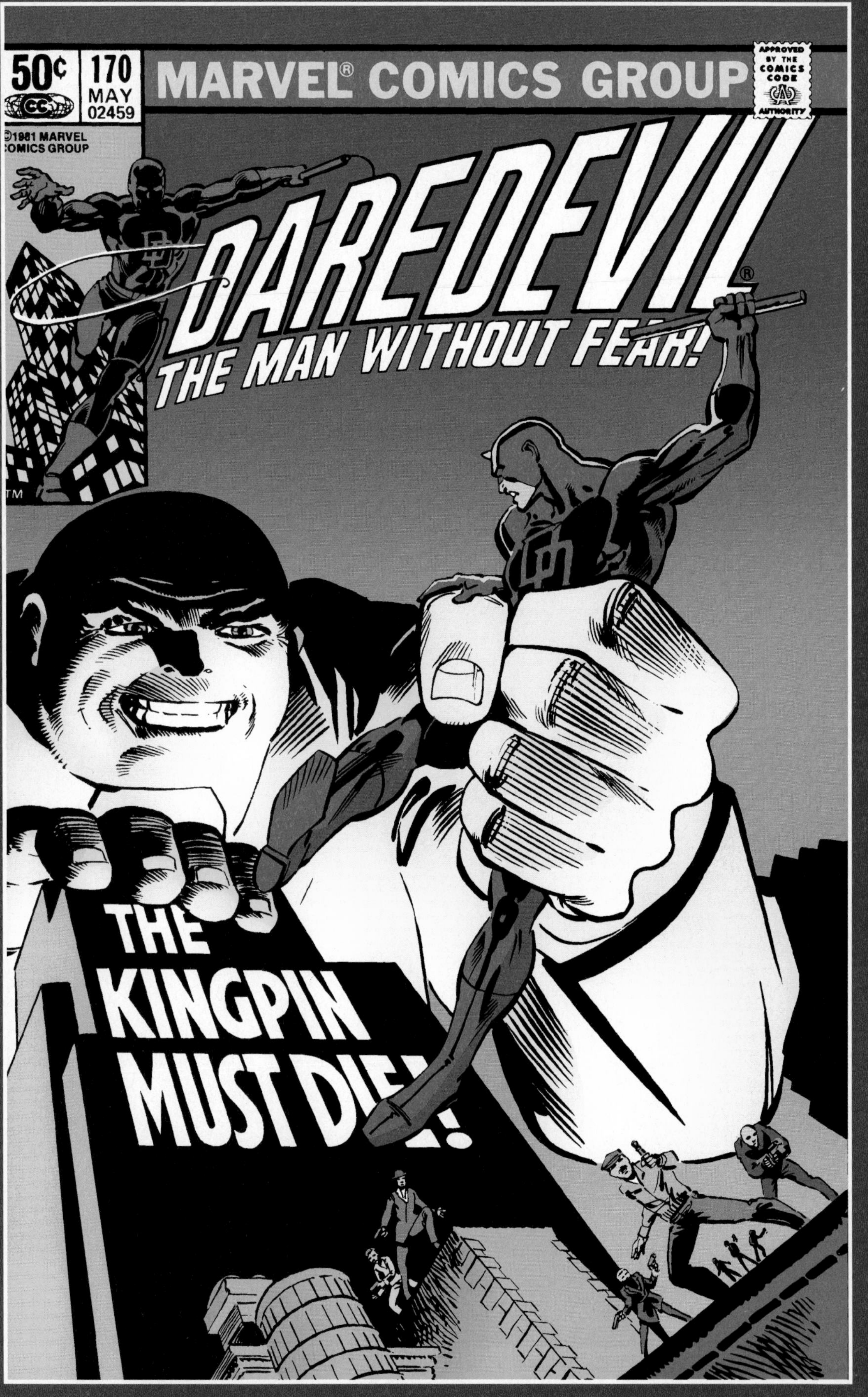
50¢
170
MAY
02459
MARVEL® COMICS GROUP
APPROVED BY THE COMICS CODE AUTHORITY
©1981 MARVEL COMICS GROUP
DAREDEVIL®
THE MAN WITHOUT FEAR!
TM
THE KINGPIN MUST DIE!

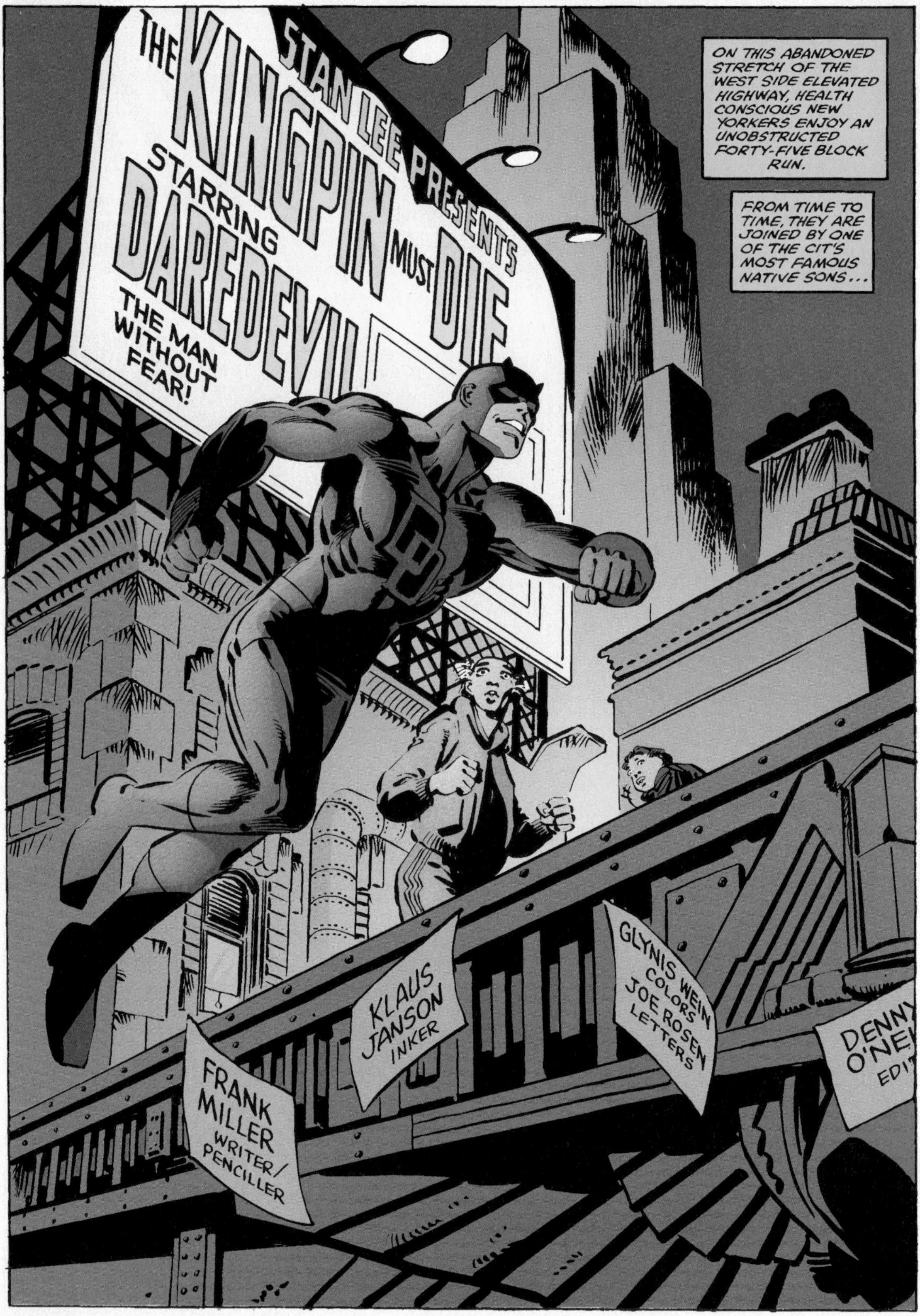

STAN LEE PRESENTS
THE KINGPIN MUST DIE
STARRING DAREDEVIL
THE MAN WITHOUT FEAR!
ON THIS ABANDONED STRETCH OF THE WEST SIDE ELEVATED HIGHWAY, HEALTH CONSCIOUS NEW YORKERS ENJOY AN UNOBSTRUCTED FORTY-FIVE BLOCK RUN.
FROM TIME TO TIME, THEY ARE JOINED BY ONE OF THE CIT'S MOST FAMOUS NATIVE SONS...
FRANK MILLER WRITER/PENCILLER
KLAUS JANSON INKER
GLYNIS WEIN COLORS
JOE ROSEN LETTERS

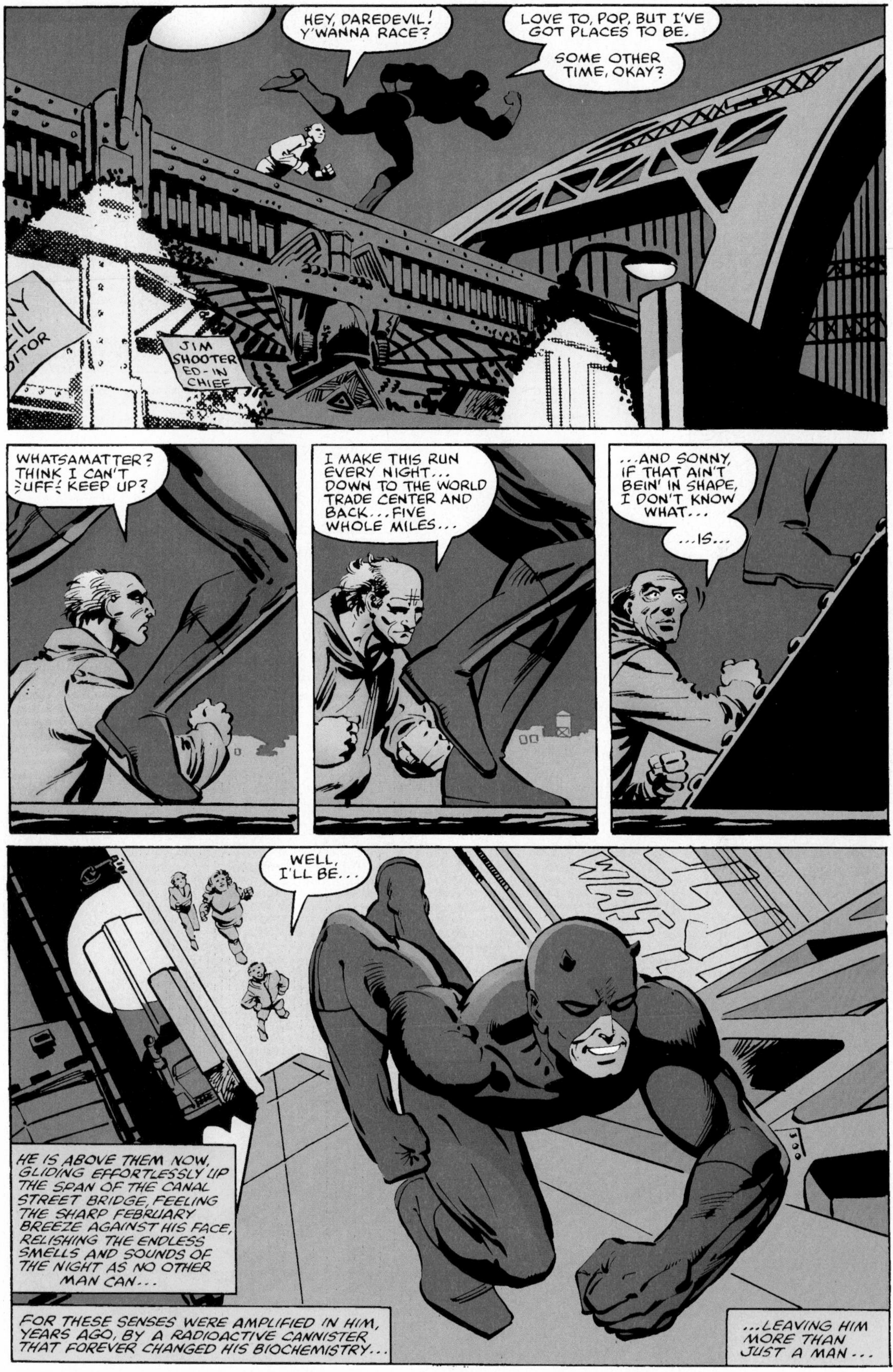
HEY, DAREDEVIL! Y'WANNA RACE?
LOVE TO, POP, BUT I'VE GOT PLACES TO BE.
SOME OTHER TIME, OKAY?
JIM SHOOTER ED-IN CHIEF
WHATSAMATTER? THINK I CAN'T ≥UFF≤ KEEP UP?
I MAKE THIS RUN EVERY NIGHT... DOWN TO THE WORLD TRADE CENTER AND BACK... FIVE WHOLE MILES...
...AND SONNY, IF THAT AIN'T BEIN' IN SHAPE, I DON'T KNOW WHAT...
...IS...
WELL, I'LL BE...
HE IS ABOVE THEM NOW, GLIDING EFFORTLESSLY UP THE SPAN OF THE CANAL STREET BRIDGE, FEELING THE SHARP FEBRUARY BREEZE AGAINST HIS FACE, RELISHING THE ENDLESS SMELLS AND SOUNDS OF THE NIGHT AS NO OTHER MAN CAN...
FOR THESE SENSES WERE AMPLIFIED IN HIM, YEARS AGO, BY A RADIOACTIVE CANNISTER THAT FOREVER CHANGED HIS BIOCHEMISTRY...
...LEAVING HIM MORE THAN JUST A MAN...

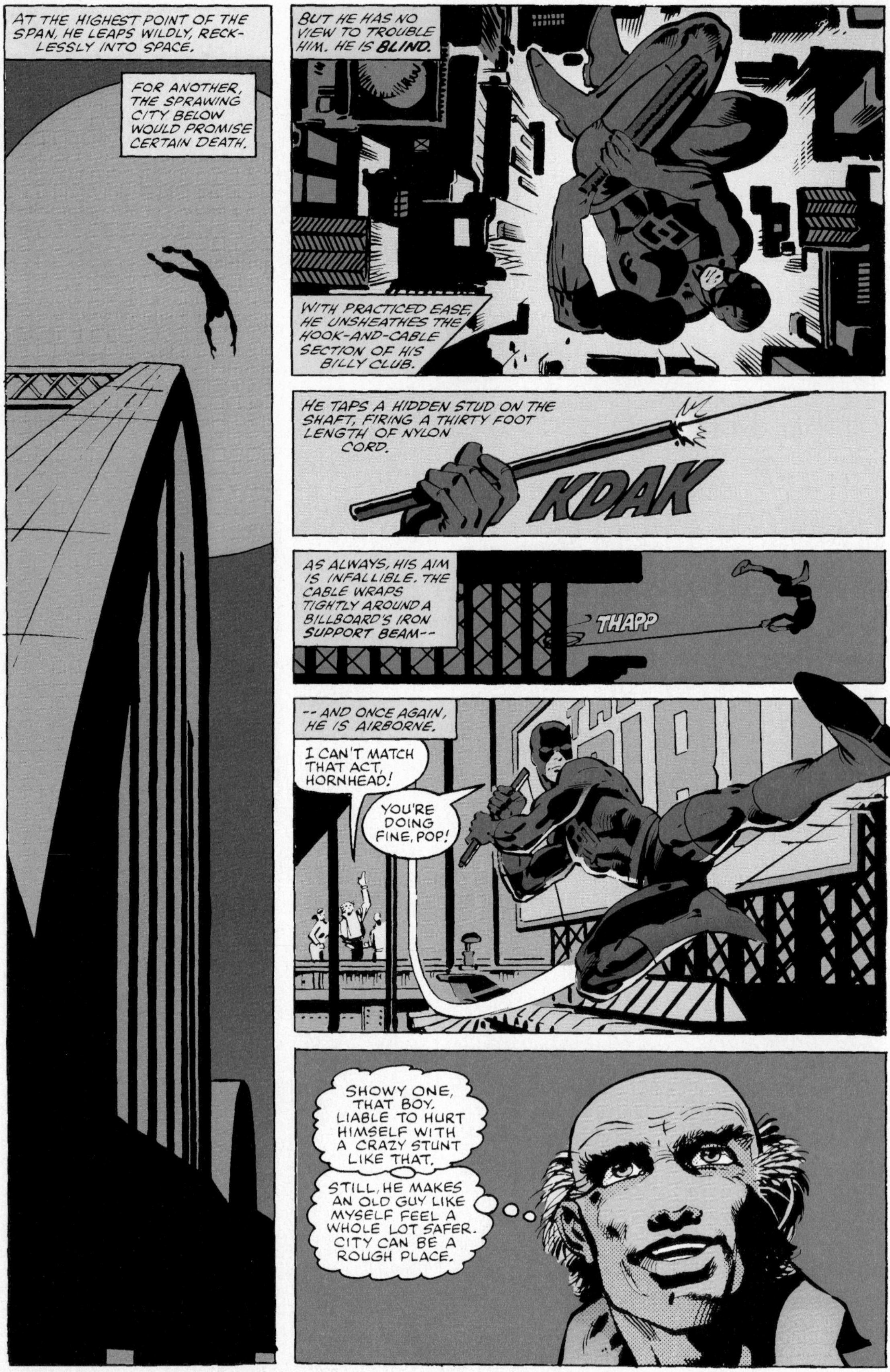
AT THE HIGHEST POINT OF THE SPAN, HE LEAPS WILDLY, RECKLESSLY INTO SPACE.
FOR ANOTHER, THE SPRAWING CITY BELOW WOULD PROMISE CERTAIN DEATH.
BUT HE HAS NO VIEW TO TROUBLE HIM. HE IS BLIND.
WITH PRACTICED EASE, HE UNSHEATHES THE HOOK-AND-CABLE SECTION OF HIS BILLY CLUB.
HE TAPS A HIDDEN STUD ON THE SHAFT, FIRING A THIRTY FOOT LENGTH OF NYLON CORD.
KDAK
AS ALWAYS, HIS AIM IS INFALLIBLE. THE CABLE WRAPS TIGHTLY AROUND A BILLBOARD'S IRON SUPPORT BEAM--
THAPP
-- AND ONCE AGAIN, HE IS AIRBORNE.
I CAN'T MATCH THAT ACT, HORNHEAD!
YOU'RE DOING FINE, POP!
SHOWY ONE, THAT BOY. LIABLE TO HURT HIMSELF WITH A CRAZY STUNT LIKE THAT.
STILL, HE MAKES AN OLD GUY LIKE MYSELF FEEL A WHOLE LOT SAFER. CITY CAN BE A ROUGH PLACE.

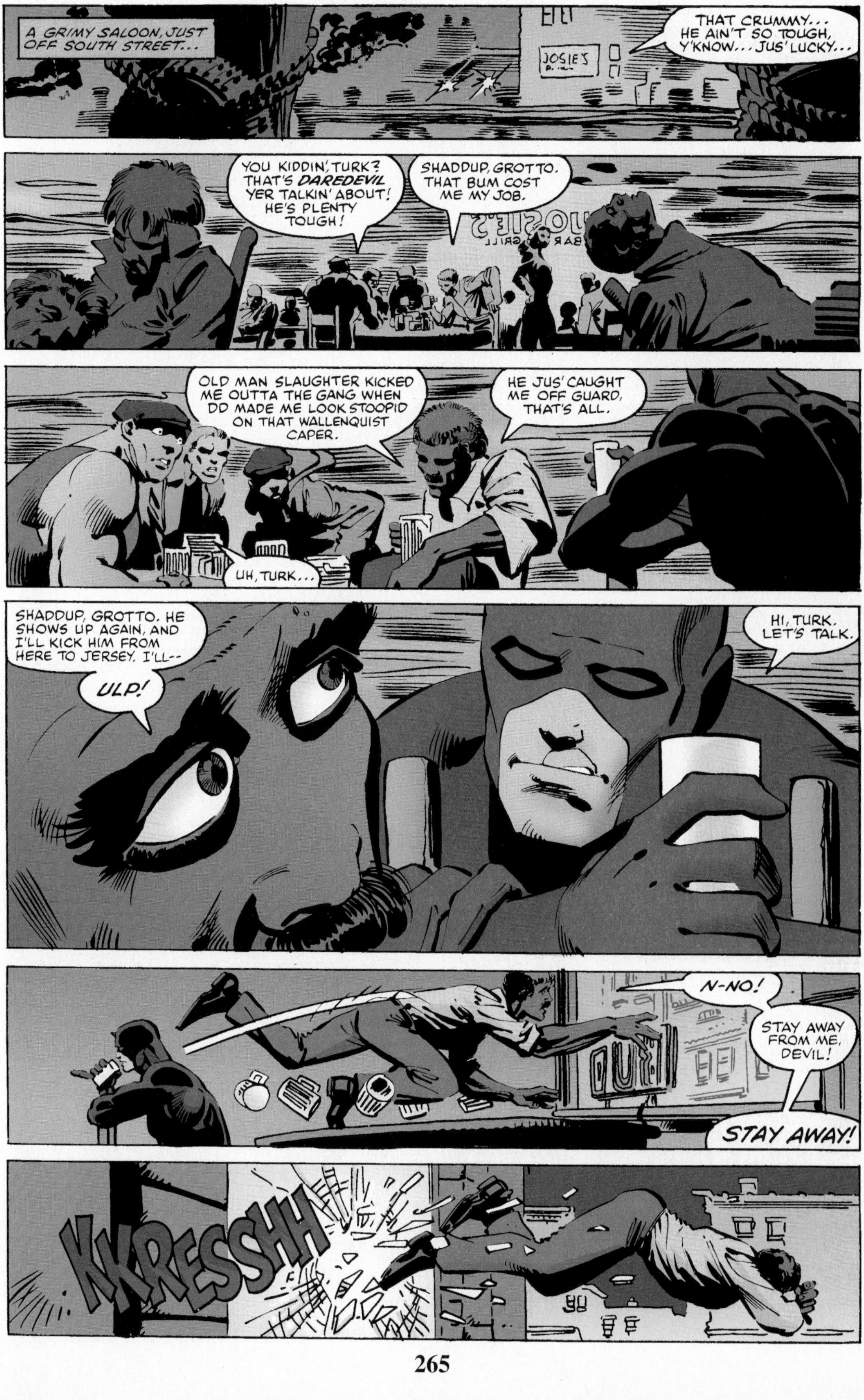
A GRIMY SALOON, JUST OFF SOUTH STREET...
JOSIE'S
THAT CRUMMY... HE AIN'T SO TOUGH, Y'KNOW... JUS' LUCKY...
YOU KIDDIN', TURK? THAT'S DAREDEVIL YER TALKIN' ABOUT! HE'S PLENTY TOUGH!
SHADDUP, GROTTO. THAT BUM COST ME MY JOB.
OLD MAN SLAUGHTER KICKED ME OUTTA THE GANG WHEN DD MADE ME LOOK STOOPID ON THAT WALLENQUIST CAPER.
HE JUS' CAUGHT ME OFF GUARD, THAT'S ALL.
UH, TURK...
SHADDUP, GROTTO. HE SHOWS UP AGAIN, AND I'LL KICK HIM FROM HERE TO JERSEY. I'LL--
ULP!
HI, TURK. LET'S TALK.
N-NO!
STAY AWAY FROM ME, DEVIL!
STAY AWAY!
KKRESSHH

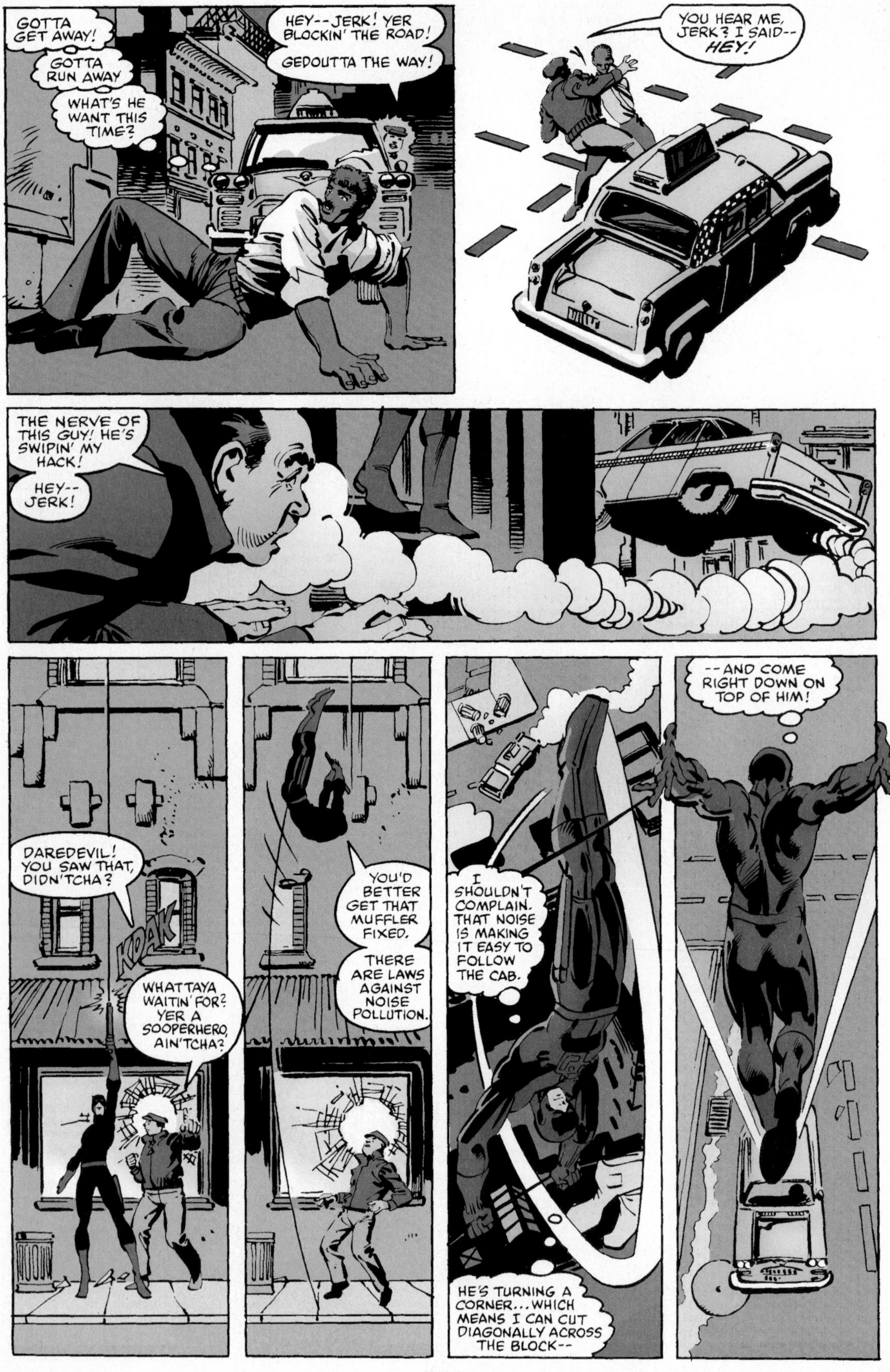
GOTTA GET AWAY!
GOTTA RUN AWAY
WHAT'S HE WANT THIS TIME?
HEY--JERK! YER BLOCKIN' THE ROAD!
GEDOUTTA THE WAY!
YOU HEAR ME, JERK? I SAID-- HEY!
THE NERVE OF THIS GUY! HE'S SWIPIN' MY HACK!
HEY-- JERK!
DAREDEVIL! YOU SAW THAT, DIDN'TCHA?
KRAK
WHATTAYA WAITIN' FOR? YER A SOOPERHERO, AIN'TCHA?
YOU'D BETTER GET THAT MUFFLER FIXED.
THERE ARE LAWS AGAINST NOISE POLLUTION.
I SHOULDN'T COMPLAIN. THAT NOISE IS MAKING IT EASY TO FOLLOW THE CAB.
HE'S TURNING A CORNER... WHICH MEANS I CAN CUT DIAGONALLY ACROSS THE BLOCK--
--AND COME RIGHT DOWN ON TOP OF HIM!

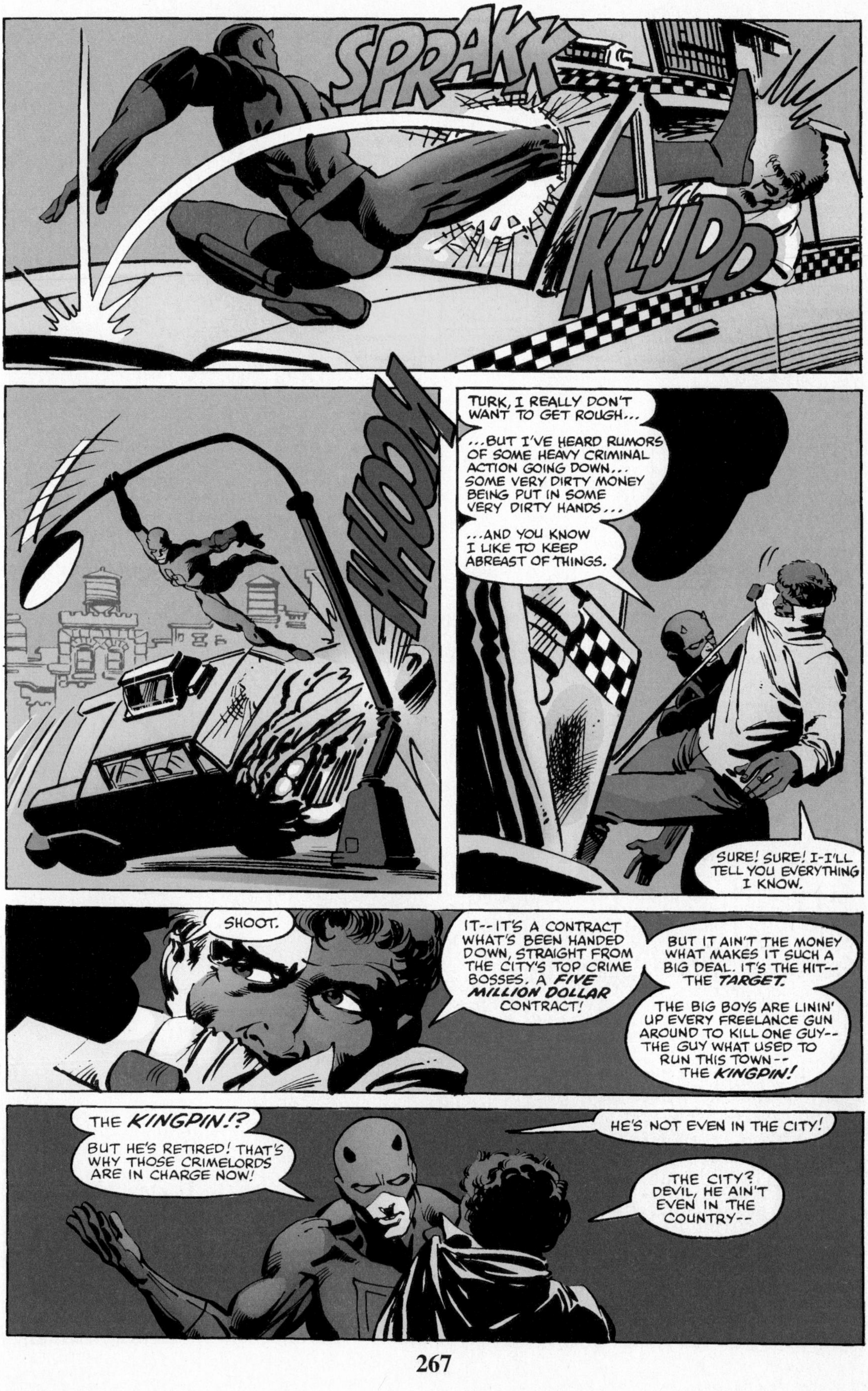
SPRAKK
KLUDD
WHOOM
TURK, I REALLY DON'T WANT TO GET ROUGH...
...BUT I'VE HEARD RUMORS OF SOME HEAVY CRIMINAL ACTION GOING DOWN... SOME VERY DIRTY MONEY BEING PUT IN SOME VERY DIRTY HANDS...
...AND YOU KNOW I LIKE TO KEEP ABREAST OF THINGS.
SURE! SURE! I-I'LL TELL YOU EVERYTHING I KNOW.
SHOOT.
IT--IT'S A CONTRACT WHAT'S BEEN HANDED DOWN, STRAIGHT FROM THE CITY'S TOP CRIME BOSSES. A *FIVE MILLION DOLLAR* CONTRACT!
BUT IT AIN'T THE MONEY WHAT MAKES IT SUCH A BIG DEAL. IT'S THE HIT-- THE *TARGET.*
THE BIG BOYS ARE LININ' UP EVERY FREELANCE GUN AROUND TO KILL ONE GUY-- THE GUY WHAT USED TO RUN THIS TOWN-- THE *KINGPIN!*
THE *KINGPIN!?*
BUT HE'S RETIRED! THAT'S WHY THOSE CRIMELORDS ARE IN CHARGE NOW!
HE'S NOT EVEN IN THE CITY!
THE CITY? DEVIL, HE AIN'T EVEN IN THE COUNTRY--

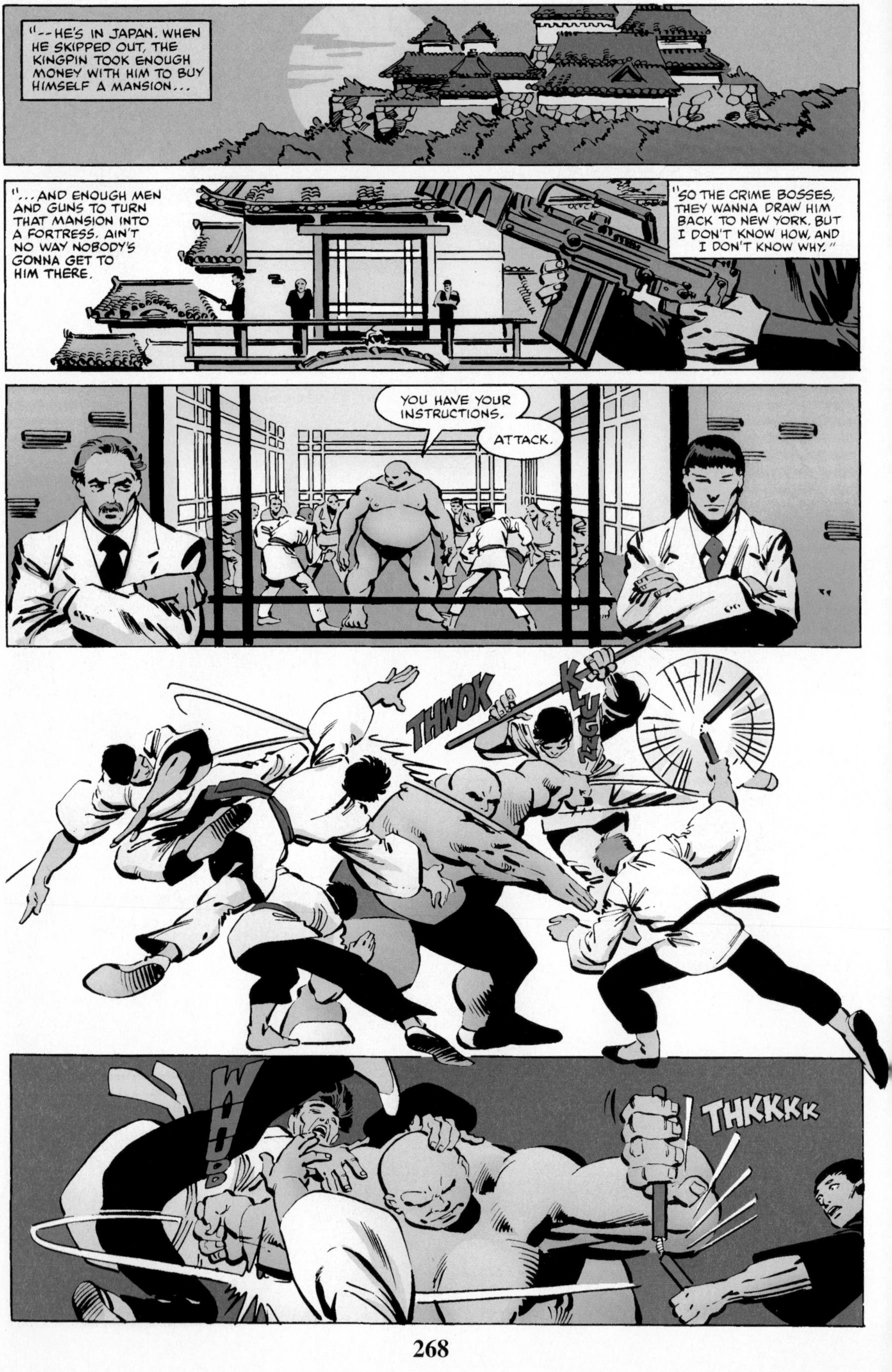
"--HE'S IN JAPAN. WHEN HE SKIPPED OUT, THE KINGPIN TOOK ENOUGH MONEY WITH HIM TO BUY HIMSELF A MANSION...
"...AND ENOUGH MEN AND GUNS TO TURN THAT MANSION INTO A FORTRESS. AIN'T NO WAY NOBODY'S GONNA GET TO HIM THERE.
"SO THE CRIME BOSSES, THEY WANNA DRAW HIM BACK TO NEW YORK. BUT I DON'T KNOW HOW, AND I DON'T KNOW WHY."
YOU HAVE YOUR INSTRUCTIONS.
ATTACK.
THWOK
KLUGN
WHUD
THKKKK

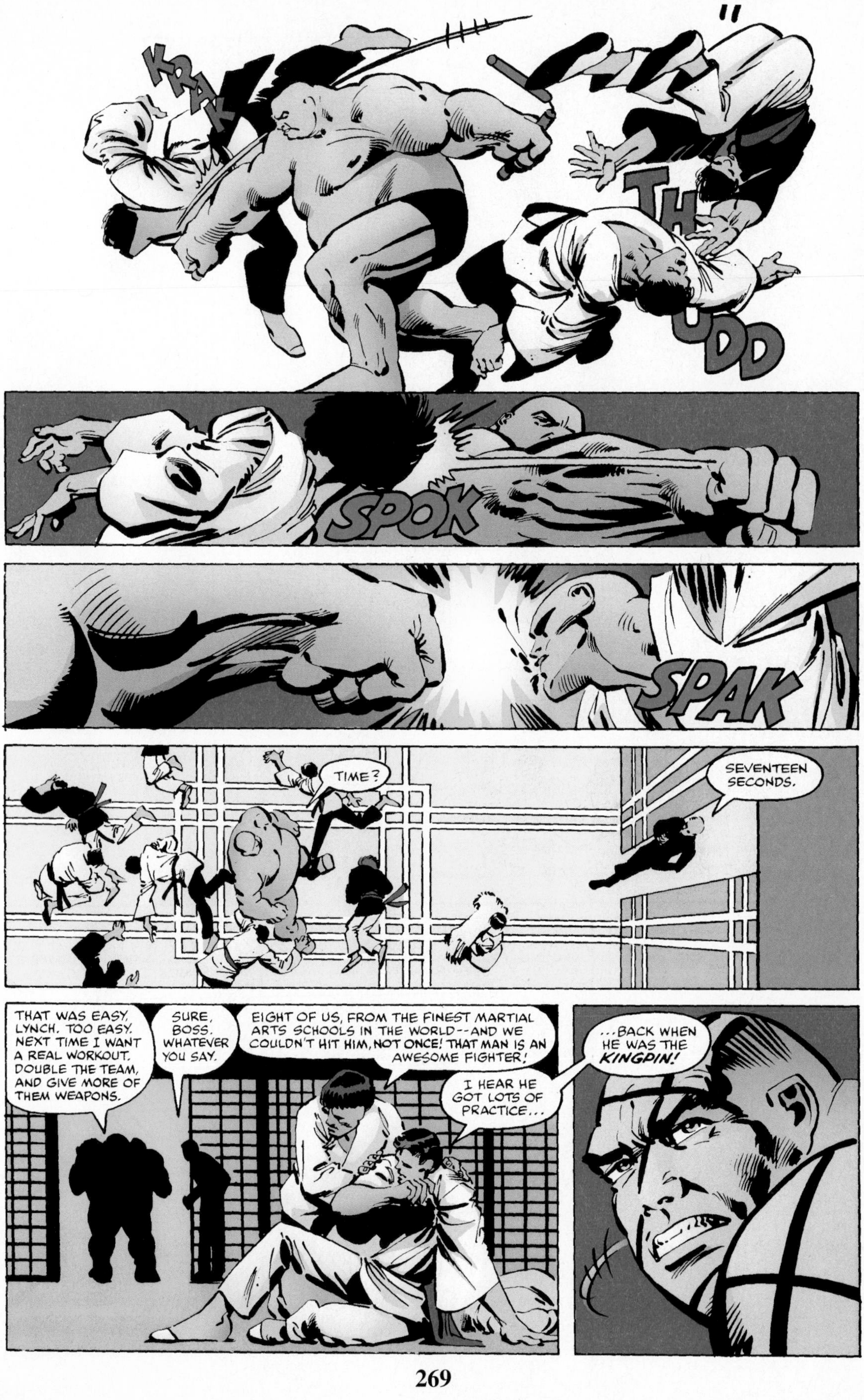
KRAK
THUDD
SPOK
SPAK
TIME?
SEVENTEEN SECONDS.
THAT WAS EASY, LYNCH. TOO EASY. NEXT TIME I WANT A REAL WORKOUT. DOUBLE THE TEAM, AND GIVE MORE OF THEM WEAPONS.
SURE, BOSS. WHATEVER YOU SAY.
EIGHT OF US, FROM THE FINEST MARTIAL ARTS SCHOOLS IN THE WORLD--AND WE COULDN'T HIT HIM, NOT ONCE! THAT MAN IS AN AWESOME FIGHTER!
I HEAR HE GOT LOTS OF PRACTICE...
...BACK WHEN HE WAS THE KINGPIN!

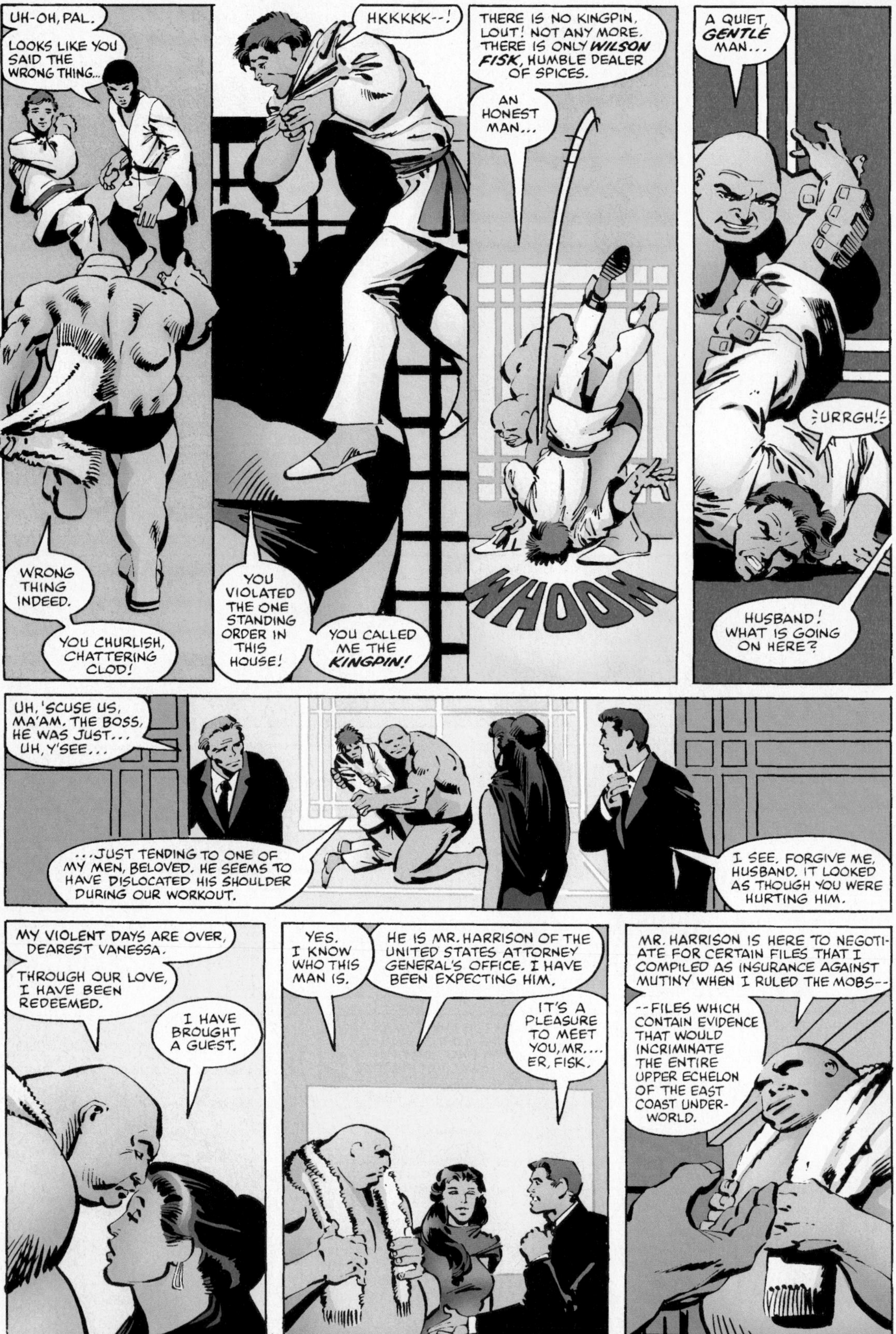
UH-OH, PAL.
LOOKS LIKE YOU SAID THE WRONG THING...
WRONG THING INDEED.
YOU CHURLISH, CHATTERING CLOD!
HKKKKK--!
YOU VIOLATED THE ONE STANDING ORDER IN THIS HOUSE!
YOU CALLED ME THE KINGPIN!
THERE IS NO KINGPIN, LOUT! NOT ANY MORE. THERE IS ONLY WILSON FISK, HUMBLE DEALER OF SPICES.
AN HONEST MAN...
WHOOM
A QUIET, GENTLE MAN...
URRGH!
HUSBAND! WHAT IS GOING ON HERE?
UH, 'SCUSE US, MA'AM. THE BOSS, HE WAS JUST... UH, Y'SEE...
...JUST TENDING TO ONE OF MY MEN, BELOVED. HE SEEMS TO HAVE DISLOCATED HIS SHOULDER DURING OUR WORKOUT.
I SEE. FORGIVE ME, HUSBAND. IT LOOKED AS THOUGH YOU WERE HURTING HIM.
MY VIOLENT DAYS ARE OVER, DEAREST VANESSA.
THROUGH OUR LOVE, I HAVE BEEN REDEEMED.
I HAVE BROUGHT A GUEST.
YES. I KNOW WHO THIS MAN IS.
HE IS MR. HARRISON OF THE UNITED STATES ATTORNEY GENERAL'S OFFICE. I HAVE BEEN EXPECTING HIM.
IT'S A PLEASURE TO MEET YOU, MR.... ER, FISK.
MR. HARRISON IS HERE TO NEGOTIATE FOR CERTAIN FILES THAT I COMPILED AS INSURANCE AGAINST MUTINY WHEN I RULED THE MOBS--
--FILES WHICH CONTAIN EVIDENCE THAT WOULD INCRIMINATE THE ENTIRE UPPER ECHELON OF THE EAST COAST UNDERWORLD.

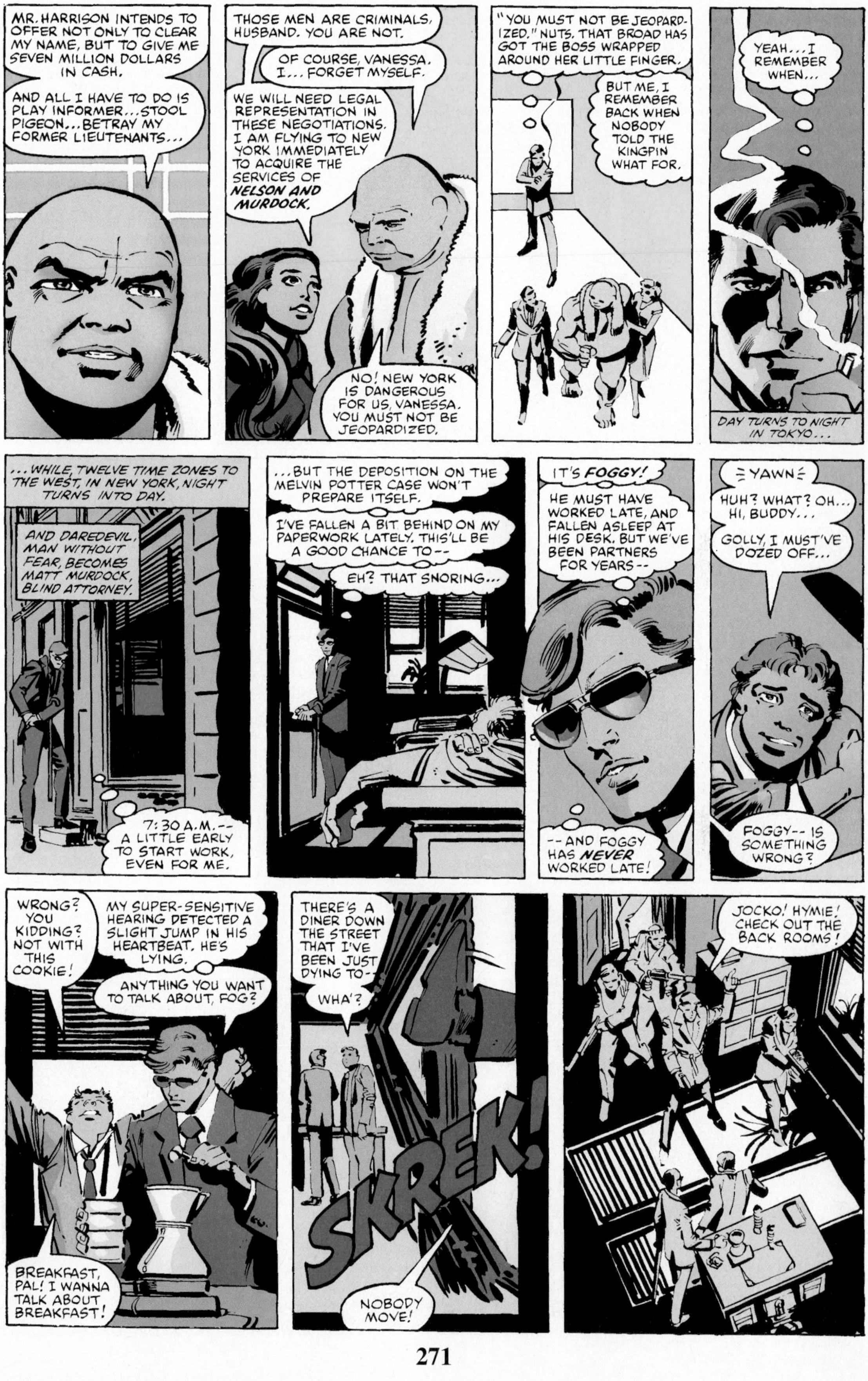
MR. HARRISON INTENDS TO OFFER NOT ONLY TO CLEAR MY NAME, BUT TO GIVE ME SEVEN MILLION DOLLARS IN CASH.
AND ALL I HAVE TO DO IS PLAY INFORMER... STOOL PIGEON... BETRAY MY FORMER LIEUTENANTS...
THOSE MEN ARE CRIMINALS, HUSBAND. YOU ARE NOT.
OF COURSE, VANESSA. I... FORGET MYSELF.
WE WILL NEED LEGAL REPRESENTATION IN THESE NEGOTIATIONS. I AM FLYING TO NEW YORK IMMEDIATELY TO ACQUIRE THE SERVICES OF NELSON AND MURDOCK.
NO! NEW YORK IS DANGEROUS FOR US, VANESSA. YOU MUST NOT BE JEOPARDIZED.
"YOU MUST NOT BE JEOPARDIZED." NUTS. THAT BROAD HAS GOT THE BOSS WRAPPED AROUND HER LITTLE FINGER.
BUT ME, I REMEMBER BACK WHEN NOBODY TOLD THE KINGPIN WHAT FOR.
YEAH... I REMEMBER WHEN...
DAY TURNS TO NIGHT IN TOKYO...
...WHILE, TWELVE TIME ZONES TO THE WEST, IN NEW YORK, NIGHT TURNS INTO DAY.
AND DAREDEVIL, MAN WITHOUT FEAR, BECOMES MATT MURDOCK, BLIND ATTORNEY.
7:30 A.M.-- A LITTLE EARLY TO START WORK, EVEN FOR ME.
...BUT THE DEPOSITION ON THE MELVIN POTTER CASE WON'T PREPARE ITSELF.
I'VE FALLEN A BIT BEHIND ON MY PAPERWORK LATELY. THIS'LL BE A GOOD CHANCE TO--
EH? THAT SNORING...
IT'S FOGGY!
HE MUST HAVE WORKED LATE, AND FALLEN ASLEEP AT HIS DESK. BUT WE'VE BEEN PARTNERS FOR YEARS--
--AND FOGGY HAS NEVER WORKED LATE!
≡YAWN≡
HUH? WHAT? OH... HI, BUDDY...
GOLLY, I MUST'VE DOZED OFF...
FOGGY-- IS SOMETHING WRONG?
WRONG? YOU KIDDING? NOT WITH THIS COOKIE!
MY SUPER-SENSITIVE HEARING DETECTED A SLIGHT JUMP IN HIS HEARTBEAT. HE'S LYING.
ANYTHING YOU WANT TO TALK ABOUT, FOG?
BREAKFAST, PAL! I WANNA TALK ABOUT BREAKFAST!
THERE'S A DINER DOWN THE STREET THAT I'VE BEEN JUST DYING TO--
WHA'?
SKREK!
NOBODY MOVE!
JOCKO! HYMIE! CHECK OUT THE BACK ROOMS!

THAT DISTINCTIVE SMELL OF CORDITE AND BLUING... WE'RE BEING HELD AT GUNPOINT!

WE'RE BEING HELD AT GUNPOINT, MATT.

STAND PAT. I'LL HANDLE THIS.

ER...AHEM...UH, ANY-THING WE CAN DO TO HELP YOU FELLOWS?

YOU KIN SHADDUP.

OKAY.

GENTLEMEN, PLEASE-- PUT AWAY YOUR WEAPONS. THIS IS A LAW FIRM, NOT A BATTLEFIELD.

YES, MA'AM.

MR. MURDOCK, MR. NELSON, PLEASE ACCEPT MY APOLOGIES. THESE MEN ARE BODYGUARDS, AS-SIGNED TO ME BY MY HUSBAND. HE TENDS TO BE OVERPROTECTIVE.

I AM VANESSA. I HAVE COME TO REQUEST YOUR AID.

SHORTLY... ...AND SO, MY HUSBAND REQUIRES THE FINEST LEGAL REPRESENTATION AVAILABLE, WE ARE PREPARED TO PAY YOU TWO HUNDRED THOUSAND DOLLARS.

TWO HUNDRED THOUSAND DOLLARS...

WHA--WHAT DO YOU SAY, MATT?

THIS EXPLAINS WHY THE CRIMELORDS WANT THE KINGPIN KILLED. THE EVIDENCE IN THOSE FILES COULD PUT THEM OUT OF BUSINESS.

I'VE BEEN ACHING TO SINK MY TEETH INTO A CASE LIKE THIS.

MR. MURDOCK?

MA'AM, I THINK WE CAN...

YEARS OF LIVING WITH DANGER HAVE TRAINED THIS MAN TO HEAR WITHOUT LISTENING--

-- TO RESPOND REFLEXIVELY TO CERTAIN SOUNDS--

--THE SOUND OF A STEEL MAGAZINE SLIDING INTO PLACE--

--A HAMMER, SHARPLY COCKED--

--A BULLET, SLIDING INTO ITS CHAMBER...

LOOK OUT!

BRAKARRAKABRAK RAKABRAKABR

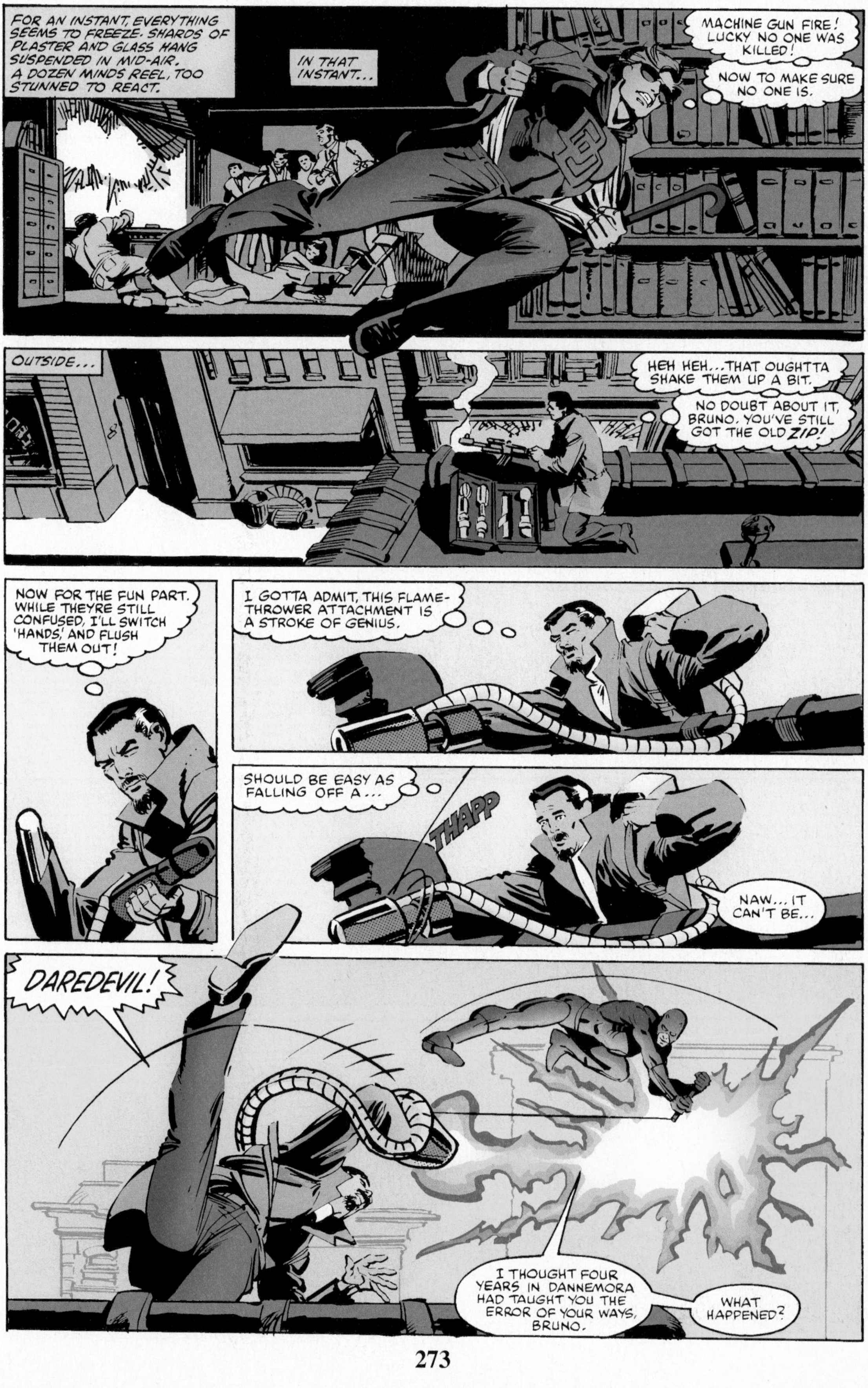

FOR AN INSTANT, EVERYTHING SEEMS TO FREEZE. SHARDS OF PLASTER AND GLASS HANG SUSPENDED IN MID-AIR. A DOZEN MINDS REEL, TOO STUNNED TO REACT.
IN THAT INSTANT...
MACHINE GUN FIRE! LUCKY NO ONE WAS KILLED!
NOW TO MAKE SURE NO ONE IS.
OUTSIDE...
HEH HEH...THAT OUGHTTA SHAKE THEM UP A BIT.
NO DOUBT ABOUT IT, BRUNO. YOU'VE STILL GOT THE OLD ZIP!
NOW FOR THE FUN PART. WHILE THEYRE STILL CONFUSED, I'LL SWITCH 'HANDS,' AND FLUSH THEM OUT!
I GOTTA ADMIT, THIS FLAME-THROWER ATTACHMENT IS A STROKE OF GENIUS.
SHOULD BE EASY AS FALLING OFF A...
THAPP
NAW... IT CAN'T BE...
DAREDEVIL!
I THOUGHT FOUR YEARS IN DANNEMORA HAD TAUGHT YOU THE ERROR OF YOUR WAYS, BRUNO.
WHAT HAPPENED?

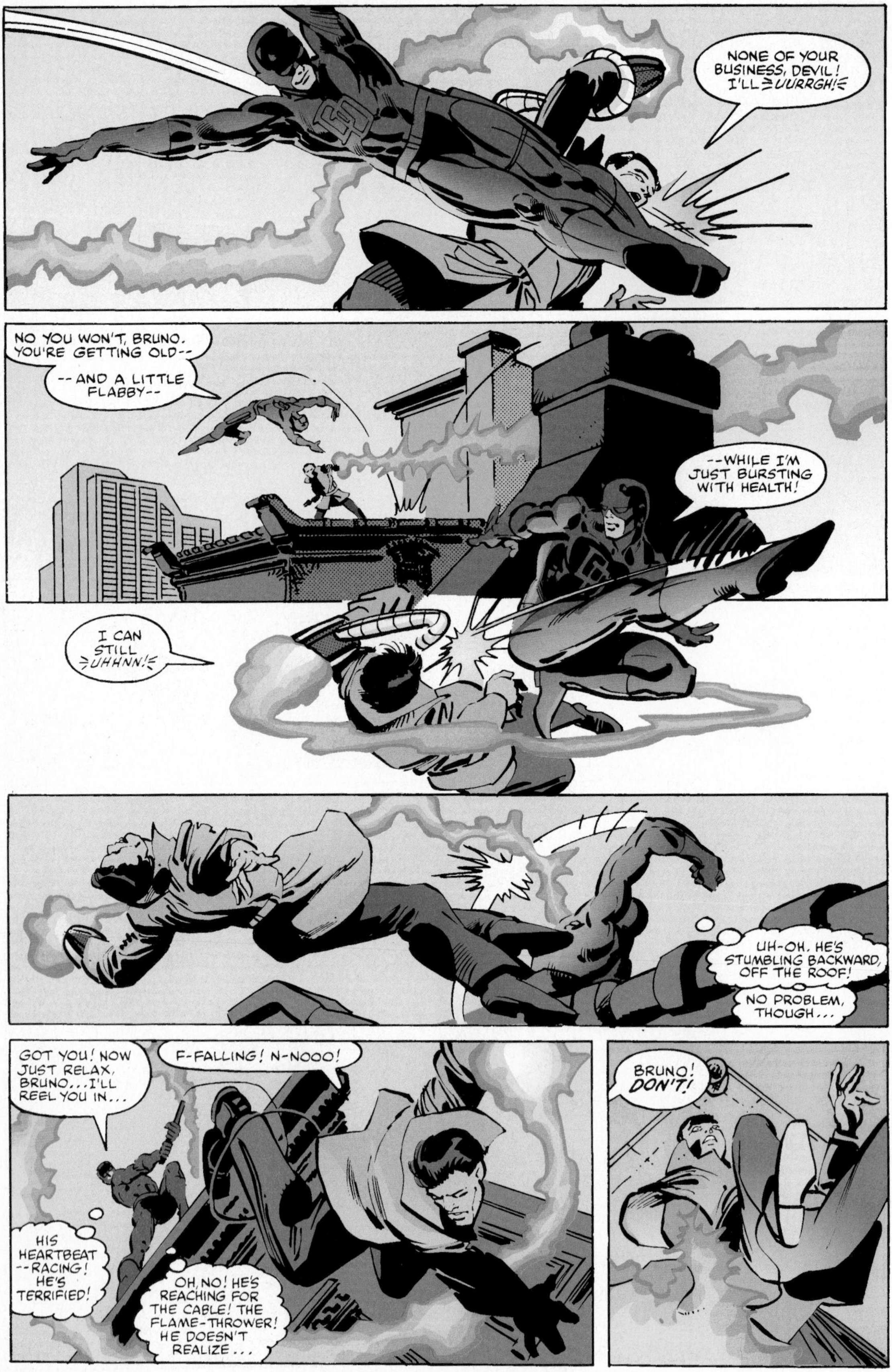

NONE OF YOUR BUSINESS, DEVIL! I'LL ≷UURRGH!≶
NO YOU WON'T, BRUNO. YOU'RE GETTING OLD--
--AND A LITTLE FLABBY--
--WHILE I'M JUST BURSTING WITH HEALTH!
I CAN STILL ≷UHHNN!≶
UH-OH. HE'S STUMBLING BACKWARD, OFF THE ROOF!
NO PROBLEM, THOUGH...
GOT YOU! NOW JUST RELAX, BRUNO... I'LL REEL YOU IN...
F-FALLING! N-NOOO!
HIS HEARTBEAT --RACING! HE'S TERRIFIED!
OH, NO! HE'S REACHING FOR THE CABLE! THE FLAME-THROWER! HE DOESN'T REALIZE...
BRUNO! DON'T!

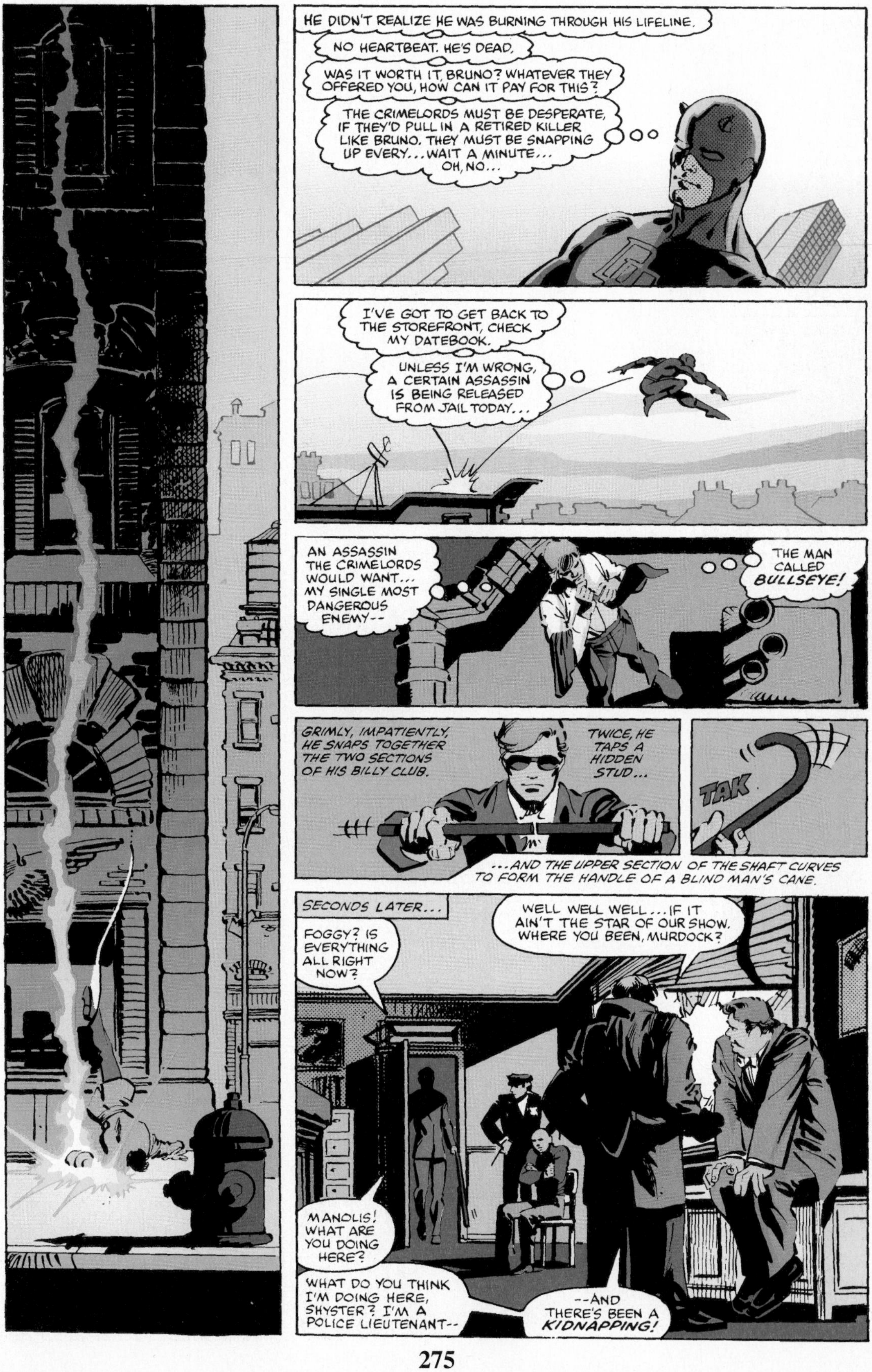

HE DIDN'T REALIZE HE WAS BURNING THROUGH HIS LIFELINE.
NO HEARTBEAT. HE'S DEAD.
WAS IT WORTH IT, BRUNO? WHATEVER THEY OFFERED YOU, HOW CAN IT PAY FOR THIS?
THE CRIMELORDS MUST BE DESPERATE, IF THEY'D PULL IN A RETIRED KILLER LIKE BRUNO. THEY MUST BE SNAPPING UP EVERY... WAIT A MINUTE... OH, NO...
I'VE GOT TO GET BACK TO THE STOREFRONT, CHECK MY DATEBOOK.
UNLESS I'M WRONG, A CERTAIN ASSASSIN IS BEING RELEASED FROM JAIL TODAY...
AN ASSASSIN THE CRIMELORDS WOULD WANT... MY SINGLE MOST DANGEROUS ENEMY--
THE MAN CALLED BULLSEYE!
GRIMLY, IMPATIENTLY, HE SNAPS TOGETHER THE TWO SECTIONS OF HIS BILLY CLUB.
TWICE, HE TAPS A HIDDEN STUD...
TAK
...AND THE UPPER SECTION OF THE SHAFT CURVES TO FORM THE HANDLE OF A BLIND MAN'S CANE.
SECONDS LATER...
FOGGY? IS EVERYTHING ALL RIGHT NOW?
WELL WELL WELL... IF IT AIN'T THE STAR OF OUR SHOW. WHERE YOU BEEN, MURDOCK?
MANOLIS! WHAT ARE YOU DOING HERE?
WHAT DO YOU THINK I'M DOING HERE, SHYSTER? I'M A POLICE LIEUTENANT--
--AND THERE'S BEEN A KIDNAPPING!

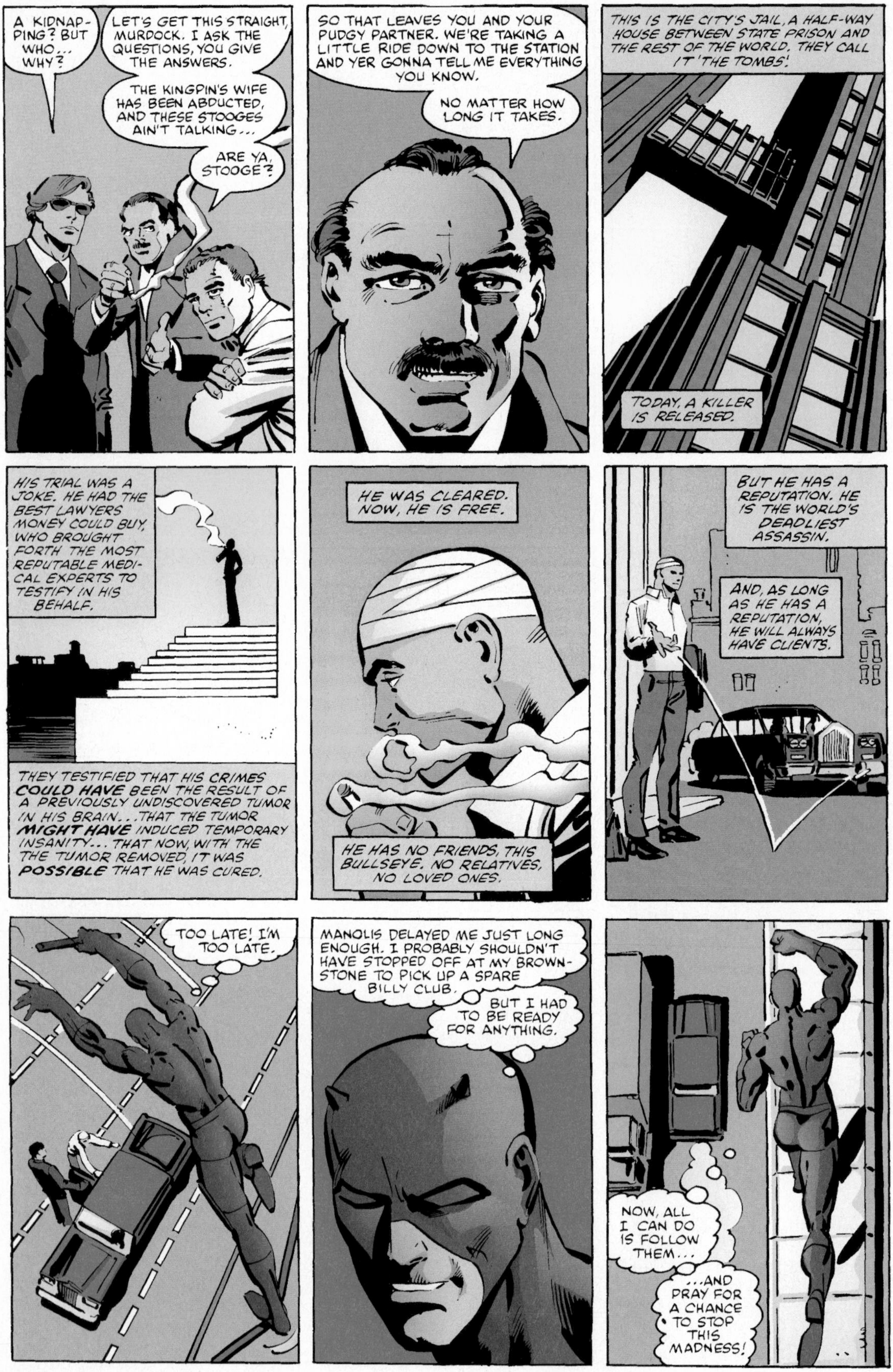
A KIDNAP-PING? BUT WHO... WHY?
LET'S GET THIS STRAIGHT, MURDOCK. I ASK THE QUESTIONS, YOU GIVE THE ANSWERS.
THE KINGPIN'S WIFE HAS BEEN ABDUCTED, AND THESE STOOGES AIN'T TALKING...
ARE YA, STOOGE?
SO THAT LEAVES YOU AND YOUR PUDGY PARTNER. WE'RE TAKING A LITTLE RIDE DOWN TO THE STATION AND YER GONNA TELL ME EVERYTHING YOU KNOW.
NO MATTER HOW LONG IT TAKES.
THIS IS THE CITY'S JAIL, A HALF-WAY HOUSE BETWEEN STATE PRISON AND THE REST OF THE WORLD. THEY CALL IT 'THE TOMBS'.
TODAY, A KILLER IS RELEASED.
HIS TRIAL WAS A JOKE. HE HAD THE BEST LAWYERS MONEY COULD BUY, WHO BROUGHT FORTH THE MOST REPUTABLE MEDICAL EXPERTS TO TESTIFY IN HIS BEHALF.
THEY TESTIFIED THAT HIS CRIMES COULD HAVE BEEN THE RESULT OF A PREVIOUSLY UNDISCOVERED TUMOR IN HIS BRAIN...THAT THE TUMOR MIGHT HAVE INDUCED TEMPORARY INSANITY... THAT NOW, WITH THE THE TUMOR REMOVED, IT WAS POSSIBLE THAT HE WAS CURED.
HE WAS CLEARED. NOW, HE IS FREE.
HE HAS NO FRIENDS, THIS BULLSEYE. NO RELATIVES, NO LOVED ONES.
BUT HE HAS A REPUTATION. HE IS THE WORLD'S DEADLIEST ASSASSIN.
AND, AS LONG AS HE HAS A REPUTATION, HE WILL ALWAYS HAVE CLIENTS.
TOO LATE! I'M TOO LATE.
MANOLIS DELAYED ME JUST LONG ENOUGH. I PROBABLY SHOULDN'T HAVE STOPPED OFF AT MY BROWN-STONE TO PICK UP A SPARE BILLY CLUB.
BUT I HAD TO BE READY FOR ANYTHING.
NOW, ALL I CAN DO IS FOLLOW THEM...
...AND PRAY FOR A CHANCE TO STOP THIS MADNESS!

THE SKY-SCRAPER STANDS PROUDLY, FIFTY STORIES OF STONE AND GLASS BATHED IN THE GLOW OF A SETTING SUN.

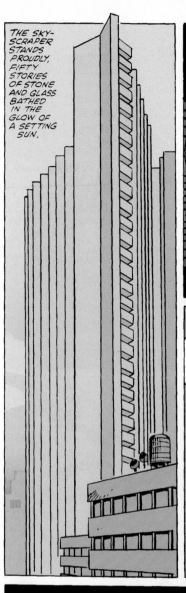

BUT ITS UPPERMOST OFFICE IS A DARK PLACE...

NOT BAD. NOT BAD AT ALL. YOU MADE THIS COSTUME EXACTLY TO MY SPECIFICATIONS.

WE TREAT OUR EMPLOYEES WELL, BULLSEYE.

IS THERE ANYTHING ELSE WE MAY PROVIDE YOU? FOOD? A DRINK, PERHAPS?

NO. LET'S GET DOWN TO BRASS TACKS.

YOU'VE KIDNAPPED THE KINGPIN'S WIFE. YOU EXPECT THAT TO DRAW HIM TO NEW YORK. YOU WANT ME TO KILL HIM. YOU WANT TO PAY ME FIVE MILLION DOLLARS. THAT'S WHAT YOU WANT.

WHAT I WANT--

--IS TEN MILLION!

TEN MILLION!? MAYBE YOU REALLY ARE STILL CRAZY! OUR RESOURCES--

--ARE NEARLY UNLIMITED, AND WE HAVE NO TIME TO QUIBBLE. TEN MILLION, THEN, BUT DON'T TRY TO...

BULLSEYE, I CAN'T LET YOU DO THIS.

I WON'T.

EH?

BULLSEYE, JUST A FEW WEEKS AGO I SAVED YOUR LIFE.

I CAN'T HELP BUT FEEL RESPONSIBLE FOR WHAT YOU DO WITH IT.

OH, WELL...

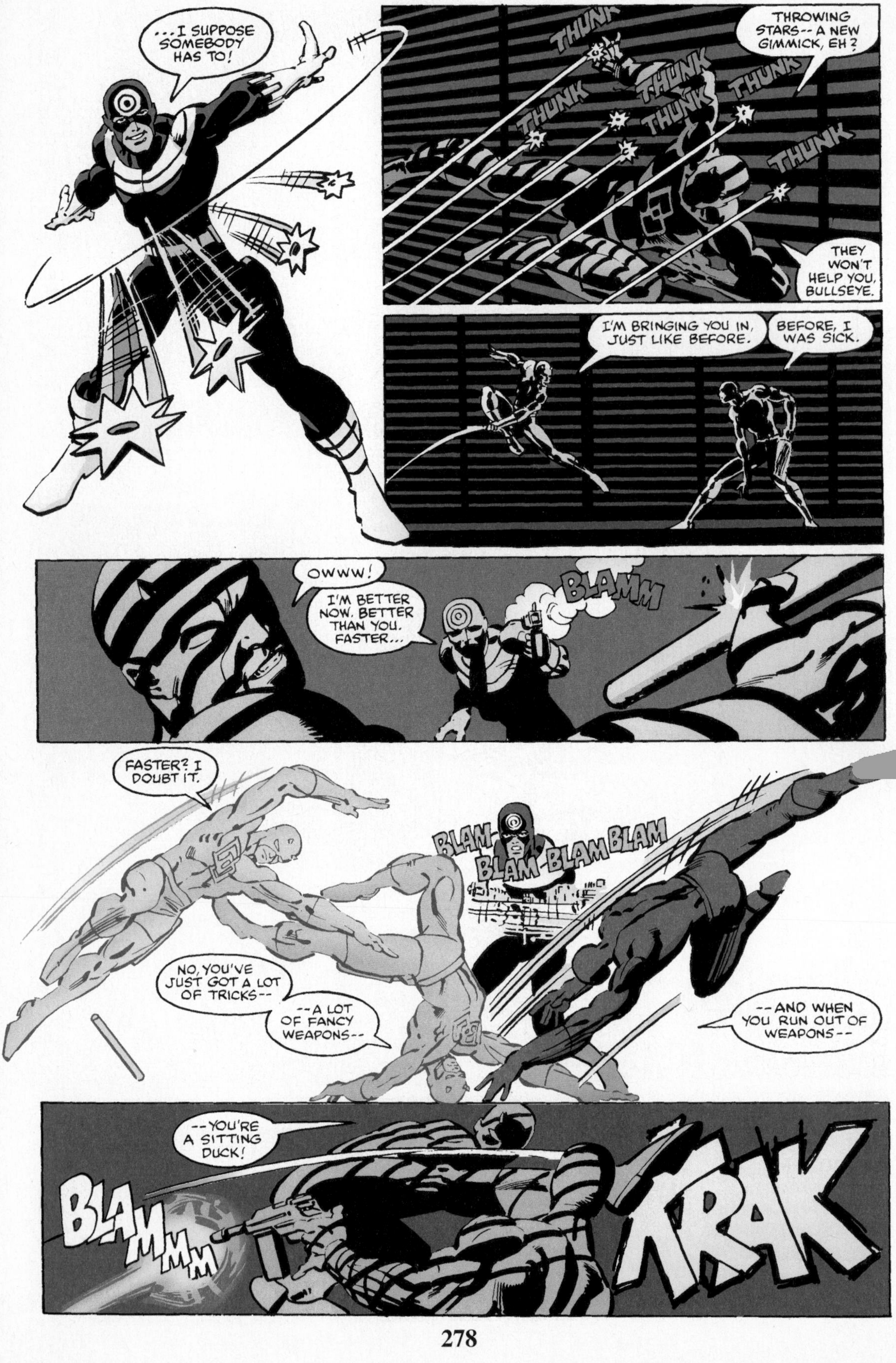

...I SUPPOSE SOMEBODY HAS TO!
THROWING STARS-- A NEW GIMMICK, EH?
THUNK
THUNK
THUNK
THUNK
THUNK
THUNK
THUNK
THEY WON'T HELP YOU, BULLSEYE.
I'M BRINGING YOU IN, JUST LIKE BEFORE.
BEFORE, I WAS SICK.
OWWW!
I'M BETTER NOW. BETTER THAN YOU. FASTER...
BLAMM
FASTER? I DOUBT IT.
BLAM
BLAM
BLAM
BLAM
NO, YOU'VE JUST GOT A LOT OF TRICKS--
--A LOT OF FANCY WEAPONS--
--AND WHEN YOU RUN OUT OF WEAPONS--
--YOU'RE A SITTING DUCK!
BLAMMMM
TRAK

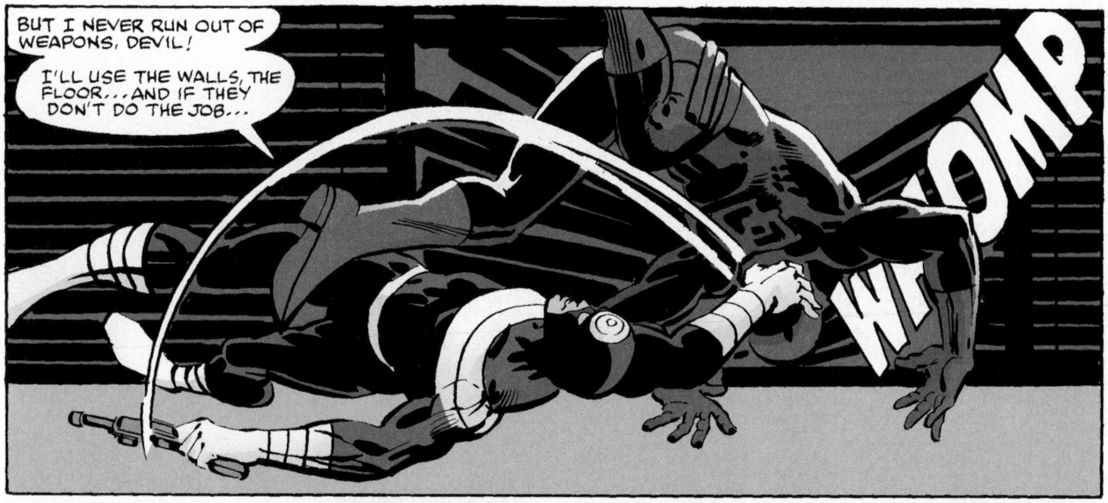
BUT I NEVER RUN OUT OF WEAPONS, DEVIL!
I'LL USE THE WALLS, THE FLOOR...AND IF THEY DON'T DO THE JOB...
WHOMP

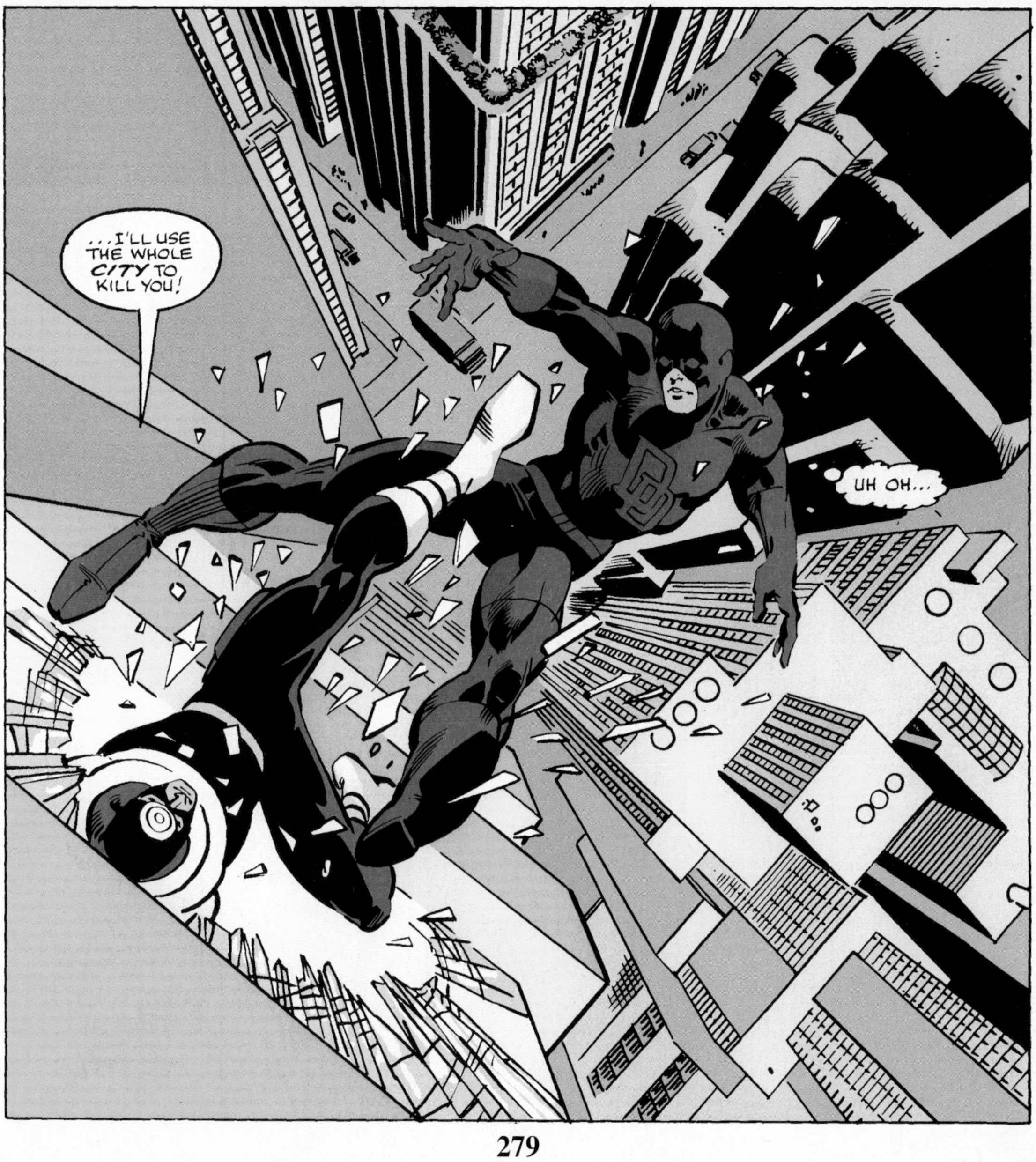
...I'LL USE THE WHOLE CITY TO KILL YOU!
UH OH...

ONCE AGAIN, SURE HANDS DRAW A LIFE-SAVING SHAFT FROM ITS SHEATH.

KOAK

THAPP

ONCE AGAIN, A NYLON CABLE IS FIRED, AND FINDS ITS TARGET.

BUT THIS TIME, THERE IS A COMPLICATION...

I WON'T LET YOU OFF THAT EASY.

HAPPY LANDINGS!

BLAMMM

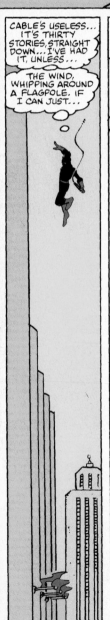

CABLE'S USELESS... IT'S THIRTY STORIES, STRAIGHT DOWN...I'VE HAD IT, UNLESS...

THE WIND, WHIPPING AROUND A FLAGPOLE. IF I CAN JUST...

NO! IT'S TOO FAR!... HAVE TO GRAB THE FLAG...HOPE IT'S STRONG ENOUGH TO...

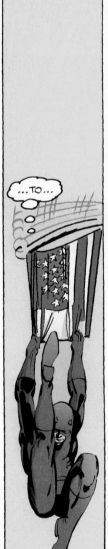

...TO...

280

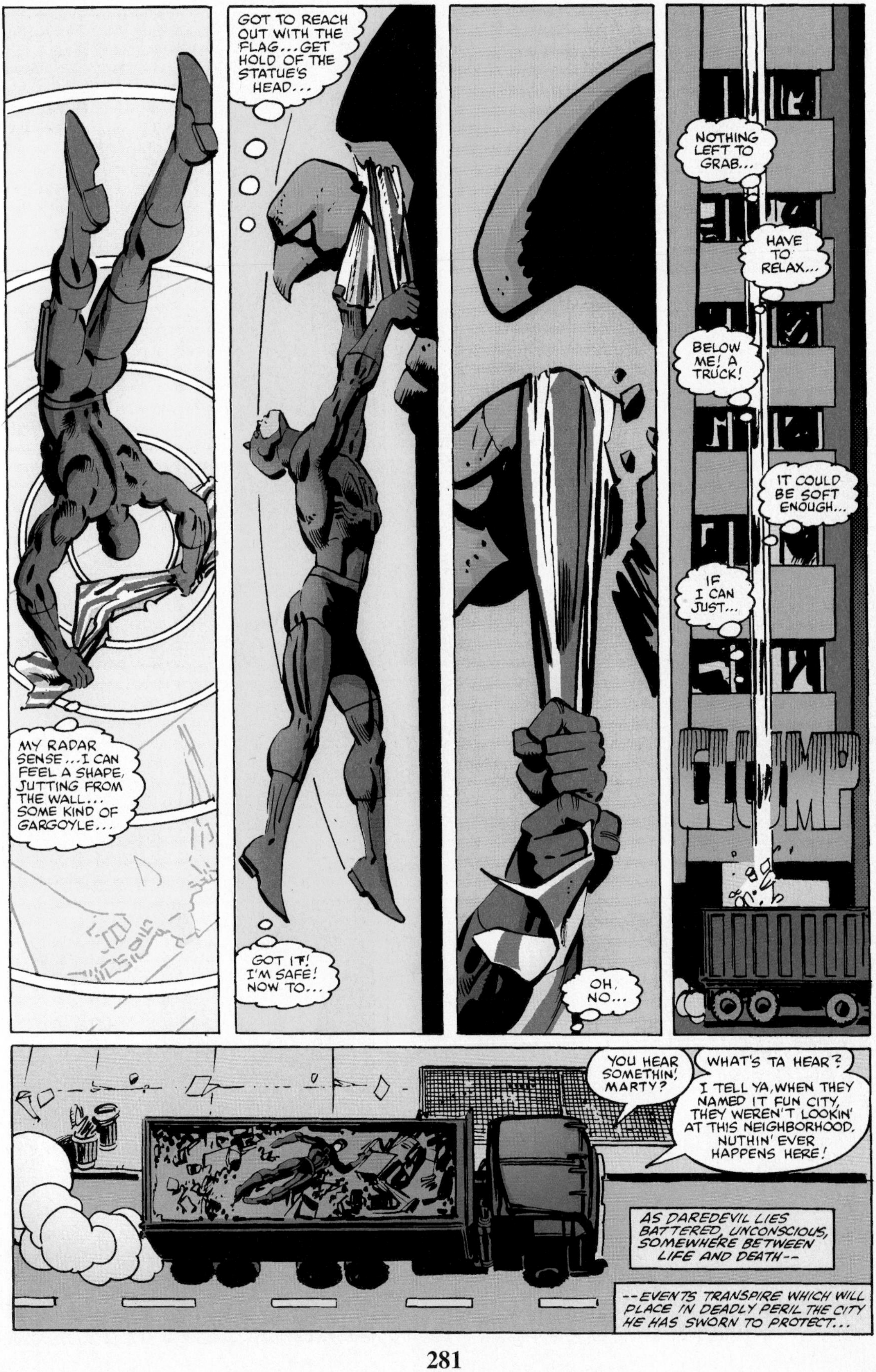
MY RADAR SENSE...I CAN FEEL A SHAPE, JUTTING FROM THE WALL... SOME KIND OF GARGOYLE...
GOT TO REACH OUT WITH THE FLAG...GET HOLD OF THE STATUE'S HEAD...
GOT IT! I'M SAFE! NOW TO...
OH, NO...
NOTHING LEFT TO GRAB...
HAVE TO RELAX...
BELOW ME! A TRUCK!
IT COULD BE SOFT ENOUGH...
IF I CAN JUST...
CLUMP
YOU HEAR SOMETHIN', MARTY?
WHAT'S TA HEAR? I TELL YA, WHEN THEY NAMED IT FUN CITY, THEY WEREN'T LOOKIN' AT THIS NEIGHBORHOOD. NUTHIN' EVER HAPPENS HERE!
AS DAREDEVIL LIES BATTERED, UNCONSCIOUS, SOMEWHERE BETWEEN LIFE AND DEATH--
--EVENTS TRANSPIRE WHICH WILL PLACE IN DEADLY PERIL THE CITY HE HAS SWORN TO PROTECT...

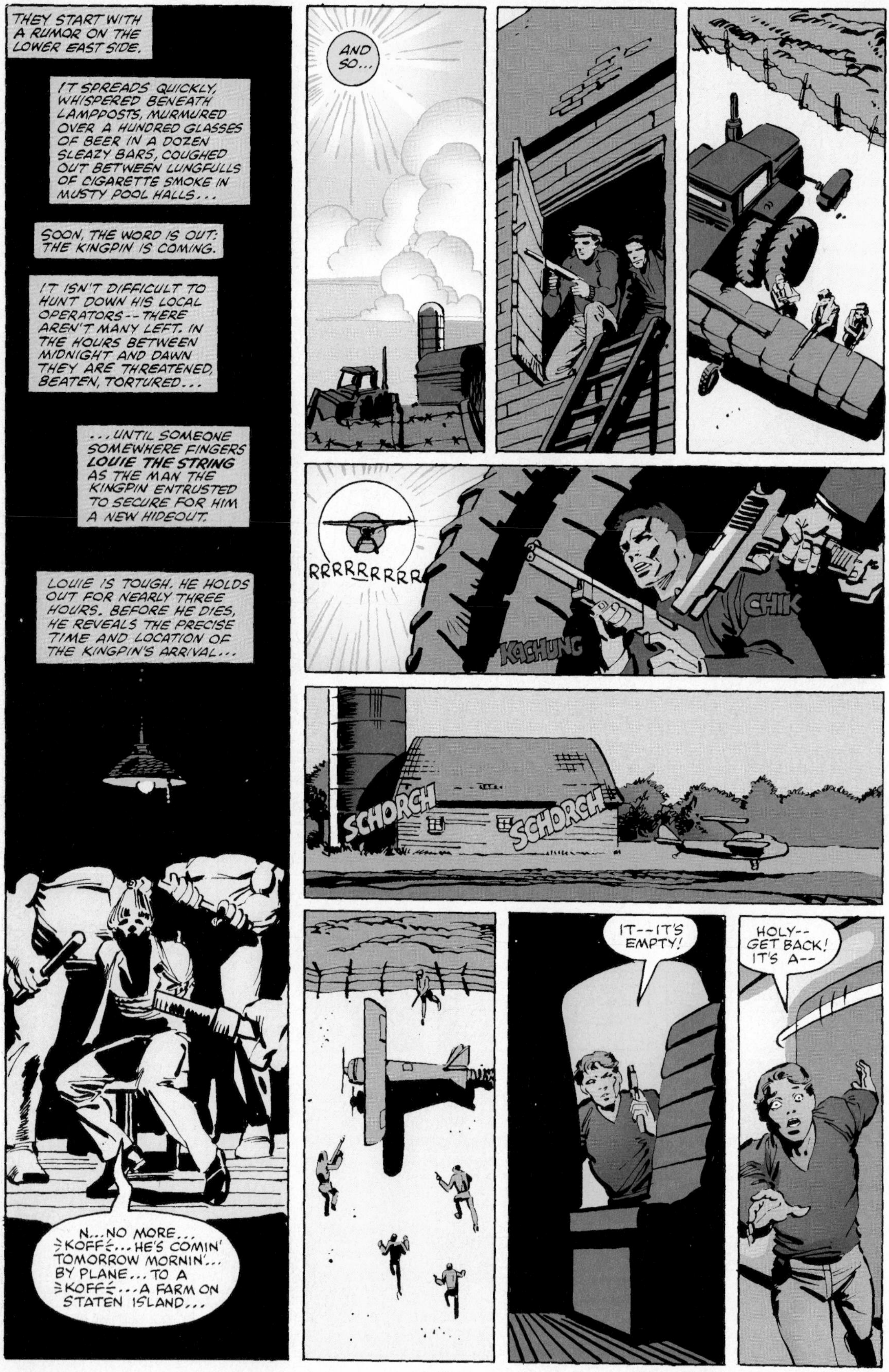
THEY START WITH A RUMOR ON THE LOWER EAST SIDE.
IT SPREADS QUICKLY, WHISPERED BENEATH LAMPPOSTS, MURMURED OVER A HUNDRED GLASSES OF BEER IN A DOZEN SLEAZY BARS, COUGHED OUT BETWEEN LUNGFULLS OF CIGARETTE SMOKE IN MUSTY POOL HALLS...
SOON, THE WORD IS OUT: THE KINGPIN IS COMING.
IT ISN'T DIFFICULT TO HUNT DOWN HIS LOCAL OPERATORS--THERE AREN'T MANY LEFT. IN THE HOURS BETWEEN MIDNIGHT AND DAWN THEY ARE THREATENED, BEATEN, TORTURED...
...UNTIL SOMEONE SOMEWHERE FINGERS LOUIE THE STRING AS THE MAN THE KINGPIN ENTRUSTED TO SECURE FOR HIM A NEW HIDEOUT.
LOUIE IS TOUGH. HE HOLDS OUT FOR NEARLY THREE HOURS. BEFORE HE DIES, HE REVEALS THE PRECISE TIME AND LOCATION OF THE KINGPIN'S ARRIVAL...
N...NO MORE... ≥KOFF≤...HE'S COMIN' TOMORROW MORNIN'... BY PLANE... TO A ≥KOFF≤...A FARM ON STATEN ISLAND...
AND SO...
RRRRRRRRR
KACHUNG
CHIK
SCHORCH
SCHORCH
IT--IT'S EMPTY!
HOLY--GET BACK! IT'S A--

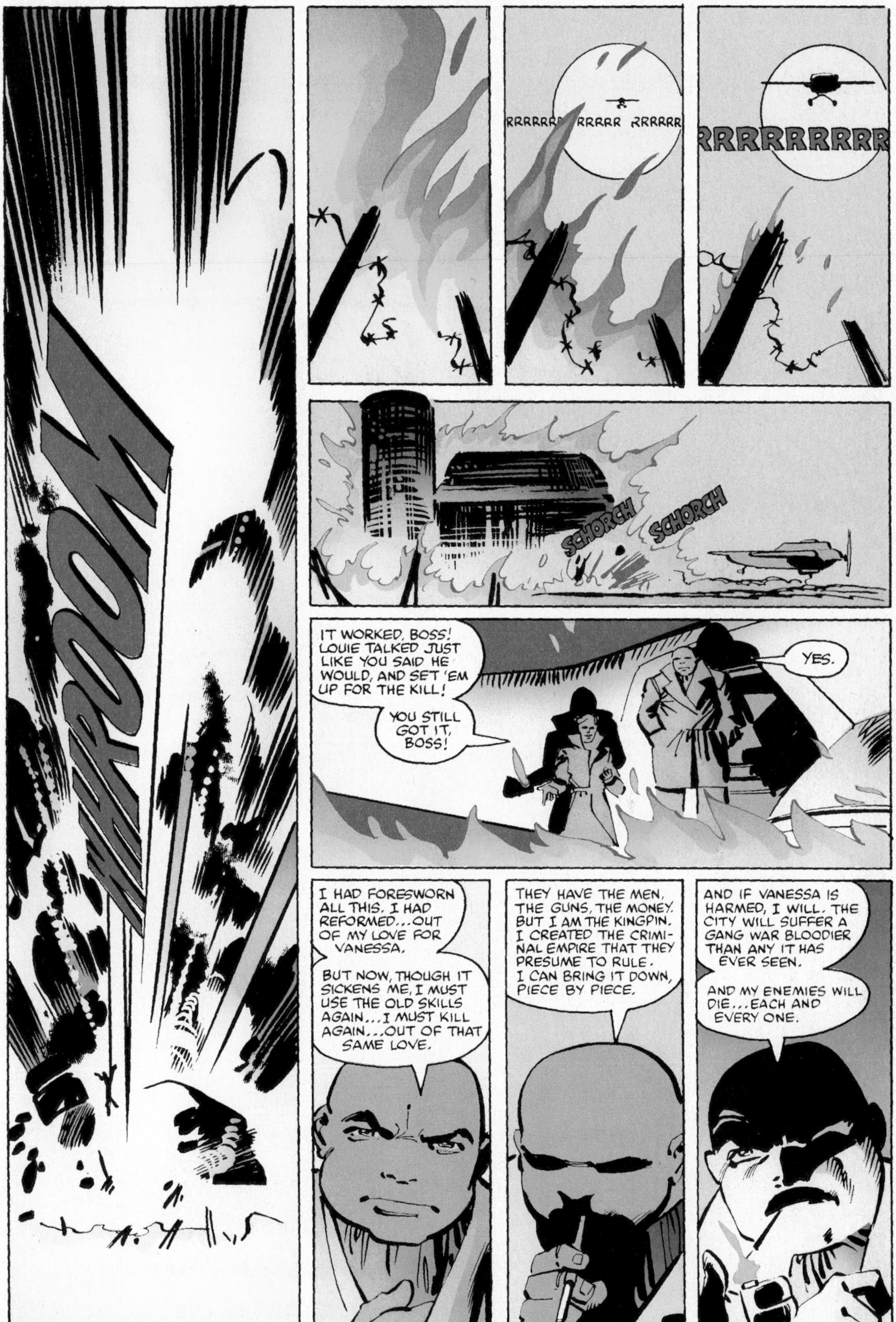
WHOOM
RRRRRR RRRRR RRRRRR
RRRRRRRRRR
SCHORCH
SCHORCH
IT WORKED, BOSS! LOUIE TALKED JUST LIKE YOU SAID HE WOULD, AND SET 'EM UP FOR THE KILL!
YOU STILL GOT IT, BOSS!
YES.
I HAD FORESWORN ALL THIS. I HAD REFORMED... OUT OF MY LOVE FOR VANESSA.
BUT NOW, THOUGH IT SICKENS ME, I MUST USE THE OLD SKILLS AGAIN... I MUST KILL AGAIN... OUT OF THAT SAME LOVE.
THEY HAVE THE MEN, THE GUNS, THE MONEY. BUT I AM THE KINGPIN. I CREATED THE CRIMINAL EMPIRE THAT THEY PRESUME TO RULE. I CAN BRING IT DOWN, PIECE BY PIECE.
AND IF VANESSA IS HARMED, I WILL. THE CITY WILL SUFFER A GANG WAR BLOODIER THAN ANY IT HAS EVER SEEN.
AND MY ENEMIES WILL DIE... EACH AND EVERY ONE.
TO BE CONTINUED!

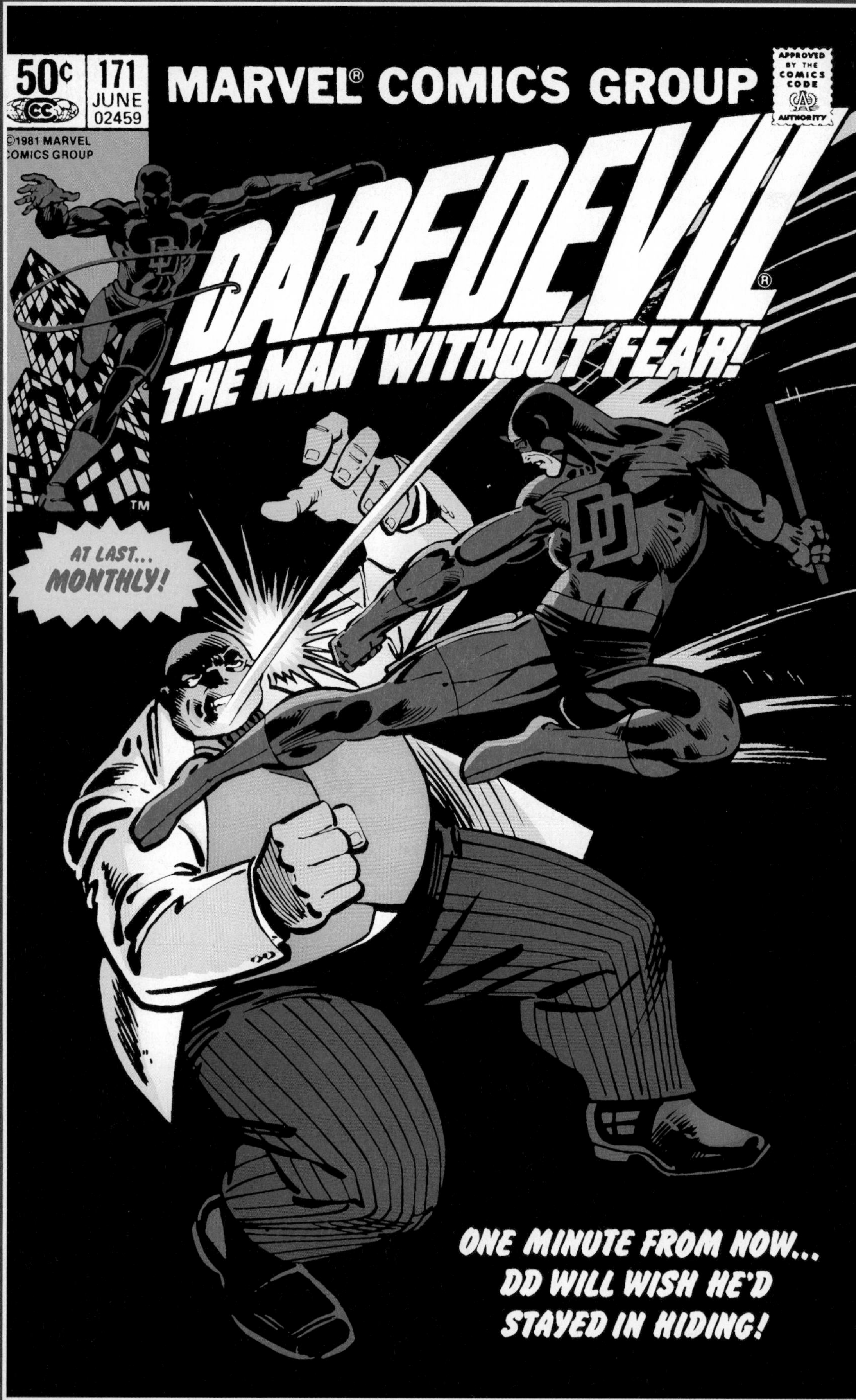

50¢
171
JUNE
02459
MARVEL® COMICS GROUP
APPROVED BY THE COMICS CODE AUTHORITY
©1981 MARVEL COMICS GROUP
DAREDEVIL®
THE MAN WITHOUT FEAR!
AT LAST... MONTHLY!
ONE MINUTE FROM NOW... DD WILL WISH HE'D STAYED IN HIDING!

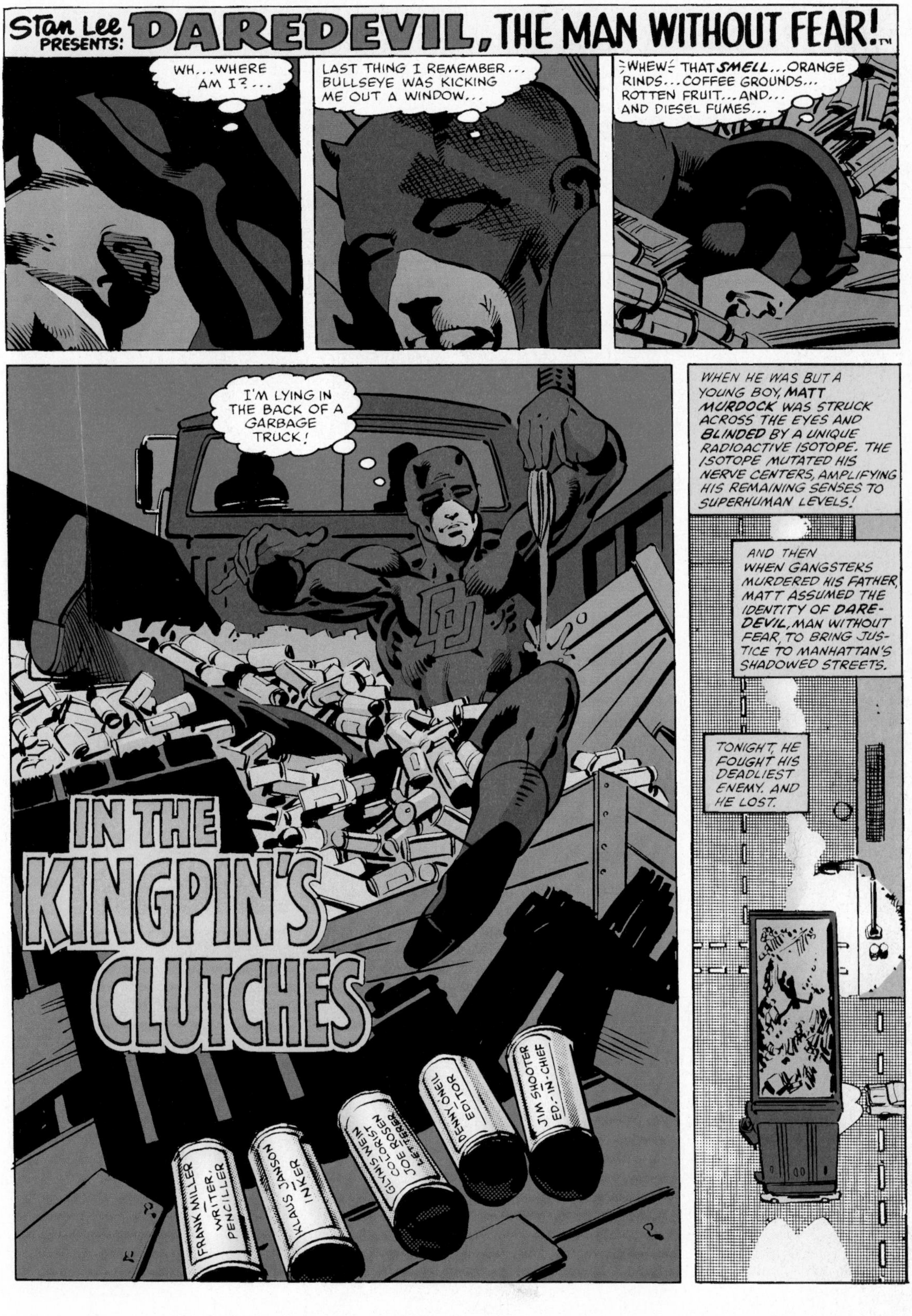

Stan Lee PRESENTS: DAREDEVIL, THE MAN WITHOUT FEAR!
WH...WHERE AM I?...
LAST THING I REMEMBER... BULLSEYE WAS KICKING ME OUT A WINDOW...
WHEW THAT SMELL...ORANGE RINDS...COFFEE GROUNDS... ROTTEN FRUIT...AND... AND DIESEL FUMES...
I'M LYING IN THE BACK OF A GARBAGE TRUCK!
WHEN HE WAS BUT A YOUNG BOY, MATT MURDOCK WAS STRUCK ACROSS THE EYES AND BLINDED BY A UNIQUE RADIOACTIVE ISOTOPE. THE ISOTOPE MUTATED HIS NERVE CENTERS, AMPLIFYING HIS REMAINING SENSES TO SUPERHUMAN LEVELS!
AND THEN WHEN GANGSTERS MURDERED HIS FATHER, MATT ASSUMED THE IDENTITY OF DAREDEVIL, MAN WITHOUT FEAR, TO BRING JUSTICE TO MANHATTAN'S SHADOWED STREETS.
TONIGHT, HE FOUGHT HIS DEADLIEST ENEMY. AND HE LOST.
IN THE KINGPIN'S CLUTCHES
FRANK MILLER WRITER, PENCILLER
KLAUS JANSON INKER
GLYNIS WEIN COLORIST
JOE ROSEN LETTERER
DENNY O'NEIL EDITOR
JIM SHOOTER ED.-IN-CHIEF

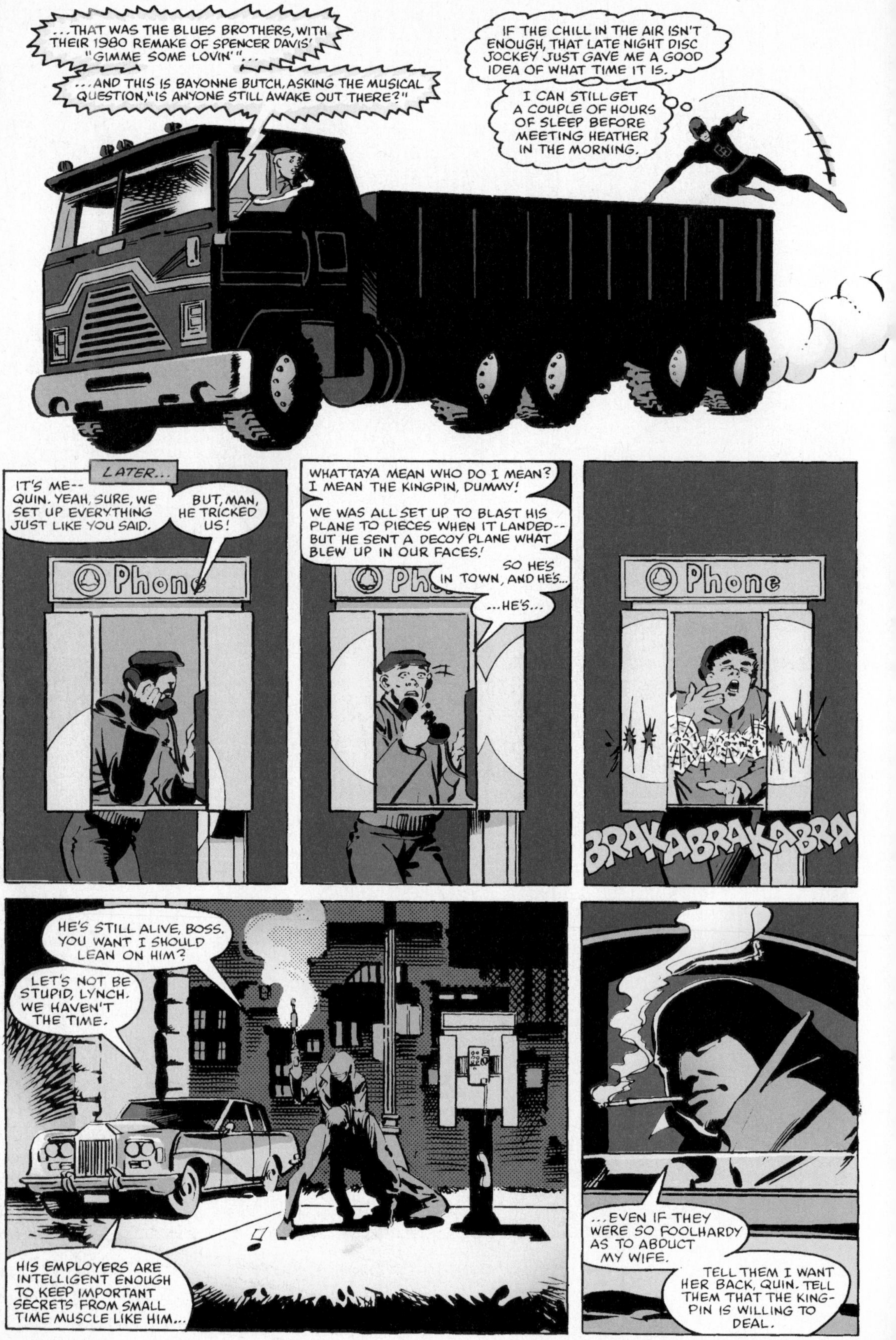
...THAT WAS THE BLUES BROTHERS, WITH THEIR 1980 REMAKE OF SPENCER DAVIS' "GIMME SOME LOVIN'"...
...AND THIS IS BAYONNE BUTCH, ASKING THE MUSICAL QUESTION, "IS ANYONE STILL AWAKE OUT THERE?"
IF THE CHILL IN THE AIR ISN'T ENOUGH, THAT LATE NIGHT DISC JOCKEY JUST GAVE ME A GOOD IDEA OF WHAT TIME IT IS.
I CAN STILL GET A COUPLE OF HOURS OF SLEEP BEFORE MEETING HEATHER IN THE MORNING.
LATER...
IT'S ME-- QUIN. YEAH, SURE, WE SET UP EVERYTHING JUST LIKE YOU SAID.
BUT, MAN, HE TRICKED US!
Phone
WHATTAYA MEAN WHO DO I MEAN? I MEAN THE KINGPIN, DUMMY!
WE WAS ALL SET UP TO BLAST HIS PLANE TO PIECES WHEN IT LANDED-- BUT HE SENT A DECOY PLANE WHAT BLEW UP IN OUR FACES!
SO HE'S IN TOWN, AND HE'S...
...HE'S...
Phone
BRAKABRAKABRA
HE'S STILL ALIVE, BOSS. YOU WANT I SHOULD LEAN ON HIM?
LET'S NOT BE STUPID, LYNCH. WE HAVEN'T THE TIME.
HIS EMPLOYERS ARE INTELLIGENT ENOUGH TO KEEP IMPORTANT SECRETS FROM SMALL TIME MUSCLE LIKE HIM...
...EVEN IF THEY WERE SO FOOLHARDY AS TO ABDUCT MY WIFE.
TELL THEM I WANT HER BACK, QUIN. TELL THEM THAT THE KING-PIN IS WILLING TO DEAL.

CENTRAL PARK...

I DON'T UNDERSTAND, MATT. JUST WHAT IS IT THAT THOSE CRIMELORDS WANT?

YOU SAY THEY'VE KIDNAPPED THE KINGPIN'S WIFE, AND DRAWN HIM BACK TO THE CITY. WHY?

THEY WANT HIS FILES, HEATHER.

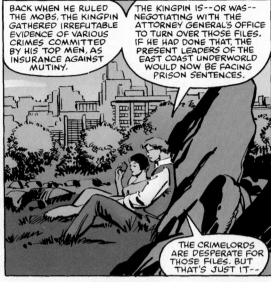

BACK WHEN HE RULED THE MOBS, THE KINGPIN GATHERED IRREFUTABLE EVIDENCE OF VARIOUS CRIMES COMMITTED BY HIS TOP MEN, AS INSURANCE AGAINST MUTINY.

THE KINGPIN IS--OR WAS-- NEGOTIATING WITH THE ATTORNEY GENERAL'S OFFICE TO TURN OVER THOSE FILES. IF HE HAD DONE THAT, THE PRESENT LEADERS OF THE EAST COAST UNDERWORLD WOULD NOW BE FACING PRISON SENTENCES.

THE CRIMELORDS ARE DESPERATE FOR THOSE FILES. BUT THAT'S JUST IT--

--SO AM I. THIS IS A CHANCE TO STRIKE A CRIPPLING BLOW TO ORGANIZED CRIME. I MUST PLAN CAREFULLY...

...PREPARE A STRATEGY THAT WILL ⸮UFF!⸮

SHOP TALK! NOTHING BUT SHOP TALK!

SOME 'SWASHBUCKLER' YOU TURNED OUT TO BE!

MILADY, YOU MISJUDGE ME!

PURE OF HEART, VIRTUOUS IN BOTH THOUGHT AND DEED, I LIVE ONLY TO SERVE THY WILL...

MY HERO!

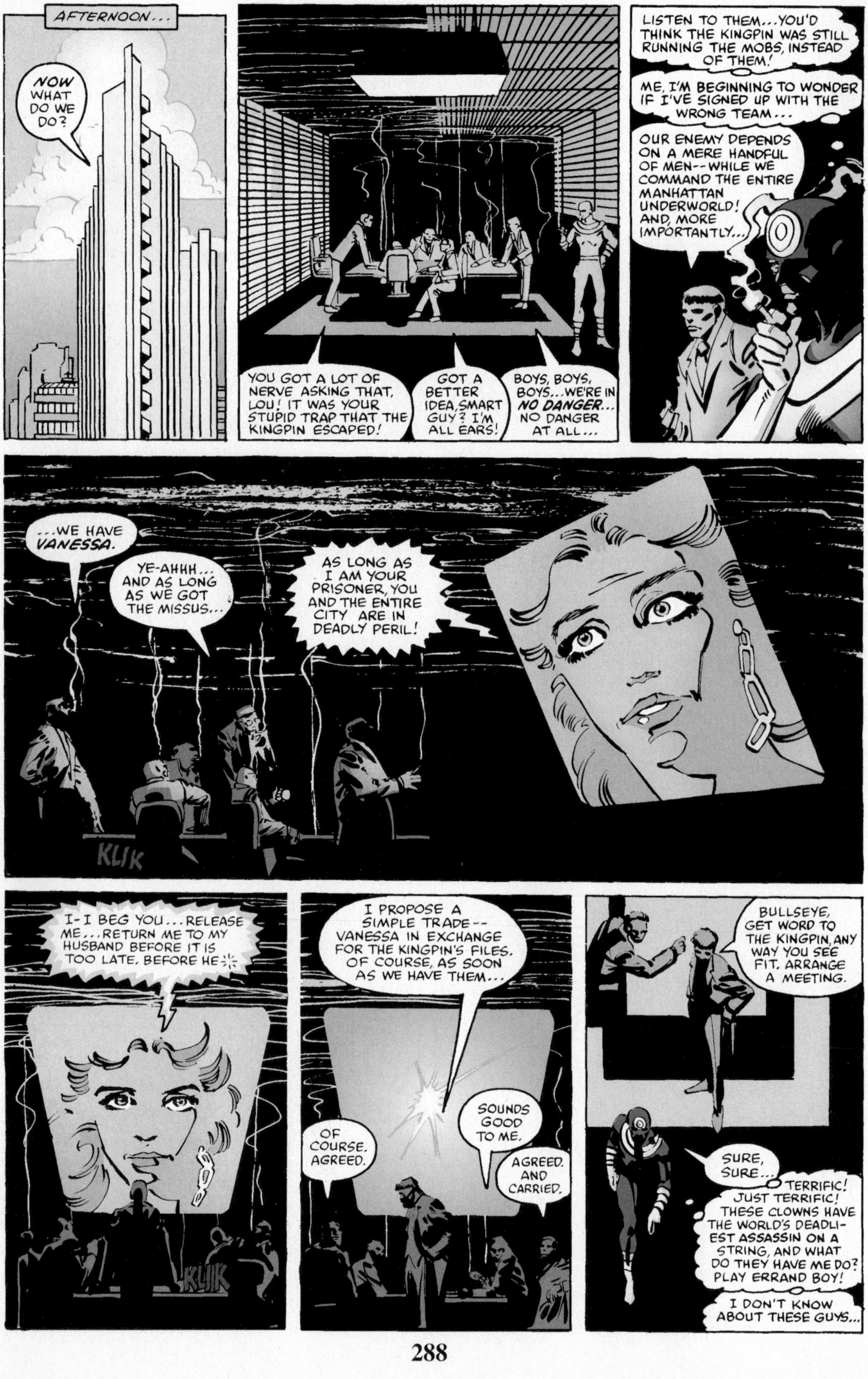
AFTERNOON...
NOW WHAT DO WE DO?
YOU GOT A LOT OF NERVE ASKING THAT, LOU! IT WAS YOUR STUPID TRAP THAT THE KINGPIN ESCAPED!
GOT A BETTER IDEA, SMART GUY? I'M ALL EARS!
BOYS, BOYS, BOYS... WE'RE IN NO DANGER... NO DANGER AT ALL...
LISTEN TO THEM... YOU'D THINK THE KINGPIN WAS STILL RUNNING THE MOBS, INSTEAD OF THEM!
ME, I'M BEGINNING TO WONDER IF I'VE SIGNED UP WITH THE WRONG TEAM...
OUR ENEMY DEPENDS ON A MERE HANDFUL OF MEN--WHILE WE COMMAND THE ENTIRE MANHATTAN UNDERWORLD! AND, MORE IMPORTANTLY...
...WE HAVE VANESSA.
YE-AHHH... AND AS LONG AS WE GOT THE MISSUS...
AS LONG AS I AM YOUR PRISONER, YOU AND THE ENTIRE CITY ARE IN DEADLY PERIL!
KLIK
I-I BEG YOU... RELEASE ME... RETURN ME TO MY HUSBAND BEFORE IT IS TOO LATE. BEFORE HE
KLIK
I PROPOSE A SIMPLE TRADE--VANESSA IN EXCHANGE FOR THE KINGPIN'S FILES. OF COURSE, AS SOON AS WE HAVE THEM...
OF COURSE. AGREED.
SOUNDS GOOD TO ME.
AGREED. AND CARRIED.
BULLSEYE, GET WORD TO THE KINGPIN, ANY WAY YOU SEE FIT. ARRANGE A MEETING.
SURE, SURE...
TERRIFIC! JUST TERRIFIC! THESE CLOWNS HAVE THE WORLD'S DEADLIEST ASSASSIN ON A STRING, AND WHAT DO THEY HAVE ME DO? PLAY ERRAND BOY!
I DON'T KNOW ABOUT THESE GUYS...

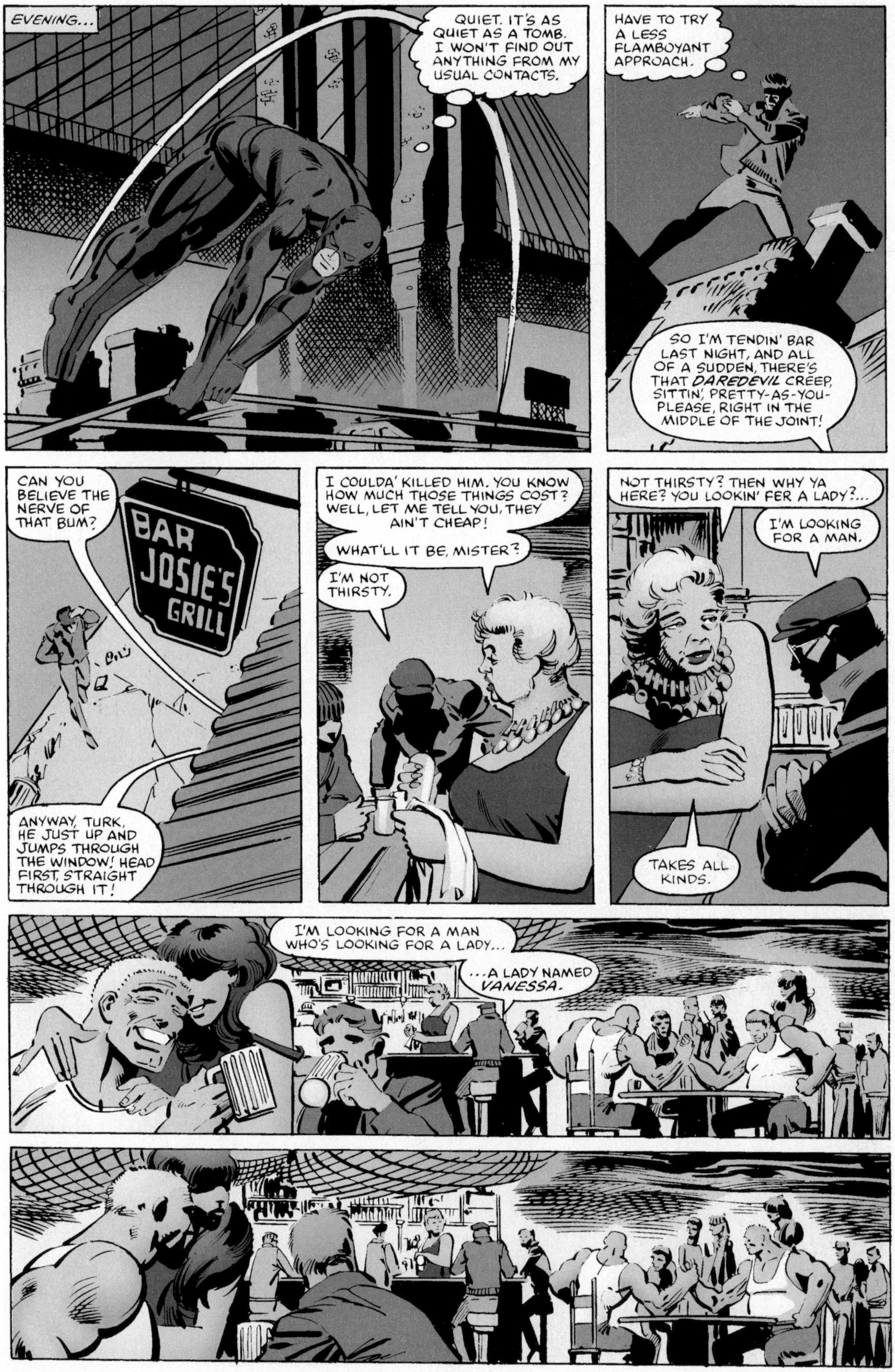
EVENING...
QUIET. IT'S AS QUIET AS A TOMB. I WON'T FIND OUT ANYTHING FROM MY USUAL CONTACTS.
HAVE TO TRY A LESS FLAMBOYANT APPROACH.
SO I'M TENDIN' BAR LAST NIGHT, AND ALL OF A SUDDEN, THERE'S THAT DAREDEVIL CREEP, SITTIN', PRETTY-AS-YOU-PLEASE, RIGHT IN THE MIDDLE OF THE JOINT!
CAN YOU BELIEVE THE NERVE OF THAT BUM?
BAR
JOSIE'S
GRILL
ANYWAY, TURK, HE JUST UP AND JUMPS THROUGH THE WINDOW! HEAD FIRST, STRAIGHT THROUGH IT!
I COULDA' KILLED HIM. YOU KNOW HOW MUCH THOSE THINGS COST? WELL, LET ME TELL YOU, THEY AIN'T CHEAP!
WHAT'LL IT BE, MISTER?
I'M NOT THIRSTY.
NOT THIRSTY? THEN WHY YA HERE? YOU LOOKIN' FER A LADY?...
I'M LOOKING FOR A MAN.
TAKES ALL KINDS.
I'M LOOKING FOR A MAN WHO'S LOOKING FOR A LADY...
...A LADY NAMED VANESSA.

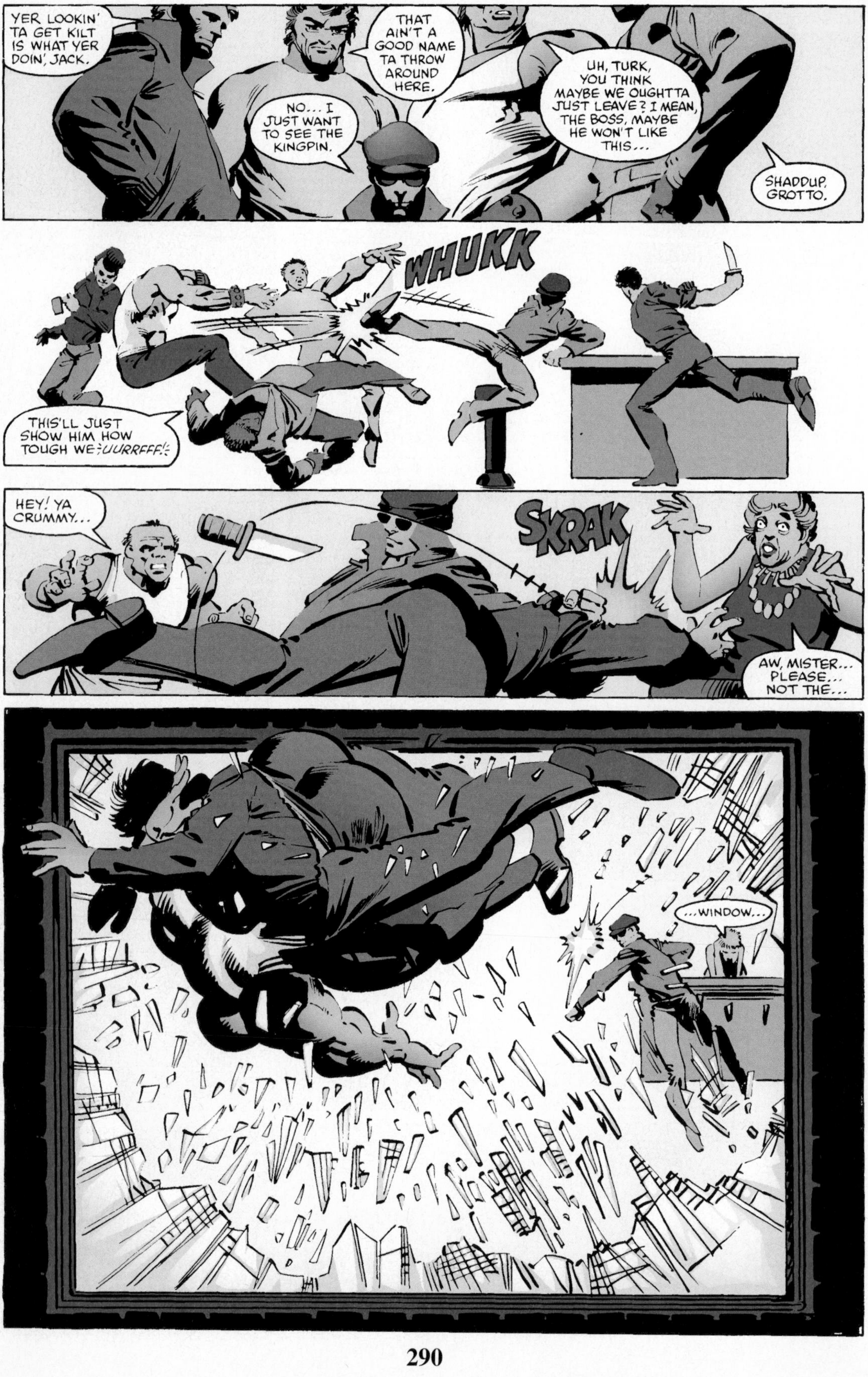
YER LOOKIN' TA GET KILT IS WHAT YER DOIN', JACK.
NO... I JUST WANT TO SEE THE KINGPIN.
THAT AIN'T A GOOD NAME TA THROW AROUND HERE.
UH, TURK, YOU THINK MAYBE WE OUGHTTA JUST LEAVE? I MEAN, THE BOSS, MAYBE HE WON'T LIKE THIS...
SHADDUP, GROTTO.
WHUKK
THIS'LL JUST SHOW HIM HOW TOUGH WE--UURRFFF!
HEY! YA CRUMMY...
SKRAK
AW, MISTER... PLEASE... NOT THE...
...WINDOW...

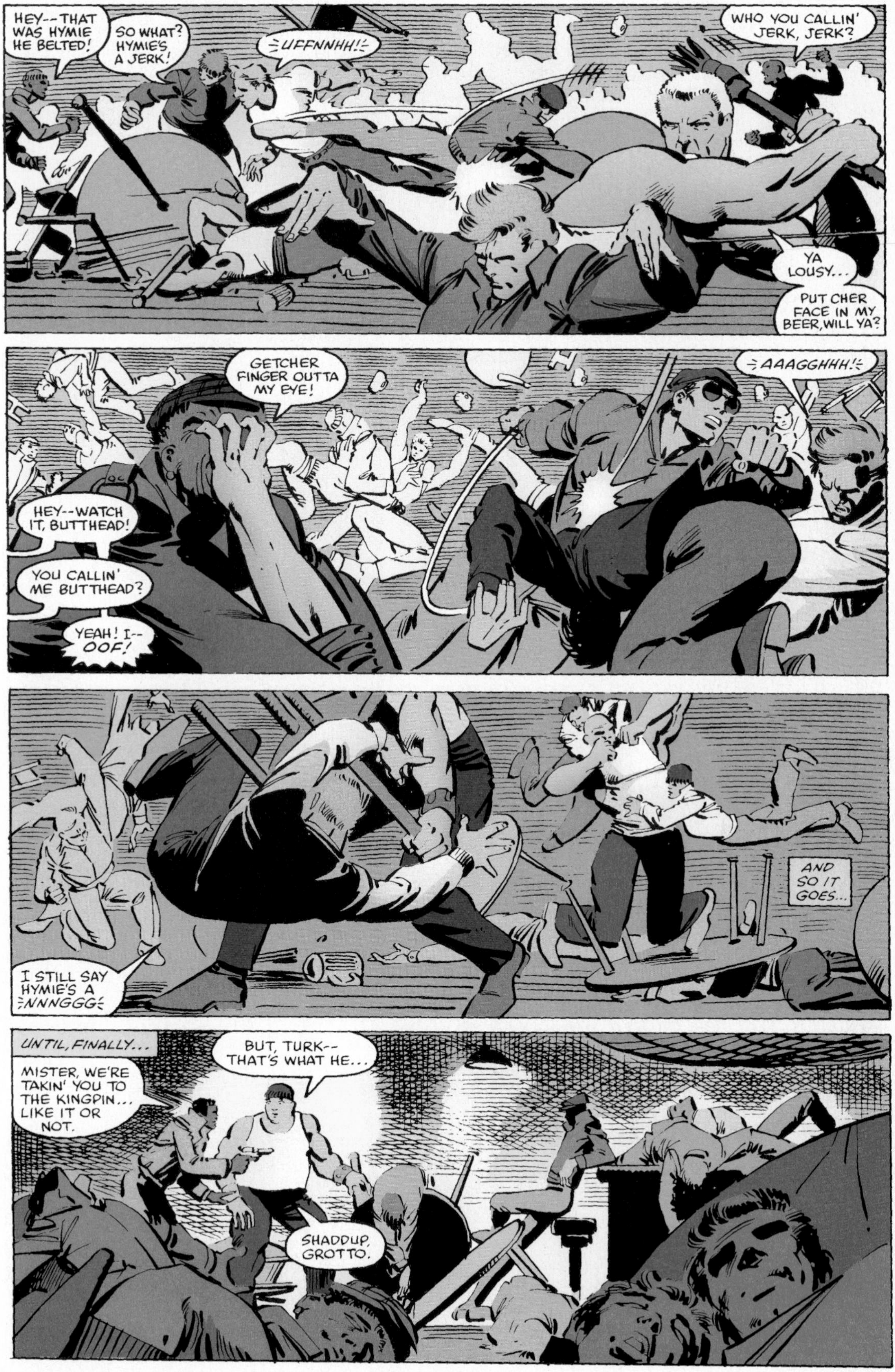
HEY--THAT WAS HYMIE HE BELTED!
SO WHAT? HYMIE'S A JERK!
UFFNNHH!
WHO YOU CALLIN' JERK, JERK?
YA LOUSY...
PUT CHER FACE IN MY BEER, WILL YA?
GETCHER FINGER OUTTA MY EYE!
AAAGGHHH!
HEY--WATCH IT, BUTTHEAD!
YOU CALLIN' ME BUTTHEAD?
YEAH! I-- OOF!
AND SO IT GOES...
I STILL SAY HYMIE'S A NNNGGG
UNTIL, FINALLY...
MISTER, WE'RE TAKIN' YOU TO THE KINGPIN... LIKE IT OR NOT.
BUT, TURK-- THAT'S WHAT HE...
SHADDUP, GROTTO.

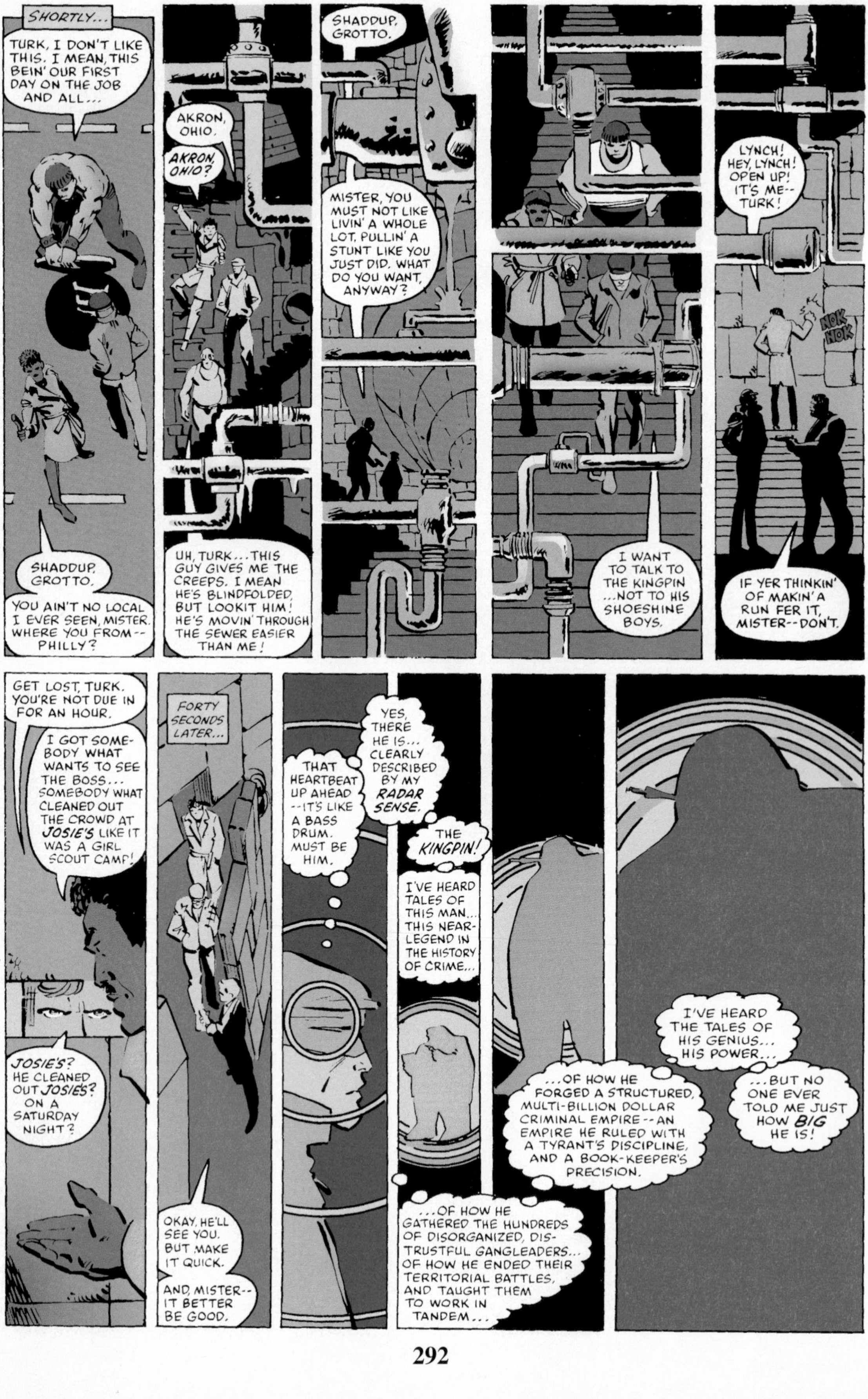
SHORTLY...
TURK, I DON'T LIKE THIS. I MEAN, THIS BEIN' OUR FIRST DAY ON THE JOB AND ALL...
SHADDUP, GROTTO.
YOU AIN'T NO LOCAL I EVER SEEN, MISTER. WHERE YOU FROM -- PHILLY?
AKRON, OHIO.
AKRON, OHIO?
UH, TURK... THIS GUY GIVES ME THE CREEPS. I MEAN HE'S BLINDFOLDED, BUT LOOKIT HIM! HE'S MOVIN' THROUGH THE SEWER EASIER THAN ME!
SHADDUP, GROTTO.
MISTER, YOU MUST NOT LIKE LIVIN' A WHOLE LOT, PULLIN' A STUNT LIKE YOU JUST DID. WHAT DO YOU WANT, ANYWAY?
I WANT TO TALK TO THE KINGPIN ...NOT TO HIS SHOESHINE BOYS.
LYNCH! HEY, LYNCH! OPEN UP! IT'S ME-- TURK!
NOK NOK
IF YER THINKIN' OF MAKIN' A RUN FER IT, MISTER-- DON'T.
GET LOST, TURK. YOU'RE NOT DUE IN FOR AN HOUR.
I GOT SOME-BODY WHAT WANTS TO SEE THE BOSS... SOMEBODY WHAT CLEANED OUT THE CROWD AT JOSIE'S LIKE IT WAS A GIRL SCOUT CAMP!
JOSIE'S? HE CLEANED OUT JOSIE'S? ON A SATURDAY NIGHT?
FORTY SECONDS LATER...
OKAY, HE'LL SEE YOU. BUT MAKE IT QUICK.
AND, MISTER-- IT BETTER BE GOOD.
THAT HEARTBEAT UP AHEAD --IT'S LIKE A BASS DRUM. MUST BE HIM.
YES, THERE HE IS... CLEARLY DESCRIBED BY MY RADAR SENSE.
THE KINGPIN!
I'VE HEARD TALES OF THIS MAN... THIS NEAR-LEGEND IN THE HISTORY OF CRIME...
...OF HOW HE GATHERED THE HUNDREDS OF DISORGANIZED, DIS-TRUSTFUL GANGLEADERS... OF HOW HE ENDED THEIR TERRITORIAL BATTLES, AND TAUGHT THEM TO WORK IN TANDEM...
...OF HOW HE FORGED A STRUCTURED, MULTI-BILLION DOLLAR CRIMINAL EMPIRE -- AN EMPIRE HE RULED WITH A TYRANT'S DISCIPLINE, AND A BOOK-KEEPER'S PRECISION.
I'VE HEARD THE TALES OF HIS GENIUS... HIS POWER...
...BUT NO ONE EVER TOLD ME JUST HOW BIG HE IS!

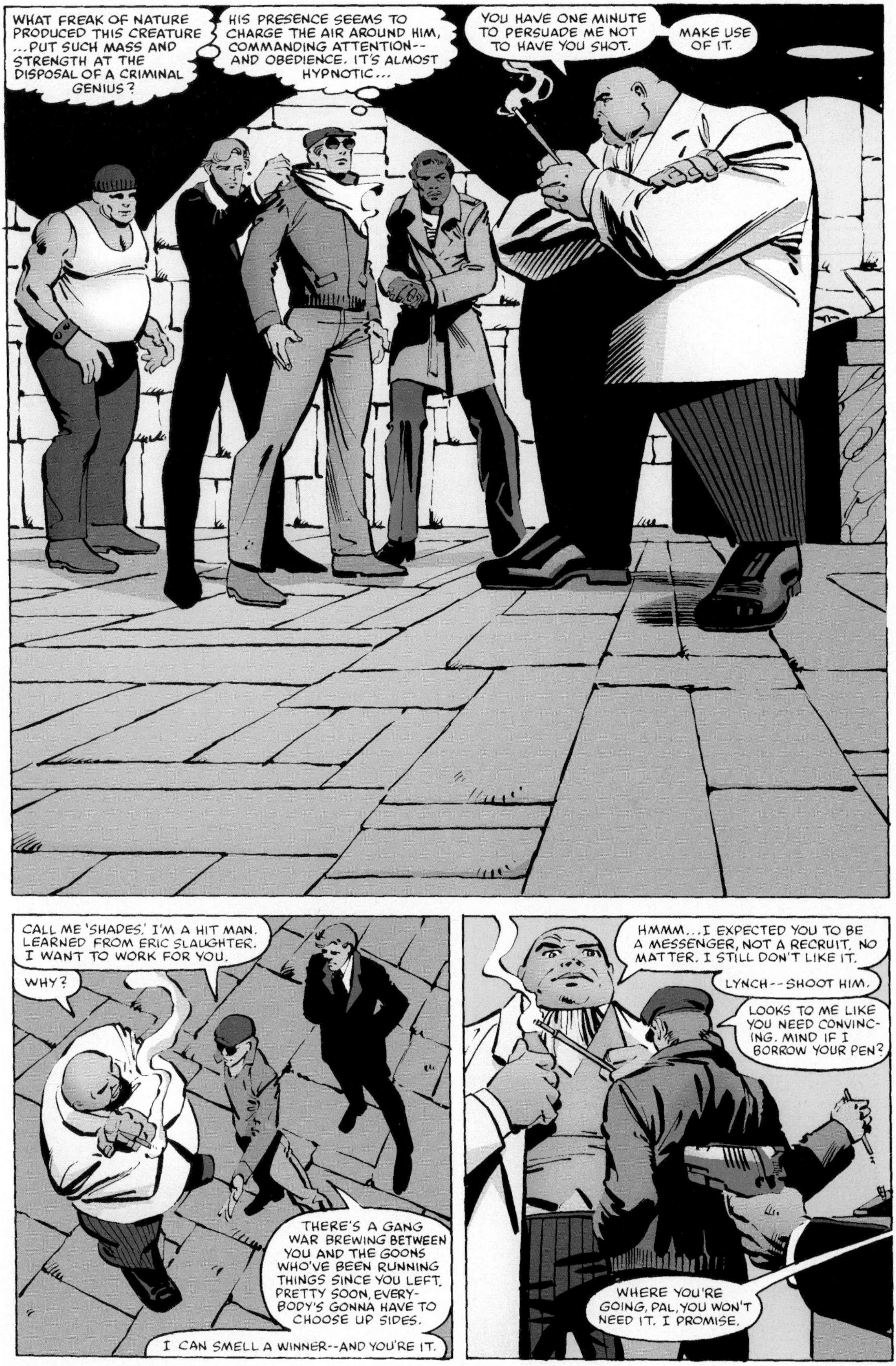
WHAT FREAK OF NATURE PRODUCED THIS CREATURE ...PUT SUCH MASS AND STRENGTH AT THE DISPOSAL OF A CRIMINAL GENIUS?
HIS PRESENCE SEEMS TO CHARGE THE AIR AROUND HIM, COMMANDING ATTENTION-- AND OBEDIENCE. IT'S ALMOST HYPNOTIC...
YOU HAVE ONE MINUTE TO PERSUADE ME NOT TO HAVE YOU SHOT.
MAKE USE OF IT.
CALL ME 'SHADES.' I'M A HIT MAN. LEARNED FROM ERIC SLAUGHTER. I WANT TO WORK FOR YOU.
WHY?
THERE'S A GANG WAR BREWING BETWEEN YOU AND THE GOONS WHO'VE BEEN RUNNING THINGS SINCE YOU LEFT. PRETTY SOON, EVERY-BODY'S GONNA HAVE TO CHOOSE UP SIDES.
I CAN SMELL A WINNER--AND YOU'RE IT.
HMMM...I EXPECTED YOU TO BE A MESSENGER, NOT A RECRUIT. NO MATTER. I STILL DON'T LIKE IT.
LYNCH--SHOOT HIM.
LOOKS TO ME LIKE YOU NEED CONVINC-ING. MIND IF I BORROW YOUR PEN?
WHERE YOU'RE GOING, PAL, YOU WON'T NEED IT. I PROMISE.

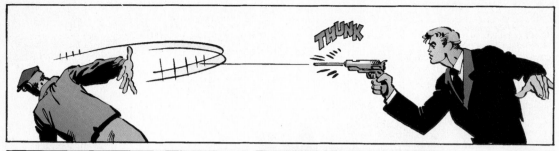

THUNK

WELL?

YOU'RE HIRED.

LORD... NEVER SAW ANYONE MOVE THAT FAST... NEVER...

EH?

IT...IT WAS *BULLSEYE*, BOSS. HE CAUGHT UP WITH ME AND THE BOYS OUTSIDE OF SWEENEY'S...

SAID...SAID HE HAD A MESSAGE... FOR YOU, BOSS...

WHAT IS IT, DUKE? QUICKLY.

HE SAYS IF...IF YOU WANT YOUR WIFE BACK...YOU GOTTA...

YOU GOTTA MEET HIS BOSSES ALONE...UN ...UNARMED...

...AT A CON...CON-STRUCTION SITE ON NINTH AVENUE AND ...AND FORTIETH... TOMORROW NIGHT... MIDNIGH...

HKKK--!

HE'S CROAKED.

SLOW ACTING POISON, NO DOUBT.

YEAH, BOSS?

THERE'S A BODY IN MY OFFICE. COME FETCH IT, AND POST ANOTHER GUARD AT THE VAULT TONIGHT.

294

BULLSEYE. YOU STRUCK AGAIN.

I SAVED YOUR LIFE, BULLSEYE, JUST A FEW WEEKS AGO. I'VE BEEN WONDERING EVER SINCE HOW I WOULD FEEL IF YOU KILLED AGAIN!

NOW I KNOW.

YOU'LL PAY FOR THIS, BULLSEYE.

THIS IS IT, BOSS-- OUR BIG CHANCE! IF WE PLAY OUR CARDS RIGHT, YOU CAN ELIMINATE THE CRIMELORDS TONIGHT--AND COME BACK AS THE KINGPIN OF CRIME!

WITLESS DOLT! YOU OVERSTEP YOUR BOUNDS!

I'VE TOLD YOU BEFORE, LYNCH-- I DON'T WANT TO RULE THE MOBS AGAIN! I DON'T WANT ANYTHING... EXCEPT VANESSA!

B-BUT, BOSS... SINCE YOU LEFT, THE ORGANIZATION'S BEEN A MESS. THE MOBS ARE ACHIN' TO HAVE YOU RUN THINGS! YOU KNOW THEY ARE!

THEY CAN HAVE THEIR STINKING MOBS! THEY CAN ROT IN HELL FOR ALL I CARE! VANESSA IS ALL THAT MATTERS--AND SHE WILL NOT BE ENDANGERED. NOT FOR A SECOND.

DO YOU UNDERSTAND ME, LYNCH?

S-SURE, BOSS. I GET IT.

YEAH, SURE, I GET IT-- BUT I DON'T LIKE IT.

I DON'T LIKE IT BECAUSE I REMEMBER THE KINGPIN BACK BEFORE HE STARTED ACTIN' LIKE A LOVESICK KID.

AND I'M THINKING MAYBE HE COULD GET SET STRAIGHT AGAIN... WITH A LITTLE SHOCK TREATMENT...

THE NEXT DAY, AT THE STORE-FRONT LAW OFFICES OF NELSON AND MURDOCK...

YES SIR, MISTER TOWER, I MEAN, NO SIR, MISTER TOWER, MISTER MURDOCK ISN'T IN TODAY.

NO SIR, I DON'T KNOW WHERE HE IS...

STOREFRONT FREE LEGAL CLINIC

READ THE ADVEN ELJE EVERY MO DAILY & B

NO SIR, MISTER NELSON ISN'T IN EITHER. YES SIR, I REALIZE THAT...YES SIR, I...

OH, EXCUSE ME, SIR.

RING RING

HELLO, NELSON AND MURDOCK. NO, HE ISN'T IN, MS. LAVENDER...NO, I DON'T KNOW WHEN... ME? I'M BECKY BLAKE ...THEIR SECRETARY...

YES, YES, I UNDER-STAND, MA'AM, BUT HE...

RING RING

OH, DEAR...

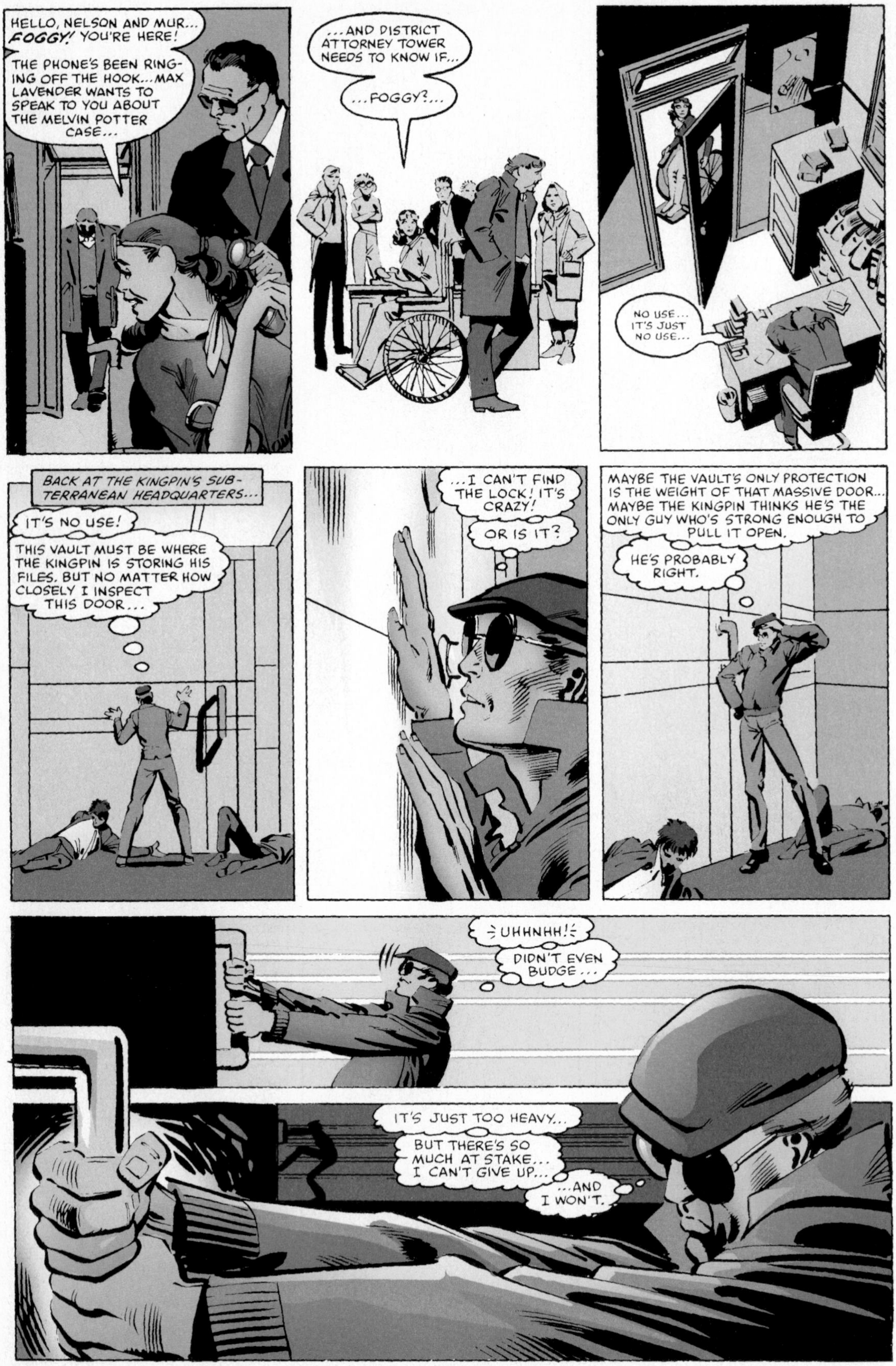
HELLO, NELSON AND MUR... FOGGY! YOU'RE HERE!
THE PHONE'S BEEN RINGING OFF THE HOOK...MAX LAVENDER WANTS TO SPEAK TO YOU ABOUT THE MELVIN POTTER CASE...
...AND DISTRICT ATTORNEY TOWER NEEDS TO KNOW IF...
...FOGGY?...
NO USE... IT'S JUST NO USE...
BACK AT THE KINGPIN'S SUBTERRANEAN HEADQUARTERS...
IT'S NO USE!
THIS VAULT MUST BE WHERE THE KINGPIN IS STORING HIS FILES. BUT NO MATTER HOW CLOSELY I INSPECT THIS DOOR...
...I CAN'T FIND THE LOCK! IT'S CRAZY!
OR IS IT?
MAYBE THE VAULT'S ONLY PROTECTION IS THE WEIGHT OF THAT MASSIVE DOOR... MAYBE THE KINGPIN THINKS HE'S THE ONLY GUY WHO'S STRONG ENOUGH TO PULL IT OPEN.
HE'S PROBABLY RIGHT.
UHHNHH!
DIDN'T EVEN BUDGE...
IT'S JUST TOO HEAVY...
BUT THERE'S SO MUCH AT STAKE... I CAN'T GIVE UP...
...AND I WON'T.

IT IS HOPELESS, HE KNOWS, SO HE DOESN'T HOPE.

HE SIMPLY PULLS--

--UNTIL HIS SHOULDER BLADES BULGE AGAINST THE KNOTTED MUSCLES OF HIS BACK--

--UNTIL HIS BREATH HISSES HOTLY THROUGH CLENCHED TEETH--

--UNTIL CORDED SINEW STRETCHES, NEAR BREAKING--

--UNTIL HIS ARMS SHAKE, AND THREATEN TO YANK FREE OF THEIR SOCKETS...

...AND SOMEHOW, SOMEWHERE BEYOND THE PAIN...

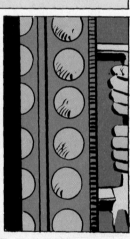

...HE FINDS THE STRENGTH HE NEEDS.

HANDS FEEL BIG AS BASKETBALLS. CAN BARELY MOVE MY ARMS. BUT THERE'S NO TIME TO RELAX.

NOW IT'S JUST A MATTER OF TAKING THESE FILES, AND GETTING OUT OF THIS PLACE ALIVE.

I WISH I WASN'T BLIND, JUST FOR AN HOUR--SO I COULD SEE DISTRICT ATTORNEY TOWER'S FACE WHEN I HAND HIM THIS!

UH-OH...STEPS, ECHOING DOWN THE HALLWAY...

BIG STEPS.

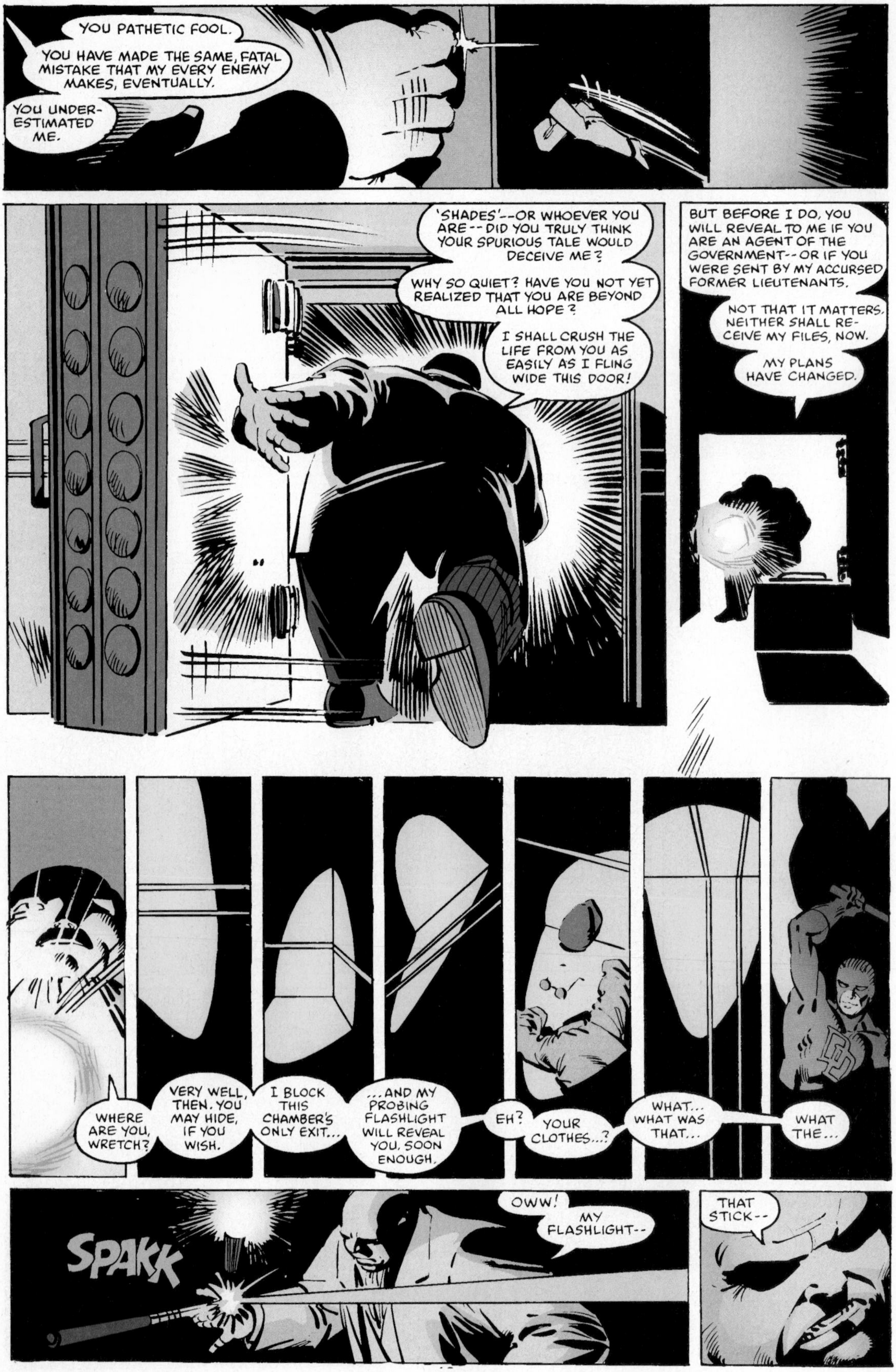
YOU PATHETIC FOOL.
YOU HAVE MADE THE SAME, FATAL MISTAKE THAT MY EVERY ENEMY MAKES, EVENTUALLY.
YOU UNDER-ESTIMATED ME.
'SHADES'--OR WHOEVER YOU ARE--DID YOU TRULY THINK YOUR SPURIOUS TALE WOULD DECEIVE ME?
WHY SO QUIET? HAVE YOU NOT YET REALIZED THAT YOU ARE BEYOND ALL HOPE?
I SHALL CRUSH THE LIFE FROM YOU AS EASILY AS I FLING WIDE THIS DOOR!
BUT BEFORE I DO, YOU WILL REVEAL TO ME IF YOU ARE AN AGENT OF THE GOVERNMENT--OR IF YOU WERE SENT BY MY ACCURSED FORMER LIEUTENANTS.
NOT THAT IT MATTERS. NEITHER SHALL RECEIVE MY FILES, NOW.
MY PLANS HAVE CHANGED.
WHERE ARE YOU, WRETCH?
VERY WELL, THEN. YOU MAY HIDE, IF YOU WISH.
I BLOCK THIS CHAMBER'S ONLY EXIT...
...AND MY PROBING FLASHLIGHT WILL REVEAL YOU, SOON ENOUGH.
EH?
YOUR CLOTHES...?
WHAT... WHAT WAS THAT...
WHAT THE...
SPAKK
OWW!
MY FLASHLIGHT--
THAT STICK--

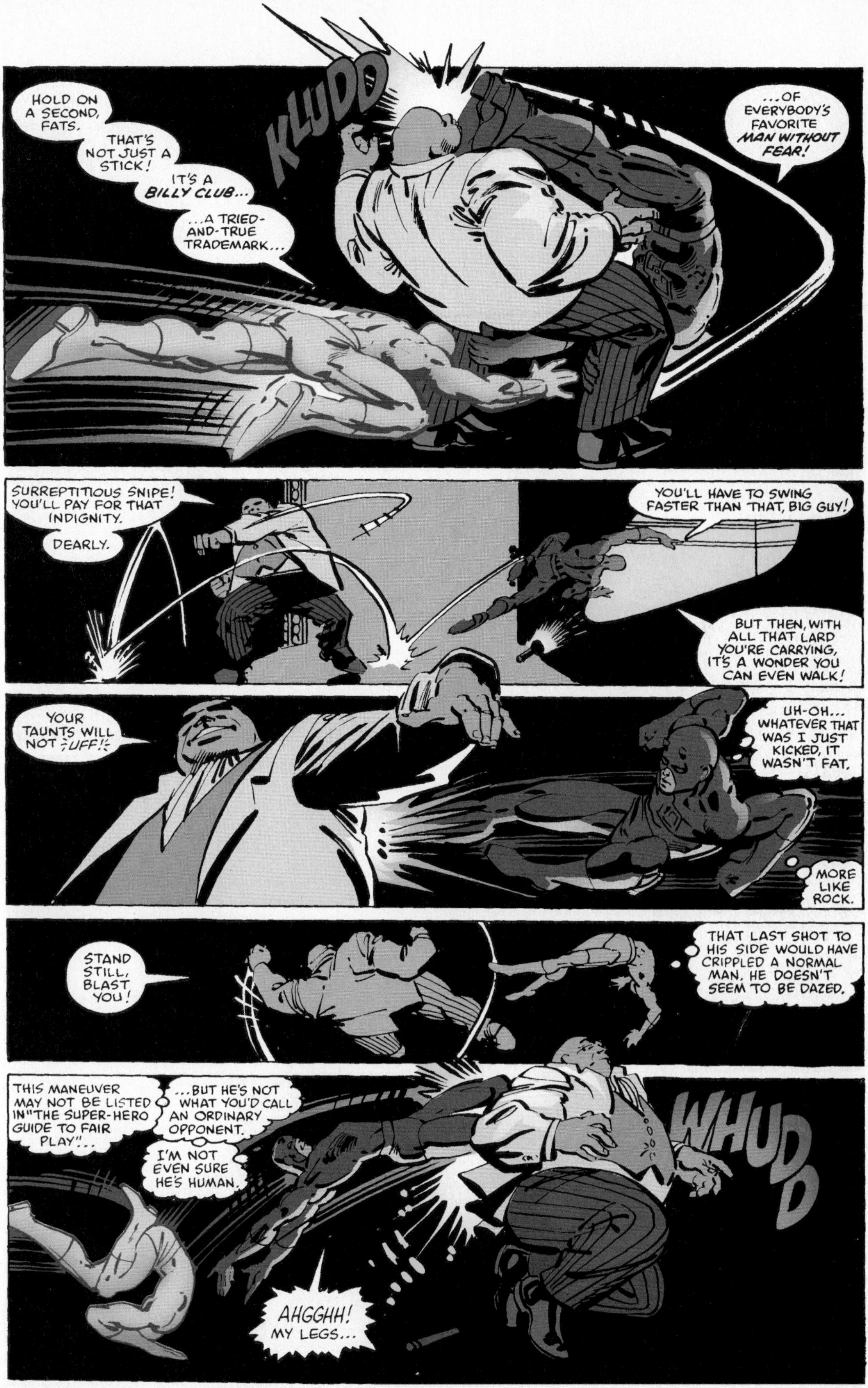
KLUDD
HOLD ON A SECOND, FATS.
THAT'S NOT JUST A STICK!
IT'S A BILLY CLUB...
...A TRIED-AND-TRUE TRADEMARK...
...OF EVERYBODY'S FAVORITE MAN WITHOUT FEAR!
SURREPTITIOUS SNIPE! YOU'LL PAY FOR THAT INDIGNITY.
DEARLY.
YOU'LL HAVE TO SWING FASTER THAN THAT, BIG GUY!
BUT THEN, WITH ALL THAT LARD YOU'RE CARRYING, IT'S A WONDER YOU CAN EVEN WALK!
YOUR TAUNTS WILL NOT -UFF!-
UH-OH... WHATEVER THAT WAS I JUST KICKED, IT WASN'T FAT.
MORE LIKE ROCK.
STAND STILL, BLAST YOU!
THAT LAST SHOT TO HIS SIDE WOULD HAVE CRIPPLED A NORMAL MAN. HE DOESN'T SEEM TO BE DAZED.
THIS MANEUVER MAY NOT BE LISTED IN "THE SUPER-HERO GUIDE TO FAIR PLAY"...
...BUT HE'S NOT WHAT YOU'D CALL AN ORDINARY OPPONENT.
I'M NOT EVEN SURE HE'S HUMAN.
WHUDD
AHGGHH! MY LEGS...

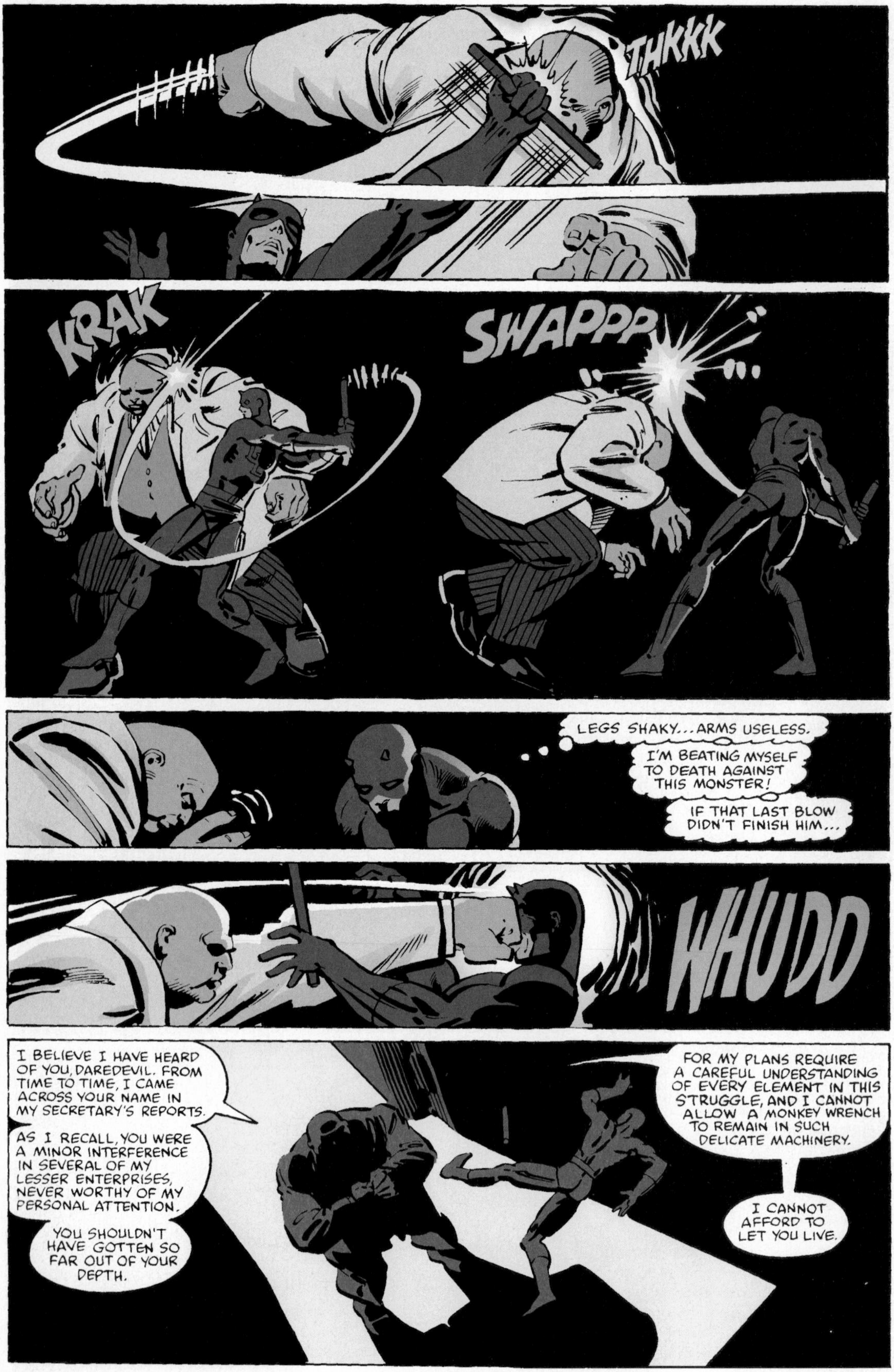
THKKK
KRAK
SWAPPP
LEGS SHAKY... ARMS USELESS.
I'M BEATING MYSELF TO DEATH AGAINST THIS MONSTER!
IF THAT LAST BLOW DIDN'T FINISH HIM...
WHUDD
I BELIEVE I HAVE HEARD OF YOU, DAREDEVIL. FROM TIME TO TIME, I CAME ACROSS YOUR NAME IN MY SECRETARY'S REPORTS.
AS I RECALL, YOU WERE A MINOR INTERFERENCE IN SEVERAL OF MY LESSER ENTERPRISES, NEVER WORTHY OF MY PERSONAL ATTENTION.
YOU SHOULDN'T HAVE GOTTEN SO FAR OUT OF YOUR DEPTH.
FOR MY PLANS REQUIRE A CAREFUL UNDERSTANDING OF EVERY ELEMENT IN THIS STRUGGLE, AND I CANNOT ALLOW A MONKEY WRENCH TO REMAIN IN SUCH DELICATE MACHINERY.
I CANNOT AFFORD TO LET YOU LIVE.

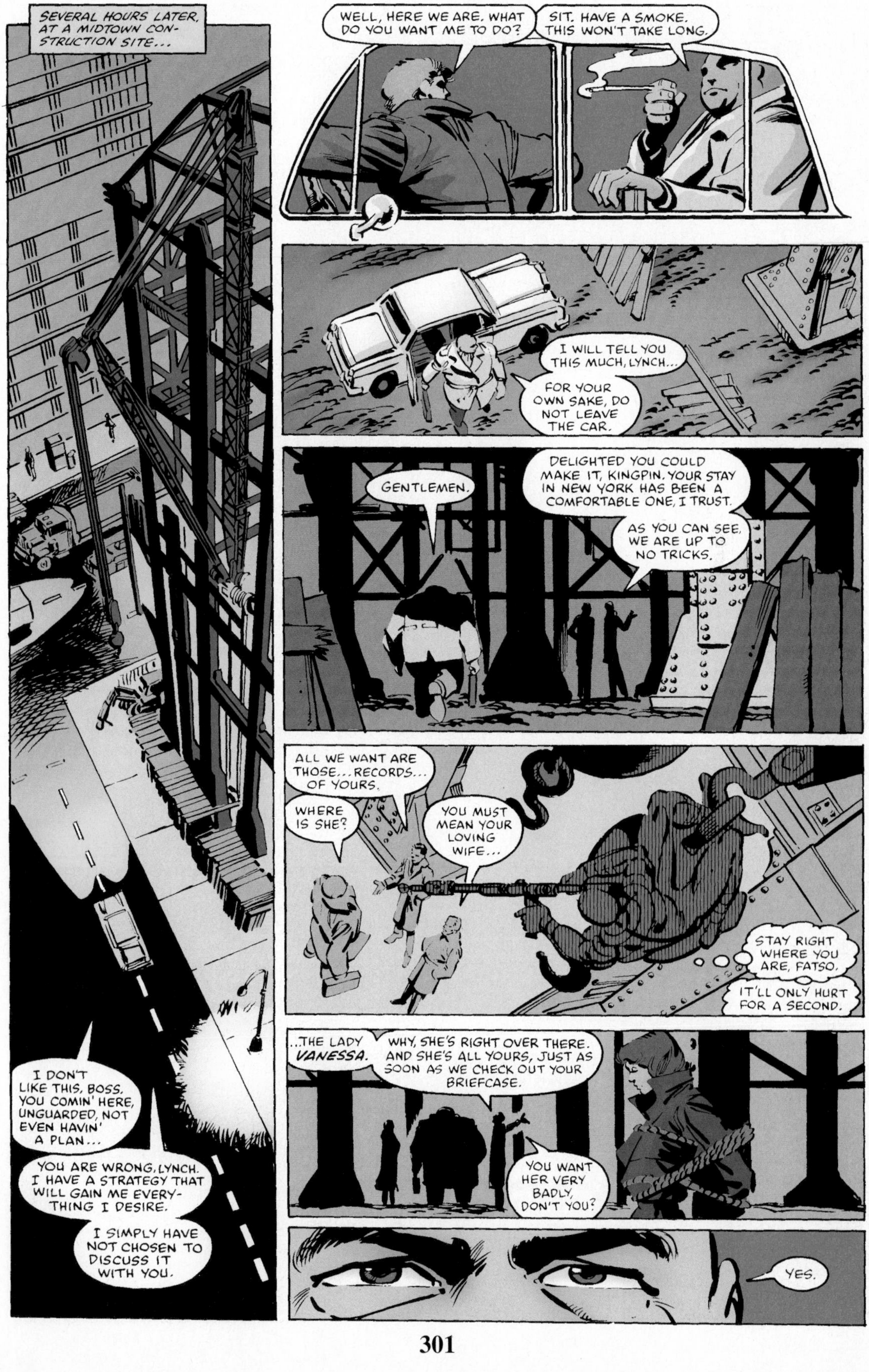
SEVERAL HOURS LATER, AT A MIDTOWN CONSTRUCTION SITE...
I DON'T LIKE THIS, BOSS. YOU COMIN' HERE, UNGUARDED, NOT EVEN HAVIN' A PLAN...
YOU ARE WRONG, LYNCH. I HAVE A STRATEGY THAT WILL GAIN ME EVERYTHING I DESIRE.
I SIMPLY HAVE NOT CHOSEN TO DISCUSS IT WITH YOU.
WELL, HERE WE ARE. WHAT DO YOU WANT ME TO DO?
SIT. HAVE A SMOKE. THIS WON'T TAKE LONG.
I WILL TELL YOU THIS MUCH, LYNCH...
FOR YOUR OWN SAKE, DO NOT LEAVE THE CAR.
GENTLEMEN.
DELIGHTED YOU COULD MAKE IT, KINGPIN. YOUR STAY IN NEW YORK HAS BEEN A COMFORTABLE ONE, I TRUST.
AS YOU CAN SEE, WE ARE UP TO NO TRICKS.
ALL WE WANT ARE THOSE... RECORDS... OF YOURS.
WHERE IS SHE?
YOU MUST MEAN YOUR LOVING WIFE...
STAY RIGHT WHERE YOU ARE, FATSO.
IT'LL ONLY HURT FOR A SECOND.
...THE LADY VANESSA.
WHY, SHE'S RIGHT OVER THERE. AND SHE'S ALL YOURS, JUST AS SOON AS WE CHECK OUT YOUR BRIEFCASE.
YOU WANT HER VERY BADLY, DON'T YOU?
YES.

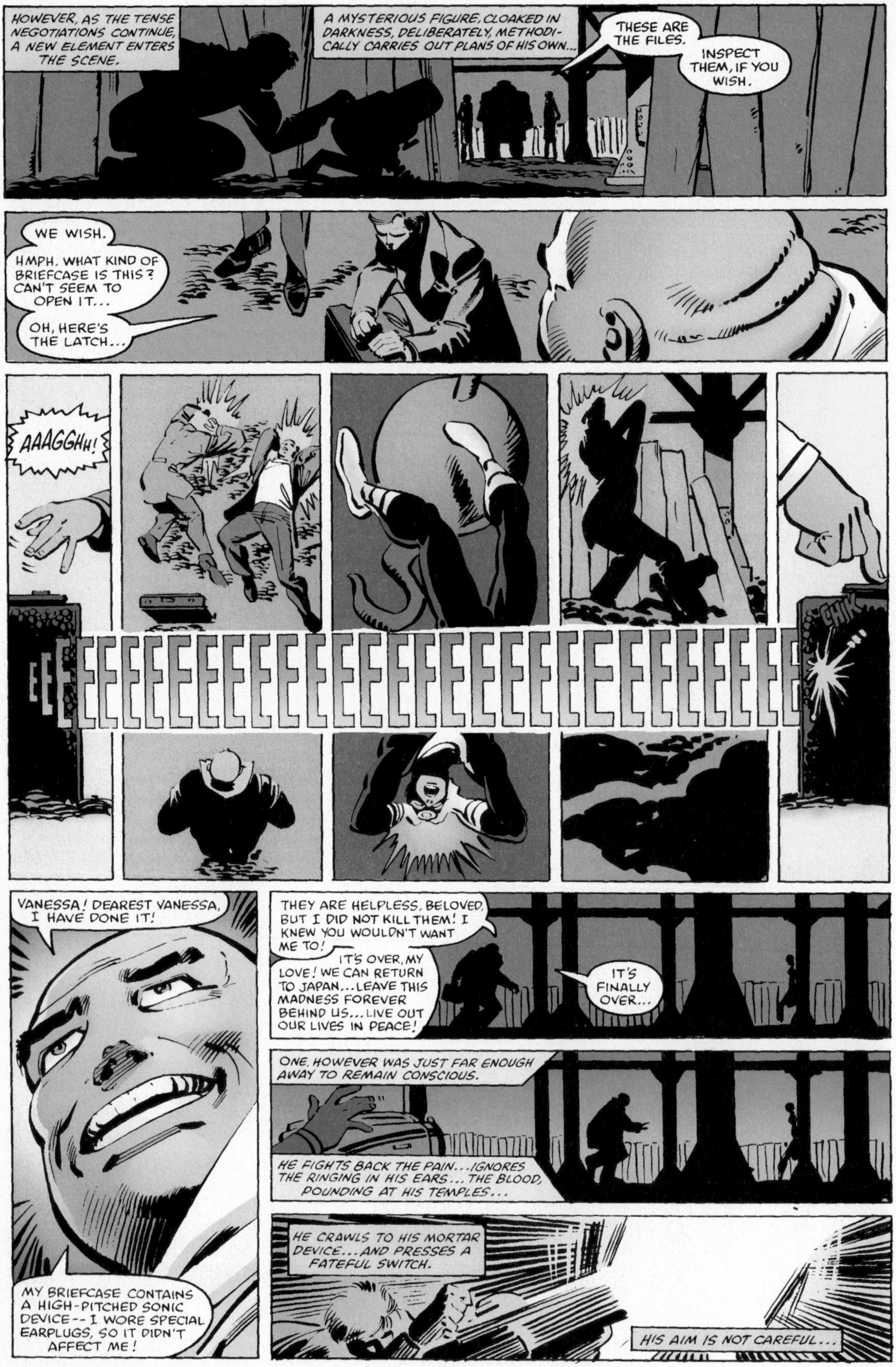
HOWEVER, AS THE TENSE NEGOTIATIONS CONTINUE, A NEW ELEMENT ENTERS THE SCENE.
A MYSTERIOUS FIGURE, CLOAKED IN DARKNESS, DELIBERATELY, METHODICALLY CARRIES OUT PLANS OF HIS OWN...
THESE ARE THE FILES.
INSPECT THEM, IF YOU WISH.
WE WISH.
HMPH. WHAT KIND OF BRIEFCASE IS THIS? CAN'T SEEM TO OPEN IT...
OH, HERE'S THE LATCH...
AAAGGHH!
EEEEEEEEEEEEEEEEEEEEEEEEEE
CHIK
VANESSA! DEAREST VANESSA, I HAVE DONE IT!
MY BRIEFCASE CONTAINS A HIGH-PITCHED SONIC DEVICE--I WORE SPECIAL EARPLUGS, SO IT DIDN'T AFFECT ME!
THEY ARE HELPLESS, BELOVED, BUT I DID NOT KILL THEM! I KNEW YOU WOULDN'T WANT ME TO!
IT'S OVER, MY LOVE! WE CAN RETURN TO JAPAN... LEAVE THIS MADNESS FOREVER BEHIND US... LIVE OUT OUR LIVES IN PEACE!
IT'S FINALLY OVER...
ONE, HOWEVER WAS JUST FAR ENOUGH AWAY TO REMAIN CONSCIOUS.
HE FIGHTS BACK THE PAIN... IGNORES THE RINGING IN HIS EARS... THE BLOOD, POUNDING AT HIS TEMPLES...
HE CRAWLS TO HIS MORTAR DEVICE... AND PRESSES A FATEFUL SWITCH.
HIS AIM IS NOT CAREFUL...

IT DOESN'T
HAVE TO BE.

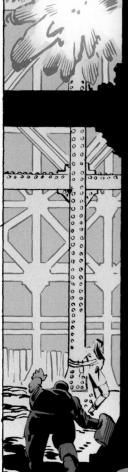

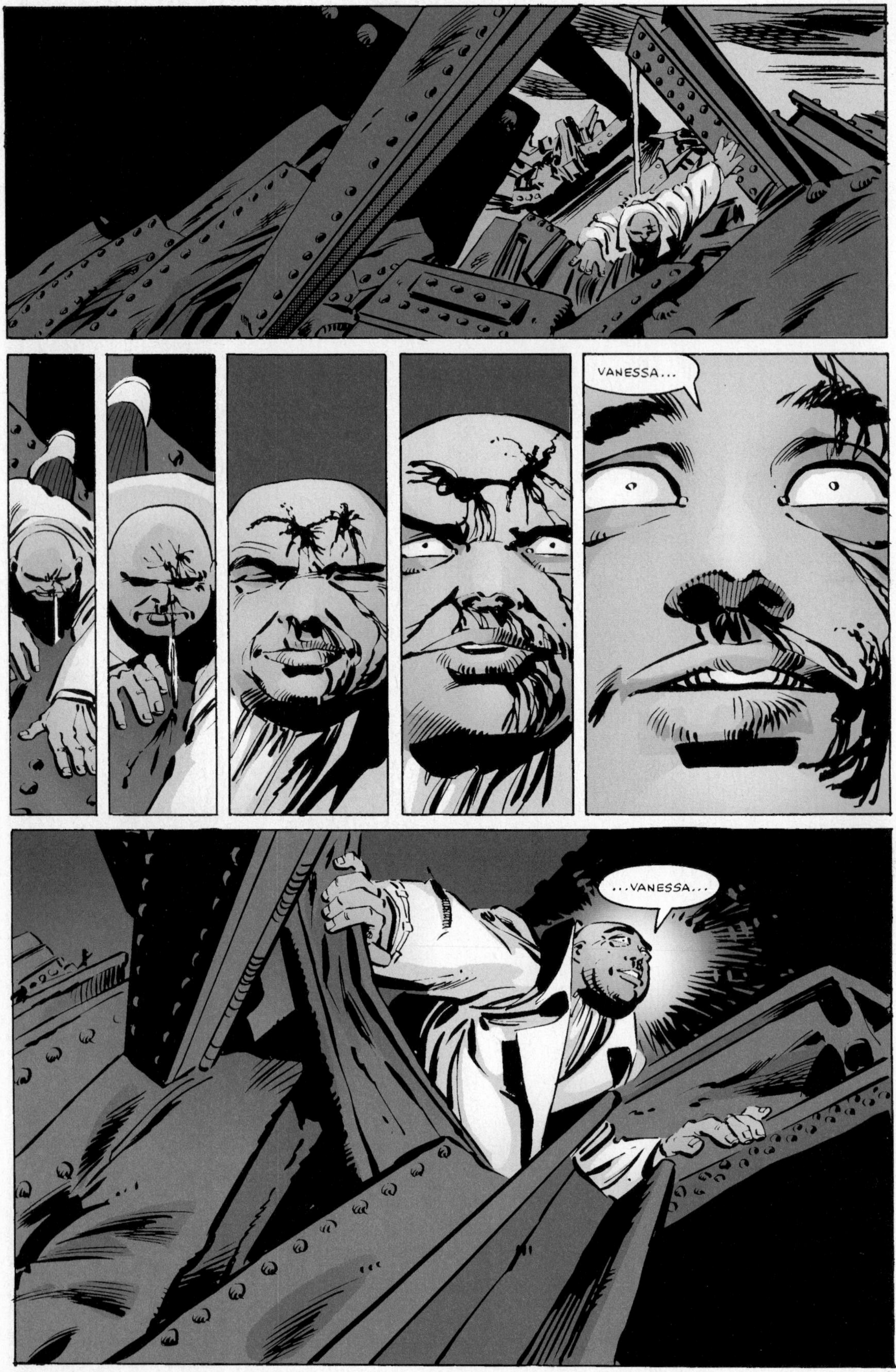
VANESSA...
...VANESSA...

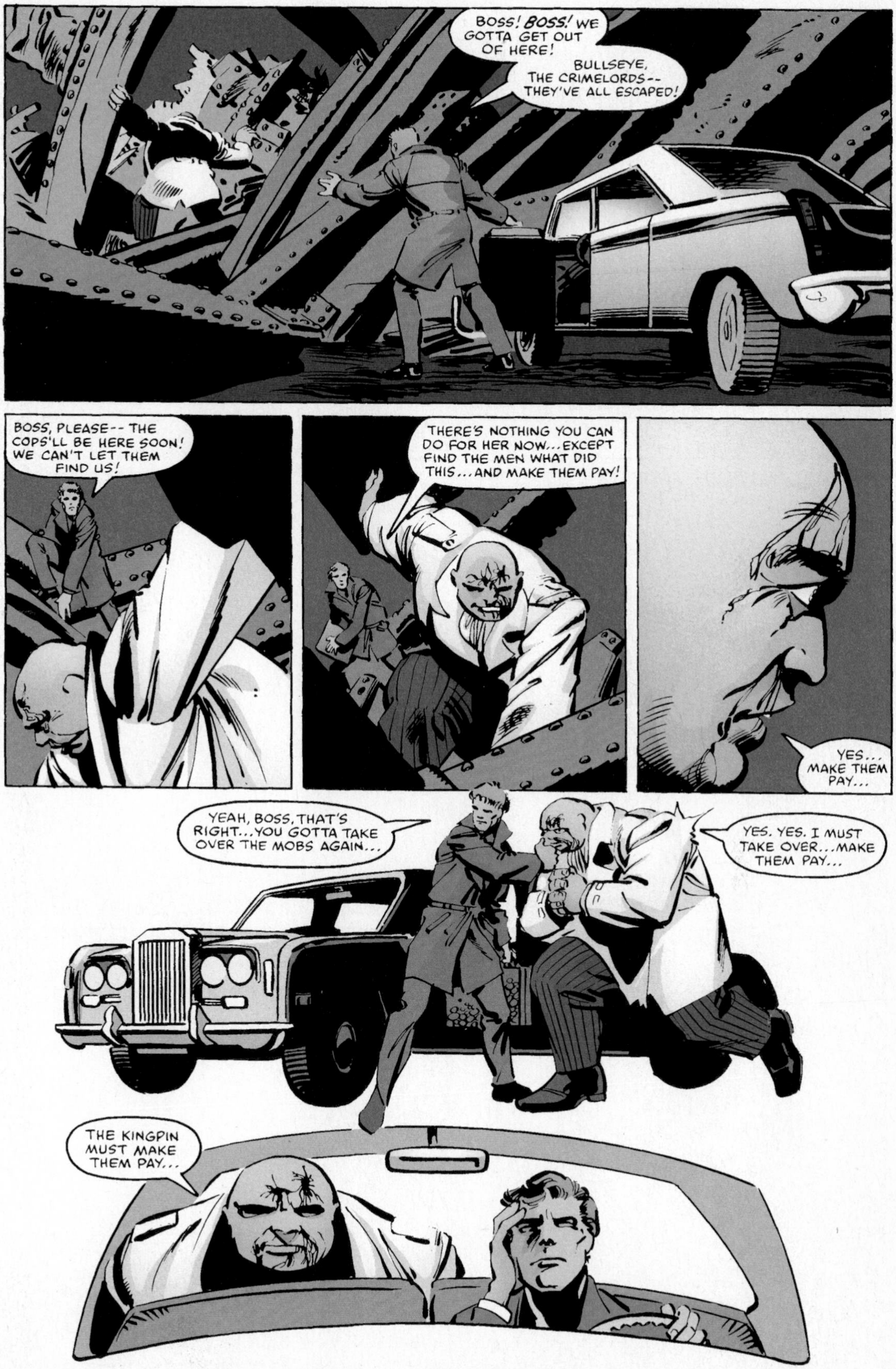
BOSS! BOSS! WE GOTTA GET OUT OF HERE!
BULLSEYE, THE CRIMELORDS-- THEY'VE ALL ESCAPED!
BOSS, PLEASE-- THE COPS'LL BE HERE SOON! WE CAN'T LET THEM FIND US!
THERE'S NOTHING YOU CAN DO FOR HER NOW... EXCEPT FIND THE MEN WHAT DID THIS... AND MAKE THEM PAY!
YES... MAKE THEM PAY...
YEAH, BOSS, THAT'S RIGHT... YOU GOTTA TAKE OVER THE MOBS AGAIN...
YES. YES. I MUST TAKE OVER... MAKE THEM PAY...
THE KINGPIN MUST MAKE THEM PAY...

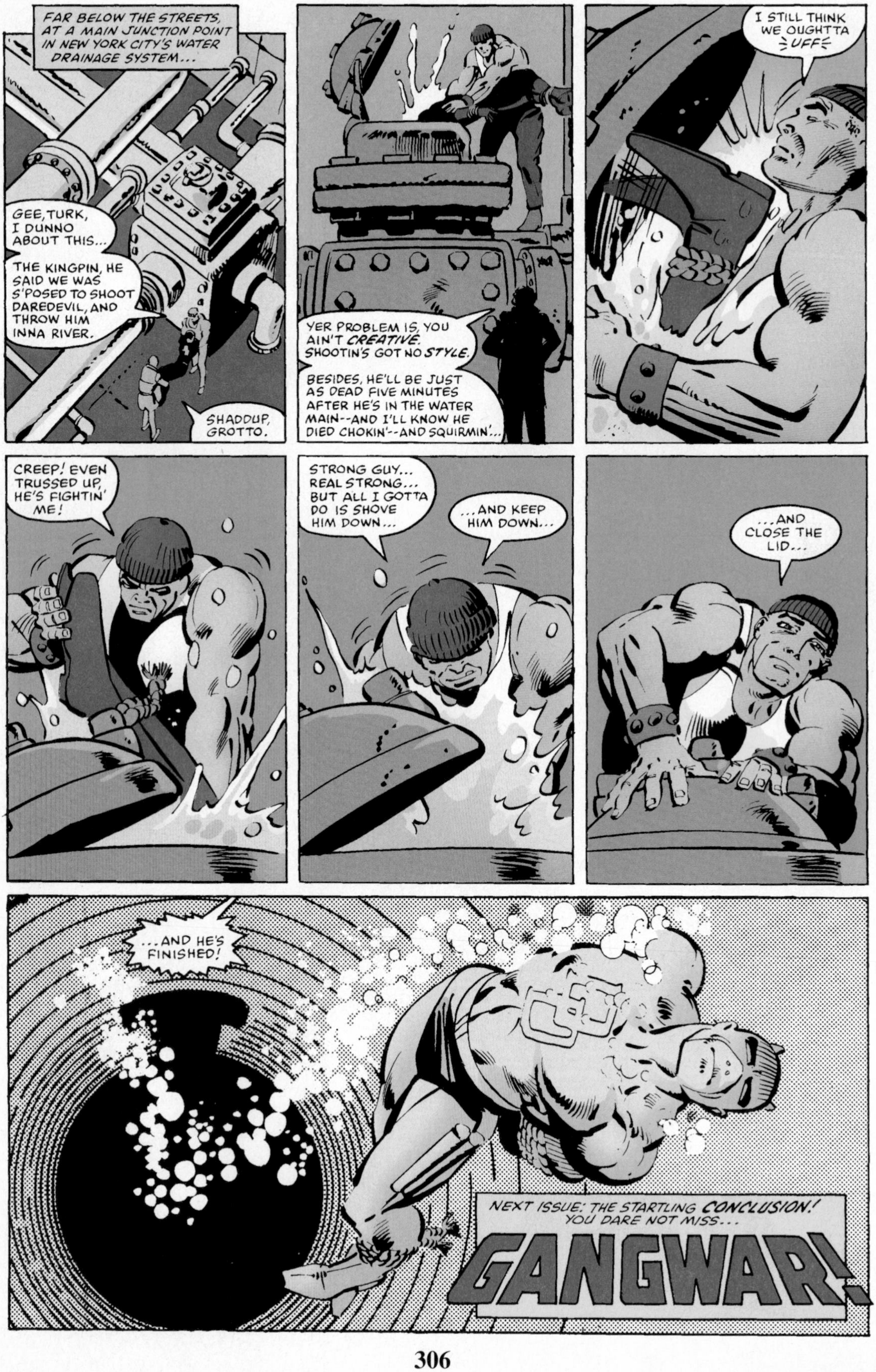

FAR BELOW THE STREETS, AT A MAIN JUNCTION POINT IN NEW YORK CITY'S WATER DRAINAGE SYSTEM...
GEE, TURK, I DUNNO ABOUT THIS...
THE KINGPIN, HE SAID WE WAS S'POSED TO SHOOT DAREDEVIL, AND THROW HIM INNA RIVER.
SHADDUP, GROTTO.
YER PROBLEM IS, YOU AIN'T CREATIVE. SHOOTIN'S GOT NO STYLE.
BESIDES, HE'LL BE JUST AS DEAD FIVE MINUTES AFTER HE'S IN THE WATER MAIN--AND I'LL KNOW HE DIED CHOKIN'--AND SQUIRMIN'...
I STILL THINK WE OUGHTTA
UFF
CREEP! EVEN TRUSSED UP, HE'S FIGHTIN' ME!
STRONG GUY... REAL STRONG... BUT ALL I GOTTA DO IS SHOVE HIM DOWN...
...AND KEEP HIM DOWN...
...AND CLOSE THE LID...
...AND HE'S FINISHED!
NEXT ISSUE: THE STARTLING CONCLUSION! YOU DARE NOT MISS...
GANGWAR!

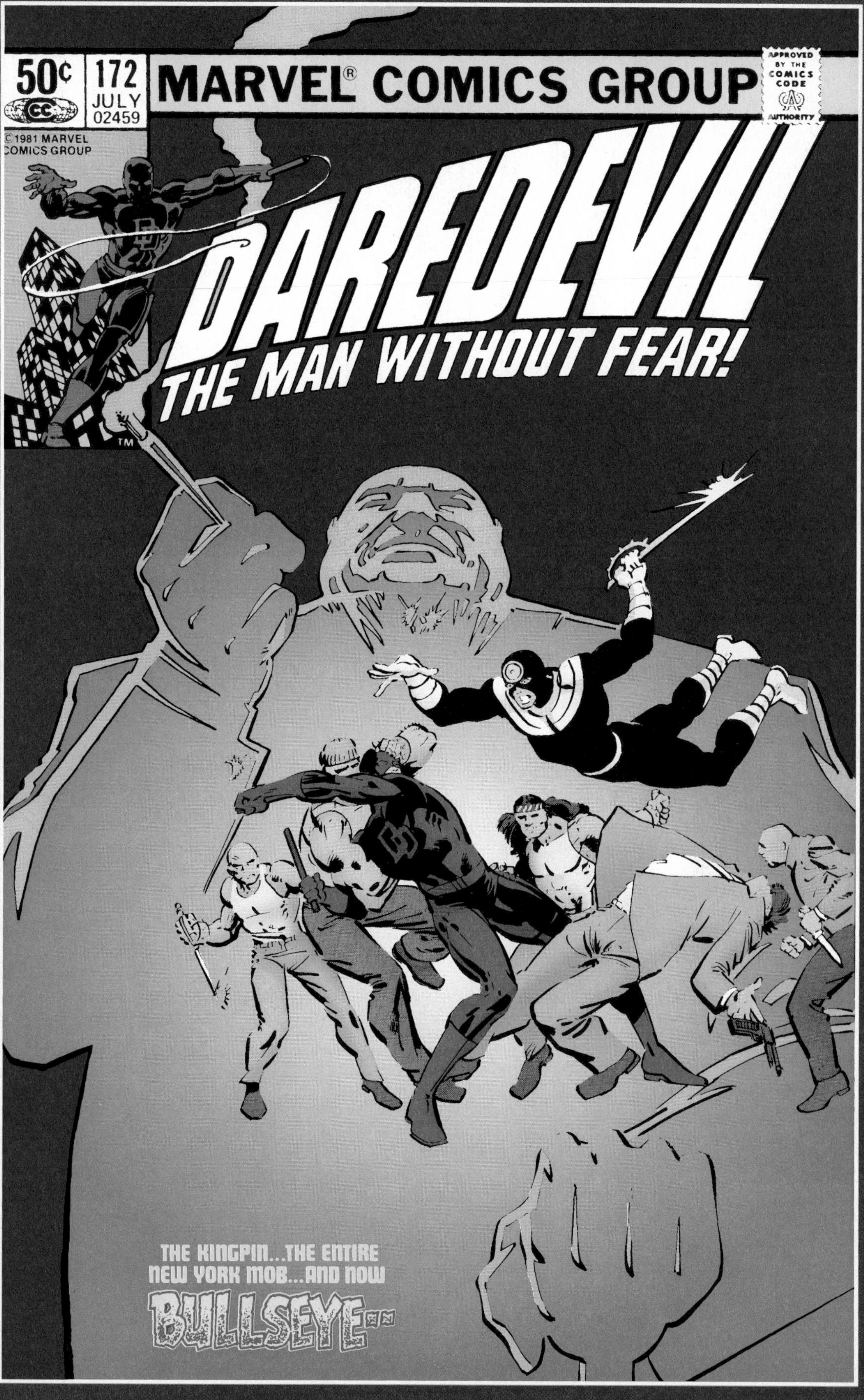

50¢
172
JULY
02459
CC
MARVEL® COMICS GROUP
APPROVED BY THE COMICS CODE AUTHORITY
©1981 MARVEL COMICS GROUP
DAREDEVIL
THE MAN WITHOUT FEAR!
TM
THE KINGPIN...THE ENTIRE
NEW YORK MOB...AND NOW
BULLSEYE--

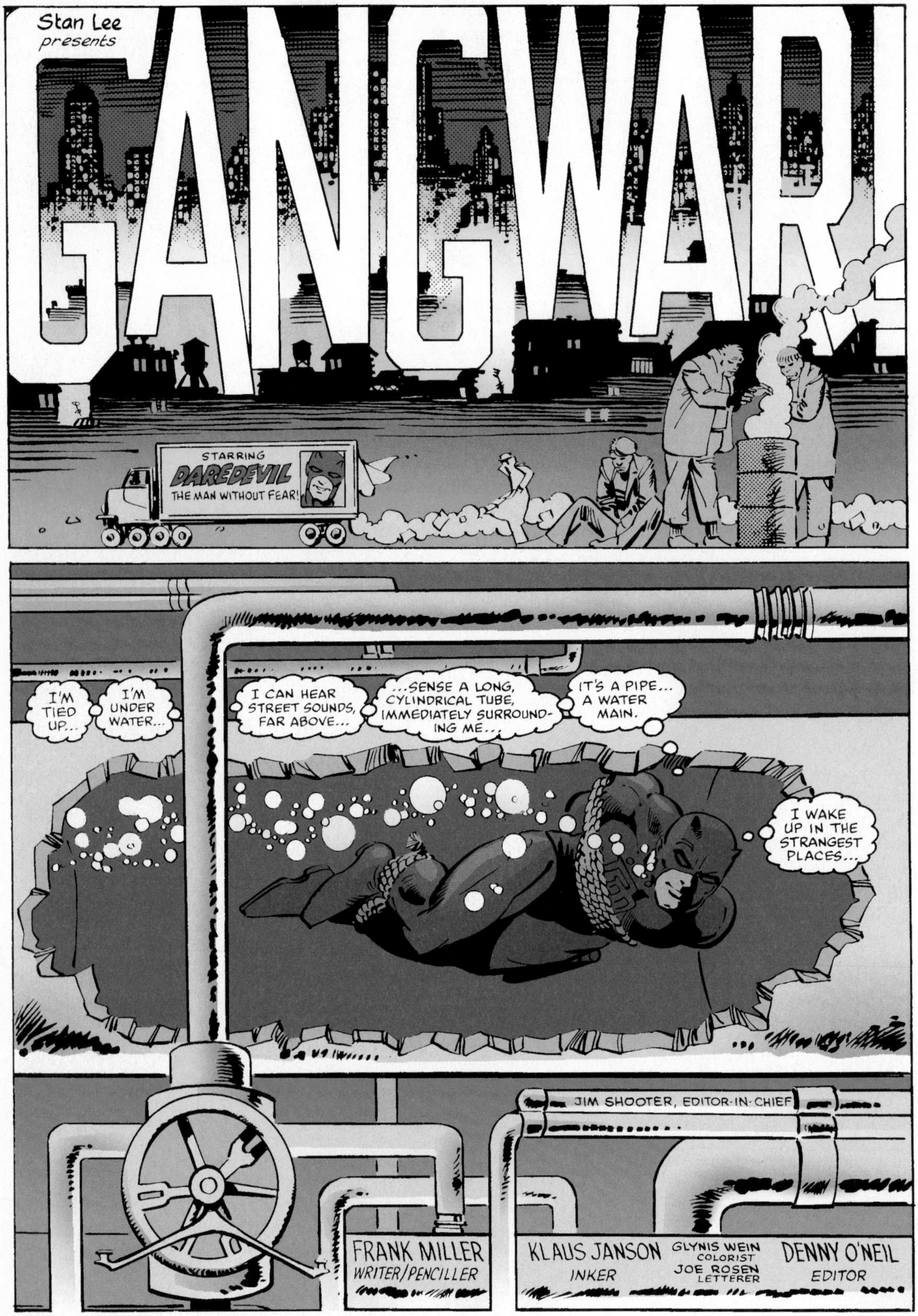
Stan Lee presents
GANGWAR!
STARRING
DAREDEVIL
THE MAN WITHOUT FEAR!
I'M TIED UP...
I'M UNDER WATER...
I CAN HEAR STREET SOUNDS, FAR ABOVE...
...SENSE A LONG, CYLINDRICAL TUBE, IMMEDIATELY SURROUNDING ME...
IT'S A PIPE... A WATER MAIN.
I WAKE UP IN THE STRANGEST PLACES...
JIM SHOOTER, EDITOR-IN-CHIEF
FRANK MILLER WRITER/PENCILLER
KLAUS JANSON INKER
GLYNIS WEIN COLORIST
JOE ROSEN LETTERER
DENNY O'NEIL EDITOR

Panel 1:

THREE MINUTES MORE OF THIS, MAYBE FOUR--

--AND I'M FINISHED.

HAVE TO MOVE SWIFTLY. CAN'T LET THE WORLD BE DEPRIVED OF ITS ONE AND ONLY BLIND SUPERHERO!

Panel 2:

OF COURSE, IF THE RADIATION THAT ROBBED MY SIGHT HADN'T HEIGHTENED MY REMAINING SENSES, I'D NEVER FIND MY WAY OUT OF HERE.

BUT THEN, I PROBABLY WOULDN'T MAKE A HABIT OF GETTING MYSELF INTO SITUATIONS LIKE THIS ONE, EITHER.

GOOD THING TURK HASN'T GOTTEN ANY BETTER AT TYING KNOTS. THERE THEY GO.

THAT TOOK ONE MINUTE.

LEAVING TWO.

Panel 3:

MY *RADAR SENSE* IS DULLED, DOWN HERE, BUT IT CAN STILL DETECT THIS JUNCTION WITH ANOTHER PIPE--

--AND I CAN FEEL THE CURRENT, PULLING ME TOWARD IT.

THIS COULD BE A WAY OUT.

Panel 4:

TIGHT SQUEEZE...

IF I WEREN'T BLIND, I MIGHT SEE A LIGHT AT THE END OF THE TUNNEL.

BUT I CAN'T. SO I JUST DON'T KNOW...

Panel 5:

I--I'M LOSING IT... BLACKING OUT...

I'LL NEVER MAKE IT...

IT'S TOO LATE...

Panel 6:

≥GASP!≤

I ≥KOFF≤ ≥KOFF≤ I DID IT!

I CAN *BREATHE*...

≥WHEW!≤ BUT THAT *SMELL*... WHAT THE...

WHO-- WHO ARE THESE PEOPLE?

Panel 7:

MONEY FOR FOOD...

MONEY FOR FOOD...

MONEY FOR FOOD...

THEY'RE VAGABONDS... LIVING HERE, BELOW THE CITY.

PLEASE-- STAY AWAY. I CAN'T HELP YOU.

I'M *SORRY*...

MONEY FOR FOOD...

LATER...

I'M *SORRY*, JOSIE. I'LL PAY THE TAB NEXT WEEK, I SWEAR!

JUS' GIMME ANOTHER BREW.

JOSIE'S BAR

THAT'S WHAT YOU SAID LAST WEEK, TURK. *AND* THE WEEK BEFORE.

THIS TIME I MEAN IT, JOSIE. HONEST.

I JUS' FINISHED A BIG JOB...

...AN' SOON AS I GET PAID, I'M GONNA BE ROLLIN' IN DOUGH!

YEAH. I'D CALL SNUFFIN' *DAREDEVIL* A BIG JOB, ALL RIGHT.

AN' IT'S GONNA MAKE ME A BIG MAN WITH THE KINGPIN, YES SIR...

AFTER THIS, NOBODY'S GONNA DARE MESS WITH ME. NOBODY WHO'S FOND OF LIVIN', ANYW--

HUH?

NAW... THAT AIN'T... HE COULDN'T...

DIDJA HAFTA, DD? DIDJA?

AW JEEZ-- HE'S HEADIN' FER THE WINDOW!

DD, PLEASE-- THAT'S THREE THIS WEEK! YOU KNOW HOW MUCH THEM THINGS COST?

DON'T WORRY, JOSIE. US DAREDEVILS COME WELL-EQUIPPED.

NOTE THE ALL-PURPOSE *BILLY CLUB*, COMPLETE WITH A THIRTY FOOT NYLON CORD.

KDAK

IT'S GOOD FOR SNAGGING LEDGES-- OR FLAGPOLES--

--OR CROOKS.

THAPP

I KILLED HIM. I *KILLED* HIM.

HOW'D HE GET AWAY THIS TIME?

HOW?

RELAX, TURK. I'M NOT ANGRY.

JUST CURIOUS.

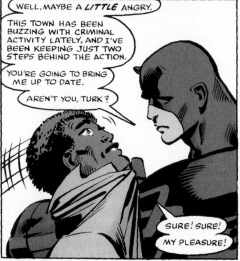

WELL, MAYBE A *LITTLE* ANGRY.

THIS TOWN HAS BEEN BUZZING WITH CRIMINAL ACTIVITY LATELY, AND I'VE BEEN KEEPING JUST TWO STEPS BEHIND THE ACTION.

YOU'RE GOING TO BRING ME UP TO DATE.

AREN'T YOU, *TURK?*

SURE! SURE! MY PLEASURE!

REMEMBER THE KINGPIN OF CRIME? HE USED TO RUN THE MOBS.

WELL, HE'S GOT THIS WIFE, *VANESSA*, WHAT CONVINCED HIM TO RETIRE AND MOVE TO JAPAN. AN' EVERYTHING WOULDA' BEEN OKAY IF THAT'S ALL HE DID. BUT IT AIN'T.

VANESSA, SHE NAGGED HIM INTA AGREEING TO TURN OVER STATE'S EVIDENCE AGAINST HIS TOP MEN--THE MEN WHAT RUN THINGS NOW THAT HE'S GONE.

THING IS, THE NEW CRIMELORDS GOT WIND OF WHAT HE WAS UP TO. SO THEY *KIDNAPPED* THE BROAD WHEN SHE CAME HERE TO HIRE A SHYSTER FER THE KINGPIN.

Y'SEE, THEY WANTED THE KINGPIN TO COME BACK, JUST SO'S THEY COULD HAVE HIM KILLED.

TO DO THAT, THEY HIRED *BULLSEYE*, CUZ WHEN IT COMES TO KILLIN', HE'S THE BEST.

ANYWAY, THE KINGPIN CAME TO NEW YORK FER HIS LADY. AN' HE BROUGHT HIS FILES.

THAT'S WHEN *YOU* DECIDED TO GET CLEVER.

YOU DISGUISED YERSELF AND GOT HIRED BY THE KINGPIN. THEN YOU TRIED TO STEAL THAT STATE'S EVIDENCE.

BUT HE WAS SMARTER THAN YOU-- SMARTER AND TOUGHER. HE DECKED YOU BUT GOOD AN' HAD ME DROP YOU INNA WATER MAIN.

THEN HE WENT TO MEET THE CRIME-LORDS AN' TRADE THE EVIDENCE FER HIS LADY.

THING IS, JUST WHEN HE'D CLOBBERED THEM AND WAS GONNA FREE THE BIM, SOMEBODY UP AND DROPPED A BUILDING ON HER.

NOW, THE KINGPIN'S OUT FER BLOOD. HE'S TAKIN' OVER THE MOBS AGAIN-- AN' AIN'T NOTHIN' GONNA STOP HIM.

WE'LL SEE.

MEANWHILE, I'M GOING TO GET MY HANDS ON THOSE FILES. AND, TURK, YOU'RE NOT WORKING FOR THE KINGPIN. NOT ANY MORE.

YOU'RE WORKING FOR ME.

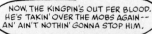

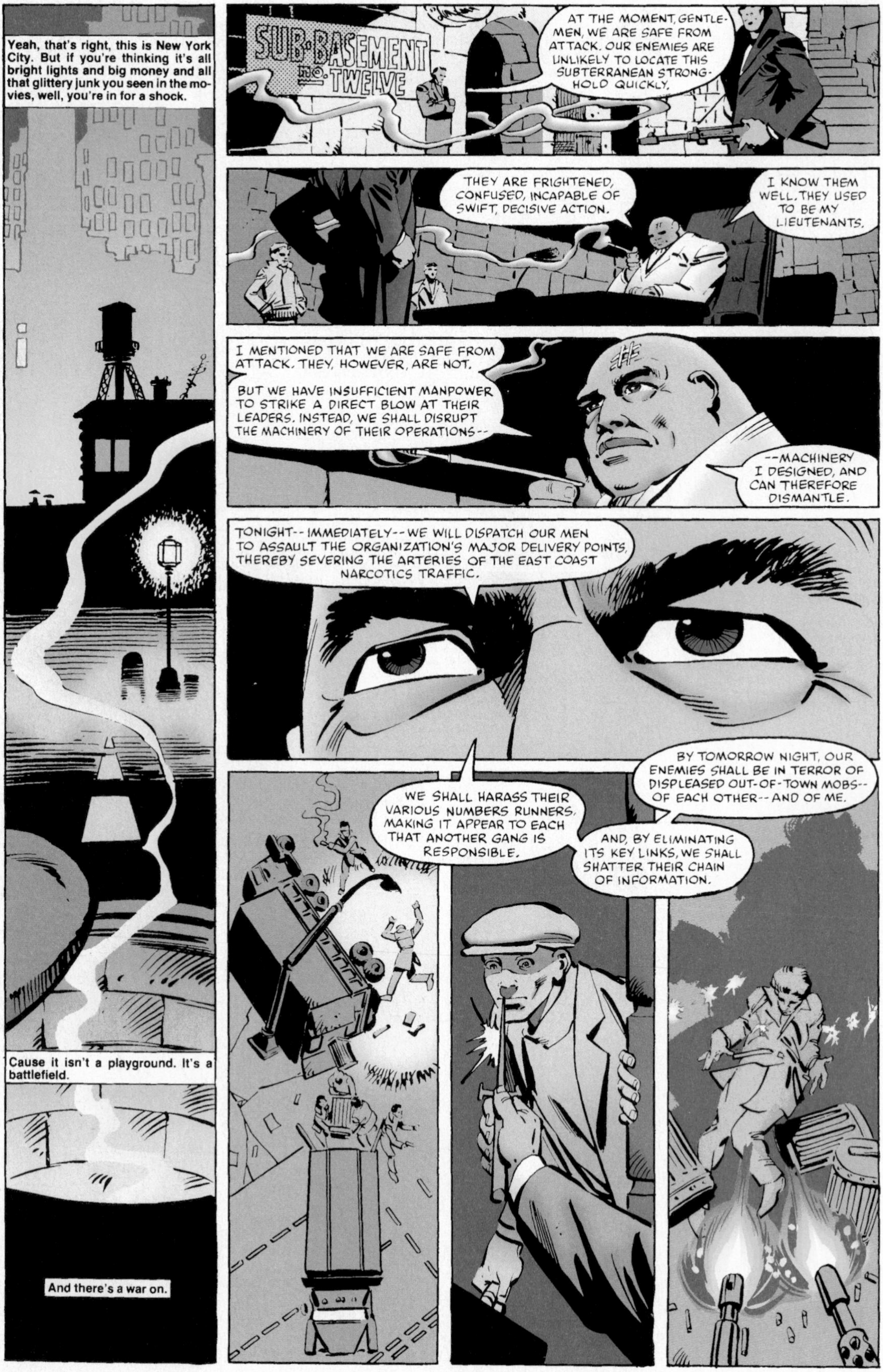

Yeah, that's right, this is New York City. But if you're thinking it's all bright lights and big money and all that glittery junk you seen in the movies, well, you're in for a shock.
SUB-BASEMENT No. TWELVE
AT THE MOMENT, GENTLEMEN, WE ARE SAFE FROM ATTACK. OUR ENEMIES ARE UNLIKELY TO LOCATE THIS SUBTERRANEAN STRONGHOLD QUICKLY.
THEY ARE FRIGHTENED, CONFUSED, INCAPABLE OF SWIFT, DECISIVE ACTION.
I KNOW THEM WELL. THEY USED TO BE MY LIEUTENANTS.
I MENTIONED THAT WE ARE SAFE FROM ATTACK. THEY, HOWEVER, ARE NOT.
BUT WE HAVE INSUFFICIENT MANPOWER TO STRIKE A DIRECT BLOW AT THEIR LEADERS. INSTEAD, WE SHALL DISRUPT THE MACHINERY OF THEIR OPERATIONS--
--MACHINERY I DESIGNED, AND CAN THEREFORE DISMANTLE.
TONIGHT-- IMMEDIATELY-- WE WILL DISPATCH OUR MEN TO ASSAULT THE ORGANIZATION'S MAJOR DELIVERY POINTS, THEREBY SEVERING THE ARTERIES OF THE EAST COAST NARCOTICS TRAFFIC.
WE SHALL HARASS THEIR VARIOUS NUMBERS RUNNERS, MAKING IT APPEAR TO EACH THAT ANOTHER GANG IS RESPONSIBLE.
AND, BY ELIMINATING ITS KEY LINKS, WE SHALL SHATTER THEIR CHAIN OF INFORMATION.
BY TOMORROW NIGHT, OUR ENEMIES SHALL BE IN TERROR OF DISPLEASED OUT-OF-TOWN MOBS-- OF EACH OTHER-- AND OF ME.
Cause it isn't a playground. It's a battlefield.
And there's a war on.

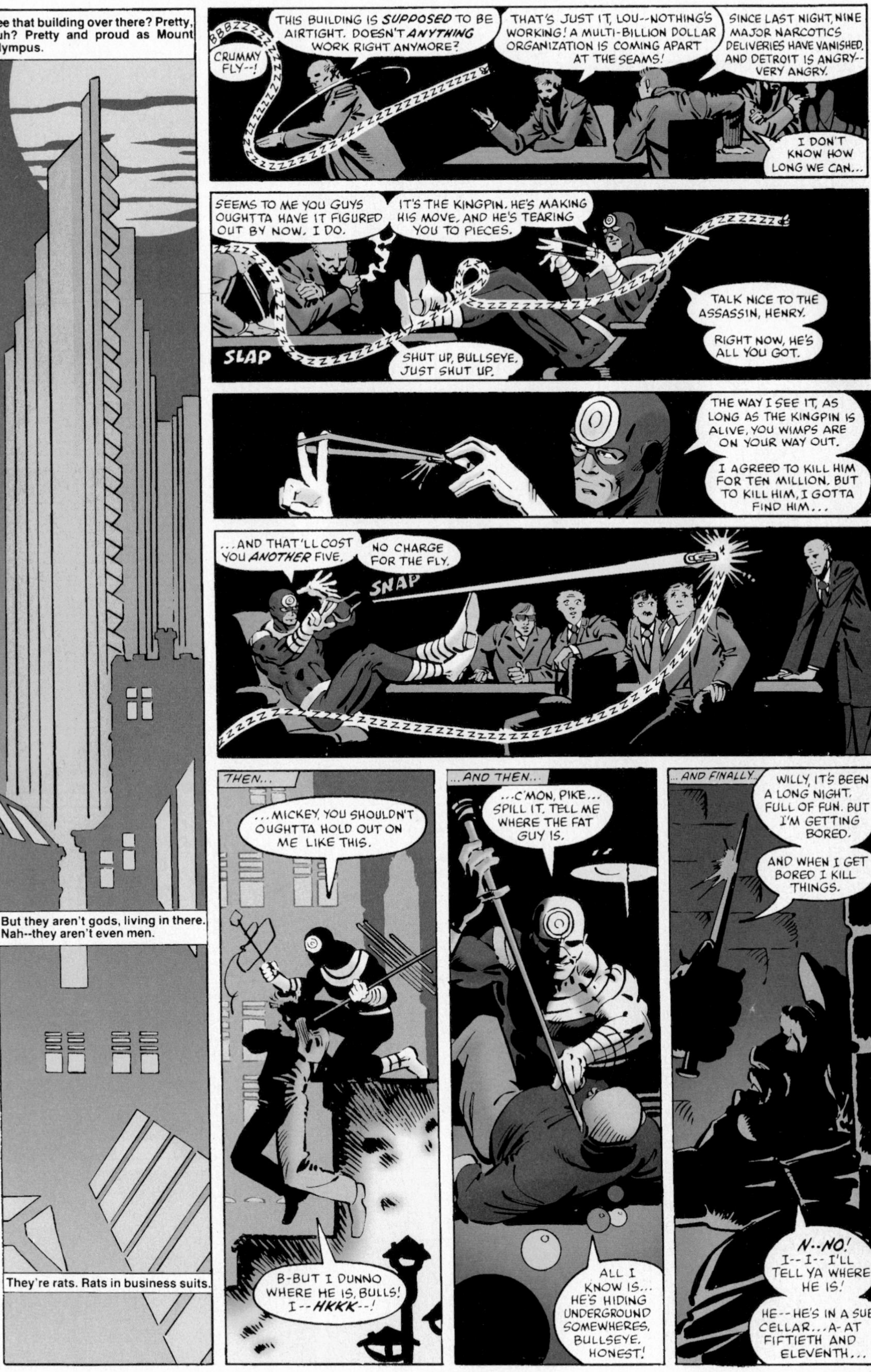

See that building over there? Pretty, huh? Pretty and proud as Mount Olympus.
But they aren't gods, living in there. Nah--they aren't even men.
They're rats. Rats in business suits.
BBBZZZZZ
CRUMMY FLY--!
THIS BUILDING IS SUPPOSED TO BE AIRTIGHT. DOESN'T ANYTHING WORK RIGHT ANYMORE?
THAT'S JUST IT, LOU--NOTHING'S WORKING! A MULTI-BILLION DOLLAR ORGANIZATION IS COMING APART AT THE SEAMS!
SINCE LAST NIGHT, NINE MAJOR NARCOTICS DELIVERIES HAVE VANISHED, AND DETROIT IS ANGRY--VERY ANGRY.
I DON'T KNOW HOW LONG WE CAN...
SEEMS TO ME YOU GUYS OUGHTTA HAVE IT FIGURED OUT BY NOW. I DO.
IT'S THE KINGPIN. HE'S MAKING HIS MOVE, AND HE'S TEARING YOU TO PIECES.
SLAP
SHUT UP, BULLSEYE, JUST SHUT UP.
TALK NICE TO THE ASSASSIN, HENRY.
RIGHT NOW, HE'S ALL YOU GOT.
THE WAY I SEE IT, AS LONG AS THE KINGPIN IS ALIVE, YOU WIMPS ARE ON YOUR WAY OUT.
I AGREED TO KILL HIM FOR TEN MILLION. BUT TO KILL HIM, I GOTTA FIND HIM...
...AND THAT'LL COST YOU ANOTHER FIVE.
NO CHARGE FOR THE FLY.
SNAP
THEN...
...MICKEY, YOU SHOULDN'T OUGHTTA HOLD OUT ON ME LIKE THIS.
B-BUT I DUNNO WHERE HE IS, BULLS! I--HKKK--!
...AND THEN...
...C'MON, PIKE... SPILL IT. TELL ME WHERE THE FAT GUY IS.
ALL I KNOW IS... HE'S HIDING UNDERGROUND SOMEWHERES, BULLSEYE. HONEST!
...AND FINALLY...
WILLY, IT'S BEEN A LONG NIGHT. FULL OF FUN. BUT I'M GETTING BORED.
AND WHEN I GET BORED I KILL THINGS.
N--NO! I-- I-- I'LL TELL YA WHERE HE IS!
HE--HE'S IN A SUB-CELLAR...A-AT FIFTIETH AND ELEVENTH...

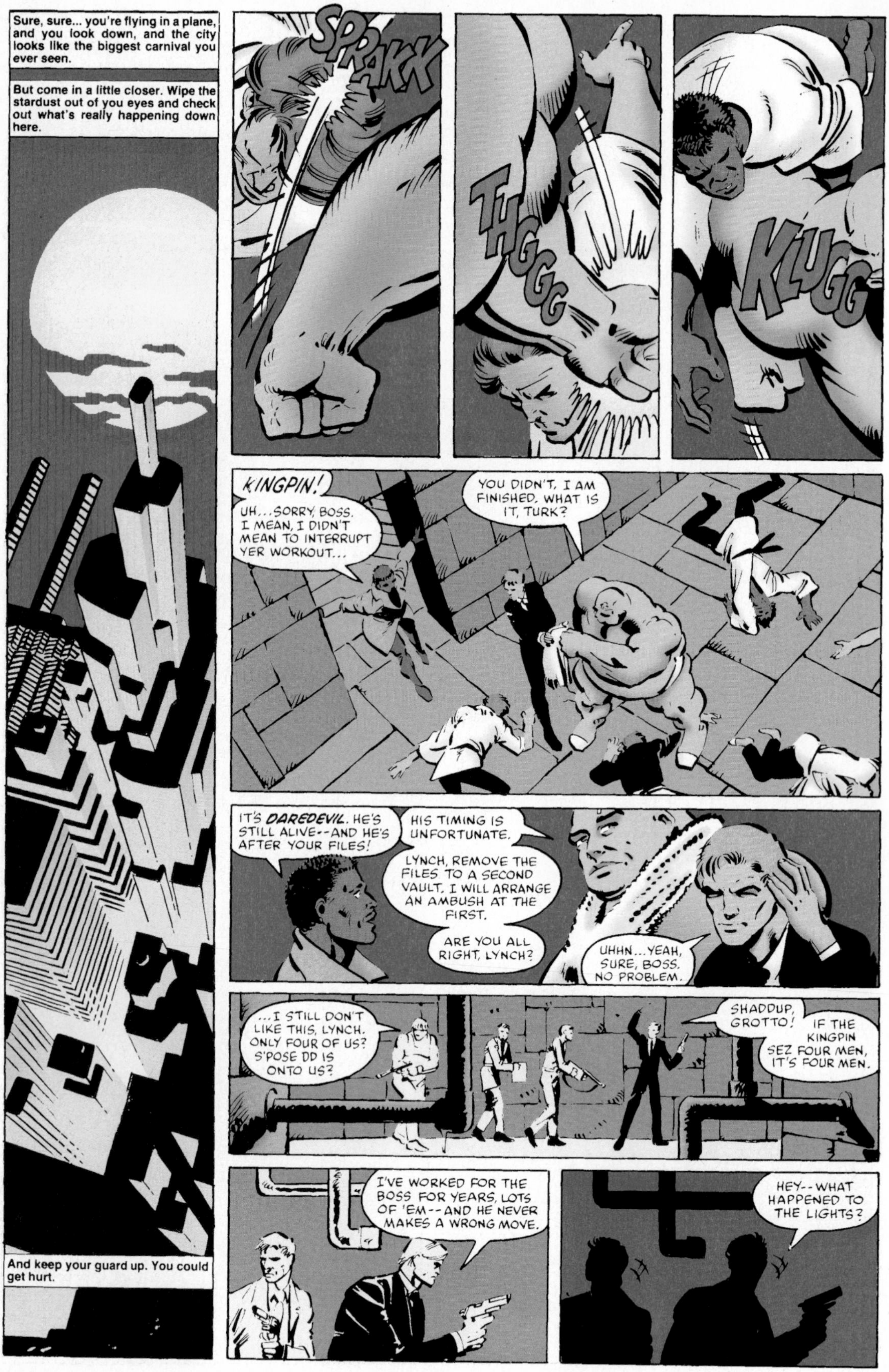

Sure, sure... you're flying in a plane, and you look down, and the city looks like the biggest carnival you ever seen.
But come in a little closer. Wipe the stardust out of you eyes and check out what's really happening down here.
SPRAKK
THGGG
KLUGG
KINGPIN!
UH... SORRY, BOSS. I MEAN, I DIDN'T MEAN TO INTERRUPT YER WORKOUT...
YOU DIDN'T. I AM FINISHED. WHAT IS IT, TURK?
IT'S DAREDEVIL. HE'S STILL ALIVE--AND HE'S AFTER YOUR FILES!
HIS TIMING IS UNFORTUNATE.
LYNCH, REMOVE THE FILES TO A SECOND VAULT. I WILL ARRANGE AN AMBUSH AT THE FIRST.
ARE YOU ALL RIGHT, LYNCH?
UHHN... YEAH, SURE, BOSS. NO PROBLEM.
...I STILL DON'T LIKE THIS, LYNCH. ONLY FOUR OF US? S'POSE DD IS ONTO US?
SHADDUP, GROTTO!
IF THE KINGPIN SEZ FOUR MEN, IT'S FOUR MEN.
I'VE WORKED FOR THE BOSS FOR YEARS, LOTS OF 'EM--AND HE NEVER MAKES A WRONG MOVE.
HEY--WHAT HAPPENED TO THE LIGHTS?
And keep your guard up. You could get hurt.

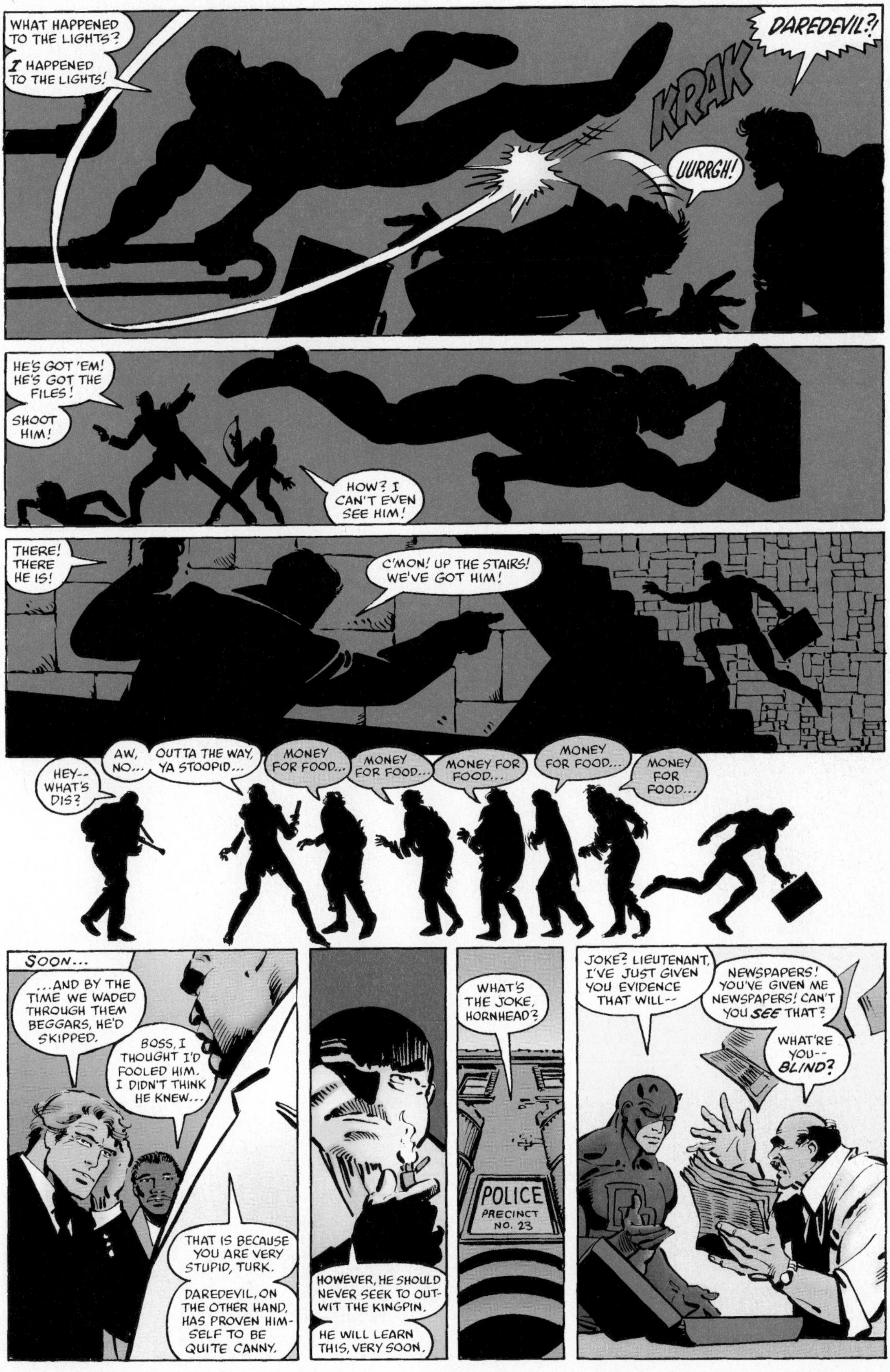
WHAT HAPPENED TO THE LIGHTS?
I HAPPENED TO THE LIGHTS!
DAREDEVIL?!
KRAK
UURRGH!
HE'S GOT 'EM! HE'S GOT THE FILES!
SHOOT HIM!
HOW? I CAN'T EVEN SEE HIM!
THERE! THERE HE IS!
C'MON! UP THE STAIRS! WE'VE GOT HIM!
HEY-- WHAT'S DIS?
AW, NO...
OUTTA THE WAY, YA STOOPID...
MONEY FOR FOOD...
MONEY FOR FOOD...
MONEY FOR FOOD...
MONEY FOR FOOD...
MONEY FOR FOOD...
SOON...
...AND BY THE TIME WE WADED THROUGH THEM BEGGARS, HE'D SKIPPED.
BOSS, I THOUGHT I'D FOOLED HIM. I DIDN'T THINK HE KNEW...
THAT IS BECAUSE YOU ARE VERY STUPID, TURK.
DAREDEVIL, ON THE OTHER HAND, HAS PROVEN HIMSELF TO BE QUITE CANNY.
HOWEVER, HE SHOULD NEVER SEEK TO OUTWIT THE KINGPIN.
HE WILL LEARN THIS, VERY SOON.
WHAT'S THE JOKE, HORNHEAD?
POLICE PRECINCT NO. 23
JOKE? LIEUTENANT, I'VE JUST GIVEN YOU EVIDENCE THAT WILL--
NEWSPAPERS! YOU'VE GIVEN ME NEWSPAPERS! CAN'T YOU SEE THAT?
WHAT'RE YOU-- BLIND?

But the bottom line is that it's still the greatest town there ever was. Anywhere.

Once you're here it'll change you-- It'll make you one of its people. You'll grow to love it.

Thing is, to love New York, you gotta know it. And to know it, you gotta take the bad with the good.

And sometimes, there's an awful lot of bad...

CRIPES, IS THIS THING HEAVY OR WHAT?

QUIET BACK THERE!

WE'RE RIGHT OUTSIDE THE KINGPIN'S SUB-CELLAR. LET'S NOT ADVERTISE THAT, OKAY?

LET'S SEE IF YOUR BOSS'S BATTLE PLAN HOLDS ANY WATER.

CA-MON! MOVE IT, WILLYA? SET UP THAT GUN WHILE YOU'RE STILL YOUNG ENOUGH TO FIRE IT.

OKAY, OKAY. IT'S READY.

THEN SHOOT IT, FER--

WHOOM

NOBODY HOME.

GOTTA GIVE FATSO CREDIT. HE'S SHARP AS A--

HEY!

TAK

WHAT THE...

THE CEILING!

IT'S COMING DOWN!

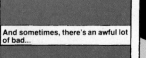

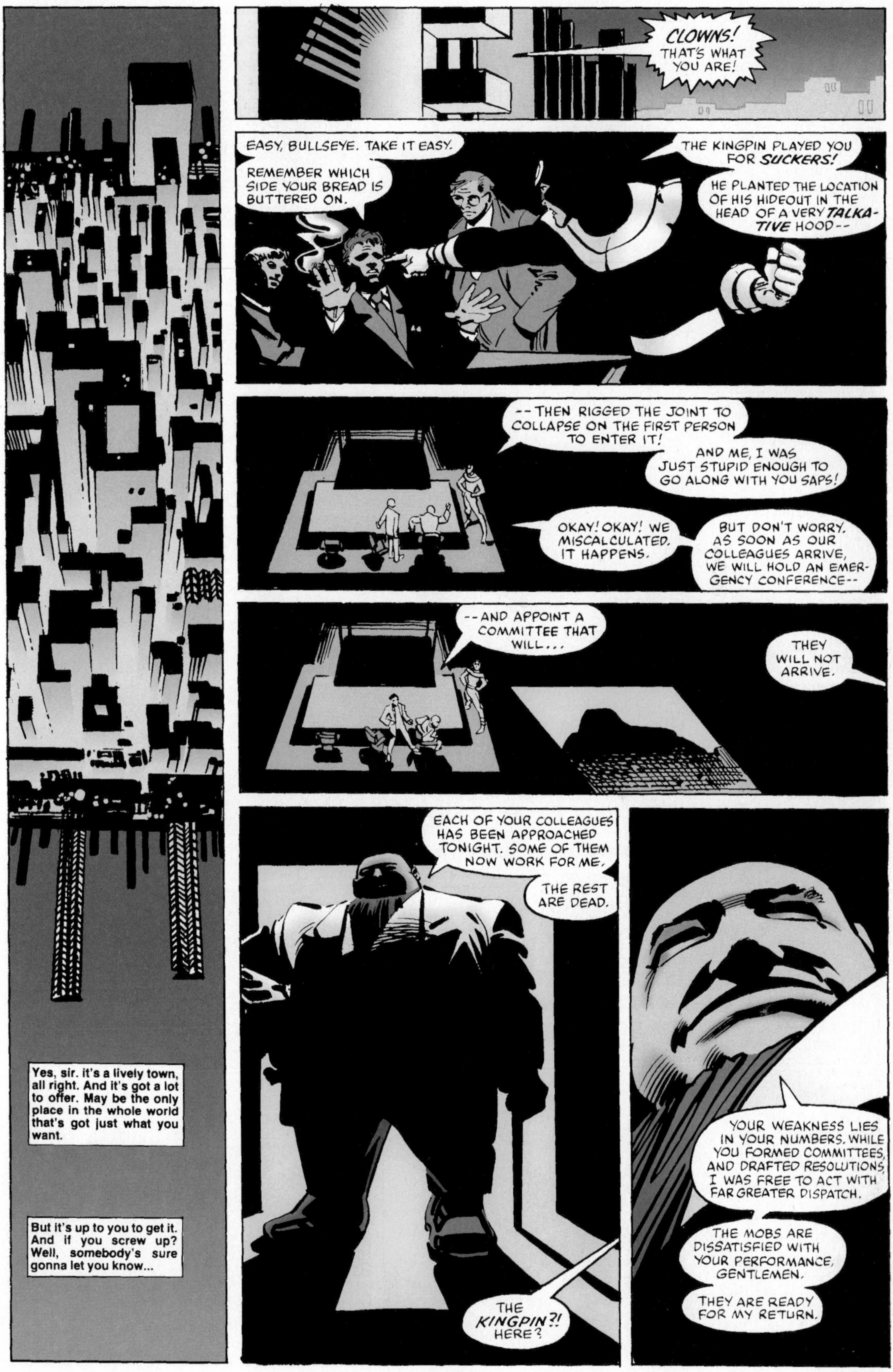

CLOWNS! THAT'S WHAT YOU ARE!
EASY, BULLSEYE. TAKE IT EASY.
REMEMBER WHICH SIDE YOUR BREAD IS BUTTERED ON.
THE KINGPIN PLAYED YOU FOR SUCKERS!
HE PLANTED THE LOCATION OF HIS HIDEOUT IN THE HEAD OF A VERY TALKATIVE HOOD--
--THEN RIGGED THE JOINT TO COLLAPSE ON THE FIRST PERSON TO ENTER IT!
AND ME, I WAS JUST STUPID ENOUGH TO GO ALONG WITH YOU SAPS!
OKAY! OKAY! WE MISCALCULATED. IT HAPPENS.
BUT DON'T WORRY. AS SOON AS OUR COLLEAGUES ARRIVE, WE WILL HOLD AN EMERGENCY CONFERENCE--
--AND APPOINT A COMMITTEE THAT WILL...
THEY WILL NOT ARRIVE.
EACH OF YOUR COLLEAGUES HAS BEEN APPROACHED TONIGHT. SOME OF THEM NOW WORK FOR ME.
THE REST ARE DEAD.
THE KINGPIN?! HERE?
YOUR WEAKNESS LIES IN YOUR NUMBERS. WHILE YOU FORMED COMMITTEES, AND DRAFTED RESOLUTIONS, I WAS FREE TO ACT WITH FAR GREATER DISPATCH.
THE MOBS ARE DISSATISFIED WITH YOUR PERFORMANCE, GENTLEMEN.
THEY ARE READY FOR MY RETURN.
Yes, sir. it's a lively town, all right. And it's got a lot to offer. May be the only place in the whole world that's got just what you want.
But it's up to you to get it. And if you screw up? Well, somebody's sure gonna let you know...

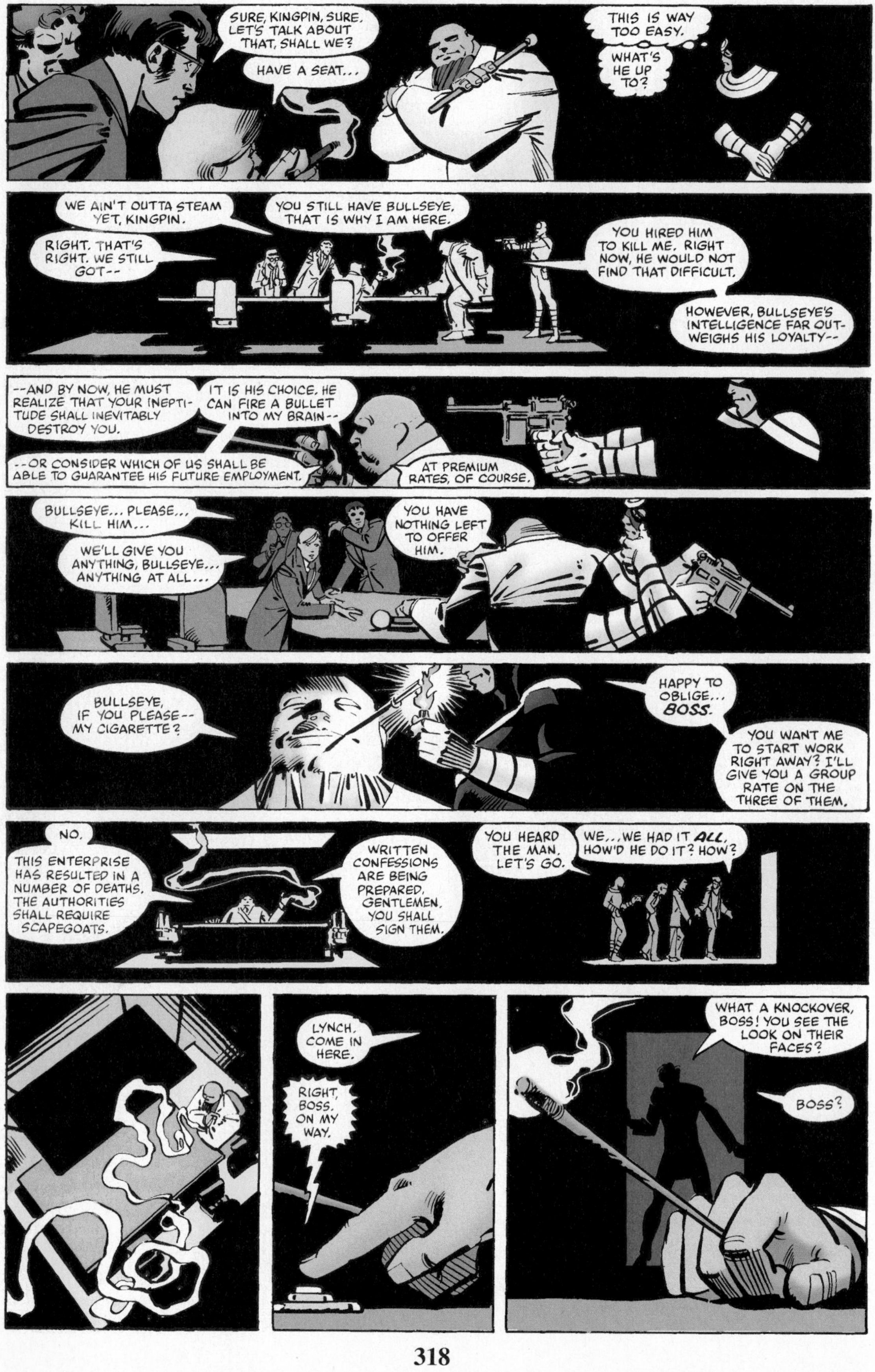
SURE, KINGPIN, SURE. LET'S TALK ABOUT THAT, SHALL WE?
HAVE A SEAT...
THIS IS WAY TOO EASY.
WHAT'S HE UP TO?
WE AIN'T OUTTA STEAM YET, KINGPIN.
RIGHT. THAT'S RIGHT. WE STILL GOT--
YOU STILL HAVE BULLSEYE. THAT IS WHY I AM HERE.
YOU HIRED HIM TO KILL ME. RIGHT NOW, HE WOULD NOT FIND THAT DIFFICULT.
HOWEVER, BULLSEYE'S INTELLIGENCE FAR OUT-WEIGHS HIS LOYALTY--
--AND BY NOW, HE MUST REALIZE THAT YOUR INEPTI-TUDE SHALL INEVITABLY DESTROY YOU.
IT IS HIS CHOICE. HE CAN FIRE A BULLET INTO MY BRAIN--
--OR CONSIDER WHICH OF US SHALL BE ABLE TO GUARANTEE HIS FUTURE EMPLOYMENT.
AT PREMIUM RATES, OF COURSE.
BULLSEYE... PLEASE... KILL HIM...
WE'LL GIVE YOU ANYTHING, BULLSEYE... ANYTHING AT ALL...
YOU HAVE NOTHING LEFT TO OFFER HIM.
BULLSEYE, IF YOU PLEASE-- MY CIGARETTE?
HAPPY TO OBLIGE... BOSS.
YOU WANT ME TO START WORK RIGHT AWAY? I'LL GIVE YOU A GROUP RATE ON THE THREE OF THEM.
NO.
THIS ENTERPRISE HAS RESULTED IN A NUMBER OF DEATHS. THE AUTHORITIES SHALL REQUIRE SCAPEGOATS.
WRITTEN CONFESSIONS ARE BEING PREPARED, GENTLEMEN. YOU SHALL SIGN THEM.
YOU HEARD THE MAN. LET'S GO.
WE... WE HAD IT ALL. HOW'D HE DO IT? HOW?
LYNCH. COME IN HERE.
RIGHT, BOSS. ON MY WAY.
WHAT A KNOCKOVER, BOSS! YOU SEE THE LOOK ON THEIR FACES?
BOSS?

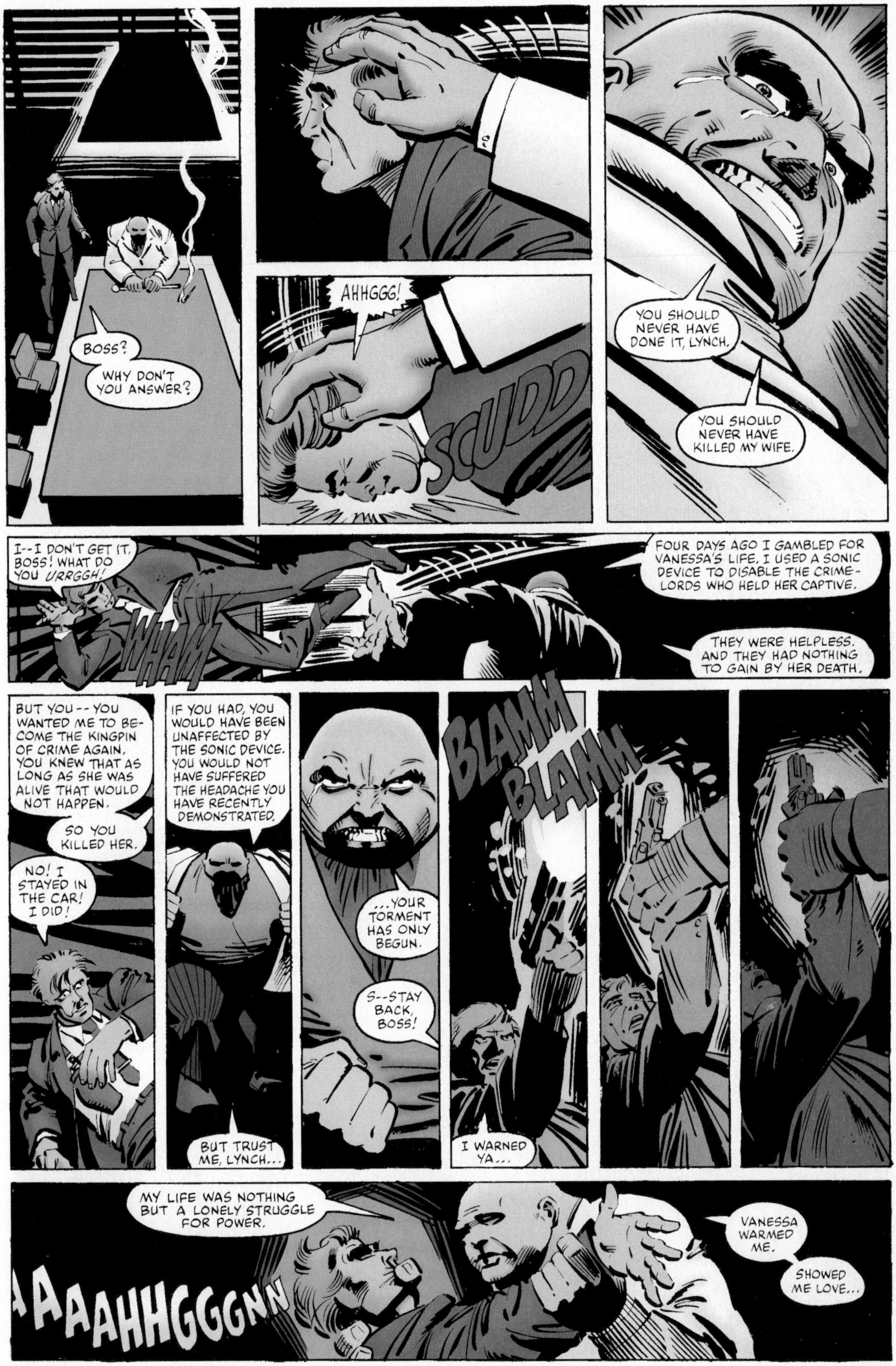
BOSS?
WHY DON'T YOU ANSWER?
AHHGGG!
SCUDD
YOU SHOULD NEVER HAVE DONE IT, LYNCH.
YOU SHOULD NEVER HAVE KILLED MY WIFE.
I--I DON'T GET IT, BOSS! WHAT DO YOU URRGGH!
WHAM
FOUR DAYS AGO I GAMBLED FOR VANESSA'S LIFE. I USED A SONIC DEVICE TO DISABLE THE CRIME-LORDS WHO HELD HER CAPTIVE.
THEY WERE HELPLESS. AND THEY HAD NOTHING TO GAIN BY HER DEATH.
BUT YOU--YOU WANTED ME TO BECOME THE KINGPIN OF CRIME AGAIN. YOU KNEW THAT AS LONG AS SHE WAS ALIVE THAT WOULD NOT HAPPEN.
SO YOU KILLED HER.
NO! I STAYED IN THE CAR! I DID!
IF YOU HAD, YOU WOULD HAVE BEEN UNAFFECTED BY THE SONIC DEVICE. YOU WOULD NOT HAVE SUFFERED THE HEADACHE YOU HAVE RECENTLY DEMONSTRATED.
BUT TRUST ME, LYNCH...
...YOUR TORMENT HAS ONLY BEGUN.
S--STAY BACK, BOSS!
BLAMM
BLAMM
I WARNED YA...
MY LIFE WAS NOTHING BUT A LONELY STRUGGLE FOR POWER.
AAAAHHGGGNN
VANESSA WARMED ME.
SHOWED ME LOVE...

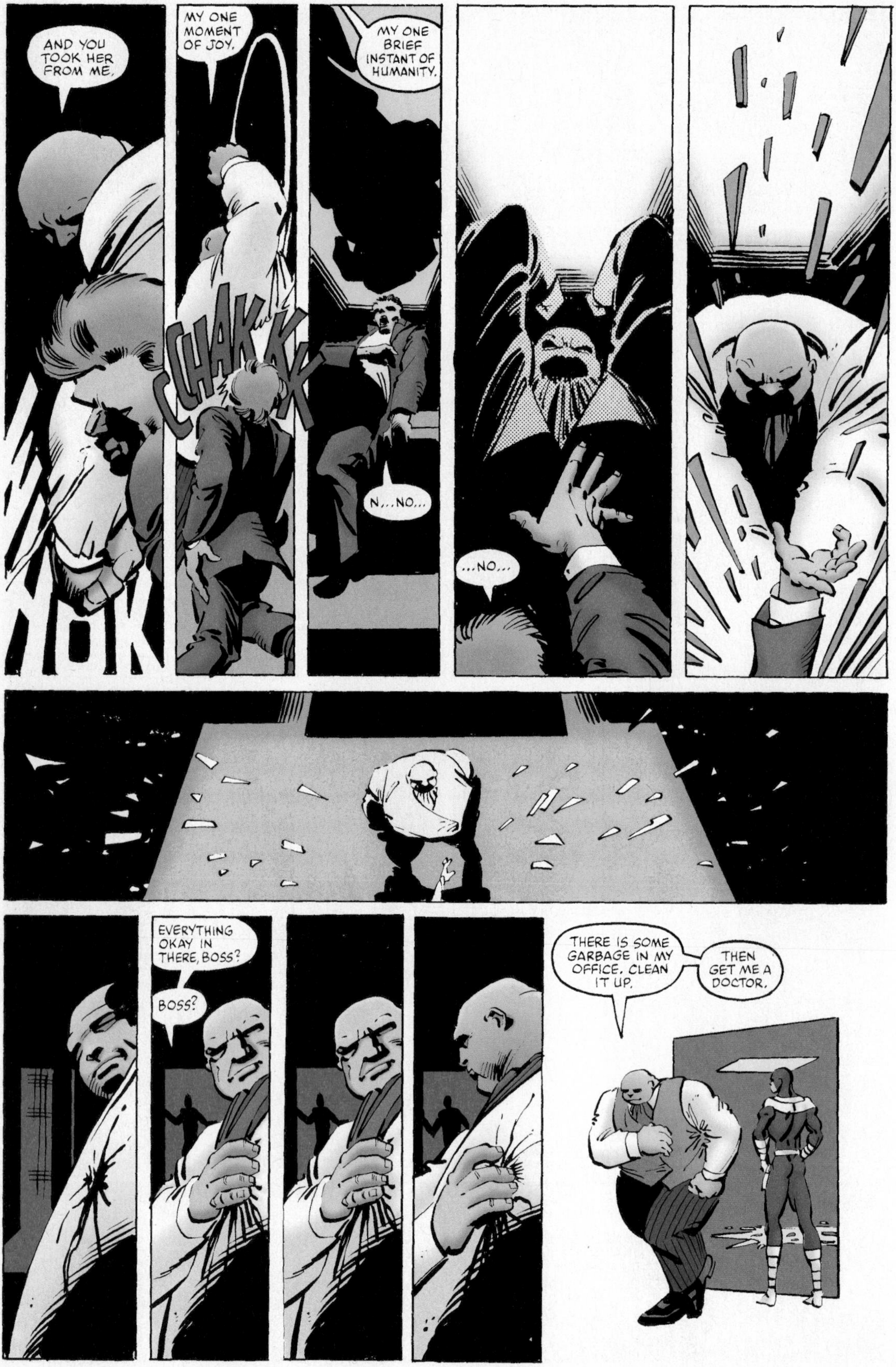
AND YOU TOOK HER FROM ME.
MY ONE MOMENT OF JOY.
CHAKKK
MY ONE BRIEF INSTANT OF HUMANITY.
N...NO...
...NO...
EVERYTHING OKAY IN THERE, BOSS?
BOSS?
THERE IS SOME GARBAGE IN MY OFFICE. CLEAN IT UP.
THEN GET ME A DOCTOR.

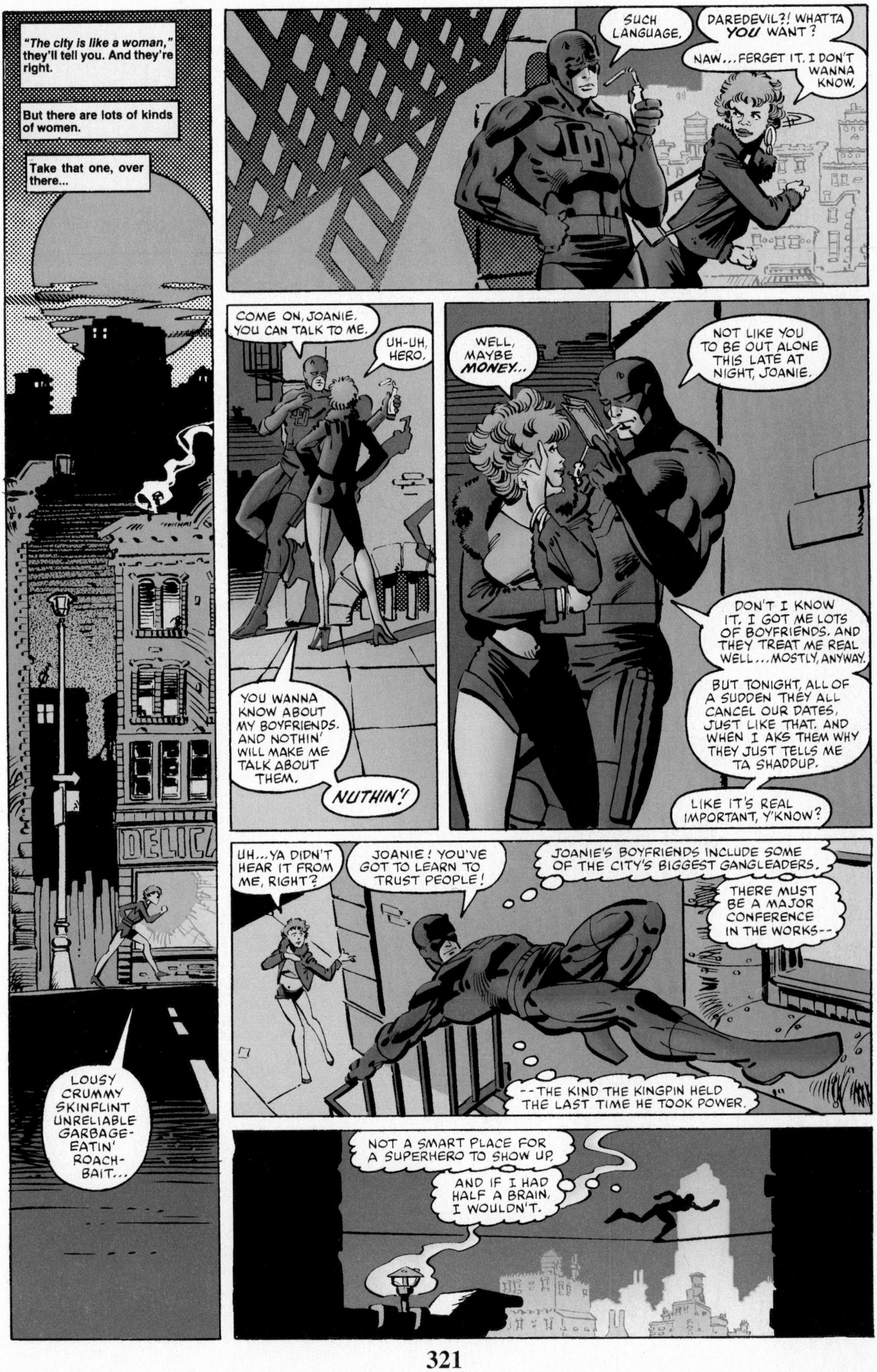
"The city is like a woman," they'll tell you. And they're right.
But there are lots of kinds of women.
Take that one, over there...
DELICA
LOUSY CRUMMY SKINFLINT UNRELIABLE GARBAGE-EATIN' ROACH-BAIT...
SUCH LANGUAGE.
DAREDEVIL?! WHATTA YOU WANT?
NAW... FERGET IT. I DON'T WANNA KNOW.
COME ON, JOANIE. YOU CAN TALK TO ME.
UH-UH, HERO.
YOU WANNA KNOW ABOUT MY BOYFRIENDS. AND NOTHIN' WILL MAKE ME TALK ABOUT THEM.
NUTHIN'!
WELL, MAYBE MONEY...
NOT LIKE YOU TO BE OUT ALONE THIS LATE AT NIGHT, JOANIE.
DON'T I KNOW IT. I GOT ME LOTS OF BOYFRIENDS. AND THEY TREAT ME REAL WELL... MOSTLY, ANYWAY.
BUT TONIGHT, ALL OF A SUDDEN THEY ALL CANCEL OUR DATES, JUST LIKE THAT. AND WHEN I AKS THEM WHY THEY JUST TELLS ME TA SHADDUP.
LIKE IT'S REAL IMPORTANT, Y'KNOW?
UH... YA DIDN'T HEAR IT FROM ME, RIGHT?
JOANIE! YOU'VE GOT TO LEARN TO TRUST PEOPLE!
JOANIE'S BOYFRIENDS INCLUDE SOME OF THE CITY'S BIGGEST GANGLEADERS.
THERE MUST BE A MAJOR CONFERENCE IN THE WORKS--
--THE KIND THE KINGPIN HELD THE LAST TIME HE TOOK POWER.
NOT A SMART PLACE FOR A SUPERHERO TO SHOW UP.
AND IF I HAD HALF A BRAIN, I WOULDN'T.

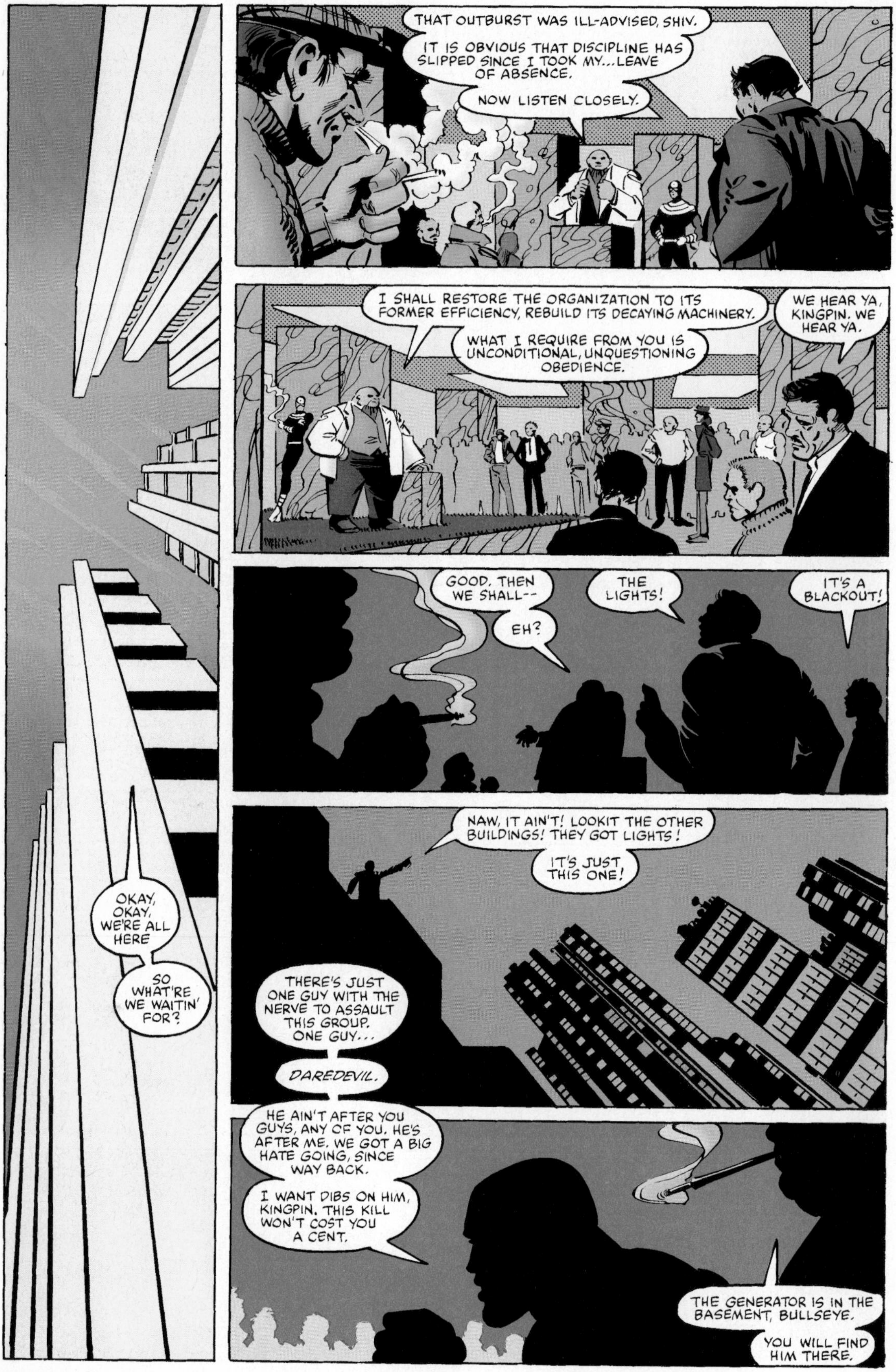
THAT OUTBURST WAS ILL-ADVISED, SHIV.
IT IS OBVIOUS THAT DISCIPLINE HAS SLIPPED SINCE I TOOK MY... LEAVE OF ABSENCE.
NOW LISTEN CLOSELY.
I SHALL RESTORE THE ORGANIZATION TO ITS FORMER EFFICIENCY, REBUILD ITS DECAYING MACHINERY.
WHAT I REQUIRE FROM YOU IS UNCONDITIONAL, UNQUESTIONING OBEDIENCE.
WE HEAR YA, KINGPIN. WE HEAR YA.
GOOD. THEN WE SHALL--
EH?
THE LIGHTS!
IT'S A BLACKOUT!
NAW, IT AIN'T! LOOKIT THE OTHER BUILDINGS! THEY GOT LIGHTS!
IT'S JUST THIS ONE!
OKAY, OKAY, WE'RE ALL HERE
SO WHAT'RE WE WAITIN' FOR?
THERE'S JUST ONE GUY WITH THE NERVE TO ASSAULT THIS GROUP. ONE GUY...
DAREDEVIL.
HE AIN'T AFTER YOU GUYS, ANY OF YOU. HE'S AFTER ME. WE GOT A BIG HATE GOING, SINCE WAY BACK.
I WANT DIBS ON HIM, KINGPIN. THIS KILL WON'T COST YOU A CENT.
THE GENERATOR IS IN THE BASEMENT, BULLSEYE.
YOU WILL FIND HIM THERE.

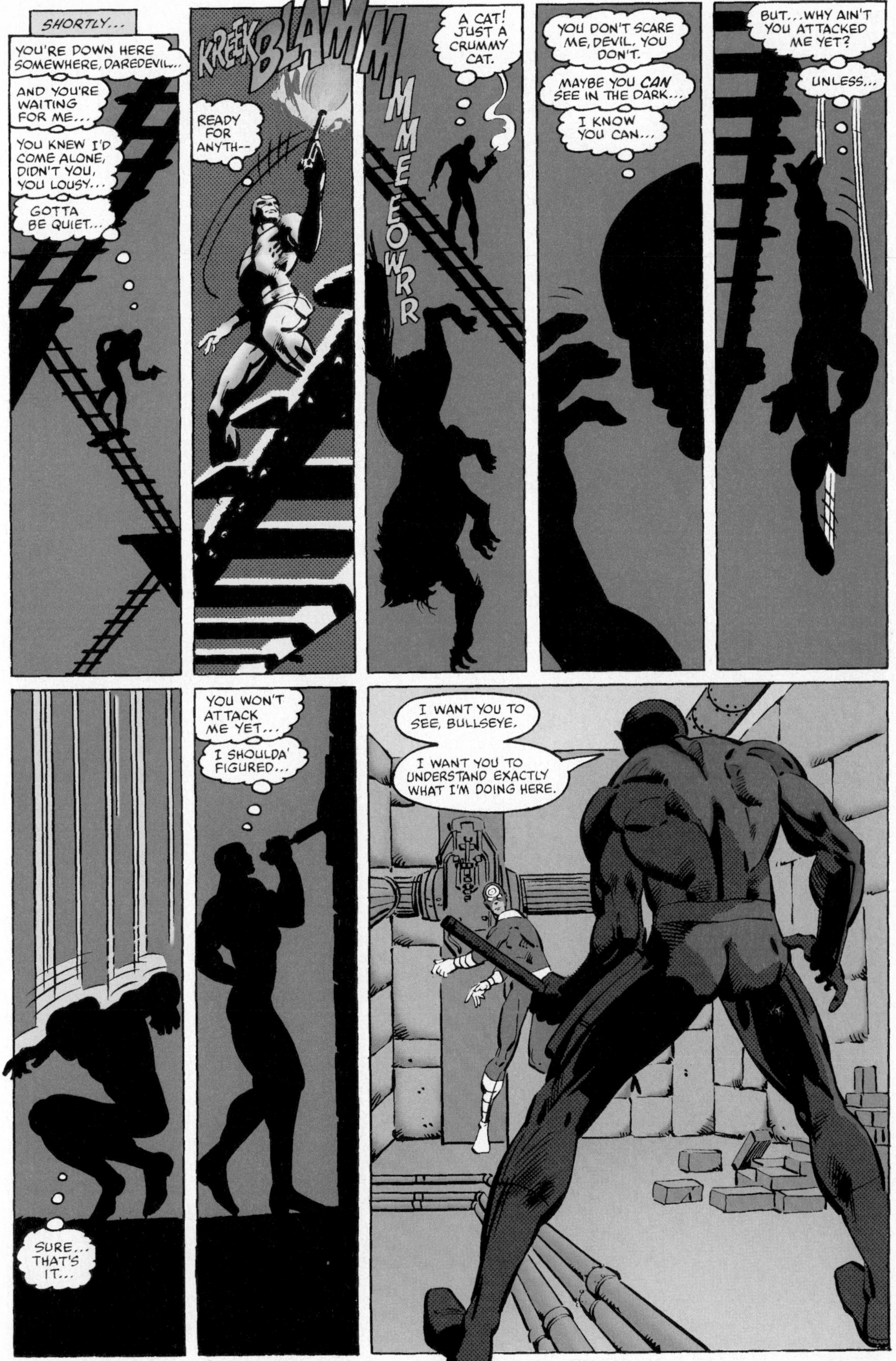
SHORTLY...
YOU'RE DOWN HERE SOMEWHERE, DAREDEVIL...
AND YOU'RE WAITING FOR ME...
YOU KNEW I'D COME ALONE, DIDN'T YOU, YOU LOUSY...
GOTTA BE QUIET...
KREEK BLAMMM
READY FOR ANYTH--
MMMEEOWRR
A CAT! JUST A CRUMMY CAT.
YOU DON'T SCARE ME, DEVIL. YOU DON'T.
MAYBE YOU CAN SEE IN THE DARK...
I KNOW YOU CAN...
BUT...WHY AIN'T YOU ATTACKED ME YET?
UNLESS...
SURE... THAT'S IT...
YOU WON'T ATTACK ME YET...
I SHOULDA' FIGURED...
I WANT YOU TO SEE, BULLSEYE.
I WANT YOU TO UNDERSTAND EXACTLY WHAT I'M DOING HERE.

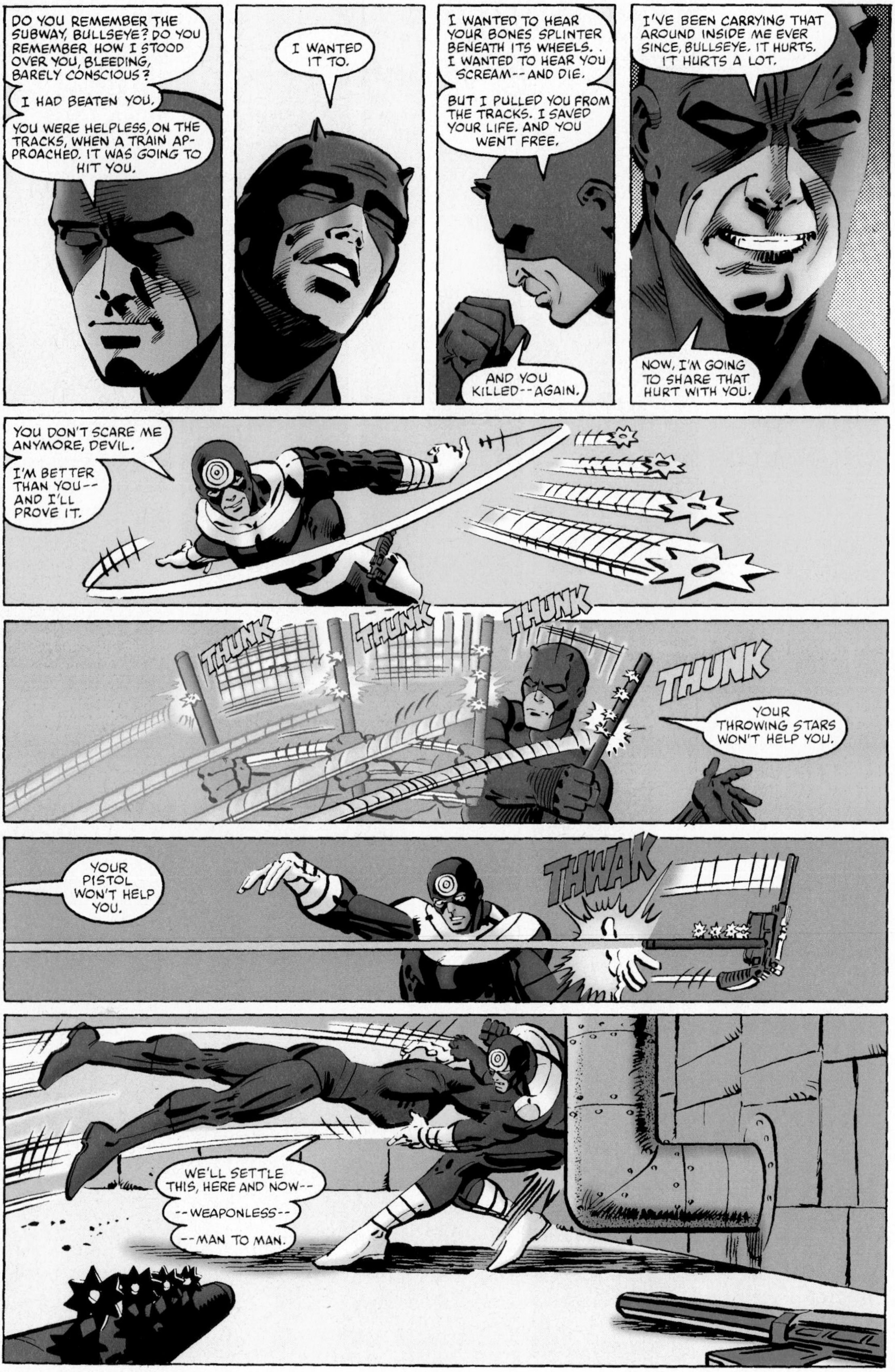
DO YOU REMEMBER THE SUBWAY, BULLSEYE? DO YOU REMEMBER HOW I STOOD OVER YOU, BLEEDING, BARELY CONSCIOUS?
I HAD BEATEN YOU.
YOU WERE HELPLESS, ON THE TRACKS, WHEN A TRAIN APPROACHED. IT WAS GOING TO HIT YOU.
I WANTED IT TO.
I WANTED TO HEAR YOUR BONES SPLINTER BENEATH ITS WHEELS. . I WANTED TO HEAR YOU SCREAM--AND DIE.
BUT I PULLED YOU FROM THE TRACKS. I SAVED YOUR LIFE. AND YOU WENT FREE.
AND YOU KILLED--AGAIN.
I'VE BEEN CARRYING THAT AROUND INSIDE ME EVER SINCE, BULLSEYE. IT HURTS. IT HURTS A LOT.
NOW, I'M GOING TO SHARE THAT HURT WITH YOU.
YOU DON'T SCARE ME ANYMORE, DEVIL.
I'M BETTER THAN YOU--AND I'LL PROVE IT.
THUNK
THUNK
THUNK
THUNK
YOUR THROWING STARS WON'T HELP YOU.
YOUR PISTOL WON'T HELP YOU.
THWAK
WE'LL SETTLE THIS, HERE AND NOW--
--WEAPONLESS--
--MAN TO MAN.

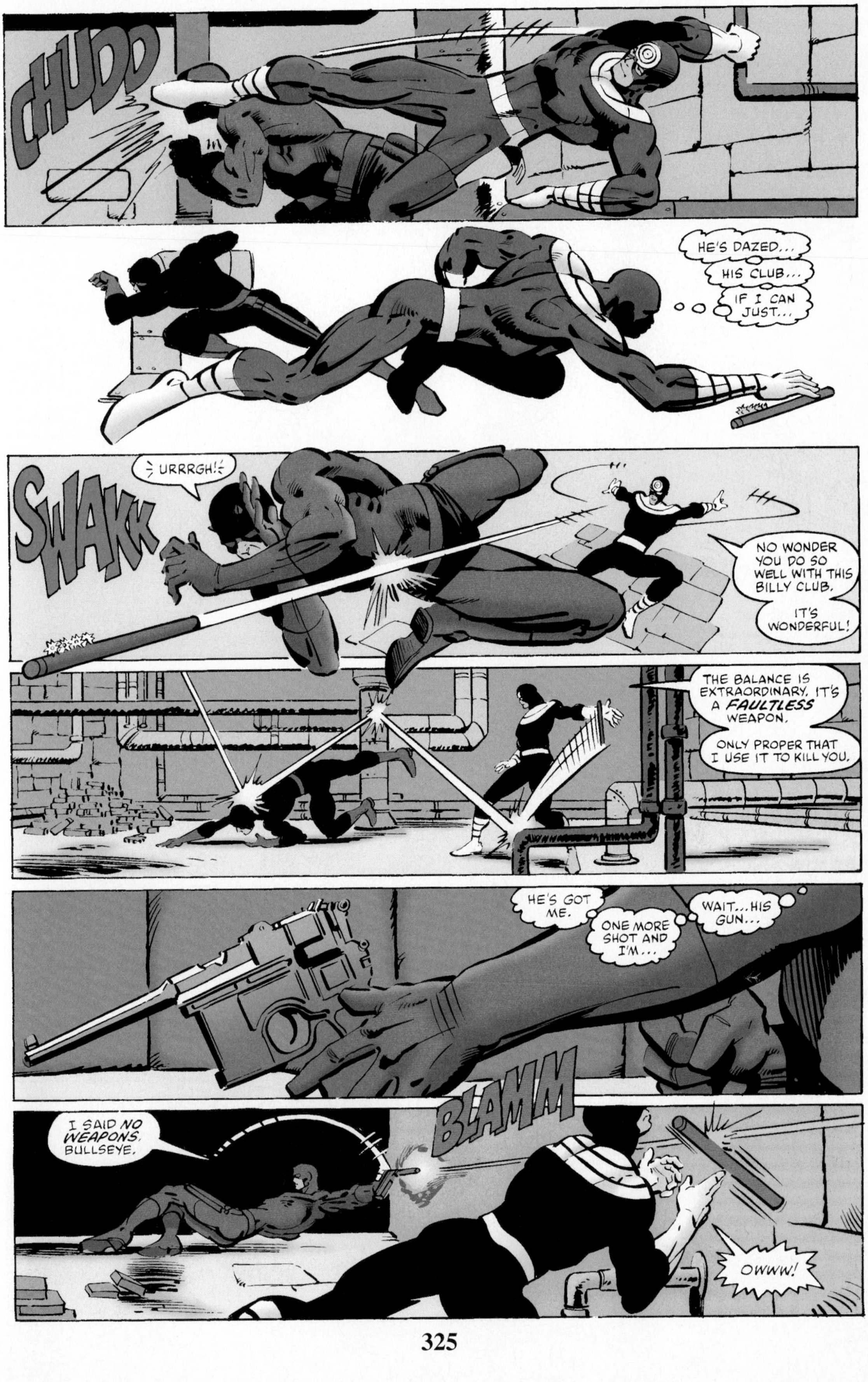
CHUDD
HE'S DAZED...
HIS CLUB...
IF I CAN JUST...
SWAKK
URRRGH!
NO WONDER YOU DO SO WELL WITH THIS BILLY CLUB.
IT'S WONDERFUL!
THE BALANCE IS EXTRAORDINARY. IT'S A FAULTLESS WEAPON.
ONLY PROPER THAT I USE IT TO KILL YOU.
HE'S GOT ME.
ONE MORE SHOT AND I'M...
WAIT... HIS GUN...
BLAMM
I SAID NO WEAPONS, BULLSEYE.
OWWW!

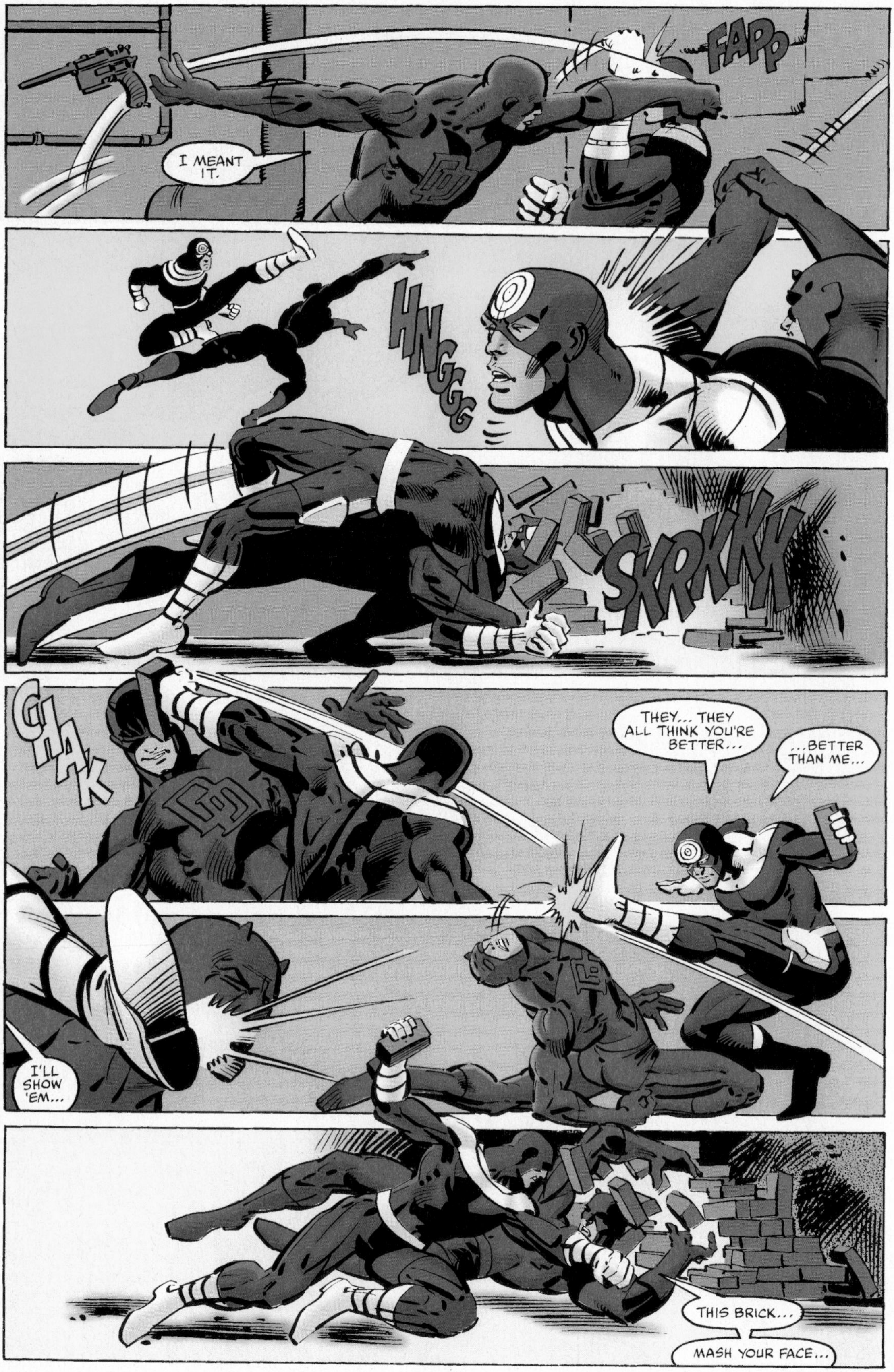
FAPP
I MEANT IT.
HNGGG
SKRKKK
CHAK
THEY... THEY ALL THINK YOU'RE BETTER...
...BETTER THAN ME...
I'LL SHOW 'EM...
THIS BRICK...
MASH YOUR FACE...

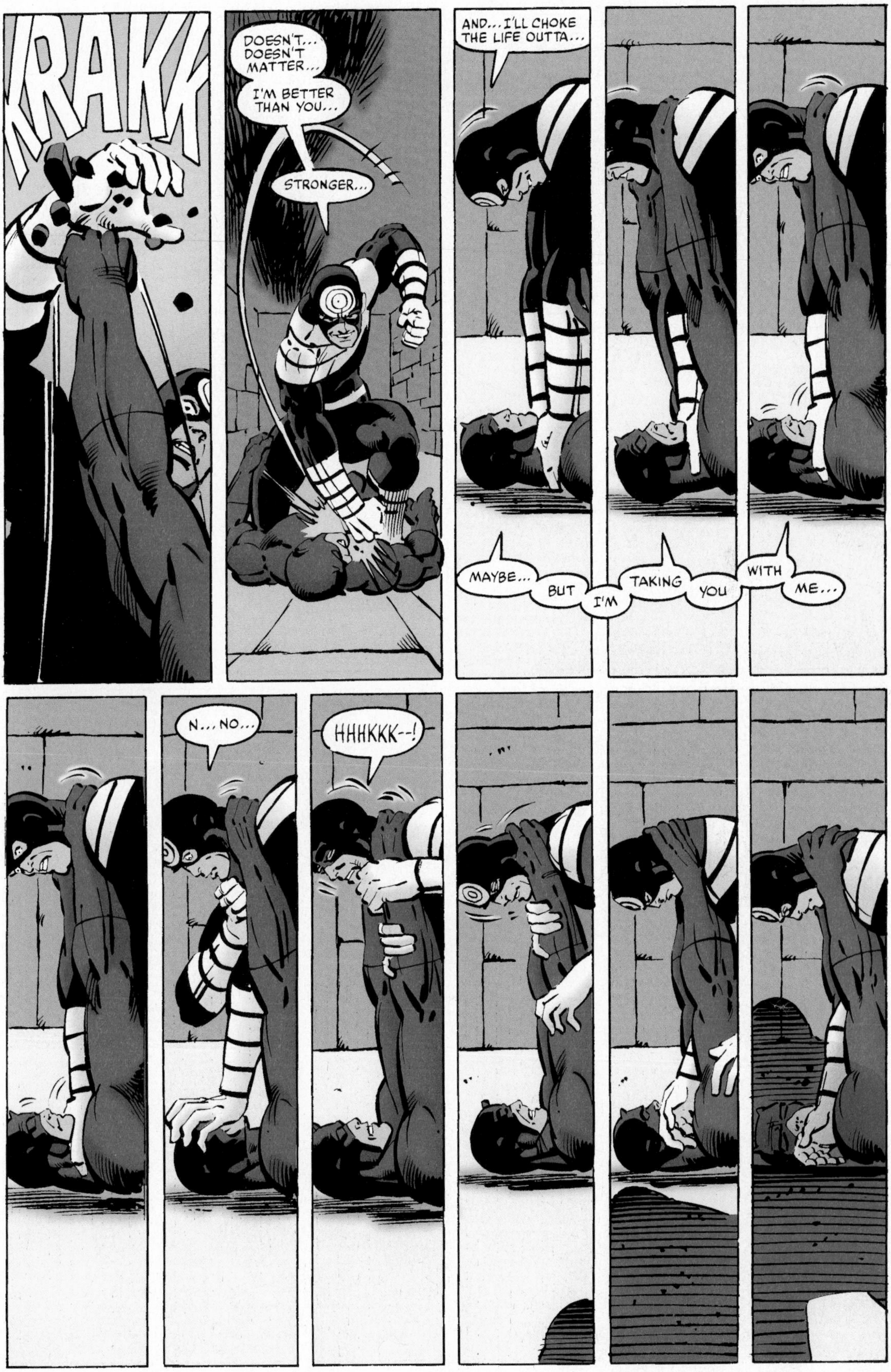
KRAKK
DOESN'T... DOESN'T MATTER...
I'M BETTER THAN YOU...
STRONGER...
AND... I'LL CHOKE THE LIFE OUTTA...
MAYBE...
BUT
I'M
TAKING
YOU
WITH
ME...
N... NO...
HHHKKK--!

DON'T TWITCH A MUSCLE.

SO FOCUSSED ON BULLSEYE... DIDN'T NOTICE THEM.

BUT THERE'S STILL A CHANCE. IF I CAN STALL THEM, JUST LONG ENOUGH FOR ME TO CATCH MY BREATH...

BULLSEYE IS STILL BREATHING. YOU MAY FINISH HIM.

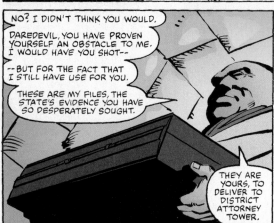

NO? I DIDN'T THINK YOU WOULD.

DAREDEVIL, YOU HAVE PROVEN YOURSELF AN OBSTACLE TO ME. I WOULD HAVE YOU SHOT--

--BUT FOR THE FACT THAT I STILL HAVE USE FOR YOU.

THESE ARE MY FILES, THE STATE'S EVIDENCE YOU HAVE SO DESPERATELY SOUGHT.

THEY ARE YOURS, TO DELIVER TO DISTRICT ATTORNEY TOWER.

MINUTES AFTER HE RECEIVES THEM, HE WILL ISSUE WARRANTS TO ARREST THE ENTIRE UPPER ECHELON OF THE EAST COAST UNDERWORLD.

SOON, THEY WILL BE IMPRISONED--

--AND I SHALL REPLACE THEM WITH MY MEN.

YOU SHALL ELIMINATE MY COMPETITION FOR ME.

I KNOW WHAT I'M THINKING, DAREDEVIL.

YOU'RE PLANNING SOME DESPERATE, FUTILE ATTACK-- YOU SEEK TO BRING ME IN, AS WELL. YOU ARE A VERY PASSIONATE MAN.

BUT IT IS NOT YOUR PASSION THAT I NOW ADDRESS. IT IS YOUR INTELLECT.

CONSIDER YOUR POSITION. YOU HAVE BULLSEYE -- I'LL THROW HIM IN AS A COURTESY--

--AND I SHALL BE LEFT WITH A SHATTERED ORGANIZATION TO REBUILD. FOR A TIME, YOUR SIDE WILL BE THAT MUCH STRONGER.

CONSIDER THE GREATER GOOD TO SOCIETY...

...AND YOU SHALL SEE THAT YOU REALLY HAVE NO CHOICE, AFTER ALL.

YOU WIN, KINGPIN. THIS TIME.

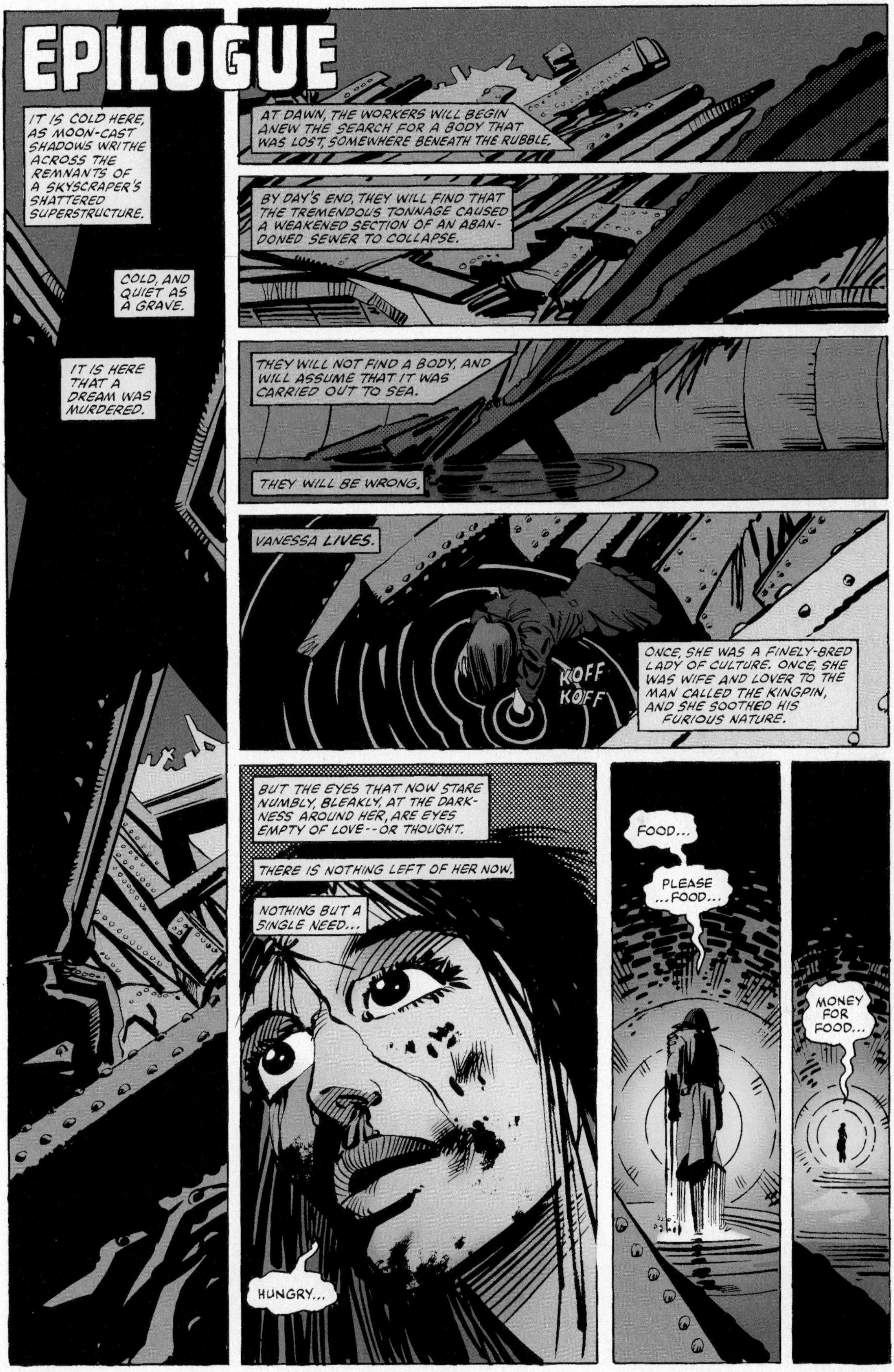
EPILOGUE
IT IS COLD HERE, AS MOON-CAST SHADOWS WRITHE ACROSS THE REMNANTS OF A SKYSCRAPER'S SHATTERED SUPERSTRUCTURE.
COLD, AND QUIET AS A GRAVE.
IT IS HERE THAT A DREAM WAS MURDERED.
AT DAWN, THE WORKERS WILL BEGIN ANEW THE SEARCH FOR A BODY THAT WAS LOST, SOMEWHERE BENEATH THE RUBBLE.
BY DAY'S END, THEY WILL FIND THAT THE TREMENDOUS TONNAGE CAUSED A WEAKENED SECTION OF AN ABANDONED SEWER TO COLLAPSE.
THEY WILL NOT FIND A BODY, AND WILL ASSUME THAT IT WAS CARRIED OUT TO SEA.
THEY WILL BE WRONG.
VANESSA LIVES.
KOFF KOFF
ONCE, SHE WAS A FINELY-BRED LADY OF CULTURE. ONCE, SHE WAS WIFE AND LOVER TO THE MAN CALLED THE KINGPIN, AND SHE SOOTHED HIS FURIOUS NATURE.
BUT THE EYES THAT NOW STARE NUMBLY, BLEAKLY, AT THE DARKNESS AROUND HER, ARE EYES EMPTY OF LOVE--OR THOUGHT.
THERE IS NOTHING LEFT OF HER NOW.
NOTHING BUT A SINGLE NEED...
HUNGRY...
FOOD...
PLEASE ...FOOD...
MONEY FOR FOOD...

**MARVEL
COMICS GROUP**

DAREDEVIL

©1979 MCG

Bible   By Frank Miller
                                                   8/19/80

575 MADISON AVENUE
NEW YORK, NEW YORK 10
212/838-7900
TELEX 238061

CADENCE
PUBLISHING

DAREDEVIL

　　　Hell's Kitchen, twenty years ago: Battlin' Murdock, an
aging heavyweight boxer, asks his ten-year-old son to promise
never to become a fighter, to become a doctor or a lawyer or
somebody - somebody with a future.　The boy makes the promise.

　　　It is a hard promise to keep.　Young Matt Murdock is a
born fighter, a natural athlete.　He sees the other boys at
school enjoying sports, scoring the touchdowns and home runs
he feels he could make, given the chance.　Matt is tormented by
his fellows, who give the quiet bookworm a cruel nickname:
DAREDEVIL.

　　　One lonely night, in a fit of anger, Matt strikes his
father's light bag and knocks it from the wall.　He looks down
at the bag, astonished at his feat of strength.　Then it hits him.

He could work out like this every day, just to keep in shape.
And his father would never know...

He grows to adolescence, driving himself to become a
straight-A student, and secretly becoming an athlete of Olympic
quality.

Fifteen years ago: Matt is walking home from high school
when he sees a truck careen from its motorcade, out of control,
toward a helpless old blind man. His secret training serves him
well as he tackles the old man, pushing him out of the way.
The truck, swerving wildly, topples on its side and bursts into
flame. Matt looks up at the truck and sees men in radiation
suits throw a heavy case from the back of the truck. He sees
the case shatter, and, flying from it, a brilliant blue cannister.
The cannister strikes him across the eyes, and he never sees
anything, ever again.

He is later to learn that the cannister contained radioactive
material which was the result of an unrepeatable laboratory
accident. He is never to learn the exact nature of the material,
nor that of the incredible effects of the radiation.

It is in the hospital that Matt feels the changes. His
remaining senses are amplified to superhuman levels. He can
hear the faintest whisper, even a heartbeat; he can taste the
exact number of grains of salt on a pretzel; he can touch a
printed page and read it feeling the vague impression of the
ink; he can smell a rose from a hundred feet away.

Most amazing of all, he develops a built-in 'radar-sense',
which guides him unerringly past every obstacle!

Permanently blind, yet strangely more capable
than a sighted man, Matt resolves to become a lawyer - the
'somebody' his father so desperately wants him to be. He
enters college.

But college costs money, lots of it, and Battlin' Murdock
is hard-pressed to meet the costs. All he knows is fighting, and
the speed and skill have long since left his fists. No legitimate
manager is willing to take a chance on him. He's an honest man,
and a proud man, but his son's career is worth more to him than
his pride. He goes to The Fixer, the most criminal fight manager
in the city, and begs for a fight.

The Fixer takes a personal interest - and delight - in
promoting the fighter who threw him out of his dressing room,

years earlier. Battlin' Murdock becomes a phenomenon in boxing,
unexpectedly winning fight after fight, actually lining up a
semi - title bout. Murdock, in his simple honesty, is the only
man in boxing who doesn't know the real reason for his success.

Before the semi-title bout, The Fixer instructs Murdock to
throw the fight. Murdock refuses. The Fixer tells him that he
either throws the fight, or dies.

Madison Square Garden, eight years ago: Matt is in the
audience as Battlin' Murdock fights the fight of his life,
and wins. Walking home that night, he is shot to death.

Battlin' Murdock's corner man tells Matt that The Fixer
had his father killed. Matt wants vengeance, but is bound by his
father's oath to lead a non-violent life. No, he thinks, Matt
Murdock can't make The Fixer pay...but someone else can...

That night, a dark, mysterious figure attacks and apprehends
The Fixer and his gang. DAREDEVIL is born!

In the years that follow, Matt and his roommate, Franklin
'Foggy' Nelson, graduate law school and open a law practice in
Manhattan. Foggy is a likable, if clumsy, friend and partner.

After a brief but brilliantly successful stint as Park Avenue
attorneys, Matt and Foggy set up a storefront law office on

Manhattan's lower east side, where they start a practice devoted
to aiding the poor and underprivileged. They hire a secretary,
Becky Blake, a young, attractive woman who is confined to a
wheelchair, but nonetheless is competent, tough, and independent.
Thus, by day Matt fights injustice as a prominent lawyer--and by
night, when the need arises, he stalks the rooftops and alleyways
of Manhattan as a crimson-clad champion of law and justice. His
unique radar sense and other super senses guide him through the
darkness with greater ease than sighted men.

His blind man's cane breaks into two pieces - one is a
hook-and-cable device that enables him to cross distances too
great for him to leap, the other a shaft of steel-reinforced
wood that he uses as a billy club.

His upper east side townhouse serves as home and headquarters.
In a hidden gym he sharpens and perfects his skills.

Like Perry Mason and Paul Drake in one, Matt Murdock is more
than a crusading lawyer. He is a terror to the underworld, a
crimson clad champion of justice. He is DAREDEVIL, The Man
Without Fear!

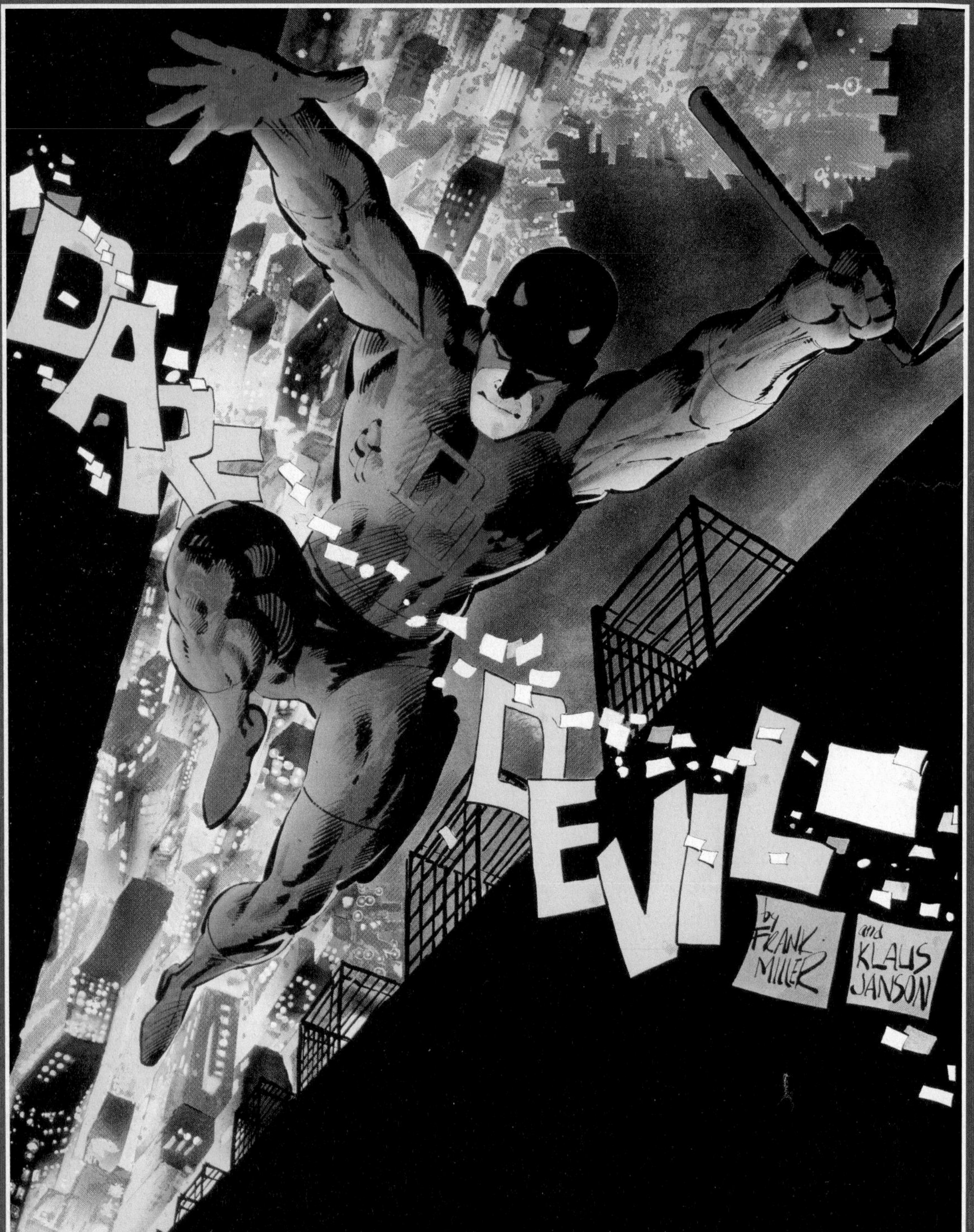
DAREDEVIL
by FRANK MILLER
and KLAUS JANSON

Daredevil Poster by Frank Miller & Klaus Janson